ASP.NET 1.0 Namespace Reference with C#

Jason Bell

Mike Clark

Andy Elmhorst

Dave Gerding

Matt Gibbs

Alex Homer

Amit Kalani

Bruce Lee

Matt Milner

John Schenken

Wrox Press Ltd. ®

ASP.NET 1.0 Namespace Reference with C#

Published by Wrox Press Ltd,
Arden House, 1102 Warwick Road, Acocks Green,
Birmingham, B27 6BH, UK
Printed in the United States
ISBN 1-86100-744-2

Trademark Acknowledgments

Credits

Authors
Jason Bell
Mike Clark
Andy Elmhorst
Dave Gerding
Matt Gibbs
Alex Homer
Amit Kalani
Bruce Lee
Matt Milner
John Schenken

Managing Editor
Louay Fatoohi

Commissioning Editor
Matthew Cumberlidge

Technical Editors
Michelle Everitt
Helen Callaghan

Project Manager
Beth Sacks

Technical Reviewers
Maxime Bombardier
Paul Churchill
Andrew Stopford
Don Lee
Sophie McQueen
Larry Schoeneman
David Schultz
Matthew Gibbs

Production Coordinator
Abbie Forletta

Index
John Collin

Cover
Natalie O'Donnell

Additional Material
Brian Patterson
Bill Forgey

Author Agent
Charlotte Smith

Proof Reader
Susan Nettleton

About the Authors

Jason Bell

Jason Bell started learning computer programming back in 1981 on his father's TI-99/4A with an incredible 16KB of RAM and a panoramic 10" display supporting resolutions of up to 256x192. After eight years of developing software for the US Air Force, Jason is now an MCSD working as a consultant for Stroudwater NHG, a Microsoft Certified Partner located in Portland, ME. When he's not busy donating out-of-date computer books to the library or reformatting his computer's hard drive to install more beta software, Jason enjoys piloting small aircraft, driving his vintage Porsche, and dreaming about going back to school someday to work toward a PhD in Physics.

Mike Clark

Mike Clark, is senior analyst at Lucin, and is responsible for www.salcentral.com the first web services brokerage. Over the past eight years he has increasingly become more involved in Internet technologies and using his expertise in multi-tier windows development sees the movement into web services as adoption of lessons learned, rather than a completely new environment. Mike now predominantly works in commercial aspects of web services, having developed the web sites www.webservicewatch.com and www.webservicelibrary.com. He is known for his distinctly aggressive style of development and still can't resist a 48 hour working session. Mike Clark can be contacted at mikec@lucin.com.

Andy Elmhorst

Andy Elmhorst is a developer and writer, who spends most of his time architecting and building web applications using Microsoft server technologies. He enjoys delving into the details of every technology he gets his hands on. Andy's currently working for Renaissance Learning, Inc. where he enjoys building cool products with cool people. Every chance he has, he gets away to the Wisconsin Northwoods with his family to enjoy the great outdoors. Andy Elmhorst can be reached at andyelmhorst@hotmail.com.

Dave Gerding

Dave Gerding is a consultant, writer, programmer,and owner of Versive LLC, an interactive solutions developer. He was the founding faculty member of the Interactive Multimedia Program at Columbia College Chicago and consulted in its development before joining the program. He is a Microsoft Certified Systems Engineer and a McCarthy Technologies Certified Core Instructor. Gerding wrote for over a dozen national and international technology publications prior to joining Columbia and continues to write in his spare time.

Matt Gibbs

Matt Gibbs is a software developer at Microsoft where he has been working on Internet technologies since 1997. He is currently working on the Mobile Internet Toolkit. Matt is looking forward to finishing his graduate studies in Computer Science at the University of Washington soon, so that he can spend more time with his wife, son, and daughter.

Alex Homer

Alex Homer is a software developer and technical author living and working in the idyllic rural surroundings of the Derbyshire Dales in England. He started playing with Microsoft's Active Server Pages technology right from the early betas of version 1.0 (remember "Denali"?) – and has watched with awe and excitement as it has evolved into probably the most comprehensive server-side Web programming environment available today. With the advent of ASP.NET, it gets even better. In fact, he's so excited about the whole new framework and application model that he once nearly referred to it as a "paradigm". In the meantime, he has to be forcibly removed from his computer three times a week for the administration of food and fresh air. You can contact Alex at alex@stonebroom.com.

Amit Kalani

Amit Kalani has been actively programming using Microsoft .NET Framework since it was introduced. He is a contributing author for *Inside ASP.NET* and *.NET Mobile Web Developer's Guide* and has also done technical reviews for several popular books on C#, VB.NET, and ASP.NET. Amit is a Bachelor of Science and is also a Microsoft-certified professional. Amit lives in Michigan with his wife Priti.

I would like to thank Priti; this book wouldn't have been possible without her immense support. Special thanks go to my editor, Matthew Cumberlidge who has done diligent work in making this work better than what I had written. My word of thanks is also for project manager, Beth Sacks and author agent, Charlotte Smith for making sure that the project was well organized. I would also like to thank Scott Worley for introducing me to Matt.

Bruce Lee

Before he went to Canada, Bruce Lee was a technical support engineer at Microsoft Taiwan. He is also an author and technical writer for a couple of Chinese books, and *Windows 2000 Magazine's* Traditional Chinese Edition. His focus has always been on Microsoft technologies, especially on operating systems, network management and web development. When not working, you can usually find him with his favorite dog, Jay-Jay, near the St. Lawrence River. You can reach him at yihcheng@hotmail.com.

Bruce wants to give special thanks to Rob Howard for giving him direction and support in his writing.

Matt Milner

Matt Milner works as a Technical Architect for BORN in Minneapolis where he designs and builds Microsoft solutions for clients in a variety of industries. Matt's primary focus has been using Windows DNA architecture, and he is excited about the move to .NET with its powerful new features. When Matt is not working at his computer, he spends his time in his woodshop, reading, or enjoying the many great natural resources of Minnesota.

John Schenken

John Schenken is currently Software Test Lead on the Visual Basic Server Enterprise Team for Microsoft. He was previously Test Lead for the Microsoft Script Debugger that shipped with the Windows NT Option Pack, and is still responsible for it in Windows 2000. He has programming experience involving MSMQ, SMTP, NT Event Log, NT Perf Counters, ASP, and ADO – basically that's wide experience writing end-to-end web applications involving business objects.

Table of Contents

Table of Contents

Table of Contents

Table of Contents

Table of Contents

Table of Contents

Table of Contents

Table of Contents

Table of Contents

ASP Today

www.asptoday.com

ASP Today

www.asptoday.com

Introduction

What Is This Book About?

This book is a complete reference to the ASP.NET namespaces for developers who are already familiar with using ASP.NET. We will not be wasting your time by hyping up ASP.NET – we assume that you are up to speed with how slick and powerful it is. We are going to concentrate on providing a neat and tidy reference to the main classes you will use as an ASP.NET developer and illustrating them with simple but useful examples.

Each chapter covers another of the ASP.NET namespaces, from `System.Web` right through to `System.Web.Services.Protocols`, with coverage of individual classes, methods, and properties presented in easy-to-use alphabetical order. We also have two very useful appendices that will help you accomplish some very common tasks in ASP.NET: working with data and working with XML.

What This Book Is

- ❑ It's a hardcore reference to the ASP.NET namespaces.

- ❑ It is rigidly organized to help you find the class, method, or property that you are looking for as easily as possible.

- ❑ It's an invaluable addition to the Microsoft documentation.

- ❑ It is a rich source of demonstrative examples, and best practice advice.

- ❑ It is presented in C#.

What This Book Is Not

- ❑ It's not an introductory tutorial to ASP.NET.

- ❑ It's not a copy of the documentation; we go much further in explaining and demonstrating those classes which matter.

- ❑ It is not a high-level discursive text, it is a down-and-dirty reference.

What This Book Covers

This book covers the following namespaces:

- ❏ `System.Web` – this namespace is essentially the base namespace, which enables all browser/server communication in ASP.NET.

- ❏ `System.Web.UI` – this namespace includes the `Control` class, which is the base class for all HTML and Web controls, which are so powerful in making your ASP.NET applications dynamic.

- ❏ `System.Web.UI.HtmlControls` – HTML server controls provide you with direct programmatic access to HTML tags on the server.

- ❏ `System.Web.UI.WebControls` – Web controls run server-side and provide the developer with easy access to extremely complex functionality, such as the Calendar control.

- ❏ `System.Web.UI.MobileControls` – Mobile controls are versions of the Web controls designed specifically for use on mobile devices, allowing for rich functionality on limited platforms.

- ❏ `System.Web.Caching` – the classes of this namespace allow you to cache frequently used resources on the server in order to provide a sleeker user experience.

- ❏ `System.Web.Configuration` – these classes allow you to configure your ASP.NET applications at a very low level.

- ❏ `System.Web.Security` – these classes, along with those from `System.Security`, provide security for your ASP.NET applications.

- ❏ `System.Web.Services` – Web Services are a new and exciting technology that allows you to expose the functionality of your components over the Internet. This namespace provides the base classes that you can leverage for this purpose.

- ❏ `System.Web.Services.Description` – these classes help you to describe the functionality and contents of your Web Services so that they can be easily consumed by third parties.

- ❏ `System.Web.Services.Protocols` – these classes allow you to control the way data is transmitted across the wire between client and Web Service.

In addition we have two extensive appendices, which overview the fundamentals of working with data and XML in ASP.NET, using plenty of efficient examples.

Who Is This Book For?

This book is for developers who have already got to grips with ASP.NET, and require a handy reference guide to the classes they already use or might like to use in the future. In other words, it's for developers who have already spent some time using ASP.NET and don't need a book that tells them the basics.

What You Need to Use This Book

We'd like to think that you have a passion for ASP.NET, though in reality there may be one or two people who just use it because they have to. Either way, ASP.NET is what this book is about, and what we expect you to be familiar with. We summarize all the requirements in the next two sections.

Prerequisite Knowledge and Experience

This book is aimed at developers who have learned about .NET, and in particular ASP.NET. It would be advisable to have already read *Professional ASP.NET 1.0 Special Edition* (ISBN 1-86100-703-5) also by Wrox Press.

Since the syntax and code examples in this book are coded in C#, knowledge of that programming language is assumed.

The sample files can be downloaded from http://www.wrox.com/.

Development Tools and Run-Time Environment

Basically, all you need is a text editor and a server running the .NET Framework. The examples are all presented as Visual Studio .NET projects, but they can just as easily be run without VS.NET. You will also need to obtain and install the Microsoft Mobile Internet Toolkit (MMIT) to be able to run the examples for Chapter 5.

To get the .NET Framework, go to http://msdn.microsoft.com/.NET/. You can get the MMIT from http://msdn.microsoft.com/vstudio/device/mitdefault.asp.

A database server is also required – though it can be on the same physical machine as your .NET Framework installation. The database servers we use in the book are Microsoft SQL Server 2000 and Access 2000.

Conventions

We've used a number of different styles of text and layout in this book to help differentiate between the different kinds of information. Here are examples of the styles we used and an explanation of what they mean.

There are many examples illustrating the various classes of the ASP.NET namespaces throughout this book. These examples are presented in easy-to-find boxes like this:

Example: A HelloWorld Example

The text and code of the example will be in here.

Code has several styles. If we're presenting a word that we're talking about in the text – for example, when discussing a `case...else` loop, it's in this font. If it's a block of code that can be typed as a program and run, then it's also in a gray box:

```
<?xml version 1.0?>
```

Sometimes we'll see code in a mixture of styles, like this:

```
<?xml version 1.0?>
<Invoice>
    <part>
        <name>Widget</name>
        <price>$10.00</price>
    </part>
</invoice>
```

In cases like this, the code with a white background is code we are already familiar with; the line highlighted in gray is a new addition to the code since we last looked at it, or code that we want to highlight for some other reason.

Occasionally, there are commands or code lines that should be presented as a single line, but can't (because of the limited width of the page). In this case, we indicate the overflow by using a ⌐ symbol, like this:

```
csc /t:exe /out:logClient.exe logClient.cs⌐
/r:system.dll,System.Runtime.Remoting.dll,../bin/logger.dll
```

Advice, hints, and background information come in this indented, italicised style.

Important pieces of information come in boxes like this.

Bullets appear indented, with each new bullet marked as follows:

- **Important words** are in a bold type font.
- Words that appear on the screen, or in menus like Open or Close, are in a similar font to the one you would see on a Windows desktop.
- Keys that you press on the keyboard like *Ctrl* and *Enter*, are in italics.

Customer Support

We value feedback from our readers, and we want to know what you think about this book: what you liked, what you didn't like, and what you think we can do better next time. You can send us your comments, either by returning the reply card in the back of the book, or by e-mail to feedback@wrox.com. Please be sure to mention the book's title and ISBN in your message.

How to Download the Sample Code for the Book

When you visit the Wrox site, http://www.wrox.com/, simply locate the title through our Search facility or by using one of the title lists. Click on Download in the Code column, or on Download Code on the book's detail page.

The files that are available for download from our site have been archived using WinZip. When you have saved the attachments to a folder on your hard-drive, you need to extract the files using a de-compression program such as WinZip or PKUnzip. When you extract the files, they should be arranged into folders. When you start the extraction process, ensure your software (WinZip, PKUnzip, etc.) is set to use folder names.

Errata

We've made every effort to make sure that there are no errors in the text or in the code. However, no one is perfect and mistakes do occur. If you find an error in one of our books, like a spelling mistake or a faulty piece of code, we would be very grateful for feedback. By sending in errata you may save another reader hours of frustration, and of course, you will be helping us to provide even higher quality information. Simply e-mail the information to support@wrox.com. We'll check the information you give us, and if appropriate, we'll post it to the errata page for that title or use it in subsequent editions of the book.

To find errata on the web site, go to http://www.wrox.com/, and locate the title through our **Advanced Search** or title list. Click on the **Book Errata** link, which is below the cover graphic on the book's detail page.

E-mail Support

If you wish to query a problem in the book directly with an expert who knows the book in detail then e-mail support@wrox.com, with the title of the book and the last four numbers of the ISBN in the subject field of the e-mail. A typical e-mail should include the following things:

❑   The **title of the book, last four digits of the ISBN (7442)**, and **page number** of the problem in the Subject field.

❑   Your **name, contact information**, and the **problem** in the body of the message.

We *won't* send you junk mail. We need the details to save your time and ours. When you send an e-mail message, it will go through the following chain of support:

❑   Customer Support – Your message is delivered to our customer support staff, who are the first people to read it. They have files on most frequently asked questions and will answer anything general about the book or the web site immediately.

❑   Editorial – Deeper queries are forwarded to the technical editor responsible for that book. They have experience with the programming language or particular product, and are able to answer detailed technical questions on the subject.

❑   The Authors – Finally, in the unlikely event that the editor cannot answer your problem, they will forward the request to the author. We do try to protect the author from any distractions to their writing; however, we are quite happy to forward specific requests to them. All Wrox authors help with the support on their books. They will e-mail the customer and the editor with their response, and again all readers should benefit.

The Wrox Support process can only offer support to issues that are directly pertinent to the content of our published title. Support for questions that fall outside the scope of normal book support is provided via the community lists of our http://p2p.wrox.com/ forum.

p2p.wrox.com

For author and peer discussion join the P2P mailing lists. Our unique system provides **programmer to programmer**™ contact on mailing lists, forums, and newsgroups, all in addition to our one-to-one e-mail support system. If you post a query to P2P, you can be confident that it will be examined by the many Wrox authors and other industry experts who are present on our mailing lists. At p2p.wrox.com you will find a number of different lists that will help you, not only while you read this book, but also as you develop your own applications.

To subscribe to a mailing list, just follow these steps:

1. Go to http://p2p.wrox.com/.

2. Choose the appropriate category from the left menu bar.

3. Click on the mailing list you wish to join.

4. Follow the instructions to subscribe and fill in your e-mail address and password.

5. Reply to the confirmation e-mail you receive.

6. Use the subscription manager to join more lists and set your e-mail preferences.

Why This System Offers the Best Support

You can choose to join the mailing lists or you can receive them as a weekly digest. If you don't have the time, or facility, to receive the mailing list, then you can search our online archives. Junk and spam mails are deleted, and your own e-mail address is protected by the unique Lyris system. Queries about joining or leaving lists, and any other general queries about lists, should be sent to listsupport@p2p.wrox.com.

System.Object Members

In order to save you having to look at tiresome repetition we have decided to extract the reference material for those members that are inherited from System.Object into this introduction. The following members are inherited by every class in the .NET Framework, and we therefore felt it was necessary to include some description but we didn't need to talk about it in every class.

System.Object Public Methods

Equals

The Equals method determines whether two object instances are equal. It returns True if the two objects are equal, otherwise False. There are two overloaded forms of the method, which take either an object or two objects as input, respectively.

```
public virtual bool Equals(object);
public static bool Equals(object, object);
```

GetHashCode

The `GetHashCode` method returns a hash code for the current object instance. Objects that you intend to group in or reference via a hash table must override this method because objects that are treated as keys in a hash table must generate their own hash code – hence this `virtual` method is provided.

```
public virtual int GetHashCode();
```

GetType

The `GetType` method returns the type of the current object, which in .NET reflection resolves to the class type name of the current object instance. You might use `GetType` while walking a control parent/child hierarchy to ensure that you access the appropriate methods or properties of a particular child control based on the returned type of the current control.

```
public Type GetType();
```

ToString

The `ToString` method returns a string representing the object. By default the fully qualified name of the type of the object is returned.

```
public virtual string ToString();
```

System.Object Protected Methods

Finalize

The `Finalize` method is basically the deconstructor method of the control object. Your cleanup code, if any, should be overridden in `Dispose`, for consistency's sake, and then simply invoked in an overridden version of `Finalize` should you choose to implement `Finalize`.

```
~Object();
```

MemberwiseClone

The `MemberwiseClone` method creates a "shallow" copy of the current object. "Shallow" copies are new instances of the original instance with matching values in the non-static member properties.

```
protected object MemberwiseClone();
```

> **In the initial listings of classes and their members in each chapter you will notice that some have been highlighted in bold text. This highlighting means that we will discuss this particular class or member in detail later in that chapter.**

1

System.Web

The `System.Web` namespace contains classes that provide the basic infrastructure for developing Web-based applications and supporting ASP.NET framework client-server communication. It includes classes like `HttpRequest` and `HttpResponse` that encapsulate the communication information passed between Web Server and client browser, yet also provides classes to access information about the application and file paths to give you detailed insight of the Web application's execution environment. Overall, the `System.Web` namespace provides you with a rich set of classes that allow you to keep your focus on building Web solutions rather than digging into the unnecessary complex details of the communication protocol and execution environment.

In this chapter we'll cover those classes in the `System.Web` namespace that are the most useful, and commonly used in ASP.NET web applications. These classes make up the bulk of the namespace and provide the majority of its functionality. Before we begin, however, we'll cover some of the basics of ASP.NET Web development.

Creating an ASP.NET Page

In classic ASP programming, server-side script was embedded directly into the HTML text of a page. The HTML content was written onto the page and the statements that need to be executed on the server side were written between <% and %> tags so that the server could catch them for processing. Certainly there were exceptions to this, for example, when a page simply redirected the user to a display screen, but for the most part, this was the case.

This mixing of code, that represents business logic or validation logic, with the HTML, that usually will only contain user interface information, produced code that was difficult to write and maintain, especially in the large development projects. More proactive development teams would take extra steps to develop coding standards to minimize this but it still could not be eliminated by root, as this was the basic nature of ASP development during those days.

With ASP.NET you can continue to mix code and layout, but there are features available in the development framework that will allow you to keep the presentation tier separate from the business logic tier. This method uses a `Code Behind` way of development where one file (the Web Form) will contain all presentation information and a separate file with a similar name (the `Code Behind` file) will contain all the server side processing information. This approach has many benefits, not least of which is improved manageability, readability, and reusability.

Here is an example Web Form, `Time.aspx`, where code and layout are mixed. The code is enclosed in `<script>` blocks. The code for this example can be found in the `Time.aspx`, which is in the code download for this chapter:

```
<%@ Page %>
<html>
<head>
  <title>Time Web Form</title>
</head>
<body>
  <script language="cs" runat="server">
    public string GetTime()
    {
      return System.DateTime.Now.ToString();
    }
  </script>
  The time at the server is
  <%=GetTime()%>
</body>
</html>
```

The first point to note here is that our page has an `.aspx` file extension. This tells the web server that it is an ASP.NET Web Form, and should be handled accordingly. Next, notice that we're using a script block to wrap a function called `GetTime` that returns the system date and time as a string value. The surrounding script block specifies the language and the location to run the script, in this case at the server. You can only use one of the supported languages on a given web page, as the entire page is compiled to a single instance of a `Page` class (discussed in Chapter 2), but different languages can be used for different pages, enabling a web application to contain several different languages within the one application.

Finally, our script returns a value using a function call and returns the following output:

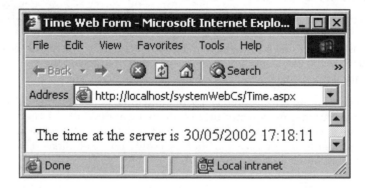

This could also have been achieved like this:

```
<h2>
    The time at the server is
    <%=System.DateTime.Now.ToString();%>
</h2>
```

The structure we've used so far will be very familiar to ASP developers. Now we're going to compose a similar example, `TimeDotNetStyle.aspx`, using the suggested ASP.NET architecture, where only the layout elements appear in the `.aspx` file:

```
<%@ Page Language="cs" Inherits="TimeDotNetStyle"
    Src="TimeDotNetStyle.aspx.cs"%>
<html>
    <head>
    <title>Time DotNet Style</title>
    </head>
    <body>
        <form id="Form1" method="post" runat="server">
            <asp:Label ID="time" Runat="server"></asp:Label>
        </form>
    </body>
</html>
```

There are a couple of important things to notice here. First, the file now contains a `@Page` directive at the top of the file, which tells the .NET runtime about the page. Its `Language` attribute tells the runtime which compiler to use on the file; in this case it's the C# compiler. Its `Src` attribute specifies the name of the file (also referred to as the Code Behind file) that contains our server-side code, and its `Inherits` attribute indicates that our `.aspx` page derives from the `TimeDotNetStyle` class.

In addition, we have used an ASP.NET `<asp:Label>` and an HTTP `<form>` element, both with their `runat` attributes set to `"server"`. This indicates that these items will be available to us as objects in our code behind file. To see how this works, let's examine that file, `TimeDotNetStyle.aspx.cs`, now:

```
public class TimeDotNetStyle : System.Web.UI.Page
{
    protected System.Web.UI.WebControls.Label time;

    private void Page_Load(object sender, System.EventArgs e)
    {
        //set the text property of our label control to the current time.
        time.Text = "The time at the server is: " +
                    System.DateTime.Now.ToString();
    }
}
```

Here we're defining a class to inherit from `System.Web.UI.Page`. Within that class we're declaring a variable called `time` of the type `System.Web.UI.WebControls.Label` that represents our `<asp:Label>` element from the Web Form. Then in the `Page_Load` event handler we're simply setting the `Text` property of our label to the value that we want to display. The output produced by `TimeDotNetStyle.aspx` is exactly the same as that produced by the former code, in `Time.aspx`.

The System.Web Namespace

Now that we've seen how to make a basic page, we'll delve into more detail about the many classes that the ASP.NET `System.Web` namespace makes available to developers. We'll be focusing primarily on classes that deal with communication between the client and the server.

The following classes are covered in the `System.Web` namespace. Those that are in bold are the classes in the `System.Web` namespace that are the most frequently used.

Class	Description
HttpApplication	An ASP.NET application is a collection of files, pages, executable pages, and so on, all stored within a virtual directory (and its sub-directories) on a single Web server. An ASP.NET Web server maintains a pool of `HttpApplication` objects for each ASP.NET application configured on the server. Once the server receives a request for an application, it will pick up an instance of `HttpApplication` object from that pool and assign it to process the incoming request. While this `HttpApplication` object is assigned to this request, it is exclusive to it and will remain actively so throughout the lifetime of this request. After the request is completed it is assigned back to the pool of objects for future reuse. Among its many properties, the object of this class is to provide you with access to important information stored in the `Request`, `Response` and `Session` objects for the current request. It is also responsible for initiating `Application_OnStart` and `Application_OnEnd` events.
HttpApplication State	The **HttpApplicationState** class objects are responsible for maintaining application-wide state for an ASP.NET application. An **HttpApplicationState** object is created when a client requests the very first resource from ASP.NET application and it will live as long as the application is active. It is therefore ideal for storing global information that should live beyond individual user sessions, requests or responses.

Class	Description
HttpBrowser Capabilities	**This class pulls the browser capability information from the HTTP request and makes this information accessible on the server. With the help of this class you can easily determine if the browser making a request for your Web Forms is capable of supporting ActiveX controls, Java Applets, JavaScript, cookies, frames, etc. You can also collect other information like browser type, version and operating system and much more.**
HttpCachePolicy	The HttpCachePolicy class allows you to have programmatic control over the Output caching mechanism of ASP.NET. HttpCachePolicy allows you to have control over the expiration of cache, dependency settings and caching parameters among other things.
HttpCacheVaryBy Headers	You can use the HttpCacheVaryByHeaders class to vary the cache output based on the list of HTTP Headers. The HttpCacheVaryByHeaders class provides a type safe way to set the HttpCachePolicy.VaryByHeaders property.
HttpCacheVaryBy Params	You can use the HttpCacheVaryByParams property to vary the cache output based on the list of parameters in a given GET or POST request. The HttpCacheVaryByparams class provides a type safe way to set the HttpCachePolicy.VaryByParams property.
HttpClient Certificate	An object of the HttpClientCertificate class will hold information about the digital certificate that the client uses to negotiate with the Web server. Using its properties like Issuer, IsValid and Certificate, among others, you can get all required information about the client certificate.
HttpCompile Exception	HttpCompileException derives from HttpException. It is thrown if there is a compiler error. You can use the properties of this class to find out more about the causes of the error.
HttpContext	**This class provides information about the current context in which the request is executing including error information or values contained within the request.**
HttpCookie	**This class allows the creation and manipulation of cookies sent to and from the client.**
HttpCookie Collection	This class provides access to a collection of cookies. An object of this type is available in both the HttpRequest and HttpResponse objects to allow access to the cookies sent with a request or to be sent with the response.
HttpException	This exception is thrown when an HTTP error occurs.
HttpFile Collection	This class provides a wrapper around a collection of posted files to make managing and working with those files as a group much easier.

Class	Description
HttpModule Collection	HttpModuleCollection is an assembly that can be created to respond to various ASP.NET or user generated events. HttpModuleCollection class is used to index and retrieve a collection of IHttpModules associated with a given ASP.NET application.
HttpParse Exception	This exception is thrown when a parse error occurs.
HttpPostedFile	**This class provides an object that represents a file posted to the server via an input tag on the browser and allows easy manipulation and saving of the file.**
HttpRequest	**This class encapsulates information and functionality surrounding the request made to the web server by the client including forms data, query strings, headers, and browser information. Essentially, it encompasses all information sent to the server in an object.**
HttpResponse	**This class encapsulates the outgoing stream from the server and allows for manipulation of the information being sent to the client including outgoing cookies, headers, HTML content, and caching information.**
HttpRuntime	**This class provides access to the Internet Information Services (IIS) run-time process and provides information on the host environment including file paths, application IDs and the ability to process a request and to close the runtime.**
HttpServer Utility	**This class encapsulates a great deal of the helper functions for working with web applications including the encoding and decoding of strings, mapping paths, executing other .aspx pages, and creating COM objects to be used in the page.**
HttpStatic Objects Collection	StaticObjects are the objects declared in the global.asax within the <object> tags with scope set to application. HttpStaticObjectsCollection provides a collection for such objects in the given ASP.NET application.
HttpUtility	HttpUtility class provides various utility methods for encoding and decoding URLs.
HttpWorker Request	HttpWorkerRequest is an abstract class that defines methods and enumerations used by ASP.NET runtime to process requests; you will only use this class when you need to implement your own hosting environment instead of using the one provided by ASP.NET.
HttpWriter	HttpWriter class can be use to send output to the clients. It is basically a TextWriter attached to an HttpResponse object.

Class	Description
ProcessInfo	ProcessInfo provides information on currently executing ASP.NET worker processes. You can get a ProcessInfo class for the currently executing ASP.NET application by using shared methods available in ProcessModelInfo class.
ProcessModelInfo	ProcessModelInfo provides two shared methods; ProcessModelInfo.GetCurrentProcessInfo and ProcessModelInfo.GetHistory. These return the ProcessInfo for the current ASP.NET worker processes.
TraceContext	The TraceContext class can be used to reveal the execution details of a Web request. This class provides two methods, warn and write that you can use for writing to the trace log. You can specify a tracing category to organize your statements.

HttpApplicationState Class

The HttpApplicationState class is responsible for maintaining application-wide state for an ASP.NET application. An HttpApplicationState object is created when a client requests the very first resource from an ASP.NET application and it exists as long as the application is active. Consequently, the application state is a good place to store the information that should live beyond individual user sessions, requests or responses. However, while this class is a natural area for global variables, these would not be shared across either a web farm or a web garden.

An HttpApplicationState object stores the state of an application in the form of a name-object pair inside a collection and provides methods to manipulate this collection. This class derives from the more general System.Collections.Specialized.NameObjectCollectionBase class (a MustInherit class), which defines some base functionality for Name-Object collection objects.

HttpApplicationState Public Methods

❑ **Add**

❑ **Clear**

❑ Equals – inherited from System.Object, see Introduction for more details

❑ **Get**

❑ **GetEnumerator**

❑ GetHashCode – inherited from System.Object, see Introduction for more details

❑ **GetKey**

❑ **GetObjectData**

❑ GetType – inherited from System.Object, see Introduction for more details

❑ **Lock**

❑ **OnDeserialization**

❑ **Remove**

- ❑ **RemoveAll**
- ❑ **RemoveAt**
- ❑ **Set**
- ❑ `ToString` – inherits from `System.Object`, see Introduction for more details
- ❑ **UnLock**

Add

The `Add` method is used to insert items into the `HttpApplicationState` collection. It takes an object as a parameter for the value, and since all items in .NET are derived from `Object`, you can, potentially, store anything in application state. However, you should seriously consider those items that you are storing and the cost of saving and retrieving that information. This will depend on the object size you have chosen for your site. Large items can degrade performance as the user load increases.

```
public void Add(string name, object value);
```

The parameter `name` specifies the key name of the item you wish to add to the collection. The parameter `value` specifies the value of the object you wish to add to the application state.

Clear

The `Clear` method can be used to remove all of the items that are currently stored in `HttpApplicationState` collection.

```
public void Clear();
```

Get

The `Get` method is used to get the object from the `HttpApplicationState` collection either by key name or the index value. This method is overloaded and exists in two versions.

```
public object Get(int index);
```

The `index` parameter represents the index number of the object that needs to be fetched. It is a zero-based index.

```
public object Get(string key);
```

The `key` parameter represents the key name of the object that needs to be fetched.

GetEnumerator

The `GetEnumerator` method allows for reading through a collection, by returning an enumerator, which will iterate through the `NameObjectCollectionBase`. This method is derived from `System.Collections.Specialized.NameObjectCollectionBase`. The enumerator cannot be used to make any changes to the collection and serves to return the keys of the collections, in string form, only. To move between keys, you will need to call `IEnumerator.MoveNext`.

```
public IEnumerator GetEnumerator();
```

GetKey

The GetKey method allows for accessing the key name of the object stored in the collection by specifying the index. This method returns the name of the object by which it was stored.

```
public string GetKey(int index);
```

The parameter index specifies the index of the object in the collection.

GetObjectData

The GetObjectData method implements the ISerializable interface and is derived from System.Collections.Specialized.NameObjectCollectionBase. It returns the data needed to serialize the HttpApplicationState. Serialization reduces an object into a more easily managed and transportable form that still bears a strong correlation to the original object.

```
public virtual void GetObjectData(SerializationInfo info,
                                  StreamingContext context);
```

The info parameter specifies the information needed to serialize an object. The context parameter refers to the source and destination of the serialized stream for this object's instance.

Lock

The Lock method applies a block on the HttpApplicationState collection. This is very helpful when you are trying to perform updates to this collection and don't want other pages to modify the application state concurrently. It's always a good practice to call this method when the application state data is modifiable by pages. However when other pages try to access the collection when this method is called they will have to wait till this lock is released using the UnLock method explained later in this section. Locking may extend application response time at the cost of data integrity so the combination of Lock and UnLock should be used judiciously to Lock as late as possible and UnLock as early as possible.

```
public void Lock();
```

OnDeserialization

The OnDeserialization method implements the System.Runtime.Serialization.ISerializable interface and is derived from System.Collections.Specialized.NameObjectCollectionBase. It raises the deserialization event when deserialization is complete.

```
public virtual void OnDeserialization(object sender);
```

The sender parameter specifies the source object of the deserialization event.

Remove

The `Remove` method allows for taking a single object out of the collection. The method is called with the key name of the object, which was created at the time of adding the object.

```
public void Remove(string name);
```

The `name` parameter specifies the name of the object that is to be removed.

RemoveAll

The `RemoveAll` method removes all the objects from the `HttpApplicationState` collection. This method makes an internal call to the `Clear` method.

```
public void RemoveAll();
```

RemoveAt

The `RemoveAt` method removes a single object out of the application state by specifying its index position.

```
public void RemoveAt(int index);
```

The `index` parameter represents the index number of the object that needs to be removed. It is a zero-based index.

Set

The `Set` method allows for updating an object that is already present in the application state.

```
public void Set(string name, object value);
```

The `name` parameter specifies the key name of the object that needs to be updated. The `value` parameter represents the new updated object.

UnLock

The `UnLock` method is used to release the lock previously applied by the `Lock` method to the `HttpApplicationState` object. Whenever `Lock` is applied, the application state object is not accessible by the other pages or objects. Therefore once the updating is done, the lock should be released using the `UnLock` method.

```
public void UnLock();
```

HttpApplicationState Protected Methods

❑ **BaseAdd**

❑ **BaseClear**

❑ **BaseGet**

❑ **BaseGetAllKeys**

- ❑ **BaseGetAllValues**
- ❑ **BaseGetKey**
- ❑ **BaseHasKeys**
- ❑ **BaseRemove**
- ❑ **BaseRemoveAt**
- ❑ **BaseSet**
- ❑ `Finalize` – inherited from `System.Object`, see Introduction for more details
- ❑ `MemberwiseClone` – inherited from `System.Object`, see Introduction for more details

BaseAdd

The `BaseAdd` method is derived from the
`System.Collections.Specialized.NameObjectCollectionBase` class. The `BaseAdd`
method is used to insert items into the collection object. It throws a `NotSupportedException` if the
collection is read-only.

```
protected void BaseAdd(string name, object value)
```

The `name` parameter specifies the key name of the item you wish to add to the collection. The `value`
parameter specifies the object that needs to be added.

BaseClear

The `BaseClear` method is derived from the
`System.Collections.Specialized.NameObjectCollectionBase` class. The `BaseClear`
method can be used to remove all of the items that are currently stored in the collection object. It throws
a `NotSupportedException` if the collection is read-only.

```
protected void BaseClear();
```

BaseGet

The `BaseGet` method is derived from the
`System.Collections.Specialized.NameObjectCollectionBase` class. The `BaseGet`
method is used to get the object from the `collection` either by key name or the index value. It is an
overloaded method.

```
protected object BaseGet(int index);
```

The `index` parameter represents the index number of the object that needs to be fetched. It is a zero-
based index.

```
protected object BaseGet(string key);
```

The `key` parameter represents the key name of the object that needs to be fetched.

BaseGetAllKeys

The `BaseGetAllKeys` method is derived from the
`System.Collections.Specialized.NameObjectCollectionBase` class. The
`BaseGetAllKeys` method is used to get all the key names from the collection in an array of strings.

```
protected string[] BaseGetAllKeys();
```

BaseGetAllValues

The `BaseGetAllValues` method is derived from the
`System.Collections.Specialized.NameObjectCollectionBase` class. The
`BaseGetAllValues` method is used to get all the values from the collection in an array. This method
is overloaded and has two versions:

```
protected object[] BaseGetAllValues();
protected object[] BaseGetAllValues(Type type);
```

The `type` parameter represents the type of the array to be returned. If the type passed is not a valid
`System.Type` object then an `ArgumentException` is thrown, or if it is passed as `null` then an
`ArgumentNullException` is thrown.

BaseGetKey

The `BaseGetKey` method is derived from the
`System.Collections.Specialized.NameObjectCollectionBase` class. The `BaseGetKey`
method allows for accessing the key name of the object stored in the collection by specifying the index.
This method returns the name of the object by which it was stored.

```
protected string BaseGetKey(int index);
```

The `index` parameter specifies the index of the object in the collection.

BaseHasKeys

The `BaseHasKeys` method is derived from the
`System.Collections.Specialized.NameObjectCollectionBase` class. The `BaseHasKeys`
method returns a `Boolean` value where `false` represents that the collection has keys that refer to
`null`.

```
protected bool BaseHasKeys();
```

BaseRemove

The `BaseRemove` method is derived from the
`System.Collections.Specialized.NameObjectCollectionBase` class. The `BaseRemove`
method allows for taking specified objects out of the collection. This method is called with the key name
of the object, which was created at the time of adding the object. It throws a
`NotSupportedException` when the collection is read-only or the collection has fixed size.

```
protected void BaseRemove(string name)
```

The name parameter specifies the name of the object that is to be removed.

BaseRemoveAt

The BaseRemoveAt method is derived from the
System.Collections.Specialized.NameObjectCollectionBase class. The
BaseRemoveAt method removes a single object out of the collection by specifying its index position. It
throws a NotSupportedException when the collection is read-only or the collection has fixed size. It
also throws an ArgumentOutOfRangeException if the index is outside the possible valid range
of indexes.

```
protected void BaseRemoveAt(int index)
```

The index parameter represents the index number of the object that needs to be removed. It is a zero-
based index.

BaseSet

The BaseSet method is derived from the
System.Collections.Specialized.NameObjectCollectionBase class. The BaseSet
method allows for updating an object that is already present in the collection. This method has two
overloaded versions.

```
protected void BaseSet(int index, object value);
```

In the method illustrated above, the index parameter represents the index number of the object that
needs to be updated. It is a zero-based index. The value parameter represents the new updated object.
The method below has the name parameter specifying the key name of the object that needs to be
updated. The value parameter represents the new updated object.

```
protected void BaseSet(string name, object value);
```

It throws a NotSupportedException when the collection is read-only and an
ArgumentOutOfRangeException if the index is outside the possible valid range of indexes.

HttpApplicationState Public Properties

All the properties of the application state are read-only.

- ❑ **AllKeys**
- ❑ **Contents**
- ❑ **Count**
- ❑ **Item**
- ❑ **Keys**
- ❑ **StaticObjects**

AllKeys

The `AllKeys` property gets all the key names available in the application state collection. A string array is returned with each item containing the key name of an object.

```
public string[] AllKeys {get;}
```

Contents

The `Contents` property just gets a reference to the `HttpApplicationState` object.

```
public HttpApplicationState Contents {get;}
```

> This property is available for backward compatibility with the earlier versions of ASP. Traditionally, this property was implemented as a collection of the **Application** object that allowed access to the contents of **Application** with a collection interface.

Count

The `Count` property gets the number of objects in the application state. The default value is 0. This property is overridden.

```
public override int Count {get;}
```

Item

The `Item` property indicates a specific object in the application state collection. This method has two overloaded versions to allow for accessing the object by name or numeric index.

```
public object this[int] {get;}
```

The `index` parameter represents the index number of the object that needs to be fetched. It is a zero-based index.

```
public object this[string] {get; set;}
```

The `key` parameter represents the key name of the object that needs to be retrieved.

Keys

The `Keys` property is derived from the `System.Collections.Specialized.NameObjectCollectionBase` class. The `Keys` property gets all the key names available in the collection. A `System.Collections.Specialized.NameObjectCollectionBase.KeysCollection` object is returned containing keys of the collection.

```
public virtual NameObjectCollectionBase.KeysCollection Keys {get;}
```

StaticObjects

The `StaticObjects` property provides access to items that were declared in the `Global.asax` file using the following syntax:

```
<object scope="Application" runat="server">
```

This property returns a special collection class that acts as a wrapper around these objects.

```
public HttpStaticObjectsCollection StaticObjects {get;}
```

HttpApplicationState Protected Properties

❑ `IsReadOnly`

IsReadOnly

The `IsReadOnly` property is derived from the `System.Collections.Specialized.NameObjectCollectionBase` class. It gets or sets a `Boolean` value indicating whether the collection is read-only or not. A value of `true` means the collection is read-only.

```
protected bool IsReadOnly {get; set;}
```

HttpBrowserCapabilities Class

Knowing the client's browser and the environment in which your pages are being viewed is very helpful in tailoring your pages to them. For example, using different stylesheets and tags for different situations gives a great deal of useful flexibility. You could make a decision about whether to use ActiveX or a Java Applet to perform some functionality based on your knowledge of what the client supports.

It is the means to make these decisions that the `HttpBrowserCapabilities` class provides. It derives from the more general `System.Web.Configuration.HttpCapabilitiesBase` class, which provides some base functionality for reading capabilities information from configuration files. This is based on the User-Agent header and server variables collection for the given request. The machine wide configuration file, `machine.config`, contains the mappings of a User-Agent string (discussed with the `HttpRequest` class) to the capabilities of a browser. Keep in mind that these capabilities only indicate what a client is capable of, not what it will actually support. For example, a user may turn off cookie support in their browser, but because the browser can support cookies in general, the `HttpBrowserCapabilities` class will indicate that the client supports cookies.

As it helps us to know the capabilities of the client's browser, this class can be accessed through the browser property of the intrinsic request object.

HttpBrowserCapablilities Public Methods

❑ `Equals` – inherited from `System.Object`, see Introduction for more details

❑ `GetHashCode` – inherited from `System.Object`, see Introduction for more details

- ❑ GetType – inherited from System.Object, see Introduction for more details
- ❑ ToString – inherited from System.Object, see Introduction for more details

HttpBrowserCapabilities Protected Methods

- ❑ Finalize – inherited from System.Object, see Introduction for more details
- ❑ MemberwiseClone – inherited from System.Object, see Introduction for more details

HttpBrowserCapabilities Public Properties

The majority of the properties of the HttpBrowserCapabilities class are Boolean values indicating if a particular technology is supported or not. If a value cannot be determined on the client requesting a resource, then the default value of false is returned. Since these properties return the capabilities of a client's browser, these are all read-only properties.

- ❑ **ActiveXControls**
- ❑ **AOL**
- ❑ **BackgroundSounds**
- ❑ **Beta**
- ❑ **Browser**
- ❑ **CDF**
- ❑ **ClrVersion**
- ❑ **Cookies**
- ❑ **Crawler**
- ❑ **EcmaScriptVersion**
- ❑ **Frames**
- ❑ **Item**
- ❑ **JavaApplets**
- ❑ **JavaScript**
- ❑ **MajorVersion**
- ❑ **MinorVersion**
- ❑ **MSDomVersion**
- ❑ **Platform**
- ❑ **Tables**
- ❑ **Type**
- ❑ **VBScript**
- ❑ **Version**

❑   **`W3CDomVersion`**

❑   **`Win16`**

❑   **`Win32`**

ActiveXControls

The `ActiveXControls` property indicates if the browser supports ActiveX controls. It is a read only property and returns a `Boolean` value. This value is `false` by default.

```
public bool ActiveXControls {get;}
```

AOL

The `AOL` property indicates whether the browser is an America Online browser. This property can be used to determine if the client is using an AOL browser and then target special features of that AOL client, or to suppress content that is not appropriate for an AOL browser. It is a read-only property and returns a `Boolean` value. The default value for this property is `false`.

```
public bool AOL {get;}
```

BackgroundSounds

The `BackgroundSounds` property indicates whether the browser supports background sounds, which are embedded links to sound files that play while the page is being displayed, without any user interaction to start them. It is a read-only property and returns a `Boolean` value. The default value for this property is `false`.

```
public bool BackgroundSounds {get;}
```

Beta

The `Beta` property indicates whether the browser is a beta version as indicated in the HTTP headers sent to the server. It is a read only property and returns a `Boolean` value. The default value for this property is `false`.

```
public bool Beta {get;}
```

Browser

The `Browser` property indicates the name of the client browser as sent to the server in the user-agent HTTP header. It is a read-only property and returns a `String` value. If you want to get a string value representing the browser and the version, use the `Type` property.

```
public string Browser {get;}
```

CDF

The CDF property indicates whether the browser supports the Channel Definition Format (CDF), which is an implementation of XML that allows for providing software channels such as those found in the Internet Explorer browser. It is a read-only property and returns a `Boolean` value. The default value for this property is `false`.

```
public bool CDF {get;}
```

ClrVersion

The `ClrVersion` property indicates the version number of the Common Language Runtime (CLR) on the client machine. Currently, this property will not be widely used, as most clients will not have the CLR installed on their computers. In the future, it will prove useful to target code to the client based on their version of the CLR. This property is only supported in browsers that are IE 5.0 or higher.

```
public Version ClrVersion {get;}
```

It is a read-only property and returns a `Version` object. The `Version` object represents the version as `MajorVersion.MinorVersion[.build[.revision]]`, where the `build` and `revision` versions are optional. If the CLR is not installed in the client's machine, the property returns `0.0.-1.-1`.

Cookies

The `Cookies` property indicates whether the client browser can support cookies. It is a read-only property and returns a `Boolean` value. This property will not tell you if the Cookies option has been turned off on the client browser. The default value for this property is `false`.

```
public bool Cookies {get;}
```

Crawler

The `Crawler` property indicates whether the client requesting the page is a search engine crawler or an Internet browser. It is a read-only property and returns a `Boolean` value. A value of `true` indicates that the client is a search engine crawler. The default value for this property is `false`.

```
public bool Crawler {get;}
```

EcmaScriptVersion

The `EcmaScriptVersion` property indicates the version of European Computer Manufacturer's Association (ECMA) script supported by the client. ECMA script is more commonly referred to as JavaScript. This property can be used in conjunction with the `JavaScript` property that determines if the browser supports JavaScript. For more information about ECMA, see their official web site at http://www.ecma.ch.

```
public Version EcmaScriptVersion {get;}
```

It is a read-only property and returns a `Version` object. The `Version` object represents the version as `MajorVersion.MinorVersion[.build[.revision]]`, where the `build` and `revision` versions are optional.

Frames

The `Frames` property indicates whether the client browser supports HTML frames. It is a read-only property and returns a `Boolean` object. The default value for this property is `false`.

```
public bool Frames {get;}
```

Item

The `Item` property gets the value of a specified property of the `HttpBrowserCapabilities` class, passed as a parameter.

```
public virtual string this[string key] {get;}
```

The `key` parameter specifies the name of the property in this class to be retrieved.

The following code displays the `EcmaScriptVersion` through the `Item` property:

```
sbText.AppendFormat("ECMA Script Version via Item property: {0}" ,
                    Request.Browser["EcmaScriptVersion"]);
```

JavaApplets

The `JavaApplets` property indicates whether the browser supports Java Applets. It is a read-only property and returns a `Boolean` object. The default value for this property is `false`.

```
public bool JavaApplets {get;}
```

JavaScript

The `JavaScript` property indicates whether the browser supports JavaScript. It is a read-only property and returns a `Boolean` object. The default value for this property is `false`. This property can be used in conjunction with the `EcmaScriptVersion` property, which provides the version number of supported scripting.

```
public bool JavaScript {get;}
```

MajorVersion

The `MajorVersion` property indicates the major version of the browser as sent to the server by the browser. A browser with a version number of 4.7, for instance, has a major version of 4. It is a read-only property and returns an `Integer` value.

```
public int MajorVersion {get;}
```

MinorVersion

The `MinorVersion` property indicates the minor, or decimal, version number of the client browser based on information passed from the browser to the server in the request. Therefore, a browser with a version number of 4.7, for instance, has a minor version of 0.7. It is a read-only property and returns a `Double` value.

```
public double MinorVersion {get;}
```

MSDomVersion

The `MSDomVersion` property returns the version of the Microsoft HTML Document Object Model (DOM) present on the client. Use this property to determine the level of HTML functionality supported on the client side. It is a read-only property and returns a `Version` object. The `Version` object represents the version as `MajorVersion.MinorVersion[.build[.revision]]`, where the `build` and `revision` versions are optional. For non-Microsoft browsers, this property will return an `MSDomVersion` of 0.0

```
public Version MSDomVersion {get;}
```

Platform

The `Platform` property indicates the operating system platform that the client is using as sent to the browser in the HTTP request. This is useful for managing stylesheets, as, for example, the Macintosh renders pages slightly differently from Windows machines.

```
public string Platform {get;}
```

This property is read-only and returns a `String` value. Possible return values are: `Unknown`, `Win16`, `Win95`, `Win98`, `WinNT` (this includes `Windows 2000` and `Windows XP`), `WinCE`, `Mac68K`, `MacPPC`, `UNIX`, and `WebTV`.

Tables

The `Tables` property indicates whether the client's browser supports HTML tables. The default value for this property is `false`.

```
public bool Tables {get;}
```

Type

The `Type` property indicates the browser name and major version number for the client browser. For example, if the client is using Internet Explorer 6, the `Type` property returns `IE6`. This property is different from the `Browser` property, which only represents the browser and not the version. It is a read-only property and returns a `String` value.

```
public string Type {get;}
```

VBScript

The VBScript property indicates whether the client supports VBScript in the browser. It is a read-only property and returns a Boolean value where true indicates that the browser supports VBScript. The default value for this property is false.

```
public bool VBScript {get;}
```

Version

The Version property indicates the version of the client browser including the major and minor numbers. It is a read-only property and returns a string representation of the browser's version.

```
public string Version {get;}
```

W3CDomVersion

The W3CDomVersion property indicates the version of the W3C XML Document Object Model (DOM) that is supported on the client. This property can be useful in determining whether or not to use certain XML elements. It is a read-only property returning a Version object. The Version object represents the version as MajorVersion.MinorVersion[.build[.revision]], where the build and revision versions are optional.

```
public Version W3CDomVersion {get;}
```

Win16

The Win16 property indicates whether the client is running on a 16-bit Windows platform. The default value for this property is false.

```
public bool Win16 {get;}
```

Win32

The Win32 property indicates whether the client is running on a 32-bit Windows platform. The default value for this property is false.

```
public bool Win32 {get;}
```

Example: Using the HttpBrowserCapabilities Class

The following code snippet shows the usage of all of the properties of the HttpBrowserCapabilities class, available in HttpBrowserCapabilitiesUsage.aspx:

```
using System;
using System.Collections;
using System.ComponentModel;
using System.Data;
using System.Drawing;
using System.Web;
using System.Web.SessionState;
```

```csharp
using System.Web.UI;
using System.Web.UI.WebControls;
using System.Web.UI.HtmlControls;
using System.Text;

namespace WebUsageCs
{
  /// <summary>
  /// Summary description for HttpBrowserCapabilitiesUsage.
  /// </summary>
  public class HttpBrowserCapabilitiesUsage : System.Web.UI.Page
  {
    protected System.Web.UI.WebControls.LinkButton LBtnBrowser;
    protected System.Web.UI.WebControls.Label LblBrowser;
    private void Page_Load(object sender, System.EventArgs e)
    {
      // Put user code to initialize the page here
    }

    #region Web Form Designer generated code
    ...

    private void LBtnBrowser_Click(object sender, System.EventArgs e)
    {
      StringBuilder sbText = new StringBuilder();

      // Get the reference to the HttpBrowserCapabilities object
      HttpBrowserCapabilities myBrowser;
      myBrowser = Request.Browser;

      // Display all the properties of the HttpBrowserCapabilities Class
      sbText.AppendFormat("ActiveX Controls Support: {0}" ,
                          myBrowser.ActiveXControls);
      sbText.Append("<br>");
      sbText.AppendFormat("AOL Client: {0}", myBrowser.AOL);
      sbText.Append("<br>");
      sbText.AppendFormat("Background Sounds Support: {0}" ,
                          myBrowser.BackgroundSounds);
      sbText.Append("<br>");
      sbText.AppendFormat("Beta Release: {0}" , myBrowser.Beta);
      sbText.Append("<br>");
      sbText.AppendFormat("Browser String: {0}" , myBrowser.Browser);
      sbText.Append("<br>");
      sbText.AppendFormat("Channel Definition Format(CDF); Support: {0}" ,
                          myBrowser.CDF);
      sbText.Append("<br>");
      sbText.AppendFormat(".NET CLR Version: {0}" , myBrowser.ClrVersion);
      sbText.Append("<br>");
      sbText.AppendFormat("Cookies Support: {0}" , myBrowser.Cookies);
      sbText.Append("<br>");
      sbText.AppendFormat("Crawler Search Engine: {0}" ,
                          myBrowser.Crawler);
      sbText.Append("<br>");
```

```
            sbText.AppendFormat("ECMA Script Version: {0}" ,
                          myBrowser.EcmaScriptVersion);
            sbText.Append("<br>");
            sbText.AppendFormat("Frames Support: {0}" , myBrowser.Frames);
            sbText.Append("<br>");
            sbText.AppendFormat("ECMA Script Version via Item property: {0}" ,
                          myBrowser["EcmaScriptVersion"]);
            sbText.Append("<br>");
            sbText.AppendFormat("Java Applet Support: {0}" ,
                          myBrowser.JavaApplets);
            sbText.Append("<br>");
            sbText.AppendFormat("JavaScript Support: {0}" ,
                          myBrowser.JavaScript);
            sbText.Append("<br>");
            sbText.AppendFormat("Browser Major Version: {0}",
                          myBrowser.MajorVersion);
            sbText.Append("<br>");
            sbText.AppendFormat("Browser Minor Version: {0}",
                          myBrowser.MinorVersion);
            sbText.Append("<br>");
            sbText.AppendFormat("Microsoft HTML Document Object Model " +
                          "Version: {0}", myBrowser.MSDomVersion);
            sbText.Append("<br>");
            sbText.AppendFormat("Client's Platform: {0}", myBrowser.Platform);
            sbText.Append("<br>");
            sbText.AppendFormat("HTML Tables Support: {0}", myBrowser.Tables);
            sbText.Append("<br>");
            sbText.AppendFormat("Browser Type - Name and Major Version: {0}",
                          myBrowser.Type);
            sbText.Append("<br>");
            sbText.AppendFormat("VBScript support: {0}", myBrowser.VBScript);
            sbText.Append("<br>");
            sbText.AppendFormat("Browser Full Version: {0}", myBrowser.Version);
            sbText.Append("<br>");
            sbText.AppendFormat("World Wide Web (W3C) XML Document Object " +
                          "Model Version: {0}", myBrowser.W3CDomVersion);
            sbText.Append("<br>");
            sbText.AppendFormat("Win16 Computer: {0}", myBrowser.Win16);
            sbText.Append("<br>");
            sbText.AppendFormat("Win32 Computer: {0}", myBrowser.Win32);
            sbText.Append("<br>");

        LblBrowser.Text=sbText.ToString();
    }
  }
}
```

The following screenshot displays the browser capabilities in an IE6 browser:

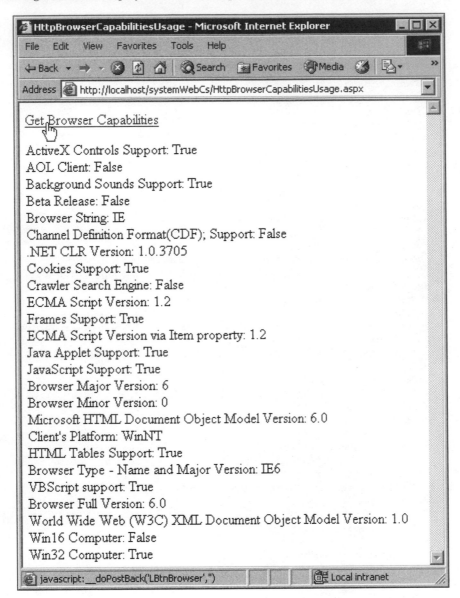

To demonstrate the differences when an alternative browser accesses a page, the screenshot below displays the browser capabilities in a Netscape 7.0 browser:

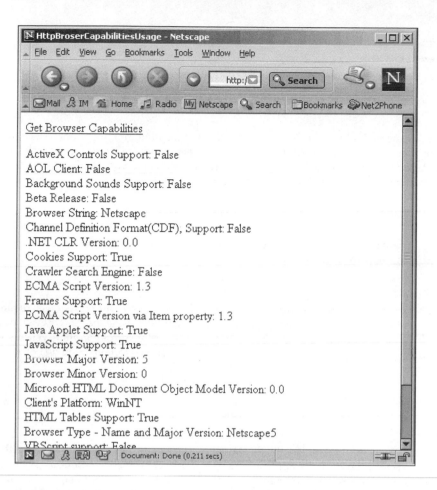

HttpContext Class

To process an HTTP Request, an ASP.NET application needs to know a considerable amount about the particular context of a request, such as the security level of the user or the configuration settings of the browser. The HttpContext class can provide all of the information about the context in which a given web request is executing.

HttpContext Public Methods

- ❏ **AddError**

- ❏ **ClearError**

- ❏ Equals – inherited from System.Object, see Introduction for more details

- ❏ **GetAppConfig**

- ❏ **GetConfig**

- ❏ GetHashCode – inherited from System.Object, see Introduction for more details

- ❑   GetType – inherited from System.Object, see Introduction for more details
- ❑   **RewritePath**
- ❑   ToString – inherited from System.Object, see Introduction for more details

AddError

The AddError method allows the developer to insert an exception into the errors collection, which can be useful if you want to make your error information more generally available. For example, if you create a user control, you may want to record exceptions that occur in your control to the error collection of the context so that other objects in the page can be aware of, and get information about, the error.

```
public void AddError(Exception error);
```

The error parameter here specifies the Exception object that contains information about the error you want to add to the collection.

ClearError

The ClearError method clears **all** errors from the errors collection of the current web request. This is especially important when you are providing custom error handling using the Error event of the page object. See ErrorPage in Chapter 2 for more information on custom error handling. When you deal with errors that arise in the context of a web request, you must clear this collection if you do not also want the ASP.NET runtime to catch and report those errors.

```
public void ClearError();
```

GetAppConfig

The GetAppConfig method allows the developer to retrieve the configuration information applicable to the current application from the application's web.config file. This method is static and the object that this returns depends on the configuration section accessed. See Chapter 7 for more information on configuration files and managing configuration information in ASP.NET.

```
public static object GetAppConfig(string key);
```

The key parameter here specifies the name of the configuration section you wish to retrieve.

GetConfig

The GetConfig method allows the developer to retrieve configuration information for the current web request. The type of object returned by this method depends on the configuration section accessed. See Chapter 7 for information on configuration files and managing configuration information in ASP.NET.

```
public object GetConfig(string key);
```

The key parameter here specifies the name of the configuration section you wish to retrieve.

RewritePath

The `RewritePath` method allows you to specify a rewrite path. This can be used to programmatically redirect the user to an alternative page. An example of the use for this could be, if you wished to personalize the page that a user is accessing; you would not wish to rewrite the page each time a user requests it so you could use the `RewritePath` property to point the request at a generic page. This page could then utilize user name information sent in the request to customize the page accessed via the `RewritePath`.

```
public void RewritePath(string path);
```

The `path` parameter here represents the path that is to be set as the rewrite path.

HttpContext Protected Methods

- ❑ `Finalize` – inherited from `System.Object`, see Introduction for more details
- ❑ `MemberwiseClone` – inherited from `System.Object`, see Introduction for more details

HttpContext Public Properties

- ❑ **AllErrors**
- ❑ **Application**
- ❑ **ApplicationInstance**
- ❑ **Cache**
- ❑ **Current**
- ❑ **Error**
- ❑ **Handler**
- ❑ **IsCustomErrorEnabled**
- ❑ **IsDebuggingEnabled**
- ❑ **Items**
- ❑ **Request**
- ❑ **Response**
- ❑ **Server**
- ❑ **Session**
- ❑ **SkipAuthorization**
- ❑ **Timestamp**
- ❑ **Trace**
- ❑ **User**

AllErrors

The `AllErrors` property returns an array of the exceptions (`System.Exception` object) that have been thrown in the processing of the current request. This property is a convenient way to collect, and act on, all of the errors that occurred during processing, either by logging them, or presenting them to the user. It is a read–only property. It returns `null` if there were no errors generated while processing the request.

```
public Exception[] AllErrors {get;}
```

Application

The `Application` property gets a reference to the `HttpApplicationState` object for the current request, which can be used to store values across sessions and requests. It is a read-only property but allows the underlying `HttpApplicationState` object to be modified.

```
public HttpApplicationState Application {get;}
```

ApplicationInstance

The `ApplicationInstance` property provides a reference to the `HttpApplication` object. This property can be used to retrieve or assign an application object for the current HTTP request. The `HttpApplication` class is the base class for applications defined and contains properties, methods and events common to all the objects in the application in the `Global.asax` file.

```
public HttpApplication ApplicationInstance {get; set;}
```

Cache

The `Cache` property accesses the `Cache` object for the current HTTP Request, allowing the developer to insert and retrieve items to the cache. This built-in `Cache` object can be extremely useful in caching data or other information that is expensive to retrieve and does not change often. It is a read-only property and returns a reference to the `System.Web.Caching.Cache` object for the current HTTP request. See Chapter 6 for detailed explanation on Caching.

```
public Cache Cache {get;}
```

Current

This shared property provides a reference to the current context (`HttpContext`) object in which the request is executing. This can be useful if you want to access the methods and properties of the context as this provides you with a reference.

```
public static HttpContext Current {get;}
```

This method can be used in the multi-tier architecture by the business layer or the database layer (`.dll`) files that need to get a reference to the current context to invoke its methods or call its properties.

Error

The Error property provides access to the first error encountered during the processing of the request. If you are just looking for the first error, perhaps to indicate the cause of further errors, then this property will give you access to that information. It is a read-only property and returns a System.Exception object.

```
public Exception Error {get;}
```

Handler

The Handler property gets or sets the IHttpHandler object (that is a Page object) for the current request. This gives a reference to the Page object in the case of web pages. Other classes that implement IHttpHandler include HttpApplication and HttpRemotingHandler.

```
public IHttpHandler Handler{get; set;}
```

IsCustomErrorEnabled

IsCustomErrorEnabled provides a Boolean value representing whether custom errors are enabled or not for the current web request. It is a read-only property and returns true if the custom errors are enabled for the HTTP request, and false otherwise.

```
public bool IsCustomErrorEnabled {get;}
```

IsDebuggingEnabled

IsDebuggingEnabled provides a Boolean value representing whether debugging is enabled or not for the current web request. It is a read-only property and returns true if the HTTP request is in debug mode and false otherwise.

```
public bool IsDebuggingEnabled {get;}
```

Items

The Items property returns an IDictionary based key-value collection that in a web request can be used to maintain and share data between an IHttpHandler based object and IHttpModule based object.

```
public IDictionary Items {get;}
```

Request

The Request property gets access to the HttpRequest object for the current web request. This property can then be accessed to call all the methods and properties of the HttpRequest class. See the HttpRequest class reference in this chapter for detailed information.

```
public HttpRequest Request {get;}
```

Response

The Response property gets access to the HttpResponse object for the current web request. This property then can be accessed to call all the methods and properties of the HttpResponse class. See HttpResponse class reference in this chapter for detailed information.

```
public HttpResponse Response {get;}
```

Server

The `Server` property gets access to the `HttpServerUtility` object for the current web request. This property then can be accessed to call all the methods and properties of the `HttpServerUtility` class. See `HttpServerUtility` class reference in this chapter for detailed information.

```
public HttpServerUtility Server {get;}
```

Session

The `Session` property gets access to the `HttpSessionState` object for the current web request. This property then can be accessed to call all the methods and properties of the `HttpSessionState` class. See `HttpSessionState` class reference in this chapter for detailed information.

```
public HttpSessionState Session {get;}
```

SkipAuthorization

The `SkipAuthorization` property allows the developer to indicate that a given request should skip the authorization process and execute without checking the user's credentials. This property is for use in advanced security schemes where there is a need to allow a user access to a page with universal access. The `Forms` authentication process uses this to allow a user access to a specified login page before being authenticated. It sets a `Boolean` value of `false` as default, which will not skip the authorization process.

```
public bool SkipAuthorization {get; set;}
```

Timestamp

The `Timestamp` property retrieves the date and time of when the current HTTP web request was initiated.

```
public DateTime Timestamp {get;}
```

Trace

The `Trace` property allows the developer to retrieve the `TraceContext` object for the current HTTP web request. This property can be used to write values into `TraceContext` object, which is useful for debugging.

```
public TraceContext Trace {get;}
```

User

The `User` property indicates the `IPrincipal` object under which the current request is executing. Using this object you can get information about the user making the request and use this information to get or set the security information. For more information on Security settings, see Chapter 8.

```
public IPrincipal User {get; set;}
```

Example: The Properties of the HttpContext Class

The following code, from `HttpContextUsage.aspx`, shows the usage of all the properties of the `HttpContext` class:

```
using System;
using System.Collections;
using System.ComponentModel;
using System.Data;
using System.Drawing;
using System.Web;
using System.Web.SessionState;
using System.Web.UI;
using System.Web.UI.WebControls;
using System.Web.UI.HtmlControls;
using System.Text;

namespace WebUsageCs
{
  /// <summary>
  /// Summary description for HttpContextUsage.
  /// </summary>
  public class HttpContextUsage : System.Web.UI.Page
  {
    protected System.Web.UI.WebControls.LinkButton LBtnContext;
    protected System.Web.UI.WebControls.Label LblContext;

    private void Page_Load(object sender, System.EventArgs e)
    {
      // Put user code to initialize the page here
    }

    #region Web Form Designer generated code
    ...

    private void LBtnContext_Click(object sender, System.EventArgs e)
    {
      StringBuilder sbText = new StringBuilder();

      sbText.Append("All Errors:");
      sbText.Append("<br>");

      Exception[] aException;
      aException = Context.AllErrors;
      if(aException != null)
      {
        //Exception myException;
        foreach(Exception myException in aException)
        {
          sbText.AppendFormat("Exception: {0}" , myException.Message);
          sbText.Append("<br>");
        }
```

```
    }

    sbText.AppendFormat("Application Items Count: {0}" ,
                        Context.Application.Count);
    sbText.Append("<br>");

    sbText.AppendFormat("Application Instance: {0}" ,
                        Context.ApplicationInstance);
    sbText.Append("<br>");

    sbText.AppendFormat("Number of Items in the Cache: {0}" ,
                        Context.Cache.Count);
    sbText.Append("<br>");

    sbText.AppendFormat("Current Context's Timestamp: {0}" ,
                        HttpContext.Current.Timestamp);
    sbText.Append("<br>");

    sbText.AppendFormat("First Error: {0}" , Context.Error);
    sbText.Append("<br>");

    sbText.AppendFormat("Get the Page Postback value via the Handler " +
                "property: {0}" , ((Page)Context.Handler).IsPostBack);
    sbText.Append("<br>");

    sbText.AppendFormat("Is Custom Error Enabled: {0}" ,
                        Context.IsCustomErrorEnabled);
    sbText.Append("<br>");

    sbText.AppendFormat("Is Debugging Enabled: {0}" ,
                        Context.IsDebuggingEnabled);
    sbText.Append("<br>");

    sbText.AppendFormat("Context Items Count: {0}" ,
                        Context.Items.Count);
    sbText.Append("<br>");

    sbText.AppendFormat("Request Content Type: {0}" ,
                        Context.Request.ContentType);
    sbText.Append("<br>");

    sbText.AppendFormat("Response Content Type: {0}" ,
                        Context.Response.ContentType);
    sbText.Append("<br>");

    sbText.AppendFormat("Server TimeOut: {0}" ,
                        Context.Server.ScriptTimeout);
    sbText.Append("<br>");

    sbText.AppendFormat("Session ID: {0}" , Context.Session.SessionID);
    sbText.Append("<br>");
```

```
            sbText.AppendFormat("Skip Authorization: {0}" ,
                            Context.SkipAuthorization);
            sbText.Append("<br>");

            sbText.AppendFormat("Timestamp: {0}" , Context.Timestamp);
            sbText.Append("<br>");

            sbText.AppendFormat("Trace Enabled: {0}" , Context.Trace.IsEnabled);
            sbText.Append("<br>");

            sbText.AppendFormat("User Identity Is Authenticated: {0}" ,
                            Context.User.Identity.IsAuthenticated);
            sbText.Append("<br>");

            LblContext.Text = sbText.ToString();

        }
    }
}
```

Here is a screenshot showing the output of the above code:

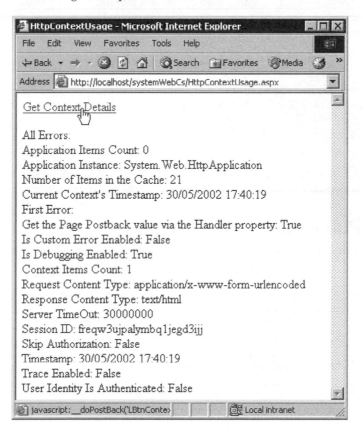

HttpCookie Class

The HTTP protocol is stateless by nature. A client sends a request to the server and receives a response. Until the client requests another page, the browser is not connected to the server. While this lightens the load on the server because the connection does not need to be maintained, it limits the ability to persist information specific to the client. Each time the client connects to the server to request a page it could be a different client, or a different user on the same machine.

Cookies, introduced in the early versions of the popular web browsers, allow the web developer to store small pieces of information on the client computer, providing that the browser has been configured to accept cookies. These "cookies" of information specify an expiration date and a URL path on the server. The client browser then sends the cookie back to the originating server each time a request is made for a resource in the path specified. In addition to having cookies that are persisted between visits to the site, in-memory cookies (also known as **Session Cookies** or **Transient Cookies**) can be created that only last until the browser is closed, which is how session has traditionally been maintained.

Using these cookies, developers are able to maintain some sense of state or "connectedness" with the client. However, many users do not like the idea of web sites storing information on their computer, so they may turn cookies off. A good web site needs to be developed with this in mind and come up with alternative methods for maintaining state. With ASP.NET, it is now possible to utilize the method used in classic ASP, where state could be maintained by passing the `SessionID` to the client but bypass the need for cookies altogether by changing just one setting in a file. This can be set in the `web.config` file, under the `sessionState` setting that is illustrated below:

```
<sessionState
    mode="InProc"
    stateConnectionString="tcpip=127.0.0.1:42424"
    sqlConnectionString="data source=127.0.0.1;user id=sa;password="
    cookieless="false"
    timeout="20"
/>
```

Where the `cookieless` state setting is set to `true` (`false` is the default value), a unique number will be randomly generated and added in front of the requested file as an identifier.

HttpCookie Public Methods

- ❑ `Equals` – inherited from `System.Object`, see Introduction for more details
- ❑ `GetHashCode` – inherited from `System.Object`, see Introduction for more details
- ❑ `GetType` – inherited from `System.Object`, see Introduction for more details
- ❑ `ToString` – inherited from `System.Object`, see Introduction for more details

HttpCookie Protected Methods

- ❑ `Finalize` – inherited from `System.Object`, see Introduction for more details
- ❑ `MemberwiseClone` – inherited from `System.Object`, see Introduction for more details

HttpCookie Public Properties

- ❑ **Domain**
- ❑ **Expires**
- ❑ **HasKeys**
- ❑ **Item**
- ❑ **Name**
- ❑ **Path**
- ❑ **Secure**
- ❑ **Value**
- ❑ **Values**

Domain

The Domain property indicates the domain name where the cookie originated and thus where it should be sent when making client requests. It is used to get or set the domain name. The default value is the current domain.

```
public string Domain {get; set;}
```

Cookies can only be sent to their originating domain. This practice protects the user because it means that your cookies from the online retailer you shop at do not get transmitted to other sites you visit. See also the Path property.

Expires

The Expires property indicates the expiration date and time of the cookie.

```
public DateTime Expires {get; set;}
```

Use this property when setting a new cookie to indicate to the browser when the cookie should no longer be sent with requests. An application of this property is when a cookie has been set to expire and its life needs to be extended.

HasKeys

Unlike a typical name/value pair, a cookie can have multiple string values. The HasKeys property indicates whether this is the case or not.

```
public bool HasKeys {get;}
```

For example, a simple cookie might have a name of color and a value of red. However, a cookie with sub keys might have a name of color and values of red, blue, or yellow.

```
<%
Response.Cookies["color"]["color1"]="red";
Response.Cookies["color"]["color2"]="blue";
Response.Cookies["color"]["color3"]="yellow";
%>
```

43

If we checked the HasKeys properties in this second case it would return true. We could then use the Values property to extract the individual values. If this property returns false, then we can use the Value property to get the one specific value.

Item

The Item property indicates a specific value in the cookie. This property would only be used on a cookie that has sub keys, as indicated by the HasKeys property. The Item property acts as a shortcut to the items in the Values collection (as distinct from the Value property).

```
public string this[string key] {get; set;}
```

The parameter key specifies the name of the item in the cookie to be retrieved.

> This property is only available for backward compatibility. Use the **Values** property in ASP.NET.

Name

The Name property indicates the name of the cookie to be set, or that has been set. The default value is null.

```
public string Name {get; set;}
```

Path

The Path property indicates the path on the server for which the cookie is valid. This property, in conjunction with the Domain attribute of the cookie, indicates to the client browser when it should send the cookie along with the request.

```
public string Path {get; set;}
```

Cookies are intended to maintain state on a given site. Because the information stored in these cookies is specific to a site, and may contain information that should not be shared, client browsers only send cookies to the domain from which they were created. Therefore, a cookie created in the www.wrox.com domain will not be sent when the user visits msdn.microsoft.com.

To further specify when, and where, the cookie should be sent, the path for a cookie can be set to indicate the directory path on the domain that should receive it. So, a cookie from the www.wrox.com domain with a path of /aspprogref would not be accessible for pages requested from http://www.wrox.com/authors, but would be available for pages requested from http://www.wrox.com/aspprogref/examples. Using a Path of "/" indicates that all directory paths on the server should have access to the cookie.

Secure

The Secure property indicates whether the cookie should be sent over a Secure Socket Layer (SSL) connection. If so the cookie will only be sent if the protocol of the request is HTTPS.

```
public bool Secure {get; set;}
```

Use this property when working on a secure site to ensure that the client does not send the cookie over an insecure connection.

Value

The `Value` property indicates the value for the cookie. Use this property to either set or get the value of the cookie.

```
public string Value {get; set;}
```

Values

The `Values` property returns a `NameValueCollection` of the values for the cookie, or allows for the setting of specific values.

```
public NameValueCollection Values {get;}
```

The majority of cookies are used as a single name and value. However, a given cookie may have more than one value. This property allows for retrieving all of the values in a cookie within one property. It can be used in conjunction with the `HasKeys` property of the `HttpCookie` object or the `HasKeys` method of the `Values` property itself.

HttpPostedFile Class

The `HttpPostedFile` class provides an object to encapsulate a file that has been posted to the server. The binary file content is included in the content body of the incoming request and traditionally required the use of a third-party component or custom code to extract. In ASP.NET we have a built-in object to work with that represents the individual file posted to the server.

HttpPostedFile Public Methods

- ❑ `Equals` – inherited from `System.Object`, see Introduction for more details
- ❑ `GetHashCode` – inherited from `System.Object`, see Introduction for more details
- ❑ `GetType` – inherited from `System.Object`, see Introduction for more details
- ❑ **`SaveAs`**
- ❑ `ToString` – inherited from `System.Object`, see Introduction for more details

SaveAs

The `SaveAs` method allows you to save a posted file to a given location on the server with a specific name.

```
public void SaveAs(string fileName);
```

The `fileName` parameter represents the physical path where the file should be saved.

The file name must be a physical path to the file. If a simple file name is given without any path information, an attempt will be made to write the file to the Windows System directory (typically `c:\winnt\system32\`), where the IIS executable resides. Since this is probably not the place you want to be collecting posted files, you should provide the file name with a full directory path.

Example: Using the HttpPostedFile Class

The following code from `HttpPostedFileUsage.aspx` shows the usage of the `SaveAs` method and some of the properties of the `HttpPostedFile` class:

```
using System;
using System.Collections;
using System.ComponentModel;
using System.Data;
using System.Drawing;
using System.Web;
using System.Web.SessionState;
using System.Web.UI;
using System.Web.UI.WebControls;
using System.Web.UI.HtmlControls;
using System.Xml;

namespace WebUsageCs
{
  /// <summary>
  /// Summary description for HttpPostedFileUsage.
  /// </summary>
  public class HttpPostedFileUsage : System.Web.UI.Page
  {
    protected System.Web.UI.WebControls.Label Label1;
    protected System.Web.UI.WebControls.Button LBtnSubmit;
    protected System.Web.UI.WebControls.Label LblMessage;
    protected System.Web.UI.HtmlControls.HtmlInputFile InputFile;

    private void Page_Load(object sender, System.EventArgs e)
    {
      // Put user code to initialize the page here
    }

    #region Web Form Designer generated code
    ...

    private void LBtnSubmit_Click(object sender, System.EventArgs e)
    {
      if(InputFile.PostedFile != null)
      {
        try
        {
          HttpPostedFile file = InputFile.PostedFile;
          LblMessage.Text += "Content Length:" + file.ContentLength +
                             "<BR>";
          LblMessage.Text += "Content Type:" + file.ContentType + "<BR>";
```

```
         LblMessage.Text += "File Name:" + file.FileName + "<BR>";

         InputFile.PostedFile.SaveAs(@"C:\new.txt");
         LblMessage.Text += @"File uploaded from the client " +
                            "successfully: C:\new.txt";
      }
      catch(Exception ex)
      {
         LblMessage.Text += "Error Uploading file: C:\new.txt" + "<br>" +
                            ex.ToString();
      }
   }
   else
      LblMessage.Text = "Please choose a file to upload";
   }
 }
}
```

This code will produce the following output:

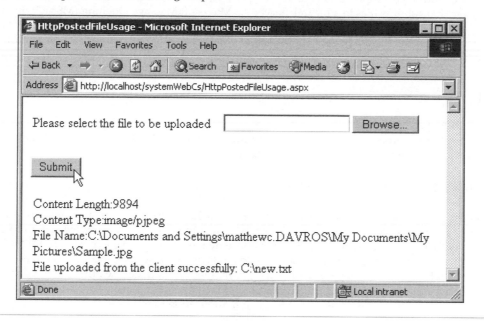

> To write files to disk, it is required that your security permissions be such that the
> account the web request is running under is allowed write access to the server. If you
> wish to allow users complete access to your site, the account under which their
> requests will be executing is the **aspnet_wp** account, by default.

47

HttpPostedFile Protected Methods

- ❑ `Finalize` – inherited from `System.Object`, see Introduction for more details
- ❑ `MemberwiseClone` – inherited from `System.Object`, see Introduction for more details

HttpPostedFile Public Properties

- ❑ **`ContentLength`**
- ❑ **`ContentType`**
- ❑ **`FileName`**
- ❑ **`InputStream`**

ContentLength

The `ContentLength` property indicates the length, in bytes, of the file that was posted to the server. This information can be important in determining actions to perform on the file. For example, you could have a page that submits files to a BizTalk Server via Microsoft Message Queuing (MSMQ). Because MSMQ has a message size limit of 2MB for Unicode files, a check of the `ContentLength` property could determine if the file can be sent via MSMQ or whether an alternative transport mechanism will need to be employed.

```
public int ContentLength {get;}
```

ContentType

The `ContentType` property indicates the Multipurpose Internet Mail Extensions (MIME) type of the file posted to the web server such as `text/HTML` or `text/XML`.

```
public string ContentType {get;}
```

The content type of the file can be extremely important to the security of your site. You may want to ensure that the files posted to your web site meet certain criteria in order to be processed, or to process files differently based on their content. For example, you may allow people to post both HTML or text files as well as image files as part of a custom content management system. Incoming images may go to one location while text files get parsed and saved to another location. On the other hand, you probably don't want a user to be able to load an executable application to your server. Therefore, if a file does not meet the requirements you have set you'll want your application to refuse it.

Some common MIME types are shown in the following table along with their file extensions.

Type	Description	FileExtensions
application/msaccess	Microsoft Access	.mdb
application/msword	Microsoft Word	.doc
application/octet-stream	Uninterpreted Binary	.bin
application/pdf	Portable Document Format	.pdf
application/postscript	Postscript file	.ps, .ai, .eps
application/vnd.ms-excel	Microsoft Excel	.xls
application/vnd.ms-powerpoint	Microsoft Powerpoint	.ppt
application/vnd.ms-project	Microsoft Project	.mpp
application/vnd.visio	Microsoft Visio	.vsd
application/vnd.wap.wmlc	Compiled WML	.wmlc
application/vnd.wap.wmlscriptc	Compiled WML script	.wmlsc
application/zip	Zip compressed file	.zip
audio/mpeg	MPEG audio file	.mpg, .mpeg
image/gif	GIF image	.gif
image/jpeg	JPEG image	.jpg, .jpeg, .jpe
image/png	PNG image file	.png
image/tiff	Tag Image File Format	.tiff, .tif
image/vnd.wap.wbmp	WAP bitmap	.wbmp
text/css	Cascading Style Sheets	.css
text/html	HyperText Markup Language	.htm, .html
text/plain	Plain text	.txt
text/richtext	Rich text	.rtx
text/sgml	Structured Generalized Markup Language	.sgml

Table continued on following page

Type	Description	FileExtensions
`text/tab-separated-values`	Tab separated text	`.tsv`
`text/vnd.wap.wml`	Wireless Markup Language	`.wml`
`text/vnd.wap.wmlscript`	Wireless Markup Language Script	`.wmls`
`text/xml`	eXtensible Markup Language	`.xml`
`text/xml-external-parsed-entity`	XML externally parsed entities	`.xml`
`video/mpeg`	MPEG video	`.mpg, .mpeg`
`video/quicktime`	Apple QuickTime video	`.mov`
`video/vnd.vivo`	VIVO movie	`.vivo`

> **For a full list of MIME types visit:**
> **ftp://ftp.isi.edu/in-notes/iana/assignments/media-types/**

FileName

The `FileName` property indicates the path of the file on the client's computer. This property matches the text that appears in the file input box on the web page. Don't be confused by this property and think that the path maps to a location on the server. Use the `SaveAs` method to save a file to a specific location on the server.

```
public string FileName {get;}
```

InputStream

The `InputStream` property indicates the stream object that the file is on, allowing access to the file as a stream. This object provides an alternative to the simpler `SaveAs` method in that we can act directly on the stream of data provided allowing for more detailed checking of content or specialized processing.

```
public Stream InputStream {get;}
```

Below is an example of reading from the input stream and writing that information out to another stream. The `FileStream` object could be replaced with almost any stream to write the data to.

```
int i;

  //loop through the posted files
  for(i = 0; i < Request.Files.Count; i++)
  {

    //create a file stream to write out the temporary file
```

```
System.IO.FileStream OutputFile =  new System.IO.FileStream("file"
         + i.ToString() + ".tmp", System.IO.FileMode.OpenOrCreate,
         System.IO.FileAccess.Write);

   //create a buffer for working with the streams
   Byte[] buffer = new Byte[64];
   //as long as we are getting data out, we'll write it to the other
   //stream.
   while(Request.Files[i].InputStream.Read(buffer, 0,
                                  buffer.Length) > 0)
   {
     OutputFile.Write(buffer, 0, buffer.Length);
   }
}
```

HttpRequest Class

The HttpRequest class represents the incoming request from a client. For example, when a user enters a URL in their browser, the browser makes a request to the server identified in the URL for a given resource. This request includes a wide variety of information pertaining to the client and the request itself. Included in this might be form data that a user has filled out, or persisted information from cookies. The ASP.NET intrinsic Request object provides a reference to HttpRequest class methods and properties.

HttpRequest Public Methods

- ❑ **BinaryRead**
- ❑ Equals – inherited from System.Object, see Introduction for more details
- ❑ GetHashCode – inherited from System.Object, see Introduction for more details
- ❑ GetType – inherited from System.Object, see Introduction for more details
- ❑ **MapImageCoordinates**
- ❑ **MapPath**
- ❑ **SaveAs**
- ❑ ToString – inherited from System.Object, see Introduction for more details

BinaryRead

The BinaryRead method reads a specified number of bytes from the request stream in an array. The number of bytes to read will most often be the size of the request in order to get the entire content sent, but can vary depending on the problem you are trying to solve.

```
public Byte[] BinaryRead(int count);
```

The parameter count represents the number of bytes to read. If this value is zero, or greater than the number of bytes available, an ArgumentException will be thrown.

When working with posted data on the request object, the bulk of development rests with reading simple text data from the posted information. However, there are cases where the information posted is not in plain text. This is where the `BinaryRead` method is useful. This method allows for the reading of binary information, such as an image or file, and working with the bytes returned. In other situations, there may be a need to capture the request in a binary format and transmit it to some other process.

> The **`BinaryRead`** method is provided for backward compatibility. For new applications use the **`InputStream`** property of the **`HttpRequest`** class to read the raw data from the request.

MapImageCoordinates

The `MapImageCoordinates` method returns an array of integers representing the map coordinates of a form image that is submitted to the server. This method works with both HTML input elements, with its type set to `image`, and with the `ImageButton` server control.

```
public  int[] MapImageCoordinates(string imageFieldName
```

The parameter `imageFieldName` specifies the field name of the image map as it is defined in the form.

Example: Using the MapImageCoordinates Method

The following code example, `MapImageCoordinates.aspx`, shows how to get the *x* and *y* coordinates of an image input control indicating where it has been clicked:

```csharp
using System;
using System.Collections;
using System.ComponentModel;
using System.Data;
using System.Drawing;
using System.Web;
using System.Web.SessionState;
using System.Web.UI;
using System.Web.UI.WebControls;
using System.Web.UI.HtmlControls;

namespace WebUsageCs
{
    /// <summary>
    /// Summary description for MapImageCoordinates.
    /// </summary>
    public class MapImageCoordinates : System.Web.UI.Page
    {
        protected System.Web.UI.WebControls.Label LblCoordinates;
        protected System.Web.UI.HtmlControls.HtmlInputImage mapimage;

        private void Page_Load(object sender, System.EventArgs e)
        {
            //get the coordinates and write them out to the response
```

```
        //if the page has been posted back
        if(IsPostBack)
        {
          int[] Coordinates;
          Coordinates = Request.MapImageCoordinates("mapimage");
          LblCoordinates.Text = "X: " + Coordinates[0] + "<br>Y: "
              + Coordinates[1];
        }
      }

      #region Web Form Designer generated code
      ...

    }
  }
```

In the Web Form we add an `<input>` element with its type set to `image`. In the code behind, we first check to make sure the page is being posted back to by using the `IsPostBack` property, and then retrieve the coordinates of the image input. In this example we simply output the coordinates for where in the square the user has clicked, but we could also determine the location of the click and respond differently depending on where the click occurred. The output from this example, `MapImageCoordinates.aspx`, is illustrated below:

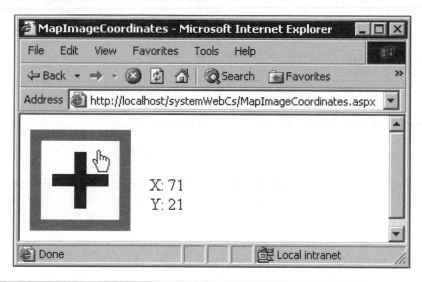

MapPath

The `MapPath` method maps a given virtual path to the physical path. It returns a string representing the physical path of the file for a specified virtual path of a web server, passed as its parameter. There are two overloaded forms of this method.

```
public string MapPath(string virtualPath);
```

In the above example, the parameter `virtualPath` represents the virtual path for which a corresponding physical path is desired.

```
public string MapPath(string virtualPath string baseVirtualDir,
                      bool allowCrossMapping);
```

Here, the `baseVirtualDir` parameter represents the base virtual directory from which the file should be mapped. The `allowCrossMapping` allows the file path to map to another application.

This method will throw an `HttpException` if there is no `HttpContext` object defined for the request. It can also throw this exception if the virtual file path belonged to another application and `allowCrossMapping` was set to `false`.

The following code snippet shows the path to the directory of another application on the server in order to reference an XML file stored there and output the text of one of the nodes:

```
//map the path to the file in the other application
string path;
path = Request.MapPath("categories.xml", @"\HelperApp", true);

//open the xml document from the path and output the first category node
XmlDocument Categories = new XmlDocument();
Categories.Load(path);
Response.Write(Categories.SelectNodes("//category").Item(0).InnerText);

//set our variable to nothing so it can be garbage collected
Categories = null;
```

SaveAs

The `SaveAs` method saves the current `HttpRequest` to a disk file.

```
public void SaveAs(string filename, bool includeHeaders);
```

The parameter `filename` specifies the physical path to the file location for saving the request. The parameter `includeHeaders` indicates whether the headers from the request should also be saved out to the file.

The `SaveAs` method allows the developer to save the client request out to a file. This can be helpful when working with requests that contain data such as XML documents or other messaging systems where the client request as a whole might be saved to a directory to be picked up by another application or if there is a need to keep a history of the requests made to the server, for security or analysis purposes.

HttpRequest Protected Methods

❑ `Finalize` – inherited from `System.Object`, see Introduction for more details

❑ `MemberwiseClone` – inherited from `System.Object`, see Introduction for more details

HttpRequest Public Properties

All `HttpRequest` class properties, except the `Filter` property, are `ReadOnly`.

- ❑ **AcceptTypes**
- ❑ **ApplicationPath**
- ❑ **Browser**
- ❑ **ClientCertificate**
- ❑ **ContentEncoding**
- ❑ **ContentLength**
- ❑ **ContentType**
- ❑ **Cookies**
- ❑ **CurrentExecutionFilePath**
- ❑ **FilePath**
- ❑ **Files**
- ❑ **Filter**
- ❑ **Form**
- ❑ **Headers**
- ❑ **HttpMethod**
- ❑ **InputStream**
- ❑ **IsAuthenticated**
- ❑ **IsSecureConnection**
- ❑ **Params**
- ❑ **Path**
- ❑ **PathInfo**
- ❑ **PhysicalApplicationPath**
- ❑ **PhysicalPath**
- ❑ **QueryString**
- ❑ **RawUrl**
- ❑ **RequestType**
- ❑ **ServerVariables**
- ❑ **TotalBytes**
- ❑ **Url**
- ❑ **UrlReferrer**
- ❑ **UserAgent**
- ❑ **UserHostAddress**
- ❑ **UserHostName**
- ❑ **UserLanguages**

AcceptTypes

The `AcceptTypes` property indicates the MIME types of files that the requesting client will accept in return. An array of string values, each representing a MIME type accepted by the browser, is returned.

```
public string[] AcceptTypes {get;}
```

Most client browsers allow a user to indicate handlers for certain document types. Using this property, the developer can determine if a client supports a specific type. For example, you could have a function on your site that outputs a Microsoft Word file. It might be useful to check that the client will accept the `application/msword` type. If not, then an alternative format, such as PDF, could be used. See the `HttpPostedFile.ContentType` property for a list of popular MIME types.

The following code snippet shows the usage of `AcceptTypes` property and then iterates through the string array returned to display all the `AcceptTypes`:

```
Response.Write("AcceptTypes:");
string[] atypes = Request.AcceptTypes;
foreach(string types in aTypes)
{
  Response.Write(types);
}
```

ApplicationPath

The `ApplicationPath` property indicates the ASP.NET application's virtual path on the server. This property is useful when you need to determine the root path of the web application in order to determine the location of other files.

```
public string ApplicationPath {get;}
```

For example, we might want to write code to be included in many different web pages. This code could load an XML file that is in a subdirectory of the application. The following code would allow us to find this file, regardless of where in the application hierarchy the code executes:

```
string XmlSettings;
XmlSettings = Request.ApplicationPath + @"/XML/settings.xml";
```

Browser

The `Browser` property returns an `HttpBrowserCapabilities` object, which allows access to the abilities and characteristics of the requesting browser. See the `HttpBrowserCapabilities` class earlier in this chapter for more details.

The following code snippet can be used to determine if the browser type is `IE6` or not:

```
if(Request.Browser.Type.Equals("IE6"))
   //perform an action for the IE browser
else
   //perform an action supported by all browsers
```

ClientCertificate

The `ClientCertificate` property indicates the certificate sent from the client for secure communications. This object can be used to get access to the information contained in that certificate.

```
public HttpClientCertificate ClientCertificate {get;}
```

The client certificate is used in secure communications, with the server using SSL technology. Being able to access this certificate allows the developer to ensure the certificate is appropriate and sufficient for the site. In the following snippet, we check to make sure the client certificate has at least 128-bit encryption. If not, we output a simple message that indicates to the user that they need a certificate with greater encryption and end the processing of the page immediately using the `End` method of the `HttpResponse` class. The `KeySize` of a certificate indicates the level of encryption. The greater the key size, the greater the encryption:

```
if(Request.ClientCertificate.KeySize < 128)
{
  Response.Write("Your certificate needs to be at least 128 bit");
  Response.End();
}
```

ContentEncoding

The `ContentEncoding` property indicates the character encoding of the client. This value indicates whether the request is ASCII text, or UTF8, or similar. For more information on the different encoding values and utility classes to convert from one encoding to another, examine the `Encoding` class in the `System.Text` namespace.

```
public Encoding ContentEncoding {get;}
```

Here is a usage of this property showing the `EncodingName`:

```
Response.Write ("Content Encoding Name: " +
                Request.ContentEncoding.EncodingName);
```

ContentLength

The `ContentLength` property indicates the length, in bytes, of the request. This information can be used when handling the content using the `BinaryRead` method or the `InputStream` property to read the data from the request.

```
public int ContentLength {get;}
```

The following code displays the value returned by this property:

```
Response.Write("Content Length: " + Request.ContentLength);
```

57

ContentType

The `ContentType` property indicates the MIME type of the incoming request such as `text/HTML`.

```
public string ContentType {get;}
```

The `ContentType` property can be used to discriminate between the types of files being posted to the server. For example, when the content type is `"multipart/form-data"`, files may be included in the posted information.

The following code displays the `ContentType` of the current request:

```
Response.Write("Content Type: " + Request.ContentType);
```

Cookies

The `Cookies` property returns all of the cookies sent to the server by the client browser. The `Cookies` collection on the request allows for accessing those cookies being sent to the server. Use the `Cookies` collection of the `HttpResponse` object to send new cookies out to the client, or update existing cookies there. This property returns an `HttpCookieCollection` object.

```
public HttpCookieCollection Cookies {get;}
```

The following code checks the `user_name` cookie property:

```
if(Request.Cookies["user_name"] == "")
   Response.Cookies["user_name"] = Request.Form.Item("user_name");
```

CurrentExecutionFilePath

The `CurrentExecutionFilePath` property indicates the virtual path to the file on the server. This property is different from the `FilePath` property, as it returns the path of the current executing page when the `HttpServerUtility.Transfer` and `HttpServerUtility.Execute` methods are called, unlike returning path of the parent page that called these methods.

```
Public ReadOnly Property CurrentExecutionFilePath As String
```

FilePath

The `FilePath` property indicates the virtual path to the file on the server.

```
public string FilePath {get;}
```

For example, given the URL http://www.wrox.com/aspprogref/chapters.aspx the `FilePath` property would return `/aspprogref/chapters.aspx`.

Files

The `Files` property indicates a collection of files posted to the web server from a client form submission.

```
public HttpFileCollection Files {get;}
```

Uploading files to a web server has come to be an important part of many custom web solutions and content management packages. In the past, the easiest way to manage all of these files was to use a third-party component that did the work of splitting out the files from the uploaded form data.

> The **Files** collection is only populated when the **ContentType** of the form is "**multipart/form-data**".

Filter

The Filter property indicates a stream object to use as a filter on the incoming request object. The incoming request will be passed through this stream as it is processed, allowing the filtering stream class to read and manipulate the incoming data. This could be used to build a sort of incoming proxy, by which the data is thoroughly examined before being dealt with in the page. It gets or sets the stream object to be used as a filter and throws an HttpException if the stream object is not valid.

```
public Stream Filter {get;}
```

Form

The Form property indicates the contents of an HTML form posted to the server. In order for form data to be accessible, the MIME type of the incoming request must be "application/x-www-form-urlencoded" or "multipart/form-data". The values in the form are returned as a collection, specifically a NameValueCollection class instance.

```
public NameValueCollection Form {get;}
```

HTML forms are one of the primary ways to allow a user to send information to a web site. The Form property allows the developer to get access to the information that was posted and handle it appropriately, perhaps saving it to a database, or performing actions based on the input.

Form values are accessed from this collection using the names given them in the HTML form at design time, including radio buttons and checkboxes. For more information on the elements in a form and their properties, see Chapters 3 to 5.

The following code snippet displays all the items in the form collection:

```
Response.Write("Form Values:");
NameValueCollection formFields = Request.Form;
string[] aFields = formFields.AllKeys;
foreach(string field in aFields)
  Response.Write(field + ":" + formFields[field]);
```

Headers

The Headers property indicates the HTML headers sent in the request. This value is returned as a collection, specifically a NameValueCollection class instance.

```
public NameValueCollection Headers {get;}
```

When a client makes a request to a server for a resource, a great deal of the information sent to the server is **Metadata** (data that describes the request and the client). The headers of a request contain information regarding the client browser, cookies, accepted types, language, and encoding. Much of this information is encapsulated in other properties of the request that may be easier to use. However, the `Headers` property allows the developer to access specialized information from the headers, and, in the `HttpResponse` object, add their own headers. For example, if we wished to view the User-Agent header, we could use the following code:

```
string UserAgent = Request.Headers["User-Agent"];
```

HttpMethod

The `HttpMethod` property indicates the method of the HTTP request being made (GET, POST, or HEAD).

```
public string HttpMethod {get;}
```

When requesting a resource from a site, there are three different methods that can be used. When typing in a URL to your browser and getting a page back, a GET request is made. When submitting a form, the POST method can be specified, which will include the information in the request itself rather than in the URL. The HEAD request specifies that only the headers that would be sent with a GET request should be returned. This property indicates in which method the data was transferred and can provide insight into where to look for specific data.

The following code displays the `HttpMethod` of the incoming request:

```
Response.Write("Http Method:" + Request.HttpMethod);
```

InputStream

The `InputStream` property indicates a stream containing the incoming HTTP request body. This read-only stream object provides access to the body of the incoming request. For example, when we post a form to the server, the values in our form show up in the body of the HTTP request and can, therefore, be seen using this stream.

```
public Stream InputStream {get;}
```

The following code snippet displays the `Length` of the stream containing the incoming HTTP request body:

```
Response.Write("Input Stream Length: " + Request.InputStream.Length);
```

IsAuthenticated

The `IsAuthenticated` property indicates whether the user has been authenticated to the site. There are several methods of authentication available to a developer when building a site in ASP.NET including Windows, Forms-based, and Passport. This property will indicate whether the client making the request has been authenticated by one of these mechanisms. In order for this property to return anything except `false`, the `<authentication>` element in the `web.config` file must be set to a value other than `none`. Similarly, you may have to change the values in the `<authorization>` element to allow and deny users. See Chapter 8 for information on forms-based authentication.

```
public bool IsAuthenticated {get;}
```

The following code displays whether the user has been authenticated or not:

```
Response.Write("Is Authenticated: " + Request.IsAuthenticated);
```

IsSecureConnection

The `IsSecureConnection` property indicates whether the user's connection is over a HTTPS (secure) connection. When creating secure sites that contain sensitive information or that will be requesting sensitive information from users, a form of data encryption is often employed to protect this information. Today, Secure Sockets Layer (SSL) is the most common security framework used to protect this data.

SSL provides a public/private key framework for ensuring that a client or server is who it says it is and assures the user that they are sending their information only where they want. A hacker cannot get access to the information because they do not have access to the public or private keys existing on the communicating servers. This security comes at a cost to performance. Encrypting and decrypting data takes time, and the size of the data that needs to be transmitted is larger as well. For this reason, it is important to use SSL only where necessary.

Use this property to determine if the client is requesting pages using SSL encryption. It might be helpful to modify a site to use low resolution images, or different formatting, knowing that the requests to the server will take longer given the increased network traffic related to encrypting and decrypting the data.

```
public bool IsSecureConnection {get;}
```

The code below displays whether the incoming request was over a HTTPS or not:

```
Response.Write("Is Secure Connection: " + Request.IsSecureConnection);
```

Params

The `Params` property is a collection combining the `Form`, `QueryString`, `Cookies`, and `ServerVariables` values into one collection object of the type `NameValueCollection`.

```
public NameValueCollection Params {get;}
```

This property allows for accessing a named parameter that might exist in a variety of locations. At times, it might be expected that a parameter will be sent to the page, but it may come in different forms. This property makes it easier to access these values without creating long conditional statements.

The following code displays all the contents stored in the `Form`, `QueryString`, `Cookies`, and `ServerVariables` by iterating through the collection object returned by the `Params` property:

```
Response.Write("Param Values contain QueryString, Form, " +
               ServerVariables and Cookies items:");
nameValueCollection param = Request.Params;
string[] aParam = param.AllKeys;

foreach(string paramKey in aParam)
  Response.Write(paramKey & ":" & params[paramKey]);
```

Path

The `Path` property indicates the path of the current request, including any information trailing the file name. This property differs from the `FilePath` in that the `FilePath` property does not include the information following the file itself. See below for more clarification on this.

```
public string Path {get;}
```

PathInfo

The `PathInfo` property indicates the information in a URL request that follows the file location.

```
public string PathInfo {get;}
```

> The **FilePath**, **Path**, and **PathInfo** properties are all closely related and can be a bit confusing. A sample to show the difference should clarify any confusion. Given the URL: **http://www.wrox.com/aspprogref.aspx/TOC**
>
> The following values would be returned for the three properties:
>
> **FilePath: http://www.wrox.com/aspprogref.aspx**
>
> **Path: http://www.wrox.com/aspprogref.aspx/TOC**
>
> **PathInfo: TOC**

PhysicalApplicationPath

The `PhysicalApplicationPath` property indicates the disk (physical) file path to the application directory.

```
Public ReadOnly Property PhysicalApplicationPath As String
```

An example return value for this property would be `"c:\inetpub\wwwroot\WebUsage\"`.

PhysicalPath

The `PhysicalPath` property indicates the physical disk path to the file requested in the URL. This differs from the above property in that it reflects the path of the actual file requested.

```
public string PhysicalPath {get;}
```

An example return value for this property would be `"c:\inetpub\wwwroot\WebUsage\HttpRequestUsage.aspx"`.

QueryString

The `QueryString` property indicates a collection of the parameters sent to the server via the URL.

```
NameValueCollection Query = HttpRequest.QueryString;
```

For example, given the URL: http://www.wrox.com/aspprogref.aspx?chap=2&section=3

`HttpRequest.QueryString["chap"]` will return the value "2".
`HttpRequest.QueryString["section"]` will return the value "3".

RawUrl

The `RawUrl` property indicates the path to the resource excluding the server and domain information, but including the query string parameters, if present.

```
public string RawUrl {get;}
```

For example, the URL http://www.wrox.com/aspprogref/examples/chap2.zip would result in the following return value: `/aspprogref/examples/chap2.zip`

RequestType

The `RequestType` property indicates the type of request made by the client (GET or POST).

```
public string RequestType {get;}
```

The following code displays the `RequestType` of the incoming request:

```
Response.Write("Request Type:" + Request.RequestType);
```

ServerVariables

The `ServerVariables` property gets a collection of the web server variables.

```
public NameValueCollection ServerVariables {get;}
```

Below is a table of the possible server variables in this collection:

Variable	Meaning
ALL_HTTP	All of the HTTP headers with their names in all caps and prefixed with HTTP_
ALL_RAW	All of the HTTP headers in the format they were sent to the server
APPL_MD_PATH	The metabase path of the web application. The metabase is the storage area for IIS configuration settings.
APPL_PHYSICAL_PATH	The physical path of the web application
AUTH_PASSWORD	The password of the user if using Basic authentication
AUTH_TYPE	The authentication type used to authenticate the user. Possible values include NTLM and basic.

Table continued on following page

Variable	Meaning
AUTH_USER	The user name of the authorized user
CERT_COOKIE	A cookie providing the ID of the certificate if one is present on the client
CERT_ISSUER	The name of the company that issued the client certificate; this matches the issuer field on the certificate
CERT_KEYSIZE	The size, in bits, of the encryption key used to encrypt data
CERT_SECRETKEYSIZE	The size, in bits, of the secret or private key on the server
CERT_SERIALNUMBER	The serial number of the client certificate
CERT_SERVER_ISSUER	The issuer field in the server certificate
CERT_SERVER_SUBJECT	The subject field of the server certificate
CERT_SUBJECT	The subject field of the client certificate
CONTENT_LENGTH	The length, in bytes, of the incoming request
CONTENT_TYPE	The MIME type of the request, such as www-url-encoded for a form being posted to the server
GATEWAY_INTERFACE	The Common Gateway Interface (CGI) supported on the server
HTTP_ACCEPT	The MIME types the client can accept
HTTP_ACCEPT_ENCODING	The compression encoding types supported by the client
HTTP_ACCEPT_LANGUAGE	The languages accepted by the client
HTTP_CONNECTION	Indicates whether the connection allows keep-alive functionality
HTTP_COOKIE	The cookies sent with a request
HTTP_HOST	The host name of the server
HTTP_USER_AGENT	Information about the browser used to connect to the server including version and type
HTTPS	Indicates whether HTTPS was used for the request. Returns "On" if the request came through SSL, or "Off" if not.
HTTPS_KEYSIZE	The number of bits in the encryption used to make the SSL connection
HTTPS_SECRETKEYSIZE	The size, in bits, of the private key on the server
HTTPS_SERVER_ISSUER	The name of the issuing authority for the server certificate as found in the Issuer field of the certificate

Variable	Meaning
HTTPS_SERVER_SUBJECT	The subject of the server certificate as found in the subject field of the certificate
INSTANCE_ID	The metabase ID of the web server instance
INSTANCE_META_PATH	The metabase path of the web server instance
LOCAL_ADDR	The IP address of the server that is handling the request
LOGON_USER	The NT user name of the user if known
PATH_INFO	The virtual path to the requested resource
PATH_TRANSLATED	The physical path to the requested resource
QUERY_STRING	A string containing any information after the name of the resource requested
REMOTE_ADDR	The IP address of the client making the request
REMOTE_HOST	The host name of the client making the request, if available
REMOTE_USER	The original NT user name sent by the client before it is modified by any authentication filters on the server
REQUEST_METHOD	The type of the HTTP request made. Possible values are "GET", "POST", and "HEAD".
SCRIPT_NAME	The virtual path to the script currently executing
SERVER_NAME	The host name of the server
SERVER_PORT	The server port to which the request was made
SERVER_PORT_SECURE	If the port is set to use SSL, this value is 1, otherwise it is 0
SERVER_PROTOCOL	The HTTP protocol and version in use on the server
SERVER_SOFTWARE	The name and version of the web server software running on the server
URL	The virtual path to the file requested

TotalBytes

The TotalBytes property indicates the total number of bytes posted to the server in the client's request.

```
public int TotalBytes {get;}
```

The following code displays the TotalBytes of the current request:

```
Response.Write("Total Bytes: " + Request.TotalBytes);
```

Url

The `Url` property indicates the Universal Resource Identifier (URI) and its associated information regarding the resource requested. For a client using a web browser, this would be the same information that appears in their browser address.

```
public Uri Url {get;}
```

The following code displays the `Url` of the current request:

```
Response.Write("Url: " + Request.Url.Tostring());
```

UrlReferrer

The `UrlReferrer` property indicates the URI of the previously accessed page that linked to the current request page. The `UrlReferrer` property can be useful for tracking information about how users arrive at your site or the path that users take when in your site. However, it is not a good idea to use this information for security purposes or any other purpose where you need to be guaranteed that a user is coming from a certain page. This property is only populated when the user is navigating to the page from a link in another web page. Therefore, if the client enters the address directly in their browser, or uses a bookmark, this object will be `null`.

```
public Uri UrlReferrer {get;}
```

The following code displays the `UrlReferrer`:

```
Response.Write("Url Referrer: " + Request.UrlReferrer.Tostring());
```

UserAgent

The `UserAgent` property indicates the browser being used by the client. It contains a raw string representing the client's browser. This property is the basis for much of the information contained in the `HttpBrowserCapabilities` object retrieved via the `Browser` property.

```
public string UserAgent {get;}
```

The following code displays the `UserAgent`:

```
Response.Write("User Agent: " + Request.UserAgent);
```

An example of a string for IE 6.0 might look like this:

Mozilla/4.0 (compatible; **MSIE 6.0**; Windows NT 5.0; .NET CLR 1.0.3705)

UserHostAddress

The `UserHostAddress` property indicates the IP address of the requesting client's machine. This can be useful if you want to determine if someone's connecting from your local network or not. It also has potential for allowing customization based on whether you know the user's network or not. For example, a company may want to have different content or navigation on their home page for employees browsing to the site from the office, versus the content that users outside the company get.

```
public string UserHostAddress {get;}
```

The following code displays the UserHostAddress:

```
Response.Write("User Host Address: " + Request.UserHostAddress);
```

UserHostName

The UserHostName property indicates the host name of the requesting client's machine.

```
public string UserHostName {get;}
```

The following code displays the UserHostName:

```
Response.Write("User Host Name: " + Request.UserHostName);
```

UserLanguages

The UserLanguages property indicates the languages preferred by the user's browser. This property returns an array of languages supported by the client. In Internet Explorer, the user can set these values via the **Internet Options** control panel. You can use this array of values to search for a preferred language to present your information in.

```
public string[] UserLanguages A
```

The following code snippet displays all the languages preferred by the requesting browser:

```
Response.Write("User Languages:");
string[] alanguages = Request.UserLanguages;
foreach(string languages in aLanguages)
  Response.Write(languages);
```

Example: The Properties of the HttpRequest class

The code shown below, HttpRequestUsage.aspx.cs, will display the values of all of the properties of the HttpRequest class:

```
using System;
using System.Collections;
using System.ComponentModel;
using System.Data;
using System.Drawing;
using System.Web;
using System.Web.SessionState;
using System.Web.UI;
using System.Web.UI.WebControls;
using System.Web.UI.HtmlControls;
using System.Text;
using System.Collections.Specialized;
```

```
namespace WebUsageCs
{
  /// <summary>
  /// Summary description for HttpRequestUsage.
  /// </summary>
  public class HttpRequestUsage : System.Web.UI.Page
  {
    protected System.Web.UI.WebControls.LinkButton LBtnRequest;
    protected System.Web.UI.WebControls.Label LblRequest;

    private void Page_Load(object sender, System.EventArgs e)
    {
      // Put user code to initialize the page here
    }

    #region Web Form Designer generated code
    ...

    private void LBtnRequest_Click(object sender, System.EventArgs e)
    {
      StringBuilder sbText = new StringBuilder();

      //Display all the properties of the HttpRequest Class
      sbText.Append("This example shows the usage of the properties of " +
                    "HttpRequest Class");
      sbText.Append("<br>");

      sbText.Append("AcceptTypes:");
      sbText.Append("<br>");
      string[] aTypes = Request.AcceptTypes;
      foreach(string types in aTypes)
      {
        sbText.Append(types);
        sbText.Append("<br>");
      }
      sbText.Append("<br>");

      sbText.AppendFormat("Application Path: {0}" ,
                          Request.ApplicationPath);
      sbText.Append("<br>");

      sbText.AppendFormat("Browser Type: {0}" , Request.Browser.Type);
      sbText.Append("<br>");

      sbText.AppendFormat("Client Certificate Subject: {0}" ,
                          Request.ClientCertificate.Subject);
      sbText.Append("<br>");

      sbText.AppendFormat("Content Encoding Name: {0}" ,
                          Request.ContentEncoding.EncodingName);
      sbText.Append("<br>");
```

```
sbText.AppendFormat("Content Length: {0}" , Request.ContentLength);
sbText.Append("<br>");

sbText.AppendFormat("Content Type: {0}" , Request.ContentType);
sbText.Append("<br>");

sbText.Append("Cookies ");
sbText.Append("<br>");
HttpCookieCollection cookiesCollection = Request.Cookies;
int cookieCount  = cookiesCollection.Count;
int i;
for(i =  0; i < cookieCount; i++)
{
  sbText.Append(cookiesCollection[i].Name + ":" +
                cookiesCollection[i].Value);
  sbText.Append("<br>");
}

sbText.Append("<br>");

sbText.AppendFormat("Current Execution File Path: {0}" ,
                    Request.CurrentExecutionFilePath);
sbText.Append("<br>");

sbText.AppendFormat("File Path: {0}" , Request.FilePath);
sbText.Append("<br>");

sbText.Append("Files ");
sbText.Append("<br>");
HttpFileCollection filesCollection = Request.Files;
int fileCount = filesCollection.Count;
int j;
for(j= 0; j < fileCount; j++)
{
  sbText.Append(filesCollection[j].FileName);
  sbText.Append("<br>");
}
sbText.Append("<br>");

sbText.AppendFormat("Filter Length: {0}" , Request.Filter.Length);
sbText.Append("<br>");

sbText.Append("Form Values:");
sbText.Append("<br>");
NameValueCollection formFields = Request.Form;
string[] aFields = formFields.AllKeys;

foreach(string field in aFields)
{
  sbText.Append(field + ":" + formFields[field]);
  sbText.Append("<br>");
}
```

```
                    sbText.Append("Header Values:");
                    sbText.Append("<br>");
          NameValueCollection headers = Request.Headers;
          string[] aHeader = headers.AllKeys;
          foreach(string headerKey in aHeader)
          {
            sbText.Append(headerKey + ":" + headers[headerKey]);
            sbText.Append("<br>");
          }
          sbText.Append("<br>");

          sbText.AppendFormat("Http Method: {0}" , Request.HttpMethod);
          sbText.Append("<br>");

          sbText.AppendFormat("Input Stream Length: {0}" ,
                              Request.InputStream.Length);
          sbText.Append("<br>");

          sbText.AppendFormat("Is Authenticated: {0}" ,
                              Request.IsAuthenticated);
          sbText.Append("<br>");

          sbText.AppendFormat("Is Secure Connection: {0}" ,
                              Request.IsSecureConnection);
          sbText.Append("<br>");

          sbText.AppendFormat("Is Secure Connection via Item Property: {0}" ,
                              Request["IsSecureConnection"]);
          sbText.Append("<br>");

          sbText.Append("Param Values contain QueryString, Form, " +
                        "ServerVariables and Cookies items:");
          sbText.Append("<br>");
          NameValueCollection param = Request.Params;
          string[] aParam = param.AllKeys;
          foreach(string paramKey in aParam)
          {
            sbText.Append(paramKey + ":" + param[paramKey]);
            sbText.Append("<br>");
          }

          sbText.Append("<br>");

          sbText.AppendFormat("Path: {0}" , Request.Path);
          sbText.Append("<br>");

          sbText.AppendFormat("Path Information: {0}" , Request.PathInfo);
          sbText.Append("<br>");

          sbText.AppendFormat("Physical Application Path: {0}" ,
                              Request.PhysicalApplicationPath);
```

```
      sbText.Append("<br>");

      sbText.AppendFormat("Physical Path: {0}" , Request.PhysicalPath);
      sbText.Append("<br>");

      sbText.Append("QueryString Values:");
      sbText.Append("<br>");
      NameValueCollection querys = Request.QueryString;
      string[] aQuery = querys.AllKeys;
      foreach(string queryKey in aQuery)
      {
        sbText.Append(queryKey + ":" + querys[queryKey]);
        sbText.Append("<br>");
      }

      sbText.Append("<br>");

      sbText.AppendFormat("Raw Url: {0}" , Request.RawUrl);
      sbText.Append("<br>");

      sbText.AppendFormat("Request Type: {0}" , Request.RequestType);
      sbText.Append("<br>");

      sbText.Append("Server Variables Values:");
      sbText.Append("<br>");
      NameValueCollection servers = Request.ServerVariables;
      string[] aServer = servers.AllKeys;
      foreach(string serverKey in aServer)
      {
        sbText.Append(serverKey + ":" + servers[serverKey]);
        sbText.Append("<br>");
      }

      sbText.Append("<br>");

      sbText.AppendFormat("Total Bytes: {0}" , Request.TotalBytes);
      sbText.Append("<br>");

      sbText.AppendFormat("Url: {0}" , Request.Url);
      sbText.Append("<br>");

      sbText.AppendFormat("Url Referrer: {0}" , Request.UrlReferrer);
      sbText.Append("<br>");

      sbText.AppendFormat("User Agent: {0}" , Request.UserAgent);
      sbText.Append("<br>");

      sbText.AppendFormat("User Host Address: {0}" ,
                          Request.UserHostAddress);
      sbText.Append("<br>");

      sbText.AppendFormat("User Host Name: {0}" , Request.UserHostName);
      sbText.Append("<br>");
```

```
        sbText.Append("User Languages:");
        sbText.Append("<br>");
        string[] alanguages = Request.UserLanguages;
        foreach(string languages in alanguages)
        {
          sbText.Append(languages);
          sbText.Append("<br>");
        }

        sbText.Append("<br>");

        LblRequest.Text=sbText.ToString();
      }
    }
  }
```

The following screenshot shows some of the output that this code produces:

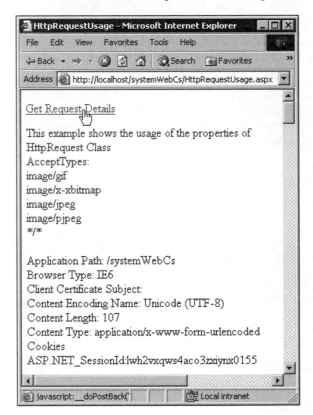

HttpResponse Class

The `HttpResponse` class encompasses all of the content getting written out to the client, including headers, cookies, and other non-UI items. Writing to this stream is equivalent to sending data to the client. The `HttpResponse` object is accessible via the intrinsic `Response` object allowing syntax like the following:

```
Response.ContentType="text/XML"
```

HttpResponse Public Methods

- ❏ **AddCacheItemDependencies**
- ❏ **AddCacheItemDependency**
- ❏ **AddFileDependencies**
- ❏ **AddFileDependency**
- ❏ **AddHeader**
- ❏ **AppendHeader**
- ❏ **AppendToLog**
- ❏ **ApplyAppPathModifier**
- ❏ **BinaryWrite**
- ❏ **Clear**
- ❏ **ClearContent**
- ❏ **ClearHeaders**
- ❏ **Close**
- ❏ **End**
- ❏ Equals – inherited from `System.Object`, see Introduction for more details
- ❏ **Flush**
- ❏ GetHashCode – inherited from `System.Object`, see Introduction for more details
- ❏ GetType – inherited from `System.Object`, see Introduction for more details
- ❏ **Pics**
- ❏ **Redirect**
- ❏ **RemoveOutputCacheItem**
- ❏ ToString – inherited from `System.Object`, see Introduction for more details
- ❏ **Write**
- ❏ **WriteFile**

AddCacheItemDependencies

The `AddCacheItemDependencies` method allows you to specify that validity of one item in the cache is dependent on a list of other items in the cache. The list of items is supplied as an `ArrayList` containing keys of the items. When the items referred to by these keys are removed from the cache, the cache response for the current item will become invalid.

```
public void AddCacheItemDependencies(ArrayList cacheKeys);
```

AddCacheItemDependency

The `AddCacheItemDependency` method allows you to specify that validity of one item in the cache is dependent on some other item in the cache. If the other item is removed from cache, the cache response of current item will become invalid.

```
public void AddCacheItemDependency(string cacheKey);
```

AddFileDependencies

The `AddFileDependencies` method allows the addition of multiple files to the list of files the current response is dependent on. These file dependencies are related to the caching mechanisms in ASP.NET as setting file dependencies indicates that a cached response is dependent on the files and the cache should be refreshed when the file(s) change. See Chapter 6 for more information on caching in ASP.NET.

```
public void AddFileDependencies(ArrayList fileNames);
```

The parameter `fileNames` represents an `ArrayList` filled with values representing the file path of the files to add.

AddFileDependency

The `AddFileDependency` method allows the addition of a single file as a dependency for the given response object. It is a quicker method to add a single file dependency than using an array of file names as above. Caching is an important part of many high volume sites and having a response that can be cached based on when a file changes is a very powerful mechanism for achieving high throughput on a web site. See Chapter 6 for more information on caching in ASP.NET.

```
public void AddFileDependency(string fileName);
```

The parameter `fileName` represents the path to the file on which this response should be dependent.

AddHeader

The `AddHeader` method allows the addition of an HTTP header to the outgoing response. See the `HttpRequest` class's `Headers` property for more information on common headers.

```
public void AddHeader(string name, string value);
```

The parameter name specifies the name of the header to add and the `value` parameter represents the value to be set for the header named in the first parameter.

> This method is only provided for backward compatibility with ASP. In ASP.NET the
> `AppendHeader` method should be used instead.

AppendHeader

The `AppendHeader` method allows the addition of a header to the outgoing response stream.

```
public void AppendHeader(string name, string value);
```

The parameter name specifies the name of the header to add and the `value` parameter represents the value to be set for the header named in the first parameter. For example, maybe we have a server web farm and want to indicate to the calling program the actual server that serviced the request. We could append a custom header indicating this value:

```
Response.AppendHeader("SERVICING_SERVER" ,
Request.ServerVariables["LOCAL_ADDR"]);
```

There are standard headers in HTTP communications with a browser, but this method allows for adding your own custom ones in addition to the standard headers.

AppendToLog

The `AppendToLog` method allows you to append information to the IIS web log entry for the request. In this way, specialized information can be included in the log based on the events of the page processing.

```
public void AppendToLog(string param);
```

The parameter `param` represents the string to be added to the IIS web log entry for this response.

Being able to extend the website log can be a powerful mechanism for performing business analysis on a web site. While the standard web logs can be useful for understanding basic traffic patterns, being able to add information to the log can allow you to understand a user's actions through adding in more information about what they're doing. The information in the logs can be imported into a database or other source to provide more powerful analysis.

ApplyAppPathModifier

The `ApplyAppPathModifier` method allows the addition of a session ID to the virtual path, returning the new virtual path with the addition of the session ID in the virtual path. This method can be used when the session state's cookieless attribute is set to `true`, as it will add the Session ID in the newly constructed virtual path.

```
public string ApplyAppPathModifier(string virtualPath);
```

The parameter `virtualPath` refers to a virtual path that needs `Session ID` to be appended and is pointing to resource.

BinaryWrite

The `BinaryWrite` method allows writing out binary data, such as an image or PDF file, to the response stream.

```
public void BinaryWrite(Byte[] buffer);
```

The parameter `buffer` represents the byte array containing the binary data to be written to the `Response` stream.

Clear

The `Clear` method allows cleaning out the response stream buffer. This might be helpful if information has been written out and the page logic requires the information not to be displayed. For example, if the request begins processing, and the logic dictates that a redirect is necessary, then this method can be used to clear the headers that have already been written to the response before redirecting the client.

```
public void Clear();
```

ClearContent

The `ClearContent` method clears out just the content portion of the buffer stream but not the header information.

```
public void ClearContent();
```

ClearHeaders

The `ClearHeaders` method clears any custom or standard headers that have been set for the response. This can be useful if you are designing pages that do not contain any user interface. For example, if you have a page that serves as an interface to another application, you may want to remove the headers for your communication between the two applications. It throws an `HttpException` object if this method is called after the headers information is sent.

```
public void ClearHeaders();
```

Close

The `Close` method closes the response object so that no other data can be written to it. In actuality the physical socket connection between the client and the server is closed.

```
public void Close();
```

End

The `End` method stops execution of the page after flushing the output buffer to the client. It also raises the `Application_EndRequest` event.

```
public void End();
```

In the middle of a page execution, a situation might arise that causes the page execution to end without completing the processing. Calling this method stops the execution at the point of call and returns the output to the client.

Flush

The `Flush` method allows for flushing all of the currently buffered content out to the client.

```
public void Flush();
```

When buffering the response (see the `BufferContent` property) the `Flush` method can be used to send the buffered content to the browser in chunks. This provides a faster display to the client. The `Flush` method is called intrinsically when the `End` method is called.

Pics

The `Pics` method allows the addition of a `Pics-label` HTTP header to the outgoing response object. This `Pics-label` identifies a content rating for the material contained in the page. Any value can be set using this method, as the .NET runtime does not set any requirements or do any checking on the value. The only restriction is that the value must be less than 255 characters. This `PICS` header is the indicator of content that is checked when you set content restrictions in Internet Explorer. For more information on PICS, visit the World Wide Web Consortium's web site at http://w3c.org/PICS/.

```
public void Pics(string value);
```

The `value` parameter specifies the value to be set for the `Pics-label` header.

Redirect

The `Redirect` method allows you to send a redirection directive to the client browser. Many browsers support this type of response and will make a new request for the specified resource. This method requires another round trip between the client and server. As such, you should, instead, try to use either the `HttpServerUtility.Transfer` method or the `HttpServerUtility.Execute` method, as neither of these methods requires the client to make a new request. The `Redirect` method has two overloads.

```
public void Redirect(string url);
```

The parameter `url` represents the URL client needs redirecting to.

```
public void Redirect(string url, bool endResponse);
```

The `endResponse` parameter indicates whether to end the current response, by implicitly calling the `End` method. The default value for this property, if only specifying the URL, is `true`. The `endResponse` parameter is useful if you want code to continue executing even if the user has been redirected. For example, if you decide at some point in your code to redirect the user, but you have code that follows in your page that still needs to execute in order for the page to successfully process, then you can set this value to `false` to ensure that the rest of the code in your page executes.

RemoveOutputCacheItem

The `RemoveOutputCacheItem` is a `static` method that removes all the cached items linked with any resource. The path is specified as a parameter to this method and it removes all cached items from the cache for the specified physical path.

```
public static void RemoveOutputCacheItem(string path);
```

The `path` represents the physical path from which the cache items need to be removed.

Write

The `Write` method allows writing output to the outgoing stream. There are several overloaded versions of this method to allow for the output of a variety of data types.

```
public void Write(char ch);
```

The parameter `ch` specifies the character to write to the output stream.

```
public void Write(object ob);
```

The parameter `ob` specifies the object to write to the output stream. It writes the object to the output stream by calling its `ToString` method intrinsically.

```
public void Write(string value);
```

The parameter `value` specifies the string value to write to the output stream.

```
public void Write(char[] buffer, int index, int count);
```

The parameter `buffer` represents the character array to write to the outgoing stream. The parameter `index` specifies the array index to begin writing from and the parameter `count` represents the number of elements to write out to the stream.

WriteFile

The `WriteFile` method writes a file out to the output stream. This file could contain HTML and other text elements that would help make up the page content. This method has four overloaded versions:

```
public void WriteFile(string fileName);
```

The parameter `fileName` specifies the name or path of the file to write out to the stream.

```
public void WriteFile(string fileName, bool readIntoMemory);
```

The parameter `fileName` specifies the name or path of the file to write out to the stream. The `readIntoMemory` parameter indicates whether the file should be read into a memory block.

```
public void WriteFile(IntPtr fileHandle, long offset, long size);
```

The parameter `fileHandle` specifies the handle to the file that should be written out to the stream. The `offset` parameter represents the starting position in the file at which reading should begin and the `size` parameter specifies the number of bytes to read and then write out to the stream.

```
public void WriteFile(string fileName, long offset, long size);
```

The parameter `fileName` specifies the name or path of the file to write out to the stream. The `offset` parameter represents the starting position in the file at which reading should begin and the `size` parameter specifies the number of bytes to read and then write out to the stream.

HttpResponse Protected Methods

- ❑ `Finalize` – inherited from `System.Object`, see Introduction for more details
- ❑ `MemberwiseClone` – inherited from `System.Object`, see Introduction for more details

HttpResponse Public Properties

- ❑ **Buffer**
- ❑ **BufferOutput**
- ❑ **Cache**
- ❑ **CacheControl**
- ❑ **Charset**
- ❑ **ContentEncoding**
- ❑ **ContentType**
- ❑ **Cookies**
- ❑ **Expires**
- ❑ **ExpiresAbsolute**
- ❑ **Filter**
- ❑ **IsClientConnected**
- ❑ **Output**
- ❑ **OutputStream**
- ❑ **Status**
- ❑ **StatusCode**
- ❑ **StatusDescription**
- ❑ **SuppressContent**

Buffer

The `Buffer` property indicates whether or not the output to the response stream will be buffered and therefore cleared before being sent to the client. It is used to return or assign a `Boolean` value where `true` represents that the output will be buffered.

```
public bool Buffer {get; set;}
```

> This method is only available for backward compatibility with ASP. Use the **BufferOutput** property instead in ASP.NET.

BufferOutput

The `BufferOutput` property indicates whether the response output should be buffered until the page has completed processing and then be sent to the client, instead of being sent as the page is processed.

```
public bool BufferOutput {get; set;}
```

It is used to return or assign a `Boolean` value where `true` represents that the output will be buffered. The default value for this property is `true`, to allow buffering. Buffering the content before it goes out to the client has several benefits. For example, because the output is buffered, if after processing a portion of the page it is determined that the response should be redirected, then there is no problem. However, if the response had not been buffered, the header would have already been sent to the client. In this case the "302" header cannot be written to the response and an error will be thrown.

Cache

The `Cache` property indicates the caching policy in effect for the page by returning a `Cache` object. This property is the preferred mechanism for setting information about page caching expirations. Caching allows for the maintenance of a copy of the page output in memory and servicing requests for the page from memory rather than processing the page again. The policy, set through the `Cache` property, indicates such parameters as when the in-memory cached data should expire and where the information can be cached (Server, Client, or Intermediate Server).

```
public HttpCachePolicy Cache {get;}
```

CacheControl

The `CacheControl` property indicates the value to set for the HTTP cache-control header. This value can be `public` or `private`; `public` indicates that the page can be cached at any point between the client and the server, such as on a server designed specifically for caching, and `private` indicates that the content can only be cached on the client.

```
public string CacheControl {get; set;}
```

> The **CacheControl** property has been deprecated. You should use the methods and properties of the **HttpCachePolicy** object exposed through the **Cache** property to set the cacheability of the page.

Charset

The `Charset` property indicates the character set to use for the output stream.

```
public string Charset {get; set;}
```

The default character set is determined by the settings in the `<globalization>` section of the `web.config` file but can be overridden by setting this property. In this section you can set the default values for many of the properties related to globalization. The sample section from a `web.config` file below shows some of the properties that can be set:

```
<globalization
    fileEncoding="utf-8"
    requestEncoding="utf-8"
    responseEncoding="utf-8"
    culture="en-US"
    uiCulture="de-DE"
/>
```

The settings listed here, with the exception of `fileEncoding` and `requestEncoding`, can also be set at the page level by placing them in a page directive.

The difference between the `CharSet` property and the `ContentEncoding` property is that the `CharSet` can be set to `null` and the content-type header will be suppressed. The `ContentEncoding` property cannot be set to `null`.

ContentEncoding

The `ContentEncoding` property indicates an `Encoding` object that represents the character set in use on the outgoing stream. This property provides a more robust, object-oriented approach for setting the character set for the outgoing response when compared with the `CharSet` property. It becomes important when working with international applications, which need to be flexible in the languages they display. Setting the `ContentEncoding` property to `null` will cause an `ArgumentException` to be thrown

```
public Encoding ContentEncoding {get; set;}
```

ContentType

The `ContentType` property indicates the MIME type (see list earlier in this chapter of MIME types) of the outgoing response stream. The default value for this property is `text/html` as the majority of content served by web servers is HTML text. If you were returning XML data directly to the client, then this property would be set to `text/xml`. The `ContentType` property will throw an `HttpException` if it is set to `null`.

```
public string ContentType {get; set;}
```

Cookies

The `Cookies` property indicates the cookies collection, which allows the addition of cookies to the outgoing stream. The `HttpCookiesCollection` (discussed earlier in the chapter) provides a wrapper for a collection of cookies. The `Cookies` property refers to the collection that is created on the server and sent to the client in the `Set-Cookie` header. The property is read-only, but the underlying collection can be used to add or manipulate the cookies sent to the client.

```
public HttpCookiesCollection Cookies {get;}
```

Expires

The `Expires` property indicates the number of minutes that the page should be cached on the client browser. It is used to set or get the number of minutes before which the cached page expires.

```
public int Expires {get; set;}
```

> The **`Expires`** property has been deprecated. You should use the methods and properties of the **`HttpCachePolicy`** object exposed through the **`Cache`** property to set the expiration for the page in ASP.NET.

ExpiresAbsolute

The `ExpiresAbsolute` property indicates the specific date and time until which the page should be cached by the client browser.

```
public DateTime ExpiresAbsolute {get; set;}
```

> The **`ExpiresAbsolute`** property has been deprecated. You should use the methods and properties of the **`HttpCachePolicy`** object exposed through the **`Cache`** property to set the absolute expiration for the page.

Filter

The `Filter` property indicates the stream applied as a filter to the outgoing response. A custom stream class can be set to filter the outgoing content and apply any changes necessary. A simple example would be a stream class that capitalizes all of the HTML tags in the output.

```
public bool Filter {get; set;}
```

IsClientConnected

The `IsClientConnected` property indicates whether the client is still connected to the server. It returns `true` if the client is connected to the server and `false` otherwise. This property can be useful when running a lengthy request. Perhaps you have a long running query, or are waiting for a response from another server. If the client is no longer connected, it does not pay to continue processing the request. In a high volume site, it's important to only process what is necessary.

```
public bool IsClientConnected {get;}
```

Output

The `Output` property indicates a `TextWriter` object that can be used to directly send output to the HTTP response stream. The `Response.Write` syntax is much more familiar for classic ASP developers, but ultimately does the same thing. Writing with the `Response.Write` or `Response.Output.Write` methods performs the same operation, and will produce the same results. The `Output` property simply allows for another mechanism of doing this and provides a `TextWriter` class as the object.

```
public TextWriter Output {get;}
```

OutputStream

The `OutputStream` property indicates a stream object that can be used to write output directly onto the response stream. This is useful if you have content that you are streaming from another source or if you are using a business object, or helper function, that requires a stream to write to. This stream is very similar to the `Response` object in that it is written to in similar ways, but this property gives you direct access to the stream as an object that derives directly from the abstract stream class. This property helps in sending binary output in the content sent to the client. It throws an `HttpException` when the output stream is not present.

```
public Stream OutputStream {get;}
```

Status

The `Status` property indicates the HTTP status that is being sent to the client. This is a string value representing both the code and text versions (for example `200 OK`). The default value is `200 OK`. An `HttpException` occurs if the `Status` is set to an invalid status code.

```
public string Status {get; set;}
```

StatusCode

The `StatusCode` property indicates the numeric representation of the status of the HTTP output sent by the server to the client. For example, a successful request is indicated by a status code `200` while a redirection is indicated by a status code of `302`. Most users are probably familiar with the `404` status code meaning that a resource was not found. These codes indicate to the web browser the outcome of the request made to the server. The default value is `200`. An `HttpException` occurs if the `StatusCode` is set after sending the HTTP headers. For a complete list of HTTP status codes, see http://www.w3.org/Protocols/HTTP/HTRESP.html.

```
public int StatusCode {get; set;}
```

StatusDescription

The `StatusDescription` property indicates the string representation of the status of the HTTP output sent by the server to the client. The default value is `OK`. An `HttpException` occurs if the `StatusDescription` is set after sending the HTTP headers.

```
public string StatusDescription {get; set;}
```

SuppressContent

The `SuppressContent` property indicates whether the content in the page should be sent to the client. A `true` value indicates that the content should be suppressed and not sent. If this property is set to `true`, and the response is being buffered, then the response to the client will be blank. If buffering is turned off and this property is set to `true`, then only that content sent to the output stream before setting this property to `true` will be sent.

```
public bool SuppressContent {get; set;}
```

HttpRuntime Class

The HttpRuntime class offers methods and properties regarding the run-time environment in which the web application is running as well as information about the runtime itself. This information can be useful for finding path information or locating files needed in processing pages, as well as in more advanced development where the programmer needs to work with the ASP.NET internals.

HttpRuntime Public Methods

- ❏ **Close**
- ❏ Equals – inherited from System.Object, see Introduction for more details
- ❏ GetHashCode – inherited from System.Object, see Introduction for more details
- ❏ GetType – inherited from System.Object, see Introduction for more details
- ❏ **ProcessRequest**
- ❏ ToString – inherited from System.Object, see Introduction for more details

Close

The Close method allows shutting down the runtime (CLR) and clearing the cache. There is no need to call this method in the normal processing of request. This method call is required when the application wishes to provide its own hosting requirement.

```
public static void Close();
```

ProcessRequest

The ProcessRequest method is the method that drives all requests made to the web site. This method is the invocation that actually starts a web request. This method call is required, like Close method, when the application wishes to provide its own hosting requirement or when the code implements its own HttpWorkerRequest to execute child requests.

```
public static void ProcessRequest(HttpWorkerRequest request);
```

The parameter request represents the actual request made by the client.

HttpRuntime Protected Methods

- ❏ Finalize – inherited from System.Object, see Introduction for more details
- ❏ MemberwiseClone – inherited from System.Object, see Introduction for more details

HttpRuntime Public Properties

All the properties of the HttpRuntime class are public, static, and readonly.

- ❏ **AppDomainAppId**
- ❏ **AppDomainAppPath**

- ❑ **AppDomainAppVirtualPath**
- ❑ **AppDomainId**
- ❑ **AspInstallDirectory**
- ❑ **BinDirectory**
- ❑ **Cache**
- ❑ **ClrInstallDirectory**
- ❑ **CodegenDir**
- ❑ **IsOnUNCShare**
- ❑ **MachineConfigurationDirectory**

AppDomainAppId

The AppDomainAppId shared property indicates a string value that represents the identification of the application within the AppDomain that the web application is currently executing in. See the AppDomainId property to get the ID for the application domain itself. An application domain is a unit of processing that is used to separate the code executing in different applications. While the runtime generally takes care of creating application domains, the domains can be created by a developer to execute code in separate spaces. AppDomainAppId is a read-only property and returns a string value.

```
public static string AppDomainAppId {get;}
```

AppDomainAppPath

The AppDomainAppPath property indicates the file path to the physical directory where the files for the current web application reside. AppDomainAppPath is a read-only property and returns a string value.

```
public static string AppDomainAppPath {get;}
```

AppDomainAppVirtualPath

The AppDomainAppVirtualPath property indicates the virtual path to the directory where the files for the web application exist in the application domain. It is a read-only property and returns a string value.

```
public static string AppDomainAppVirutalPath {get;}
```

AppDomainId

The AppDomainId property indicates the identification (ID) of the AppDomain in which the web application is running. AppDomainId is a read-only property and returns a string value.

```
public static string AppDomainId {get;}
```

AspInstallDirectory

The `AspInstallDirectory` property indicates the physical path to the directory where the ASP.NET runtime is installed. It is a read-only property and returns a string value representing the physical path.

```
public static string AspInstallDirectory {get;}
```

BinDirectory

The `BinDirectory` property indicates the `bin` directory for the current web application. This directory is where all assemblies used in the application, other than those in the Global Application Cache (GAC), are located. It is a read-only property and returns a string value representing the bin directory path.

```
public static string BinDirectory {get;}
```

Cache

The `Cache` property indicates a `Cache` object that allows the developer to insert and retrieve items to be cached. This built-in `Cache` object can be extremely useful in caching data or other information that is expensive to retrieve and does not change often. It is a read-only property and returns a reference to `System.Web.Caching.Cache` object.

```
public static Cache Cache {get;}
```

The `Cache` object can be used to cache frequently used information in a web application. This helps in improving the performance of the application. See Chapter 6 for an example of using the `Cache` object to cache data from a database. These `Cache` objects can also have dependencies, such as a file dependency. For example, we might load information from an XML document and store it in the `Cache` object. This cache can be dependent on the file we loaded our data from, so that when our file changes, the cache can be updated.

ClrInstallDirectory

The `ClrInstallDirectory` property indicates the physical path to the file system directory where the Common Language Runtime binary files are located. It is a read-only property and returns a string value.

```
public static string ClrInstallDirectory {get;}
```

CodegenDir

The `CodegenDir` property indicates the physical path to the directory on the file system that acts as the default location for assemblies generated dynamically. It is a read-only property and returns a string value.

```
public static string CodegenDir {get;}
```

One of the benefits of ASP.NET over classic ASP programming is that the code and web pages are compiled as opposed to being interpreted. This compilation allows faster execution of the code. When a page is requested, if it has not been compiled, it is compiled at that time and the compiled files are accessed from that point on. This property provides the path to the directory where these compiled files are created.

IsOnUNCShare

The IsOnUNCShare property indicates whether the application files are located on a UNC (Universal Naming Convention) share as opposed to being located locally on the web server. It is a read-only property and returns a Boolean value, with true indicating that the application files are located on a UNC share.

```
public static bool IsOnUNCShare {get;}
```

MachineConfigurationDirectory

The MachineConfigurationDirectory property indicates the physical path to the directory where the machine configuration (machine.config) file for the current application is located. It is a read-only property and returns a string value.

```
public static string MachineConfigurationDirectory {get;}
```

The machine configuration file contains configuration information that covers the entire machine. This information acts as the base configuration information for the machine, which can be overridden by more specific files such as the web.config file. See Chapter 7, for more information on using the configuration files in ASP.NET.

Example: The Properties of the HttpRuntime Class

The code example, HttpRuntimeUsage.aspx.cs, shown below demonstrates the usage for all of the properties of the HttpRuntime class:

```
using System;
using System.Collections;
using System.ComponentModel;
using System.Data;
using System.Drawing;
using System.Web;
using System.Web.SessionState;
using System.Web.UI;
using System.Web.UI.WebControls;
using System.Web.UI.HtmlControls;
using System.Text;

namespace WebUsageCs
{
    /// <summary>
    /// Summary description for HttpRuntimeUsage.
    /// </summary>
```

```csharp
public class HttpRuntimeUsage : System.Web.UI.Page
{
  protected System.Web.UI.WebControls.LinkButton LBtnRuntime;
  protected System.Web.UI.WebControls.Label LblRuntime;

  private void Page_Load(object sender, System.EventArgs e)
  {
    // Put user code to initialize the page here
  }

  #region Web Form Designer generated code
  ...

  private void LBtnRuntime_Click(object sender, System.EventArgs e)
  {
    StringBuilder sbText = new StringBuilder();

    // Display all the properties of the HttpRuntime Class
    sbText.AppendFormat("Application Identification of Application " +
                        "Domain: {0}" , HttpRuntime.AppDomainAppId);
    sbText.Append("<br>");
    sbText.AppendFormat("Physical Path of the Application " +
                        "Directory: {0}" , HttpRuntime.AppDomainAppPath);
    sbText.Append("<br>");
    sbText.AppendFormat("Virtual Path of the Application " +
                "Directory: {0}" , HttpRuntime.AppDomainAppVirtualPath);
    sbText.Append("<br>");
    sbText.AppendFormat("Application Domain Identification: {0}" ,
                        HttpRuntime.AppDomainId);
    sbText.Append("<br>");
    sbText.AppendFormat("ASP.NET Executable Files Install " +
                "Directory: {0}" , HttpRuntime.AspInstallDirectory);
    sbText.Append("<br>");
    sbText.AppendFormat("Bin Files Directory: {0}" ,
                        HttpRuntime.BinDirectory);
    sbText.Append("<br>");
    sbText.AppendFormat("Current Application Cache: {0}" ,
                        HttpRuntime.Cache);
    sbText.Append("<br>");
    sbText.AppendFormat("CLR Executable Files Install Directory: {0}" ,
                        HttpRuntime.ClrInstallDirectory);
    sbText.Append("<br>");
    sbText.AppendFormat("ASP.NET Code Generated Files Directory: {0}" ,
                        HttpRuntime.CodegenDir);
    sbText.Append("<br>");
    sbText.AppendFormat("ASP.NET Files located on UNC Share: {0}" ,
                        HttpRuntime.IsOnUNCShare);
    sbText.Append("<br>");
    sbText.AppendFormat("machine.config File Directory: {0}" ,
                        HttpRuntime.MachineConfigurationDirectory);
    sbText.Append("<br>");
    LblRuntime.Text=sbText.ToString();
  }
```

```
    }
  }
```

The following screenshot displays the output:

HttpServerUtility Class

The `HttpServerUtility` class provides helper functions that can be used in your application. These methods and properties are available through the intrinsic `Server` object of the `Page` class and can be referenced from within a page as in the following example:

```
Server.HtmlDecode(string);
```

HttpServerUtility Public Methods

- ❑ **ClearError**
- ❑ **CreateObject**
- ❑ **CreateObjectFromClsid**
- ❑ Equals – inherited from System.Object, see Introduction for more details
- ❑ **Execute**
- ❑ GetHashCode – inherited from System.Object, see Introduction for more details
- ❑ **GetLastError**
- ❑ GetType – inherited from System.Object, see Introduction for more details
- ❑ **HtmlDecode**
- ❑ **HtmlEncode**
- ❑ **MapPath**
- ❑ ToString – inherited from System.Object, see Introduction for more details
- ❑ **Transfer**
- ❑ **UrlDecode**
- ❑ **UrlEncode**
- ❑ **UrlPathEncode**

ClearError

The ClearError method enables you to clear the last exception. The exception still needs to be caught, but this method clears it from memory so that it does not appear that there have been, or are currently, errors with the application.

```
public void ClearError();
```

CreateObject

The CreateObject method enables the creation of COM objects using their PROGID or using the type of the object. This method is similar to the Server.CreateObject method in classic ASP. There are two overloaded versions of this method.

```
public object CreateObject(string progID);
```

The progID parameter here represents the Programmatic Identifier of the COM object to be created as it is found in the registry.

```
public object CreateObject(Type type);
```

The type parameter here represents the System.Type of the Object to be created as a COM object.

This method creates a COM object on the server and returns an object reference to it allowing the developer to program against the object calling its methods and properties.

One thing to keep in mind when working with COM components is that apartment-threaded components are not creatable by default. In order to be able to use these components, such as the `Scripting.Dictionary` object, the `AspCompat` attribute of the page directive must be set to `true`.

```
<%@ Page AspCompat=true %>
```

This indicates to the runtime that this page should be allowed to run on a Single-Threaded Apartment (STA) thread. This offers the benefit of being able to call apartment-threaded components and components in COM+ that need access to the ASP.NET intrinsic objects or object context.

CreateObjectFromClsid

The `CreateObjectFromClsid` method enables the creation of a COM object from its Class ID (`CLSID`) as it appears in the registry.

```
public object CreateObjectFromClsid(string clsid);
```

The `clsid` parameter represents the string representation of the class ID of the object to be created.

This method allows for the creation of COM objects on the server based on the `CLSID` of these objects. This allows for interoperability between .NET managed code and unmanaged COM code, written in C++ or VB, for example.

Execute

The `Execute` method executes an `.aspx` page from within the current page and, optionally, returns the output of that page. This method passes the current `HttpRequest` and `HttpResponse` to the executing page, so it will be able to access the information about the request, and write to the response as if it were requested directly. There are two overloaded versions of this method as outlined below.

```
public void Execute(string path);
```

The `path` parameter here specifies the `URL` of the page to execute.

```
public void Execute(string path, TextWriter writer);
```

The `path` parameter here specifies the `URL` of the page to execute. The `writer` parameter represents the `TextWriter` object into which the executing page writes its output.

It is often the case that a web site using classic ASP is designed with UI pages and action pages. For example, there might be a page that contains a form and another that processes it. The UI page could still be called and pass execution to the processing page, even returning the UI output to the client. The example below demonstrates how ASP.NET might handle this:

```
<%@ Page language="cs" %>
<html>
<body>
```

```
<h2>Thank you for your response.</h2>

<script runat="server">

  private void BtnSubmit_Click(object sender, System.EventArgs e)
  {
    //execute the processing page and return the output to the response
    //object
    Server.Execute("processing.aspx", Response.Output);
  }

</script>
</body>
</html>
```

GetLastError

The GetLastError method allows the developer to get the last exception that was thrown. It returns the Exception object representing the last exception. If there were no exceptions generated, then the method will return null. Therefore the returned Exception object must be always first verified against null, or a run-time NullReferenceException is thrown.

```
public Exception GetLastError();
```

HtmlDecode

The HtmlDecode method enables decoding strings that have been previously encoded for sending safely over HTTP to a browser. It returns the decoded string. This method has two overloaded versions:

```
public string HtmlDecode(string encodedString);
```

The encodedString parameter here specifies the encoded string to be decoded.

```
public void HtmlDecode(string encodedString, TextWriter writer);
```

The writer parameter represents the TextWriter object into which the decoded string will be written.

HtmlEncode

The HtmlEncode method enables strings to be encoded so that they are safe for transmitting over HTTP to a web browser. There are two overloaded versions of this method:

```
public string HtmlEncode(string inputString)
```

The inputString parameter here specifies the string to be encoded for delivery to the browser.

```
public void HtmlEncode(string inputString, TextWriter writer);
```

The `writer` parameter represents the `TextWriter` object into which the encoded string will be written.

When working with URL strings it is important to ensure that the browser can interpret them correctly. URL strings are therefore encoded with replacement characters so that the browser can achieve this. An example of this would be the string "Priced < $50", which becomes "Priced < $50" after being encoded. Notice that the "<" symbol was replaced as it has special meaning to the HTML rendering engines in web browsers. The `HtmlEncode` and `HtmlDecode` methods provide an easy way to manipulate strings so they are safe to pass to the browser.

MapPath

The `MapPath` method allows mapping of the physical path of the file given the virtual path. It returns a `String` object representing the physical path of the file for a specified virtual path of a web server, passed as its parameter.

```
public string MapPath(string path);
```

The parameter `path` represents the virtual path for which a corresponding physical path is desired.

Transfer

The `Transfer` method allows the transfer of a page execution from the current page to another page on the server. Unlike the `Redirect` method, this method transfers execution to a new page that returns a result to the browser.

```
public void Transfer(string path);
```

The parameter `path` specifies the URL to transfer the execution to. This resource must reside on the same server and the URL must not contain any query strings.

```
public void Transfer(string path, bool preserveForm);
```

The `preserveForm` parameter indicates whether the forms and query string collection should be preserved so they may be accessed from the receiving page.

In ASP 2.0, we had access to the `Response.Redirect` method that would send a directive to the client browser with a `302` status code that indicated to the browser that it should request a different resource. In ASP 3.0 and now in ASP.NET, we also have the ability to transfer execution of a page to another page without this round trip to the client. Not only is this faster, but it creates a smoother experience for the user.

UrlDecode

The `UrlDecode` method enables the decoding of a URL string that has been encoded to allow for special characters in the URL. This method has two overloaded versions:

```
public string UrlDecode(string url);
```

The parameter `url` specifies the URL to be decoded.

```
public void UrlDecode(string url, TextWriter writer);
```

The `writer` object represents the `TextWriter` object to which the decoded string will be written.

UrlEncode

The `UrlEncode` method enables the encoding of a URL string so that the string becomes safe to be transmitted over HTTP. This method has two overloaded versions.

```
public string UrlEncode(string url);
```

The parameter `url` specifies the URL to be encoded.

```
public void UrlEncode(string url, TextWriter writer);
```

The `writer` object represents the `TextWriter` object to which the encoded string will be written.

Given the URL http://www.mysite.com/default.aspx?name=my site, the `UrlEncode` method would return:

```
http%3a%2f%2fwww.mysite.com%2fdefault.aspx%3fname%3dMy+site.
```

All spaces and special characters in the string are replaced with character codes so that the string is safe to be passed to the browser.

UrlPathEncode

The `UrlPathEncode` method allows for encoding the directory path portion of a URL. This method does not encode the resource name itself, the path info, or query string parameters.

```
public string UrlPathEncode(string url);
```

The parameter `url` specifies the URL to be encoded.

Given the URL http://www.mysite.com/default.aspx?name=my site the `UrlPathEncode` method would return:

```
http%3a%2f%2fwww.mysite.com%2fdefault.aspx?name=Mysite.
```

Notice that while all spaces and special characters in the URL are replaced with special characters, as in the `UrlEncode` method, the information following the page name is not encoded.

HttpServerUtility Protected Methods

❑ `Finalize` – inherited from `System.Object`, see Introduction for more details

❑ `MemberwiseClone` – inherited from `System.Object`, see Introduction for more details

HttpServerUtility Public Properties

- ❑ **MachineName**
- ❑ **ScriptTimeout**

MachineName

The MachineName property returns the name of the server that hosts the application. The property throws an HttpException if the server name could not be found.

```
public string MachineName {get;}
```

ScriptTimeout

The ScriptTimeout property indicates the number of seconds that are allowed to elapse before the processing of a page will be terminated and a timeout error is sent to the client. Therefore it allows you to set or get the request timeout.

```
public int ScriptTimeout {get; set;}
```

A script running in IIS may encounter issues that keep it from continuing execution, such as waiting for a database query to return. This property indicates how long the script will run before being cancelled. If a script needs a long time to run, for example you know the query will take a long time and will probably wish to avoid the timeout; this property should be set higher in this situation. Be sure to alert your users that the action they are about to take is going to take some time as many users will not wait more than a few seconds for a response from a web server.

HttpSessionState Class

While the HttpSessionState class is not part of the System.Web namespace (it belongs to the System.Web.SessionState namespace), maintaining state is an integral part of many web developers' core activities. As such, it makes sense to talk briefly about this class and how to use it. First, it should be noted that Session in ASP.NET has grown considerably from the ASP 3.0 days. In classic ASP, the session object allowed the storage of name-value pairs. These items are stored in memory and were accessible only for a given client and for a specified duration, the client's "session". Two big problems with maintaining state using the session object in classic ASP were that storing a value in session tied a user to a given server so load balancing and server farms could not take full advantage of spreading the web hits across multiple servers. Second, storing objects in session could cause nightmarish performance problems when the object was not free-threaded, as it caused a given session not only to be tied to a machine, but also to be tied to a specific thread on that machine. So, when the user made a request, if the thread they needed was busy, they would have to wait until it was ready to process their request.

With .NET, the first problem is solved by providing several different storage mechanisms and improvements to the way session information is handled and the second is less of an issue with .NET as components are thread-safe and have the ability to easily serialize themselves to a persistent storage medium.

In ASP.NET we have three options for storing session values. A description of each appears in the table below along with some of the benefits and drawbacks of each.

Mode	Description	Benefits	Drawbacks
InProc	Session data is stored in memory on the web server. This is comparable to the session object in classic ASP. This is the default setting.	Fastest access to items in session of the three options	The drawbacks are the same as they always have been for session: a user is tied to a single server so this is not as scalable as other modes
Sql Server	Session data is stored in a SQL Server database. An SQL script is provided to set up the database.	This provides a scalable solution in that it does not tie a user to a given server for their requests. This method has the ability to provide failure recovery, as the database is a persistent and transactional system that can recover the state if necessary.	While this method does not tie a client to a given web server, performance is degraded a bit by the overhead of reading and writing to the database
State Server	Session data is stored in memory on a specified server. An NT service runs on a central server and state data is sent to and retrieved from this service, which keeps the data in memory.	This method provides a bit more scalability in that clients are not tied to a given server, but there is some added overhead involved in traversing the network to read and write values.	Like the InProc method, this option does not have any disaster recovery. If the StateServer crashes or hangs for some reason, all session data is lost and the site will not be able to continue to work with session data.

In choosing an option for session state you should consider the needs of your application and what the most important factors are. In general, session state management in ASP.NET is greatly improved. In addition to the options for the storage location, session state is processed on separate threads so that a crash of an application does not mean a loss of state information. And, for those browsers that do not support cookies, there is a cookieless session mechanism that utilizes the query string to pass the session ID back to the server.

This class allows for access to the mechanisms for storing information for a given user session. (This class actually belongs to the System.Web.SessionState namespace.)

In order to set the mode for session, you will need to edit the `web.config` file. The three examples below show typical settings for the three different modes.

InProc

```
<sessionState mode="InProc"
    cookieless="false"
    timeout="20" />
```

SqlServer

```
<sessionState mode="SqlServer"
    sqlConnectionString="data source=127.0.0.1;database=state;user id=sa;
        password="
    cookieless="false"
    timeout="20" />
```

StateServer

```
<sessionState mode="StateServer"
    stateConnectionString="tcpip=127.0.0.1:42424"
    cookieless="false"
    timeout="20" />
```

One final note on session: if you are not using session in your application, disable it. Like many of the other features of ASP.NET, session can be very powerful, but if it is not being used, it adds extra overhead to the processing on the server.

HttpSessionState Public Methods

❑ **Abandon**

❑ **Add**

❑ **Clear**

❑ **CopyTo**

❑ Equals – inherited from System.Object, see Introduction for more details

❑ **GetEnumerator**

❑ GetHashCode – inherited from System.Object, see Introduction for more details

❑ GetType – inherited from System.Object, see Introduction for more details

❑ **Remove**

❑ **RemoveAll**

❑ **RemoveAt**

❑ ToString – inherited from System.Object, see Introduction for more details

Abandon

The `Abandon` method terminates the session removing all values from it. Essentially, this method notifies the session handlers to drop the session and all of its contents. You can use this method to force a session to be dropped, rather than waiting for a user to close their browser or the timeout to be reached. This can be used to provide "sign out" functionality in which the user indicates they are done working on the site and allows you to cancel their session to recover server resources.

```
public void Abandon();
```

Add

The `Add` method is used to insert items into an `HttpSessionState` collection. It takes an object as a parameter for the value, and since all items in .NET are derived from `Object`, you can, potentially, store anything in session state. However, you should seriously consider those items that you are storing and the cost of saving and retrieving that information. This will depend on the object size you have chosen for your site. Large items can degrade performance as the user load increases.

```
public void Add(string name, object value);
```

The parameter `name` specifies the key name of the item you wish to add to the collection. The parameter `value` specifies the object you wish to add to the session state.

Clear

The `Clear` method can be used to remove all of the items that are currently stored in the `HttpSessionState` collection.

```
public void Clear();
```

CopyTo

The `CopyTo` method copies the session state values collection to a single-dimensional array at the specified index.

```
public void CopyTo(Array array, int index);
```

The `array` parameter specifies the array in which the values collection is copied and the `index` parameter specifies the starting index to copy from in the array.

GetEnumerator

The `GetEnumerator` method allows reading through the session state collection, by letting it iterate through the Name–Object collection. It does not allow modifying the underlying collection. It returns keys of the collection as strings and lets you move to the next key through the `IEnumerator.MoveNext` method.

```
public IEnumerator GetEnumerator();
```

Remove

The Remove method deletes a single object out of the session-state collection. This method is called with the key name of the object, which was created at the time of adding the object.

```
public void Remove(string name);
```

The parameter name specifies the name of the object that is to be removed.

RemoveAll

The RemoveAll method removes all the objects from the HttpSessionState collection. This method makes an internal call to the Clear method.

```
public void RemoveAll();
```

RemoveAt

The RemoveAt method removes a single object out of the session state by specifying its index position.

```
public void RemoveAt(int index);
```

The parameter index represents the index number of the object that needs to be removed. It is zero-based index.

HttpSessionState Protected Methods

- ❑ Finalize – inherited from System.Object, see Introduction for more details
- ❑ MemberwiseClone – inherited from System.Object, see Introduction for more details

HttpSessionState Public Properties

All the properties of the session state are read-only.

- ❑ CodePage
- ❑ Contents
- ❑ Count
- ❑ IsCookieLess
- ❑ IsNewSession
- ❑ IsReadOnly
- ❑ IsSynchronized
- ❑ Item
- ❑ Keys
- ❑ LCID
- ❑ Mode

- ❑ `SessionID`
- ❑ `StaticObjects`
- ❑ `SyncRoot`
- ❑ `Timeout`

CodePage

The `CodePage` property gets or sets the character set or code page identifier used for displaying dynamic content, for the current session.

```
public int CodePage {get; set;}
```

> The `CodePage` property is provided for compatibility versions with previous versions of ASP. You should use `Response.ContentEncoding.CodePage` instead.

Contents

The `Contents` property just gets a reference to the `HttpSessionState` object.

```
public HttpSessionState Contents {get;}
```

> This property is available for backward compatibility with the earlier versions of ASP. Traditionally, this property was implemented as a collection of the `Session` object that allowed access to the contents of `Session` with a collection interface.

Count

The `Count` property gets the number of objects in the session state. The default value is 0. This property is overridden.

```
public int Count {get;}
```

IsCookieLess

The `IsCookieLess` property returns a `Boolean` value indicating whether the session mechanism is operating in a cookieless fashion. For those browsers with cookie support disabled, or that do not support cookies, the Session ID is passed to the server as part of the query string. This property can be used to determine if the session is using cookies so a developer can make decisions about interacting with the client.

```
public bool IsCookieLess {get;}
```

IsNewSession

The IsNewSession property returns a Boolean value indicating whether the session was created with the current request.

```
public bool IsNewSession {get;}
```

IsReadOnly

The IsReadOnly property returns a Boolean value indicating whether the session object is read-only.

```
public bool IsReadOnly {get;}
```

IsSynchronized

The IsSynchronized property returns a Boolean value indicating whether the session object is synchronized or not.

```
public bool IsSynchronized {get;}
```

Item

The Item property indicates a specific object in the session state collection. This method has two overloaded versions to allow for accessing the object by name or numeric index.

```
public object this[int] {get; set;}
```

The parameter index represents the index number of the object that needs to be fetched. It is zero-based index.

```
public object this[string] {get; set;}
```

The parameter key represents the key name of the object that needs to be retrieved.

Keys

The Keys property gets all the key names available in the collection. A SystemCollections.Specialized.NameObjectCollectionBase.KeysCollection object is returned containing keys of the collection.

```
public NameObjectCollectionBase.KeysCollection Keys {get;}
```

LCID

The LCID property gets or sets the locale identifier of the current session.

```
public int LCID {get; set;}
```

Mode

The `Mode` property returns an enumerated value indicating the storage mechanism for the session. These options were discussed in the introduction of this section.

```
public SessionStateMode Mode {get;}
```

The possible values for the `Mode` property are indicated below:

Value	Meaning
Off	Session is disabled and therefore not available for storage of values
InProc	Session is being maintained on the local machine in memory
SqlServer	Session is using a SQL Server database to store values
StateServer	Session is being stored using the out-of-process NT service state server

SessionID

The `SessionID` returns the unique session identifier that identifies the current session.

```
public string SessionID {get;}
```

StaticObjects

The `StaticObjects` property provides access to items that were declared in the `Global.asax` file using the following syntax:

```
<object runat="server" scope="Session" >
```

This property returns a special collection class that acts as a wrapper around these objects.

```
public HttpStaticObjectsCollection StaticObjects {get;}
```

SyncRoot

The `SyncRoot` property returns an object to be used to synchronize access to the session-state collection.

```
public object SyncRoot {get;}
```

Timeout

The `Timeout` property indicates the time, in minutes, that is allowed between requests from a client before the session is destroyed. The default value for this property is `20`. This is important because a session is defined as a single user's interaction with your web site. Once that user has stopped interacting with your site, their session is still taking up valuable memory on the server. In a high volume site this can have an impact on performance. On the other hand, if you set this property too low, a user may not have completed working on your site and come back to their computer to find that all of the work they have done is lost and they must start all over again.

You should be sure to consider the ramifications and the needs of your site before changing this value. It can also be set for an application in the `web.config` file.

```
public int Timeout {get; set;}
```

2

System.Web.UI

The System.Web.UI namespace includes the foundation classes for all user interface generation in ASP.NET. Literally everything that is rendered to the client browser is encapsulated within a class or child class of the System.Web.UI namespace.

In this chapter we will be looking in depth at several core classes of the System.Web.UI namespace, namely:

❑ Control Class – represents the base class for all UI elements in a Web Form. It is the basis for pages, user controls, server controls, HTML controls, and literal text controls.

❑ TemplateControl Abstract Class – provides common functionality for the page and user control classes.

❑ Page Class – represents a single page, or Web Form, in a web application and houses all objects found on the page. Each page that a developer creates derives from the Page class and therefore has all the functionality of this class.

❑ UserControl Class – represents small reusable parts of a web page that can be compiled separately and inserted in any page.

The Control Hierarchy

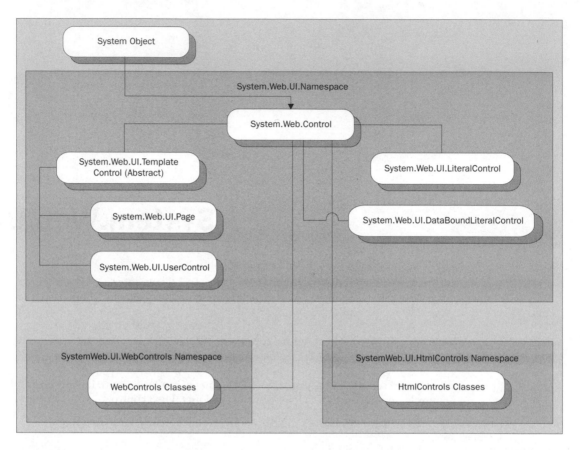

In ASP.NET, everything conforms to the object-oriented programming model. In fact all programmatic entities in the .NET run-time are children of the `System.Object` base class. When you create an ASP.NET web page it may arrive on the browser as plain HTML text but on the server it lived as an instance of the `System.Web.UI.Page` class referenced above. In fact, every single user interface element of that page, from the text to the drop-down menu, spent an instant instantiated as some version of a **control object**.

Microsoft calls user interface elements **controls**. All the controls in the page live in a hierarchy or "tree" of control objects. The parent control of every ASP.NET web page lives on the server as a `Page` class instance. All other controls for that page are children to that `Page` class instance and these children can, in turn, have child controls. So, during server processing of a browser request every item in the page, including the page itself, is instantiated as one of the following objects:

❑ **Page object** – this object represents the web page itself and as such acts as a container to all of the other controls on the page.

- **Literal Controls** – a Literal Control is any literal text or HTML element on a page that is not processed in some way by the server. Even though literal text and HTML are not processed by the server, they are allocated a Literal Control object to handle their rendering to the browser at the time the page is processed.

- **Server Controls** – unlike literal controls, Server Controls *are* processed on the server before text is rendered to the browser. When an .aspx page is called the server controls in it are fully programmatic entities on the server, real objects that have associated methods and properties, can fire and respond to events and even maintain state. On the .aspx page server controls look almost identical to standard HTML entities, but unlike HTML entities, server controls are fully accessible by your server-side code. (See the next three chapters for details on the Server Controls built in to ASP.NET.)

- **User Controls** – a UserControl object represents a group of related controls and text that you design. A User Control lets you build custom user interface "snap-ins" that you can reuse in pages across your application.

Consider the following page:

Example: hierarchy.aspx

```
<%@ Page language="c#"  %>
<HTML>
  <HEAD id="head">
    <title id="title">Hierarchy Display</title>
  </HEAD>
  <body id="body">
    <form id="Hierarchy" method="post" runat="server">
      <h2 id="heading2">
        A calendar control
      </h2>
      <asp:Calendar ID="cal" runat="server" />
      <a href="hierarchy.aspx" runat="server" ID="A1">This is my link</a>
    </form>
  </body>
</HTML>
```

Every HTML element or entity in the page above will be instantiated at run time as an object subordinate to a `Page` instance. This nested grouping of controls is often referred to as the **control hierarchy**. If we could see the control hierarchy generated at run time on the server it would look like this:

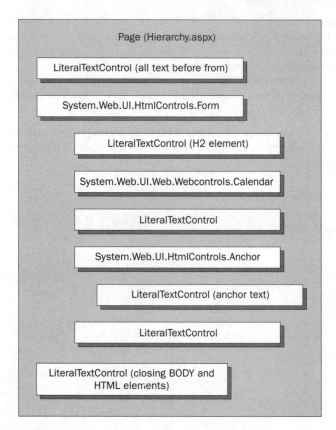

When working with a control (remember this includes `Page` objects), we can get access to the controls collection for each item, and add new controls or work with the controls contained in the parent control. See the section later on the `Controls` property of the `Control` class.

Another important point to note is that the `Page` and `UserControl` classes derive from the abstract class `TemplateControl`. This is appropriate as both `Page` and `UserControl` objects are "freestanding" user interface abstractions. Pages encapsulate a web form with embedded controls. User Controls are also "freestanding" and reusable user interface objects that, once built or acquired by you, can be plugged into any ASP.NET page.

The Control Lifecycle

From the time the browser request is received until the response has been processed, completed and returned by the server, controls are instantiated and eventually destroyed on the server, creating a "control lifecycle".

The various stages of this lifecycle are shown along with the common activities that occur at each stage. To hook into this process, you either handle the event directly, or override the method shown in the right-hand column.

Stage	Purpose	Event or Method
Initialize	Initialize the control's state, setting up variables needed for the duration of processing.	`Init` event (`OnInit` method)
Load View State	State information is restored for the control by loading it from the view state or a custom mechanism.	`LoadViewState` method
Process PostBack Data	Incoming form data is processed and control properties are updated accordingly.	`IPostBackDataHandler. LoadPostData`
Load	Perform processing common to all requests. All controls are populated and accessible at this time.	`Load` event (`OnLoad` method)
Send PostBack Notifications	Controls implementing the `IPostBackDataHandler` interface are notified of changes to their state.	`IPostBackDataHandler. RaisePostDataChanged Event`
Handle PostBack Events	Controls that participate in postback events, such as the button control, handle events associated with the action that initiated the postback.	`IPostBackEventHandler. RaisePostBackEvent`
PreRender	Any final updates are made to the control before it is rendered. This is the very last opportunity to make changes to the state of the control.	`PreRender` event (`OnPreRender` method)
Save State	The control state is saved and persisted to a string, which is sent to the client in a hidden form field.	`SaveViewState` method
Render	The control is written to the output stream to be sent to the client.	`Render` method
Commit/Abort Transaction (page)	For pages run in transactions, any cleanup required after the transaction completes.	`CommitTransaction/ AbortTransaction` events

Stage	Purpose	Event or Method
Unload	The control has completed processing and can be removed from memory.	`Unload` Event
Dispose	Final cleanup before the control is released from memory.	`Dispose` method

As controls go through this lifecycle, we can override methods or handle events to run custom code that augments the processing of the control.

Classes of the System.Web.UI Namespace

In many respects the classes within the `System.Web.UI` Namespace represent the day to day building blocks of ASP.NET application development. All user interface functionality and features for ASP.NET are provided in the `System.Web.UI` namespace. The most important of these from a developer's standpoint and the most commonly used classes include:

❑   `Control`

❑   `Page`

❑   `Template Control`

❑   `User Control`

The detailed coverage of each of these four classes provides a substantial foundation for understanding and a reference for user interface development in ASP.NET. The complete class listing of the `System.Web.UI` namespace includes the following:

Class	Description
`AttributeCollection`	The `AttributeCollection` is an object representing the opening tag of a server control element and cannot be inherited.
`BasePartialCachingControl`	The `BasePartialCachingControl` is the base class for `StaticPartialCachingControl` and `PartialCachingControl` classes. It cannot be inherited.
`ConstructorNeedsTagAttribute`	The `ConstructorNeedsTagAttribute` class indicates that a server control needs a tag name in its constructor.
`Control`	**The `Control` class is the base class for all ASP.NET server controls, providing them with common functionality.**
`ControlBuilder`	The `ControlBuilder` class helps the page parser build a control.

Class	Description
ControlBuilderAttribute	The ControlBuilderAttribute class refers to a ControlBuilder object used to help the page parser build a control. It cannot be inherited.
ControlCollection	The ControlCollection class acts as an aggregator for control objects and is typified by the Control.Controls property.
CssStyleCollection	The CssStyleCollection class aggregates the inline CSS style attributes for an HTML server control. It cannot be inherited.
DataBinder	This class provides support for RAD development environments like Visual Studio .NET and is not used in day to day development.
DataBinding	This class provides support for RAD development environments like Visual Studio .NET and is not used in day to day development.
DataBindingCollection	This class provides support for RAD development environments like Visual Studio .NET and is not used in day to day development.
DataBindingHandlerAttribute	This class provides support for RAD development environments like Visual Studio .NET and is not used in day to day development.
DataBoundLiteralControl	DataBoundLiteralControl allows for the handling of data-binding expressions expressed in <%#...%> syntax that are processed by the server. It cannot be inherited.
EmptyControlCollection	EmptyControlCollection is derived from ControlCollection and represents an "empty" version of the parent class.
Html32TextWriter	Html32TextWriter is derived from System.Web.UI.HtmlTextWriter and renders HTML content for 3.2 compliant browsers.
HtmlTextWriter	HtmlTextWriter is derived from System.IO.TextWriter and renders HTML content for browsers. It should be rendered as an output stream when you override server control methods that write HTML like Control.Render.
ImageClickEventArgs	ImageClickEventArgs is derived from System.EventArgs and encapsulates the data generated by clicks on HtmlInputImage, ImageButtons, etc.

Class	Description
LiteralControl	LiteralControl supports literal text destined for the client that is *not* processed or referenced on the server, including static HTML elements, text and miscellaneous strings.
Page	**The Page control class represents a single web page.**
Pair	Pair is provided to allow more convenient storage handling of view state elements by allowing coupled ("pair") object storage. There is a nearly identical class called Triplet that allows three-element grouping.
ParseChildrenAttribute	ParseChildrenAttribute specifies metadata that defines an attribute to be used to indicate properties that are declaratively referenced for a control. This class lets you define whether XML elements inside a control's tags are to be handled like properties of the control or child controls in their own right. This class cannot be inherited.
PartialCachingAttribute	User controls that use the @OutputCache declaration generate a PartialCachingAttribute object at run time which indicates that they participate in caching and should be cached.
PartialCachingControl	User controls that use the @OutputCache declaration generate a PartialCachingControl object at run time.
PersistChildrenAttribute	The PersistChilrenAttribute is used at design time to determine whether child controls should be persisted as nested inner controls.
PersistenceModeAttribute	The PersistenceModeAttribute class is metadata specifying the persistence mode of a control and how the control is persisted to an ASP.NET page. It cannot be inherited.
StateBag	The StateBag class is responsible for storing view state data in a control. It cannot be inherited.
StateItem	The StateItem class is an element within a statebag that stores the property and associated name of the property of a control. This class cannot be inherited.
StaticPartialCachingControl	StaticPartialCachingControl derives from System.Web.UI.Control and encapsulates a control that has been declaratively referenced in a page or control and that is participating in output caching.
TagPrefixAttribute	The TagPrefixAttribute class derives from System.Attribute and has the duty of specifying the tag prefix used declaratively in the page to identify a custom control. It cannot be inherited.

Class	Description
TemplateContainerAttribute	The TemplateContainerAttribute class indicates the INamingContainer type that will contain the template for a control.
TemplateControl	**The TemplateControl class is the base class for the UserControl objects you create as well as the Page class.**
ToolboxDataAttribute	This class provides support for RAD development environments like Visual Studio .NET and is not used in day to day development.
Triplet	The Triplet class is used to make the storage of values in a control's view state more convenient for values that are stored in threes, like RGB color values for HTML colorspace definitions. The sibling Pair class efficiently stores pairs of objects in a control's view state.
UserControl	**The UserControl class is the base class for custom user interface components that are reusable in various pages.**
UserControlControlBuilder	This undocumented class appears to provide support for RAD development environments like Visual Studio .NET and is not used in day to day development.
ValidationPropertyAttribute	The ValidationPropertyAttribute is the metadata that a control uses to identify a validation property. It cannot be inherited
ValidatorCollection	The ValidationCollection class acts as an aggregator of validation controls and contains an array of IValidator references, each a reference to a validator control. It cannot be inherited.

Control Class

The Control class represents the base class for the User Interface elements in ASP.NET. As a base class, the Control class methods, properties and events are common to *all* the user interface controls that ASP.NET provides for building interfaces, including the System.Web.UI.HTMLControls and System.Web.UI.WebControls namespaces which you will use most often as you build your pages. Furthermore, since your custom user controls and even the ASP.NET Page object itself derive from Control, understanding the Control base class is critical to building ASP.NET pages and user interface experiences.

Control Public Methods

- ❏ **DataBind**
- ❏ **Dispose**
- ❏ Equals – inherited from System.Object, see Introduction for details.
- ❏ **FindControl**
- ❏ GetHashCode – inherited from System.Object, see Introduction for details.
- ❏ GetType – inherited from System.Object, see Introduction for details.
- ❏ **HasControls**
- ❏ **RenderControl**
- ❏ **ResolveUrl**
- ❏ ToString – inherited from System.Object, see Introduction for details.

DataBind

The DataBind method binds a specified data source to the control and all its child controls. Binding causes the data elements in the data source to "inhabit" the related properties of the control, such as populating a list control with the contents of a data set. If you are building your own custom or template-based controls you will need to override this method if your control binds to a data source.

```
public virtual void DataBind();
```

Dispose

The Dispose method enables a control to do any final housekeeping, such as releasing resources, before it is removed from memory by the garbage collector. Dispose is the method you need to override and invoke if you want to handle cleanup for your control. Microsoft recommends against duplicating your cleanup code in Finalize (see below) and instead Finalize should simply invoke the Dispose method. This is because Dispose is meant to be called explicitly but Finalize may be called in a "non-deterministic" manner by the garbage collection process.

Remember, you must call Dispose before you release your last reference to the Control or the resources held by the Control will be unavailable until garbage collection calls the Control object's destructor. If you know the control is leaving scope, Dispose it. If a Control has children, call their Dispose method too from within the parent Dispose method.

```
public virtual void Dispose();
```

FindControl

The FindControl method takes a string as input and returns a reference to a child control that has the same name in the current **naming container**. If no child control is found the method returns Null. The NamingContainer and related ID property are discussed in the *Properties* section of this class description.

```
public virtual Control FindControl(string);
```

HasControls

The `HasControls` method indicates whether the current control has child controls. Child controls are controls living within the current control. You should use `HasControls` when checking for the existence of controls instead of using the `ControlCollection` class' `Count` property because `HasControls` is faster. If, however, you need the actual count of children controls then the `Count` property is required.

```
public virtual bool HasControls();
```

RenderControl

The `RenderControl` method takes an `HtmlTextWriter` as input and causes a control to output its content to the `HtmlTextWriter` that is provided by value as input. `RenderControl` also retrieves trace information when tracing is turned on. In contrast, the protected version of the `Render` method cannot retrieve trace information. Both public and protected methods can be overridden to create custom controls for the rendering process. Remember, if you create a custom control and override this method, do not forget to call the `RenderControl` method separately for each child control of the parent.

```
public void RenderControl(HtmlTextWriter writer);
```

ResolveUrl

The `ResolveUrl` method takes a string as input and resolves a relative URL to the corresponding absolute URL, which is returned as a string. This method differs from the more common `MapPath` in that it returns a URL as opposed to a physical path to a file. This method can be helpful when you need to provide the client with a path to a resource that resides on the server but you don't have prior knowledge of the whole path, or you want your code to be flexible enough to run from multiple locations. Since the returned URL is intended for the client, this method also returns the session cookie value embedded in the URL if you have configured your web application to maintain session state without cookies.

```
public string ResolveUrl(string relativeUrl);
```

Example: Walking the Control Hierarchy

The following `.aspx` page and code-behind class (`walkingHierarchy.aspx` and `walkingHierarchy.aspx.cs` respectively in the code download) demonstrate navigating the control hierarchy, and uses the `GetType`, `ToString`, `HasControls` methods and the `uniqueID` and `Controls` properties of the control class.

The page is a follows:

```
<%@ Page language="c#" AutoEventWireup="false"
        Codebehind="walkingHierarchy.aspx.cs"
        Inherits="wroxRef1.walkingHierarchy" %>
<HTML>
  <HEAD id="head">
    <title id="title">Walking the Control Hierarchy</title>
```

```
</HEAD>
  <body id="body">
    <form id="formHierarchy" method="post" runat="server">
      <h1>Walking the Control Hierarchy
      </h1>
      <P><asp:table id="tableSample" runat="server"
                    GridLines="Both" BackColor="Transparent"
                    BorderWidth="1" BorderStyle="Ridge">
        <asp:TableRow>
          <asp:TableCell Text="1"></asp:TableCell>
          <asp:TableCell Text="2"></asp:TableCell>
          <asp:TableCell Text="3"></asp:TableCell>
        </asp:TableRow>
      </asp:table></P>
    <P>
        <asp:Label id="labelControlHierarchy"
                   runat="server"></asp:Label></P>
    </form>
  </body>
</HTML>
```

The code-behind class renders the control hierarchy as HTML and demonstrates various methods and properties of the control class:

```
using System;
using System.Collections;
using System.ComponentModel;
using System.Data;
using System.Drawing;
using System.Web;
using System.Web.SessionState;
using System.Web.UI;
using System.Web.UI.WebControls;
using System.Web.UI.HtmlControls;

namespace wroxRef1
{
  /// <summary>
  /// Summary description for walkingHierarchy.
  /// </summary>
  public class walkingHierarchy : System.Web.UI.Page
  {
    protected System.Web.UI.WebControls.Table tableSample;
    protected System.Web.UI.WebControls.Label labelControlHierarchy;

    private void Page_Load(object sender, System.EventArgs e)
    {
      labelControlHierarchy.Text += "<ul>";
      walkAndRenderControlHierarchy(Page);
      labelControlHierarchy.Text += "</ul>";
    }
```

...

```
    private void walkAndRenderControlHierarchy(Control thisControl)
    {
      // this method recursively renders the control hierarchy
      // information to a label control
      labelControlHierarchy.Text += "<li>" + thisControl.UniqueID +
              "/" + thisControl.GetType().ToString();

      // this is a way of checking type and accessing control contents
      // for literalControls
      if(thisControl.GetType().ToString() ==
                                      "System.Web.UI.LiteralControl")
      {
        LiteralControl tempLiteralControl = (LiteralControl)thisControl;
        labelControlHierarchy.Text += "   <b>(" +
                Server.HtmlEncode(tempLiteralControl.Text) + ")</b>";
      }

      if(thisControl.GetType().ToString() ==
                                      "System.Web.UI.WebControls.TableCell")
      {
        TableCell tempTableCell = (TableCell)thisControl;
        labelControlHierarchy.Text += "   <b>(" +
                Server.HtmlEncode(tempTableCell.Text) + ")</b>";
      }

      labelControlHierarchy.Text += "<br/>";

      if(thisControl.HasControls())
      {
        labelControlHierarchy.Text += "<ul>";

        foreach(Control controlItem in thisControl.Controls)
        {
          walkAndRenderControlHierarchy(controlItem);
        }
        labelControlHierarchy.Text += "</ul>";
      }
    }
  }
}
```

The output of this example code is as follows:

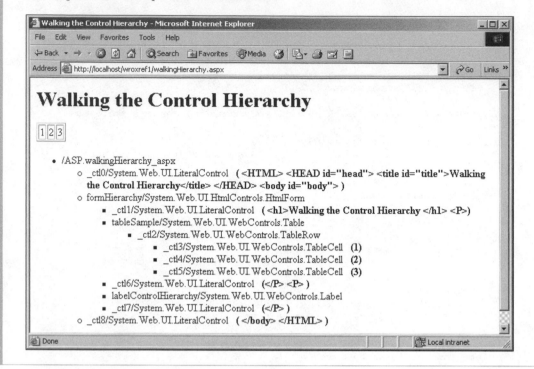

Control Protected Methods

❑ **AddParsedSubObject**

❑ **ClearChildViewState**

❑ **CreateChildControls**

❑ **CreateControlCollection**

❑ **EnsureChildControls**

❑ Finalize – inherited from System.Object, see Introduction for details.

❑ **IsLiteralContent**

❑ **LoadViewState**

❑ **MapPathSecure**

❑ MemberwiseClone – inherited from System.Object, see Introduction for details.

❑ **OnBubbleEvent**

❑ **OnDataBinding**

- ❑ **OnInit**
- ❑ **OnLoad**
- ❑ **OnPreRender**
- ❑ **OnUnload**
- ❑ **RaiseBubbleEvent**
- ❑ **Render**
- ❑ **RenderChildren**
- ❑ **SaveViewState**
- ❑ **TrackViewState**

AddParsedSubObject

The `AddParsedSubObject` method takes an `Object` as input and allows the addition of further parsed content, such as parsed HTML or XML, to the controls collection of the given control. Unless you override it, this method automatically adds `LiteralControl` objects to the server control's `ControlCollection` object. This method should be overridden for custom controls for which you wish to inhibit such a feature. For example, if you created a control and did not want users to be able to add their own literal controls to it, then you would override this method with an empty implementation. This is especially important when working with databound templated controls.

```
protected virtual void AddParsedSubObject(object obj);
```

ClearChildViewState

The `ClearChildViewState` method clears the view state of all child controls contained in the referenced control. If, for example, you have a control that allows databinding, then you would use this method to clear the state information of child controls before binding new data to them. View state is turned on by default, so it is important to clear the view state of the child controls in situations where you don't want latent data to persist.

```
protected void ClearChildViewState();
```

CreateChildControls

The `CreateChildControls` method is called by a control to determine if it should create any child controls that it is to contain. If you develop container controls or templated controls, you must override this method to handle the creation of your child controls.

```
protected virtual void CreateChildControls();
```

An example of creating child controls follows. We have a User Control that creates some literal text, an `<H3>` element, a label object, and an ASP.NET textbox adding each to its collection of controls. This is an example of adding such items dynamically rather than declaratively from the designer tool, but the two forms can be intermingled if desired.

Example: CreateChildControls

Assume we have a user control, `createChildren.ascx`, templated as follows:

```
<%@ Control Language="c#" AutoEventWireup="false"
            Codebehind="createChildren.ascx.cs"
            Inherits="wroxRef1.createChildren" %>
<ASP:LABEL id="staticlabel" runat="server">
  This is my static label</ASP:LABEL>
```

Now we code behind for the control as follows:

```
namespace wroxRef1
{
  using System;
  using System.Data;
  using System.Drawing;
  using System.Web;
  using System.Web.UI.WebControls;
  using System.Web.UI.HtmlControls;
  using System.Web.UI;

  /// <summary>
  /// Summary description for createChildren1.
  /// </summary>
  public abstract class createChildren : System.Web.UI.UserControl
  {
    protected System.Web.UI.WebControls.Label staticlabel;

    private void Page_Load(object sender, System.EventArgs e)
    {
      // Put user code to initialize the page here
    }

    protected override void CreateChildControls()
    {
      this.Controls.Add(new LiteralControl("<h3>Dynamically Added Child" +
                                           "Control</h3>"));

      // create a label and add it to the controls
      Label TextLabel = new Label();
      TextLabel.ID = "label";
      TextLabel.Text = "Enter your name: ";
      this.Controls.Add(TextLabel);

      // Add a text box to the controls
      TextBox Input = new TextBox();
      Input.Text = "HERE";
      this.Controls.Add(Input);

      Button Button1 = new Button();
      Button1.Click += new System.EventHandler(Button1_OnClick);
```

```
      this.Controls.Add(Button1);

      // Indicate that we have created the child controls
      this.ChildControlsCreated = true;
    }

    protected void Button1_OnClick(object sender, EventArgs e)
    {
      if(!this.ChildControlsCreated)
        this.Controls.Add(new LiteralControl("Am I going to show up?"));
      else
        ((Label)this.FindControl("label")).Text = "Controls already " +
                                                  "created";
    }

  ...
  }
}
```

While the template for the user control includes only static text controls, the overridden
CreateChildControls represented above generates new controls at run time, resulting in
the following HTML output:

CreateControlCollection

The CreateControlCollection method creates a collection of the child controls contained by the
given control. This method is helpful if the Controls property of the control is not adequate, or if there
is a need to work with a separate control collection. For example, if you have a custom control that
creates a collection object based on the ControlCollection class you should do that instantiation
within an override of this method.

```
protected virtual ControlCollection CreateControlCollection();
```

EnsureChildControls

The `EnsureChildControls` method checks the control to make sure it contains child controls. If it does not, then the method creates a child `LiteralControl` based on the literal text contained in the control. Call this method first when your code must, for example, refer to the first control in the controls collection and you want to ensure that doing so will not result in an exception because the control doesn't exist.

```
protected virtual void EnsureChildControls();
```

IsLiteralContent

The `IsLiteralContent` method tests whether a control is a literal control. A literal control contains only literal text and does not contain any server controls. This method can be useful when working with collections of controls to sort those you wish to perform actions on.

```
protected bool IsLiteralContent();
```

LoadViewState

The `LoadViewState` method takes an `Object` as input and allows restoration of the state of a control as previously stored by the `SaveViewState` method. Generally, this method will not need to be called explicitly, but may be overridden if you require custom routines for maintaining state. For example, if you are building a custom control to act as a container of other controls, you may want to provide an implementation for this method that loads the state of the contained controls, and also sets values for the current control itself.

```
protected virtual void LoadViewState(object savedState);
```

Additionally, if a control customizes storage of property data in View State, like handling custom types via serialization or via a `TypeConverter`, the control *must* provide a custom implementation for restoring property values from data stored in View State via overloaded `LoadViewState` and `SaveViewState` methods.

MapPathSecure

This method takes a string as input and maps the relative file path specified to its absolute path, but only if the control has sufficient security permissions to read the file. Therefore, if you map a file that has security restrictions such that would not enable the user to read it, then this method will fail throwing an `HttpException`.

```
protected string MapPathSecure(string virtualPath);
```

OnBubbleEvent

The `OnBubbleEvent` method takes an `Object` and `EventArgs` as input and is called when a child control event propagates up to this control. In handling the event, the control can indicate that it has handled it, or bubble the event up to its parent control, or both.

A control participates in event bubbling through either `OnBubbleEvent` or its sibling, `RaiseBubbleEvent`.

There is no defined `Bubble` event, as this event simply allows for passing other events up the control hierarchy. This is why the source needs to be specified in the method signature. This bubbling mechanism passes events up the control hierarchy so that parent controls have the opportunity to act on events as well. In this way, a parent control, such as a page or user control, can listen for events from all of its child controls and act accordingly.

```
protected virtual bool OnBubbleEvent(object source, EventArgs args);
```

Example: OnBubble Event User Control

As an example, let's create a user control that bubbles its post-back event up to the parent page once it has acted on the event itself. Assume a bubbler control, `bubbler.ascx`, templated as follows:

```
<%@ Control Language="c#" AutoEventWireup="false"
            Codebehind="bubbler.ascx.cs"
            Inherits="wroxRef1.bubbler" %>
<ASP:BUTTON id="Button1" text="Button" runat="server"></ASP:BUTTON>
<BR>
<ASP:LABEL id="Label1" runat="server">
   Label</ASP:LABEL>
```

The user control interface consists of a simple button and label, which both run at the server. In the code behind our control, we handle the post-back event of the button and modify the label. In the handler, we deal with the event, in this case changing the label text, and then bubble the event up so the parent control can also react to the event. As you will see below, in the code behind for a page containing the above control, we can then deal with this event when it bubbles up to page level:

```
namespace wroxRef1
{
   using System;
   using System.Data;
   using System.Drawing;
   using System.Web;
   using System.Web.UI.WebControls;
   using System.Web.UI.HtmlControls;

   /// <summary>
   /// Summary description for bubbler.
   /// </summary>
   public abstract class bubbler : System.Web.UI.UserControl
   {
      protected System.Web.UI.WebControls.Button Button1;
      protected System.Web.UI.WebControls.Label Label1;
```

```
      private void Page_Load(object sender, System.EventArgs e)
      {
        // Put user code to initialize the page here
      }

      private void Button1_Click(object sender, System.EventArgs e)
      {
        // handle the event as it pertains to the control
        Label1.Text = "Thanks for clicking!";

        // bubble the event so the parent can also respond
        this.RaiseBubbleEvent(sender, e);
      }



      ...
    }
  }
```

In the parent page, we override the OnBubbleEvent to handle incoming events from child
controls ourselves. In this case, we update a label and then return true to indicate that we have
handled the event. Returning false would allow the event to continue bubbling up the
control hierarchy.

```
using System;
using System.Collections;
using System.ComponentModel;
using System.Data;
using System.Drawing;
using System.Web;
using System.Web.SessionState;
using System.Web.UI;
using System.Web.UI.WebControls;
using System.Web.UI.HtmlControls;

namespace wroxRef1
{
  /// <summary>
  /// Summary description for bubblerPage.
  /// </summary>
  public class bubblerPage : System.Web.UI.Page
  {
    protected System.Web.UI.WebControls.Label Label1;
    private void Page_Load(object sender, System.EventArgs e)
    {
      // Put user code to initialize the page here
    }

    protected override bool OnBubbleEvent(object sender,
                                          System.EventArgs e)
    {
      Label1.Text = ((Control)sender).ID;
```

```
        return true;
    }

    ...
}
}
```

The output is as follows:

Event bubbling architecture is extremely powerful and lets you handle events at any level above the point in the control hierarchy at which the event originated.

OnDataBinding

The OnDataBinding method takes an EventArgs as input and enables a control to handle any work associated with binding the control to a data source. Override this method if you are developing a control that will support data binding to perform the appropriate actions to enumerate the data source and add contents to your control.

```
protected virtual void OnDataBinding(EventArgs e);
```

OnInit

The OnInit method takes an EventArgs as input. This method is used to handle any initialization for your control. At this point in the control lifecycle the sequencing of control initialization is not determined, which means you cannot access any other controls using this method, not even the parent of the control. Remember, only use OnInit to handle initialization specific to internal properties of this control.

```
protected virtual void OnInit(EventArgs e);
```

OnLoad

The `OnLoad` method takes an `EventArgs` as input and is invoked later in the control lifecycle than `OnInit`. It signifies that the control should prepare itself for rendering. Unlike at the `Init` stage, overloaded `OnLoad` methods can safely access other controls in the hierarchy to which they have access because they have been initialized. Databinding is typically facilitated at this stage of the control lifecycle.

```
protected virtual void OnLoad(EventArgs e);
```

OnPreRender

The `OnPreRender` method takes an `EventArgs` object as input and fires the `PreRender` event. `PreRender` is a few steps later in the control lifecycle than `Load`. During `PreRender`, via an overloaded `OnPreRender` method, the control should perform any actions required immediately before the view state is saved and the content is rendered to the client. At this point in the control lifecycle, the state of the control can still be saved. Beyond this point, after the control has been rendered, this ability is lost.

```
protected virtual void OnPreRender(EventArgs e);
```

OnUnload

The `OnUnload` method takes an `EventArgs` object as input and fires the `Unload` event. `Unload` is the last step in the lifecycle prior to `Dispose`, at which point the control is released from memory. `Unload` signifies the control has completed processing, therefore expensive resources such as database connections or files should be released at this time so that they do not have to wait to be garbage collected.

```
protected virtual void OnUnload(EventArgs e);
```

RaiseBubbleEvent

The `RaiseBubbleEvent` method takes an `Object` and `EventArg` objects as input. The method raises or passes a given event up the control hierarchy to the control's parent. In this way `RaiseBubbleEvent` is fundamental to event bubbling because it causes the `OnBubbleEvent` method of the parent to be invoked. See the *OnBubble* example from earlier in the chapter for details.

```
protected void RaiseBubbleEvent(object source, EventArgs args);
```

Render

The `Render` method takes an `HtmlTextWriter` object as input and is the point in the control lifecycle when text is rendered via the output stream to the client browser. It's important to note that if you would like to enable your control to participate in tracing for debugging purposes then the `RenderControl` method must be used instead. Both the `Render` and `RenderControl` methods require that you call `RenderChildren` to render all children. If you want to specify the order in which the child controls are rendered or do work between the rendering of specific controls you must use the `Controls` property of `FindControl` to call `RenderControl` method for each child control.

```
protected virtual void Render(HtmlTextWriter writer);
```

RenderChildren

The `RenderChildren` method takes an `HtmlTextWriter` as input and writes the content of the server control's child controls to the output stream. Whenever you override the `Render` or `RenderControl` methods, you should include a call to `RenderChildren`. This method loops through the child control's hierarchy calling the `RenderControl` method on each. Alternatively, for greater control in the rendering process you may call `RenderControl` individually for each child control to handle child control rendering.

```
protected virtual void RenderChildren(HtmlTextWriter writer);
```

Example: Rendering

The following example shows a page control that overrides the `Render` method to handle its own display. On this `.aspx` page we have simply placed a button control:

```
<%@ Page language="c#" Codebehind="rendering.aspx.cs"
        AutoEventWireup="false"
        Inherits="wroxRef1.rendering" %>
<!DOCTYPE HTML PUBLIC "-//W3C//DTD HTML 4.0 Transitional//EN" >
<HTML>
  <HEAD>
    <title>rendering</title>
    <meta name="GENERATOR" Content="Microsoft Visual Studio 7.0">
    <meta name="CODE_LANGUAGE" Content="C#">
    <meta name="vs_defaultClientScript" content="JavaScript">
    <meta name="vs_targetSchema"
        content="http://schemas.microsoft.com/intellisense/ie5">
  </HEAD>
  <body MS_POSITIONING="GridLayout">
    <form id="rendering" method="post" runat="server">
    </form>
  </body>
</HTML>
```

The code behind for the web page is as follows:

```
using System;
using System.Collections;
using System.ComponentModel;
using System.Data;
using System.Drawing;
using System.Web;
using System.Web.SessionState;
using System.Web.UI;
using System.Web.UI.WebControls;
using System.Web.UI.HtmlControls;

namespace wroxRef1
{
  /// <summary>
  /// Summary description for rendering.
  /// </summary>
```

```
public class rendering : System.Web.UI.Page
  {
    private void Page_Load(object sender, System.EventArgs e)
    {
      // Put user code to initialize the page here
    }

    protected override void Render(HtmlTextWriter writer)
    {
      // do our custom rendering of the parent control
      writer.Write("<h2>Custom Rendering</h2>");

      // Commenting out the following line will result in only
      // the above text being displayed by the client
      this.RenderChildren(writer);
    }

  ...
  }
}
```

In the `Render` method, we use the `HtmlTextWriter` passed as an argument to write any content that we wish to render on the client. We then call the `RenderChildren` method, passing the same `HtmlTextWriter` used to render the current control. The important thing to understand is the precedence or sequence consequences of overriding `Render`. The previous example generates the following HTML, which you can view by selecting View | Source:

```
<h2>Custom Rendering</h2>
<!DOCTYPE HTML PUBLIC "-//W3C//DTD HTML 4.0 Transitional//EN" >
<HTML>
  <HEAD>
    <title>rendering</title>
    <meta name="GENERATOR" Content="Microsoft Visual Studio 7.0">
    <meta name="CODE_LANGUAGE" Content="C#">
    <meta name="vs_defaultClientScript" content="JavaScript">
    <meta name="vs_targetSchema"
          content="http://schemas.microsoft.com/intellisense/ie5">
  </HEAD>
  <body MS_POSITIONING="GridLayout">
    <form name="rendering" method="post" action="rendering.aspx"
          id="rendering">
      <input type="hidden" name="__VIEWSTATE"
             value="dDwtMTI3OTMzNDM4NDs7PuPMjr3Ua1yxQudYYs7zagCqsnSp" />
    </form>
  </body>
</HTML>
```

The output from this example should look as below:

Notice how the `<h2>Custom Rendering</h2>` element is rendered *before* the standard doctype declarations and other introductory HTML? This is exactly what is supposed to happen – the render method we overrode *preceded* the standard page object rendering and thus our method's text made it to the client first. Keep rendering sequence at top of mind when overloading `Render`.

SaveViewState

The `SaveViewState` method returns an object that represents the view state for the control. This view state is a string that allows information between page calls to persist, stores control property values between round-trips and is rendered to the client in a hidden input field. In this way ASP.NET encourages stateless server-side constructs, resulting in greater scalability.

```
protected virtual object SaveViewState();
```

TrackViewState

The `TrackViewState` method initiates the tracking of changes in the view state for the control. These changes can then be stored in the server control's `StateBag` object. This method is used when creating templated databound controls to ensure that their state is properly monitored for view state.

```
protected virtual void TrackViewState();
```

Example: Databound Templated Control

This example uses a simple databound control to demonstrate some basic features of the `Control` class. Most importantly, this example shows a custom implementation for saving and loading view state. The control created provides an `ItemTemplate` and an `AlternatingItemTemplate` which allow the developer to specify different templates according to the position of the element in the data source. In addition, the style for the `ItemTemplate` and `AlternatingItemTemplate` can be specified.

There are two important classes in this example. The ViewStateControl class provides a very simple, incomplete databound control example, which is interesting in part because it is derived as a component rather than as a standard user control. The ViewStateContainer class provides, naturally, a container class for the ItemTemplate and AlternatingItemTemplate objects.

The hosting page below, viewStateControlPage.aspx, hosts several controls:

```
<%@ Page language="c#" Codebehind="viewStateControlPage.aspx.cs"
        AutoEventWireup="false"
        Inherits="wroxRef1.viewStateControlPage" %>
<%@ Register TagPrefix="WROX" namespace="wroxRef1" Assembly="wroxRef1"%>
<%@ Register TagPrefix="WROX" TagName="Binding" Src="Binding.ascx" %>
<!DOCTYPE HTML PUBLIC "-//W3C//DTD HTML 4.0 Transitional//EN">
<HTML>
  <HEAD>
    <title>viewStateControlPage</title>
  </HEAD>
  <body MS_POSITIONING="FlowLayout">
    <form id="Form1" method="post" runat="server">
      <WROX:BINDING id="binding" runat="server"></WROX:BINDING>
      <BR>
      <BR>
      <!-- place holder for the state view -->
      <ASP:REPEATER id="repeat" runat="server"></ASP:REPEATER>
      <BR>
      <BR>
      <WROX:VIEWSTATECONTROL id="StateControl" runat="server">
        <ITEMTEMPLATE>Item Color:
                <%# Container.DataItem %><BR></ITEMTEMPLATE>
        <ITEMSTYLE backcolor="gray"></ITEMSTYLE>
        <ALTERNATINGITEMTEMPLATE>Alternating Item Color:
             <%# Container.DataItem %><BR></ALTERNATINGITEMTEMPLATE>
        <ALTERNATINGITEMSTYLE backcolor="Yellow"></ALTERNATINGITEMSTYLE>
      </WROX:VIEWSTATECONTROL>
      <ASP:BUTTON id="postbackbutton" runat="server"
                  text="post back"></ASP:BUTTON>
    </form>
  </body>
</HTML>
```

Notice that our Register directive near the top of the page indicates that we are loading a control from an assembly rather than a User Control file (.ascx). This allows us to create element tag names with the given prefix that correspond to a control class in our assembly. In this case, WROX:ViewStateControl points to the ViewStateControl class defined in our code, which we'll see in a moment.

The Page_Load method in the code behind for the above web page creates a data source that will be used by the templated control, in this case an array of colors. It then sets the data sources for the controls, loads a template for the repeating control and binds the data to the controls.

```csharp
using System;
using System.Collections;
using System.ComponentModel;
using System.Data;
using System.Drawing;
using System.Web;
using System.Web.SessionState;
using System.Web.UI;
using System.Web.UI.WebControls;
using System.Web.UI.HtmlControls;

namespace wroxRef1
{
  /// <summary>
  /// Summary description for viewStateControlPage.
  /// </summary>
  public class viewStateControlPage : System.Web.UI.Page
  {
    protected Repeater repeat;
    protected Button postbackbutton;
    protected ViewStateControl StateControl;

    private void Page_Load(object sender, System.EventArgs e)
    {
      //create a collection for our data source
      ArrayList List = new ArrayList(3);
      List.Add("Red");
      List.Add("Blue");
      List.Add("Orange");

      //set the datasource property of our control
      //and call databind
      ((Binding)FindControl("binding")).DataSource = List;

      //set the repeater control's datasource to the list
      //created above
      repeat.DataSource = List;

      //load the item template from a file
      repeat.ItemTemplate = LoadTemplate("viewStateTemplate.ascx");

      //set the datasource of the custom control
      StateControl.DataSource = List;

      //call databind to cause the page and all of its controls
      //to bind to their data sources
      DataBind();

    }

    ...

  }
}
```

In the code file itself, `ViewStateControl.cs`, we build a fairly complex control that allows for this templating and styling along with databinding and state management. Note that this file is not a code-behind file, but rather a standalone C# code file.

```
using System;
using System.ComponentModel;
using System.Web.UI;
using System.Collections;
using System.Web.UI.WebControls;

namespace wroxRef1
{
  /// <summary>
  /// Summary description for ViewStateControl.
  /// </summary>
  [DefaultProperty("Text")]
  [ToolboxData("<{0}:ViewStateControl runat=server>" +
               "</{0}:ViewStateControl>")]
  public class ViewStateControl :
                                  System.Web.UI.WebControls.WebControl,
                                  INamingContainer

  {
```

To begin with, we define some private variables and their corresponding property accessors to allow consumers of our control to set templates for items and alternating items as well as their styles. The container for this template is defined in the `ViewStateContainer` class reference, providing both `ItemTemplate` and `AlternatingItemTemplate` functionality:

```
//variables for the templates and datasource
private ITemplate m_ItemTemplate;
private ITemplate m_AlternatingItemTemplate;
private IEnumerable m_DataSource;

//style variables
private Style m_ItemStyle;
private Style m_AlternatingItemStyle;
public ViewStateControl()
  {

//datasource property allowing for a collection
//to be bound to the control
public IEnumerable DataSource
{
  get
  {
    return m_DataSource;
  }
  set
  {
    m_DataSource = value;
  }
}
```

Now we add an `ItemTemplate` property which allows an `ItemTemplate` to be specified in the HTML. The container for this template is indicated as the `ViewStateContainer` that we will define in a moment:

```
//The ItemTemplate property allowing for an ItemTemplate
//to be specified in the HTML. The container for this
//template is indicated as the ViewStateContainer defined below
[TemplateContainer(typeof(ViewStateContainer))]
public ITemplate ItemTemplate
{
  get
  {
    return m_ItemTemplate;
  }
  set
  {
    m_ItemTemplate = value;
  }
}


//alternating item template property
[TemplateContainer(typeof(ViewStateContainer))]
public ITemplate AlternatingItemTemplate
{
  get
  {
    return m_AlternatingItemTemplate;
  }
  set
  {
    m_AlternatingItemTemplate = value;
  }
}

public Style ItemStyle
{
  get
  {
    return m_ItemStyle;
  }
  set
  {
    m_ItemStyle = value;
  }
}

public Style AlternatingItemStyle
{
  get
  {
    return m_AlternatingItemStyle;
  }
```

```
    set
        {
            m_AlternatingItemStyle = value;
        }
    }
```

The control is databound, and provides a public `DataSource` property that allows a collection to be set as the source for the control's information. We override the `DataBind` method to instantiate our templates, and begin by clearing the child controls and any child control view state to ensure that the new data we apply will be the only data in the controls. Next, we create an instance of our simple container class with a single property, and we instantiate our template in this class.

```
//overridden databind method which creates instances of the
//container class and instantiates the template in the
//container
public override void DataBind()
{
    base.OnDataBinding(EventArgs.Empty);

    // clear any controls and their state
    Controls.Clear();
    ClearChildViewState();

    //make sure we have a datasource and at least one template
    if((m_DataSource != null) && (m_ItemTemplate != null))
    {
        IEnumerator Item;
        Item = m_DataSource.GetEnumerator();
        int Counter = 1;

        while(Item.MoveNext())
        {
            ViewStateContainer m_Container = new ViewStateContainer(this,
                                                        Item.Current);
            if((Counter % 2) != 0)
            {
                m_ItemTemplate.InstantiateIn(m_Container);
                m_Container.ApplyStyle(m_ItemStyle);
            }
            else
            {
                if(m_AlternatingItemTemplate != null)
                {
                    m_AlternatingItemTemplate.InstantiateIn(m_Container);
                    m_Container.ApplyStyle(m_AlternatingItemStyle);
                }
                else
                {
                    m_ItemTemplate.InstantiateIn(m_Container);
                    m_Container.ApplyStyle(m_ItemStyle);
                }
            }
        }
```

Once our template is loaded into the container, we apply the style indicated and call the `DataBind` method on the container.

```
        //make sure the container binds the data and add it to
        //the controls collection
        m_Container.DataBind();
        Controls.Add(m_Container);
        Counter++;
      }
    }
```

Now we indicate that we have created the child controls, and ensure that view state is tracked for our control, by the `TrackViewState` method:

```
    //indicate that we have created our child controls and that
    //view state should be tracked for our control
    ChildControlsCreated = true;
    TrackViewState();
  }


//override the saveviewstate method to manage the saving
//of our object state
protected override object SaveViewState()
{
  object basestate = base.SaveViewState();

  object ItemStyleState;
  if(m_ItemStyle != null)
    ItemStyleState = ((IStateManager)m_ItemStyle).SaveViewState();
  else
    ItemStyleState = null;

  object AlternatingItemStyleState;
  if(m_AlternatingItemStyle != null)
    AlternatingItemStyleState =
            ((IStateManager)m_AlternatingItemStyle).SaveViewState();
  else
    AlternatingItemStyleState = null;

  object[] thisstate = new object[3];
  thisstate[0] = basestate;
  thisstate[1] = ItemStyleState;
  thisstate[2] = AlternatingItemStyleState;

  return thisstate;
}
```

Finally we override the `LoadViewState` method to control the loading of our style information:

```
    //override the loadviewstate method to control the
    //loading of our style information
    protected override void LoadViewState(object state)
    {
      if(state != null)
      {
        object[] innerstate = (object[])state;

        if(innerstate[0] != null)
          base.LoadViewState(innerstate[0]);

        if(innerstate[1] != null)
      ((IStateManager)m_AlternatingItemStyle).LoadViewState(innerstate[1]);

        if(innerstate[2] != null)
          ((IStateManager)m_ItemStyle).LoadViewState(innerstate[2]);
      }
    }
  }
}
```

In this example we have overridden the `LoadViewState` and `SaveViewState` methods in order to customize the way state is persisted. For the purposes of the sample, we are simply putting the styles for our templates into the view state along with the base class state. We then load this same state and apply it to the styles for the control. Here is the output for the `viewStateControlPage.aspx` page:

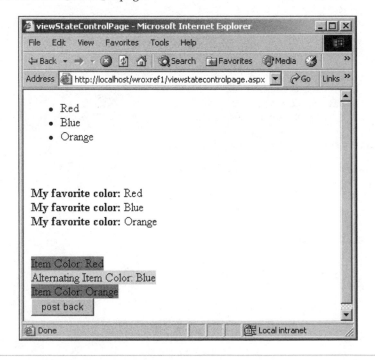

Control Public Properties

- ❑ **ClientID**
- ❑ **Controls**
- ❑ **EnableViewState**
- ❑ **ID**
- ❑ **NamingContainer**
- ❑ **Page**
- ❑ **Parent**
- ❑ **Site**
- ❑ **TemplateSourceDirectory**
- ❑ **UniqueID**
- ❑ **Visible**

ClientID

The `ClientID` property is the ID generated by ASP.NET for the control. The `ClientID` is generated even when you don't specify an ID property in the ASP.NET page. If you do specify an ID attribute explicitly then this ID will override the `ClientID` value that would have been generated and the two values will be identical.

```
public virtual string ClientID {get;}
```

Controls

The `Controls` property returns a `ControlCollection` object representing the child controls of the current control. This property is useful when you need to iterate through, manipulate or access child controls. Remember, you can also add and remove objects from the `ControlCollection` with the `Controls` property. For example here is the syntax for adding a child control into the `ControlCollection` object:

```
Controls.Add(New LiteralControl("<h1>SomeHeading: "))
```

This will add the control as a child to the current control.

```
public virtual ControlCollection Controls {get;}
```

EnableViewState

The `EnableViewState` property determines whether the `ViewState` is enabled or disabled for the control; the default is `true`.

While in most cases ViewState is desirable, you can improve performance by disabling ViewState in the right circumstances. If your control is populated by a database request, consider setting this property to false. If you don't, resources may be wasted loading ViewState into the server control that will only be overridden by the database query on the next call. Naturally, this needs to be weighed against the potential alternative performance strategy of calling the database request on the first call to the control, then using IsPostBack to determine whether to fetch the data again or use the ViewState. You need to consider the appropriate technique depending on the dynamic nature of the data being rendered into the control.

```
public virtual bool EnableViewState {get; set;}
```

ID

The ID property indicates the ID for the control. The value in this property corresponds to the ID attribute of the control as it appears in the HTML of a web form. This ID will also match the name of the variable in the code behind file that implements the control. Remember, you cannot include spaces in this property because it will generate a parser error. The ClientID is automatically generated by ASP.NET regardless of whether an ID property has been set. However, any new name assigned to a Server control by the ID property will override the ClientID value, allowing programmatic access to a particular control.

```
public virtual string ID {get; set;}
```

NamingContainer

The NamingContainer property is a reference to the control's "naming container". A naming container is the parent control of the current control contextualized in a sort of namespace to ensure all controls on the page have a unique indentifier. Many controls are created with generic names such as ctrl0 if you use Visual Studio .NET and User Controls could easily have items with an ID identical to an item on the containing page. Naming containers provide one mechanism for reducing such naming collisions. The control returned by this property will be the first control above this one in the hierarchy of the INamingContainer interface. This property can be useful for finding other controls being processed, such as other controls on a particular level of a page. You can retrieve the naming container for the control and then use the FindControl method on the naming container to find another control in this "namespace".

```
public virtual Control NamingContainer {get;}
```

Page

The Page property is a reference to the Page control in which the current control resides. At run time all controls, even custom controls, are subordinate to one page control instance.

```
public virtual Page Page {get; set;}
```

Parent

The `Parent` property returns a reference to the parent control of the current control.

```
public virtual Control Parent {get;}
```

Site

The `Site` property returns a `Site` object for communication between a component and its container. The `Site` object also allows an object to manage the controls it contains. This property determines where a control is being hosted, for instance in a designer such as Visual Studio .NET's Web Forms designer.

```
public ISite Site {get; set;}e
```

TemplateSourceDirectory

The `TemplateSourceDirectory` property indicates the virtual directory holding the page or server control that is the parent of the current control. This can be especially useful when designing User Controls as it identifies the location of the page file in which a control is housed. Remember, if you subsequently use `MapPathSecure` your control will need the appropriate file permissions to access the source file and or directories or an `HttpException` will be generated.

```
public virtual string TemplateSourceDirectory {get;}
```

UniqueID

`UniqueID` property indicates the fully qualified unique name for a control. This includes the naming container ID, the client ID, and the control's own ID. With naming containers, the `UniqueID` property of a control is the concatenation of the naming containers in which it resides followed by the control's ID. A server-side label control with an ID of "outputlabel" residing in a `DataList` with an ID of "List" would have a `UniqueID` of "List:ctrl0:outputlabel", where "ctrl0" is the templated control from the `DataList`.

Remember, in order for your control to be a naming container, a control must implement the `INamingContainer` interface. The good news is that this interface does not define any public methods or properties, but simply serves to indicate that the control acts as a naming container.

```
public virtual string UniqueID {get;}
```

Visible

The `Visible` property indicates whether a control is meant to be visible on the rendered page. The default value is set to `true`.

```
public virtual bool Visible {get; set;}
```

Control Protected Properties

- **ChildControlsCreated**
- **Context**
- **Events**
- **HasChildViewState**
- **IsTrackingViewState**
- **ViewState**
- **ViewStateIgnoresCase**

ChildControlsCreated

The `ChildControlsCreated` property indicates whether the child controls of the control have been created. With your own controls you must make sure to set this property to `true` once you have created the child controls. Likewise, unless you particularly wish to add a new set of controls, you should check the value of this property before creating any child controls. Following this guideline will ensure that child controls are only created once.

```
protected bool ChildControlsCreated {get; set;}
```

Context

The `Context` property gives your control access to the `HttpContext` object for the current Web request. For those who are experienced with ASP, most of the familiar intrinsic ASP objects are represented here as object properties of `Context`, including `Application`, `Session`, `Request`, `Response`, and others, including error handling and security, associated with the current HTTP request.

```
protected virtual HttpContext Context {get;}
```

Events

The `Events` property gets a list of event delegates for the current control. The retrieved list is an `EventHandlerList` – a rather inefficient structure for searching, so it may be slow if you have a lot of event handlers. This property allows the developer to access the delegates assigned to the events in the control and call them if required.

```
protected EventHandlerList Events {get;}
```

HasChildViewState

The `HasChildViewState` property is `true` if any of the child controls have saved view state information. You can speed up your code and avoid calling `ClearChildViewState` when it isn't necessary by checking this property. If the property is `false`, `ClearChildViewState` is unnecessary.

```
protected bool HasChildViewState {get;}
```

IsTrackingViewState

The `IsTrackingViewState` property returns a `Boolean` indicating whether the control is saving changes to the view state.

```
protected bool IsTrackingViewState {get;}
```

ViewState

The `ViewState` property is a reference to a `StateBag` object that contains the properties for the control as preserved in the round-trip to and from the server and client. If you needed to persist control values in the `ViewState` programmatically you can implement properties for your control as follows:

```
public string UserName
{
  get
  {
    return(string) ViewState["UserName"];
  }
  set
  {
    ViewState["UserName"] = value;
  }
}
```

Obviously, you can use similar syntax to directly read values from the `StateBag` for your control.

```
protected virtual StateBag ViewState {get;}
```

ViewStateIgnoresCase

The `ViewStateIgnoresCase` property defaults to `true` and indicates the case sensitivity of the control in terms of how it saves view state information. If you create a custom control that *is* case-sensitive, such as the case-sensitivity to the *key* portion of the key/value pairs in the `StateBag`, make sure you override this property and set it to `false` in your control.

```
protected virtual bool ViewStateIgnoresCase {get;}
```

Control Public Events

- ❑ **DataBinding**
- ❑ **Disposed**
- ❑ **Init**
- ❑ **Load**
- ❑ **PreRender**
- ❑ **Unload**

DataBinding

The DataBinding event is fired to tell a control it is time to perform any data binding that has been defined for the control, typically the DataBind method.

```
public event EventHandler DataBinding;
```

Example: Databinding

Here we specify a simple User Control that uses the DataBind method to handle the DataBinding event. The code for this example can be found in Binding.ascx.cs in the code download. The first thing we do is to create a DataSource property that allows a user to provide a collection from which we can build our control. We also create an internal variable to hold it. Next, we define our Page_DataBind method, which will act as event handler. This method resets the child control values, then walks through the items in the data source creating list items for each, and adding them to the child control collection.

```csharp
namespace wroxRef1
{
  using System;
  using System.Data;
  using System.Drawing;
  using System.Web;
  using System.Web.UI.WebControls;
  using System.Web.UI.HtmlControls;
  using System.Web.UI;
  using System.Collections;

  /// <summary>
  /// Summary description for Binding.
  /// </summary>
  public abstract class Binding : System.Web.UI.UserControl
  {

    //our internal variable
    protected IEnumerable mDataSource;

    //create a property to allow for setting the datasource
    public IEnumerable DataSource
    {
      get
      {
        return mDataSource;
      }
      set
      {
        mDataSource = value;
      }
    }
    private void Page_Load(object sender, System.EventArgs e)
    {
      //make sure the datasource has been set before acting on it
```

```
    if(mDataSource != null)
    {
        //clear any child controls and child view state
        ClearChildViewState();
        Controls.Clear();

        //start an unordered list for items
        Controls.Add(new LiteralControl("<ul>"));

        //get an enumerator from our datasource so we can walk
        //the collection
        IEnumerator Enumerator = mDataSource.GetEnumerator();

        //while we still have data, move to the next item
        while(Enumerator.MoveNext())
        {
          //add a literal control which is a list item containing the data
          //item
          Controls.Add(new LiteralControl("<li>" +
                                            Enumerator.Current.ToString()));
        }

        //add the closing tag for our list as a literal control
        Controls.Add(new LiteralControl("</ul>"));
    }
  }

  ...
  }
}
```

To bind data to this control, the hosting page's code behind, bindingPage.aspx.cs , needs to provide data for the control as an ArrayList and bind that data to the DataSource property of the new control defined above. The code is written as an event handler for the Databinding event and in the page's Page_Load we simply call DataBind, which triggers the event for the page and all the child controls, including our user control. The Page_Load and Page_DataBind methods used to test the new control in a page are as follows:

```
using System;
using System.Collections;
using System.ComponentModel;
using System.Data;
using System.Drawing;
using System.Web;
using System.Web.SessionState;
using System.Web.UI;
using System.Web.UI.WebControls;
using System.Web.UI.HtmlControls;

namespace wroxRef1
```

```
{
  /// <summary>
  /// Summary description for bindingPage.
  /// </summary>
  public class bindingPage : System.Web.UI.Page
  {
    private void Page_Load(object sender, System.EventArgs e)
    {
      DataBind();
    }

    private void Data_Bind(object sender, System.EventArgs e)
    {

      //Create Sample datasource to bind to the control
      //In your code this could be xml, db, etc...
      ArrayList List = new ArrayList(3);

      List.Add("Red");
      List.Add("Blue");
      List.Add("Orange");

      //now set the datasource property of our control
      //We use the findcontrol method and the id of the control
      //to get the reference and assign the value in one
      //compact statement

      ((Binding)FindControl("binding1")).DataSource = List;
    }

    ...

  }
}
```

Disposed

The `Disposed` event is fired as the last step in the control lifecycle. In this event handler, all resources such as database connections or open files should be released so that they do not have to wait until garbage collection before being made available again. On a high traffic site, this step is critical as it releases resources much sooner than the garbage collection process.

```
public event EventHandler Disposed;
```

Init

The `Init` event fires the `OnInit` event handler and is called upon the creation of a control. You can think of `Init` as the constructor for your control, however, you cannot reference any other controls at this stage in the event lifecycle. "Start-up" or set-up code that refers to *other* controls *must* be handled in `Load` because you cannot assume that the other controls have been initialized when your code received the `Init` event.

```
public event EventHandler Init;
```

Load

The `Load` event fires the `OnLoad` event handler and is called after basic initialization of the control. Any setup code that refers to other controls or deals with external data such as datasources, files, and so on, should be handled in the `OnLoad` event handler.

```
public event EventHandler Load;
```

PreRender

The `PreRender` event fires an `OnPreRender` event handler and is used to handle any final, necessary updates to your control prior to the content being rendered to the browser. If, for example, your control depends on a property in another control that may change *after* the `Load` event for that control you could use `OnPreRender` to synchronize your control with the other just before it is rendered.

```
public event EventHandler PreRender;
```

Unload

The `Unload` event is fired after the control has completed rendering and processing and is preparing to unload from memory. `Unload` is actually called before `Dispose`, and since there is the danger of developers treating them equally (they are confusingly similar in function), it is probably better practice to make a habit of putting your cleanup code in `Dispose` and then calling `Dispose` both from an `Unload` handler and from a `Finalize` handler. In this way you can be certain that your code is unloaded at the earliest possible moment and that your code cleanup strategy is consistent across all controls.

```
public event EventHandler Unload;
```

Page Class

The Page control class represents a single web page. While a Page object represents a single web page instance, it includes a wide variety of methods and properties that recognize that an `.aspx` page typically lives in the broader context of an **application**. As such, provisions for error handling, state management, debugging, security and caching are found in addition to the likely candidates of Request and Response.

Page Public Methods

- ❑ DataBind – inherited from Control, see Control Class reference for details.
- ❑ Dispose – inherited from Control, see Control Class reference for details.
- ❑ Equals – inherited from System.Object, see Introduction for details.
- ❑ FindControl – inherited from Control, see Control Class reference for details.
- ❑ GetHashCode – inherited from System.Object, see Introduction for details.
- ❑ **GetPostBackClientEvent**
- ❑ **GetPostBackClientHyperlink**
- ❑ **GetPostBackEventReference**
- ❑ GetType – inherited from System.Object, see Introduction for details.
- ❑ **GetTypeHashCode**
- ❑ HasControls – inherited from Control, see Control Class reference for details.
- ❑ **IsClientScriptBlockRegistered**
- ❑ **IsStartUpScriptRegistered**
- ❑ LoadControl – inherited from TemplateControl, see TemplateControl Class reference for details.
- ❑ LoadTemplate – inherited from TemplateControl, see TemplateControl Class reference for details.
- ❑ **MapPath**
- ❑ ParseControl – inherited from TemplateControl, see TemplateControl Class reference for details.
- ❑ **RegisterArrayDeclaration**
- ❑ **RegisterClientScriptBlock**
- ❑ **RegisterHiddenField**
- ❑ **RegisterOnSubmitStatement**
- ❑ **RegisterRequiresPostBack**
- ❑ **RegisterRequiresRaiseEvent**
- ❑ **RegisterStartupScript**
- ❑ **RegisterViewStateHandler**

- ❏ `RenderControl` – inherited from `Control`, see `Control` Class reference for details.
- ❏ `ResolveUrl` – inherited from `Control`, see `Control` Class reference for details.
- ❏ `ToString` – inherited from `System.Object`, see Introduction for details.
- ❏ **Validate**
- ❏ **VerifyRenderingInServerForm**

GetPostBackClientEvent

The `GetPostBackClientEvent` method takes a `Control` and `String` as input and returns a string that contains the client-side script equivalent for the post-back event of a given control. This is with a JScript.NET prefix if the browser making the request is identified as Internet Explorer version 4 or higher. This is useful when you need to render client-side script dynamically based on a targeted control that may change at run time.

```
public string GetPostBackClientEvent(Control control, string argument);
```

GetPostBackClientHyperlink

The `GetPostBackClientHyperlink` method returns a `String` and a `Control` as input where the string represents a hyperlink to the client-side script call, which initiates the post-back process.

```
public string GetPostBackClientHyperlink(Control control, string argument);
```

GetPostBackEventReference

The `GetPostBackEventReference` method takes a `Control` and a `String` as input and returns a string that represents a client-side script that, when called, initiates the post-back process.

```
public string GetPostBackEventReference(Control);
public string GetPostBackEventReference(Control, string);
```

Example: Client Side Event Method Generation

We can use the postback event methods defined above to gain a high degree of control over the way client-side code generates postback events. Consider the following example, `postBackPage.aspx` in the code download for this chapter:

```
<%@ Page language="c#" Codebehind="postBackPage.aspx.cs"
        AutoEventWireup="false"
        Inherits="wroxRef1.postBackPage" %>
<!DOCTYPE HTML PUBLIC "-//W3C//DTD HTML 4.0 Transitional//EN">
<HTML>
  <HEAD>
    <title>postBackPage</title>
    <meta content="Microsoft Visual Studio.NET 7.0" name="GENERATOR">
    <meta content="C#" name="CODE_LANGUAGE">
    <meta content="JavaScript" name="vs_defaultClientScript">
    <meta content="http://schemas.microsoft.com/intellisense/ie5"
```

```
         name="vs_targetSchema">
    </HEAD>
    <body id="body">
      <form id="Form1" method="post" runat="server">
        <h1>Client Event Binding and Generation Demo</h1>
        <p>ASP.NET gives you a lot of control over how event generation
           is handled on the client. You can even fake event generation.
           For example, clicking on the hyperlink below the control fires
           the TextChanged event for the textbox even though it actually
           hasn't changed. These methods are useful when you have custom
           control where you need more control over the client-side script
           generated.</p>
        <h2>A Submit Control and a Link</h2>
        <P><asp:button id="Button1" runat="server"
                       Text="Button"></asp:button><br>
          <asp:hyperlink id="HyperLinkButton"
                         runat="server">HyperLink</asp:hyperlink></P>
        <h2>Some Runtime Generated Client-Side Event Script Generated</h2>
        <p>Click the links or the button to generate client-side event
           script...</p>
        <P><asp:label id="labelGetPostbackClientEvent"
                      runat="server">GetPostBackClientEvent:</asp:label></P>
      </form>
    </body>
</HTML>
```

With a code-behind file, `postBackPage.aspx.cs`, like this:

```
using System;
using System.Collections;
using System.ComponentModel;
using System.Data;
using System.Drawing;
using System.Web;
using System.Web.SessionState;
using System.Web.UI;
using System.Web.UI.WebControls;
using System.Web.UI.HtmlControls;

namespace wroxRef1
{
  /// <summary>
  /// Summary description for postBackPage.
  /// </summary>
  public class postBackPage : System.Web.UI.Page
  {
    protected Label labelGetPostbackClientEvent;
    protected Label labelGetPostbackEventReference;
    protected Button Button1;
    protected HyperLink HyperLinkButton;

    private void Page_Load(object sender, System.EventArgs e)
```

```
{
        //grab and set the client-side event handler
        //Set the link's URL to client-side script that fires event
        //for the Button1
        //In this way we can superimpose event generation
        //arbitrarily, binding one control to another... etc..
        HyperLinkButton.NavigateUrl = GetPostBackClientHyperlink(Button1,
                                                    "submit");

        string script = "<script>" + "\n" + "<!-- function client()" + "\n";
        script += "{" + "\n" + "alert(";
        script += '"';
        script += "Generated function";
        script += '"';
        script += ");" + "\n" + "}";
        script += "-->" + "\n" + "</script>";
        RegisterClientScriptBlock("uniqueKey", script);
          //"<script><!--" +  "function client()" +
          //"{alert(""generated function"");" +  "}" + "--></script>");

        if(IsPostBack)
          labelGetPostbackClientEvent.Text =
            GetPostBackClientEvent(HyperLinkButton, "Some Argument");

    }

    private void Button1_Click(object sender, System.EventArgs e)
    {
      //handle the event as it pertains to the control
      Button1.Text = "Thanks for clicking the button... or did you" +
                                              "click the link?";
    }

    ...

    private void InitializeComponent()
    {
      this.Load += new System.EventHandler(this.Page_Load);
      this.Button1.Click += new
                    System.EventHandler(this.Button1_Click);

    }
  }
}
```

When used this way, the event fired by the hyperlink is indistinguishable on the server-side from the event generated by clicking the button:

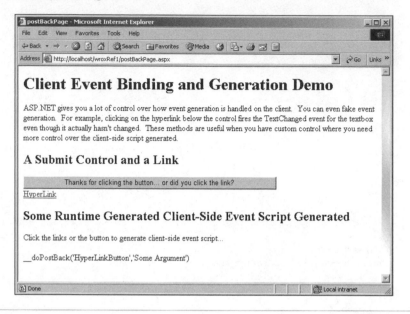

GetTypeHashCode

The `GetTypeHashCode` method returns an integer value representing the hash code for the page. The `Page` object generates the hash code at run time and constitutes a unique ID for the page.

```
public virtual int GetTypeHashCode();
```

IsClientScriptBlockRegistered

The `IsClientScriptBlockRegistered` method takes a `String` as input and determines if a given client script, as indexed by the key, has already been registered. Client-side scripts are "registered" at run time to avoid sending duplicate script blocks to the browser. If the script has already been generated and registered by using this method you can avoid the expense of generating the script. It is especially important to call this method before you call the `RegisterClientScriptBlock` method, if your script generation is resource intensive, perhaps involving database calls, and so on. See the `RegisterClientScriptBlock` method description for more information.

```
public bool IsClientScriptBlockRegistered(string key);
```

IsStartUpScriptRegistered

The `IsStartUpScriptRegistered` method takes a `String` representing a client-side script key and returns a `Boolean` indicating whether or not the startup script has been registered. A startup script may be created by the developer and registered with the Runtime. (See the *Client-Side Registration* example for details and practical application of this and related methods).

```
public bool IsStartUpScriptRegistered(string key);
```

MapPath

The `MapPath` method takes a `String` representing a virtual path on the server and returns a string representing the equivalent physical path on the server.

```
public string MapPath(string virtualPath);
```

RegisterArrayDeclaration

The `RegisterArrayDeclaration` method takes two strings as input and creates a client-side script block that declares an array. In addition, you can add an element to the array. Subsequent calls to this method using the same array name add further elements to the array. In this way, controls in a page request can add themselves or elements of their content to this array. For example this code:

```
RegisterArrayDeclaration("someArray", "1")
RegisterArrayDeclaration("someArray", "2")
RegisterArrayDeclaration("someArray", "3")
```

generates the following script on the client side:

```
<script language="javascript">
<!--
  var someArray =  new Array(1, 2, 3);
// -->
</script>
```

This results in an array with three elements valued 1, 2, and 3. (See the `Client-Side Registration` example for details and practical application of this and related methods)

```
public void RegisterArrayDeclaration(string arrayName,
                                     string arrayValue);
```

RegisterClientScriptBlock

The `RegisterClientScriptBlock` takes two strings as input; `key` represents a named index to the script and `script` contains the literal text of the script source. You use this method to write client-side script while ensuring that only one copy of a given script will be sent to the client. For example, a page and a user control may both have scripts with the same declaration. If the page has registered its scripts, then the user control will not be able to overwrite them. Remember, if multiple controls register the same block of script, they are assumed to be the same and the first block registered will take precedence.

The following code:

```
string script = "<script>" + "\n" + "<!-- function client()" + "\n";
script += "{" + "\n" + "alert(";
script += '"';
script += "Generated function";
script += '"';
script += ");" + "\n" + "}";
script += "-->" + "\n" + "</script>";
RegisterClientScriptBlock("uniqueKey" script);
```

Generates the resulting client-side script:

```
<script> <!--
  function client()
  {
    alert("generated function");
  }
--></script>
```

(See the *Client-Side Registration* example for details and practical application of this and related methods)

```
public virtual void RegisterClientScriptBlock(string key,string script);
```

RegisterHiddenField

The `RegisterHiddenField` method takes two strings as input; `hiddenFieldName` acts as the name or key of the name/value pair and `hiddenFieldInitialValue` represents the value. On rendering, the form will include a hidden field with the name/value pair specified here. Registering hidden fields enables a way to uniformly manage client-side variables to be used or shared by registered client-side scripts. Remember, once the name/value pair is set at run time, subsequent calls to this method with the `hiddenFieldName` will have no effect and the initial field and value will remain.

```
public void RegisterHiddenField(string hiddenFieldName,
                                string hiddenFieldInitialValue);
```

RegisterOnSubmitStatement

The `RegisterOnSubmitStatement` method takes two strings as input; `key` acts as a named index to the submit related script and `script` contains the script to be rendered to the client. The script you include here would typically include your custom client-side form validation code. (See the *Client-Side Registration* example for details and practical application of this and related methods)

```
public void RegisterOnSubmitStatement(string key, string script);
```

RegisterRequiresPostBack

The `RegisterRequiresPostBack` takes a server-side control as input and registers the fact with the Runtime that the control must be notified of postback events. Only a few objects require postback handling, including `Button` and `ImageButton`. This method allows the developer to extend that collection. Remember that too many postbacks will significantly degrade the user experience due to latency introduced by round-trips to the server.

```
public void RegisterRequiresPostBack(Control control);
```

RegisterRequiresRaiseEvent

The `RegisterRequiresRaiseEvent` is used for a specific control that is to have events raised when it is processed on the server. This means that as the control is initialized, loaded and processed, it will raise events to indicate its current stage of processing.

```
public virtual void RegisterRequiresRaiseEvent(IPostBackEventHandler
                                               control);
```

RegisterStartupScript

The `RegisterStartupScript` method takes two strings, `key` and `script`, as input. The `Key` serves as a text index to the script at run time and `script` holds the literal text of the client-side script. This script block is written inline with the page code. This differs from `RegisterClientScriptBlock` in that the scripts registered with this method are intended to be run when the page is first processed by the client application, essentially serving as client-side initialization script. Remember, script registered with this method should *not* include any function declarations.

```
public virtual void RegisterStartupScript(string key, string script);
```

RegisterViewStateHandler

The `RegisterViewStateHandler` method takes no input and it is usually the `HtmlForm` server control for the page that will call this method. If this method is *not* called the page will not save the view state during page processing. Server controls call this method to calculate the view state for their containing page.

```
public void RegisterViewStateHandler();
```

Example: Client-Side Registration

This example pulls together many of the methods of the `Page` class that allow registering client-side code such as scripts and arrays. The ability to register these items to avoid collisions and ensure that all client-side code gets created is important when creating controls that have their own client-side script. If a User Control exists more than once on a given page, using these methods ensures that a related client-side element will only get created one time.

In the following page, `ClientCodeRegistrationPage.aspx`, we have several controls defined to use with our client-side script. The button **Button1** serves as the submit button for our form, while the link anchor element `postbacklink` will be dynamically set to initiate the post back. The next anchor tag references a JavaScript function that will be registered on the server and rendered to the client by the code behind. The text boxes serve as targets for the `ChangeText` script function.

```
<%@ Page language="c#" Codebehind="ClientCodeRegistrationPage.aspx.cs"
        AutoEventWireup="false"
        Inherits="wroxRef1.ClientCodeRegistrationPage" %>
<!DOCTYPE html public "-//w3c//dtd html 4.0 transitional//en" >
<HTML>
  <HEAD>
```

153

```
<TITLE>Client side registration examples</TITLE>
  </HEAD>
  <BODY ms_positioning="FlowLayout">
    <FORM id="ClientCodeRegistration" method="post" runat="server">
      <BR>
      <ASP:TEXTBOX id="TextBoxSingle" runat="server"
                   textmode="SingleLine"></ASP:TEXTBOX>
      <BR>
      <asp:button id="Button1" runat="server" text="Button"></asp:button>
      <BR>
      <A href="" id="postbacklink"
                 runat="server">Dynamically generated postback</A>
      <BR>
      <BR>
      <A href="javascript:ChangeText()">Change Text Boxes</A>
      <BR>
      <asp:TextBox id="TextBox1" runat="server"></asp:TextBox>
      <BR>
      <asp:TextBox id="TextBox2" runat="server"></asp:TextBox>
      <BR>
    </FORM>
  </BODY>
</HTML>
```

The code behind class does the work script generation and registration as follows:

```
using System;
using System.Collections;
using System.ComponentModel;
using System.Data;
using System.Drawing;
using System.Web;
using System.Web.SessionState;
using System.Web.UI;
using System.Web.UI.WebControls;
using System.Web.UI.HtmlControls;
using System.Text;

namespace wroxRef1
{
  /// <summary>
  /// Summary description for ClientCodeRegistrationPage.
  /// </summary>
  public class ClientCodeRegistrationPage : System.Web.UI.Page
  {
    protected Button Button1;
    protected TextBox TextBoxSingle;
    protected TextBox TextBox1;
    protected TextBox TextBox2;
    protected HtmlAnchor postbacklink;

    private void Page_Load(object sender, System.EventArgs e)
```

```
{
        //we use a string builder to build our string
        //and provide constants for the opening and closing
        //script tags.
        StringBuilder Builder = new StringBuilder(1024);

        string ScriptStart = "<script language=" + '"' + "javascript"
                                    + '"' + ">" + "\n" + "<!-- ";
        string EndScript = "\n" + "-->" + "\n" + "</script>";

        //register an array on the client containing
        //ids of the textbox controls to be used by one
        //of the client-side scripts
        RegisterArrayDeclaration("TextBoxes", "'TextBox1'");
        RegisterArrayDeclaration("TextBoxes", "'TextBox2'");

        //register new client script block
        //which dynamically fills two text boxes
        //using the array registered earlier
        Builder.Append(ScriptStart);
        Builder.Append("\n" + "function ChangeText()" + "\n");
        Builder.Append("\n" +
                "{document.getElementById(TextBoxes[0]).value='dynamic'");
        Builder.Append("\n" +
                "document.getElementById(TextBoxes[1]).value='dynamic'");
        Builder.Append("\n" + "}");
        Builder.Append(EndScript);

        RegisterClientScriptBlock("DynamicScript", Builder.ToString());

        //clear string builder
        Builder.Remove(0, Builder.Length);

        //register startup script which sets the status bar
        //text to a message.
        Builder.Append(ScriptStart);
        Builder.Append("\n" + "window.status='Client-Side Registrations" +
                                            "Example'" + "\n");
        Builder.Append(EndScript);

        RegisterStartupScript("StatusStartup", Builder.ToString());

        //set the click event for the dynamic link to postback
        //this simulates posting back with this control as the
        //source of the event and with the arguments specified
        //which in this case is an empty string.
        postbacklink.HRef = GetPostBackClientHyperlink(postbacklink, "");

        //register a hidden field to be manipulated in the
        //submit script.
        RegisterHiddenField("HiddenFormField", "Initialized");
```

```
//register a submit script which sets the hidden field just
    //registered
    Builder.Remove(0, Builder.Length);
    Builder.Append(ScriptStart);
    Builder.Append("\n" + "function SubmitMethod()" + "\n");
    Builder.Append("\n" + "\t" + "{document.all.item(" + '"' +
                   "HiddenFormField" + '"' + ").value=" + '"' +
                   "Set Value" + '"');
    Builder.Append("\n" + "return true" + "\n" + "}");
    Builder.Append(EndScript);

    RegisterClientScriptBlock("SubmitMethod", Builder.ToString());

    //register the call to the above method when the form submits
    RegisterOnSubmitStatement("SubmitMethod", "SubmitMethod()");

    //print out our hidden form field to show that it was
    //changed when we submitted the form.
    if(Request.Form["HiddenFormField"] != null)
      Response.Write("Hidden Field:" + Request.Form["HiddenFormField"]);
    }
  }
}
```

The output for this code would be as follows:

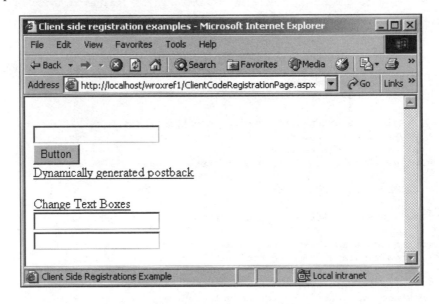

After clicking on the hyperlink, the value of `HiddenFormField` changes from `Initialized` to `Set Value`. The Textbox values are updated by clicking on the **Change Text Boxes** link. If you then click on the **Dynamically generated postback** link, the value of `HiddenFormField` returns to `Initialized`.

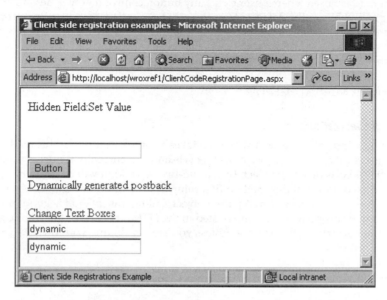

In our code behind, we first create a `StringBuilder` to do our string manipulation. This is the preferred method for string concatenation as the class is designed to optimally manage the memory demands of these operations. We also create constant string values for the opening and closing tags of our script blocks. Next, we register a client-side array that contains the ID values of our two text boxes. While these controls were declared in our page, they could have just as easily been dynamically added to the page or a control at run time. **It's important to note that because we declare the array twice, with the same name, we end up with one array of two elements.** We then create and register the `ChangeText` function on the client, which will dynamically change the text in the two textboxes by referencing the registered array.

A startup script is an inline script in a page, and therefore runs when the page loads. We have created and registered a startup script, which changes the status bar of the browser to display a message. We then use the `GetPostBackClientHyperlink` method to set the `HREF` property of the HTML anchor element to call the `__doPostback` function, passing in the element itself as the target and empty event arguments. Finally, we register a hidden form field and create a function that changes the field's value. The call to this function is then set as the `OnSubmitStatement` event handler for the page.

The potential utility of a structured system of client-side script registration can't be overstated. Consider, for example, an inherited base class for `Page` that uses overridden methods to render common client-script to all pages in the application. The script registration system would enable instances of that `Page` class to add their own inline script while preserving the script used by all pages in the application. This is just one of the many uses of these methods.

Validate

The `Validate` method takes no input and triggers the validation routines for any validation controls in the page. The method is raised when a user clicks any button control that has the `CausesValidation` property set to `true`, which is the default. After `Validate` is called, the `IsValid` property of the page will indicate whether any of the validation controls found errors in the input. Remember, if you happen to check the `IsValid` property before `Validate` has been called, the result will be useless because the validation controls will not have validated the submitted information.

```
public virtual void Validate();
```

VerifyRenderingInServerForm

The `VerifyRenderingInServerForm` method takes a control as input. If this method is called when the `Page` object is *not* in the render phase of its lifecycle and *also* currently rendering controls subordinate to the server-side `Form` object, then a run-time exception will be thrown. You can make a habit of having your controls call this method first thing in their `Render` method. Since controls won't work outside the context of an `HtmlForm` parent object, calling this method is good practice to ensure that your controls were properly placed and nested in the HTML version of the web page. Microsoft recommends against overriding this method unless you are developing your own `Page` framework model.

```
public virtual void VerifyRenderingInServerForm(Control control);
```

Page Protected Methods

- ❏ `AddParsedSubObject` – inherited from `Control`, see `Control` Class reference for details.
- ❏ `ClearChildViewState` – inherited from `Control`, see `Control` Class reference for details.
- ❏ `Construct` – inherited from `TemplateControl`, see `TemplateControl` Class reference for details.
- ❏ `CreateChildControls` – inherited from `Control`, see `Control` Class reference for details.
- ❏ `CreateControlCollection` – inherited from `Control`, see `Control` Class reference for details.
- ❏ **`CreateHtmlTextWriter`**
- ❏ **`DeterminePostBackMode`**
- ❏ `EnsureChildControls` – inherited from `Control`, see `Control` Class reference for details.
- ❏ `Finalize` – inherited from `System.Object`, see `Introduction` for details.
- ❏ `IsLiteralContent` – inherited from `Control`, see `Control` Class reference for details.
- ❏ **`LoadPageStateFromPersistenceMedium`**
- ❏ `LoadViewState` – inherited from `Control`, see `Control` Class reference for details.
- ❏ `MapPathSecure` – inherited from `Control`, see `Control` Class reference for details.
- ❏ `MemberwiseClone` – inherited from `System.Object`, see `Introduction` for details.

- ❑ OnAbortTransaction – inherited from `TemplateControl`, see `TemplateControl` Class reference for details.

- ❑ OnBubbleEvent – inherited from `Control`, see `Control` Class reference for details.

- ❑ OnCommitTransaction – inherited from `TemplateControl`, see `TemplateControl` Class reference for details.

- ❑ OnDataBinding – inherited from `Control`, see `Control` Class reference for details.

- ❑ OnError – inherited from `TemplateControl`, see `TemplateControl` Class reference for details.

- ❑ OnInit – inherited from `Control`, see `Control` Class reference for details.

- ❑ OnLoad – inherited from `Control`, see `Control` Class reference for details.

- ❑ OnPreRender – inherited from `Control`, see `Control` Class reference for details.

- ❑ OnUnload – inherited from `Control`, see `Control` Class reference for details.

- ❑ RaiseBubbleEvent – inherited from `Control`, see `Control` Class reference for details.

- ❑ **RaisePostBackEvent**

- ❑ **Render**

- ❑ **RenderChildren**

- ❑ **SavePageStateToPersistenceMedium**

- ❑ **SaveViewState**

- ❑ **TrackViewState**

CreateHtmlTextWriter

The `CreateHtmlTextWriter` method takes a `TextWriter` object as input and returns an `HtmlTextWriter` instance. If the output has been targeted at `downlevel` browsers, then an `Html32TextWriter` will be created instead. This method can be overridden and is useful when you want to pass an `HtmlTextWriter` to a function or business object so that it can write to the output stream directly.

```
protected virtual HtmlTextWriter CreateHtmlTextWriter(TextWriter tw);
```

DeterminePostBackMode

The `DeterminePostBackMode` method returns a `NameValueCollection` object representing the form values submitted during `postback`. If the GET method was used, then the values are extracted from the query string, whereas, if the values are sent using the POST method, they are extracted from the `Form` collection of the request. If the page is being requested for the first time there is no `postback` and the method will return `null`. Make sure your code handles the possibility of a null return or you will generate an exception on the first call to the page.

It's important to note that this method will only work for server-side forms used with the postback mechanism. Also, the method of the request can also be determined from the `Headers` property of the `HttpRequest` class.

```
protected virtual NameValueCollection DeterminePostBackMode();
```

LoadPageStateFromPersistenceMedium

The `LoadPageStateFromPersistenceMedium` method lets you do custom handling of loading page state. Typically this method uses hidden fields in the page as the data source for state. If you want to use something other than hidden fields as the storage medium you will also have to override the `SavePageStateToPersistenceMedium` method.

```
protected virtual object LoadPageStateFromPersistenceMedium();
```

RaisePostBackEvent

The `RaisePostBackEvent` method takes a control that implements `IPostBackEventHandler` and a `String` as input. The `RaisePostBackEvent` method raises the `Postback` event of a particular control.

When a button is clicked and posts back to the server, an event handler can be assigned in the button control to handle that event. While that handler is executing, the control can then invoke the `RaisePostBackEvent` method with another control specified as an argument. This allows us to respond to a single action from the user with multiple events. It is important to remember that `Postback` is raised after the `Load` phase of the controls change notification has completed, but before `PreRendering` occurs.

```
protected virtual void RaisePostBackEvent(IPostBackEventHandler
                                sourceControl, string eventArgument);
```

Example: RaisePostBack

As an example, the web form below, `RaisePostBack.aspx`, has a standard button and a link button. When the standard button is clicked, the event handlers for both are carried out. However, if the link button is clicked then only its own event handler is called.

```
<%@ Page language="c#" Codebehind="RaisePostBack.aspx.cs"
        AutoEventWireup="false"
        Inherits="wroxRef1.RaisePostBack" %>
<!DOCTYPE HTML PUBLIC "-//W3C//DTD HTML 4.0 Transitional//EN">
<HTML>
  <HEAD>
    <META name="GENERATOR" content="Microsoft Visual Studio 7.0">
    <META name="CODE_LANGUAGE" content="C#">
    <META name="vs_defaultClientScript" content="JavaScript (ECMAScript)">
    <META name="vs_targetSchema"
    content="http://schemas.microsoft.com/intellisense/ie5">
  </HEAD>
  <BODY ms_positioning="FlowLayout">
    <FORM id="Form1" method="post" runat="server">
      <ASP:BUTTON id="MainButton" runat="server"
                text="Main Button"></ASP:BUTTON>
      <BR>
```

```
<ASP:LINKBUTTON id="TriggeredLink"
                     runat="server">Triggered Link</ASP:LINKBUTTON>
     <BR>
     <ASP:LABEL id="Message" runat="server"></ASP:LABEL>
     <BR>
   </FORM>
 </BODY>
</HTML>
```

The page above creates a pair of controls for demonstration purposes, including `MainButton` and `TriggeredLink`, the latter of which is a `LinkButton`. Here is the code behind for this page, `RaisePostBack.aspx.cs`:

```
using System;
using System.Collections;
using System.ComponentModel;
using System.Data;
using System.Drawing;
using System.Web;
using System.Web.SessionState;
using System.Web.UI;
using System.Web.UI.WebControls;
using System.Web.UI.HtmlControls;

namespace wroxRef1
{
  /// <summary>
  /// Summary description for RaisePostBack.
  /// </summary>
  public class RaisePostBack : System.Web.UI.Page
  {
    protected Button MainButton;
    protected System.Web.UI.WebControls.LinkButton TriggeredLink;
    protected Label Message;

    private void Page_Load(object sender, System.EventArgs e)
    {
      //start each request with an empty label
      Message.Text = string.Empty;
    }

    //event handler for the main button
    private void MainButton_Click(object sender, System.EventArgs e)
    {
      //output a message and then raise the event from the other button
      Message.Text = Message.Text + "Main Button Clicked <BR>";
      RaisePostBackEvent(TriggeredLink, "");
    }

    //event handler for the triggered link (link button)
    private void TriggeredLink_Click(object sender, System.EventArgs e)
    {
      //output a message
```

```
Message.Text = Message.Text + "Triggered Link Clicked";
        }

    ...

    }
}
```

Then, using the code behind above, we create an event handler for `MainButton` that raises the `Postback` event for the `TriggeredLink` *within* `MainButton`'s `Click` event handler. The result is that a single control event can invoke the post back event handlers of one or more related controls. The examples below illustrate the resultant page for when `MainButton` is clicked, followed by the page for when `TriggeredLink` is clicked.

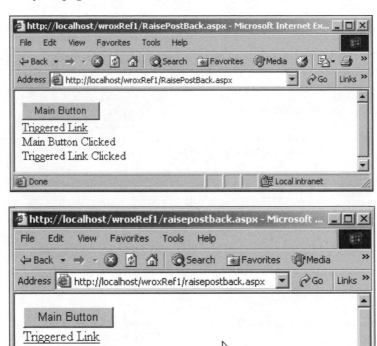

Render

The `Render` method takes an `HtmlTextWriter` object as input and is the point in the control lifecycle when text is rendered via the output stream to the client browser. It's important to note that if you would like to enable your control to participate in tracing for debugging purposes then the `RenderControl` method must be used instead. Both the `Render` and `RenderControl` methods require that you call `RenderChildren` to render all children. If you want to specify the order in which the child controls are rendered or do work between the rendering of specific controls you must use the `Controls` property of `FindControl` to call `RenderControl` method for each child control.

```
protected virtual void Render(HtmlTextWriter writer);
```

RenderChildren

The RenderChildren method takes an HtmlTextWriter as input and writes the content of the server-control's child controls to the output stream. Whenever you override the Render or RenderControl methods, you should include a call to RenderChildren. This method loops through the child control's hierarchy calling the RenderControl method on each. Alternatively, for greater control in the rendering process you may call RenderControl individually for each child control to handle child control rendering.

```
protected virtual void RenderChildren(HtmlTextWriter writer);
```

SavePageStateToPersistenceMedium

The SavePageStateToPersistenceMedium method saves any view state information for the page to something other than a hidden field.

```
protected virtual void SavePageStateToPersistenceMedium(object viewState);
```

SaveViewState

The SaveViewState method returns an object that represents the view state for the control. This view state is a string that allows information between page calls to persist, stores control property values between round-trips and is rendered to the client in a hidden input field. In this way ASP.NET encourages stateless server-side constructs, resulting in greater scalability.

```
protected virtual object SaveViewState();
```

TrackViewState

The TrackViewState method initiates the tracking of changes in the view state for the control. These changes can then be stored in the server control's StateBag object. This method is used when creating templated databound controls to ensure that their state is properly monitored for view state.

```
protected virtual void TrackViewState();
```

Page Public Properties

- ❑ **Application**
- ❑ **Cache**
- ❑ **ClientID**
- ❑ **ClientTarget**
- ❑ **Controls**
- ❑ **EnableViewState**
- ❑ **ErrorPage**
- ❑ ID – inherited from Control, see Control Class reference for details.
- ❑ **IsPostBack**
- ❑ **IsValid**

- ❏ `NamingContainer` – inherited from `Control`, see `Control` Class reference for details.
- ❏ `Page` – inherited from `Control`, see `Control` Class reference for-details.
- ❏ `Parent` – inherited from `Control`, see `Control` Class reference for details.
- ❏ **Request**
- ❏ **Response**
- ❏ **Server**
- ❏ **Session**
- ❏ `Site` – inherited from `Control`, see `Control` Class reference for details.
- ❏ **SmartNavigation**
- ❏ `TemplateSourceDirectory` – inherited from `Control`, see `Control` Class reference for details.
- ❏ **Trace**
- ❏ `UniqueID` – inherited from `Control`, see `Control` Class reference for details.
- ❏ **User**
- ❏ **Validators**
- ❏ `Visible` – inherited from `Control`, see `Control` Class reference for details.

Application

The `Application` property returns the `Application` object (of `HttpApplicationState` type) for the current page and web request. This object is similar in functionality to the intrinsic `Application` object of classic ASP in that `HttpApplicationState` contains state data for the web application in which the `Page` is running. The `Application` acts as a collection of key-value pairs where any object type can be stored and shared among pages. (For details on configuration options that can affect the scalability of applications that maintain state in the `Application` or `Session` properties see Chapter 7)

```
public HttpApplicationState Application {get;}
```

Because objects in the application are shared among all its users, the `HttpApplicationState` object supports locking in order to maintain thread synchronization and eliminate concurrency problems. This mechanism ensures that only one thread at a time can work with the application's state values. Because this locking prevents other threads accessing the object, it is important to release the lock as soon as possible by calling the `Unlock` method. Below is an example that updates values of the `Application` object. Notice that we lock the values first so that another thread cannot update the `SharedValue` member before we get a chance to update our second value.

```
Application.Lock()
  Application.Item("SharedValue") = "Value to be shared"
  Application.Item("SharedValueCount") =
                    Application.Item("SharedValue").ToString().Length
Application.Unlock()
```

Cache

The Cache property allows access to the application's Cache object. Caching affords opportunities to dramatically increase the efficiency, speed, and scalability of ASP.NET applications by caching the text output pages and controls, and simply returning the cached text rather than loading and executing the pages. Naturally, a fine degree of control is allowed to set the conditions regarding how and when cache hits should fire instead of related code. See Chapter 6 for more information on the Cache object.

```
public Cache Cache {get;}
```

ClientID

The ClientID property is inherited from Control. See Control Class reference for details.

```
public virtual string ClientID {get;}
```

ClientTarget

The ClientTarget property reflects the browser type by brand and version number of the requesting client. Assuming you've made the appropriate additions to Web.Config (see Chapter 7 for details), setting ClientTarget to ie4, for example, will force the HttpBrowserCapabilities object associated with the page to use the values for Internet Explorer 4.0 regardless of which browser software made the request.

```
public string ClientTarget {get; set;}
```

The ClientTarget property can also be set in the Page declaration of an .aspx file, as here:

```
<%@ Page language="c#" Codebehind="someForm.aspx.c#"
        ClientTarget="downlevel" Inherits="Wrox.WebForm1"%>
```

Use this property to override the default behavior of the page and user controls, if, for example, you want your page to always produce downlevel content, even when the client is Internet Explorer 5+. Forcing client output can create a common look and feel across pages and, more importantly, reduce the number of variables associated with medium or large-scale application testing requirements.

Controls

The Controls property is inherited from Control. See Control Class reference for details.

```
public virtual ControlCollection Controls {get;}
```

EnableViewState

The EnableViewState property is a Boolean value indicating whether ViewState is enabled for roundtrips to the server. Disabling ViewState prevents controls from maintaining state between web page requests and those controls not responsible for the postback will not maintain their state and corresponding information may have to be re-entered by the user. The default value of this property is true.

```
public virtual bool EnableViewState {get; set;}
```

ErrorPage

The `ErrorPage` property is a string value that is a path to a page to which redirects should be forwarded in the event of unhandled page exceptions. This simple and powerful property finally affords an easy way to aggregate baseline error-handling for your application in a single page.

```
public string ErrorPage {get; set;}
```

It's important to note that responses will only be directed to this page when the `CustomErrors` element in the `Web.config` file has its `mode` attribute set to `On` or `RemoteOnly`. The options for the `CustomErrors mode` attribute include `On`, which allows custom error pages to be shown, `RemoteOnly`, which allows custom errors to be shown only to clients other than the local machine, and `Off`, indicating that custom errors will not be displayed for any user.

IsPostBack

The `IsPostBack` property is a `Boolean` value that indicates that the page was instantiated as a result of a `PostBack` event originating on the client. Certain controls, such as buttons, image buttons, and so on, automatically post back to the server. When they do so, their `PostBack` event, such as a button click, is fired and can be handled.

It is important to check this property when loading the page to avoid any processing that only needs to be done on the first request for the page. For example, if you load data into a `Datagrid`, by only doing so when the page is first loaded, you save the cost of connecting to the database and querying it for every subsequent request that uses the same data.

Conversely, when `IsPostBack` is `false`, the page is being loaded for the first time and should be processed appropriately.

```
public bool IsPostBack {get;}
```

IsValid

The `IsValid` property returns a `Boolean` value indicating whether or not the page form value validation succeeded. `IsValid` itself is only valid after either `Page.Validate` has been called explicitly by you or the `CausesValidation` property for the control that fired the postback to the server is `true`.

```
public bool IsValid {get;}
```

Request

The `Request` property returns an object of type `HttpRequest` and should be familiar to classic ASP users in that it encapsulates the inbound request from the client browser. This object allows access to returned forms, cookie information, browser capabilities, and more. See Chapter 1, *System.Web*, for more information on the `HttpRequest` object.

```
public HttpRequest Request {get;}
```

Response

The Response property returns an object of type HttpResponse and, similar to its Request counterpart, should be familiar to classic ASP users in that it encapsulates the outbound response destined for the client browser. Response is used for operations such as setting cookies and creating UI elements. See Chapter 1, *System.Web,* for more information.

```
public HttpRespone Response {get;}
```

Server

The Server property returns an object of type HttpServerUtility and is the updated version of the traditional intrinsic Server object found in classic ASP. Server is used to encapsulate the server on which the ASP.NET application is running. Typical uses of Server include COM object instantiation. See Chapter 1 for more information on the ServerUtility class.

```
public HttpServerUtility Server {get;}
```

Session

The Session property returns an object of type HttpSessionState and is used to maintain state for individual users of the ASP.NET application. For more information on the HttpSessionState class see Chapter 1.

```
public virtual HttpSessionState Session {get;}
```

SmartNavigation

The SmartNavigation property is a Boolean value indicating whether SmartNavigation is enabled or disabled. SmartNavigation uses advanced browser-level HTML/Javascript features to offer a smoother UI experience. This is done by posting back just IFrames and other sections of the page necessary to retrieve only those parts of the page that are to be refreshed. IFrames are only supported fully on the very latest browsers and results are likely to be inconsistent or unusable on anything but late model Internet Explorer versions. Also, Microsoft recommends against setting this value in code and instead recommends setting the value using the Page directive.

```
public bool SmartNavigation {get; set;}
```

Trace

The Trace property returns a TraceContext instance that encapsulates execution information for the current page – in other words, a call stack, control hierarchy and other information can be accessed, which is invaluable for debugging.

```
public TraceContext Trace {get;}
```

To enable tracing on the page use the following directive:

```
<%@ Page Trace="True" %>
```

You can also enable tracing for all pages in the application via the `Web.Config` file with the following example:

```
<Trace enabled="true" requestLimit="10" pageOutput="true"
       traceMode="SortByTime" localOnly="true" />
```

Example: Page-Level Tracing

The following fragment is a rendering of a "hello world" ASP.NET page trace, as implemented in the `helloTracing.aspx` page in the code download. Please note that you will have to enable tracing in the `Web.config` file in order to see this output. As you can see the control lifecycle of the page is rendered along with execution times for each stage, and so on. Tracing is a powerful optimizing tool:

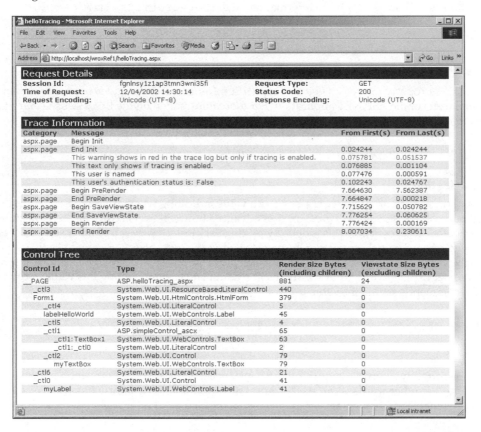

More importantly, `Trace.Write` allows you to render values to the screen that will only appear if Tracing is currently enabled for the page. For example:

```
Trace.Warn("This warning shows in red in the trace log but only if" +
           " tracing is enabled.")
Trace.Write("This text only shows if tracing is enabled.")
```

User

The `User` property returns an `IPrincipal` instance that encapsulates information about the user that requested the page. Specifically, an `IPrincipal` object represents the security context of the user for whom the code is executing. Both identity and role information is available. For more information on using `User` in a web application see Chapter 8.

```
public IPrinicipal User {get;}
```

Some examples of using `User` include:

```
Trace.Write("This user is named " + User.Identity.Name.ToString());
Trace.Write("This user's authentication status is: " +
            User.Identity.IsAuthenticated.ToString());
```

Validators

The `Validators` property returns a `ValidatorCollection` instance that encapsulates all validation controls of the current page. When you need to iterate through or manage validation controls on a page, without any foreknowledge of the controls available in a specific page instance, `Validators` provides a convenient collection.

```
public ValidatorCollection Validators {get;}
```

Page Protected Properties

❑ `ChildControlsCreated` – inherited from `Control`, see `Control` Class reference for details.

❑ **Context**

❑ `Events` – inherited from `Control`, see `Control` Class reference for details.

❑ `HasChildViewState` – inherited from `Control`, see `Control` Class reference for details.

❑ `IsTrackingViewState` – inherited from `Control`, see `Control` Class reference for details.

❑ `ViewState` – inherited from `Control`, see `Control` Class reference for details.

❑ `ViewStateIgnoresCase` – inherited from `Control`, see `Control` Class reference for details.

Context

The `Context` property is of type `HttpContext`. The `Context` for the request allows access to configuration information, error collections, and the like. See Chapter 1 for details of the `HttpContext` class.

```
protected override HttpContext Context {get;}
```

In the following example, we use the Context object to return a collection of the exceptions that occurred during the request for error tracking or reporting.

```
int i;
Exception[] ex = Context.AllErrors;
for(i=0; i < ex.Length; i++)
  Response.Write(ex[i].Message);
```

Page Public Events

❑ AbortTransaction – inherited from Control, see Control Class reference for details.

❑ CommitTransaction – inherited from TemplateControl, see TemplateControl Class reference for details.

❑ DataBinding – inherited from Control, see Control Class reference for details.

❑ Disposed – inherited from Control, see Control Class reference for details.

❑ Error – inherited from TemplateControl, see TemplateControl Class reference for details.

❑ Init – inherited from Control, see Control Class reference for details.

❑ **Load**

❑ PreRender – inherited from Control, see Control Class reference for details.

❑ Unload – inherited from Control, see Control Class reference for details.

Load

The Load event fires the OnLoad event handler and is called after basic initialization of the control. Any setup code that refers to other controls or deals with external data such as datasources, files, and so on, should be handled in the OnLoad event handler.

```
public event EventHandler Load;
```

TemplateControl Class

The TemplateControl class represents the base class for the UserControl objects you create and the Page class. All pages and User Controls inherit first from System.Web.UI.TemplateControl, which is an abstract class that is itself derived from System.Web.Control referenced earlier in this chapter. As such, the vast majority of methods and properties belonging to this class are inherited. The benefits of having a common base class include improved code manageability and modularity.

Like the Control class, TemplateControl is fundamental to a thorough understanding of user interface development in ASP.NET. This class is an abstract class, which means that it cannot be created explicitly. However, it *must* be inherited from in order to gain the functionality it exposes.

TemplateControl Public Methods

❏ `DataBind` – inherited from `Control`, see `Control` Class reference for details.

❏ `Dispose` – inherited from `Control`, see `Control` Class reference for details.

❏ `Equals` – inherited from `System.Object`, see Introduction for details.

❏ `FindControl` – inherited from `Control`, see `Control` Class reference for details.

❏ `GetHashCode` – inherited from `System.Object`, see Introduction for details.

❏ `GetType` – inherited from `System.Object`, see Introduction for details.

❏ `HasControls` – inherited from `Control`, see `Control` Class reference for details.

❏ **LoadControl**

❏ **LoadTemplate**

❏ **ParseControl**

❏ `RenderControl` – inherited from `Control`, see `Control` Class reference for details.

❏ `ResolveUrl` – inherited from `Control`, see `Control` Class reference for details.

❏ `ToString` – inherited from `System.Object`, see Introduction for details.

LoadControl

The `LoadControl` method takes a virtual path to a control as a string input. The method returns a reference to a `UserControl` by loading the file that contains the control definition. This means that a User Control, defined in a file with the extension `.ascx`, can be loaded dynamically at run time, as opposed to declaratively inserting the control in the HTML of the web form, providing greater flexibility in your design.

```
public Control LoadControl(string virtualPath);
```

For example, if we have a textbox control defined in `simpleControl.ascx`, we can load it then add it to the child controls in the page using the following code:

```
private void Form_Load(object sender, System.EventArgs e)
{
  uc = (UserControl)LoadControl("simpleControl.ascx");
  Form1.Controls.Add(uc);
}
```

The critical thing to note here is that we are creating the control within the `Load` event handler we provided for the server-side `Form` control. Remember, server-side controls can *only* live within the context of a form parent. If we try to use `LoadControl` elsewhere, like inside the `Page_Load` handler, the code will throw an exception and fail. (The preceding example can be found in `helloTracing.aspx`.)

LoadTemplate

The `LoadTemplate` method takes a string as input and loads a control template from a file. A template is an object implementing the `ITemplate` interface. Templates allow you to define the layout for the contents of a server control in a familiar HTML-like format. The `LoadTemplate` method loads the template definition, comprising HTML and text, from a file at run time rather than specifying it in the page or control at design time.

Only a few of the controls that ship with ASP.NET support templates, including the `Repeater`, `DataList`, and `DataGrid`. For example, the `DataGrid` has both a Header Template and a Footer Template to allow the developer to specify the layout for the header and footer of the grid.

Take a look at the following code extract from our *DataBound Templated Control* example earlier in this chapter that shows how to use an Item Template with a `Repeater` control:

```
private void Page_Load(object sender, System.EventArgs e)
{
  //create a datasource
  ArrayList List = new ArrayList(3);
  List.Add("Red");
  List.Add("Blue");
  List.Add("Orange");

  //set the datasource of the repeater item to
  //the array list created above
  repeat.DataSource = List;

  //load the item template from a file
  repeat.ItemTemplate = LoadTemplate("Template.ascx");

  //call DataBind to cause the page and all of its controls to execute
  //their data binding event handlers.
  DataBind();

}
```

For a fully functional demonstration that includes other important issues refer to the `viewStateControlPage.aspx` web form we use in the *DataBound Templated Control* example earlier in the chapter.

```
public ITemplate LoadTemplate(string virtualPath);
```

ParseControl

The `ParseControl` method takes a `String` as input and parses the specified string into a control. This enables the creation of `Control` objects that are dynamically based on the text in the string. A similar process is performed to parse the elements in a web form into `Control` objects in a page. The string parameter should contain a User Control in the same syntax as required in an `.ascx` file but can't include code because this method doesn't do actual run-time compilation of the code.

```
public Control ParseControl(string content);
```

Remember, server-side controls, like buttons or text boxes, must reside in the context of a server-side form control. So the following code,

```
Controls.Add(ParseControl("<asp:textBox id='myTextBox' " +
                          "runat='server'>This is a textbox</asp:textBox>"))
```

will fail in the Page_Load method. But if we include a server-side form control and catch the form's Load event with the following,

```
private void Form_Load(object sender, System.EventArgs e)
{
  UserControl uc;
  uc = (UserControl)LoadControl("simpleControl.ascx");
  Form1.Controls.Add(uc);

  Form1.Controls.Add(ParseControl("<asp:textBox id='myTextBox'" +
                          "runat='server'>This is a textbox</asp:textBox>"));
}
```

the text box will appear in the form.

TemplateControl Protected Methods

❑ AddParsedSubObject – inherited from Control, see Control Class reference for details.

❑ ClearChildViewState – inherited from Control, see Control Class reference for details.

❑ **Construct**

❑ CreateChildControls – inherited from Control, see Control Class reference for details.

❑ CreateControlCollection – inherited from Control, see Control Class reference for details.

❑ EnsureChildControls – inherited from Control, see Control Class reference for details.

❑ Finalize – inherited from System.Object, see Introduction for details.

❑ IsLiteralContent – inherited from Control, see Control Class reference for details.

❑ LoadViewState – inherited from Control, see Control Class reference for details.

❑ MapPathSecure – inherited from Control, see Control Class reference for details.

❑ MemberwiseClone – inherited from System.Object, see Introduction for details.

❑ **OnAbortTransaction**

❑ **OnCommitTransaction**

❑ OnDataBinding – inherited from Control, see Control Class reference for details.

❑ **OnError**

❑ OnInit – inherited from Control, see Control Class reference for details.

❑ OnLoad – inherited from Control, see Control Class reference for details.

- ❑ OnPreRender – inherited from `Control`, see `Control` Class reference for details.
- ❑ **OnUnload**
- ❑ `RaiseBubbleEvent` – inherited from `Control`, see `Control` Class reference for details.
- ❑ `Render` – inherited from `Control`, see `Control` Class reference for details.
- ❑ `RenderChildren` – inherited from `Control`, see `Control` Class reference for details.
- ❑ `SaveViewState` – inherited from `Control`, see `Control` Class reference for details.
- ❑ `TrackViewState` – inherited from `Control`, see `Control` Class reference for details.

Construct

The `Construct` method allows page and User Control authors to handle construction time for their control without authoring a true constructor for the control.

```
protected virtual void Construct();
```

OnAbortTransaction

The `OnAbortTransaction` method takes an `EventArgs` as input and raises the `AbortTransaction` event. Transactions constitute application behavior that is "atomic", that is it either must happen in its entirety or, in the event the transaction fails, the application must be rolled back to its pre-transaction state. As freestanding units of an application, templated controls are ideal candidates for participation in transactions. `OnAbortTransaction` and related methods are provided to enable templated controls to act as "atomic" members of execution in a transaction.

```
protected virtual void OnAbortTransaction(EventArgs e);
```

This event handling method is called at the end of processing the page, only when the transaction property of the page has been set to `Requires` or `Requires New`. This allows the developer to respond to the result of the transaction appropriately by notifying the user of the result of their request. Because the page must have completed its processing, these events are fired directly before the `Unload` and `Disposed` events, and after all content has been rendered.

OnCommitTransaction

The `OnCommitTransaction` method takes an `EventArgs` object as input and raises the `CommitTransaction` event. This and related methods are provided to enable templated controls to act as "atoms" or members of execution in a transaction. `CommitTransaction` means the transaction has been successful and can conclude.

```
protected virtual void OnCommitTransaction(EventArgs e);
```

OnError

The `OnError` method takes `EventArgs` as input and raises the `Error` event to indicate that an error has occurred in processing the control. Use this method in conjunction with the `Error` event to centralize your response to errors. You should use exception handling in your methods that catch `Error` events and provide an appropriate response for the user interface. It is important to note that after handling the errors in the `Error` event, you need to empty out the `Error` collection by calling the `ClearError` method of the `HttpContext` class.

In addition to this error handling mechanism, the `ErrorPage` property of the `Page` object can be used for page redirection to provide custom error messages.

```
protected virtual void OnError(EventArgs e);
```

OnUnload

The `OnUnload` method takes an `EventArgs` object as input and fires the `Unload` event. `Unload` is the last step in the lifecycle prior to `Dispose`, at which point the control is released from memory. `Unload` signifies the control has completed processing, therefore expensive resources such as database connections or files should be released at this time so that they do not have to wait to be garbage collected.

```
protected virtual void OnUnload(EventArgs e);
```

TemplateControl Public Properties

❑ `ClientID` – inherited from `Control`, see `Control` Class reference for details.

❑ `Controls` – inherited from `Control`, see `Control` Class reference for details.

❑ `EnableViewState` – inherited from `Control`, see `Control` Class reference for details.

❑ `ID` – inherited from `Control`, see `Control` Class reference for details.

❑ `NamingContainer` – inherited from `Control`, see `Control` Class reference for details.

❑ `Page` – inherited from `Control`, see `Control` Class reference for details.

❑ `Parent` – inherited from `Control`, see `Control` Class reference for details.

❑ `Site` – inherited from `Control`, see `Control` Class reference for details.

❑ `TemplateSourceDirectory` – inherited from `Control`, see `Control` Class reference for details.

❑ `UniqueID` – inherited from `Control`, see `Control` Class reference for details.

❑ `Visible` – inherited from `Control`, see `Control` Class reference for details.

TemplateControl Protected Properties

❑ `ChildControlsCreated` – inherited from `Control`, see `Control` Class reference for details.

❑ `Context` – inherited from `Control`, see `Control` Class reference for details.

❑ `Events` – inherited from `Control`, see `Control` Class reference for details.

❑ `HasChildViewState` – inherited from `Control`, see `Control` Class reference for details.

❑ `IsTrackingViewState` – inherited from `Control`, see `Control` Class reference for details.

❑ `ViewState` – inherited from `Control`, see `Control` Class reference for details.

❑ `ViewStateIgnoresCase` – inherited from `Control`, see `Control` Class reference for details.

TemplateControl Public Events

- ❑ AbortTransaction – inherited from Control, see Control Class reference for details.
- ❑ **CommitTransaction**
- ❑ DataBinding – inherited from Control, see Control Class reference for details.
- ❑ Disposed – inherited from Control, see Control Class reference for details.
- ❑ **Error**
- ❑ Init – inherited from Control, see Control Class reference for details.
- ❑ Load – inherited from Page, see Page Class reference for details.
- ❑ PreRender – inherited from Control, see Control Class reference for details.
- ❑ Unload – inherited from Control, see Control Class reference for details.

CommitTransaction

The CommitTransaction event is raised when a transaction completes.

```
public event EventHandler CommitTransaction;
```

Error

The Error event is raised when an unhandled exception is thrown by the runtime.

```
public event EventHandler Error;
```

You can handle an Error event with an event handler. For example, your page can respond to unhandled exceptions by providing the following method in the code behind for your page.

```
private void Page_Load(object sender, System.EventArgs e)
{
  // Put user code to initialize the page here
  int x = 3;
  int y = 0;

  x = (x / y);
}

private void Page_Error(object sender, System.EventArgs eArgs)
{

  //write a message to the UI with some information about the error
  Response.Write("Error occurred:" + Context.Error.Message);

  //clear the error so the framework does not also handle it
  Context.ClearError();
}
```

Naturally, divide by zero is still impossible, even in .NET. Running this code throws an exception that is caught by the event handler resulting in screen output like the following:

Error occurred:Arithmetic operation resulted in an overflow.

UserControl Class

The `UserControl` class is the base class for custom user interface components that are reusable in various pages. `UserControl` is based on the abstract class `System.Web.UI.TemplateControl`, which in turn is based on `System.Web.Control`. While similar to classic ASP `Include` files, which allow text or code from an external file to be inserted into a page at run time, the `UserControl` is much more powerful as it has all of the functionality of the `Control` and `ControlTemplate` class.

User Controls are used to form parts of a page, including text, HTML, and even other controls. User Controls and their `.ascx` files, like `.aspx` pages, typically have their own code behind page. And much like the built-in server controls, they can be added to a page using HTML style tags and attributes to set their properties. We've seen plenty of examples of this throughout this chapter, so we won't repeat them here.

A User Control can only exist in the scope of a page. That is, a User Control cannot be requested directly by the client. By default, the `machine.config` file defines an HTTP handler, of type `System.Web.HttpForbiddenHandler`, to handle requests for User Controls so that the run-time does not attempt to process the file outside the scope of a page request.

UserControl Public Methods

- ❑ `DataBind` – inherited from `Control`, see `Control` Class reference for details.
- ❑ `Dispose` – inherited from `Control`, see `Control` Class reference for details.
- ❑ `Equals` – inherited from `System.Object`, see Introduction for details.
- ❑ `FindControl` – inherited from `Control`, see `Control` Class reference for details.
- ❑ `GetHashCode` – inherited from `System.Object`, see Introduction for details.
- ❑ `GetType` – inherited from `System.Object`, see Introduction for details.
- ❑ `HasControls` – inherited from `Control`, see `Control` Class reference for details.
- ❑ **`InitializeAsUserControl`**
- ❑ `LoadControl` – inherited from `TemplateControl`, see `TemplateControl` Class reference for details.
- ❑ `LoadTemplate` – inherited from `TemplateControl`, see `TemplateControl` Class reference for details.
- ❑ **`MapPath`**
- ❑ `ParseControl` – inherited from `TemplateControl`, see `TemplateControl` Class reference for details.
- ❑ `RenderControl` – inherited from `Control`, see `Control` Class reference for details.
- ❑ `ResolveUrl` – inherited from `Control`, see `Control` Class reference for details.
- ❑ `ToString` – inherited from `System.Object`, see Introduction for details.

InitializeAsUserControl

The `InitializeAsUserControl` method takes a `Page` object as input and initializes a user control that has been created declaratively inside a `Page` object. As mentioned above, the `UserControl` is like a `Page` object except that it cannot be created on its own, so this method can ensure that the control is created properly and instantiated in the control tree of the `Page` object.

```
public void InitializeAsUserControl(Page page);
```

The syntax is straightforward and requires the control reference itself, as in:

```
improvedDataGrid.InitializeAsUserControl(Me)
```

MapPath

The `MapPath` method takes a `String` as input and returns a physical path, absolute or relative, for the given virtual path.

```
public string MapPath(string virtualPath);
```

UserControl Protected Methods

- ❑ `AddParsedSubObject` – inherited from `Control`, see `Control` Class reference for details.
- ❑ `ClearChildViewState` – inherited from `Control`, see `Control` Class reference for details.
- ❑ **Construct**
- ❑ `CreateChildControls` – inherited from `Control`, see `Control` Class reference for details.
- ❑ `CreateControlCollection` – inherited from `Control`, see `Control` Class reference for details.
- ❑ `EnsureChildControls` – inherited from `Control`, see `Control` Class reference for details.
- ❑ `Finalize` – inherited from `System.Object`, see Introduction for details.
- ❑ `IsLiteralContent` – inherited from `Control`, see `Control` Class reference for details.
- ❑ **LoadViewState**
- ❑ `MapPathSecure` – inherited from `Control`, see `Control` Class reference for details.
- ❑ `MemberwiseClone` – inherited from `System.Object`, see Introduction for details.
- ❑ `OnAbortTransaction` – inherited from `Control`, see `Control` Class reference for details.
- ❑ `OnBubbleEvent` – inherited from `Control`, see `Control` Class reference for details.
- ❑ `OnCommitTransaction` – inherited from `TemplateControl`, see `TemplateControl` Class reference for details.
- ❑ `OnDataBinding` – inherited from `Control`, see `Control` Class reference for details.
- ❑ `OnError` – inherited from `TemplateControl`, see `TemplateControl` Class reference for details.
- ❑ `OnInit` – inherited from `Control`, see `Control` Class reference for details.

- ❑ OnLoad – inherited from Control, see Control Class reference for details.
- ❑ OnPreRender – inherited from Control, see Control Class reference for details.
- ❑ OnUnload – inherited from Control, see Control Class reference for details.
- ❑ RaiseBubbleEvent – inherited from Control, see Control Class reference for details.
- ❑ Render – inherited from Control, see Control Class reference for details.
- ❑ RenderChildren – inherited from Control, see Control Class reference for details.
- ❑ **SaveViewState**
- ❑ TrackViewState – inherited from Control, see Control Class reference for details.

Construct

The Construct method allows Page and UserControl authors to handle construction time for their control without authoring a true constructor for the control.

```
protected virtual void Construct();
```

LoadViewState

The LoadViewState method takes an Object as input and causes the UserControl to retrieve its view state and apply it appropriately. For example, when this method is called on a control, that control retrieves its view state information and is then able to set text for labels or alter other control states. The method should be overridden when you wish to intervene in the process of loading view state. You generally will not need to override this method unless you have referenced the control's Statebag directly to store custom information and/or you have overridden the control's SaveViewState method to do custom control state persistence techniques.

```
protected override void LoadViewState(object savedState);
```

SaveViewState

The SaveViewState method causes the UserControl to save its current state so that it can be retrieved later during a subsequent request. This method returns an Object that contains the state of the User Control. Typically this method is not overridden unless you need to customize what properties of the control are persisted or the way they are persisted in the state view. If you override this method you must create complementary code in an overridden version of the LoadViewState method for your control to function properly.

```
protected override object SaveViewState();
```

UserControl Public Properties

- ❑ **Application**
- ❑ **Attributes**
- ❑ **Cache**
- ❑ ClientID – inherited from Control, see Control Class reference for details.

- ❑ `Controls` – inherited from `Control`, see `Control` Class reference for details.
- ❑ `EnableViewState` – inherited from `Control`, see `Control` Class reference for details.
- ❑ `ID` – inherited from `Control`, see `Control` Class reference for details.
- ❑ **IsPostBack**
- ❑ `NamingContainer` – inherited from `Control`, see `Control` Class reference for details.
- ❑ `Page` – inherited from `Control`, see `Control` Class reference for details.
- ❑ `Parent` – inherited from `Control`, see `Control` Class reference for details.
- ❑ **Request**
- ❑ **Response**
- ❑ **Server**
- ❑ **Session**
- ❑ `Site` – inherited from `Control`, see `Control` Class reference for details.
- ❑ `TemplateSourceDirectory` – inherited from `Control`, see `Control` Class reference for details.
- ❑ **Trace**
- ❑ **UniqueID**
- ❑ `Visible` – inherited from `Control`, see `Control` Class reference for details.

Application

The `Application` property holds the `HttpApplicationState` object that represents the application context in which the `UserControl` is running. The object returned allows information to be shared among pages of the application.

```
public HttpApplicationState Application {get;}
```

The application-scoped state management routines are easy to use and nearly identical to those provided in classic ASP. For example:

```
// These name/value pairs will be maintained as long as
// the application is active and will be available
// to all controls across the application
myControl.Application.Add("FirstName","Davey")
myControl.Application.Add("LastName", "Jones")
```

Attributes

The `Attributes` property holds an `AttributeCollection` object that represents the name and value pairs for the User Control as declared in the HTML elements of the User Control `.ascx` file. Attributes on a `UserControl` declaration, in an `.aspx` file, are often directly mapped to special properties or public member variables. However, if there is no corresponding property or field for the attributes, or there is a need to access the entire set of attributes, this method provides access to the entire collection.

```
public AttributeCollection Attributes {get;}
```

Cache

The Cache property holds a reference to a Cache object that controls the way in which all HTML content generated by the control is cached on the server such that subsequent requests may simply be emitted from the cache. Cache "hits" like this offer staggering performance and scalability improvements. See Chapter 6 for details on utilizing caching and the Cache object.

```
public Cache Cache {get;}
```

IsPostBack

The IsPostBack property is a Boolean value that indicates whether the current request for the page is the result of a postback, returning true when the page request is the result of a postback action from a server control. Essentially if the postback value is false, the control is rendering "clean" for the first time. If it is true then the control is rendering in response to a user-driven event, such as clicking a submit button.

```
public bool IsPostBack {get;}
```

Request

The Request property returns an object of type HttpRequest and should be familiar to classic ASP users in that it encapsulates the inbound request from the client browser. This object allows access to returned forms, cookie information, browser capabilities, and more. See Chapter 1, *System.Web,* for more information on the HttpRequest object.

```
public HttpRequest Request {get;}
```

Response

The Response property returns an object of type HttpResponse and, similar to its Request counterpart, should be familiar to classic ASP users in that it encapsulates the outbound response destined for the client browser. Response is used for operations such as setting cookies and creating UI elements. See Chapter 1 for more information.

```
public HttpResponse Response {get;}
```

Server

The Server property returns an object of type HttpServerUtility and is the updated version of the intrinsic Server object found in classic ASP. Server is used to encapsulate the server on which the ASP.NET application is running. Typical uses of Server include COM object instantiation.

```
public HttpServerUtility Server {get;}
```

Session

The Session property returns an object of type HttpSessionState and is used to maintain state for individual users of the ASP.NET application. For more information on the HttpSessionState class see Chapter 1.

```
public HttpSessionState Session {get;}
```

Trace

The Trace property refers the TraceContext object that encapsulates the current web request.

```
public TraceContext Trace {get;}
```

UniqueID

UniqueID property indicates the fully qualified unique name for a control. This includes the naming container ID, the client ID, and the control's own ID.

```
public virtual string UniqueID {get;}
```

UserControl Protected Properties

❑ CreateChildControls – inherited from Control, see Control Class reference for details.

❑ Context – inherited from Control, see Control Class reference for details.

❑ Events – inherited from Control, see Control Class reference for details.

❑ HasChildViewState – inherited from Control, see Control Class reference for details.

❑ IsTrackingViewState – inherited from Control, see Control Class reference for details.

❑ ViewState – inherited from Control, see Control Class reference for details.

❑ ViewStateIgnoresCase – inherited from Control, see Control Class reference for details.

UserControl Public Events

❑ AbortTransaction – inherited from TemplateControl, see TemplateControl Class reference for details.

❑ CommitTransaction – inherited from TemplateControl, see TemplateControl Class reference for details.

❑ DataBinding – inherited from Control, see Control Class reference for details.

❑ Disposed – inherited from Control, see Control Class reference for details.

❑ Error – inherited from TemplateControl, see TemplateControl Class reference for details.

❑ Init – inherited from Control, see Control Class reference for details.

❑ Load – inherited from Control, see Control Class reference for details.

❑ PreRender – inherited from Control, see Control Class reference for details.

❑ Unload – inherited from Control, see Control Class reference for details.

3

System.Web.UI.HtmlControls

This chapter is about HTML server controls. These are very easy to use and, if you already know some native HTML tags, then you already know most of the syntax for HTML controls. HTML server controls appear very like HTML tags but have, in addition, the `runat="server"` attribute at the end of the HTML element. These server controls give the web developer the functionality of the Web Form's page framework while retaining the familiarity and ease of use of HTML tags, as they not only create an HTML element on a web page, but also create an instance of a server control.

The advantages of HTML server controls over native HTML tags are illustrated in the example below:

```
<input type="button" id="button1" value="Click"
        runat="server">
```

Without the `runat="server"` attribute, this line of HTML would be parsed into a standard HTML button. With the `runat="server"` attribute, it will be parsed into an HTML server control. Once a server control is created, you can access its properties, methods, and events through server-side code, and it can obtain input from, as well as provide feedback to, the user. This interaction cannot be achieved with simple HTML. This is why HTML server controls are so useful for building ASP.NET web applications.

The `System.Web.UI.HtmlControls` namespace provides the functionality to create HTML server controls, which can then be programmatically accessed on a Web Forms page. It includes the following three main classes: `HtmlImage` for image handling, `HtmlInputControl` for input controls, and `HtmlContainerControl` for block elements.

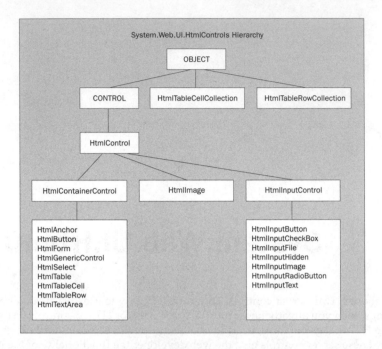

System.Web.UI.HtmlControls Hierarchy

OBJECT

CONTROL   HtmlTableCellCollection   HtmlTableRowCollection

HtmlControl

HtmlContainerControl   HtmlImage   HtmlInputControl

HtmlAnchor
HtmlButton
HtmlForm
HtmlGenericControl
HtmlSelect
HtmlTable
HtmlTableCell
HtmlTableRow
HtmlTextArea

HtmlInputButton
HtmlInputCheckBox
HtmlInputFile
HtmlInputHidden
HtmlInputImage
HtmlInputRadioButton
HtmlInputText

As you can see from the above diagram, all **HtmlControls** inherit from **System.Web.UI.Control**, so we are not going to waste your time by repeating the listing of all the members that are discussed in the previous chapter for every class in this namespace. We will only give a full listing of all the new members that the HTML controls add over and above those inherited from **Control**, and those members which are overridden.

Here is a list of the classes available in the System.Web.UI.HtmlControls namespace. Those in bold will be discussed in greater detail within this chapter:

Class	Description
HtmlAnchor	This class provides programmatic access to the **<a>** anchor element on the server. This class creates a hyperlink that allows navigation.
HtmlButton	This class provides programmatic access to the **<button>** element on the server. It is a container control, so you can place HTML inside the element instead of just text. This element is defined in HTML 4.0, and therefore it is supported by IE browsers (IE 4.0 or later) but not by Navigator or Opera.
HtmlContainer Control	This class inherits from **HtmlControl** and does not correspond to any specific HTML element, but defines methods, properties and events for all block type HTML controls (that is, the controls that require a closing tag). Because it is only used for 'container' elements that can themselves have content, it adds more useful properties that allow us to read and set this content.

Class	Description
HtmlControl	The **HtmlControl** class provides all the methods, properties and events that are common to all HTML server controls in the ASP.NET framework.
HtmlForm	The **HtmlForm** class provides programmatic access to the **<form>** element on the server. This **HtmlForm** container class contains all the server controls that need to be posted to the server.
HtmlGeneric Control	The **HtmlGenericControl** class provides a class for those HTML elements that do not already have a specified class. The class contains methods, properties and events defined for such controls. This enables us to use all HTML controls as server controls.
HtmlImage	The **HtmlImage** class provides programmatic access to the **<img>** element on the server.
HtmlInput Button	The **HtmlInputButton** class provides programmatic access to all input buttons, such as **<input type="button">**, **<input type="submit">** and **<input type="reset">** on the server.
HtmlInput CheckBox	The **HtmlInputCheckBox** class provides programmatic access to the **<input type="checkbox">** element on the server.
HtmlInput Control	The **HtmlInputControl** class defines methods, properties and events for all the HTML **<input>** controls.
HtmlInputFile	The **HtmlInputFile** control provides programmatic access to the **<file>** element on the server. This control can be used to upload files on the server.
HtmlInput Hidden	The **HtmlInputHidden** class provides programmatic access to the **<input type="hidden">** element on the server. This control stores the state information for a form.
HtmlInput Image	The **HtmlInputImage** class provides programmatic access to the **<input type="image">** element on the server. This control acts like a button combined with embedded images.
HtmlInput RadioButton	The **HtmlRadioButton** class provides programmatic access to the **<input type="radio">** element on the server. This control displays a button that can be turned on or off.
HtmlInputText	The **HtmlInputText** class provides programmatic access to the **<input type="text">** and **<input type="password">** elements on the server. These controls allow data to be edited by the user.
HtmlSelect	The **HtmlSelect** class provides programmatic access to the **<select>** element on the server. This class provides a list of values to select from. There can be single as well as multiple selections.
HtmlTable	The **HtmlTable** class provides programmatic access to the **<table>** element on the server. It creates a table control, which helps to display data in a formatted manner.
HtmlTableCell	The **HtmlTableCell** class provides programmatic access to the **<td>** and **<th>** elements on the server. This class creates a single cell in a table row.
HtmlTableCell Collection	This class provides a collection of HtmlTableCell objects that relate to a single row in the <table> element.

Class	Description
`HtmlTableRow`	The **HtmlTableRow** class provides programmatic access to the **\<tr\>** elements in the **\<table\>** element on the server.
`HtmlTableRow Collection`	This class provides a collection of `HtmlTableRow` objects that relate to all of the rows in the \<table\> element. This creates a single row in the table.
`HtmlTextArea`	The **HtmlTextArea** class provides programmatic access to the **\<textarea\>** element on the server. This can be used to display or edit large quantities of text.

> As you can see in the diagram above, every control in this namespace inherits from the base class **HtmlControl**. Therefore, in this chapter we will explain all the methods, properties, and events of the **HtmlControl** class, and to avoid repetition, we will just describe in detail those members of classes which are new or which override members of **HtmlControl**.

HtmlAnchor Class

The `HtmlAnchor` class provides programmatic access to the \<a\> (anchor) element on the server. It can be utilized in two ways; it can be used as a hyperlink just like the HTML \<a\> tag, using the `Href` property for navigation or it can perform a set of operations at server-side when the user clicks on the link, with the help of the `ServerClick` event, which it supports.

The `HtmlAnchor` class is inherited from `System.Web.UI.HtmlControls.HtmlContainerControl`.

It has the following syntax:

```
<a id="id_name"
   href="URL"
   name="bookmark"
   target="target_option"
   title="tooltip name"
   onserverclick="event_handler_name"
   runat="server">
Hyperlink_Text
</a>
```

HtmlAnchor Class Public Methods

The `HtmlAnchor` class adds no new public methods over those inherited from the `Control` class. See Chapter 2 for details.

HtmlAnchor Class Protected Methods

❑ **OnServerClick**

OnServerClick

The `OnServerClick` method raises the `ServerClick` event. This method notifies the server of the actions to be performed when the `anchor` element is clicked. Therefore, the method is executed at the server-side and requires a round-trip to the server. The `OnClick` method can be used to handle the click event at the client side. This method allows derived classes to handle the `ServerClick` event without attaching to the delegate.

```
protected virtual void OnServerClick(EventArgs e);
```

The parameter `e` refers to an `EventArgs` object that contains the server click event data.

HtmlAnchor Class Public Properties

❑ `Attributes` – inherited from `System.Web.UI.HtmlControls.HtmlControl`, see the `HtmlControl` class reference for details.

❑ `Disabled` – inherited from `System.Web.UI.HtmlControls.HtmlControl`, see the `HtmlControl` class reference for details.

❑ **Href**

❑ `InnerHtml` – inherited from `System.Web.UI.HtmlControls.HtmlContainerControl`, see the `HtmlContainerControl` class for details.

❑ `InnerText` – inherited from `System.Web.UI.HtmlControls.HtmlContainerControl`, see the `HtmlContainerControl` Class for details.

❑ **Name**

❑ `Style` – inherited from `System.Web.UI.HtmlControls.HtmlControl`, see the **HtmlControl** class reference for details.

❑ `TagName` – inherited from `System.Web.UI.HtmlControls.HtmlControl`, see the `HtmlControl` class reference for details.

❑ **Target**

❑ **Title**

HRef

The `HRef` property gets or sets the URL target of the link specified in the `HtmlAnchor` server control. It specifies the URL that should be displayed in the target window or frame. The `HRef` property corresponds to the `href` attribute in the `<a>` element.

```
public string HRef {get; set;}
```

Name

The `Name` property gets or sets the bookmark name defined in the `HtmlAnchor` server control. This property acts as a unique identifier for the control and can be used to link to a marked section on a web page. The anchor control can link to the bookmark name by setting its `HRef` property to the name of the anchor element preceded with a # symbol, in the following format:

```
<a HRef= "#AnchorElement"/>
```

The `Name` property corresponds to the `name` attribute in the `<a>` element.

```
public string Name {get; set;}
```

Target

The `Target` property indicates the target window or frame where the linked web page content will be displayed. The `Target` property corresponds to the `target` attribute in the `<a>` element.

```
public string Target {get; set;}
```

The `Target` property can have four values, as follows:

Value	Description
`_blank`	Renders the web page to a new and unframed browser window.
`_parent`	Renders the web page in the immediate frameset parent in the same browser window.
`_self`	Renders the web page in the current frame in the same browser window. (Default value).
`_top`	Renders the web page in the full and unframed window in the same browser.

Title

The `Title` property gets or sets the `ToolTip` text. This `ToolTip` is the text that is displayed when the user hovers the cursor over the anchor control, which could be information or simply the name of the control. This is a very helpful property that can provide a description of the anchor at run-time.

```
public string Title {get; set;}
```

HtmlAnchor Class Protected Properties

The `HtmlAnchor` class adds no new protected properties over those inherited from the `Control` class. See Chapter 2 for details.

HtmlAnchor Class Public Events

❑ **ServerClick**

ServerClick

When a user clicks on the text of the `HtmlAnchor` instance on a web page, the browser will navigate to the location that is specified in the `HRef` property of the control. ASP.NET has the ability to react whenever a user clicks this link, by firing the `ServerClick` event. You can write an event handler that intercepts this event and runs some code whenever the event is fired.

```
public event EventHandler ServerClick;
```

Example: The HtmlAnchor Class

Let's see the main properties and `ServerClick` event of the `HtmlAnchor` class in the following example. This code, `HtmlAnchorUsage.aspx`, is available for download:

```
<%@ Page Language="c#" AutoEventWireup="false"
        Codebehind="HtmlAnchorUsage.aspx.cs"
        Inherits="systemWebUIHTMLControlsCS.HtmlAnchorUsage" %>
<!DOCTYPE HTML PUBLIC "-//W3C//DTD HTML 4.0 Transitional//EN">
<HTML>
  <HEAD>
    <title>HtmlAnchorUsage</title>
    <meta name="GENERATOR" content="Microsoft Visual Studio.NET 7.0">
    <meta name="CODE_LANGUAGE" content="C#">
    <meta name="vs_defaultClientScript" content="JavaScript">
    <meta name="vs_targetSchema"
        content="http://schemas.microsoft.com/intellisense/ie5">
  </HEAD>
  <body MS_POSITIONING="GridLayout">
    <form id="FrmAnchor" method="post" runat="server"
        title="Click here to visit Wrox Website in a new window">
      <a id="AWrox" name="AWrox" runat="server" href="http://www.wrox.com"
        target="_blank">
          <B>WROX.COM</B></a>
      <br>
      <br>
      <a id="ARefBook" name="ARefBook" runat="server"
        title="ASP.NET Programmer's Reference Book "
        onServerClick="ARefBook_ServerClick">
      <B>ASP.NET Programmer's Reference</B></a>
      <div id="Message" runat="server"></div>
    </form>
  </body>
</HTML>
```

191

The code-behind for this example, `HtmlAnchorUsage.aspx.cs`, is shown below:

```
public class HtmlAnchorUsage : System.Web.UI.Page
  {
    protected System.Web.UI.HtmlControls.HtmlAnchor AWrox;
    protected System.Web.UI.HtmlControls.HtmlAnchor ARefBook;
    protected System.Web.UI.HtmlControls.HtmlGenericControl Message;

    private void Page_Load(object sender, System.EventArgs e)
    {
      // Put user code to initialize the page here
    }

    protected void ARefBook_ServerClick(object sender, System.EventArgs e)
    {
      Message.InnerHtml = "Thanks for buying this book!";
    }
  }
```

Here is the output screenshot showing the `ToolTip` for the anchor element:

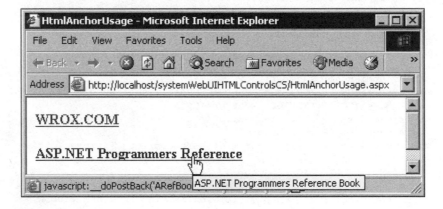

HtmlButton Class

The `HtmlButton` class creates an HTML button, `<button>` tag, on the server. Although the simple HTML `<button>` is defined in the HTML 4.0 specification, it is only supported by Internet Explorer 4.0 and above. The `HtmlButton` class is used to create rich button controls that can contain embedded special controls including other server controls.

The `HtmlButton` class is inherited from `System.Web.UI.HtmlControls.HtmlContainerControl`. It has the following syntax:

```
<button id="id_name"
        onserverclick="event_handler_name"
        runat="server">
Button_name, Button_image, or Button_control
</button>
```

HtmlButton Class Public Methods

The `HtmlButton` class adds no new public methods over those inherited from the `Control` class. See Chapter 2 for details.

HtmlButton Class Protected Methods

❑ `OnServerClick`

OnServerClick

The `OnServerClick` method raises the `ServerClick` event. This method notifies the server that the actions are to be performed when the button element is clicked. Therefore the method is executed at the server-side and requires a round-trip to the server. The `OnClick` method can be used to handle the click event at the client-side. This method allows derived classes to handle the `ServerClick` event without attaching to a delegate.

```
protected virtual void OnServerClick(EventArgs e);
```

The parameter e refers to an `EventArgs` object that contains the server click event data.

HtmlButton Class Public Properties

❑ `Attributes` – inherited from `System.Web.UI.HtmlControls.HtmlControl`, see `HtmlControl` in this chapter for details.

❑ **`CausesValidation`**

❑ `Disabled` – inherited from `System.Web.UI.HtmlControls.HtmlControl`, see `HtmlControl` in this chapter for details.

❑ `InnerHtml` – inherited from `System.Web.UI.HtmlControls.HtmlContainerControl`, see the `HtmlContainerControl` class for details.

❑ `InnerText` – inherited from `System.Web.UI.HtmlControls.HtmlContainerControl`, see the `HtmlContainerControl` class for details.

❑ `Style` – inherited from `System.Web.UI.HtmlControls.HtmlControl`, see `HtmlControl` in this chapter for details.

❑ `TagName` – inherited from `System.Web.UI.HtmlControls.HtmlControl`, see `HtmlControl` in this chapter for details.

CausesValidation

The `CausesValidation` property is used to specify whether validation should be performed when the `HtmlInputButton` control is clicked. The validation is performed by the ASP.NET validation controls (if there are any) associated with the input server controls in the page. Therefore this property causes the validation controls to perform a validation test if set to `true`, which is the default value. Sometimes it is necessary to submit the page without validation; for example in the event of the cancel or reset button being clicked. This property, when `true` may perform validations at both the client and server level depending on the browser capability and the setting of the `clienttarget` attribute in the `Page` directive.

```
public bool CausesValidation {get; set;}
```

HtmlButton Class Protected Properties

The HtmlButton class adds no new protected properties over those inherited from the Control class. See Chapter 2 for details.

HtmlButton Class Public Events

❑ **ServerClick**

ServerClick

The ServerClick event is raised when a user clicks on the HtmlButton instance on a web page. This event is represented on the control by an attribute, onserverclick, which attaches an event handler to the event. We can then write an event handler method that intercepts this event and runs some code whenever the event is fired.

```
public event EventHandler ServerClick;
```

Example: Using the Main Properties of the HtmlButton Class

Let's see the main properties of the HtmlButton class in the following example. This code is available for download with the filename HtmlButtonUsage.aspx:

```
<%@ Page Language="c#" AutoEventWireup="false"
        Codebehind="HtmlButtonUsage.aspx.cs"
        Inherits="systemWebUIHTMLControlsCS.HtmlButtonUsage" %>
<!DOCTYPE HTML PUBLIC "-//W3C//DTD HTML 4.0 Transitional//EN">
<HTML>
  <HEAD>
    <title>HtmlButtonUsage</title>
    <meta content="Microsoft Visual Studio.NET 7.0"
          name="GENERATOR">
    <meta content="C#" name="CODE_LANGUAGE">
    <meta content="JavaScript"
          name="vs_defaultClientScript">
    <meta content="http://schemas.microsoft.com/intellisense/ie5"
          name="vs_targetSchema">
  </HEAD>
  <body>
    <form id="FrmButton" method="post" runat="server">
      <div>Enter your Name:</div>
      <input id="TxtName" type="text" runat="server">
      <asp:requiredfieldvalidator id="ReqValTxtName"
              runat="server"
              Display="Dynamic" ControlToValidate="TxtName"
              ErrorMessage="Please enter Name">
              </asp:requiredfieldvalidator><br>
      <br>
      <button id="BtnSubmit" type="button" runat="server"
   onServerClick="BtnSubmit_ServerClick"
```

```
                        causesvalidation="true">
                Submit With Validation</button>
          <buttonid="BtnSubmitWithoutValidation"
                    type="button"
                    runat="server"
                    onServerClick="BtnSubmit_ServerClick">Submit
                    Without Validation</button>
          <br>
          <br>
          <br>
          <button id="BtnWrox" name="BtnWrox" type="button"
                    runat="server"
                    onserverclick="BtnWrox_ServerClick"
                    CausesValidation="false">
            <IMG style="WIDTH: 42px; HEIGHT: 43px"
                 height="43"
                 src="wroxlogo.gif" width="42">
          </button> <br>
          <br>
          <button id="BtnFancy"
                    onmouseover="this.style.backgroundColor='#3D59AB'"
                    style="BORDER-LEFT-COLOR: black;
                    BORDER-BOTTOM-COLOR: black;
                    FONT: bold 10pt verdana; WIDTH: 182px;
                    COLOR: silver;
                    BORDER-TOP-COLOR: black; HEIGHT: 28px;
                    BACKGROUND-COLOR: teal;
                     BORDER-RIGHT-COLOR: black; FORE-COLOR: white"
                     onmouseout="this.style.backgroundColor='teal'"
                     runat="server">
            Cool Fancy Button
          </button>
          <br>
          <div id="Message" runat="server"></div>
      </form>
    </body>
</HTML>
```

The above code first displays two buttons. Then, the next button, `BtnWrox`, shows how a button control can have embedded images. The last control is a fancy button control created with style properties that changes the color of the button when the mouse hovers over it.

The code-behind file, `HtmlButtonUsage.aspx.cs`, shows how to set the `CausesValidation` property at run-time:

```
public class HtmlButtonUsage : System.Web.UI.Page
  {
    protected System.Web.UI.WebControls.RequiredFieldValidator
                                                  ReqValTxtName;
    protected System.Web.UI.HtmlControls.HtmlInputText TxtName;
    protected System.Web.UI.HtmlControls.HtmlButton BtnSubmit;
    protected System.Web.UI.HtmlControls.HtmlButton
                                    BtnSubmitWithoutValidation;
```

```
protected System.Web.UI.HtmlControls.HtmlButton BtnWrox;
protected System.Web.UI.HtmlControls.HtmlButton BtnFancy;
protected System.Web.UI.HtmlControls.HtmlGenericControl Message;

private void Page_Load(object sender, System.EventArgs e)
{
  BtnSubmit.CausesValidation = true;
  BtnSubmitWithoutValidation.CausesValidation = false;
}


...

private void InitializeComponent()
{
  this.BtnSubmit.ServerClick += new
                  System.EventHandler(this.BtnSubmit_ServerClick);
  this.BtnWrox.ServerClick += new
                    System.EventHandler(this.BtnWrox_ServerClick);
  this.BtnFancy.ServerClick += new
                    System.EventHandler(this.BtnFancy_ServerClick);
  this.Load += new System.EventHandler(this.Page_Load);

}

protected void BtnSubmit_ServerClick(object sender, System.EventArgs e)
{
  Message.InnerHtml = "You entered " + TxtName.Value;
}

protected void BtnWrox_ServerClick(object sender, System.EventArgs e)
{

}

protected void BtnFancy_ServerClick(object sender, System.EventArgs e)
{

}
```

Here is a screenshot showing what happens if we try to submit the form with the validation button and we haven't entered a value into the text box:

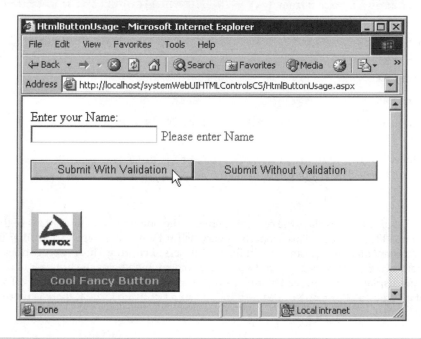

HtmlContainerControl Class

The `HtmlContainerControl` class does not correspond to any specific HTML element, but defines methods, properties and events for all block type HTML controls, that is, the controls that require a closing tag (for example: `<span>`, `<div>`, `<form>`, `<table>`, `<tr>`, `<td>`, `<a>`). These controls inherit from this class and can use the features of this class to manipulate the contents embedded between the opening and closing tag. There are two new main properties defined by the `HtmlContainerControl` class; `InnerHtml` and `InnerText`.

The `HtmlContainerControl` class is inherited from `System.Web.UI.HtmlControls.HtmlControl`.

HtmlContainerControl Class Public Methods

The `HtmlContainerControl` class adds no new public methods over those inherited from the `Control` class. See Chapter 2 for details.

HtmlContainerControl Class Protected Methods

The `HtmlContainerControl` class adds no new protected methods over those inherited from the `Control` class. See Chapter 2 for details.

HtmlContainerControl Class Public Properties

- ❏ `Attributes` – inherited from `System.Web.UI.HtmlControls.HtmlControl`, see the `HtmlControl` class reference for details.

- ❏ `Disabled` – inherited from `System.Web.UI.HtmlControls.HtmlControl`, see the `HtmlControl` class reference for details.

- ❏ **InnerHtml**

- ❏ **InnerText**

- ❏ `Style` – inherited from `System.Web.UI.HtmlControls.HtmlControl`, see the `HtmlControl` class reference for details.

- ❏ `TagName` – inherited from `System.Web.UI.HtmlControls.HtmlControl`, see the `HtmlControl` class reference for details.

InnerHtml

The `InnerHtml` property displays the contents between the opening and closing tags of the container server control in a HTML mode. This property is very helpful when it is necessary to alter the HTML data between the opening and closing tags of the HTML server control. This property does not encode special characters like < and > as < and > and so on, which helps the browser to detect the HTML text and display it in formatted manner. An `HttpException` is thrown if the HTML server control is not a `LiteralControl` or `DataBoundLiteralControl` and if there is more than one HTML server control.

```
public virtual string InnerHtml {get; set;}
```

InnerText

The `InnerText` property displays the contents between the opening and closing tags of the container server control in text mode. This property is very helpful when text data with special characters is to be assigned between the opening and closing tags of the HTML server control. This property does encode special characters like < and > as < and >, enabling the browser to display output in a textual manner. Therefore if the contents have any special characters, they would appear the same when it is displayed. An `HttpException` is thrown if the HTML server control is not a `LiteralControl` or `DataBoundLiteralControl` and if there is more than one HTML server control.

```
public virtual string InnerText {get; set;}
```

Example: Using the InnerHtml and InnerText Properties

Let's see the `InnerHtml` and `InnerText` properties in action. This code is available for download, under the filename `HtmlContainerControlUsage.aspx`:

```
<%@ Page Language="c#" AutoEventWireup="false"
        Codebehind="HtmlContainerControlUsage.aspx.cs"
        Inherits="systemWebUIHTMLControlsCS.HtmlContainerControlUsage" %>
<!DOCTYPE HTML PUBLIC "-//W3C//DTD HTML 4.0 Transitional//EN">
<HTML>
  <HEAD>
```

```
<title>HtmlContainerControl</title>
    <meta name="GENERATOR"
        content="Microsoft Visual Studio.NET 7.0">
    <meta name="CODE_LANGUAGE" content="C#">
    <meta name="vs_defaultClientScript"
        content="JavaScript">
    <meta name="vs_targetSchema"
        content="http://schemas.microsoft.com/intellisense/ie5">
  </HEAD>
  <body MS_POSITIONING="GridLayout">
    <form id="FrmContainerControl" method="post"
        runat="server">
      <span id="SpnInnerHtml" runat="server"></span>
      <hr>
      <span id="SpnInnerText" runat="server"></span>
    </form>
  </body>
</HTML>
```

The code-behind, `HtmlContainerControlUsage.aspx.cs`, is shown next;

```
public class HtmlContainerControlUsage : System.Web.UI.Page
  {
    protected System.Web.UI.HtmlControls.HtmlGenericControl SpnInnerHtml;
    protected System.Web.UI.HtmlControls.HtmlGenericControl SpnInnerText;

    private void Page_Load(object sender, System.EventArgs e)
    {
      SpnInnerHtml.InnerHtml = "<font size=+2>InnerHtml</font>";
      SpnInnerText.InnerText = "<font size=+2>InnerText</font>";
    }
  }
```

The following screenshot shows the output:

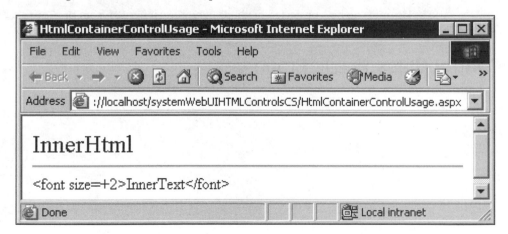

199

From the above screenshot we can clearly see what the difference is between `InnerHtml` and `InnerText`. The `InnerHtml` property tells our control to take everything between the quotes and interpret it as HTML and parse it as such. The `InnerText` property tells our control to interpret everything between the quotes as text, and to produce HTML code behind the scenes that will output the required content as it is displayed in our code. For example, each instance of a `<` character is converted to `&lt;` behind the scenes.

HtmlContainerControl Class Protected Properties

The `HtmlContainerControl` class adds no new protected properties over those inherited from the `Control` class. See Chapter 2 for details.

HtmlContainerControl Class Public Events

The `HtmlContainerControl` class adds no new public events over those inherited from the `Control` class. See Chapter 2 for details.

HtmlControl Class

The `HtmlControl` class provides basic properties that are inherited by all of the HTML server controls. It inherits from the `Control` class of the `System.Web.UI` namespace. The `HtmlControl` class itself belongs to `System.Web.UI.HtmlControls` namespace where it provides the methods, properties, and events that are inherited by all HTML server control classes.

HtmlControl Class Public Methods

The `HtmlControl` class adds no new public methods over those inherited from the `Control` class. See Chapter 2 for details.

HtmlControl Class Protected Methods

The `HtmlControl` class adds no new protected methods over those inherited from the `Control` class. See Chapter 2 for details.

HtmlControl Class Public Properties

- ❑ **Attributes**
- ❑ **Disabled**
- ❑ **Style**
- ❑ **TagName**

Attributes

The `Attributes` property gets all of the attribute name-value pairs expressed on a server control tag within an ASP.NET page. This property returns the name-value pairs as a `System.Web.UI.AttributeCollection` object that can be used by the code to access attributes of the `HTML` server control. These attributes are stored in the `ViewState`. The property is read-only, but the underlying `AttributeCollection` can be used to manipulate the attributes.

```
public AttributeCollection Attributes {get;}
```

Disabled

The `Disabled` property gets or sets `true` or `false` to indicate whether the control is enabled for user input and is submitted with the form or not. The default value is `false`.

```
public bool Disabled {get; set;}
```

Style

The `Style` property gets all of the cascading style sheet (CSS) properties that are applied to a specific HTML server control in a web page. It gets all style sheet properties in a `CssStyleCollection` object.

```
public CssStyleCollection Style {get;}
```

TagName

The `TagName` property displays the name of an HTML tag that contains the `runat="server"` attribute. This property can be helpful in giving the name of the HTML server control at run-time.

```
public virtual string TagName {get;}
```

HtmlControl Class Protected Properties

The `HtmlControl` class adds no new protected properties over those inherited from the `Control` class. See Chapter 2 for details.

HtmlControl Class Public Events

The `HtmlControl` class adds no new public events over those inherited from the `Control` class. See Chapter 2 for details.

Example: Using the Main Properties of HTMLControl

The following code from `HtmlControlUsage.aspx` shows the usage of all four of the main properties of the `HtmlControl` class: `Attributes`, `Disabled`, `Style` and `TagName`. The following code shows how to set the `Style` property.

```
<%@ Page Language="c#" AutoEventWireup="false"
        Codebehind="HtmlControlUsage.aspx.cs"
        Inherits="systemWebUIHTMLControlsCS.HtmlControlUsage" %>
<!DOCTYPE HTML PUBLIC "-//W3C//DTD HTML 4.0 Transitional//EN">
<HTML>
  <HEAD>
    <title>HtmlControlsProperties</title>
    <meta content="Microsoft Visual Studio.NET 7.0"
          name="GENERATOR">
    <meta content="C#" name="CODE_LANGUAGE">
    <meta content="JavaScript"
          name="vs_defaultClientScript">
    <meta content="http://schemas.microsoft.com/intellisense/ie5"
          name="vs_targetSchema">
  </HEAD>
  <body MS_POSITIONING="GridLayout">
    <form id="FrmHtmlControl" method="post" runat="server">
        Delivery Date <input type="text" runat="server"
        id="TxtDate"
        name="TxtDate" style="FONT-SIZE: 12px;
        FONT-FAMILY: Arial">
        <br>
        Method of Shipment
        <select id="Shipping" name="Shipping"
                runat="server">
          <option selected>UPS</option>
          <option>USPS</option>
          <option>FEDEX</option>
        </select>
        <br>
        <br>
        <input type="button" runat="server"
                id="BtnAttributes"
                name="BtnAttributes" value="Attributes">
        <input type="button" runat="server"
                id="BtnDisabled"
                name="BtnDisabled" value="Disabled">
        <input type="button" runat="server" id="BtnStyle"
                name="BtnStyle"
                value="Style">
        <input type="button" runat="server"
                id="BtnTagName"
                name="BtnTagName" value="TagName">
        <br>
        <br>
        <span id="Message" runat="server"></span>
      </form>
```

```
</body>
</HTML>
```

The code-behind, `HtmlControlUsage.aspx.cs`, below shows how the `Attributes` and `Style` properties can be manipulated at run-time. It also includes `ServerClick` handlers for all the buttons. The `BtnAttributes_ServerClick` iterates through the `AttributeCollection` and displays each one of them; the `BtnDisabled_ServerClick` checks if the controls are disabled and, if not, then disables them, or enables them if they are disabled. The `BtnStyle_ServerClick` iterates through the style collection and displays each one of them, and the `BtnTagName_ServerClick` event handler displays the tag of the server controls.

```
public class HtmlControlUsage : System.Web.UI.Page
  {
    protected System.Web.UI.HtmlControls.HtmlInputText TxtDate;
    protected System.Web.UI.HtmlControls.HtmlSelect Shipping;
    protected System.Web.UI.HtmlControls.HtmlInputButton BtnAttributes;
    protected System.Web.UI.HtmlControls.HtmlInputButton BtnDisabled;
    protected System.Web.UI.HtmlControls.HtmlInputButton BtnStyle;
    protected System.Web.UI.HtmlControls.HtmlInputButton BtnTagName;
    protected System.Web.UI.HtmlControls.HtmlGenericControl Message;

    private void Page_Load(object sender, System.EventArgs e)
    {
      TxtDate.Style.Add("color", "Teal");
      Shipping.Style.Add("color", "Teal");

      TxtDate.Attributes.Add("MaxLength", "10");
      Shipping.Attributes.Add("Value", "USPS");
    }


    ...

    private void InitializeComponent()
    {
      this.BtnAttributes.ServerClick += new
                  System.EventHandler(this.BtnAttributes_ServerClick);
      this.BtnDisabled.ServerClick += new
                    System.EventHandler(this.BtnDisabled_ServerClick);
      this.BtnStyle.ServerClick += new
                      System.EventHandler(this.BtnStyle_ServerClick);
      this.BtnTagName.ServerClick += new
                    System.EventHandler(this.BtnTagName_ServerClick);
      this.Load += new System.EventHandler(this.Page_Load);

    }

    private void BtnTagName_ServerClick(object sender, System.EventArgs e)
    {
      Message.InnerHtml = "TagName:" + "<br>";
      Message.InnerHtml += "Delivery Date:" + TxtDate.TagName + "<br>";
      Message.InnerHtml += "Shipping Method:" + Shipping.TagName + "<br>";
    }
```

```csharp
    private void BtnAttributes_ServerClick(object sender,
                                           System.EventArgs e)
{
  Message.InnerHtml = "Attributes:" + "<br>";
  Message.InnerHtml += "Delivery Date" + "<br>";
  IEnumerator datekeys  = TxtDate.Attributes.Keys.GetEnumerator();
  while(datekeys.MoveNext())
  {
    string key = (string)datekeys.Current;
    Message.InnerHtml += key + ":" + TxtDate.Attributes[key] + "<br>";
  }

  Message.InnerHtml += "Shipping Method" + "<br>";
  IEnumerator shipkeys  = TxtDate.Attributes.Keys.GetEnumerator();
  while(shipkeys.MoveNext())
  {
    string key = (string)shipkeys.Current;
    Message.InnerHtml += key + ":" + Shipping.Attributes[key] + "<br>";
  }

}

private void BtnDisabled_ServerClick(object sender, System.EventArgs e)
{
  if(TxtDate.Disabled == true)
  {
    TxtDate.Disabled = false;
    Shipping.Disabled = false;
  }
  else
  {
    TxtDate.Disabled = true;
    Shipping.Disabled = true;
  }
}

private void BtnStyle_ServerClick(object sender, System.EventArgs e)
{
  Message.InnerHtml = "Style:" + "<br>";
  Message.InnerHtml += "Delivery Date" + "<br>";
  IEnumerator datekeys  = TxtDate.Style.Keys.GetEnumerator();
  while(datekeys.MoveNext())
  {
    string key = (string)datekeys.Current;
    Message.InnerHtml += key + ":" + TxtDate.Style[key] + "<br>";
  }

  Message.InnerHtml += "Shipping Method" + "<br>";
  IEnumerator shipkeys = TxtDate.Style.Keys.GetEnumerator();
  while(shipkeys.MoveNext())
  {
    string key = (string)shipkeys.Current;
    Message.InnerHtml += key + ":" + Shipping.Style[key] + "<br>";
```

```
        }
      }
    }
```

Here is a screenshot showing the output when the Button labeled **Style** is clicked:

HtmlForm Class

The HtmlForm class creates a server-side HTML form, `<form>` tag on the server. There can be only one `<form runat="server">` element on a web page and all the HTML and ASP.NET server controls should be placed inside this control, if they want to be accessed at the server-side.

The HtmlForm class is inherited from `System.Web.UI.HtmlControls.HtmlContainerControl` and is the container of all server controls on a web page.

It has the following syntax:

```
<form id = "id_name"
      method= "POST | GET"
      enctype = "Encoding_Type_Name"
      action = "target_page_filename"
      runat = "server">
      (Other controls, input forms, and so on.)
</form>
```

It's worth noting that the `HtmlForm` class doesn't support the `action` attribute, but the HTML `<form>` tag does. The `action` attribute is used to pass values to other Web Form pages. So, if `action` is no longer supported, how should we pass values between Web Form pages? Generally speaking, you can consider the following three ways.

First, using `Querystring`, which will gather the information you want, append it to a URL, passing this in a GET request to retrieve a specific resource that can be cached or reused. However, when using this method, all of the information we are requesting is visible in the address line of the browser. While this is useful if, for example, we're doing a search on a search engine, where the results can be cached and reused, it's definitely not what we want for passing around things that are more security-sensitive, which will need to be encapsulated in POST requests.

The second method uses `Session`, which will keep all the information you want in memory in the user's current session. Before it expires, you can read the information from session variables from other Web Form pages. The advantage with this is that all Web Form pages in a web site can read the session information, but the disadvantage is that this method uses a considerable amount of the session's memory.

The third method is to use custom page properties and then redirect from the original page to the target page in such a way that you can still read values in the old page.

HtmlForm Class Public Methods

The `HtmlForm` class adds no new public methods over those inherited from the `Control` class. See Chapter 2 for details.

HtmlForm Class Protected Methods

The `HtmlForm` class adds no new protected methods over those inherited from the `Control` class. See Chapter 2 for details.

HtmlForm Class Public Properties

- ❏ `Attributes` – inherited from `System.Web.UI.HtmlControls.HtmlControl`, see the `HtmlControl` class reference for details.
- ❏ `Disabled` – inherited from `System.Web.UI.HtmlControls.HtmlControl`, see the `HtmlControl` Class reference for details.
- ❏ **`Enctype`**
- ❏ `InnerHtml` – inherited from `System.Web.UI.HtmlControls.HtmlContainerControl`, see the `HtmlContainerControl` class for details.
- ❏ `InnerText` – inherited from `System.Web.UI.HtmlControls.HtmlContainerControl`, see the `HtmlContainerControl` class for details.
- ❏ **`Method`**
- ❏ **`Name`**
- ❏ `Style` – inherited from `System.Web.UI.HtmlControls.HtmlControl`, see the `HtmlControl` class reference for details.
- ❏ `TagName` – inherited from `System.Web.UI.HtmlControls.HtmlControl`, see the `HtmlControl` class reference for details.
- ❏ **`Target`**

Enctype

The Enctype property specifies the encoding type used by the browsers when they post form's data to the server. The Enctype property indicates to the server the type of data that is posted back by the client's browser. The Enctype property corresponds to the enctype attribute in the <form> element. The supported encoding types are:

❑ application/x-www-form-urlencoded (standard encoding type, Internet media type)

❑ multipart/form-data (form contains multiple type of data)

❑ text/plain (text or plain content)

❑ image/jpeg(image file)

If you use the HtmlInputFile control or a normal <input type="file"> element, you must set the enctype attribute yourself to allow files to be uploaded to the server. The multipart/form-data encoding type is required when the HtmlInputFile control is used, and is coded as follows;

```
<input type=file id=loFile enctype="multipart/form-data"
```

Usually the encoding type will be application/x-www-form-urlencoded.

```
public string Enctype {get; set;}
```

Method

The Method property indicates how the form will send its data to the server. This can be done in two ways: GET and POST. In the GET method, the form forms a querystring, which contains a server control's id and values in the format (id=value), separated from one another with the ampersand (&) symbol. This querystring is then attached to the URL by separating the URL address and querystring with a question mark (?) symbol. This is illustrated in the following example:

http://www.wrox.com/bookpage.aspx?book=aspnetprogref&page=codedownload

The GET method has certain limitations, such as a size limit on the amount of data that can be sent by it. Further, the contents are sent as a querystring attached with the URL so sensitive data should not be sent to the server via this method. Also, it can affect PostBack and state management features built into the .NET framework. Therefore, the GET method should be used only if insensitive data and small amounts of data need to be sent without any PostBack and state management capability.
The other method is POST, which is the default method of sending the data to the server. The POST method sends the data to the server encapsulated in a Request object. The Method property corresponds to the method attribute in the <form> element.

```
public string Method {get; set;}
```

Name

The Name property retrieves the HTML name attribute that will be rendered to the browser.

```
public string Name {get; set;}
```

Target

The `Target` property indicates the target window or frame where the results of the browser request will be displayed. It gets or sets the target location where the results fetched back from the server will be rendered. The `Target` property corresponds to the `target` attribute in the `<form>` element. This property can be used to redirect the results to another browser window or frame.

```
public virtual string Target {get; set;}
```

The `Target` property can have four values as follows:

Value	Description
_blank	Renders the results to a new and unframed browser window.
_parent	Renders the results of the immediate frameset parent in the same browser window.
_self	Renders the results of the current frame in the same browser window.
_top	Renders the results of the full and unframed window in the same browser.

HtmlForm Class Protected Properties

The `HtmlForm` class adds no new protected properties over those inherited from the `Control` class. See Chapter 2 for details.

HtmlForm Class Public Events

The `HtmlForm` class adds no new public events over those inherited from the `Control` class. See Chapter 2 for details.

Example: Setting Form Properties Using HtmlForm

The following code from `HtmlFormUsage.aspx` shows the usage of the `HtmlForm` control properties:

```
<%@ Page Language="c#" AutoEventWireup="false"
        Codebehind="HtmlFormUsage.aspx.cs"
        Inherits="systemWebUIHTMLControlsCS.HtmlFormUsage" %>
<!DOCTYPE HTML PUBLIC "-//W3C//DTD HTML 4.0 Transitional//EN">
<HTML>
  <HEAD>
    <title>HtmlFormUsage</title>
    <meta content="Microsoft Visual Studio.NET 7.0"
        name="GENERATOR">
    <meta content="C#" name="CODE_LANGUAGE">
    <meta content="JavaScript"
        name="vs_defaultClientScript">
```

```
<meta content="http://schemas.microsoft.com/intellisense/ie5"
        name="vs_targetSchema">
  </HEAD>
  <body MS_POSITIONING="GridLayout">
    <form id="FrmForm" name="FrmForm" method="post"
        target="_self"
        encType="application/x-www-form-urlencoded"
        runat="server">
      <h3>Fill out the details
      </h3>
      <table>
        <tr>
          <td>Name
          </td>
          <td><input id="TxtName" type="text" name="TxtName"
                    runat="server">
          </td>
        </tr>
        <tr>
          <td>Address
          </td>
          <td><textarea id="TxtAddress" _
                    name="TxtAddress" rows="6"
                    cols="50" runat="server"></textarea>
          </td>
        </tr>
        <tr>
          <td><input id="BtnSubmit" type="submit"
                    value="Submit"
                    name="BtnSubmit" runat="server">
          </td>
        </tr>
      </table>
      <div id="Message" runat-"server"></div>
    </form>
  </body>
</HTML>
```

The following screenshot shows how the form controls will be displayed:

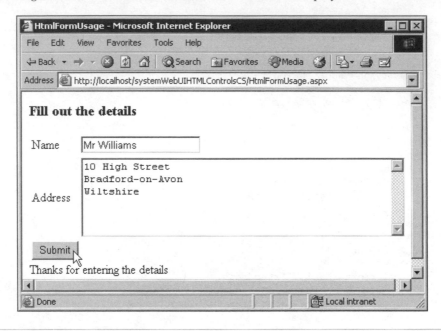

HtmlGenericControl Class

There are around 100 elements currently defined in HTML, although some are browser-specific. Rather than provide a distinct class for each of these, the .NET Framework contains specific classes for only a few of the HTML elements. These mainly include those elements that we use on an HTML `<form>`, or which we use to build interactive parts of a page (such as hyperlinks or images) and contains methods, properties and events defined for these generic controls such as `<body>`, `<font>`, `<span>`, `<div>`, `<h1>`, or `<h2>`.

This doesn't mean that we can't use other HTML controls as server controls. If there is no specific class for an element, the framework substitutes the `System.Web.UI.HtmlControls.HtmlGenericContol` class instead. This is not a base class, but a public class designed for use with elements for which there is no specific class. The `HtmlGenericControl` class is inherited from `System.Web.UI.HtmlControls.HtmlContainerControl`.

In the example below, you can see that we have defined the `<div>` as being a server control (it includes the `runat="server"` attribute), and this allows us to use the XML-style shorthand syntax of specifying a forward slash instead of a closing tag.

```
<div id="divResult" runat="server" />
...
void Page_Load()
{  ...
  divResult.InnerHtml = strResult;
}
```

To display the result, we simply set the `InnerHtml` property on the server. So, if the value of `strResult` is "This is the result", the page output will contain:

```
<div id="divResult">This is the result</div>
```

As the `HtmlGenericControl` is based on the `HtmlContainerControl` base class (which itself inherits from `HtmlControl`), it exposes the same list of members (properties, methods, and events) that we described earlier for these classes.

HtmlGenericControl Class Public Methods

The `HtmlGenericControl` class adds no new public methods over those inherited from the `Control` class. See Chapter 2 for details.

HtmlGenericControl Class Protected Methods

The `HtmlGenericControl` class adds no new protected methods over those inherited from the `Control` class. See Chapter 2 for details.

HtmlGenericControl Class Public Properties

❏ `Attributes` – inherited from `System.Web.UI.HtmlControls.HtmlControl`, see the `HtmlControl` class reference for details.

❏ `Disabled` – inherited from `System.Web.UI.HtmlControls.HtmlControl`, see the `HtmlControl` class reference for details.

❏ `InnerHtml` – inherited from `System.Web.UI.HtmlControls.HtmlContainerControl`, see the `HtmlContainerControl` class for details.

❏ `InnerText` – inherited from `System.Web.UI.HtmlControls.HtmlContainerControl`, see the `HtmlContainerControl` class for details.

❏ `Style` – inherited from `System.Web.UI.HtmlControls.HtmlControl`, see the `HtmlControl` class reference for details.

Example: Using the HtmlGenericControl Class

The following code from `HtmlGenericControlUsage.aspx` demonstrates the properties of `HtmlGenericControl` class:

```
<%@ Page Language="c#" AutoEventWireup="false"
        Codebehind="HtmlGenericControlUsage.aspx.cs"
        Inherits="systemWebUIHTMLControlsCS.HtmlGenericControlUsage" %>
<!DOCTYPE HTML PUBLIC "-//W3C//DTD HTML 4.0 Transitional//EN">
<HTML>
  <HEAD>
    <title>HtmlGenericControlUsage</title>
    <meta name="GENERATOR"
        content="Microsoft Visual Studio.NET 7.0">
    <meta name="CODE_LANGUAGE" content="C#">
    <meta name="vs_defaultClientScript"
```

```
               content="JavaScript">
    <meta name="vs_targetSchema"
          content="http://schemas.microsoft.com/intellisense/ie5">
  </HEAD>
  <body id="Body" runat="server">
    <form id="Form1" method="post" runat="server">
      <h2 id="H2" runat="server"></h2>
    </form>
  </body>
</HTML>
```

The code-behind file, `HtmlGenericControlUsage.aspx.cs`, sets the message box that appears when this application is run:

```
public class HtmlGenericControlUsage : System.Web.UI.Page
  {
    protected System.Web.UI.HtmlControls.HtmlGenericControl H2;
    protected System.Web.UI.HtmlControls.HtmlGenericControl Body;

    private void Page_Load(object sender, System.EventArgs e)
    {
      Body.Attributes.Add("onload" , "javascript:alert('"
                          + Body.TagName + "');");
      H2.InnerHtml = "Generic Control Usage";
    }
  }
```

The output from this application would be as follows:

HtmlGenericControl Class Protected Properties

The `HtmlGenericControl` class adds no new protected properties over those inherited from the `Control` class. See Chapter 2 for details.

HtmlGenericControl Class Public Events

The `HtmlGenericControl` class adds no new public events over those inherited from the `Control` class. See Chapter 2 for details.

HtmlImage Class

The `HtmlImage` class provides programmatic access to the `<img>` image element on the server and displays an image. The `HtmlImage` control doesn't require a closing tag like the HTML `<img>`.

The `HtmlImage` class is inherited from `System.Web.UI.HtmlControls.HtmlControl`.

It has the following syntax:

```
<img id="id_name"
     alt = "alternative text"
     align = "alignment of image"
     border = "border width"
     height = "height of image"
     src = "URI of image"
     width = "width of image"
     runat = "server">
```

HtmlImage Class Public Methods

The `HtmlImage` class adds no new public methods over those inherited from the `Control` class. See Chapter 2 for details.

HtmlImage Class Protected Methods

The `HtmlImage` class adds no new protected methods over those inherited from the `Control` class. See Chapter 2 for details.

HtmlImage Class Public Properties

❑ **Align**

❑ **Alt**

❑ Attributes – inherited from `System.Web.UI.HtmlControls.HtmlControl`, see the `HtmlControl` class reference for details.

❑ **Border**

❑ Disabled – inherited from `System.Web.UI.HtmlControls.HtmlControl`, see the `HtmlControl` class reference for details.

❑ **Height**

❑ Style – inherited from `System.Web.UI.HtmlControls.HtmlControl`, see the `HtmlControl` class reference for details.

❑ TagName – inherited from `System.Web.UI.HtmlControls.HtmlControl`, see the `HtmlControl` class reference for details.

Align

The `Align` property gets or sets the alignment of an image relative to the other web page elements. The image is aligned to the `left`, `center` or `right` of the web page, when assigned one of these values. The default for this property is `bottom`.

```
public string Align {get; set;}
```

Alt

The `Alt` property gets or sets an alternative caption that the browser displays if the image is either unavailable or has not been downloaded yet. The `Alt` property is also displayed as a `Tooltip` of the image in newer versions of browsers.

```
public string Alt {get; set;}
```

Border

The `Border` property is used to create a border frame for an image, having specified the number of pixels as its width. This property can be used to get or set the width of border of an image in pixels.

```
public int Border {get; set;}
```

Height

The `Height` property gets or sets the height of an image. By default, the height is set in pixels; it can be also set as the percentage of the size of the window. It is always a good programming practice to set the `Height` value of the image. This avoids using the browser to calculate the height of the image before displaying, and thus, the image is loaded faster. Therefore, although the `Height` property can be used to scale images at run-time, it is always a good practice to scale the images to the desired size if possible at the design time itself.

```
public int Height {get; set;}
```

Src

The `Src` property gets or sets the path and filename of an image that will be displayed. If the image resides in the current directory, then the path need not be set; thus it allows both relative and absolute paths. The shortcut to the virtual root directory "~/" can be used here. All the relative paths are converted to absolute paths automatically when the control is rendered.

```
public string Src {get; set;}
```

Width

The `Width` property gets or sets the width of an image. By default, the width is set in pixels; it can be also set as the percentage of the size of the window. It is always good programming practice to set the `Width` value of the image. This avoids using the browser to calculate the width of the image before displaying, and the image is loaded faster, thus, although the `Width` property can be used to scale images at runtime, it is always good practice to scale the images to the desired size if possible at the design time itself.

```
public int Width {get; set;}
```

Example: Using the Properties of HtmlImage

Let's see a simple example that shows how the properties can be easily assigned at design time and run-time. Here the book images can be changed at the click of a button. The code is available in `HtmlImageUsage.aspx`:

```
<<%@ Page Language="c#" AutoEventWireup="false"
         Codebehind="HtmlImageUsage.aspx.cs"
         Inherits="systemWebUIHTMLControlsCS.HtmlImageUsage" %>
<!DOCTYPE HTML PUBLIC "-//W3C//DTD HTML 4.0 Transitional//EN">
<HTML>
  <HEAD>
    <title>HtmlImageUsage</title>
    <meta content="Microsoft Visual Studio.NET 7.0"
          name="GENERATOR">
    <meta content="C#" name="CODE_LANGUAGE">
    <meta content="JavaScript"
          name="vs_defaultClientScript">
    <meta content="http://schemas.microsoft.com/intellisense/ie5"
          name="vs_targetSchema">
  </HEAD>
  <body MS_POSITIONING="GridLayout">
    <form id="FrmImage" method="post" runat="server">
      <table>
        <tr>
          <td>
            <img id="ImgBook" name="ImgBook" runat="server"
                 align="absMiddle" border="2"
                 src="ProfASPNET.gif"
                 height="150" width="120"
                 alt="Professional ASP.NET Programming">
          </td>
          <td>
            <input type="submit" runat="server"
                   id="BtnSubmit"
                   name="BtnSubmit" value="Change Image">
          </td>
        </tr>
      </table>
    </form>
  </body>
</HTML>
```

The code-behind file, `HtmlImageUsage.aspx.cs`, for this is shown below:

```
public class HtmlImageUsage : System.Web.UI.Page
  {
    protected System.Web.UI.HtmlControls.HtmlImage ImgBook;
    protected System.Web.UI.HtmlControls.HtmlInputButton BtnSubmit;

    private void Page_Load(object sender, System.EventArgs e)
    {
      // Put user code to initialize the page here
```

```
    }

    private void BtnSubmit_ServerClick(object sender, System.EventArgs e)
    {
      if(ImgBook.Src=="ProfASPNET.gif")
      {
        ImgBook.Src="ASPNETWeb.gif";
        ImgBook.Alt="ASP.NET Website Programming";
      }
      else
      {
        ImgBook.Src="ProfASPNET.gif";
        ImgBook.Alt="Professional ASP.NET";
      }
    }
```

Here is a screenshot showing the output of the above code:

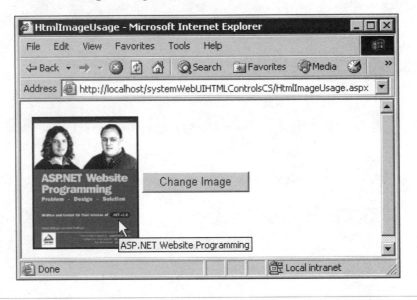

HtmlImage Class Protected Properties

The `HtmlImage` class adds no new protected properties over those inherited from the `Control` class. See Chapter 2 for details.

HtmlImage Class Public Events

The `HtmlImage` class adds no new public events over those inherited from the `Control` class. See Chapter 2 for details.

HtmlInputButton Class

The `HtmlInputButton` class allows programmatic access to the HTML `<input type=button>`, `<input type=submit>`, and `<input type=reset>` tags on the server. Note that `HtmlInputButton` does not require a closing tag, and thus is not a `Container Control` and cannot have embedded server controls like `HtmlButton` class object.

The `HtmlInputButton` class is inherited from `System.Web.UI.HtmlControls.HtmlInputControl`.

It has the following syntax:

```
<input id="id_name"
       type = "button | submit | reset"
       onserverclick = "onserverclick handler"
       runat = "server">
```

HtmlInputButton Class Public Methods

The `HtmlInputButton` class adds no new public methods over those inherited from the `Control` class. See Chapter 2 for details.

HtmlInputButton Class Protected Methods

❑ **OnServerClick**

OnServerClick

The `OnServerClick` method raises the `ServerClick` event. This method notifies the server of the actions to be performed when the `InputButton` element is clicked. Therefore, the method is executed at the server-side and requires a round-trip to the server. The `OnServerClick` method can be used to handle the click event at the client-side. This method allows derived classes to handle the `ServerClick` event without attaching to a delegate.

```
protected virtual void OnServerClick(EventArgs e);
```

The parameter e refers to an `EventArgs` object that contains the server click event data.

HtmlInputButton Class Public Properties

❑ `Attributes` – inherited from `System.Web.UI.HtmlControls.HtmlControl`, see the `HtmlControl` class reference for details.

❑ **CausesValidation**

❑ `Disabled` – inherited from `System.Web.UI.HtmlControls.HtmlControl`, see the `HtmlControl` class reference for details.

❑ `Name` – inherited from `System.Web.UI.HtmlControls.HtmlInputControl`, see the `HtmlInputControl` for details.

❑ `Style` – inherited from `System.Web.UI.HtmlControls.HtmlControl`, see the `HtmlControl` class reference for details.

- ❑ TagName – inherited from `System.Web.UI.HtmlControls.HtmlControl`, see the `HtmlControl` class reference for details.

- ❑ Type – inherited from `System.Web.UI.HtmlControls.HtmlInputControl`, see the `HtmlInputControl` for details.

- ❑ Value – inherited from `System.Web.UI.HtmlControls.HtmlInputControl`, see the `HtmlInputControl` for details.

CausesValidation

The `CausesValidation` property is used to specify whether validation should be performed when the `HtmlInputButton` control is clicked. The validation is performed by the ASP.NET validation controls (if any) associated with the input server controls in the page. Therefore this property causes the validation controls to perform a validation test if set to `true`, and if set to `false` no validation occurs. The default value is `true`. Sometimes, it is necessary to submit the page without validation like, for example, in the event of a cancel or reset button clicked. This property, when `true`, may perform validations at both client and server level depending on the browser capability and the setting of the `clienttarget` attribute in the `Page` directive.

```
public bool CausesValidation {get; set;}
```

HtmlInputButton Class Protected Properties

The `HtmlInputButton` class adds no new protected properties over those inherited from the `Control` class. See Chapter 2 for details.

HtmlInputButton Class Public Events

- ❑ **ServerClick**

ServerClick

The `ServerClick` event is raised when a user clicks on the `HtmlInputButton` instance on a web page. This event is represented on the control by an attribute, `onserverclick`, which attaches an event handler to the event. We can then write an event handler method that captures this event and runs some code whenever the event is fired.

```
public event EventHandler ServerClick;
```

Example: Using the Main Properties of HtmlInputButton

Let's see the main properties and `ServerClick` event of all three types of `HtmlInputButton` objects in the following example. This code is available for download under the filename `HtmlInputButtonUsage.aspx`:

```
<%@ Page Language="c#" AutoEventWireup="false"
        Codebehind="HtmlInputButtonUsage.aspx.cs"
        Inherits="systemWebUIHTMLControlsCS.HtmlInputButtonUsage" %>
<!DOCTYPE HTML PUBLIC "-//W3C//DTD HTML 4.0 Transitional//EN">
```

```
<HTML>
  <HEAD>
    <title>HtmlInputButtonUsage</title>
    <meta name="GENERATOR"
          content="Microsoft Visual Studio.NET 7.0">
    <meta name="CODE_LANGUAGE" content="C#">
    <meta name="vs_defaultClientScript"
          content="JavaScript">
    <meta name="vs_targetSchema"
          content="http://schemas.microsoft.com/intellisense/ie5">
  </HEAD>
  <body MS_POSITIONING="GridLayout">
    <form id="FrmInputButton" method="post" runat="server">
     <table>
      <tr>
        <td>
          Name
        </td>
        <td>
          <input type="text" runat="server" id="TxtName"
                 name="TxtName">
        </td>
      </tr>
      <tr>
        <td>
            Email
        </td>
        <td>
          <input type="text" runat="server" id="TxtEmail"
                 name="TxtEmail">
          <asp:RequiredFieldValidator ID="ReqValTxtEmail"
                 runat="server" ControlToValidate="TxtEmail"
                 ErrorMessage="Please Enter Email Address">
          </asp:RequiredFieldValidator>
        </td>
      </tr>
      <tr>
        <td>
          Zip Code
        </td>
        <td>
          <input type="text" runat="server" id="TxtZipCode"
                 name="TxtZipCode">
        </td>
        </tr>
        <tr>
        <td>
          <input type="submit" runat="server"
                 value="Submit"
                 id="BtnSubmit" name="BtnSubmit">
        </td>
        <td>
          <input type="reset" runat="server"
                 value="Reset"
```

```
                    id="BtnReset"
                    name="BtnReset"> <input type="button"
                    runat="server"
                    value="Display" id="BtnDisplay"
                    name="BtnDisplay"
                    CausesValidation="false">
        </td>
      </tr>
        </table>
    <div id="Message" runat="server"></div>
    </form>
  </body>
</HTML>
```

The code-behind file, `HtmlInputButtonUsage.aspx.cs`, is shown below:

```
public class HtmlInputButtonUsage : System.Web.UI.Page
  {
    protected System.Web.UI.WebControls.RequiredFieldValidator
                                        ReqValTxtEmail;
    protected System.Web.UI.HtmlControls.HtmlInputText TxtName;
    protected System.Web.UI.HtmlControls.HtmlInputText TxtEmail;
    protected System.Web.UI.HtmlControls.HtmlInputText TxtZipCode;
    protected System.Web.UI.HtmlControls.HtmlInputButton BtnSubmit;
    protected System.Web.UI.HtmlControls.HtmlInputButton BtnReset;
    protected System.Web.UI.HtmlControls.HtmlInputButton BtnDisplay;
    protected System.Web.UI.HtmlControls.HtmlGenericControl Message;

    private void Page_Load(object sender, System.EventArgs e)
    {
      // Put user code to initialize the page here
    }


    private void BtnSubmit_ServerClick(object sender, System.EventArgs e)
    {
      if((TxtName.Value != "") && (TxtEmail.Value != "") &&
        (TxtZipCode.Value != ""))
        Message.InnerText="Thank you for entering the information";
      else
        Message.InnerText = "Please enter all the information";
    }

    private void BtnDisplay_ServerClick(object sender, System.EventArgs e)
    {
      Message.InnerHtml = "You have entered:" + "<br>";
      Message.InnerHtml += TxtName.Value + "<br>";
      Message.InnerHtml += TxtEmail.Value + "<br>";
      Message.InnerHtml += TxtZipCode.Value + "<br>";
    }
  }
```

Here is a screenshot displaying the output when the user has selected Display:

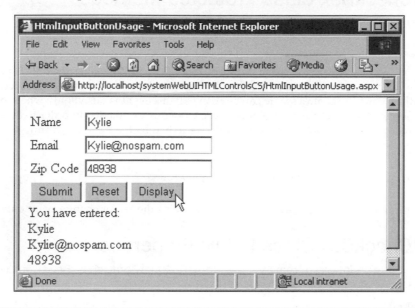

HtmlInputCheckBox Class

The HtmlInputCheckBox class allows programmatic access to the HTML <input type="checkbox"> tag on the server. This control provides a box to the user, which can be checked or unchecked, and is usually used to select a true or false state. Note that the HtmlInputCheckBox class does **not** require a closing tag. The checkbox control does not provide a built-in attribute to assign a caption but literal text can be inserted at the desired place in the web page to create a caption.

The HtmlInputCheckBox class is inherited from System.Web.UI.HtmlControls.HtmlInputControl.

It has the following syntax:

```
<input id="id_name"
       type = "checkbox"
       checked
       runat = "server">
  Caption_Text
```

HtmlInputCheckBox Class Public Methods

The HtmlInputCheckBox class adds no new public methods over those inherited from the Control class. See Chapter 2 for details.

HtmlInputCheckBox Class Protected Methods

❑ **OnServerChange**

OnServerChange

The OnServerChange method raises the ServerChange event. Whenever the data is posted to the server, if there is a change in the state of the checkbox since the previous post to the server, this event is raised. Note, that while the control's state can be changed, this event is raised only when the data is posted to the server. The checkbox control must have ViewState enabled in order to be able to raise this event correctly. This method allows derived classes to handle the ServerChange event directly without attaching to a delegate.

```
protected virtual void OnServerChange(EventArgs e);
```

The parameter e refers to an EventArgs object that contains the server change event data.

HtmlInputCheckBox Class Public Properties

❑ Attributes – inherited from System.Web.UI.HtmlControls.HtmlControl, see the HtmlControl class reference for details.

❑ **Checked**

❑ Disabled – inherited from System.Web.UI.HtmlControls.HtmlControl, see the HtmlControl class reference for details.

❑ Name – inherited from System.Web.UI.HtmlControls.HtmlInputControl, see the HtmlInputControl for details.

❑ Style – inherited from System.Web.UI.HtmlControls.HtmlControl, see the HtmlControl class reference for details.

❑ TagName – inherited from System.Web.UI.HtmlControls.HtmlControl, see the HtmlControl class reference for details.

❑ Type – inherited from System.Web.UI.HtmlControls.HtmlInputControl, see the HtmlInputControl for details.

❑ Value – inherited from System.Web.UI.HtmlControls.HtmlInputControl, see the HtmlInputControl for details.

Checked

The Checked property is used to assign or determine whether the input checkbox is checked. This property returns true if the checkbox is checked and false otherwise. This is the main property of the checkbox and provides the state of the checkbox.

```
public bool Checked {get; set;}
```

HtmlInputCheckBox Class Protected Properties

The `HtmlInputCheckBox` class adds no new protected properties over those inherited from the `Control` class. See Chapter 2 for details.

HtmlInputCheckBox Class Public Events

❑   **`ServerChange`**

ServerChange

The `ServerChange` event is raised when a web page is posted to the server. Note, this event does not fire when there is a change in the state and no new post to the server. The controls state can be changed but the event is raised only when the data is posted to the server, and at that time the state is different from the previous post. The checkbox control must have `ViewState` enabled in order to be able to raise this event correctly. This event is represented on the control by an attribute, `onserverchange`, which attaches an event handler to the event. We can then write an event handler method that intercepts this event and run some code whenever the event is fired.

```
public event EventHandler ServerChange;
```

Example: Using the Main Properties of the HtmlInputCheckBox Class

Let's see the main properties and `ServerChange` event of `HtmlInputCheckBox` class in the following example. This code is available for download with the filename `HtmlInputCheckBoxUsage.aspx`:

```
<%@ Page Language="c#" AutoEventWireup="false"
        Codebehind="HtmlInputCheckBoxUsage.aspx.cs"
        Inherits="systemWebUIHTMLControlsCS.HtmlInputCheckBoxUsage" %>
<!DOCTYPE HTML PUBLIC "-//W3C//DTD HTML 4.0 Transitional//EN">
<HTML>
  <HEAD>
    <title>HtmlInputCheckBoxUsage</title>
    <meta name="GENERATOR"
        content="Microsoft Visual Studio.NET 7.0">
    <meta name="CODE_LANGUAGE" content="C#">
    <meta name="vs_defaultClientScript"
        content="JavaScript">
    <meta name="vs_targetSchema"
        content="http://schemas.microsoft.com/intellisense/ie5">
  </HEAD>
  <body MS_POSITIONING="GridLayout">
    <form id="FrmCheckBox" method="post" runat="server">
      <b>Choose your favorite Programming Languages:</b>
      <br>
      <br>
      <input type="checkbox" id="CSharp" name="C#"
          runat="server" value="C#"
          onserverchange="Language_ServerChange">C#
             
```

```
            <input type="checkbox" id="VB"
                   name="VB.NET" runat="server" value="VB.NET"
                   checked onserverchange="Language_ServerChange">
               VB.NET    
            <input type="checkbox"
                   id="Java" name="Java" runat="server" value="Java"
                   onserverchange="Language_ServerChange">
               Java    
            <input type="checkbox"
                   id="VBScript" name="VB Script" runat="server"
                   value="VBScript"
                   onserverchange="Language_ServerChange">
               VB Script    
            <input type="checkbox"
                   id="JavaScript" name="JavaScript" runat="server"
                   value="JavaScript"
                   onserverchange="Language_ServerChange">
               JavaScript
            <br>
            <br>
            <input type="submit" runat="server" value="Submit">
            <br>
            <br>
            <div id="Message" runat="server"></div>
         </form>
      </body>
</HTML>
```

As you can see, a single event handler handles the `ServerChange` event for all the checkboxes:

```
public class HtmlInputCheckBoxUsage : System.Web.UI.Page
  {
    protected System.Web.UI.HtmlControls.HtmlInputCheckBox CSharp;
    protected System.Web.UI.HtmlControls.HtmlInputCheckBox VB;
    protected System.Web.UI.HtmlControls.HtmlInputCheckBox Java;
    protected System.Web.UI.HtmlControls.HtmlInputCheckBox VBScript;
    protected System.Web.UI.HtmlControls.HtmlInputCheckBox JavaScript;
    protected System.Web.UI.HtmlControls.HtmlInputButton Submit1;
    protected System.Web.UI.HtmlControls.HtmlGenericControl Message;

    private void Page_Load(object sender, System.EventArgs e)
    {
      // Put user code to initialize the page here
    }

    protected void Language_ServerChange(object sender, System.EventArgs e)
    {
      Message.InnerHtml = "You have chosen:" + "<br>";
      if(CSharp.Checked == true)
        Message.InnerHtml += CSharp.Value + "<br>";
      if(VB.Checked == true)
        Message.InnerHtml += VB.Value + "<br>";
      if(Java.Checked == true)
```

```
        Message.InnerHtml += Java.Value + "<br>";
      if(VBScript.Checked == true)
        Message.InncrHtml += VBScript.Value + "<br>";
      if(JavaScript.Checked == true)
        Message.InnerHtml += JavaScript.Value + "<br>";
    }
```

Here is a screenshot showing the output:

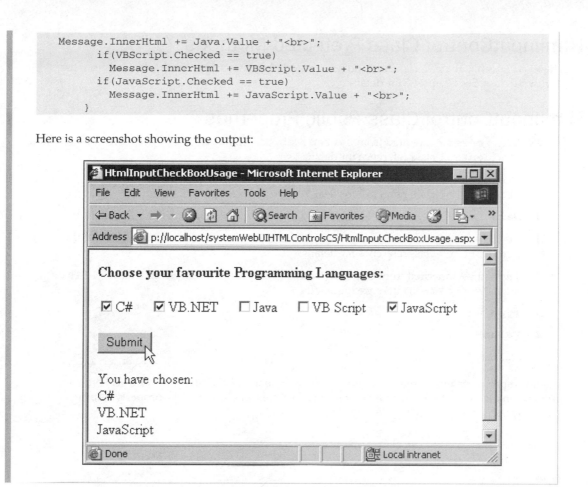

HtmlInputControl Class

The HtmlInputControl class does not correspond to any specific HTML element, but defines methods, properties and events for all HTML input controls, such as `<input type="text">`, `<input type="button">`, `<input type="radio">`, for example. These controls inherit from this class and use the features of this class. There are three new main properties defined by the HtmlInputControl class, which are Name, Type and Value.

The HtmlInputControl class is inherited from System.Web.UI.HtmlControls.HtmlControl.

HtmlInputControl Class Public Methods

The HtmlInputControl class adds no new public methods over those inherited from the Control class. See Chapter 2 for details.

HtmlInputControl Class Protected Methods

The `HtmlInputControl` class adds no new protected methods over those inherited from the `Control` class. See Chapter 2 for details.

HtmlInputControl Class Public Properties

- ❏ `Attributes` – inherited from `System.Web.UI.HtmlControls.HtmlControl`, see the `HtmlControl` class reference for details.

- ❏ `Disabled` – inherited from `System.Web.UI.HtmlControls.HtmlControl`, see the `HtmlControl` class reference for details.

- ❏ **Name**

- ❏ `Style` – inherited from `System.Web.UI.HtmlControls.HtmlControl`, see the `HtmlControl` class reference for details.

- ❏ `TagName` – inherited from `System.Web.UI.HtmlControls.HtmlControl`, see the `HtmlControl` class reference for details.

- ❏ **Type**

- ❏ **Value**

Name

The `Name` property gets or sets a unique identifier name for all HTML input controls. The `Name` property maps to the `name` attribute of the `<input>` control element. This property returns a `Control.UniqueID` value.

```
public virtual string Name {get; set;}
```

Type

The `Type` property gets the type of an HTML input control. The `Type` property maps to the `type` attribute of the `<input>` control.

```
public string Type {get;}
```

One of the most common types is the 'Submit' input button. The following table shows all of the different types of HTML input controls:

Type	Description
Button	A command button: `<input type="button" runat="server">`
Checkbox	The checkbox type, which can be either `True` or `False`: `<input type="checkbox" runat="server">`

Type	Description
file	In ASP.NET, this is a new function for uploading files from client-side to server-side: `<input type="file" runat="server">`
hidden	The field is hidden so that you can persist information between posts to the server without the user knowing: `<input type="hidden" runat="server">`
image	Acts like an image button: `<input type="image" runat="server">`
password	A textbox which masks user input: `<input type="password" runat="server">`
radio	You can only select one of these buttons from its group: `<input type="radio" runat="server">`
reset	Clears the values in the HTML input controls within a form and acts like a button for cleaning up: `<input type="reset" runat="server">`
submit	A button that submits information to the server: `<input type="submit" runat="server">`
Text	A text box for data entry: `<input type="text" runat="server">`

Value

The Value property is used to get or set the value of the associated input control. The Value property maps to the value attribute of the `<input>` control element.

```
public virtual string Value {get; set;}
```

Example: Using HtmlInputControl

The following code from HtmlInputControlUsage.aspx shows the usage of the three main properties, Name, Type and Value of HtmlInputControl class by its inherited classes:

```
<%@ Page Language="c#" AutoEventWireup="false"
        Codebehind="HtmlInputControlUsage.aspx.cs"
        Inherits="systemWebUIHTMLControlsCS.HtmlInputControlUsage" %>
<!DOCTYPE HTML PUBLIC "-//W3C//DTD HTML 4.0 Transitional//EN">
<HTML>
  <HEAD>
    <title>HtmlInputControlUsage</title>
    <meta name="GENERATOR"
          content="Microsoft Visual Studio.NET 7.0">
    <meta name="CODE_LANGUAGE" content="C#">
    <meta name="vs_defaultClientScript"
```

```
              content="JavaScript">
          <meta name="vs_targetSchema"
                content="http://schemas.microsoft.com/intellisense/ie5">
      </HEAD>
      <body MS_POSITIONING="GridLayout">
        <form id="FrmInputControl" method="post" runat="server">
          <table>
           <tr>
             <td>
               Name
             </td>
             <td>
               <input type="text" runat="server"
                      name="TxtName" id="TxtName">
             </td>
           </tr>
           <tr>
             <td>
               Is ASP.NET Interesting
             </td>
             <td>
               <input type="checkbox" runat="server"
                      id="ChkInteresting" name="ChkInteresting"
                      value="ASP.NET">
             </td>
           </tr>
           <tr>
             <td>
               <input type="submit" runat="server"
                      id="BtnSubmit" name="BtnSubmit"
                      value="Submit"
                      onserverclick="BtnSubmit_ServerClick">
             </td>
           </tr>
          </table>
          <span id="Message" runat="server"></span>
        </form>
      </body>
    </HTML>
```

The code in the code-behind file, `HtmlInputControlUsage.aspx.cs`, is as follows:

```
public class HtmlInputControlUsage : System.Web.UI.Page
  {
    protected System.Web.UI.HtmlControls.HtmlInputText TxtName;
    protected System.Web.UI.HtmlControls.HtmlInputCheckBox ChkInteresting;
    protected System.Web.UI.HtmlControls.HtmlInputButton BtnSubmit;
    protected System.Web.UI.HtmlControls.HtmlGenericControl Message;

    private void Page_Load(object sender, System.EventArgs e)
    {
      // Put user code to initialize the page here
    }
```

```
protected void BtnSubmit_ServerClick(object sender,
                                     System.EventArgs e)
{
    Message.InnerHtml = "Name:" + TxtName.Name + "Type:"
                     + TxtName.Type + " Value:"
                     + TxtName.Value + "<br>";
    Message.InnerHtml += "Name:" + BtnSubmit.Name + " Type:"
                     + BtnSubmit.Type + " Value:"
                     + BtnSubmit.Value  + "<br>";
    Message.InnerHtml += "Name:" + ChkInteresting.Name + " Type:"
                     + ChkInteresting.Type + " Value:"
                     + ChkInteresting.Value + " Checked:"
                     + ChkInteresting.Checked  + "<br>";
}
```

Here is a screenshot showing the output:

HtmlInputControl Class Protected Properties

The `HtmlInputControl` class adds no new protected properties over those inherited from the `Control` class. See Chapter 2 for details.

HtmlInputControl Class Public Events

The `HtmlInputControl` class adds no new public events over those inherited from the `Control` class. See Chapter 2 for details.

HtmlInputFile Class

The `HtmlInputFile` class allows programmatic access to the HTML `<input type="file">` tag on the server. This control helps in uploading binary and text files from a client browser to the server. This control works with Internet Explorer 3.2 or above.

This is arguably one of the most complex and powerful classes of the `System.Web.UI.HtmlControl` namespace. Note that this control does not require a closing tag. To upload files to the server, the `EncType` property of the `<form>` control should be set to `"multipart/form-data"`.

The `HtmlInputFile` class is inherited from `System.Web.UI.HtmlControls.HtmlInputControl`.

It has the following syntax:

```
<input id = "id_name"
       type = "file"
       accept = "MIME encodings"
       maxlength = "Maximum length of path"
       size = "width of file-path textbox"
       postedfile = "uploaded file"
       runat = "server">
```

HtmlInputFile Class Public Methods

The `HtmlInputFile` class adds no new public methods over those inherited from the `Control` class. See Chapter 2 for details.

HtmlInputFile Class Protected Methods

The `HtmlInputFile` class adds no new protected methods over those inherited from the `Control` class. See Chapter 2 for details.

HtmlInputFile Class Public Properties

❑ **Accept**

❑ `Attributes` – inherited from `System.Web.UI.HtmlControls.HtmlControl`, see the `HtmlControl` class reference for details.

❑ `Disabled` – inherited from `System.Web.UI.HtmlControls.HtmlControl`, see the `HtmlControl` class reference for details.

❑ **MaxLength**

❑ `Name` – inherited from `System.Web.UI.HtmlControls.HtmlInputControl`, see the `HtmlInputControl` for details.

❑ **PostedFile**

❑ **Size**

- ❑ Style – inherited from `System.Web.UI.HtmlControls.HtmlControl`, see the `HtmlControl` class reference for details.

- ❑ TagName – inherited from `System.Web.UI.HtmlControls.HtmlControl`, see the `HtmlControl` class reference for details.

- ❑ Type – inherited from `System.Web.UI.HtmlControls.HtmlInputControl`, see the `HtmlInputControl` for details.

- ❑ Value – inherited from `System.Web.UI.HtmlControls.HtmlInputControl`, see the `HtmlInputControl` for details.

Accept

The `Accept` property gets or sets a comma-separated list of MIME encodings that can be used to constrain the file types that the browser lets the user select.

```
public string Accept {get; set;}
```

The following code example demonstrates how you would restrict all but Image file types.

```
accept="image/*"
```

MaxLength

The `MaxLength` property gets or sets the maximum length of the path of a file that will be uploaded from a client to the server.

```
public int MaxLength {get; set;}
```

PostedFile

The `PostedFile` property gets access to the file that is uploaded from a client. The property returns an `HttpPostedFile` object. The `System.Web.UI.HttpPostedFile` class provides methods and properties to enable uploading of files to the server. See the `HttpPostedFile` class reference in Chapter 1 for detailed information.

```
public HttpPostedFile PostedFile {get;}
```

Size

The `Size` property gets or sets the width of the textbox that is used to accept the file path.

```
public int Size {get; set;}
```

The following code, from `HtmlInputFileUsage.aspx`, utilizes the properties of the `HtmlInputFile` class:

```
<%@ Page Language="c#" AutoEventWireup="false"
        Codebehind="HtmlInputFileUsage.aspx.cs"
        Inherits="systemWebUIHTMLControlsCS.HtmlInputFileUsage" %>
<!DOCTYPE HTML PUBLIC "-//W3C//DTD HTML 4.0 Transitional//EN">
<HTML>
  <HEAD>
    <title>HtmlInputFileUsage</title>
    <meta content="Microsoft Visual Studio.NET 7.0"
        name="GENERATOR">
    <meta content="C#" name="CODE_LANGUAGE">
    <meta content="JavaScript"
        name="vs_defaultClientScript">
    <meta content="http://schemas.microsoft.com/intellisense/ie5"
        name="vs_targetSchema">
  </HEAD>
  <body MS_POSITIONING="GridLayout">
    <form id="FrmInputFile" encType="multipart/form-data"
        runat="server">
      Please select the file to be uploaded:
      <input id="InputFile" type="file" runat="server" size="40"
          maxlength="40">
      <br>
      <br>
      Please enter the target file name:
      <input id="TxtFileName" type="text" name="TxtFileName"
          runat="server">
      <input id="BtnSubmit" type="submit"
          value="Upload" name="BtnSubmit" runat="server">
      <br>
      <br>
      <div id="Message" runat="server"></div>
    </form>
  </body>
</HTML>
```

Here is the code-behind, `HtmlInputFileUsage.aspx.cs`, for this application:

```
public class HtmlInputFileUsage : System.Web.UI.Page
  {
    protected System.Web.UI.HtmlControls.HtmlInputFile InputFile;
    protected System.Web.UI.HtmlControls.HtmlInputText TxtFileName;
    protected System.Web.UI.HtmlControls.HtmlInputButton BtnSubmit;
    protected System.Web.UI.HtmlControls.HtmlGenericControl Message;

    private void Page_Load(object sender, System.EventArgs e)
    {
      // Put user code to initialize the page here
    }
    private void BtnSubmit_ServerClick(object sender, System.EventArgs e)
```

```
{
  if(TxtFileName.Value == "")
  {
    Message.InnerHtml = "Please enter a target file name";
    return;
  }
  if(InputFile.PostedFile != null)
  {
    try
    {
      Message.InnerHtml = "Max Length:" + InputFile.MaxLength + "<BR>";
      Message.InnerHtml += "Name:" + InputFile.Name + "<BR>";
      Message.InnerHtml += "Type:" + InputFile.Type + "<BR>";
      Message.InnerHtml += "Value:" + InputFile.Value + "<BR>";
      Message.InnerHtml += "Size:" + InputFile.Size + "<BR>";
      Message.InnerHtml += "Content Length:"
                        + InputFile.PostedFile.ContentLength + "<BR>";
      Message.InnerHtml += "Content Type:"
                          + InputFile.PostedFile.ContentType + "<BR>";
      Message.InnerHtml += "File Name:"
                          + InputFile.PostedFile.FileName + "<BR>";

      InputFile.PostedFile.SaveAs(@"C:\temp\" + TxtFileName.Value);
      Message.InnerHtml += @"File uploaded from the client"
                  + " successfully: C:\temp\" + TxtFileName.Value;
    }
    catch(Exception ex)
    {
      Message.InnerHtml += @"Error Uploading file: C:\temp\"
                    + TxtFileName.Value + "<br>" + ex.ToString();
      return;
    }
  }
  else
    Message.InnerHtml = "Please choose a file to upload";
}
}
```

233

Here is a screenshot showing the successful upload of the file to the server:

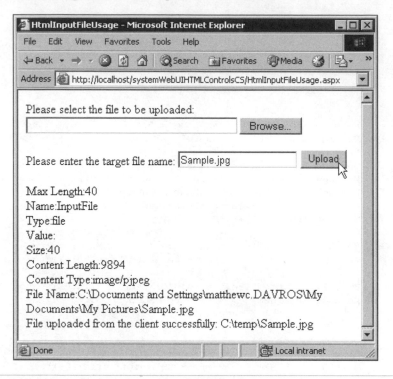

HtmlInputFile Class Protected Properties

The HtmlInputFile class adds no new protected properties over those inherited from the Control class. See Chapter 2 for details.

HtmlInputFile Class Public Events

The HtmlInputFile class adds no new public events over those inherited from the Control class. See Chapter 2 for details.

HtmlInputHidden Class

The HtmlInputHidden class allows programmatic access to the HTML <input type="hidden"> tag on the server. Note that the HtmlInputHidden class does not require a closing tag. We often use <input type="hidden"> to pass an embedded, non-visible piece of information when a user performs a post-back action.

You won't actually see a hidden object in a browser, so these hidden controls can be used to contain a string of information that you want to trigger by an action. Of course, you can hide information that you don't want to show in a page, and pass it to another page in a normal 'form' action. The HtmlInputHidden class can also save ViewState information across requests using hidden text fields.

The `HtmlInputHidden` class is inherited from
`System.Web.UI.HtmlControls.HtmlInputControl`.

It has the following syntax:

```
<input id = "id_name"
       type = "hidden"
       value = "hidden content"
       OnServerChange = "Method name"
       runat = "server">
```

HtmlInputHidden Class Public Methods

The `HtmlInputHidden` class adds no new public methods over those inherited from the `Control` class. See Chapter 2 for details.

HtmlInputHidden Class Protected Methods

❑ **OnServerChange**

OnServerChange

The `OnServerChange` method raises the `ServerChange` event. Whenever the data is posted to the server, if there is a change in the state of the hidden text from the previous post to the server, this event is raised. Note that this event is raised only when the data is posted to the server. The control's state can be changed but the event is raised only when the data is posted to the server, and if, at that time, the state is different. The hidden text control must have `ViewState` enabled in order to be able to raise this event correctly. This method allows derived classes to handle the `ServerChange` event directly without attaching to a delegate.

```
protected virtual void OnServerChange(EventArgs e);
```

The parameter e refers to an `EventArgs` object that contains the server change event data.

HtmlInputHidden Class Public Properties

❑ `Attributes` – inherited from `System.Web.UI.HtmlControls.HtmlControl`, see the `HtmlControl` class reference for details.

❑ `Disabled` – inherited from `System.Web.UI.HtmlControls.HtmlControl`, see the `HtmlControl` class reference for details.

❑ `Name` – inherited from `System.Web.UI.HtmlControls.HtmlInputControl`, see the `HtmlInputControl` for details.

❑ `Style` – inherited from `System.Web.UI.HtmlControls.HtmlControl`, see the `HtmlControl` class reference for details.

❑ `TagName` – inherited from `System.Web.UI.HtmlControls.HtmlControl`, see the `HtmlControl` class reference for details.

- ❑ Type – inherited from System.Web.UI.HtmlControls.HtmlInputControl, see the HtmlInputControl for details.

- ❑ Value – inherited from System.Web.UI.HtmlControls.HtmlInputControl, see the HtmlInputControl for details.

Example: Using HtmlInputHidden to Store Information

The following code from HtmlInputHiddenUsage.aspx shows how hidden control can be used to store information between posts to the server:

```
<%@ Page Language="c#" AutoEventWireup="false"
        Codebehind="HtmlInputHiddenUsage.aspx.cs"
        Inherits="systemWebUIHTMLControlsCS.HtmlInputHiddenUsage" %>
<!DOCTYPE HTML PUBLIC "-//W3C//DTD HTML 4.0 Transitional//EN">
<HTML>
  <HEAD>
    <title>HtmlInputHiddenUsage</title>
    <meta content="Microsoft Visual Studio.NET 7.0"
         name="GENERATOR">
    <meta content="C#" name="CODE_LANGUAGE">
    <meta content="JavaScript"
         name="vs_defaultClientScript">
     <meta content="http://schemas.microsoft.com/intellisense/ie5"
          name="vs_targetSchema">
  </HEAD>
  <body MS_POSITIONING="GridLayout">
    <form id="FrmInputHidden" method="post" runat="server">
      Enter Some Data:
      <input type="text" runat="server"
            id="TxtData" name="TxtData">
      <input type="hidden"
            id="Data" name="Data" runat="server">
      <input type="submit" value="Submit" runat="server"
            onserverClick="BtnSubmit_ServerClick"
            id="BtnSubmit" name="BtnSubmit">
      <br>
      <br>
      <div id="Message" runat="server"></div>
    </form>
  </body>
</HTML>
```

The code-behind file, HtmlInputHiddenUsage.aspx.cs, follows below:

```
public class HtmlInputHiddenUsage : System.Web.UI.Page
  {
    protected System.Web.UI.HtmlControls.HtmlInputText TxtData;
    protected System.Web.UI.HtmlControls.HtmlInputHidden Data;
    protected System.Web.UI.HtmlControls.HtmlInputButton BtnSubmit;
    protected System.Web.UI.HtmlControls.HtmlGenericControl Message;
```

```
    private void Page_Load(object sender, System.EventArgs e)
    {
      if(Page.IsPostBack)
        Message.InnerHtml = " You Previously Entered, " + Data.Value;
    }



    protected void BtnSubmit_ServerClick(object sender,
                                        System.EventArgs e)
    {
      Data.Value = TxtData.Value;
    }
  }
}
```

The following screenshot shows how the hidden field contains the value which was entered before in the last PostBack to the server:

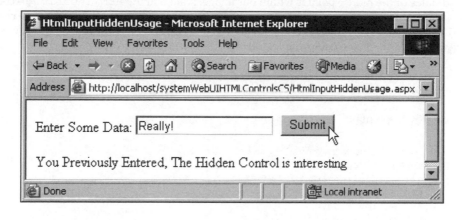

HtmlInputHidden Class Protected Properties

The Html InputHidden class adds no new protected properties over those inherited from the Control class. See Chapter 2 for details.

HtmlInputHidden Class Public Events

❑ **ServerChange**

ServerChange

The `ServerChange` event is raised whenever there is a change in the state of the hidden text between posts to the server. Note that this event does not fire when there is a change in the state and no post to the server. The controls state can be changed but the event is raised only when the data is posted to the server, and only at that time if the state is different from the previous post. The hidden text control must have `ViewState` enabled in order to be able to raise this event correctly. This event is represented on the control by an attribute, `onserverchange`, which attaches an event handler to the event. We can then write an event handler method that intercepts this event and run some code whenever the event is fired.

```
public event EventHandler ServerChange;
```

HtmlInputImage Class

The `HtmlInputImage` class allows programmatic access to the HTML `<input type="image">` tag on the server. When this is clicked, the form containing the element is submitted to the server along with the coordinates of the mouse pointer within our image. Note that the `HtmlInputImage` control offers greater support for down-level browsers than the `HtmlButton` control. With the `ServerClick` event, an `HtmlInputImage` can change its alignment dynamically and have the same behavior as a button. It also can use DHTML events, for example `OnMouseOver` and `OnMouseOut`.

The `HtmlInputImage` class is inherited from `System.Web.UI.HtmlControls.HtmlInputControl`.

It has the following syntax:

```
<input id = "id_name"
       type = "image"
       align = "alignment of image"
       alt = "text of alert"
       src = "image path"
       width = "image width"
       onserverclick = "onserverclick handler"
       runat = "server">
```

HtmlInputImage Class Public Methods

The `HtmlInputImage` class adds no new public methods over those inherited from the `Control` class. See Chapter 2 for details.

HtmlInputImage Class Protected Methods

❑ **OnServerClick**

OnServerClick

The `OnServerClick` method raises the `ServerClick` event. When the user clicks on the input image control, the `ServerClick` event is raised. With the `ServerClick` event, an `HtmlInputImage` can change its alignment dynamically and have the same behavior as a button. This method allows derived classes to handle the `ServerClick` event directly without attaching to a delegate.

```
protected virtual void OnServerClick(ImageClickEventArgs e);
```

The parameter e refers to an `EventArgs` object that contains the server click event data.

HtmlInputImage Class Public Properties

- ❑ **Align**

- ❑ **Alt**

- ❑ Attributes – inherited from `System.Web.UI.HtmlControls.HtmlControl`, see the `HtmlControl` class reference for details.

- ❑ **Border**

- ❑ **CausesValidation**

- ❑ Disabled – inherited from `System.Web.UI.HtmlControls.HtmlControl`, see the `HtmlControl` class reference for details.

- ❑ Name – inherited from `System.Web.UI.HtmlControls.HtmlInputControl`, see the `HtmlInputControl` for details.

- ❑ **Src**

- ❑ Style – inherited from `System.Web.UI.HtmlControls.HtmlControl`, see the `HtmlControl` class reference for details.

- ❑ TagName – inherited from `System.Web.UI.HtmlControls.HtmlControl`, see the `HtmlControl` class reference for details.

- ❑ Type – inherited from `System.Web.UI.HtmlControls.HtmlInputControl`, see the `HtmlInputControl` for details.

- ❑ Value – inherited from `System.Web.UI.HtmlControls.HtmlInputControl`, see the `HtmlInputControl` for details.

Align

The `Align` property gets or sets the alignment of an image relative to the other web page elements. The image is aligned to the `left` or `right` of the web page, when assigned one of these values. The other values can be `top`, `bottom` or `middle`. In the case of `top`, the upper edge of the image is aligned with the upper edge of the highest element on the same line. Similarly for `bottom`, the lower edge is aligned with the lower edge of the lowest element on the same line. In the case of `middle`, the control is aligned with the lower edge of the first line of text.

```
public string Align {get; set;}
```

Alt

The `Alt` property gets or sets an alternative caption that the browser displays if the image is either unavailable or has not been downloaded yet. The `Alt` property is also displayed as a `Tooltip` of the image in newer versions of browsers.

```
public string Alt {get; set;}
```

Border

The Border property is used to create a border frame for an image having a specified number of pixels as its width. This property can be used to get or set the width of border of an image in pixels.

```
public int Border {get; set;}
```

CausesValidation

The CausesValidation property is used to specify whether validation should be performed when the HtmlInputImage control is clicked. The validation is performed by the ASP.NET validation controls (if any) associated with the input server controls in the page. Therefore this property causes the validation controls to perform validation test if set to true, or false if no validation occurs. The default value is true. Sometimes, it is necessary to submit the page without validation, for example in the event of a cancel or reset button being clicked. This property, when true may perform validations at both client and server level depending on the browser capability and the setting of the clienttarget attribute in the Page directive.

```
public bool CausesValidation {get; set;}
```

Src

The Src property gets or sets the path and filename of an input image that will be displayed. If the image resides in the current directory, then the path need not be set. Thus it allows both relative and absolute paths. The shortcut to the virtual root directory "~/" can be used here. All the relative paths are converted to absolute paths automatically when the control is rendered.

```
public string Src {get; set;}
```

Example: Using the HtmlInputImage Control

Let's see a simple example that shows the X and Y co-ordinates where the click has occurred. The code is available in HtmlInputImageUsage.aspx:

```
<%@ Page Language="c#" AutoEventWireup="false"
        Codebehind="HtmlInputImageUsage.aspx.cs"
        Inherits="systemWebUIHTMLControlsCS.HtmlInputImageUsage" %>
<!DOCTYPE HTML PUBLIC "-//W3C//DTD HTML 4.0 Transitional//EN">
<HTML>
  <HEAD>
    <title>HtmlInputImageUsage</title>
    <meta content="Microsoft Visual Studio.NET 7.0"
        name="GENERATOR">
    <meta content="C#" name="CODE_LANGUAGE">
    <meta content="JavaScript"
        name="vs_defaultClientScript">
    <meta content="http://schemas.microsoft.com/intellisense/ie5"
        name="vs_targetSchema">
  </HEAD>
  <body MS_POSITIONING="GridLayout">
    <form id="FrmInputImage" method="post" runat="server">
      <input type="image" runat="server" id="ImgWrox"
```

```
                 name="ImgWrox" align="top" border="1"
                 src="wroxlogo.gif"
                 onserverclick="ImgWrox_ServerClick">
      <div id="Message" runat="server"></div>
    </form>
  </body>
</HTML>
```

The code-behind file, `HtmlInputImageUsage.aspx.cs`, is shown next:

```
public class HtmlInputImageUsage : System.Web.UI.Page
  {
    protected System.Web.UI.HtmlControls.HtmlInputImage ImgWrox;
    protected System.Web.UI.HtmlControls.HtmlGenericControl Message;

    private void Page_Load(object sender, System.EventArgs e)
    {
      // Put user code to initialize the page here
    }

    protected void ImgWrox_ServerClick(object sender,
                                    System.Web.UI.ImageClickEventArgs e)
    {
      Message.InnerText = "You have clicked at X:" + e.X + " and Y:" + e.Y;
    }
  }
```

The output from this code is demonstrated below:

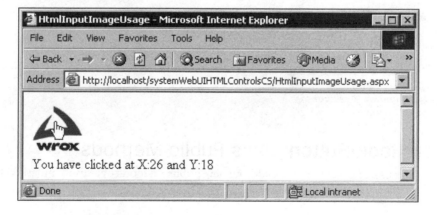

HtmlInputImage Class Protected Properties

The `HtmlInputImage` class adds no new protected properties over those inherited from the `Control` class. See Chapter 2 for details.

HtmlInputImage Class Public Events

❏ **ServerClick**

ServerClick

The ServerClick event is raised whenever the input image control is clicked. With the ServerClick event, an HtmlInputImage can change its alignment dynamically and have the same behavior as a button. This event is represented on the control by an attribute, onserverclick, which attaches an event handler to the event. We can then write an event handler method that intercepts this event and run some code whenever the event is fired.

```
public event ImageClickEventHandler ServerClick;
```

HtmlInputRadioButton Class

The HtmlInputRadioButton class allows programmatic access to the HTML <input type="radio"> tag on the server. This control provides a button to the user, which can be turned on or off, and is usually used to select a true or false state. The radio button generally implies only one item can be selected in a group of items. This is achieved with the help of the Name property that indicates the name of the group that the radio button is associated with. The HtmlInputRadioButton class does require a closing tag. The radio button control does not provide a built-in attribute to assign a caption but literal text can be inserted at the desired place in the web page to create a caption.

The HtmlInputRadioButton class is inherited from System.Web.UI.HtmlControls.HtmlInputControl.

It has the following syntax:

```
<input id="id_name"
        type = "radio"
        name = "radio group"
        checked
        runat = "server">
    Caption_Text
```

HtmlInputRadioButton Class Public Methods

The HtmlInputRadioButton class adds no new public methods over those inherited from the Control class. See Chapter 2 for details.

HtmlInputRadioButton Class Protected Methods

❏ **OnServerChange**

OnServerChange

The `OnServerChange` method raises the `ServerChange` event. Whenever the data is posted to the server, if there is a change in the state of the radio button from the previous post to the server, this event is raised. Note, that this event is raised only when the data is posted to the server. The control's state can be changed but the event is raised only when the data is posted to the server, and at that time, only if the state is different. The radio button control must have `ViewState` enabled in order to be able to raise this event correctly. This method allows derived classes to handle the `ServerChange` event directly without attaching to a delegate.

```
protected virtual void OnServerChange(EventArgs e);
```

The parameter e refers to an `EventArgs` object that contains the server change event data.

HtmlInputRadioButton Class Public Properties

- ❑ `Attributes` – inherited from `System.Web.UI.HtmlControls.HtmlControl`, see the `HtmlControl` class reference for details.

- ❑ **Checked**

- ❑ `Disabled` – inherited from `System.Web.UI.HtmlControls.HtmlControl`, see the `HtmlControl` class reference for details.

- ❑ **Name**

- ❑ `Style` – inherited from `System.Web.UI.HtmlControls.HtmlControl`, see the `HtmlControl` class reference for details.

- ❑ `TagName` – inherited from `System.Web.UI.HtmlControls.HtmlControl`, see the `HtmlControl` class reference for details.

- ❑ `Type` – inherited from `System.Web.UI.HtmlControls.HtmlInputControl`, see the `HtmlInputControl` for details.

- ❑ **Value**

Checked

The `Checked` property is used to assign or determine whether the input radio button is selected. This property returns `true` if the radio button is selected and `false` otherwise. This property is the main property and gives the state of the radio button.

```
public bool Checked {get; set;}
```

Name

The `Name` property gets or sets the name of the group with which the radio button control is associated. The radio button control allows only one item to be selected in a list of items if they are grouped together. The `Name` property groups those items together by assigning the same value to all of the radio buttons `Name` property, so that only one of them can be selected.

```
public override string Name {get; set;}
```

Value

The `Value` property retrieves or determines the value for the `HtmlInputRadioButton`.

```
public override string Value {get; set;}
```

HtmlInputRadioButton Class Protected Properties

The `HtmlInputRadioButton` class adds no new protected properties over those inherited from the `Control` class. See Chapter 2 for details.

HtmlInputRadioButton Class Public Events

❑ `ServerChange`

ServerChange

The `ServerChange` event is raised whenever there is a change in the state of the radio button between posts to the server. It does require, though, that the data is posted to the server. The control's state can be changed but the event is raised only when the data is posted to the server, and at that time, only if the state is different from the previous post. The radio button control must have `ViewState` enabled in order to be able to raise this event correctly. This event is represented on the control by an attribute, `onserverchange`, which attaches an event handler to the event. We can then write an event handler method that intercepts this event and run some code whenever the event is fired.

```
public event EventHandler ServerChange;
```

Example: The HtmlInputRadioButton class

Let's see the main properties and the `ServerChange` event of the `HtmlInputRadioButton` class in the following example. This code is available for download with the filename `HtmlInputRadioButtonUsage.aspx`:

```
<%@ Page Language="c#" AutoEventWireup="false"
        Codebehind="HtmlInputRadioButtonUsage.aspx.cs"
        Inherits="systemWebUIHTMLControlsCS.HtmlInputRadioButtonUsage" %>
<!DOCTYPE HTML PUBLIC "-//W3C//DTD HTML 4.0 Transitional//EN">
<HTML>
  <HEAD>
    <title>HtmlInputRadioButtonUsage</title>
    <meta name="GENERATOR"
          content="Microsoft Visual Studio.NET 7.0">
    <meta name="CODE_LANGUAGE" content="C#">
    <meta name="vs_defaultClientScript"
          content="JavaScript">
    <meta name="vs_targetSchema"
          content="http://schemas.microsoft.com/intellisense/ie5">
  </HEAD>
  <body MS_POSITIONING="GridLayout">
    <form id="FrmRadioButton" method="post" runat="server">
      <h3>
Select Mode of Payment:
```

```
            </h3>
            <input type="radio" id="RBtnCheck" name="Mode"
                   runat="server" value="Check" checked
                   onserverchange="RBtnMode_ServerChange">
              Personal Check
            <input type="radio" id="RBtnCC" name="Mode"
                   runat="server" value="CC"
                   onserverchange="RBtnMode_ServerChange">
              Credit Card
            <br>
            <br>
            <input type="submit" value="Submit">
            <br>
            <br>
            <span id="SpnBank" runat="server"
                  Visible="true">
              Bank Details:
            <textarea id="TxtBank"
                      name="TxtBank" runat="server" Rows="4"
                      cols="50">
            </textarea>
            </span>
            <br>
            <span id="SpnCC" runat="server"
                  Visible="false">
              Credit Card Number:
            <input type="text" id="TxtCC" name="TxtCC" runat="server">
            </span>
        </form>
    </body>
</HTML>
```

As you can see a single event handler handles the ServerChange event for all of the radio buttons. The code-behind file for this example, HtmlInputRadioButton.aspx.cs, is shown below:

```
public class HtmlInputRadioButtonUsage : System.Web.UI.Page
  {
    protected System.Web.UI.HtmlControls.HtmlInputRadioButton RBtnCheck;
    protected System.Web.UI.HtmlControls.HtmlInputRadioButton RBtnCC;
    protected System.Web.UI.HtmlControls.HtmlGenericControl SpnBank;
    protected System.Web.UI.HtmlControls.HtmlTextArea TxtBank;
    protected System.Web.UI.HtmlControls.HtmlGenericControl SpnCC;
    protected System.Web.UI.HtmlControls.HtmlInputText TxtCC;

    private void Page_Load(object sender, System.EventArgs e)
    {
      // Put user code to initialize the page here
    }

    ...

    private void InitializeComponent()
    {
```

245

```
        this.RBtnCheck.ServerChange += new
                        System.EventHandler(this.RBtnMode_ServerChange);
        this.RBtnCC.ServerChange += new
                        System.EventHandler(this.RBtnMode_ServerChange);
        this.Load += new System.EventHandler(this.Page_Load);

    }

    protected void RBtnMode_ServerChange(object sender, System.EventArgs e)
    {
        if(RBtnCheck.Checked == true)
        {
            SpnBank.Visible = true;
            SpnCC.Visible = false;
        }
        else
        {
            SpnBank.Visible = false;
            SpnCC.Visible = true;
        }
    }
}
```

Here is a screenshot showing the output:

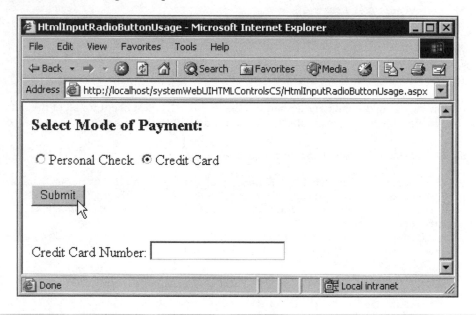

HtmlInputText Class

The `HtmlInputText` class allows programmatic access to the HTML `<input type="text">` and `<input type="password">` tag on the server. Note that it does not require a closing tag. This control is used for the input of textual and sensitive information from the user using input text and input password respectively.

The `HtmlInputText` class is inherited from `System.Web.UI.HtmlControls.HtmlInputControl`.

It has the following syntax:

```
<input id="id_name
        type = "text | password"
        maxlength = "Maximum length of content"
        size = "width of textbox"
        value = "content of textbox"
        runat = "server">
```

HtmlInputText Class Public Methods

The `HtmlInputText` class adds no new public methods over those inherited from the `Control` class. See Chapter 2 for details.

HtmlInputText Class Protected Methods

❏ **OnServerChange**

OnServerChange

The `OnServerChange` method raises the `ServerChange` event. Whenever the data is posted to the server, if there is a change in the state of the text from the previous post to the server, this event is raised. Note, that this event is raised only when the data is posted to the server. The control's state can be changed but the event is raised only when the data is posted to the server, and at that time, only if the state is different. The text control must have `ViewState` enabled in order to be able to raise this event correctly. This method allows derived classes to handle the `ServerChange` event directly without attaching to a delegate.

```
protected virtual void OnServerChange(EventArgs e);
```

The parameter e refers to an `EventArgs` object that contains the server change event data.

HtmlInputText Class Public Properties

❏ `Attributes` – inherited from `System.Web.UI.HtmlControls.HtmlControl`, see the `HtmlControl` class reference for details.

❏ `Disabled` – inherited from `System.Web.UI.HtmlControls.HtmlControl`, see the `HtmlControl` class reference for details.

- ❏ **MaxLength**
- ❏ Name – inherited from `System.Web.UI.HtmlControls.HtmlInputControl`, see the `HtmlInputControl` for details.
- ❏ **Size**
- ❏ Style – inherited from `System.Web.UI.HtmlControls.HtmlControl`, see the `HtmlControl` Class reference for details.
- ❏ TagName – inherited from `System.Web.UI.HtmlControls.HtmlControl`, see the `HtmlControl` Class reference for details.
- ❏ Type – inherited from `System.Web.UI.HtmlControls.HtmlInputControl`, see the `HtmlInputControl` for details.
- ❏ Value – inherited from `System.Web.UI.HtmlControls.HtmlInputControl`, see the `HtmlInputControl` for details.

MaxLength

The `MaxLength` property is used to get or set the maximum number of characters that can be allowed in the input text (Textbox) control. This property is helpful when we don't want the user to enter information more than a specified length.

```
public int MaxLength {get; set;}
```

Size

The `Size` property is used to set the width of the textbox. This property, when specified sets the width of the textbox to accommodate the specified number of characters.

```
public int Size {get; set;}
```

HtmlInputText Class Protected Properties

The `HtmlInputText` class adds no new protected properties over those inherited from the `Control` class. See Chapter 2 for details.

HtmlInputText Class Public Events

- ❏ **ServerChange**

ServerChange

The `ServerChange` event is raised whenever there is a change in the state of the text between posts to the server. Note that this event does not fire when there is a change in the state if there is no post to the server. It requires that the data is posted to the server. The control's state can be changed but the event is raised only when the data is posted to the server, and at that time, only if the state is different from the previous post. The text control must have `ViewState` enabled in order to be able to raise this event correctly. This event is represented on the control by an attribute, `onserverchange`, which attaches an event handler to the event. We can then write an event handler method that intercepts this event and run some code whenever the event is fired.

```
public event EventHandler ServerChange;
```

Example: Using the HtmlInputText Class

Let's see the main properties and `ServerChange` event of `HtmlInputText` class in the following example. This code is available for download with the filename `HtmlInputTextUsage.aspx`:

```
<%@ Page Language="C#" AutoEventWireup="false"
        Codebehind="HtmlInputTextUsage.aspx.cs"
        Inherits="systemWebUIHTMLControlsCS.HtmlInputTextUsage" %>
<!DOCTYPE HTML PUBLIC "-//W3C//DTD HTML 4.0 Transitional//EN">
<HTML>
  <HEAD>
    <title>HtmlInputTextUsage</title>
    <meta name="GENERATOR"
          content="Microsoft Visual Studio.NET 7.0">
    <meta name="CODE_LANGUAGE" content="C#">
    <meta name="vs_defaultClientScript"
          content="JavaScript">
    <meta name="vs_targetSchema"
          content="http://schemas.microsoft.com/intellisense/ie5">
  </HEAD>
  <body MS_POSITIONING="GridLayout">
    <form id="FrmInputText" method="post" runat="server">
      <table>
        <tr>
          <td>
            UserName
          </td>
          <td>
            <input type="text" id="TxtUserName"
                   runat="server" name="TxtUserName"
                   size="25">
          </td>
        </tr>
        <tr>
          <td>
            Password
          </td>
          <td>
            <input type="password" id="TxtPassword"
                   runat="server" name="TxtPassword"
                   maxlength="8" size="15"
                   onServerChange="TxtPassword_ServerChange">
          </td>
        </tr>
      </table>
      <input type="submit" value="Submit" runat="server"
             id="BtnSubmit" name="BtnSubmit">
      <div id="Message" runat="server"></div>
    </form>
  </body>
</HTML>
```

The following code-behind file, `HtmlInputTextUsage.aspx.cs`, displays the `ServerChange` event handler for the `TxtPassword` control. The `TxtPassword_ServerChange` event handler prompts the user to select a different password if the password is the same as the username. The `BtnSubmit_ServerClick` event handler displays the username and password entered:

```
public class HtmlInputTextUsage : System.Web.UI.Page
  {
    protected System.Web.UI.HtmlControls.HtmlInputText TxtUserName;
    protected System.Web.UI.HtmlControls.HtmlInputText TxtPassword;
    protected System.Web.UI.HtmlControls.HtmlInputButton BtnSubmit;
    protected System.Web.UI.HtmlControls.HtmlGenericControl Message;

    private void Page_Load(object sender, System.EventArgs e)
    {
      // Put user code to initialize the page here
    }

    protected void TxtPassword_ServerChange(object sender,
                                      System.EventArgs e)
    {
      if(TxtUserName.Value == TxtPassword.Value)
        Message.InnerText = "Please enter a different password. "
                      + "It is same as your user name";
    }

    protected void BtnSubmit_ServerClick(object sender, System.EventArgs e)
    {
      Message.InnerHtml += "<br>" + "<I> You entered "
                      + TxtUserName.Value + " and "
                      + TxtPassword.Value ;
    }
  }
```

Here is a screenshot showing the output:

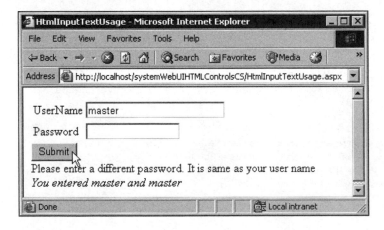

HtmlSelect Class

HTML defines only one way to create list box controls; the HTML `<select>` element. This is implemented as the server control named `HtmlSelect`. The `HtmlSelect` class allows programmatic access to an HTML `<select>` element on the server. Each item is listed as an `<option>` element within the `<select>` tags and is represented as a `Webcontrol.ListItem`. To assign values to these listed items, you can use the `ListItem.Text` property assigned to that item. Other properties of the `ListItem` can be used to further manipulate it.

The `HtmlSelect` class is inherited from `System.Web.UI.HtmlControls.HtmlContainerControl`.

It has the following syntax:

```
<select id="select_id"
        datasource = "databindingsource name"
        datamember = "data member in the datasource to bind"
        datatextfield = "field to databind option"
        datavaluefield = "field to databind option"
        multiple
        items = "a collection of options"
        selectindex = "index of current selecteditem"
        size = "number of visible items"
        value = "current item value"
        runat = "server">
  <option value="option1_value"> option1_name </option>
  <option value="option2_value"> option2_name </option>
</select>
```

HtmlSelect Class Public Methods

The `HtmlSelect` class adds no new public methods over those inherited from the `Control` class. See Chapter 2 for details.

HtmlSelect Class Protected Methods

❑ **OnServerChange**

OnServerChange

The `OnServerChange` method raises the `ServerChange` event. Whenever the data is posted to the server, if there is a change in the state of the selected items of the `HtmlSelect` control from the previous post to the server, this event is raised. Note, that this event is raised only when the data is posted to the server. The items can be selected or deselected at anytime but the event is raised only when the data is posted to the server, and if, at that time, the state is different. The `HtmlSelect` control must have `ViewState` enabled in order to be able to raise this event correctly. This method allows derived classes to handle the `ServerChange` event directly without attaching to a delegate.

```
protected virtual void OnServerChange(EventArgs e);
```

The parameter e refers to an `EventArgs` object that contains the server change event data.

HtmlSelect Class Public Properties

- ❏ `Attributes` – inherited from `System.Web.UI.HtmlControls.HtmlControl`, see the `HtmlControl` Class reference for details.

- ❏ **`DataMember`**

- ❏ **`DataSource`**

- ❏ **`DataTextField`**

- ❏ **`DataValueField`**

- ❏ `Disabled` – inherited from `System.Web.UI.HtmlControls.HtmlControl`, see the `HtmlControl` class reference for details.

- ❏ `InnerHtml` – inherited from `System.Web.UI.HtmlControls.HtmlContainerControl`, see the `HtmlContainerControl` Class for details.

- ❏ `InnerText` – inherited from `System.Web.UI.HtmlControls.HtmlContainerControl`, see the `HtmlContainerControl` class for details.

- ❏ **`Items`**

- ❏ **`Multiple`**

- ❏ **`Name`**

- ❏ **`SelectedIndex`**

- ❏ **`Size`**

- ❏ `Style` – inherited from `System.Web.UI.HtmlControls.HtmlControl`, see the `HtmlControl` class reference for details.

- ❏ `TagName` – inherited from `System.Web.UI.HtmlControls.HtmlControl`, see the `HtmlControl` class reference for details.

- ❏ **`Value`**

DataMember

The `DataMember` property indicates the data member of the datasource that the `HtmlSelect` control is bound to. This property is very helpful when the `DataSource` has multiple sets of members to bind to. For example, a `DataSet` object can be a `DataSource` and a specific table in the `Dataset` can become the `DataMember` of the `HtmlSelect` control.

```
public virtual string DataMember {get; set;}
```

DataSource

The `DataSource` property gets or sets the data source to bind to the `HtmlSelect` control. The `<option>` elements will be filled with the data available in the `DataSource`. The `DataSource` should be either a `System.Collections.IEnumerable` object or a `System.ComponentModel.IListSource` object, otherwise an `ArgumentException` occurs. If the `DataSource` has multiple sets of members to bind to, then the `DataMember` property can be used to indicate the desired member name.

```
public virtual object DataSource {get; set;}
```

DataTextField

The DataTextField property gets or sets the field in the data source that provides the text for an <option> element. The <option> element maps to the ListItem object and this property maps to the ListItem.Text property. This property is displayed in the HtmlSelect control. This property is used to indicate the specific member of the DataSource or DataMember to bind with. For example, a table in a DataSet may contain many columns. This can be used to specify the column whose values should be displayed in the HtmlSelect control.

```
public virtual string DataTextField {get; set;}
```

DataValueField

The DataValueField property gets or sets the field in the data source that provides the value for an <option> element. The <option> element maps to the ListItem object and this property maps to the ListItem.Value property. This property is not displayed in the HtmlSelect control but is stored as a value for the <option> element. This property is very helpful when we want to show descriptive, user-friendly text to the user, but want to associate the text with a value that, while it is programmatically very useful, can't be understood or displayed to the user. For example: to select if we want to show the Products name in the HtmlSelect control but wish to manipulate the code with the ProductID, then the ProductID can be bound with this control. Thus when the user selects a particular product, the associated ProductID can be known very easily.

```
public virtual string DataValueField {get; set;}
```

Items

The Items property gets or sets the collection of <option> items. The option items are returned as ListIemCollection objects. The ListItemCollection object can modify the list of <option> items for the HtmlSelect server control, with the following properties:

❑   Add – adds a new option item

❑   Clear – clears all option items

❑   Remove – deletes a selected option item

❑   Count – lists the total number of option items

```
public ListItemCollection Items {get;}
```

Multiple

The Multiple property gets or sets a Boolean value indicating whether multiple <option> items can be selected from the <select> list. The default value is false. If this property is set to true, the SelectedIndex property returns the index of the first item selected in the control. Hence you need to iterate the Items collection and test whether the ListItem.Selected property is true. If this property is set to true, the HtmlSelect control will be displayed as a listbox, to allow multiple selections.

```
public bool Multiple {get; set;}
```

Name

The Name property assigns or returns a unique identifier for the select control. The Name property corresponds to the name attribute in the <select> element.

```
public string Name {get; set;}
```

SelectedIndex

The SelectedIndex property gets or sets the zero-based index of the selected <option> item. If there are no items selected, then the SelectedIndex returns –1. If multiple items are selected, SelectedIndex holds the index of the first item selected in the list. Hence you need to iterate through the Items collection and test whether the ListItem.Selected property is true.

```
public virtual int SelectedIndex {get; set;}
```

Size

The Size property is used to assign or get the height of the HtmlSelect control in rows. If the Size has a value of more than one, the HtmlSelect control will be displayed as a List Box control; otherwise it will be a drop-down ListBox control. If the Size property is less then the number of the items in the HtmlSelect control, the HtmlSelect control will have scrollbars to navigate and select.

```
public int Size {get; set;}
```

Value

The Value property is used to set or get the selected item value in the HtmlSelect control. The Value property sets the SelectedIndex property to the index of the first Item in the HtmlSelect control. If no Item is selected in the HtmlSelect control, this property returns an empty string.

```
public string Value {get; set;}
```

HtmlSelect Class Protected Properties

The HtmlSelect class adds no new protected properties over those inherited from the Control class. See Chapter 2 for details.

HtmlSelect Class Public Events

❑   **ServerChange**

ServerChange

The ServerChange event is raised whenever there is a change in the state of the selected items of the list control between posts to the server. Note that this event does not fire when there is a change in the state and no post to the server. The control's state can be changed but the event is raised only when the data is posted to the server, and if the state is different from the previous post. The HtmlSelect control must have ViewState enabled in order to be able to raise this event correctly. This event is represented on the control by an attribute, onserverchange, which attaches an event handler to the event. We can then write an event handler method that intercepts this event and run some code whenever the event is fired.

```
public event EventHandler ServerChange;
```

Example: Using the HtmlSelect Class

Let's see how to work with the main properties and `ServerChange` event of the `HtmlSelect`
class in the following example. This code is available for download with the filename
`HtmlSelectUsage.aspx`:

```
<%@ Page Language="c#" AutoEventWireup="false"
        Codebehind="HtmlSelectUsage.aspx.cs"
        Inherits="systemWebUIHTMLControlsCS.HtmlSelectUsage" %>
<!DOCTYPE HTML PUBLIC "-//W3C//DTD HTML 4.0 Transitional//EN">
<HTML>
  <HEAD>
    <title>HtmlSelectUsage</title>
    <meta content="Microsoft Visual Studio.NET 7.0"
        name="GENERATOR">
    <meta content="C#" name="CODE_LANGUAGE">
    <meta content="JavaScript"
        name="vs_defaultClientScript">
    <meta content="http://schemas.microsoft.com/intellisense/ie5"
        name="vs_targetSchema">
  </HEAD>
  <body MS_POSITIONING="GridLayout">
    <form id="FrmSelect" method="post" runat="server">
      How often do you take a holiday:
      <select id="Holiday" runat="server">
        <option value="Y" selected>Yearly</option>
        <option value="H">Half Yearly</option>
        <option value="Q">Quarterly</option>
      </select>
      <br>
      <br>
      Select your Food Category:
      <select id="Food" runat="server" multiple="true"
            size="5" onserverchange="Food_ServerChange">
      </select>
      <br>
      <br>
      <input type="submit" runat="server" id="BtnSubmit"
            value="Submit Information" name="BtnSubmit"
            onserverclick="BtnSubmit_ServerClick">
      <br>
      <br>
      <div id="Message1" runat="server"></div>
      <br>
      <div id="Message2" runat="server"></div>
    </form>
  </body>
</HTML>
```

The following code is from the code-behind file, `HtmlSelectUsage.aspx.cs`:

```
public class HtmlSelectUsage : System.Web.UI.Page
  {
    protected System.Web.UI.HtmlControls.HtmlSelect Holiday;
    protected System.Web.UI.HtmlControls.HtmlSelect Food;
    protected System.Web.UI.HtmlControls.HtmlInputButton BtnSubmit;
    protected System.Web.UI.HtmlControls.HtmlGenericControl Message1;
    protected System.Data.SqlClient.SqlConnection sqlConnection1;
    protected System.Web.UI.HtmlControls.HtmlGenericControl Message2;

    private void Page_Load(object sender, System.EventArgs e)
    {
      if (!IsPostBack)
      {
        Holiday.Items.Add(new ListItem("Monthly", "M"));
        Holiday.Items.Add(new ListItem("Fortnight" , "F"));
        Holiday.Value="M";

        sqlConnection1.Open();
        SqlDataAdapter sqlDataAdapter1 = new
         SqlDataAdapter("select categoryid, categoryname from Categories",
                     sqlConnection1);

        // Create a dataset to store the Category data.
        DataSet ds  = new DataSet();
        sqlDataAdapter1.Fill(ds, "FoodCategory");

        // Assign the Data Properties of the List control
        Food.DataSource = ds;
        Food.DataMember = "FoodCategory";
        Food.DataTextField = "categoryname";
        Food.DataValueField = "categoryid";
        Food.DataBind();

      }

    }

    ...

    private void InitializeComponent()
    {
      this.sqlConnection1 = new System.Data.SqlClient.SqlConnection();
      this.Food.ServerChange += new
                         System.EventHandler(this.Food_ServerChange);
      this.BtnSubmit.ServerClick += new
                      System.EventHandler(this.BtnSubmit_ServerClick);
      //
      // sqlConnection1
      //
      this.sqlConnection1.ConnectionString =
           "data source=(local);initial catalog=Northwind;uid=sa;pwd=;";
      this.Load += new System.EventHandler(this.Page_Load);

    }
```

```
protected void Food_ServerChange(object sender, System.EventArgs e)
{
  Message2.InnerHtml = "Food Category Selected:" + "<br>";
  foreach(ListItem foodItem in Food.Items)
  {
    if(foodItem.Selected == true)
      Message2.InnerHtml += foodItem.Text
                      + " (" + foodItem.Value + ") <br>" ;
  }
}

protected void BtnSubmit_ServerClick(object sender, System.EventArgs e)
{
  Message1.InnerHtml = "You take a holiday "
                    + Holiday.Items[Holiday.SelectedIndex].Text
                    + " (" + Holiday.Value + ")";
}
}
```

The above code, in the `Page_Load` procedure, shows how the `Food` list control is populated with the data from the Northwind database and shows the `Food` Category from the `Categories` table. The `DataTextField` and `DataValueField` properties contain the values `categoryname` and `categoryid` respectively. This example also shows how to add items to the control at run time and set the `Value` property.

The `Food_ServerChange` event handler iterates through the `Items` collection to get the values selected by the user. The `BtnSubmit_ServerClick` event handler displays the selected item in the `Holiday` list.

The following screenshot shows the output:

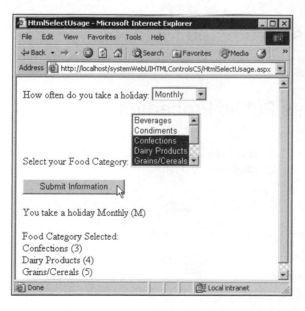

HtmlTable Class

The `HtmlTable` class provides programmatic access to the `<table>` element on the server. This creates a table control, which helps to display data in a formatted manner. You can bind the `<table>` server control and add rows and columns to a table by methods within the `HtmlTableRowCollection` and `HtmlTableCellCollection` classes.

The `HtmlTable` class is inherited from `System.Web.UI.HtmlControls.HtmlContainerControl`.

It has the following syntax:

```
<table id="table_id"
       align = "left | center | right"
       bgcolor = "background_color"
       border = "border_width"
       bordercolor = "border_color"
       cellpadding = "spacing_width_within_cell"
       cellspacing = "spacing_width_between_cells"
       height = "table_height"
       rows = "number_of_rows"
       width = "table_width"
       runat="server">
  <tr><td><td></tr>
</table>
```

HtmlTable Class Public Methods

The `HtmlTable` class adds no new public methods over those inherited from the `Control` class. See Chapter 2 for details.

HtmlTable Class Protected Methods

The `HtmlTable` class adds no new protected methods over those inherited from the `Control` class. See Chapter 2 for details.

HtmlTable Class Public Properties

❑ **Align**

❑ Attributes – inherited from `System.Web.UI.HtmlControls.HtmlControl`, see the `HtmlControl` class reference for details.

❑ **BgColor**

❑ **Border**

❑ **BorderColor**

❑ **CellPadding**

❑ **CellSpacing**

- ❑ Disabled – inherited from System.Web.UI.HtmlControls.HtmlControl, see the HtmlControl class reference for details.

- ❑ **Height**

- ❑ InnerHtml – inherited from System.Web.UI.HtmlControls.HtmlContainerControl, see the HtmlContainerControl class for details.

- ❑ InnerText – inherited from System.Web.UI.HtmlControls.HtmlContainerControl, see the HtmlContainerControl class for details.

- ❑ **Rows**

- ❑ Style – inherited from System.Web.UI.HtmlControls.HtmlControl, see the HtmlControl class reference for details.

- ❑ TagName – inherited from System.Web.UI.HtmlControls.HtmlControl, see the HtmlControl class reference for details.

- ❑ **Width**

Align

The Align property gets or sets the alignment of a table relative to the other web page elements. The table is aligned to the Left, Center or Right of the web page, when assigned one of these values. The default value is an empty string, which indicates that the value is not set.

```
public string Align {get; set;}
```

BgColor

The BgColor property gets or sets the background colors of a table. The default value is an empty string, which indicates that the value is not set. The BgColor property can be set by assigning one of the sixteen predefined color names, as listed below:

- ❑ Black
- ❑ Blue
- ❑ Cyan
- ❑ Gray
- ❑ Green
- ❑ Lime
- ❑ Magenta
- ❑ Maroon
- ❑ Navy
- ❑ Olive
- ❑ Purple
- ❑ Red
- ❑ Silver

- ❏ Teal
- ❏ White
- ❏ Yellow

It can also be set using hexadecimal notation preceded by the # symbol. By using a hexadecimal number, any custom color can be assigned to the background color of the table.

```
public string BgColor {get; set;}
```

Border

The Border property is used to create a border frame for an image having specified number of pixels as its width. This property can be used to get or set the width of border of an image in pixels.

```
public int Border {get; set;}
```

BorderColor

The BorderColor property gets or sets the border colors of a table. The BorderColor property can be set by assigning one of the predefined sixteen color names (see list above) or by using hexadecimal notation preceded by the # symbol. Through using a hexadecimal number, any custom color can be assigned to the border color of the table.

```
public string BorderColor {get; set;}
```

CellPadding

The CellPadding property gets or sets the quantity of space between the cell's border and its contents in pixels. The CellPadding property is applied to all the cells of the table; an individual cell's padding cannot be specified.

```
public int CellPadding {get; set;}
```

CellSpacing

The CellSpacing property gets or sets the quantity of space between the cells of the table in pixels. This quantity of space appears in adjacent cells horizontally and vertically.

```
public int CellSpacing {get; set;}
```

Height

The Height property gets or sets the height of a table. By default, the height is set in pixels but it can be also set as the percentage of the size of the window. When the Height property is set as a percentage, the table expands and contracts depending on the size of the browser automatically. If the Height property specified is less than the height required to display the contents of the table, the property is ignored.

```
public string Height {get; set;}
```

Rows

The `Rows` property returns a `System.Web.UI.HtmlControls.HtmlTableRowCollection` object that contains all of the rows in a table. An empty `HtmlTableRowCollection` is returned if no table rows, `<tr>` elements, are contained within the table. With the help of the `HtmlTableRowCollection` class properties and methods, the rows and cells of a table can be added, updated or deleted.

```
public virtual HtmlTableRowCollection Rows {get;}
```

Width

The `Width` property gets or sets the width of a table. By default, the width is set in pixels; it can also be set as the percentage of the size of the window. When the `Width` property is set as a percentage, the table expands and contracts depending on the size of the window automatically. If the `Width` property specified is less than the width required to display the contents of the table, the property is ignored.

```
public string Width {get; set;}
```

Example: Using the HtmlTable Class

The following code, taken from `HtmlTableUsage.aspx`, shows the usage of the `HtmlTable`, `HtmlTableRow` and `HtmlTableCell` class properties.

```
<%@ Page Language="c#" AutoEventWireup="false"
        Codebehind="HtmlTableUsage.aspx.cs"
        Inherits="systemWebUIHTMLControlsCS.HtmlTableUsage" %>
<!DOCTYPE HTML PUBLIC "-//W3C//DTD HTML 4.0 Transitional//EN">
<HTML>
  <HEAD>
    <title>HtmlTableUsage</title>
    <meta name="GENERATOR"
          content="Microsoft Visual Studio.NET 7.0">
    <meta name="CODE_LANGUAGE" content="C#">
    <meta name="vs_defaultClientScript"
          content="JavaScript">
    <meta name="vs_targetSchema"
          content="http://schemas.microsoft.com/intellisense/ie5">
  </HEAD>
  <body>
    <form id="Form1" method="post" runat="server">
      <table id="TblMain" runat="server" align="left"
             border="0" bordercolor="#3d59ab"
             cellpadding="2" cellspacing="1" height="100"
             width="300">
        <tr>
          <td>
            Rows:
          </td>
          <td>
            <INPUT type="text" id="TxtRow" runat="server"
                   NAME="TxtRow">
```

```
        </td>
        </tr>
        <tr>
          <td>
            Cells Per Row
          </td>
          <td>
            <INPUT type="text" id="TxtCell" runat="server"
                  NAME="TxtRow">
          </td>
        </tr>
        <tr id="TblRNew" runat="server">
          <td id="TblCNew" runat="server" colspan="2">
          </td>
        </tr>
      </table>
      <br>
      <br>
      <INPUT type="submit" value="Submit" id="BtnSubmit"
            runat="server" NAME="BtnSubmit">
    </form>
  </body>
</HTML>
```

The following code, HtmlTableUsage.aspx.cs, shows how the properties of these classes can be manipulated programmatically:

```
public class HtmlTableUsage : System.Web.UI.Page
  {
    protected System.Web.UI.HtmlControls.HtmlTable TblMain;
    protected System.Web.UI.HtmlControls.HtmlInputText TxtRow;
    protected System.Web.UI.HtmlControls.HtmlInputText TxtCell;
    protected System.Web.UI.HtmlControls.HtmlTableRow TblRNew;
    protected System.Web.UI.HtmlControls.HtmlTableCell TblCNew;
    protected System.Web.UI.HtmlControls.HtmlInputButton BtnSubmit;

    private void Page_Load(object sender, System.EventArgs e)
    {
      // Put user code to initialize the page here
    }


    private void BtnSubmit_ServerClick(object sender, System.EventArgs e)
    {
      HtmlTable TblNew = new HtmlTable();
      HtmlTableRow Row;
      HtmlTableCell Cell;

      int r,c;
      for(r = 1; r <= Convert.ToInt16(TxtRow.Value); r++)
      {
        Row = new HtmlTableRow();
        if(r % 2 == 0)
```

262

```
          Row.BgColor="#cfe2f1";
          for(c = 1; c <= Convert.ToInt16(TxtCell.Value); c++)
          {
            Cell = new HtmlTableCell();
            Cell.InnerHtml = "<I>Cell (" + r +"," + c + ")<I>";
            Row.Cells.Add(Cell);
          }
          TblNew.Rows.Add(Row);
        }
        TblNew.Border = 1;
        TblNew.BorderColor = "#3d59ab";
        TblNew.BgColor = "White";
        TblNew.Align = "center";
        TblCNew.Controls.Add(TblNew);
        TblMain.Border=1;
      }
   }
```

The above code adds rows and cells to an empty table. Here is a screenshot showing the new table created:

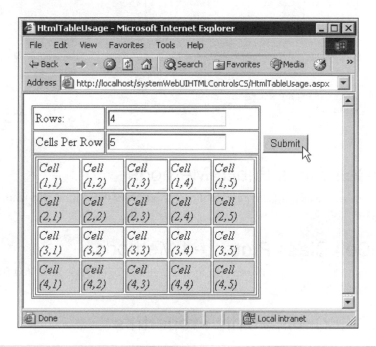

HtmlTable Class Protected Properties

The `HtmlTable` class adds no new protected properties over those inherited from the `Control` class. See Chapter 2 for details.

HtmlTable Class Public Events

The HtmlTable class adds no new public events over those inherited from the Control class. See Chapter 2 for details.

HtmlTableCell Class

The HtmlTableCell class allows programmatic access on the server to individual HTML <td> and <th> tags. You can dynamically add, remove, and insert cells to an HtmlTableRow server control. Please refer to HtmlTable class explanation for an example of the usage of this class.

The HtmlTableCell class is inherited from System.Web.UI.HtmlControls.HtmlContainerControl.

It has the following syntax:

```
<td or th id="id_name"
        align = "horizontal alignment of content in a cell"
        bgcolor = "background color of cell"
        bordercolor = "border color of cell"
        colspan = "the number of columns cell spans"
        height = "height of cell"
        nowrap = "true | false"
        rowspan = "the number of rows cell spans"
        valign = "vertical alignment of cell content"
        width = "the width of cell"
        runat="server">
    Content of cell
</td or /th>
```

HtmlTableCell Class Public Methods

The HtmlTableCell class adds no new public methods over those inherited from the Control class. See Chapter 2 for details.

HtmlTableCell Class Protected Methods

The HtmlTableCell class adds no new protected methods over those inherited from the Control class. See Chapter 2 for details.

HtmlTableCell Class Public Properties

- ❑ **Align**
- ❑ Attributes – inherited from System.Web.UI.HtmlControls.HtmlControl, see the HtmlControl class reference for details.
- ❑ **BgColor**
- ❑ **BorderColor**
- ❑ **ColSpan**

❑ `Disabled` – inherited from `System.Web.UI.HtmlControls.HtmlControl`, see the `HtmlControl` class reference for details.

❑ **Height**

❑ `InnerHtml` – inherited from `System.Web.UI.HtmlControls.HtmlContainerControl`, see the `HtmlContainerControl` class for details.

❑ `InnerText` – inherited from `System.Web.UI.HtmlControls.HtmlContainerControl`, see the `HtmlContainerControl` class for details.

❑ **NoWrap**

❑ **RowSpan**

❑ `Style` – inherited from `System.Web.UI.HtmlControls.HtmlControl`, see the `HtmlControl` class reference for details.

❑ `TagName` – inherited from `System.Web.UI.HtmlControls.HtmlControl`, see the `HtmlControl` class reference for details.

❑ **Valign**

❑ **Width**

Align

The `Align` property gets or sets the horizontal alignment of the cell contents in a table cell. The table cell contents are aligned to the `Left`, `Center` or `Right` of the cell, when assigned one of these values. The default value is an empty string, if no value has been set. This property can also be set to `Justify` and `Char`, although these are not supported by some of the browsers.

```
public string Align {get; set;}
```

BgColor

The `BgColor` property gets or sets the background color of a table cell. The `BgColor` property can be set by assigning one of the sixteen predefined color names or by using hexadecimal notation preceded by the # symbol. By using a hexadecimal number, any custom color can be assigned to the background color of the table cell.

```
public string BgColor {get; set;}
```

BorderColor

The `BorderColor` property gets or sets the border color of a table cell. The `BorderColor` property can be set by assigning predefined sixteen color names or by using hexadecimal notation preceded by the # symbol. By using a hexadecimal number, any custom color can be assigned to the border color of the table cell.

```
public string BorderColor {get; set;}
```

265

ColSpan

The ColSpan property returns the number of columns occupied by a single table cell. The default value is −1 to indicate that it is not set. This property can be helpful in certain circumstances, for example if you needed to assign a heading which is common to two columns, then you can use the ColSpan=2 property to make that heading column span for two columns.

```
public int ColSpan {get; set;}
```

Height

The Height property gets or sets the height of a table cell in pixels. The largest height specified by a cell is taken and then all the cells in that row have this height. If the Height property specified is less than the height required to display the contents of the table row, this property is ignored.

```
public string Height {get; set;}
```

NoWrap

The NoWrap property gets or sets a value indicating whether text within a cell should be wrapped. Possible values are true and false. true indicates that the value should not be wrapped. false allows wrapping of the contents in the cell and is the default value.

```
public bool NoWrap {get; set;}
```

RowSpan

The RowSpan property returns or sets the number of rows occupied by a single table cell. The default value is −1 to indicate that it is not set. This property can be helpful in certain circumstances, for example, if you need to place some contents that need more than a row to display, then you can use the RowSpan property to make that cell span for two rows or more.

```
public int RowSpan {get; set;}
```

VAlign

The VAlign property gets or sets the vertical alignment of the cells in a table cell. The table cell contents are aligned to the upper, center, lower edge of the cell when assigned to the Top, Middle or Bottom values respectively. The default value is an empty string, indicating that the value has not been set. This property can also be set to BaseLine, although some browsers do not support this value.

```
public string VAlign {get; set;}
```

Width

The Width property gets or sets the height of a table cell in pixels. The largest width specified by a cell is taken and then all the cells in the same column have this width. If the Width property specified is less than the width required to display the contents of the table cell, the property is ignored.

```
public string Width {get; set;}
```

HtmlTableCell Class Protected Properties

The `HtmlTableCell` class adds no new protected properties over those inherited from the `Control` class. See Chapter 2 for details.

HtmlTableCell Class Public Events

The `HtmlTableCell` class adds no new public events over those inherited from the `Control` class. See Chapter 2 for details.

HtmlTableRow Class

The `HtmlTableRow` class provides programmatic access to the `<tr>` (table) element on the server. This class represents a row in the table. Please refer to the `HtmlTable` class explanation for an example on the usage of this class.

The `HtmlTableRow` class is inherited from `System.Web.UI.HtmlControls.HtmlContainerControl`.

It has the following syntax:

```
<tr id="id_name"
    align = "horizontal alignment of content in a row"
    bgcolor = "background color of row"
    bordercolor = "border color of row"
    height = "height of table row"
    cells = "collection of table cells"
    valign = "the vertical alignment of row content"
    runat = "server">
  <td>Content of cell</td>
</tr>
```

HtmlTableRow Class Public Methods

The `HtmlTableRow` class adds no new public methods over those inherited from the `Control` class. See Chapter 2 for details.

HtmlTableRow Class Protected Methods

The `HtmlTableRow` class adds no new protected methods over those inherited from the `Control` class. See Chapter 2 for details.

HtmlTableRow Class Public Properties

❑ **Align**

❑ `Attributes` – inherited from `System.Web.UI.HtmlControls.HtmlControl`, see the `HtmlControl` class reference for details.

❑ **BgColor**

❑ **BorderColor**

- ❏ **Cells**

- ❏ Disabled – inherited from `System.Web.UI.HtmlControls.HtmlControl`, see the `HtmlControl` class reference for details.

- ❏ **Height**

- ❏ InnerHtml – inherited from `System.Web.UI.HtmlControls.HtmlContainerControl`, see the `HtmlContainerControl` class for details.

- ❏ InnerText – inherited from `System.Web.UI.HtmlControls.HtmlContainerControl`, see the `HtmlContainerControl` class for details.

- ❏ Style – inherited from `System.Web.UI.HtmlControls.HtmlControl`, see the `HtmlControl` class reference for details.

- ❏ TagName – inherited from `System.Web.UI.HtmlControls.HtmlControl`, see the `HtmlControl` class reference for details.

- ❏ **VAlign**

Align

The `Align` property gets or sets the horizontal alignment of the cells in a table row. The cell contents of a row are aligned to the `Left`, `Center` or `Right` of the cell, when assigned one of these values. The default value is an empty string, indicating that the value is not set. This property can also be set to `Justify` and `Char`, although these are not supported by some of the browsers.

```
public string Align {get; set;}
```

BgColor

The `BgColor` property gets or sets the background color of a table row. The `BgColor` property can be set by assigning one of the predefined sixteen color names or by using a hexadecimal notation preceded by the # symbol. Using a hexadecimal number, any custom color can be assigned to the background color of the table row.

```
public string BgColor {get; set;}
```

BorderColor

The `BorderColor` property gets or sets the border color of a table row. The `BorderColor` property can be set by assigning one of the sixteen predefined color names or by using hexadecimal notation preceded by the # symbol. By using a hexadecimal number, any custom color can be assigned to the border color of the table row.

```
public string BorderColor {get; set;}
```

Cells

The `Cells` property returns a `System.Web.UI.HtmlColtrols.HtmlTableCellCollection` object that contains all of the cells in a table row. An empty `HtmlTableCellCollection` is returned if there are no `Cell` elements within the table row. With the help of the `HtmlTableCellCollection` class properties and methods, the cells of a table row can be added, updated or deleted.

```
public virtual HtmlTableCellCollection Cells {get;}
```

Height

The Height property gets or sets the height of a table row in pixels. If the Height property specified is less than the height required to display the contents of the table row, the property is ignored.

```
public string Height {get; set;}
```

VAlign

The VAlign property gets or sets the vertical alignment of the cells in a table row. The cell contents of a row are aligned to the upper, center, lower edge of the cell when assigned to Top, Middle or Bottom values respectively. The default value is an empty string, indicating that the value is not set. This property can also be set to BaseLine, although some browsers do not support this value.

```
public string VAlign {get; set;}
```

HtmlTableRow Class Protected Properties

The HtmlTableRow class adds no new protected properties over those inherited from the Control class. See Chapter 2 for details.

HtmlTableRow Class Public Events

The HtmlTableRow class adds no new public events over those inherited from the Control class. See Chapter 2 for details.

HtmlTextArea Class

The HtmlTextArea class allows programmatic access to the HTML <textarea> element on the server. This can be used to display or edit large quantities of text. The HtmlTextArea class is inherited from System.Web.UI.HtmlControls.HtmlContainerControl.

It has the following syntax:

```
<textarea id="id_name"
          cols = "number of columns in textarea"
          name = "name of the textarea"
          rows = "number of rows in textarea"
          value = "value of the textarea"
          runat = "server">
   TextArea_Content
</textarea>
```

HtmlTextArea Class Public Methods

The `HtmlTextArea` class adds no new public methods over those inherited from the `Control` class. See Chapter 2 for details.

HtmlTextArea Class Protected Methods

❑ `OnServerChange`

OnServerChange

The `OnServerChange` method raises the `ServerChange` event. Whenever the data is posted to the server, if there is a change in the state of the text area from the previous post to the server, this event is raised. Note, that this event is raised only when the data is posted to the server. The controls state can be changed but the event is raised only when the data is posted to the server, and at that time, if the state is different. The `HtmlTextArea` control must have `ViewState` enabled in order to be able to raise this event correctly. This method allows derived classes to handle the `ServerChange` event directly without attaching to a delegate.

```
protected virtual void OnServerChange(EventArgs e);
```

The parameter e refers to an `EventArgs` object that contains the server change event data.

HtmlTextArea Class Public Properties

❑ `Attributes` – inherited from `System.Web.UI.HtmlControls.HtmlControl`, see the `HtmlControl` class reference for details.

❑ **`Cols`**

❑ `Disabled` – inherited from `System.Web.UI.HtmlControls.HtmlControl`, see the `HtmlControl` class reference for details.

❑ `InnerHtml` – inherited from `System.Web.UI.HtmlControls.HtmlContainerControl`, see the `HtmlContainerControl` class for details.

❑ `InnerText` – inherited from `System.Web.UI.HtmlControls.HtmlContainerControl`, see the `HtmlContainerControl` class for details.

❑ **`Name`**

❑ **`Rows`**

❑ `TagName` – inherited from `System.Web.UI.HtmlControls.HtmlControl`, see the `HtmlControl` class reference for details.

❑ **`Value`**

Cols

The `Cols` property indicates the width in characters of a `HtmlTextArea`. The default value, if nothing is set, is -1. If the text entered is more than the `Cols` property, then the characters will automatically continue on the next line of the control. The `Cols` property corresponds to the `cols` attribute in the `<textarea>` element.

```
public int Cols {get; set;}
```

Name

The Name property assigns or returns a unique identifier for the textarea control. The Name property corresponds to the name attribute in the `<textarea>` element.

```
public virtual string Name {get; set;}
```

Rows

The Rows property indicates the height, in characters, of an HtmlTextArea. The default value is -1. which indicates that no value has been set for this property. If the text entered is more than the rows set in the HtmlTextArea control then scrollbars are enabled. The Rows property corresponds to the rows attribute in the `<textarea>` element.

```
public int Rows {get; set;}
```

Value

The Value property gets or sets the contents of an HtmlTextArea. If there is no text entered in the HtmlTextArea, it returns an empty string object.

```
<textarea value="contents" runat="server">...</textarea>
```

Note that this is equal to `<textarea runat="server">contents</textarea>`.

```
public string Value {get; set;}
```

HtmlTextArea Class Protected Properties

The HtmlTextArea class adds no new protected properties over those inherited from the Control class. See Chapter 2 for details.

HtmlTextArea Class Public Events

❑   **ServerChange**

ServerChange

The ServerChange event is raised whenever there is a change in the state of the HtmlTextArea between posts to the server. Note that this event does not fire when there is a change in the state and no post to the server. The control's state can be changed but the event is raised only when the data is posted to the server, and if at that time the state is different from the previous post. The HtmlTextArea control must have ViewState enabled in order to be able to raise this event correctly. This event is represented on the control by an attribute, onserverchange, which attaches an event handler to the event. We can then write an event handler method that intercepts this event and run some code whenever the event is fired.

```
public event EventHandler ServerChange;
```

Example: Using the HtmlTextArea Class

Let's see the main properties and `ServerChange` event of `HtmlTextArea` class in the following example. This code is available for download with the filename `HtmlTextAreaUsage.aspx`:

```
<%@ Page Language="c#" AutoEventWireup="false"
        Codebehind="HtmlTextAreaUsage.aspx.cs"
        Inherits="systemWebUIHTMLControlsCS.HtmlTextAreaUsage" %>
<!DOCTYPE HTML PUBLIC "-//W3C//DTD HTML 4.0 Transitional//EN">
<HTML>
  <HEAD>
    <title>HtmlTextAreaUsage</title>
    <meta name="GENERATOR"
        content="Microsoft Visual Studio.NET 7.0">
    <meta name="CODE_LANGUAGE" content="C#">
    <meta name="vs_defaultClientScript"
        content="JavaScript">
    <meta name="vs_targetSchema"
        content="http://schemas.microsoft.com/intellisense/ie5">
  </HEAD>
  <body MS_POSITIONING="GridLayout">
    <form id="Form1" method="post" runat="server">
      <div>Please Enter your Hobbies:</div>
      <textarea id="TxtHobby" runat="server" name="TxtHobby"
                Cols="50" Rows="6"
                onServerChange="TxtHobby_ServerChange">
      </textarea>
      <br>
      <input type="submit" runat="server" value="Submit">
      <br>
      <br>
      <div id="Message" runat="server"></div>
    </form>
    </body>
</HTML>
```

The code-behind file, `HtmlTextAreaUsage.aspx.cs`, uses the `TxtHobby_ServerChange` event handler to convert the entered text into uppercase:

```
public class HtmlTextAreaUsage : System.Web.UI.Page
  {
    protected System.Web.UI.HtmlControls.HtmlTextArea TxtHobby;
    protected System.Web.UI.HtmlControls.HtmlInputButton Submit1;
    protected System.Web.UI.HtmlControls.HtmlGenericControl Message;

    private void Page_Load(object sender, System.EventArgs e)
    {
      // Put user code to initialize the page here
    }

    protected void TxtHobby_ServerChange(object sender, System.EventArgs e)
    {
```

```
TxtHobby.Value = TxtHobby.Value.ToUpper();
    }
```

Here is a screenshot showing the output:

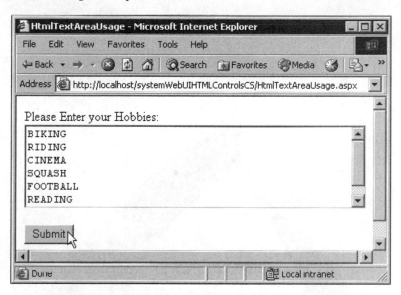

4

System.Web.UI.WebControls

The System.Web.UI.WebControls namespace provides the classes that constitute the major elements in user interface development in most ASP.NET applications. The classes in this namespace are also frequently referred to as Web server controls or just Web controls. In the previous chapter we presented a reference for HTML server controls, the server-side equivalent of the corresponding HTML tags. In this chapter you will find that Web controls duplicates the majority of the functionality provided by HTML server controls as well as providing a whole bunch of extra capabilities. You will wonder, why this duplication? This is because, unlike the HTML server controls, the Web server controls do not drag the HTML legacy with them. The Web server controls provide a much cleaner and intuitive programming model for user interface programming. For example, the HTML controls mix two distinct user interface elements in a single tag (<input type="checkbox"> and <input type="button"> to represent a checkbox and a button respectively). On the other hand, in the Web controls, we can use their names directly: <asp:Checkbox> and <asp:Button>, for example. Having this intuitive arrangement can simplify the process of creating interactive web pages.

All of the Web controls are used by simply adding the asp: namespace prefix (upper and lower case are equally acceptable) to indicate that the control belongs to the System.Web.UI.WebControls namespace. Like the HTML controls in the previous chapter, there's no need to import any namespaces into your .aspx page to use these controls. Note that, as with any other XML element, all web controls must have well-formed names that don't overlap – controls must have either an ending slash within the tag or a separate closing tag: <asp:Checkbox runat="server" /> or <asp:Checkbox runat="server">...</asp:Checkbox>, for example.

> This chapter differs in its format from the other chapters in that we are not going to provide a complete listing of every inherited member for each derived class. We are going to concentrate our coverage on those new members that the derived classes add. There is a detailed listing of all members of the **WebControl** class, and because all Web controls inherit from that class you should look there for a complete list of every inherited member for every control.

Here is a list of the classes available in the `System.Web.UI.WebControls` namespace:

Class	Description
AdCreatedEventArgs	This class provides data for the `AdCreated` event of the `AdRotator` control. It is a sealed class.
AdRotator	The **AdRotator** class provides a convenient mechanism for displaying advertisements randomly on a web page. It selects the images from a list stored in an XML file and is capable of changing the images every time the page is loaded. It makes advertisement management much easier and more practical.
BaseCompareValidator	Serves as the abstract base class for validation controls that perform typed comparisons.
BaseDataList	This is the base class from which all data listing controls, such as the **DataList** and **DataGrid**, are inherited.
BaseValidator	The **BaseValidator** class is a base class for the validation controls. This class defines the properties, methods and events common to all validation controls. Validation controls are used to validate input controls. Different types of validation controls can be associated with an input control and the associated input control's value can be validated against different types of validation.
BoundColumn	Creates columns bound to a field in the data source. A `BoundColumn` will depict each item in the bound field as text, and is the default column type of the `DataGrid` control.
Button	A **Button** control renders a clickable push-button on a Web page. The **Button** Web control submits the form to the server and it can raise an event that fires the appropriate event code in server-side script.
ButtonColumn	Displays a command button for each item in a `ButtonColumn` of the `DataGrid` control.
Calendar	The **Calendar** control displays a lively month-by-month calendar control on the web page. It allows easy navigation to select a particular day, week, and month or even selecting a range of days. It also allows you to customize the appearance of the control and even add custom content for each day.
CalendarDay	Represents a particular date in the `Calendar` control.
CheckBox	The **CheckBox** class displays a checkbox on a web page to let the user select either **true** or **false** for a given value.
CheckBoxList	The **CheckBoxList** control represents a list of checkboxes, allowing for multiple selection of the checkboxes in the list.

Class	Description
CommandEventArgs	Provides data for the Command event.
CompareValidator	**The CompareValidator control is used to compare a input control's value against another value. The CompareValidator control when associated with an input control ensures that the associated control has a valid value eliminating the need to write validation logic to check for comparisons of datat ypes or against some value.**
CustomValidator	**The CustomValidator control allows you to build a validation control with your own specification. The validation controls provided by ASP.NET handle a wide variety of validations. However, every application has its own custom requirements for validation. Those validations can be easily covered by using the CustomValidator class.**
DataGrid	**A data-bound list control that allows us to easily show, edit, page, and sort our data on a web page.**
DataGridColumn	The base class for the different column types of the DataGrid control.
DataGridColumnCollection	A collection of DataGridColumn objects representing the columns in a DataGrid control. This class cannot be inherited.
DataGridCommandEventArgs	Provides data for the CancelCommand, DeleteCommand, EditCommand, ItemCommand, and UpdateCommand events of the DataGrid control. This class cannot be inherited.
DataGridItem	Represents one row in a DataGrid control.
DataGridItemCollection	Represents a collection of DataGridItem objects in a DataGrid control.
DataGridItemEventArgs	Provides data for the ItemCreated and ItemDataBound events of the DataGrid control. This class cannot be inherited.
DataGridPageChangedEvent Args	Provides data for the PageIndexChanged event of the DataGrid control. This class cannot be inherited.
DataGridPagerStyle	Allows you to change the way pagination is rendered in a DataGrid control. This class cannot be inherited.
DataGridSortCommandEvent Args	Provides data for the SortCommand event of the DataGrid control. This class cannot be inherited.
DataKeyCollection	Represents a collection containing the key for each record in a data source. This class cannot be inherited.
DataList	**Displays data in a table form that can be edited and selected by the user, and you can configure how the control should appear by using templates.**

Class	Description
DataListCommandEventArgs	Provides data for the CancelCommand, DeleteCommand, EditCommand, ItemCommand, and UpdateCommand events of the DataList control. This class cannot be inherited.
DataListItem	Represents an item in the DataList control.
DataListItemCollection	Represents the collection of DataListItem objects in the DataList control. This class cannot be inherited.
DataListItemEventArgs	Provides data for the ItemCreated and ItemDataBound events of a DataList control. This class cannot be inherited.
DayRenderEventArgs	Provides data for the DayRender event of the Calendar control. This class cannot be inherited.
DropDownList	**The DropDownList control allows the user to select a single item from a drop-down list.**
EditCommandColumn	Displays a column with editing capability in the DataGrid control.
FontInfo	Encapsulates the font properties of text. This class cannot be inherited.
FontNamesConverter	Converts a string containing a list of font names to an array of strings containing the individual names. It also performs the reverse function.
FontUnitConverter	Converts a FontUnit to an object with another data type. It also converts an object with another data type to a FontUnit.
HyperLink	**The HyperLink control displays a link on a Web page that allows navigation to another page (URL). The link can be an image or a text. The HyperLink control does not post the form to the server.**
HyperLinkColumn	These types of columns in a DataGrid control display the contents of the items they contain as hyperlinks.
HyperLinkControlBuilder	Interacts with the parser to build a HyperLink control.
Image	**The Image control displays an image on a web page or alternate text if the image is not available.**
ImageButton	**The ImageButton control enables you to click an image on a web page as if it was a Button control. It submits the form to the server and it can raise an event that fires the appropriate event code in the server-side script.**
Label	**The Label control displays static text on a web page and allows you to manipulate it programmatically.**
LabelControlBuilder	Interacts with the parser to build a Label control.

278

Class	Description
LinkButton	The LinkButton control has the appearance of a HyperLink but acts like a Button control. The LinkButton web control submits the form to the server and it can raise an event that fires the appropriate event code in the server-side script.
LinkButtonControlBuilder	Interacts with the parser to build a LinkButton control.
ListBox	The ListBox control represents a list of items in a list box. It allows the user to select multiple items in the list enabling multiple and single item selection.
ListControl	The Listcontrol class is the base class for all the list-type controls. This class defines the properties, methods and events common to all inherited list controls like CheckBoxList, DropDownList, ListBox, and RadioButtonList. List controls are used to present a list of data to the user from which the user can select. This can be multiple as well as single selection.
ListItem	Represents a data item in a data-bound list control. This class cannot be inherited.
ListItemCollection	A collection of ListItem objects in a list control. This class cannot be inherited.
ListItemControlBuilder	Interacts with the parser to build a ListItem control.
Literal	The Literal control displays static text on a web page and allows you to manipulate it programmatically.
LiteralControlBuilder	Interacts with the parser to build a Literal control.
MonthChangedEventArgs	Provides data for the VisibleMonthChanged event of a Calendar. This class cannot be inherited.
PagedDataSource	Encapsulates the properties of the DataGrid control that allow it to perform paging. This class cannot be inherited.
Panel	The Panel class acts as a container for other controls. The Panel class can be used to control the visibility of its child controls. It can also be used to load its child controls programmatically.
PlaceHolder	The PlaceHolder control reserves an area of a web page in which you may add, insert, and remove items programmatically via the Control.Controls collection of a PlaceHolder instance.
PlaceHolderControl Builder	Interacts with the parser to build a PlaceHolder control.
RadioButton	The RadioButton control represents radio buttons on a Web page, which allows the user to select one of a set of mutually exclusive choices.
RadioButtonList	The RadioButtonList control represents a list of RadioButton controls. It allows the user to select only a single radio button from the list.

Class	Description
RangeValidator	The **RangeValidator** control is used to check whether the input control's value is within the specified range of values.
RegularExpression Validator	Extends the abstract BaseValidator class to check that the value of ControlToValidate falls within a specified range.
Repeater	This is like a simplified **DataList** control in that it only allows for displaying data, and doesn't support any editing, paging, or sorting.
RepeaterCommandEventArgs	Provides data for the ItemCommand event of a Repeater. This class cannot be inherited.
RepeaterItem	Represents an item in the Repeater control.
RepeaterItemCollection	Represents a collection of RepeaterItem objects in the Repeater control. This class cannot be inherited.
RepeaterItemEventArgs	Provides data for the ItemCreated and ItemDataBound events of a Repeater.
RepeatInfo	Encapsulates the information used to render a list control that repeats a list of items. This class cannot be inherited.
RequiredFieldValidator	The **RequiredFieldValidator** control ensures that the **ControlToValidate** has a value. It does not perform any validation on the control's value, merely verifying that a value has been provided.
SelectedDatesCollection	Encapsulates a collection of System.DateTime objects that represent the selected dates in a Calendar control. This class cannot be inherited.
ServerValidateEventArgs	Provides data for the ServerValidate event of the CustomValidator control. This class cannot be inherited.
Style	Represents the style of a Web server control as defined in a CSS file.
Table	The **Table** control allows you to build a table on a web page and set its properties. This helps you present data in tabular format.
TableCell	The **TableCell** control allows you to create an individual cell in a **Table** control.
TableCellCollection	Encapsulates a collection of TableHeaderCell and TableCell objects that make up a row in a Table control. This class cannot be inherited.
TableCellControlBuilder	Interacts with the parser to build a TableCell control.
TableHeaderCell	Represents a heading cell within a Table control.
TableItemStyle	Represents the style properties for an element of a control that renders as a TableRow or TableCell.
TableRow	The **TableRow** control represents a row in a **Table** control.

Class	Description
TableRowCollection	Encapsulates a collection of TableRow objects that represent a single row in a Table control. This class cannot be inherited.
TableStyle	Represents the style for a table control, encapsulating the properties which can control a Table control's appearance.
TargetConverter	Converts a value representing the location (target) to display the content resulting from web navigation to a string. It also converts a string to a target value.
TemplateColumn	Allows you to customize the layout of controls in a particular column of a DataGrid.
TextBox	**The TextBox control displays a textbox on a web page for user input. However, it can also be used to display text that is read-only. The textbox can render three different forms of input controls. It can be rendered as the HTML \<input type=text\>, \<input type=password\> and \<textarea\>, depending on the setting of its** TextMode **property.**
TextBoxControlBuilder	Interacts with the parser to build a TextBox control.
UnitConverter	Converts a Unit to an object of another data type. It also converts an object of another data type to a Unit.
ValidatedControl Converter	Converts a control to a string ready for validation by a Validation control.
ValidationSummary	**The ValidationSummary control displays a summary of all validation errors. It can display a summary in a web page or message box or both. This control is very helpful as it can provide a group of errors for the user to fix instead of confronting them with one error message at a time.**
WebColorConverter	Converts a predefined color name or an RGB color value to and from a System.Drawing.Color object.
WebControl	**The WebControl class acts as a base class for all Web controls and provides basic properties, methods and events that are inherited by all ASP.NET Web server controls.**
Xml	**The Xml control displays an unformatted XML document or a formatted XML document using an XSL Transformation on a web page.**

AdRotator Class

The `AdRotator` class provides a convenient mechanism for displaying advertisements randomly on a web page. It selects the images from a list stored in an XML file and changes the images every time the page is loaded. It makes advertisement management much easier and more practical. In the previous incarnation of ASP, we had to use an `ActiveX` object to achieve rich features. In ASP.NET, the `AdRotator` control is a dream for developers and administrators alike. The advertisements are detailed in an XML-based file, and thanks to the `PostBack` feature of .NET, when an advertisement is clicked, functions on the server can be executed to perform whatever task is appropriate to that advertisement.

```
<asp:AdRotator id = "id_name"
    AdvertisementFile = "XML file of advertisement"
    KeyWordFilter = "KeyWord"
    Target = "Display type"
    OnAdCreated = "AdCreatedEventHandler"
    Runat = "server" />
```

AdRotator Class Public Methods

The `AdRotator` class adds no new public methods to those inherited from the `WebControl` class. See the `WebControl` class reference for a complete listing.

AdRotator Class Protected Methods

❑ **OnAdCreated**

OnAdCreated

The `OnAdCreated` method raises the `AdCreated` event. This method notifies the server of the actions to be performed when the `AdRotator` control is created but before it is rendered in the web page. This method allows derived classes to handle the `AdCreated` event without attaching to a delegate.

```
protected virtual void OnAdCreated(AdCreatedEventArgs e);
```

The parameter e refers to an `AdCreatedEventArgs` object that contains the event-related data. Please refer to the `AdCreated` event for detailed information on the `AdCreatedEventArgs` object.

AdRotator Class Public Properties

❑ **AdvertisementFile**

❑ **KeywordFilter**

❑ **Target**

AdvertisementFile

The `AdvertisementFile` property gets or sets the path of the XML advertisement file that contains the list of advertisements (images) to be displayed.

```
public string AdvertisementFile {get; set;}
```

A typical advertisement file is shown below to illustrate the format that is followed (it's also part of advertisements.xml, which you can find in the code download for this chapter):

```
<Advertisements>
  <Ad>
    <ImageUrl>wrox.gif</ImageUrl>
    <NavigateUrl>http://www.wrox.com</NavigateUrl>
    <AlternateText>Wrox Press</AlternateText>
    <Impressions>50</Impressions>
    <Keyword>Books</Keyword>
  </Ad>
  <Ad>
    <ImageUrl>asptoday.gif</ImageUrl>
    <NavigateUrl>http://www.asptoday.com</NavigateUrl>
    <AlternateText>ASP Today</AlternateText>
    <Impressions>40</Impressions>
    <Keyword>Online Resources</Keyword>
    <AnnualSubscription>99</AnnualSubscription>
  </Ad>
</Advertisements>
```

The <Advertisements> tag is the root element of the XML file. The details of each advertisement are stored in an <Ad> element. Let's summarize the XML elements for a particular advertisement, as contained within a single <Ad> element:

Element	Description
<ImageUrl>	The URL of the image file to be displayed as an advertisement. This can be either the absolute or relative path to the URL of the image.
<NavigateUrl>	The URL of the page that is displayed when the advertisement image is clicked. If this is not set, then the advertisement is shown without a link.
<AlternateText>	If the image is not available for whatever reason, then this text is shown in the place of the image. For Internet Explorer, this attribute also behaves like a ToolTip property.
<Keyword>	The Keyword attribute can be used to organize related advertisements into groups by giving all advertisements of a certain type the same keyword. This keyword can then be used to filter out other advertisement types using the KeywordFilter property.
<Impressions>	A weighting indicating how often the image should be displayed on a web page relative to the other advertisements in the XML file.

In addition to the above elements, you can also add custom tags to include custom properties. For example, the advertisement file we show above contains an `<AnnualSubscription>` custom tag for the `ASPToday` advertisement to hold the annual subscription amount. We can access the custom tag with the help of the `AdProperties` property of the `AdCreatedEventArgs` object. Please refer to the *AdCreated Event* reference for detailed information.

KeywordFilter

The `KeywordFilter` property relates to the `<Keyword>` element of the XML advertisement file. The `Keyword` attribute is used to organize related advertisements into groups by giving all advertisements of a certain type the same keyword. You can set the `KeywordFilter` property and filter for advertisements with a matching `Keyword` element. The default is an empty string.

```
public string KeywordFilter {get; set;}
```

For example, the following code will set the `KeywordFilter` to `OnlineResources` resulting in the `AdRotator` control only displaying those advertisements for which the `Keyword` element is set to `OnlineResources`:

```
<asp:adrotator id="AdWrox" runat="server" Width="200px" Height="60px"
    AdvertisementFile="advertisements.xml"
    KeywordFilter="Online Resources"></asp:adrotator>
```

Target

The `Target` property gets or sets the name of the browser window or frame to be used to display the contents of the linked web page when the `AdRotator` control is clicked. The value of this property is case-insensitive and must begin with an alphabetical character (a-z) except for some special values that begin with the underscore symbol.

```
public string Target {get; set;}
```

The following table summarizes what the special values mean in the context of the `Target` property:

Value	Description
_blank	A new and unframed browser window is used to render the content.
_parent	The immediate frameset parent in the same browser is used to render the content.
_self	The current frame in the same browser window renders the content.
_top	The full and unframed window in the same browser renders the content.

The default value is an empty string, meaning that the new page will display in the current frame or window.

AdRotator Class Protected Properties

The AdRotator class adds no new protected properties to those inherited from the WebControl class. See the WebControl class reference for a complete listing.

AdRotator Class Public Events

❏ **AdCreated**

AdCreated

The AdCreated event is raised once per round-trip to the server after the creation of the control, but before the page is rendered. It is raised before the advertisement is rendered and after the advertisement is retrieved from the advertisement XML file.

```
public event AdCreatedEventHandler AdCreated;
```

The event handler receives information related to the event through the AdCreatedEventArgs object, passed as its argument. The following table details the properties of AdCreatedEventArgs:

Property	Description
AdProperties	Gets an object that contains all the advertisement properties for the currently displayed advertisement. This object represents a collection of key-value pairs and also includes custom properties, if any defined.
AlternateText	If the image is not available, then this text appears in the place of the image on the page. For Internet Explorer, this attribute is just like the ToolTip property.
ImageUrl	The URL of the image file to be displayed as the advertisement banner on the Web page.
NavigateUrl	The URL of the page to be displayed when the advertisement image is clicked.

Example: Using the AdRotator Control

The following example shows how to set the properties of the AdRotator control. It also shows how custom elements in the advertisement file can be used. You can find this code in the download for this chapter in AdRotatorUsage.aspx. Here is the user interface:

```
<asp:AdRotator id="AdWrox"
               runat="server"
               Width="200px"
               Height="60px"
               AdvertisementFile="advertisements.xml"
               Target="_blank"></asp:AdRotator>
<asp:Label id="LblSubscription"
           runat="server"
           Width="196px">
```

Chapter 4: System.Web.UI.WebControls

```
    </asp:Label>
```

When the advertisement image is clicked on the page a new window pops up and displays the web site that the advertisement is for. The `advertisements.xml` file contains a custom element `<AnnualSubscription>` to hold the subscription amount:

```xml
<?xml version="1.0" ?>
<Advertisements>
  <Ad>
    <ImageUrl>wrox.gif</ImageUrl>
    <NavigateUrl>http://www.wrox.com</NavigateUrl>
    <AlternateText>Wrox Press</AlternateText>
    <Impressions>50</Impressions>
    <Keyword>Books</Keyword>
  </Ad>
  <Ad>
    <ImageUrl>asptoday.gif</ImageUrl>
    <NavigateUrl>http://www.asptoday.com</NavigateUrl>
    <AlternateText>ASP Today</AlternateText>
    <Impressions>40</Impressions>
    <Keyword>Online Resources</Keyword>
    <AnnualSubscription>99</AnnualSubscription>
  </Ad>
  <Ad>
    <ImageUrl>csharptoday.gif</ImageUrl>
    <NavigateUrl>http://www.csharptoday.com</NavigateUrl>
    <AlternateText>CSharp Today</AlternateText>
    <Impressions>40</Impressions>
    <Keyword>Online Resources</Keyword>
    <AnnualSubscription>99</AnnualSubscription>
  </Ad>
</Advertisements>
```

The following code shows how we can hook into the `AdCreated` event to get access to the custom element we created:

```csharp
private void AdWrox_AdCreated(object sender,
                    System.Web.UI.WebControls.AdCreatedEventArgs e)
{
    if(((string)e.AdProperties["AnnualSubscription"]) != null)
      LblSubscription.Text = "The Annual Subscription is $"
                    + (string)e.AdProperties["AnnualSubscription"];
}
```

Here is a screenshot showing the `AnnualSubscription` property when the advertisement containing the `<AnnualSubscription>` element is shown. It also shows the `AlternateText` and `NavigateUrl` attributes in action:

BaseDataList Class

The `MustInherit BaseDataList` class is a base class for the data listing controls and is itself inherited from `System.Web.UI.WebControls.WebControl`. This class defines the properties, methods and events common to its inherited `DataGrid` and `DataList` controls. Data listing controls are used to display and manipulate the records of a data source on a web page.

BaseDataList Class Public Methods

❏ **DataBind**

❏ **IsBindableType**

DataBind

The `DataBind` method binds the data listing control and its child controls to the data source specified by the `DataSource` property.

```
public override void DataBind();
```

IsBindableType

The static `IsBindableType` method determines whether the data type can be bound to a list control that derives from the `BaseDataList` class. This method will return a `Boolean` value, `true` meaning that binding is allowed, or `false` meaning that binding will not work, depending on whether the data type is supported. Supported data types are `Boolean`, `Byte`, `SByte`, `Int16`, `UInt16`, `Int32`, `UInt32`, `Int64`, `UInt64`, `Char`, `Double`, `Single`, `DateTime`, `Decimal`, and `String`.

```
public static bool IsBindableType(Type type);
```

The parameter `type` refers to the data type to test.

BaseDataList Class Protected Methods

- ❑ `OnSelectedIndexChanged`

OnSelectedIndexChanged

The `OnSelectedIndexChanged` method will raise the `SelectedIndexChanged` event when the selection in the data listing control is changed between posts to the server. This method allows derived classes to handle the `SelectedIndexChanged` event directly without attaching to a delegate.

```
protected virtual void OnSelectedIndexChanged(EventArgs e);
```

The parameter e contains the event data to be passed in.

BaseDataList Class Public Properties

- ❑ `CellPadding`
- ❑ `CellSpacing`
- ❑ `Controls`
- ❑ `DataKeyField`
- ❑ `DataKeys`
- ❑ `DataMember`
- ❑ `DataSource`
- ❑ `GridLines`

ellPadding

The `CellPadding` property gets or sets the width in pixels between the border of a cell and the contents of a cell in the data list control. The default value is −1 indicating that the property is not set. The `CellPadding` is applied to all the four sides of the contents of the cell. Because all cells in a particular column or row share the same cell width or height, the `CellPadding` will always be the same as the widest or tallest cell in that column or row.

```
public virtual int CellPadding {get; set;}
```

CellSpacing

The `CellSpacing` property gets or sets the width in pixels between the individual cells in the data list control. The default value is 0. The `CellSpacing` is applied both horizontally and vertically in a uniform manner to cells in the control, and it is not possible to set values for `CellSpacing` between individual cells.

```
public virtual int CellSpacing {get; set;}
```

Controls

The `Controls` property returns a collection of all the child controls in the data listing control. This property returns a `System.Web.UI.ControlCollection` object that represents a collection of child controls. This collection object can then be used to add, remove or update child controls in the data listing control.

```
public override ControlCollection Controls {get;}
```

DataKeyField

The `DataKeyField` property gets or sets the name of the primary key field of the data source. This property allows you to store the key field without displaying it in the data list control. This property is stored in the `DataKeyCollection` that contains the `DataKeyField` objects for all the records in the data list control. This property can then be used to retrieve the primary key field value in the event handler. This would help us to know the record for which the particular event was raised.

```
public virtual string DataKeyField {get; set;}
```

DataKeys

The `DataKeys` property gets a collection of key fields from the data source. It returns a `DataKeyCollection` object that contains the `DataKeyField` for all the records in the data list control. This property is mostly used to fetch the key values of each record in a data listing control.

```
public DataKeyCollection DataKeys {get;}
```

DataMember

The `DataMember` property indicates the data member of the data source with which the data list control is bound. This property is very helpful when the `DataSource` has multiple sets of members to bind to. For example, a `DataSet` object can be a `DataSource`, and a specific table in the `DataSet` can become the `DataMember` of the data list control.

```
public string DataMember {get; set;}
```

DataSource

The `DataSource` property gets or sets the data source to which you want to bind the data list control. The individual item elements in the data list control will be filled with the data available in the `DataSource`. The `DataSource` property should contain an object which implements `System.Collections.IEnumerable`. The default value is `null`. If the `DataSource` has multiple sets of members to bind to, then the `DataMember` property can be used to indicate the desired member name.

```
public virtual object DataSource {get; set;}
```

Gridlines

The `Gridlines` property gets or sets the border between the cells of the data list control to be displayed. The valid values of this property belong to the `GridLines` enumeration:

- ❑ `Horizontal` – only horizontal grid lines appear
- ❑ `Vertical` – only vertical grid lines appear
- ❑ `None`
- ❑ `Both` (Default value of this property)

```
public virtual GridLines GridLines {get; set;}
```

HorizontalAlign

This property gets or sets the horizontal alignment of a control with respect to its container. The valid values of this property belong to the `HorizontalAlign` enumeration. They are:

- ❑ `Center`
- ❑ `Justify`
- ❑ `Left`
- ❑ `NotSet` (Default value for this property)
- ❑ `Right`

```
public virtual HorizontalAlign HorizontalAlign {get; set;}
```

BaseDataList Class Protected Properties

The `BaseDataList` class adds no new protected properties to those inherited from the `WebControl` class. See the `WebControl` class reference for a complete listing.

BaseDataList Class Public Events

- ❑ **SelectedIndexChanged**

SelectedIndexChanged

The `SelectedIndexChanged` event occurs whenever a selection in the data list control changes between posts to the server. The data list control raises this event if a different selection is made from the previous post to the server.

```
public event EventHandler SelectedIndexChanged;
```

The event handler receives information related to the event through the `EventArgs` object, passed as its argument.

BaseValidator Class

The `MustInherit BaseValidator` class is a base class for the validation controls. This class is inherited from the `System.Web.UI.WebControls.Label` class. This class defines the properties, methods and events common to all validation controls. Validation controls are used to validate the values that a user puts into input controls on a Web Form. Different types of validation controls can be associated with an input control and the associated input control's value can be validated against different validatory values. Validation controls perform validation both at the server and client side. However, validation at the client side depends on the capabilities of the browser and the setting of the `ClientTarget` attribute in the `Page` directive of the Web Form. Client-side validation is performed if the browser supports ECMAScript 1.2 or later and the browser supports the Internet Explorer Document Object Model 4.0 or later.

BaseValidator Class Public Methods

- ❑ **GetValidationProperty**
- ❑ **Validate**

GetValidationProperty

The `GetValidationProperty` method is a helper function that returns the validation property of the control to be validated specified by the `ControlToValidate` property. It returns a `PropertyDescriptor` object that represents the validation property of the associated input control.

```
public static PropertyDescriptor GetValidationProperty(object component);
```

The parameter `component` represents the control whose validation property is to be retrieved.

Validate

The `Validate` method performs validation on the input control specified by the `ControlToValidate` property and then updates the `IsValid` property. This method allows you to perform validation programmatically.

```
public void Validate();
```

BaseValidator Class Protected Methods

- ❑ **CheckControlValidationProperty**
- ❑ **ControlPropertiesValid**
- ❑ **DetermineRenderUpLevel**
- ❑ **EvaluateIsValid**
- ❑ **GetControlRenderID**
- ❑ **GetControlValidationValue**
- ❑ **RegisterValidatorCommonScript**
- ❑ **RegisterValidatorDeclaration**

CheckControlValidationProperty

The `CheckControlValidationProperty` method is a helper function called mainly by the `ControlPropertiesValid` method to verify whether the specified control is on the page and contains validation properties. This method does not return anything, instead it throws an `HttpException` when verification fails.

```
protected void CheckControlValidationProperty(string name,
                                              string propertyName);
```

The parameter `name` specifies the control to be validated.

ControlPropertiesValid

The `ControlPropertiesValid` returns `true` or `false` indicating whether the input control to be validated is valid.

```
protected virtual bool ControlPropertiesValid();
```

DetermineRenderUpLevel

The `DetermineRenderUpLevel` method determines whether the validation control can be rendered as an uplevel browser. It returns `true` if the browser supports uplevel rendering for validation controls, `false` otherwise.

```
protected virtual bool DetermineRenderUplevel();
```

EvaluateIsValid

The `EvaluateIsValid` method is used to determine whether the control to be validated contains a valid value. It returns `true` if the input control is valid and `false` otherwise.

```
protected abstract bool EvaluateIsValid();
```

GetControlRenderID

The `GetControlRenderID` method gets the `ClientID` of the control passed as its argument.

```
protected string GetControlRenderID(string name);
```

GetControlValidationValue

The `GetControlValidationValue` method gets the value of the input control passed as its argument.

```
protected string GetControlValidationValue(string name);
```

RegisterValidatorCommonScript

The `RegisterValidatorCommonScript` method registers the code on the web page for client-side validation.

```
protected void RegisterValidatorCommonScript();
```

RegisterValidatorDeclaration

The `RegisterValidatorDeclaration` method registers an `ECMAScript` array declaration with `Page_Validators` as the array name.

```
protected virtual void RegisterValidatorDeclaration();
```

BaseValidator Class Public Properties

- ❑ **`ControlToValidate`**
- ❑ **`Display`**
- ❑ **`EnableClientScript`**
- ❑ **`ErrorMessage`**
- ❑ **`ForeColor`**
- ❑ **`IsValid`**
- ❑ **`Text`**

ControlToValidate

The `ControlToValidate` property specifies the ID of the input control that needs to be validated. The ID of the input control must refer to a control within the same naming container as the validation control. In the case of templated controls, both the controls must be within the same template. The ID must refer to a valid input control's ID for all validation controls otherwise an `Exception` will be thrown. However for `CustomValidator` this property can be left blank.

```
public string ControlToValidate {get; set;}
```

Display

The `Display` property specifies how to display the error message of a validation control contained in the `Text` property. The valid values for this property belong to the `ValidatorDisplay` enumeration. An `ArgumentException` is thrown if this property is set with a value other than one of the `ValidatorDisplay` values. The possible values of the `ValidatorDisplay` enumeration are:

Alignment	Description
Dynamic	If the validation fails, the space for the error message inline is dynamically added.
None	The validation message is never displayed inline.
Static	The space for the message is added when the validation control is rendered.

```
public ValidatorDisplay Display {get; set;}
```

EnableClientScript

The `EnableClientScript` property enables or disables client-side validation. The default value is `true` indicating that client-side validation is enabled; a value of `false` indicates client-side validation is disabled.

```
public bool EnableClientScript {get; set;}
```

Enabled

The `Enabled` property gets or sets a `Boolean` value indicating whether a validation control is enabled. The default value is `true` indicating that the validation control is enabled; a value of `false` indicates the validation control is disabled and no validation will occur.

```
public override bool Enabled {get; set;}
```

ErrorMessage

The `ErrorMessage` property specifies error message text that is displayed when the validation fails. Normally the `Text` property is used to display the error message produced by the validation control. However, if the `Text` property is not set, then the validation control displays the value of this property. The `ErrorMessage` property is displayed by the `ValidationSummary` control if the summary control has been added to the web page.

```
public string ErrorMessage {get; set;}
```

ForeColor

The `ForeColor` property specifies the fore color of the message displayed when the validation fails. This property is overridden here. The default value is `Color.Red`. This property can be set to any custom color using the `System.Drawing.Color` structure.

```
public override Color ForeColor {get; set;}
```

IsValid

The `IsValid` gets or sets the validation test result. If the validation succeeds it has a value of `true`, otherwise `false`. The default value is `true`; the value gets changed after validation depending on whether the associated input control passed the validation. This property can also be used to set the validation result.

```
public bool IsValid {get; set;}
```

Text

The `Text` property specifies the text of the error message that is displayed by the validation control. The validation summary control displays the value of the `ErrorMessage` property if the summary control is added to the web page. This property is inherited from the `System.Web.UI.WebControls.Label` class.

```
public virtual string Text {get; set;}
```

BaseValidator Class Protected Properties

❑ **PropertiesValid**

❑ **RenderUpLevel**

PropertiesValid

The `PropertiesValid` property returns a value that indicates the validity of the input control specified by the `ControlToValidate` property. If the `ControlToValidate` is not specified or if the ID specified does not exist in the page then an `HttpException` occurs.

```
protected bool PropertiesValid {get;}
```

RenderUpLevel

The `RenderUpLevel` property returns a value that indicates whether the browser supports uplevel rendering. That means it supports client-side scripting version 1.2 or higher and Internet Explorer Document Object Model 4.0 or higher. A value of `true` indicates that the browser supports uplevel rendering, `false` otherwise.

```
protected bool RenderUplevel {get;}
```

BaseValidator Class Public Events

The `BaseValidator` class adds no new public events to those inherited from the `WebControl` class. See the `WebControl` class reference for a complete listing.

Button Class

A `Button` control renders a clickable push-button on a Web page. The `Button` web control submits the form to the server and it can raise an event that fires the appropriate event code in our server-side script. It is inherited from the `System.Web.UI.WebControls.WebControl` class.

It corresponds to the `<input type="submit">` in HTML controls. It has the following syntax:

```
<asp: Button id="id_name"
    Text = "button's caption"
    CommandName = "Command name"
    CommandArgument = "Command argument"
    Onclick = "event name" | OnCommand = "event name"
    Runat = "server" />
```

You can create either a Submit button or a Command button on a web page with the `Button` control. When you don't specify a `CommandName` property, the button is by default a Submit button. You can provide an event handler for the `Click` event to programmatically control the actions performed when the Submit button is clicked.

A button with a command name is called a Command button. You can create Command buttons by specifying the `CommandName` property, which is used to programmatically determine the button that was clicked. You can also provide additional information in the `CommandArgument` property for a button. Furthermore, you can specify an event handler for the `Command` event that programmatically controls the action performed when the Command button is clicked.

Button Class Public Methods

The `Button` class adds no new public methods to those inherited from the `WebControl` class. See the `WebControl` class reference for a complete listing.

Button Class Protected Methods

❑ **OnClick**

❑ **OnCommand**

OnClick

The `OnClick` method will raise a 'Click' event when a button is clicked. This method notifies to the server the actions to be performed when the button control is clicked and the form is submitted to the server. This method allows derived classes to handle the `Click` event without attaching to a delegate.

```
protected virtual void OnClick(EventArgs e);
```

OnCommand

The `Command` event is raised when a Command button is clicked. A Command button must have the `CommandName` and `CommandArgument` properties specified. This method notifies to the server the actions to be performed when the Command button control is clicked and the form is submitted to the server. This method allows derived classes to handle the `Command` event without attaching to a delegate.

```
protected virtual void OnCommand(CommandEventArgs e);
```

The parameter e receives information related to the event through the `CommandEventArgs` object. This object contains the `CommandName` and `CommandArgument` properties.

Button Class Public Properties

❑ **CausesValidation**

❑ **CommandArgument**

❑ **CommandName**

❑ **Text**

CausesValidation

The `CausesValidation` property is used to specify whether validation should be performed when the `Button` control is clicked. The validation is performed by the ASP.NET validation controls (if any) associated with the server controls in the page. This property therfore causes the validation controls to perform a validation test if set to `true`; if set to `false` no validation occurs. The default value is `true`. Sometimes, it is necessary to submit the page without validation, for example in the event of a cancel or reset button being clicked. This property when `true` may perform validation at both client and server-side depending on the browser's capabilities and the setting of the `ClientTarget` attribute in the `Page` directive.

```
public bool CausesValidation {get; set;}
```

CommandArgument

The `CommandArgument` property gets or sets an argument for a Command Button. When you set the `CommandName` property indicating that the button is a Command button, then this property provides the means for passing arguments to a `Command` event. The default value is an empty string. If this property is set, then it passes its value to the `Command` event when the button is clicked.

```
public string CommandArgument {get; set;}
```

CommandName

The `CommandName` property gets or sets the name of the command associated with the `Button` control. This value is passed to the `Command` event when the button is clicked. This command name can be used on the server to determine which button control was triggered. The default value is an empty string.

```
public string CommandName {get; set;}
```

Text

The `Text` property gets or sets the caption text for the button. The default value is an empty string.

```
public string Text {get; set;}
```

Button Class Protected Properties

The `Button` class adds no new protected properties to those inherited from the `WebControl` class. See the `WebControl` class reference for a complete listing.

Button Class Public Events

❑ **Click**

❑ **Command**

Click

The `Click` event will occur when a button control is clicked and the form is submitted to the server. The event is only raised for Submit buttons. A Submit button is a button control that does not have `CommandName` and `CommandArgument` properties specified.

```
public event EventHandler Click;
```

The event handler receives information related to the event through the `EventArgs` object, passed as its argument.

Command

The `Command` event will occur when a `Button` control is clicked and the form is submitted to the server. The event is only raised for Command buttons. Command buttons specify `CommandName` and `CommandArgument` properties for the button control.

```
public event CommandEventHandler Command;
```

The event handler receives information related to the event through the `CommandEventArgs` object, passed as its argument. This object contains the `CommandName` and `CommandArgument` properties to get the `CommandName` and `CommandArgument` property values.

Example: Using a Command Button

The following code example from `ButtonUsage.aspx` in the code download shows how to use `Submit` and `Command` buttons. This example allows you to generate either five random numbers through a Command button or any number of random numbers desired through a Submit button. The Command button also has its `CausesValidation` property set to `false` which results in no validation occurring when the button is clicked:

```
<form id="FrmButtonUsage" method="post" runat="server">
  <h3>Generate Random Numbers</h3>
  <table>
    <tr>
      <td>How many:</td>
      <td><asp:TextBox ID="TxtNumber" Runat="server"></asp:TextBox>
        <asp:RequiredFieldValidator ID="ReqValTxtNumber"
            Runat="server" ControlToValidate="TxtNumber"
            ErrorMessage="Please enter the number">
        </asp:RequiredFieldValidator></td>
    </tr>
    <tr>
      <td><asp:Button ID="BtnSubmit" Text="Submit" Runat="server">
        </asp:Button></td>
      <td><asp:Button ID="BtnCommand" CommandArgument="5"
                  CommandName="Random" runat="server"
                  CausesValidation="false"
                  Text="Generate 5 Random Numbers">
        </asp:Button>
      </td>
    </tr>
  </table>
  <p><span id="Message" runat="server"></span></p>
```

The BtnCommand_Command event handler code below shows how the CommandName and CommandArgument property can be accessed:

```csharp
private void BtnCommand_Command(object sender,
                    System.Web.UI.WebControls.CommandEventArgs e)
{
  Message.InnerHtml = e.CommandName + "Numbers:" + "<BR>";
  GenerateRandomNumbers(Convert.ToInt32(e.CommandArgument));
}

void GenerateRandomNumbers(int numbersCount)
{
  // Generate Random Numbers
  Random rand = new Random();
  int counter;
  for(counter = 1; counter <= numbersCount; counter++)
    Message.InnerHtml += rand.Next() + "<BR>";


}
private void BtnSubmit_Click(object sender, System.EventArgs e)
{
  Message.InnerHtml= "";
  GenerateRandomNumbers(Convert.ToInt32(TxtNumber.Text));
}
```

The following screenshot shows the output when the command button is clicked:

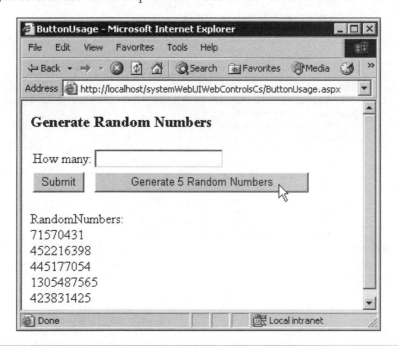

Calendar Class

The Calendar control displays a lively month-by-month calendar control on the web page. It allows for the selection of the particular day, week, and month or even selecting a range of days. It allows you to customize the appearance of the control and even add custom content for each day.

The Calendar control is an extremely sophisticated and powerful tool for web application development. One common example of where a Calendar control can be useful is in an events scheduling web application. With the Calendar control, it takes very little code to write a very professional-quality web schedule application for your users. Do remember of course that as the Calendar control posts back to the server for event processing, users may sometimes have to wait.

It is inherited from the System.Web.UI.WebControls.WebControl class. It has the following syntax:

```
<asp:Calendar id = "id_name"
            CellPadding = "pixels"
            CellSpacing = "pixels"
            DayNameFormat = "The format of day name"
            FirstDayOfWeek = "The first day of a week"
            NextMonthText = "HTML text"
            NextPrevFormat = "The format of Next Previous"
            PrevMonthText = "HTML text"
            SelectedDate = "date"
            SelectionMode = "None | Day | DayWeek | DayWeekMonth"
            SelectMonthText = "HTML text"
            SelectWeekText = "HTML text"
            ShowDayHeader = "true | false"
            ShowGridLines = "true | false"
            ShowNextPrevMonth = "true | false"
            ShowTitle = "true | false"
            TitleFormat = "Month | MonthYear"
            TodaysDate = "date"
            VisibleDate = "date"
            OnDayRender = "OnDayRenderEventHandler"
            OnSelectionChanged = " OnSelectionChangedEventHandler"
            OnVisibleMonthChanged = "OnVisibleMonthChangedEventHandler"
            Runat = "server">
            <TodayDayStyle property = "value" />
            <DayHeaderStyle property = "value" />
            <DayStyle property = "value" />
            <NextPrevStyle property = "value" />
            <OtherMonthDayStyle property = "value" />
            <SelectedDayStyle property = "value" />
            <SelectorStyle property = "value" />
            <TitleStyle property = "value" />
            <TodayDayStyle property = "value" />
            <WeekendDayStyle property = "value" />
</asp:Calendar>
```

Calendar Class Public Methods

The Calendar class adds no new public methods to those inherited from the WebControl class. See the WebControl class reference for a complete listing.

Calendar Class Protected Methods

❑ **OnDayRender**

❑ **OnSelectionChanged**

❑ **OnVisibleMonthChanged**

OnDayRender

The OnDayRender method raises the DayRender event of a Calendar control. The Calendar control does not support data binding, but it is possible for us to change the contents and format of the date cell in a Calendar control. The DayRender event is raised when the date cells in the Calendar control are created. This method allows derived classes to handle the DayRender event directly without attaching to a delegate.

```
protected virtual void OnDayRender(TableCell cell, CalendarDay day);
```

The parameter cell property gets the reference to the TableCell object that represents the cell where the day is being rendered. The paramter day represents the calendar day that is being rendered in the Calendar control. These two parameters allow you to customize the content and format of the date cell and date programmatically. You can also customize the contents of a cell by dynamically adding controls to the Control.Controls collection of the Cell property.

OnSelectionChanged

The OnSelectionChanged method raises the SelectionChanged event when the user clicks a day, a week, or a month. The user selects a day, week or month using the date selector controls. This method allows derived classes to handle the SelectionChanged event directly without attaching to a delegate.

```
protected virtual void OnSelectionChanged();
```

OnVisibleMonthChanged

The OnVisibleMonthChanged method raises the VisibleMonthChanged event when the user clicks the next or previous month navigational element to move to the next or previous month. This method allows derived classes to handle the SelectionChanged event directly without attaching to a delegate.

```
protected virtual void OnVisibleMonthChanged(DateTime newDate,
                                             DateTime previousDate);
```

The newDate parameter represents the month that will be next displayed, and the prevDate parameter is the month that was previously displayed.

Calendar Class Public Properties

- ❏ `CellPadding`
- ❏ `CellSpacing`
- ❏ `DayHeaderStyle`
- ❏ `DayNameFormat`
- ❏ `DayStyle`
- ❏ `FirstDayOfWeek`
- ❏ `NextMonthText`
- ❏ `NextPrevFormat`
- ❏ `NextPrevStyle`
- ❏ `OtherMonthDayStyle`
- ❏ `PrevMonthText`
- ❏ `SelectedDate`
- ❏ `SelectedDates`
- ❏ `SelectedDayStyle`
- ❏ `SelectionMode`
- ❏ `SelectMonthText`
- ❏ `SelectorStyle`
- ❏ `SelectWeekText`
- ❏ `ShowDayHeader`
- ❏ `ShowGridLines`
- ❏ `ShowNextPrevMonth`
- ❏ `ShowTitle`
- ❏ `TitleFormat`
- ❏ `TitleStyle`
- ❏ `TodayDayStyle`
- ❏ `TodaysDate`
- ❏ `VisbileDate`
- ❏ `WeekendDayStyle`

CellPadding

The `CellPadding` property gets or sets the distance between the contents of a cell and the cell's border. Its unit is pixels and the default value is 2. The space specified by this property is applied to all four sides of the cell.

```
public int CellPadding {get; set;}
```

CellSpacing

The `CellSpacing` property gets or sets the space between cells. Its unit is pixels and the default value is 0. The space specified by this property is applied both horizontally and vertically.

```
public int CellSpacing {get; set;}
```

DayHeaderStyle

The `DayHeaderStyle` property gets the style properties for the section where the weekdays are displayed. The default value is empty. The style properties are returned as a `TableItemStyle` object. This property only applies when the `ShowDayHeader` property is set to `true`.

```
public TableItemStyle DayHeaderStyle {get;}
```

DayNameFormat

The `DayNameFormat` property gets or sets the name format for the display of the day of the week. The format of the days of the week is encapsulated in the `DayNameFormat` enumeration. The valid values are `FirstLetter`, `FirstTwoLetters`, `Full`, and `Short`.The default value is `Short`, which means that the first three characters of the name of each day will be displayed. For example, Sunday is `Sun`, Monday is `Mon`, and so on. An `ArgumentException` is thrown if the property is set to a value other than one of the values of the `DayNameFormat` enumeration.

```
public DayNameFormat DayNameFormat {get; set;}
```

DayStyle

The `DayStyle` property gets the style properties for the days. The default value is empty. The style properties are returned as a `TableItemStyle` object.

```
public TableItemStyle DayStyle {get;}
```

FirstDayOfWeek

The `FirstDayOfWeek` property gets or sets the day of the week to display in the first day column in the `Calendar` control. The valid values are `Default`, `Monday`, `Tuesday`, `Wednesday`, `Thursday`, `Friday`, `Saturday`, and `Sunday`. The default value is `Default`, which means that the value is determined by the system settings. An `ArgumentException` is thrown if the property is set to a value other than the values of the `FirstDayOfWeek` enumeration.

```
public FirstDayOfWeek FirstDayOfWeek {get; set;}
```

NextMonthText

The `NextMonthText` property gets or sets the text for the navigational element to select the next month. The text format is HTML, and the default value is `&gt;` which denotes the "greater than" sign. This property is only applicable if the `ShowNextPrevMonth` property is set to `true`.

```
public string NextMonthText {get; set;}
```

NextPrevFormat

The NextPrevFormat property gets or sets the text format for the navigational elements that select the next and previous months for the Calendar control. The valid values are ShortMonth, FullMonth, and CustomText. The default value is CustomText, which means that the text specified in the NextMonthText and PrevMonthText properties is used. ShortMonth will display the first three characters of the month. For example, December is Dec. FullMonth will display the whole name of the month. An ArgumentException is thrown if the property is set to a value other than the values of the NextPrevFormat enumeration.

```
public NextPrevFormat NextPrevFormat {get; set;}
```

NextPrevStyle

The NextPrevStyle property gets the style properties for the next and previous month navigational elements. The style properties are returned as a TableItemStyle object. This property is only applicable if the ShowNextPrevMonth property is set to true.

```
public TableItemStyle NextPrevStyle {get;}
```

OtherMonthDayStyle

The OtherMonthDayStyle property gets the style properties for dates that are not in the month in focus in the Calendar. For example, if a Calendar control shows August, then we will see the last few days of July and the first few of September on the calendar as well. The OtherMonthDayStyle property contains sub-properties for formatting these dates. The style properties are returned as a TableItemStyle object.

```
public TableItemStyle OtherMonthDayStyle {get;}
```

PrevMonthText

The PrevMonthText property gets or sets the text for the navigational element to select the previous month. The text format is HTML, and the default value is < which denotes the "less than" sign. This property is only applicable if the ShowNextPrevMonth property is set to true.

```
public string PrevMonthText {get; set;}
```

SelectedDate

The SelectedDate property gets or sets the date selected by the user. It is in the DateTime format, for example 12:12:00 AM, 11/17/2000. A System.DateTime object represents the selected date. The default value is DateTime.MinValue. When the SelectionMode allows multiple selections, that is, it is not set to SelectionMode.Day, then this property returns the first date selected by the user. When a user selects a date, the SelectionChanged event is raised.

```
public DateTime SelectedDate {get; set;}
```

SelectedDates

The `SelectedDates` property gets a collection of `System.DateTime` objects that represent the selected dates. It is a collection of `System.DateTime` objects and the default value is an empty `SelectedDatesCollection`. This property is used when the `SelectionMode` property is set to `DayWeek` or `DayWeekMonth`.

When a user selects a week or a month, the `SelectionChanged` event is raised. The user cannot only select a week or a month, but also some special days can be selected in a `Calendar` control. For example, the user could select the range from the 10th to the 19th of a month, or a random selection of days. We can achieve this with the `SelectedDates` collection. We can use the `Add`, `Remove`, `Clear`, and `SelectRange` methods to programmatically manipulate the selected dates in the `SelectedDatesCollection`.

```
public SelectedDatesCollection SelectedDates {get;}
```

Example: Selecting a Range of Dates in a Calendar Control

The following example from `CalendarUsage1.aspx` shows how to select a range of dates. The user-interface code is:

```
<form id="FrmCalendarUsage1" method="post" runat="server">
  <asp:Calendar ID="CalSelect" runat="server"
              SelectionMode="DayWeekMonth" />
  <br>
  Start Date:
  <asp:dropdownlist id="DDLstStartDate" runat="server">
    <asp:Listitem text="1" value="1" />
    <asp:Listitem text="2" value="2" />
    <asp:Listitem text="3" value="3" />
    <asp:Listitem text="4" value="4" />
  </asp:dropdownlist><br>
  End Date:
  <asp:dropdownlist id="DDLstEndDate" runat="server">
    <asp:Listitem text="11" value="11" />
    <asp:Listitem text="12" value="12" />
    <asp:Listitem text="13" value="13" />
    <asp:Listitem text="14" value="14" />
  </asp:dropdownlist><br>
  <asp:Button id="BtnSelect" text="Select range" runat="server" />
</form>
```

The code snippet below shows how to access the `SelectedDates` property and then set the selected range programmatically by calling the `SelectRange` method of the `SelectedDatesCollection`:

```
private void Page_Load(object sender, System.EventArgs e)
  {
    if(!Page.IsPostBack)
      CalSelect.VisibleDate = CalSelect.TodaysDate;
  }
```

```
private void BtnSelect_Click(object sender, System.EventArgs e)
{
  int current_month = CalSelect.VisibleDate.Month;
  int current_year  = CalSelect.VisibleDate.Year;
  DateTime Begin_Date = new DateTime(current_year, current_month,
                  Convert.ToInt32(DDLstStartDate.SelectedItem.Text));
  DateTime End_Date = new DateTime(current_year, current_month,
                  Convert.ToInt32(DDLstEndDate.SelectedItem.Text));
  CalSelect.SelectedDates.Clear();
  CalSelect.SelectedDates.SelectRange(Begin_Date, End_Date);
}
```

The screenshot below shows the output:

SelectedDayStyle

The SelectedDayStyle property gets the style properties for the days selected by a user. The style properties are returned as a TableItemStyle object.

```
public TableItemStyle SelectedDayStyle {get;}
```

SelectionMode

The SelectionMode property gets or sets the selection mode, allowing users to select either one day, one week, or one month. The valid values are None, Day, DayWeek, and DayWeekMonth from the CalendarSelectionMode enumeration. The default value is Day. An ArgumentException is thrown if the property is set to a value other than the values of the CalendarSelectionMode enumeration.

```
public CalendarSelectionMode SelectionMode {get; set;}
```

SelectMonthText

The SelectMonthText property gets or sets the text displayed for the month selection element in the selector column. The text format is HTML and the default value is ">>" which means two "greater than" signs. The property is only applicable when the SelectionMode property is set to DayWeekMonth.

```
public string SelectMonthText {get; set;}
```

SelectorStyle

The SelectorStyle property gets the style properties for the week and month selector column. The style properties are returned as a TableItemStyle object. The property works only when SelectionMode is set to DayWeek or DayWeekMonth.

```
public TableItemStyle SelectorStyle {get;}
```

SelectWeekText

The SelectWeekText property gets or sets the text displayed for the week selection element in the selector column. The text format is HTML and the default value is ">" which means a "greater than" sign. The property is only applicable when SelectionMode is set to DayWeek or DayWeekMonth.

```
public string SelectWeekText {get; set;}
```

ShowDayHeader

The ShowDayHeader property gets or sets a value that indicates whether the name of a day of a week displays in the Calendar control. The valid values are true and false and the default value is true.

```
public bool ShowDayHeader {get; set;}
```

ShowGridLines

The ShowGridLines property gets or sets a value that indicates whether grid lines exist between day cells in the Calendar control. The valid values are true and false and the default value is false.

```
public bool ShowGridLines {get; set;}
```

ShowNextPrevMonth

The ShowNextPrevMonth property gets or sets a value that indicates whether the text or sign of the next and previous month navigational elements display in the Calendar control. The valid values are true and false and the default value is true.

```
public bool ShowNextPrevMonth {get; set;}
```

ShowTitle

The `ShowTitle` property gets or sets a value that indicates whether the title of the `Calendar` control displays. The `Title` section includes next and previous month navigation elements and the name of the current month and year. The valid values are `true` and `false` and the default value is `true`.

```
public bool ShowTitle {get; set;}
```

TitleFormat

The `TitleFormat` property gets or sets the format of the `Title` section in a `Calendar` control. The valid values are `Month` and `MonthYear`: the `TitleFormat` enumeration. The default value is `MonthYear`. This property is only applicable when the `ShowTitle` property is set to `true`.

```
public TitleFormat TitleFormat {get; set;}
```

TitleStyle

The `TitleStyle` property gets the style properties for the `Title` section in a `Calendar` control. The style properties are returned as a `TableItemStyle` object. The `TitleStyle` property is only applicable when the `ShowTitle` property is set to `true`.

```
public TableItemStyle TitleStyle {get;}
```

TodayDayStyle

The `TodayDayStyle` property gets the style properties for today's date in a `Calendar` control. The style properties are returned as a `TableItemStyle` object. The settings of the `TodayDayStyle` property will override the settings of the `DayStyle` property.

```
public TableItemStyle TodayDayStyle {get;}
```

TodaysDate

The `TodaysDate` property gets or sets a value for today's date. The default value is the system time on the computer. This property is set using a `System.DateTime` object.

```
public DateTime TodaysDate {get; set;}
```

VisibleDate

The `VisibleDate` property gets or sets the date that specifies the month to display on the `Calendar` control. You can programmatically generate a calendar by inputting a year and month. The `VisibleDate` property is updated before the `VisibleMonthChanged` event is raised.

```
public DateTime VisibleDate {get; set;}
```

Example: Using the VisibleDate Property

The following example from `CalendarUsage2.aspx` shows the `VisibleDate` property in action. The user interface code is:

```
<form id="FrmCalendarUsage2" method="post" runat="server">
  <asp:Calendar id="CalSelect" runat="server" />
  <hr>
  Year :
  <asp:DropDownList id="DDLstYear" runat="server">
    <asp:ListItem>1991</asp:ListItem>
    <asp:ListItem>1992</asp:ListItem>
    <asp:ListItem>1993</asp:ListItem>
    <asp:ListItem>1994</asp:ListItem>
    <asp:ListItem>1995</asp:ListItem>
    <asp:ListItem>1996</asp:ListItem>
    <asp:ListItem>1997</asp:ListItem>
    <asp:ListItem>1998</asp:ListItem>
    <asp:ListItem>1999</asp:ListItem>
    <asp:ListItem>2000</asp:ListItem>
    <asp:ListItem>2001</asp:ListItem>
    <asp:ListItem>2002</asp:ListItem>
  </asp:DropDownList>
  <br>
  Month :
  <asp:DropDownList id="DDLstMonth" runat="server">
    <asp:ListItem>1</asp:ListItem>
    <asp:ListItem>2</asp:ListItem>
    <asp:ListItem>3</asp:ListItem>
    <asp:ListItem>4</asp:ListItem>
    <asp:ListItem>5</asp:ListItem>
    <asp:ListItem>6</asp:ListItem>
    <asp:ListItem>7</asp:ListItem>
    <asp:ListItem>8</asp:ListItem>
    <asp:ListItem>9</asp:ListItem>
    <asp:ListItem>10</asp:ListItem>
    <asp:ListItem>11</asp:ListItem>
    <asp:ListItem>12</asp:ListItem>
  </asp:DropDownList>
  <Br>
  <asp:Button id="BtnCreate" Text="Create" runat="server" />
</form>
```

Here is the code that sets the `VisibleDate` property specifying the month and year to be displayed:

```
private void BtnCreate_Click(object sender, System.EventArgs e)
  {
    int year;
    int month;
    year = Convert.ToInt32(DDLstYear.SelectedItem.Text);
    month = Convert.ToInt32(DDLstMonth.SelectedItem.Text);
    CalSelect.VisibleDate = new DateTime(year, month, 1);
```

The screenshot shows the `Calendar` displaying the selected month and year:

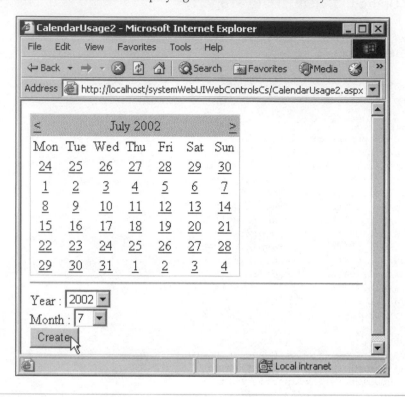

WeekendDayStyle

The `WeekendDayStyle` property gets the style properties for Saturday and Sunday. The style properties are returned as a `TableItemStyle` object. When the `WeekendDayStyle` property is set, it will override the settings of the `DayStyle` property. When the `TodayDayStyle` property is set, it will override the settings of the `WeekendDayStyle` property if today is Saturday or Sunday.

```
public TableItemStyle WeekendDayStyle {get;}
```

Calendar Class Protected Properties

The `Calendar` class adds no new protected properties to those inherited from the `WebControl` class. See the `WebControl` class reference for a complete listing.

Calendar Class Public Events

- ❑ **DayRender**
- ❑ **SelectionChanged**
- ❑ **VisibleMonthChanged**

DayRender

The DayRender event occurs when each day is created in the Calendar control. This event is generated for each date cell before it is rendered, so the event handler can be used to format individual date cells.

```
public event DayRenderEventHandler DayRender;
```

The event handler receives an argument of type DayRenderEventArgs that contains two main properties: Cell and Day. The Cell property gets the reference to the TableCell object that represents the cell where the day is being rendered. The Day property represents the calendar day that is being rendered in the Calendar control. These two parameters allow you to create the content and format of the date cell and date programmatically. You can also customize the contents of a cell by dynamically adding controls to the Control.Controls collection of the Cell property.

In the DayRender event, you cannot set any control that will raise an event. Therefore, you can only add static controls in the DayRender event. For example, an Image control, a Literal control and so on.

Example: Customizing Individual Day Cells in a Calendar Control

This example, CalendarUsage3.aspx, shows how to customize the contents of a day cell in the Calendar control. The user interface code is:

```
<form id="FrmCalendarUsage3" method="post" runat="server">
  <h3>Calendar DayRender Event Example</h3>
  <asp:Calendar id="Calendar1" runat="server"></asp:Calendar>
</form>
```

We define a sample holiday string in the Page_Load event. When the Calendar control is created, the DayRender event is fired. We use DateTime objects to add named holidays into the date cells of the Calendar control.

```
string[,] Holidays = new string[12,31];
  private void Page_Load(object sender, System.EventArgs e)
  {
    Holidays[0,0] = "<br<font size--1>New Year<font>";
    Holidays[6,3] = "<br><font size=-1>Independence Day<font>";
  }

  private void Calendar1_DayRender(object sender, DayRenderEventArgs e)
  {
      e.Cell.Controls.Add(new LiteralControl(Holidays[e.Day.Date.Month-1,
                                      e.Day.Date.Day-1]));
  }
```

The following screenshot shows the specially formatted cell for Independence Day:

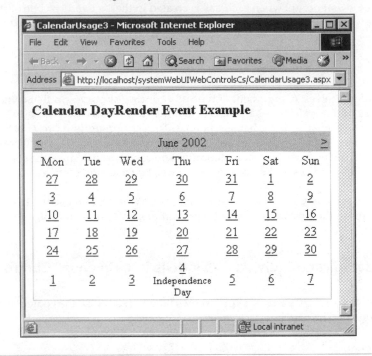

SelectionChanged

The `SelectionChanged` event occurs when the user clicks a day, a week, or a month in the `Calendar` control. The user selects day, week and month using the date selector controls.

```
public event EventHandler SelectionChanged;
```

The event handler receives an argument of type `EventArgs` that contains event related data.

Example: Hooking into the SelectionChanged Event

The following example from `CalendarUsage4.aspx` demonstrates the `SelectionChanged` event and the `SelectedDayStyle` property. The user interface code is:

```
<form id="FrmCalendarUsage4" method="post" runat="server">
  <h3>Calendar SelectionChanged Example</h3>
  Select a date or dates:<br>
  <asp:Calendar ID="CalSelect" runat="server"
                SelectionMode="DayWeekMonth">
    <SelectedDayStyle BackColor="Yellow"
                      ForeColor="Red">
    </SelectedDayStyle>
  </asp:Calendar>
```

```
<hr>
  <asp:Label id="LblMessage" runat="server" />
</form>
```

Here is the `SelectionChanged` event handler in the code-behind:

```
private void CalSelect_SelectionChanged(object sender, EventArgs e)
{
    if(CalSelect.SelectedDates.Count == 1)
        LblMessage.Text = "You selected:<br>" + CalSelect.SelectedDate;
    else
    {
        LblMessage.Text = "You selected:<br>";
        int i;
        for(i = 0; i < CalSelect.SelectedDates.Count; i++)
            LblMessage.Text += CalSelect.SelectedDates[i] + "<br>";
    }
}
```

The following screenshot shows the output when the dates are selected by clicking on the "greater than" sign to the left of a particular week in the calendar. The `SelectionChanged` event handler displays all the selected dates:

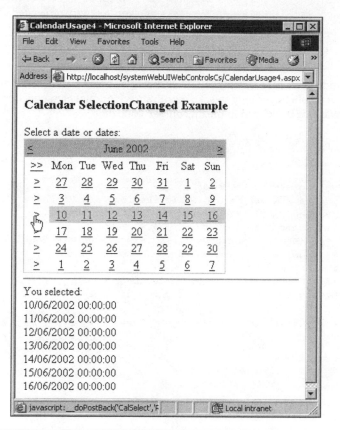

VisibleMonthChanged

The `VisibleMonthChanged` event occurs when the user clicks the navigational element that selects the next or previous month.

```
public event MonthChangedEventHandler VisibleMonthChanged;
```

The event handler receives an argument of type `MonthChangedEventArgs` containing data related to this event. There are two properties contained in the `MonthChangedEventArgs`: `NewDate` and `PreviousDate`. The `NewDate` property represents the month that will be displayed next, and the `PreviousDate` property is the month that was previously displayed.

Example: Hooking into the VisibleMonthChanged Event

The following code example from `CalendarUsage5.aspx` displays the `VisibleMonthChanged` event in action. The user interface code is:

```
<form id="FrmCalendarUsage5" method="post" runat="server">
  <h3>Calendar VisibleMonthChanged Event Example</h3>
  Click the next or previous month's navigational element:<br>
  <asp:Calendar id="CalSelect" runat="server"></asp:Calendar>
  <hr>
  <asp:Label id="LblMessage" runat="server" />
</form>
```

The following code shows the `VisibleMonthChanged` event handler that displays a different message to the user whenever they select a month's navigational elements depending on whether they are moving forward or backward in the `Calendar` control:

```
private void CalSelect_VisibleMonthChanged(object sender,
                                    MonthChangedEventArgs e)
{
  // From January to December
  if((e.NewDate.Month == 12) && (e.PreviousDate.Month == 1))
    LblMessage.Text = "You moved one month backwards.";
  // From December to January
  else if((e.NewDate.Month == 1) && (e.PreviousDate.Month == 12))
    LblMessage.Text = "You moved one month forward.";
  // All other months
  else if(e.NewDate.Month > e.PreviousDate.Month)
    LblMessage.Text = "You moved one month forward.";
  else
    LblMessage.Text = "You moved one month backwards.";
}
```

The following code displays the output when the next month is selected:

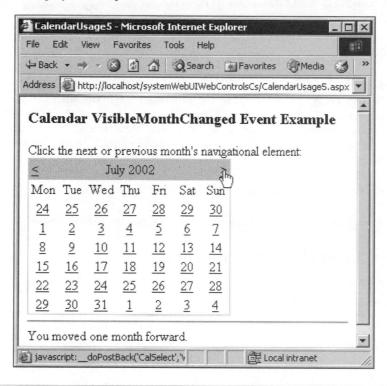

CheckBox Class

The CheckBox class displays a checkbox on a Web page to let the user select either true or false for a given value. It is inherited from the System.Web.UI.WebControls.WebControl class.

It corresponds to the <input type="checkbox"> element from the HTML controls. It has the following syntax:

```
<asp:Checkbox id = "id_name"
              AutoPostBack = "true | false"
              Text = "Label for check box"
              TextAlign = "Right | Left"
              Checked = "true | false"
              OnCheckedChanged = "CheckedChangedEventHandler"
              Runat = "server" />
```

CheckBox Class Public Methods

The CheckBox class adds no new public methods to those inherited from the WebControl class. See the WebControl class reference for a complete listing.

CheckBox Class Protected Methods

❑ **OnCheckedChanged**

OnCheckedChanged

The `OnCheckedChanged` method will raise the `CheckedChanged` event when the state of the `CheckBox` control is changed by the user clicking it. If the `AutoPostBack` property of the checkbox is set to `true` the page is then posted to the server; otherwise not. In the latter case, the `CheckedChanged` event is raised whenever there is a change in the state of the checkbox between posts to the server. The checkbox control must have viewstate enabled in order to be able to raise this event correctly. This method allows derived classes to handle the `CheckedChanged` event directly without attaching to a delegate.

```
protected virtual void OnCheckedChanged(EventArgs e);
```

The parameter e refers to an `EventArgs` object that contains the `CheckedChange` event data.

CheckBox Class Public Properties

❑ **AutoPostBack**

❑ **Checked**

❑ **Text**

❑ **TextAlign**

AutoPostBack

The `AutoPostBack` property gets or sets a value to determine whether the state of the `CheckBox` should be posted back to the server automatically when the `CheckBox` is clicked. When set to `true`, the form which contains the `Checkbox` is posted to the server automatically whenever there is a change in the state of a `CheckBox`. The default value is `false` and indicates that the postback will not occur unless the page is posted back to the server (through the click of a button or another control having its `AutoPostBack` property set to `true`). The `AutoPostBack` property requires that client-side scripting is enabled for it to function properly. This property will not post the page to the server if the browser does not support JavaScript or if client-side scripting is disabled.

```
public virtual bool AutoPostBack {get; set;}
```

Checked

The `Checked` property gets or sets a value indicating whether the `CheckBox` control is checked. The default value is `false` meaning that the `CheckBox` is unchecked by default. When this property is set to `true` the `CheckBox` is checked. The property reflects the current state of the `CheckBox`, and changes immediately as the user selects or deselects it.

```
public virtual bool Checked {get; set;}
```

Text

The Text property gets or sets the text label associated with the CheckBox control. The default is an empty string. This property can be used to associate a text label with the Checkbox.

```
public virtual string Text {get; set;}
```

TextAlign

The TextAlign property is used to get or set the alignment of the text label associated with the CheckBox control. The valid values are Right and Left. The default value is Right. An ArgumentException is thrown if the property is set to a value other than the values of the TextAlign enumeration.

```
public virtual TextAlign TextAlign {get; set;}
```

CheckBox Class Protected Properties

The CheckBox class adds no new protected properties to those inherited from the WebControl class. See the WebControl class reference for a complete listing.

CheckBox Class Public Events

❏ **CheckedChanged**

CheckedChanged

The CheckedChanged event occurs when the Checked property is changed. If the AutoPostBack property is not set to true, this event will not immediately post back to the server; rather this event will only be raised if there is a change in the state of the checkbox between the previous post to the server and the next time the data is posted to the server. However, if the AutoPostBack property is set to true, then whenever there is a change in the Checked property of the CheckBox control, this event will be raised and the page will be immediately posted to the server. The Checkbox control must have viewstate enabled in order to be able to raise this event correctly.

```
public event EventHandler CheckedChanged;
```

The event handler receives information related to the event through the EventArgs object, passed as its argument.

Example: Using the Properties of CheckBox

The following code example from CheckBoxUsage.aspx shows how to set the various CheckBox properties and how to hook into the CheckedChanged event. Here is the user interface that sets the properties:

```
<form id="FrmCheckBoxUsage" method="post" runat="server">
  <h3>Mode Of Communication</h3>
  <asp:CheckBox ID="ChkMail" Runat="server" Text="Postal Mail"
              TextAlign="Left" AutoPostBack="true"
```

317

```
                ToolTip="Does AutoPostBack">
  </asp:CheckBox>    <br>
  <asp:CheckBox ID="ChkEmail" runat="server" Text="Electronic Mail"
    TextAlign="Left"
    ToolTip="Does Not AutoPostBack (Click Submit Button ⅂
    or change the state of the Postal Mail CheckBox for the postback to ⅂
    occur)" >
  </asp:CheckBox>
  <br>
  <asp:Button ID="BtnSubmit" Runat="server" Text="Submit">
  </asp:Button>
  <br><br> <Span id="Message1" runat="server"></Span>
  <br><Span id="Message2" runat="server"></Span>
</form>
```

The above code displays two checkboxes, where the Postal Mail check box has its AutoPostBack property set to true. Whenever the user checks or unchecks this checkbox, the page is posted to the server. However, when the user checks or unchecks the other checkbox the page is not immediately posted. The event is raised only when the page is posted. The event handler code looks like this:

```
private void ChkMail_CheckedChanged(object sender, System.EventArgs e)
  {
    if(ChkMail.Checked == true)
      Message1.InnerHtml = "Postal Mail";
    else
      Message1.InnerHtml = "";
  }

private void ChkEmail_CheckedChanged(object sender, System.EventArgs e)
  {
    if(ChkEmail.Checked == true)
      Message2.InnerHtml = "Electronic Mail";
    else
      Message2.InnerHtml = "";
  }
```

The following screenshot shows the output when both the checkboxes are checked and the button is pressed:

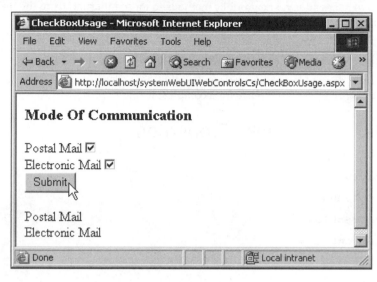

CheckBoxList Class

The `CheckBoxList` control represents a list of checkboxes, where each checkbox in the list represents a single `CheckBox` control. It allows the user to select multiple checkboxes in the list allowing multiple and single selections. Checkboxes in the list can be added either at design time using the `<asp:ListItem>` element or at run-time by manipulating with the `ListItemCollection`. The items can also be added by data-binding the `CheckBoxList` with the `DataSource`.

This class is inherited from the `System.Web.UI.WebControls.ListControl` class. It has the following syntax:

```
<asp:CheckBoxList id = "id_name"
                  AutoPostBack = "true | false"
                  CellPadding = "Pixels"
                  CellSpacing = "Pixels"
                  DataSource = "name of data source"
                  DataTextField = "DataSourceField"
                  DataValueField = "DataSourceField"
                  RepeatColumns = "ColumnCount"
                  RepeatDirection = "Vertical | Horizontal"
                  RepeatLayout = "Flow | Table"
                  TextAlign = "Right | Left"
                  OnSelectedIndexChanged = "Method for selected ⅂
                                          index changed"
                  Runat = "server">
   <asp:ListItem value="value of ListItem" >
     Content text
   </asp:ListItem>
</asp:CheckBoxList>
```

ckBoxList Class Public Methods

CheckBoxList class adds no new public methods to those inherited from the WebControl class. the WebControl class reference for a complete listing.

CheckBoxList Class Protected Methods

The CheckBoxList class adds no new protected methods to those inherited from the WebControl class. See the WebControl class reference for a complete listing.

CheckBoxList Class Public Properties

❑ **CellPadding**

❑ **CellSpacing**

❑ **RepeatColumns**

❑ **RepeatDirection**

❑ **RepeatLayout**

❑ **TextAlign**

CellPadding

The CellPadding property gets or sets the width in pixels between the border and a checkbox in the CheckBoxList. The default value is −1 that indicates that the property is not set. The CellPadding is applied to all four sides of the checkbox.

```
public virtual int CellPadding {get; set;}
```

CellSpacing

The CellSpacing property gets or sets the width in pixels between the individual checkboxes in the CheckBoxList. The default value is −1 that indicates and the property is not set. The CellSpacing is applied both horizontally and vertically to individual checkboxes.

```
public virtual int CellSpacing {get; set;}
```

RepeatColumns

The RepeatColumns property gets or sets the number of columns used to display checkboxes in the CheckBoxList. The default value is 0 and indicates that the property is not set. An ArgumentOutOfRangeException is thrown if this property is set to a negative value.

```
public virtual int RepeatColumns {get; set;}
```

RepeatDirection

The `RepeatDirection` property gets or sets a value that indicates the direction of the layout of checkboxes in the `CheckBoxList` control. The checkboxes can be displayed either vertically or horizontally. The valid values are from the `RepeatDirection` enumeration: either `Vertical` or `Horizontal`. The default value is `Vertical`. An `ArgumentException` is thrown if this property is set to a value other than the `RepeatDirection` enumeration values.

```
public virtual RepeatDirection RepeatDirection {get; set;}
```

`Vertical` layout is as follows:

CheckBox 1	CheckBox 3
CheckBox 2	CheckBox 4

`Horizontal` layout is as follows:

CheckBox 1	CheckBox 2
CheckBox 3	CheckBox 4

RepeatLayout

The `RepeatLayout` property gets or sets the layout of checkboxes in a `CheckBoxList` control. The valid values are from the `RepeatLayout` enumeration, and may be either `Flow` or `Table`. The default value is `Table`, which ensures the checkboxes are displayed in a table structure. When this property is set to `Flow`, the output is displayed without a table structure. An `ArgumentException` is thrown if this property is set to a value other than the `RepeatLayout` enumeration values.

```
public virtual RepeatLayout RepeatLayout {get; set;}
```

TextAlign

The `TextAlign` property is used to get or set the alignment of the text label associated with individual `CheckBox` controls in the `CheckBoxList`. The valid values are `Right` and `Left`, specified by the `TextAlign` enumeration. An `ArgumentException` is thrown if the property is set to a value other than the values of the `TextAlign` enumeration. A value of `Left` means that the text of the associated checkbox will be flush with the left-hand side of the control, while `Right` means that the text of the associated checkbox appears flush with the right-hand side of the control. The default value is `Right`.

```
public virtual TextAlign TextAlign {get; set;}
```

Example: Using the Properties of the CheckBoxList Control

The code from `CheckBoxListUsage.aspx` here illustrates the usage of most of the properties of the `CheckBoxList` control. Here is the user interface code:

```
<form id="FrmCheckBoxList" method="post" runat="server">
  Select your favourite programming languages:<br>
  <asp:CheckBoxList id="CBLstProgLang" runat="server" CellPadding="2"
                    CellSpacing="2" RepeatColumns="2"
                    RepeatDirection="Horizontal">
```

```
    sp:ListItem Value="VB.NET" Text="VB.NET"></asp:ListItem>
    sp:ListItem Value="C#" Text="C#"></asp:ListItem>
    sp:ListItem Value="VBScript" Text="VBScript"></asp:ListItem>
    sp:ListItem Value="JavaScript" Text="JavaScript"></asp:ListItem>
    >:CheckBoxList><br>
    t your favourite Book Shippers:<br>
    CheckBoxList id="CBLstShippers" Runat="server" RepeatLayout="Flow"
                 TextAlign="Left"
                 AutoPostBack="true"></asp:CheckBoxList>
   <br>
   <asp:Button ID="BtnSubmit" runat="server" Text="Submit"></asp:Button>
   <hr>
   <asp:Label ID="LblLanguages" Runat="server"></asp:Label><br>
   <asp:Label ID="LblShippers" Runat="server"></asp:Label>
 </form>
```

The code below shows the code for the Page_Load event where the databound Shippers
CheckBoxList is populated from the **Northwind** database. In order for this to work you will need to
alter the connection string to point to your instance of SQL Server. It also shows the code for the
SelectedIndexChanged event handler of both the checkboxes:

```
private void Page_Load(object sender, System.EventArgs e)
  {
    if(!Page.IsPostBack)
    {
      //Add an Item programmatically to the Languages CheckBoxList
      CBLstProgLang.Items.Add(new ListItem("J#", "J#"));

      // Create a SqlConnection and SqlDataAdapter object
      string ConnectionString =
            @"User ID=sa;Initial Catalog=Northwind;Data Source=(local);";
      SqlConnection cnn = new SqlConnection(ConnectionString);
      SqlDataAdapter da = new SqlDataAdapter(
                                      "select * from Shippers", cnn);

      // Create a dataset to store the Shippers data.
      DataSet ds = new DataSet();
      da.Fill(ds, "Shippers");

      CBLstShippers.DataSource = ds;
      CBLstShippers.DataMember = "Shippers";
      CBLstShippers.DataTextField = "CompanyName";
      CBLstShippers.DataValueField = "ShipperID";
      CBLstShippers.DataBind();
    }

  }

private void CBLstShippers_SelectedIndexChanged(object sender,
                                            EventArgs e)
  {
    LblShippers.Text = "Selected Book Shippers:" + "<br>";
    foreach(ListItem shipperItem in CBLstShippers.Items)
    {
```

```
        if(shipperItem.Selected == true)
            LblShippers.Text += shipperItem.Text + " (" + shipperItem.Value
                             + ") <br>";
    }
  }

private void CBLstProgLang_SelectedIndexChanged(object sender,
                                              System.EventArgs e)
  {
    LblLanguages.Text = "Selected Programming Languages:" + "<br>";
    foreach(ListItem languageItem in CBLstProgLang.Items)
    {
      if(languageItem.Selected == true)
        LblLanguages.Text += languageItem.Text + " (" + languageItem.Value
                           + ") <br>";
    }
  }
```

We iterate through the `Items` property of the `CheckBoxList` to display all the selected items. The following screenshot shows the output of this code:

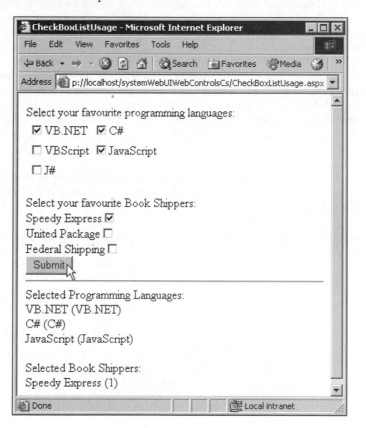

CheckBoxList Class Protected Properties

The `CheckBoxList` class adds no new protected properties to those inherited from the `WebControl` class. See the `WebControl` class reference for a complete listing.

CheckBoxList Class Public Events

The `CheckBoxList` class adds no new public events to those inherited from the `WebControl` class. See the `WebControl` class reference for a complete listing.

CompareValidator Class

The `CompareValidator` control is used to compare an input control's value against another value. The value to be compared against can be another control's value or a fixed value. When a web page is submitted some of the controls in the form are required to have a certain valid value by the server (for example, you might want the Quantity field to be greater than zero in a Shopping page). Therefore, to ensure valid data is sent to the server, there is a need to validate the data the user puts in before sending it to the server. The `CompareValidator` control, when associated with an input control, ensures that the associated control has a valid value eliminating the need to write validation logic to check for comparisons of data types or against some value. This control performs compare field validation both at the server and client side. However, validation on the client side depends on the capabilities of the browser and the setting of the `ClientTarget` attribute in the `Page` directive of the Web Form.

The `CompareValidator` control can be used to check whether the associated input control contains data in a particular data type. Therefore it can be used in places where there is a need to check that the value entered is a valid `Date`, `Currency`, `Double`, `Integer` or `String`. Further, this control can be used to compare the value entered using comparison operators like `Equal`, `NotEqual`, `GreaterThan`, `GreaterThanEqual`, and so on, against different data types like `Date`, `Currency`, `String`, and so on.

Note that if the user is supposed to be obliged to enter a value for the input control, then a `RequiredFieldValidator` should be associated with the control as only this control checks whether the user has actually entered a value.

This class is inherited from the `System.Web.UI.WebControls.BaseCompareValidator` class. It has the following syntax:

```
<asp:CompareValidator id = "id_name"
                      runat = "server"
                      ControlToValidate = "programmatic ID of Server ⌐
                                       Control to validate"
                      ValueToCompare="value to compare"
                      Type="DataType"
                      Operator="operator"
                      ErrorMessage="The error message"
                      ForeColor = "forecolor"
                      BackColor = "background color">
                      Text = "some text"
</asp:CompareValidator>
```

324

CompareValidator Class Public Methods

The `CompareValidator` class adds no new public methods to those inherited from the `WebControl` and `BaseValidator` classes. See those class references for a complete listing.

CompareValidator Class Protected Methods

The `CompareValidator` class adds no new protected methods to those inherited from the `WebControl` and `BaseValidator` classes. See those class references for a complete listing.

CompareValidator Class Public Properties

- ❑ **ControlToCompare**
- ❑ **Operator**
- ❑ **Type**
- ❑ **ValueToCompare**

ControlToCompare

The `ControlToCompare` property gets or sets the input control against whose value the associated input control is to be validated. The default value is an empty string. This property is used when the input control's value is to be validated against another input control's value. For example, in an air ticket registration application, we might have two textboxes that get the `Start Date` and `End Date` of the trip respectively. The `End Date` should be greater than the `Start Date`. Therefore, the `EndDate` can have a `CompareValidator` associated with its control to make this check. The `CompareValidator` will assign the `Start Date` textbox to the `ControlToCompare` and set the `Operator` to `GreaterThanEqual` and `Type` to `Date`. This `CompareValidator` will ensure that the user enters an `End Date` which is later than the trip `Start Date`. You should not set both the `ControlToCompare` and the `ValueToCompare` property at the same time in a `CompareValidator`. However, if both the properties are set, the `ControlToCompare` takes precedence.

```
public string ControlToCompare {get; set;}
```

Operator

The `Operator` property gets or sets the comparison operation to perform. The `CompareValidator` can be used to perform a variety of comparisons defined by the `ValidationCompareOperator` enumeration. The default value is `Equal`. An `ArgumentException` is thrown if a value other than one of the `ValidationCompareOperator` enumeration values is assigned to this property. The following table lists the valid values of the comparison operators:

Operator	Description
Equal	=
NotEqual	<>
GreaterThan	>
GreaterThanEqual	>=
LessThan	<
LessThanEqual	<=
DataTypeCheck	DataType comparison is performed. The data type can be one of String, Integer, Double, Date or Currency.

If the DataTypeCheck operator is used then the ControlToCompare and ValueToCompare properties are ignored. The input control's value is converted into the specified DataType, if it succeeds the validation succeeds otherwise the validation fails.

```
public ValidationCompareOperator Operator {get; set;}
```

Type

The Type property specifies the data type to be used when comparing data. The Type property is inherited from the BaseCompareValidator class. The values to be compared are first converted to this data type and then the comparison is performed. The valid data types are defined by the ValidationDataType enumeration. The default value is String. An ArgumentException is thrown if a value other than the ValidationDataType enumeration values is assigned to this property. The following table lists the valid data types:

Type	Description
Currency	A currency data type
Date	A date data type
Double	A double precision floating point data type
Integer	A 32 bit signed integer data type
String	A string data type. (The default.)

```
public ValidationDataType Type {get; set;}
```

ValueToCompare

The `ValueToCompare` property gets or sets the value against which the associated input control is to be validated. The default value is an empty `String`. This property is used when the input control's value is to be validated against a fixed value. For example, in an Orders Entry page, you might want the `Quantity` of the items desired to be greater than zero. Therefore, the `Quantity` field can have a `CompareValidator` associated with its control to make this check. The `CompareValidator` will assign the `ValueToCompare` to be `0`, and set the `Operator` to `GreaterThan` and the `Type` to `Integer`. This `CompareValidator` will ensure that the user enters a `Quantity` greater than 0. You should not set both the `ControlToCompare` and the `ValueToCompare` property at the same time on a `CompareValidator`. However, if both the properties are set, the `ControlToCompare` takes precedence.

```
public string ValueToCompare {get; set;}
```

Example: Using CompareValidator to Compare the Values of Controls

The following code example from `CompareValidatorUsage1.aspx` shows how to use a `CompareValidator` to compare with the value of another input control:

```
<form id="FrmCompareValidatorUsage1" method="post" runat="server">
<h3>Change Password</h3>
<table cellSpacing="2" cellPadding="2" border="0">
<tr><td>
<asp:Label id="LblScreenName" runat="server" Text="Screen Name">
</asp:Label></td>
<td>
<asp:TextBox id="TxtScreenName" runat="server" ReadOnly="true"
            Text="master" >
</asp:TextBox></td></tr>
<tr><td>
<asp:Label id="LblOldPassword" runat="server"
            Text="Old Password">
</asp:Label></td>
<td>
<asp:TextBox id="TxtOldPassword" runat="server"
            TextMode="Password">
</asp:TextBox>
</td></tr>
<tr><td>
<asp:Label id="LblNewPassword" runat="server"
            Text="New Password" >
</asp:Label></td>
<td>
<asp:TextBox id="TxtNewPassword" runat="server"
            TextMode="Password">
</asp:TextBox>
<asp:comparevalidator id="ComValTxtNewPassword" runat="server"
                        CssClass="ErrorText"
                        ControlToValidate="TxtNewPassword"
                        ControlToCompare="TxtOldPassword"
                        Operator="NotEqual"
```

```
                        Type="String"
                        ErrorMessage="Please select a different new ⅂
                            password, it matches with the old password"
                        display="dynamic"  Text="*">
</asp:comparevalidator></td></tr>
<tr><td>
<asp:Label id="LblReNewPassword" runat="server"
        Text="Re-enter New Password" >
</asp:Label></td>
<td>
<asp:TextBox id="TxtReNewPassword" runat="server"
            TextMode="Password" >
</asp:TextBox>
<asp:comparevalidator id="ComValTxtReNewPassword" runat="server"
                    ControlToValidate="TxtReNewPassword"
                    Operator="Equal"
                    ControlToCompare="TxtNewPassword" Type="String"
                    ErrorMessage="Please re-enter the new password, ⅂
                                it does not match with the new ⅂
                                password entered above"
                    display="dynamic" Text="*">
</asp:comparevalidator></td></tr>
</table><br>
<asp:button id="BtnUpdPassword" runat="server" CssClass="BoldText"
            Text="Change Password">
</asp:button>
<br>
<br>
<span id="Message" runat="server"></span>
<asp:validationsummary id="VSumPassword" runat="Server"
                    DisplayMode="BulletList">
</asp:validationsummary>
</form>
```

The code for the `BtnUpdPassword_Click` calls the `Page.IsValid` method to ensure that validation was successful:

```
private void BtnUpdPassword_Click(object sender, System.EventArgs e)
{
  if(Page.IsValid)
    // Book the Tour
    Message.InnerHtml = "Congratulations! You have successfully "
                      + "changed the password";
}
```

The following screenshot shows the error messages generated by the CompareValidator controls when validation fails:

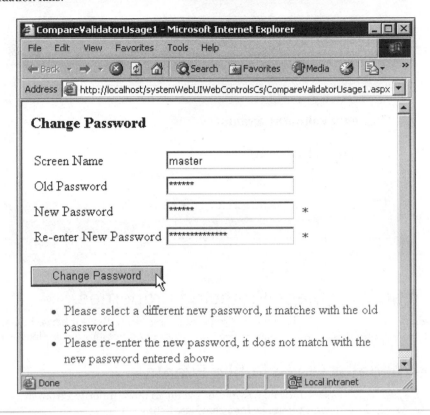

Example: Using CompareValidator with a Fixed Value

The next example, CompareValidatorUsage2.aspx, shows how to compare the control with a constant value using the ValueToCompare property:

```
<form id="FrmCompareValidatorUsage2" method="post" runat="server">
  <h3>CompareValidator Example</h3>
  Input a number less than 100:
  <br>
  <asp:textbox id="TxtNumber" runat="server"></asp:textbox>
  <asp:comparevalidator id="ComValTxtNumber" runat="server" type="Integer"
                        Errormessage="The number is greater than 100"
                        operator="lessthan" valueToCompare="100"
                        controltovalidate="TxtNumber">
  </asp:comparevalidator><BR>
  <asp:button id="BtnSumbit" runat="server"
              text="Compare">
  </asp:button><hr>
</form>
```

The following screenshot shows the error message generated when validation fails:

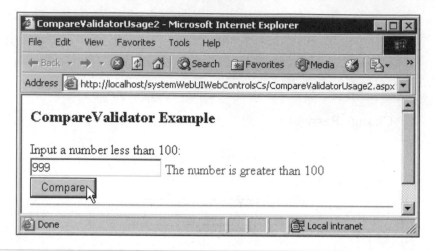

CompareValidator Class Protected Properties

The `CompareValidator` class adds no new protected properties to those inherited from the `WebControl` and `BaseValidator` classes. See those class references for a complete listing.

CompareValidator Class Public Events

The `CompareValidator` class adds no new public events to those inherited from the `WebControl` class. See the `WebControl` class reference for a complete listing.

CustomValidator Class

The `CustomValidator` control allows you to build a validation control with your own specification. The validation controls provided by ASP.NET handle a wide variety of validations. However, every application has its own custom requirements for validation, and those validations can easily be covered by using the `CustomValidator` class.

This class is inherited from the `System.Web.UI.WebControls.BaseValidator` class. It has the following syntax:

```
<asp:CustomValidator id="id_name"
                ControlToValidate = "id of control"
                ClientValidationFunction = "function for validation"
                OnServerValidate = "ServerValidateID"
                ErrorMessage = "Error message"
                runat="server" />
```

Note that if the user is supposed to compulsorily enter a value for the input control, then a `RequiredFieldValidator` should be associated with the control as only this control checks whether the user has entered a value.

CustomValidator Class Public Methods

The `CustomValidator` class adds no new public methods to those inherited from the `WebControl` and `BaseValidator` classes. See those class references for a complete listing.

CustomValidator Class Protected Methods

❑ **OnServerValidate**

OnServerValidate

The `OnServerValidate` method raises the `ServerValidate` event when validation is performed at the server. The event represents the custom validation function that is executed for validation on the server.

```
protected virtual bool OnServerValidate(string value);
```

The method returns `true` if validation succeds, otherwise `false`. The `value` parameter holds the value that is to be validated.

CustomValidator Class Public Properties

❑ **ClientValidationFunction**

ClientValidationFunction

The `ClientValidationFunction` property gets or sets the name of the custom client script function used for validation. The default is an empty string. Only the name of the function without any parameters should be passed in. The client-side function passed here will be executed for validation on the client side. The client-side validation function referred has two aruguments. The first argument contains the `CustomValidator` object and the second argument contains an object with two properties: `IsValid` and `Value`. The `IsValid` property is used to return the result of validation, either `true` or `false` and the `Value` property holds the value that is to be validated.

```
public string ClientValidationFunction {get; set;}
```

CustomValidator Class Protected Properties

The `CustomValidator` class adds no new protected properties to those inherited from the `WebControl` and `BaseValidator` classes. See those class references for a complete listing.

CustomValidator Class Public Events

❑ **ServerValidate**

ServerValidate

The ServerValidate event is raised when validation is performed at the server. The event represents the custom validation function that is executed for validation on the server.

```
public event ServerValidateEventHandler ServerValidate;
```

The event handler receives information related to the event through the ServerValidateEventArgs object, passed as its argument. The ServerValidateEventArgs object contains two properties IsValid and Value. The IsValid property holds the value of the result of validation, either true or false, and the Value property holds the value of the control that is to be validated.

Example: The ServerValidate Event of the CustomValidator Control

The following example, CustomValidatorUsage.aspx, shows how to work with the ServerValidate event. Here is the user interface code:

```
<form id="FrmCustomValidatorUsage" method="post" runat="server">
  <h3>CustomValidator Example</h3>
  Input an odd number:<Br>
  Number :
  <asp:textbox id="TxtNumber" runat="server" />
  <br>
  <br>
  <asp:button text="Validate" id="BtnValidate" runat="server" />
  <br>
  <asp:customvalidator id="CusValTxtNumber" ControlToValidate="TxtNumber"
                       runat="server"
                       ErrorMessage="Please enter an odd number" >
  </asp:customvalidator><br>
  <asp:Label ID="LblMessage" Runat="server"></asp:Label>
</form>
```

Here is the ServerValidate event handler code:

```
private void CusValTxtNumber_ServerValidate(object source,
                                            ServerValidateEventArgs args)
  {
    if(Convert.ToInt32(args.Value) % 2 != 0)
      args.IsValid = true;
    else
      args.IsValid = false;
  }
```

The following screenshot shows the output when you enter an even number by mistake, that is when validation fails:

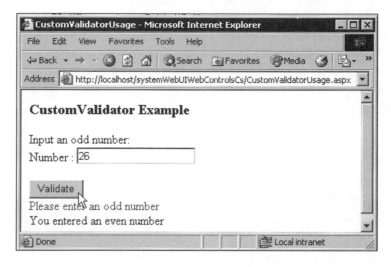

DataGrid Class

The `DataGrid` control is a very complex control, full of features for selecting, editing, deleting, paging, and sorting the data it contains. The `DataGrid` control displays records from a data table. It allows for the formatting of them and manipulating the contents of records with great ease.

This class is inherited from `System.Web.UI.WebControls.BaseDataList` class. It has the following syntax:

```
<asp:DataGrid id = "id_name" runat=server
            DataSource='name of data source'
            AllowPaging = "true | false"
            AllowSorting = "true | false"
            AutoGenerateColumns = "true | false"
            BackImageUrl = "URL of background image"
            DataKeyField = "DataSourceKeyField"
            GridLines = "None | Horizontal | Vertical | Both"
            HorizontalAlign = "Center | Justify | Left | NotSet | Right"
            PageSize = "ItemCount"
            ShowFooter = "true | false"
            ShowHeader = "true | false"
            VirtualItemCount = "ItemCount"
            OnCancelCommand = "OnCancelCommandMethod"
            OnDeleteCommand = "OnDeleteCommandMethod"
            OnEditCommand = "OnEditCommandMethod"
            OnItemCommand = "OnItemCommandMethod"
            OnItemCreated = "OnItemCreatedMethod"
            OnPageIndexChanged = "OnPageIndexChangedMethod"
```

```
                OnSortCommand = "OnSortCommandMethod"
                OnUpdateCommand = "OnUpdateCommandMethod">

   <AlternatingItemStyle property="value"/>
   <EditItemStyle property="value"/>
   <FooterStyle property="value"/>
   <HeaderStyle property="value"/>
   <ItemStyle property="value"/>
   <PagerStyle property="value"/>
   <SelectedItemStyle property="value"/>


</asp:DataGrid>
```

or:

```
<asp:DataGrid id = "id_name" runat=server
                DataSource = 'name of data source'
                AutoGenerateColumns = "false"
                'Other properties'

   <AlternatingItemStyle property="value"/>
   <EditItemStyle property="value"/>
   <FooterStyle property="value"/>
   <HeaderStyle property="value"/>
   <ItemStyle property="value"/>
   <PagerStyle property="value"/>
   <SelectedItemStyle property="value"/>

   <Columns>
     <asp:BoundColumn DataField = "DataSourceField"
                      DataFormatString = "FormatString"
                      FooterText = "FooterText"
                      HeaderImageUrl = "url"
                      HeaderText = "HeaderText"
                      ReadOnly = "true | false"
                      SortField = "DataSourceFieldToSortBy"
                      Visible = "true | false"
                      FooterStyle-property = "value"
                      HeaderStyle-property = "value"
                      ItemStyle-property = "value"/>

     <asp:ButtonColumn ButtonType = "LinkButton | PushButton"
                       Command = "BubbleText"
                       DataTextField = "DataSourceField"
                       DataTextFormatS tring="FormatString"
                       FooterText="FooterText"
                       HeaderImageUrl="url"
                       HeaderText = "HeaderText"
                       ReadOnly = "true | false"
                       SortField="DataSourceFieldToSortBy"
                       Text="ButtonCaption"
                       Visible = "true | false"/>

     <asp:EditCommandColumn ButtonType = "LinkButton | PushButton"
                            CancelText="CancelButtonCaption"
```

```
                          EditText="EditButtonCaption"
                          FooterText="FooterText"
                          HeaderImageUrl="url"
                          HeaderText="HeaderText"
                          ReadOnly="true|false"
                          SortField="DataSourceFieldToSortBy"
                          UpdateText="UpdateButtonCaption"
                          Visible = "true | false"/>

        <asp:HyperLinkColumn DataNavigateUrlField="DataSourceField"
                          DataNavigateUrlFormatString="FormatExpression"
                          DataTextField="DataSourceField"
                          DataTextFormatString="FormatExpression"
                          FooterText="FooterText"
                          HeaderImageUrl="url"
                          HeaderText="HeaderText"
                          NavigateUrl="url"
                          ReadOnly = "true | false"
                          SortField="DataSourceFieldToSortBy"
                          Target="window"
                          Text="HyperLinkText"
                          Visible = "true | false"/>

        <asp:TemplateColumn FooterText="FooterText"
                          HeaderImageUrl="url"
                          HeaderText="HeaderText"
                          ReadOnly="true|false"
                          SortField="DataSourceFieldToSortBy"
                          Visible = "true | false">

          <HeaderTemplate>
            Header template HTML
          </HeaderTemplate >
          <ItemTemplate>
            ItemTemplate HTML
          </ItemTemplate>
          <EditItemTemplate>
            EditItem template HTML
          </EditItemTemplate>
          <FooterTemplate>
            Footer template HTML
          </FooterTemplate>

        </asp:TemplateColumn>
      </Columns>

    </asp:DataGrid>
```

DataGrid Class Public Methods

The `DataGrid` class adds no new public methods to those inherited from the `WebControl` and `BaseDataList` classes. See those class references for a complete listing.

335

DataGrid Class Protected Methods

- ❏ **OnCancelCommand**
- ❏ **OnDeleteCommand**
- ❏ **OnEditCommand**
- ❏ **OnItemCommand**
- ❏ **OnItemCreated**
- ❏ **OnItemDataBound**
- ❏ **OnPageIndexChanged**
- ❏ **OnSortCommand**
- ❏ **OnUpdateCommand**

OnCancelCommand

The `OnCancelCommand` method raises the `CancelCommand` event when the `Cancel` button is clicked for an item in the `DataGrid` control. This method allows derived classes to handle the `CancelCommand` event directly without attaching to a delegate.

```
protected virtual void OnCancelCommand(DataGridCommandEventArgs e);
```

The parameter e contains event data as a `DataGridCommandEventArgs` object containing four properties: `CommandArgument`, `CommandName`, `CommandSource` and `Item`.

OnDeleteCommand

The `OnDeleteCommand` method raises the `DeleteCommand` event when the `Delete` button is clicked for an item in the `DataGrid` control. This method allows derived classes to handle the `DeleteCommand` event directly without attaching to a delegate.

```
protected virtual void OnDeleteCommand(DataGridCommandEventArgs e);
```

The parameter e contains event data as a `DataGridCommandEventArgs` object containing four properties: `CommandArgument`, `CommandName`, `CommandSource` and `Item`.

OnEditCommand

The `OnEditCommand` method raises the `EditCommand` event when the `Edit` button is clicked for an item in the `DataGrid` control. This method allows derived classes to handle the `EditCommand` event directly without attaching to a delegate.

```
protected virtual void OnEditCommand(DataGridCommandEventArgs e);
```

The parameter e contains event data as a `DataGridCommandEventArgs` object containing four properties: `CommandArgument`, `CommandName`, `CommandSource` and `Item`.

OnItemCommand

The `OnItemCommand` method raises the `ItemCommand` event when any button is clicked for an item in the `DataGrid` control. This method can be used to handle the clicking of buttons with a custom command name. This method allows derived classes to handle the `ItemCommand` event directly without attaching to a delegate.

```
protected virtual void OnItemCommand(DataGridCommandEventArgs e);
```

The parameter e contains event data as a `DataGridCommandEventArgs` object containing four properties: `CommandArgument`, `CommandName`, `CommandSource` and `Item`.

OnItemCreated

The `ItemCreated` event is raised when an item in the `DataGrid` control is created. This method allows derived classes to handle the `ItemCreated` event directly without attaching to a delegate.

```
protected virtual void OnItemCreated(DataGridItemEventArgs e);
```

The parameter e represents a `DataGridItemEventArgs` object that contains a single `Item` property. The `Item` property gets the referenced item in the `DataGrid` control when the event is raised.

OnItemDataBound

The `ItemDataBound` event is raised when an item is data bound to the `DataGrid` control. This method allows derived classes to handle the `ItemDataBound` event directly without attaching to a delegate.

```
protected virtual void OnItemDataBound(DataGridItemEventArgs e);
```

The parameter e represents a `DataGridItemEventArgs` object that contains single `Item` property. The `Item` property gets the referenced item in the `DataGrid` control when the event is raised.

OnPageIndexChanged

The `OnPageIndexChanged` method raises the `PageIndexChanged` event when any paged element is selected in the `DataGrid` control. This method allows derived classes to handle the `PageIndexChanged` event directly without attaching to a delegate.

```
protected virtual void OnPageIndexChanged(DataGridPageChangedEventArgs e);
```

The parameter e represents a `DataGridPageChangedEventArgs` object that contains two properties `CommandSource` and `NewPageIndex`. The `NewPageIndex` property gets the index number of the page of the `DataGrid` control selected by the user, and the `CommandSource` property gets the source of the command which raised the event.

OnSortCommand

The `OnSortCommand` method raises the `SortCommand` event which occurs when the text in the header cell of the column is clicked; that is, when a column is sorted. This method allows derived classes to handle the `SortCommand` event directly without attaching to a delegate.

```
protected virtual void OnSortCommand(DataGridSortCommandEventArgs e);
```

The parameter e contains event data as a DataGridSortCommandEventArgs object containing two properties CommandSource and SortExpression. The most important argument is SortExpression, which contains the text displayed in the header cell in the current column of the DataGrid control. It can then be used to sort the datagrid based on this value. The CommandSource property gets the source of the command which raised the event.

OnUpdateCommand

The OnUpdateCommand method raises the UpdateCommand event when the Update button is clicked for an item in the DataGrid control. This method allows derived classes to handle the UpdateCommand event directly without attaching to a delegate.

```
protected virtual void OnUpdateCommand(DataGridCommandEventArgs e);
```

The parameter e contains event data as a DataGridCommandEventArgs object containing four properties: CommandArgument, CommandName, CommandSource and Item.

DataGrid Class Public Properties

- ❑ **AllowCustomPaging**
- ❑ **AllowPaging**
- ❑ **AllowSorting**
- ❑ **AlternatingItemStyle**
- ❑ **AutoGenerateColumns**
- ❑ **BackImageUrl**
- ❑ **Columns**
- ❑ **CurrentPageIndex**
- ❑ **EditItemIndex**
- ❑ **EditItemStyle**
- ❑ **FooterStyle**
- ❑ **HeaderStyle**
- ❑ **Items**
- ❑ **ItemStyle**
- ❑ **PageCount**
- ❑ **PagerStyle**
- ❑ **PageSize**
- ❑ **ShowFooter**
- ❑ **ShowHeader**
- ❑ **VirtualItemCount**

AllowCustomPaging

The `AllowCustomPaging` property gets or sets a `Boolean` value indicating whether custom paging is enabled. A value of `true` indicates that custom paging is enabled, `false` indicates custom paging is disabled. The default for `AllowCustomPaging` is `false`. It is only relevant when the `AllowPaging` property is set to `true`.

The `Paging` functionality of the `DataGrid` control is aimed at situations where a large amount of data needs to be displayed, and it allows us to divide the data rows from the data source into sub-sections that are much more manageable for display on a web page. When we move forward or back between sub-sections, the data source will be re-bound to the `DataGrid` control as appropriate. If the data source is extremely large, the binding process will consume more computer resources, and the whole thing becomes increasingly inefficient, which is where the `AllowCustomPaging` property comes into its own. The `AllowCustomPaging` property lets us load only the sub-section that will be displayed in the `DataGrid` control. For example, if we want to view the eleventh to twentieth items, only the required ten items will be loaded.

```
public virtual bool AllowCustomPaging {get; set;}
```

AllowPaging

The `AllowPaging` property gets or sets a `Boolean` value indicating whether paging is to be enabled. If you have many data rows in a data source, then you may wish to divide them into groups that will be displayed one group at a time on the web page. This property must be set to `true` if you wish to split data in this way.

```
public virtual bool AllowPaging {get; set;}
```

AllowSorting

The `AllowSorting` property gets or sets a `Boolean` value indicating whether data sorting is enabled. The default value is `false`. Set to `true` to make the heading section of each column within a grid show as a `LinkButton` control. This property works with the `SortExpression` property and the `SortCommand` event.

```
public virtual bool AllowSorting {get; set;}
```

AlternatingItemStyle

The `AlternatingItemStyle` property returns the style properties for every other item from the data source. The properties are returned as a `TableItemStyle` object. The default value is an empty `TableItemStyle` object meaning no style is defined.

```
public virtual TableItemStyle AlternatingItemStyle {get;}
```

AutoGenerateColumns

The `AutoGenerateColumns` property gets or sets a `Boolean` value that indicates whether `BoundColumn` objects are automatically created and displayed in the `DataGrid` control for each field in the data source. The default value is `true`. Explicitly declared columns may be used in conjunction with such columns. When using both, explicitly declared columns will be rendered first, followed by the automatically generated ones. Note that automatically generated columns are not added to the `Columns` collection.

```
public virtual bool AutoGenerateColumns {get; set;}
```

BackImageUrl

The `BackImageUrl` property gets or sets the URL of the background image that will appear in the background of the `DataGrid` control. If the size of the background image is smaller than the `DataGrid` control, then the background image will be tiled.

```
public virtual string BackImageUrl {get; set;}
```

Columns

The `Columns` property gets the collection of objects that represents the columns of the `DataGrid`. The object returned is a `DataGridColumnCollection` that represents a collection of `DataGridColumn` objects. The `DataGridColumn` class is the `MustInherit` base class for different column types. The different column type classes that inherit from the `DataGridColumn` class are:

❑   BoundColumn

❑   ButtonColumn

❑   EditCommandColumn

❑   HyperLinkColumn

❑   TemplateColumn

```
public virtual DataGridColumnCollection Columns {get;}
```

CurrentPageIndex

The `CurrentPageIndex` property gets or sets the index number of the currently displayed page in the `DataGrid` control when paging is enabled for the `DataGrid` control. For example, say there are 100 data rows in your data source and you have set the `AllowPaging` property to `true`. You will then have ten items displayed in the `DataGrid` control at any one time, and the index number for the first page displayed by the `DataGrid` control will be 0. By setting the `CurrentPageIndex` property to 0, you will force the control to display the first ten items from the data source in the area allocated to it on the web page.

```
public int CurrentPageIndex {get; set;}
```

EditItemIndex

The `EditItemIndex` property gets or sets the index number representing the current row selected in the `DataGrid` control for editing. The index is zero-based. For example, say you want to edit the tenth item of a DataGrid then this property should be set to 9.

```
public virtual int EditItemIndex {get; set;}
```

EditItemStyle

The `EditItemStyle` property returns the style properties for the row selected for editing in the `DataGrid` control. The style properties are returned as a `TableItemStyle` object. The default value is an empty `TableItemStyle` object meaning no style is defined.

```
public virtual TableItemStyle EditItemStyle {get;}
```

FooterStyle

The FooterStyle property returns the style properties for the footer section of the DataGrid control. The style properties are returned as a TableItemStyle object. The default value is an empty TableItemStyle object meaning no style is defined.

```
public virtual TableItemStyle FooterStyle {get;}
```

HeaderStyle

The HeaderStyle property returns the style properties for the header section of the DataGrid control. The style properties are returned as a TableItemStyle object. The default value is an empty TableItemStyle object meaning no style is defined.

```
public virtual TableItemStyle HeaderStyle {get;}
```

Items

The Items property returns a collection of the DataGridItem objects that represent the individual data items in the DataGrid control. The header, footer and separator items are not included in the collection. The DataGridItemCollection returned does not provide any methods to add or remove DataGridItem objects. These objects are closely bound to DataSource.

```
public virtual DataGridItemCollection Items {get;}
```

ItemStyle

The ItemStyle property returns the style properties for data grid items from the data source. The properties are returned as a TableItemStyle object. The default value is an empty TableItemStyle object meaning no style is defined.

```
public virtual TableItemStyle ItemStyle {get;}
```

PageCount

The PageCount property retrieves the total number of pages spanned by the DataGrid control. If we want to use this property, we must ensure that paging for the DataGrid control is enabled by setting the AllowPaging property to true.

```
public int PageCount {get;}
```

PagerStyle

The PagerStyle property lets us set the style properties for the paging section of the DataGrid control when paging is enabled. The properties are returned as a DataGridPagerStyle object. The default value is an empty DataGridPagerStyle object meaning no style is defined.

```
public virtual DataGridPagerStyle PagerStyle {get;}
```

PageSize

The `PageSize` property lets us set how many items should be displayed per page of the `DataGrid` control. The default value is `10`; so set this property to specify how many items you wish the `DataGrid` to display at any one time. This property is only relevant when the `AllowPaging` property is set to `true`.

```
public virtual int PageSize {get; set;}
```

SelectedIndex

The `SelectedIndex` property lets us get or set an index number for a selected item in the `DataGrid` control. If you want to de-select the item, you need to set this property to `-1`. This property is important for editing and deleting items in a `DataGrid` control.

```
public virtual int SelectedIndex {get; set;}
```

SelectedItem

The `SelectedItem` property returns the `DataGridItem` object that represents the currently selected item in the `DataGrid` control.

```
public virtual DataGridItem SelectedItem {get;}
```

SelectedItemStyle

The `SelectedItemStyle` property returns the style properties for the currently selected item in the `DataGrid` control. The style properties are returned as a `TableItemStyle` object. The default value is an empty `TableItemStyle` object meaning no style is defined.

```
public virtual TableItemStyle SelectedItemStyle {get;}
```

ShowFooter

The `ShowFooter` property lets us get or set a `Boolean` value that indicates whether the footer section in the `DataGrid` control is to be displayed. The default is `false` meaning the footer section is not displayed.

```
public virtual bool ShowFooter {get; set;}
```

ShowHeader

The `ShowHeader` property lets us get or set a `Boolean` value that indicates whether the header section in the `DataGrid` control is to be displayed. The default is `true` meaning that a header section is by default displayed.

```
public virtual bool ShowHeader {get; set;}
```

VirtualItemCount

When we set the `AllowCustomPaging` property to `false`, then all the items in the data source will be bound to the `DataGrid` control at once. If the `AllowCustomPaging` property is set to `true`, then the number of items bound to the `DataGrid` control at any one time is given by the `VirtualItemCount` property. This property is the key to letting us get or set the number of items to show in a `DataGrid` control when we are using custom paging.

```
public virtual int VirtualItemCount {get; set;}
```

Example: Binding to a DataGrid

The following example, `DataGridUsage1.aspx`, shows how to bind a `DataGrid` with the data and also apply styles to change its appearance. The user interface code is as follows:

```
<form id="FrmDataGridUsage1" method="post" runat="server">
  <h3>Binding Records to a DataGrid</h3>
  <asp:DataGrid id="DGrdProducts" runat="server" CellPadding="2"
               CellSpacing="2">
    <AlternatingItemStyle BackColor="yellow"></AlternatingItemStyle>
    <HeaderStyle BackColor="darksalmon"></HeaderStyle>
  </asp:DataGrid>
</form>
```

The following code binds the data with the `DataGrid`. The data here is the `Products` table from the Northwind database (note that you will need to change the connection string to point to your instance of SQL Server):

```
private void Page_Load(object sender, System.EventArgs e)
{
    // Create a SqlConnection and SqlDataAdapter object
    string ConnectionString =
            @"User ID=sa;Initial Catalog=Northwind;Data Source=(local)";
    SqlConnection cnn = new SqlConnection(ConnectionString);
    SqlDataAdapter da = new SqlDataAdapter("select * from products", cnn);

    // Create a dataset to store the Products data.
    DataSet ds = new DataSet();
    da.Fill(ds, "Products");
    // And then bind the Dataset with DataGrid
    DGrdProducts.DataSource = ds;
    DGrdProducts.DataMember = "Products";
    DGrdProducts.DataBind();
}
```

Here is a screenshot showing how the `DataGrid` is rendered:

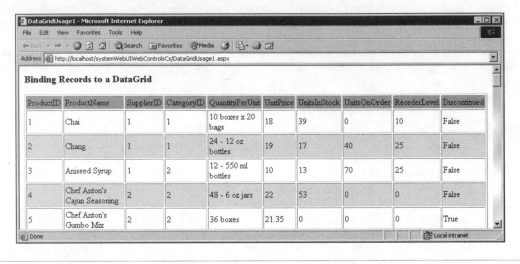

DataGrid Class Protected Properties

The `DataGrid` class adds no new protected properties to those inherited from the `WebControl` class. See the `WebControl` class reference for a complete listing.

DataGrid Class Public Events

- ❑ **CancelCommand**
- ❑ **DeleteCommand**
- ❑ **EditCommand**
- ❑ **ItemCommand**
- ❑ **ItemCreated**
- ❑ **ItemDataBound**
- ❑ **PageIndexChanged**
- ❑ **SortCommand**
- ❑ **UpdateCommand**

CancelCommand

The `CancelCommand` event occurs when the Cancel button is clicked for an item in the `DataGrid` control.

```
public event DataGridCommandEventHandler CancelCommand;
```

The event handler receives an argument of type `DataGridCommandEventArgs` containing four properties:

Property	Description
CommandArgument	The argument of the command
CommandName	The name of the command
CommandSource	The source of the command
Item	The selected item in the `DataGrid` control

DeleteCommand

The `DeleteCommand` event occurs when the Delete button is clicked for an item in the `DataGrid` control.

```
public event DataGridCommandEventHandler DeleteCommand;
```

The event handler receives an argument of type `DataGridCommandEventArgs` containing four properties: `CommandArgument`, `CommandName`, `CommandSource` and `Item`.

EditCommand

The `EditCommand` event occurs when the Edit button is clicked for an item in the `DataGrid` control.

```
public event DataGridCommandEventHandler EditCommand;
```

The event handler receives an argument of type `DataGridCommandEventArgs` containing four properties: `CommandArgument`, `CommandName`, `CommandSource` and `Item`.

Example: Creating an Editable DataGrid

The following code from `DataGridUsage2.aspx` shows how to enable editing and deleting in a `DataGrid`. The user interface code is:

```
<form id="FrmDataGridUsage2" method="post" runat="server">
  <h3>Editing and Deleting a record in DataGrid</h3>
  <asp:DataGrid id="DGrdProducts" runat="server"
              Width="588px" Height="354px"
              DataKeyField="ProductID" AutoGenerateColumns="false">
    <Columns>
      <asp:EditCommandColumn ButtonType="LinkButton" HeaderText="Edit"
                           UpdateText="Update" CancelText="Cancel"
                           EditText="Edit">
      </asp:EditCommandColumn>
      <asp:ButtonColumn HeaderText="Delete" Text="Delete"
                      CommandName="Delete">
      </asp:ButtonColumn>
      <asp:BoundColumn HeaderText="Product Name"
                     DataField="ProductName">
```

```
        </asp:BoundColumn>
        <asp:BoundColumn HeaderText="Quantity Per Unit"
                          DataField="QuantityPerUnit">
        </asp:BoundColumn>
      </Columns>
    </asp:DataGrid>
  </form>
```

The code for all the EditCommand, DeleteCommand, CancelCommand and UpdateCommand event handlers enables editing and deleting records in the DataGrid (again, you will need to alter the connection string according to your SQL Server instance):

```
private void Page_Load(object sender, System.EventArgs e)
  {
    if(!Page.IsPostBack)
      BindDGrdProducts();
  }

  private void BindDGrdProducts()
  {
    // Create a SqlConnection and SqlDataAdapter object
    string ConnectionString  =
            @"User ID=sa;Initial Catalog=Northwind;Data Source=(local);";
    SqlConnection cnn = new SqlConnection(ConnectionString);
    SqlDataAdapter da = new SqlDataAdapter("select * from products", cnn);

    // Create a dataset to store the Products data.
    DataSet ds = new DataSet();
    da.Fill(ds, "Products");
    // And then bind the Dataset with DataGrid

    DGrdProducts.DataSource = ds;
    DGrdProducts.DataMember = "Products";
    DGrdProducts.DataBind();
  }
```

Here is a screenshot of the output showing the effect when the Edit button is clicked:

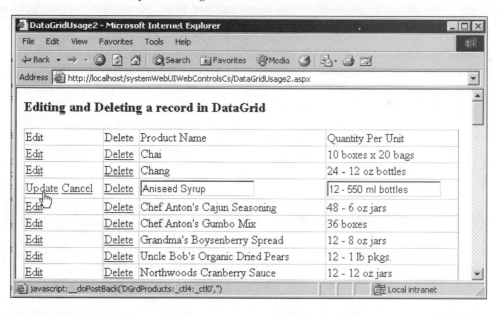

ItemCommand

The ItemCommand event occurs when any button is clicked in the DataGrid control. This event can be used to handle those buttons that have a custom command name.

```
public event DataGridCommandEventHandler ItemCommand;
```

The event handler receives an argument of type DataGridCommandEventArgs containing four properties: CommandArgument, CommandName, CommandSource and Item.

ItemCreated

The ItemCreated event occurs on the server when an item in the DataGrid control is created.

```
public event DataGridItemEventHandler ItemCreated;
```

The event handler receives an argument of type DataGridItemEventArgs that contains a single Item property. The Item property gets the referenced item in the DataGrid control when the event is raised.

ItemDataBound

The ItemDataBound event occurs when an item is data-bound to the DataGrid control.

```
public event DataGridItemEventHandler ItemDataBound;
```

The event handler receives an argument of type `DataGridItemEventArgs` that contains a single `Item` property. The `Item` property gets the referenced item in the `DataGrid` control when the event is raised.

PageIndexChanged

The `PageIndexChanged` event will be raised when a pager element is selected.

```
public event DataGridPageChangedEventHandler PageIndexChanged;
```

The event handler receives an argument of type `DataGridPageChangedEventArgs` that contains two properties: `CommandSource` and `NewPageIndex`. The `NewPageIndex` property gets the index number of the page of the `DataGrid` control selected by the user. The `CommandSource` property gets the source of the command which caused the event to fire.

Example: Enabling Paging in a DataGrid

The following code example, `DataGridUsage3.aspx`, shows how to enable paging in a `DataGrid`:

```
<form id="FrmDataGridUsage3" method="post" runat="server">
  <h3>Paging with DataGrid</h3>
  <asp:DataGrid id="DGrdProducts" runat="server"
              AllowPaging="true">
  </asp:DataGrid>
</form>
```

The code below handles the `PageIndexChanged` event (again, you will need to customize the connection string according to your settings):

```
private void Page_Load(object sender, System.EventArgs e)
  {
    if(!Page.IsPostBack)
      BindDGrdProducts();

    DGrdProducts.PagerStyle.Mode = PagerMode.NumericPages;
    DGrdProducts.PagerStyle.PageButtonCount = 3;
    DGrdProducts.PagerStyle.Position = PagerPosition.Top;
  }

private void BindDGrdProducts()
  {
    // Create a SqlConnection and SqlDataAdapter object
    string ConnectionString =
          @"User ID=sa;Initial Catalog=Northwind;Data Source=(local);";
    SqlConnection cnn = new SqlConnection(ConnectionString);
    SqlDataAdapter da = new SqlDataAdapter("select * from products", cnn);

    // Create a dataset to store the Products data.
    DataSet ds = new DataSet();
    da.Fill(ds, "Products");
```

```
    // And then bind the Dataset with DataGrid

  DGrdProducts.DataSource = ds;
  DGrdProducts.DataMember = "Products";
  DGrdProducts.DataBind();
}

private void DGrdProducts_PageIndexChanged(object source,
                                           DataGridPageChangedEventArgs e)
{
  DGrdProducts.CurrentPageIndex = e.NewPageIndex;
  BindDGrdProducts();
}
```

The following screenshot shows paging in action:

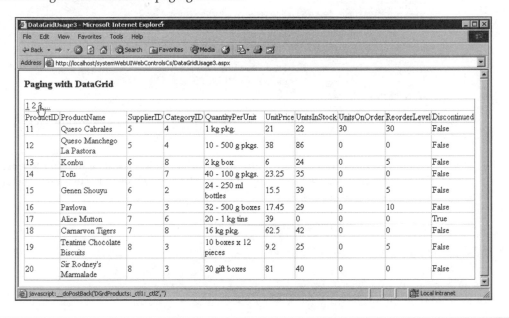

SortCommand

The SortCommand event requires that the AllowSorting property is set to true. It occurs when the text in the header cell of the column is clicked, meaning that the column is sorted.

```
public event DataGridSortCommandEventHandler SortCommand;
```

The event handler receives an argument of type DataGridSortCommandEventArgs containing two properties: CommandSource and SortExpression. The most important argument is SortExpression, which contains the text displayed in the header cell in the current column of the DataGrid control. It can then be used to sort the DataGrid based on this value.

Example: Enabling Sorting on a DataGrid

The following code from `DataGridUsage4.aspx` shows how to set up a `DataGrid` so it can be sorted. The user interface code is:

```
<form id="FrmDataGridUsage4" method="post" runat="server">
  <h3>Sorting records in DataGrid</h3>
  <asp:DataGrid id="DGrdProducts" runat="server" Width="500px"
                Height="354px" DataKeyField="ProductID"
                AutoGenerateColumns="false" AllowSorting="true">
    <Columns>
      <asp:BoundColumn DataField="ProductName" HeaderText="Product Name"
                    SortExpression="ProductName">
      </asp:BoundColumn>
      <asp:BoundColumn DataField="QuantityPerUnit"
                    HeaderText="Quantity Per Unit"
                    SortExpression="QuantityPerUnit">
      </asp:BoundColumn>
      <asp:BoundColumn DataField="UnitPrice" HeaderText="UnitPrice"
                    SortExpression="UnitPrice">
      </asp:BoundColumn>
    </Columns>
  </asp:DataGrid>
</form>
```

The fieldname on which the records are currently sorted is stored in viewstate in order to retain it on page reloads. The code below shows the sorting logic in action (you'll need to customize the connection string according to your settings):

```
private void Page_Load(object sender, System.EventArgs e)
{
  if(!Page.IsPostBack)
  {
    BindDGrdProducts();
    ViewState["SortID"] = "ProductName";
  }
}

private void BindDGrdProducts()
{
  // Create a SqlConnection and SqlDataAdapter object
  string ConnectionString  =
          @"User ID=sa;Initial Catalog=Northwind;Data Source=(local);";
  SqlConnection cnn = new SqlConnection(ConnectionString);
  SqlDataAdapter da = new SqlDataAdapter(
                "select * from products order by ProductName", cnn);

  // Create a dataset to store the Products data.
  DataSet ds = new DataSet();
  da.Fill(ds, "Products");

  // Create the DataView
```

```
DataView dvProducts = ds.Tables["Products"].DefaultView;

    // Set the Sort Property of the DataView
    if((string)ViewState["sortID"]  != "ProductName")
      dvProducts.Sort = (string)ViewState["SortID"];

    // And then bind the Dataset with DataGrid

    DGrdProducts.DataSource = dvProducts;
    DGrdProducts.DataBind();
}

private void DGrdProducts_SortCommand(object source,
                                      DataGridSortCommandEventArgs e)
{
  ViewState["SortID"]=e.SortExpression;
    BindDGrdProducts();
}
```

The screenshot shows the `DataGrid` sorted on the `QuantityPerUnit` field:

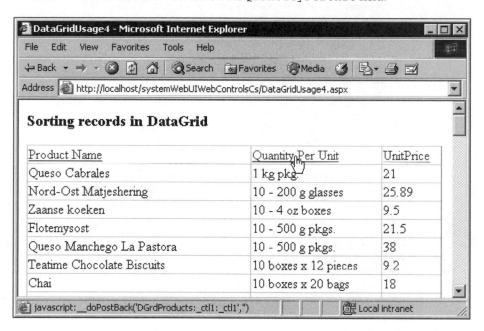

UpdateCommand

The `UpdateCommand` event occurs when the Update button is clicked for an item in the `DataGrid` control.

```
public event DataGridCommandEventHandler UpdateCommand;
```

351

The event handler receives an argument of type `DataGridCommandEventArgs` containing four properties: `CommandArgument`, `CommandName`, `CommandSource` and `Item`.

DataList Class

The `DataList` control displays data in a table in a form that can be edited and selected by the user, and you can configure how the control should appear. The `DataList` control provides seven templates for displaying data. However, the `DataList` control doesn't support paging and sorting as the `DataGrid` control does. `DataGrid` provides a complete range of features for displaying and editing data, making it suitable for applications that require complex data processing to generate the output for a web page. Although the `DataList` control does provide editing functionality, it isn't as powerful as the `DataGrid`, and data is displayed in a table rather than a grid. The `DataList` focuses primarily on the formatting of data for display, and the seven templates it provides are for this purpose.

This class is inherited from the `System.Web.UI.WebControls.BaseDataList` class. It has the following syntax:

```
<asp:DataList id="id_name"
              DataKeyField = "DataSourceKeyField"
              DataSource = "name of data source"
              ExtractTemplateRows = "true | false"
              GridLines = "None | Horizontal | Vertical | Both"
              RepeatColumns="ColumnCount"
              RepeatDirection = "Vertical | Horizontal"
              RepeatLayout = "Flow | Table"
              ShowFooter = "true | false"
              ShowHeader = "true | false"
              OnCancelCommand = "OnCancelCommandMethod"
              OnDeleteCommand = "OnDeleteCommandMethod"
              OnEditCommand = "OnEditCommandMethod"
              OnItemCommand = "OnItemCommandMethod"
              OnItemCreated = "OnItemCreatedMethod"
              OnUpdateCommand = "OnUpdateCommandMethod"
              Runat = "server">

  <AlternatingItemStyle property="value"/>
  <EditItemStyle property="value"/>
  <FooterStyle property="value"/>
  <HeaderStyle property="value"/>
  <ItemStyle property="value"/>
  <SelectedItemStyle property="value"/>
  <SeparatorStyle property="value"/>

  <HeaderTemplate>
    Header template HTML
  </HeaderTemplate>
  <ItemTemplate>
    Item template HTML
  </ItemTemplate>
  <AlternatingItemTemplate>
    Alternating item template HTML
  </AlternatingItemTemplate>
```

```
<EditItemTemplate>
  Edited item template HTML
</EditItemTemplate>
<SelectedItemTemplate>
  Selected item template HTML
</SelectedItemTemplate>
<SeparatorTemplate>
  Separator template HTML
</SeparatorTemplate>
<FooterTemplate>
  Footer template HTML
</FooterTemplate>

</asp:DataList>
```

Note that some members of this class have the same functionality as the `DataGrid` members, so those members are not explained again and you are referred to the `DataGrid` class reference.

DataList Class Public Methods

The `DataList` class adds no new public methods to those inherited from the `WebControl` and `BaseDataList` classes. See those class references for a complete listing.

DataList Class Protected Methods

❑ `OnDeleteCommand` – see `DataGrid` class reference for details.

❑ `OnEditCommand` – see `DataGrid` class reference for details.

❑ `OnItemCommand` – see `DataGrid` class reference for details.

❑ `OnItemCreated` – see `DataGrid` class reference for details.

❑ `OnItemDataBound` – see `DataGrid` class reference for details.

❑ `OnUpdateCommand` – see `DataGrid` class reference for details.

DataList Class Public Properties

❑ `AlternatingItemStyle` – see `DataGrid` class reference for details.

❑ **`AlternatingItemTemplate`**

❑ `EditItemIndex` – see `DataGrid` class reference for details.

❑ `EditItemStyle` – see `DataGrid` class reference for details.

❑ **`EditItemTemplate`**

❑ **`ExtractTemplateRows`**

❑ `FooterStyle` – see `DataGrid` class reference for details.

❑ **`FooterTemplate`**

❑ `GridLines` – see `DataGrid` class reference for details.

- ❏ HeaderStyle – see DataGrid class reference for details.
- ❏ **HeaderTemplate**
- ❏ Items – see DataGrid class reference for details.
- ❏ ItemStyle – see DataGrid class reference for details.
- ❏ **ItemTemplate**
- ❏ **RepeatColumns**
- ❏ **RepeatDirection**
- ❏ **RepeatLayout**
- ❏ SelectedIndex – see DataGrid class reference for details.
- ❏ SelectedItem – see DataGrid class reference for details.
- ❏ SelectedItemStyle – see DataGrid class reference for details.
- ❏ **SelectedItemTemplate**
- ❏ **SeparatorStyle**
- ❏ **SeparatorTemplate**
- ❏ ShowFooter – see DataGrid class reference for details.
- ❏ ShowHeader – see DataGrid class reference for details.

AlternatingItemTemplate

This property provides the content and layout to apply to every other item in the DataList control. All other elements are formatted according to the current ItemTemplate. If this template is not defined, then the ItemTemplate is used for all elements in the DataList control.

```
public virtual ITemplate AlternatingItemTemplate {get; set;}
```

EditItemTemplate

This provides the content and layout for the items in the DataList control selected for editing. If this template is not defined, then the ItemTemplate will be used to determine the content and layout for such items.

```
public virtual ITemplate EditItemTemplate {get; set;}
```

FooterTemplate

This provides the content and layout for the footer section in the DataList control. If this template is not defined, then no footer section will be displayed for the DataList control.

```
public virtual ITemplate FooterTemplate {get; set;}
```

HeaderTempate

This provides the content and layout for the header section in the DataList control. If this template is not defined, then no header section will be displayed for the DataList control.

```
public virtual ITemplate HeaderTemplate {get; set;}
```

ItemTemplate

This template **must** be defined. It provides the content and layout for all items in the `DataList` control.

```
public virtual ITemplate ItemTemplate {get; set;}
```

RepeatColumns

This gets or sets the number of columns that the `DataList` control should display. The default value is 0, indicating that the `DataList` only has a single row or column depending on the value of the `RepeatDirection` property.

```
public virtual int RepeatColumns {get; set;}
```

RepeatDirection

This gets or sets whether the contents of the `DataList` should be displayed horizontally or vertically. It can take either of the values from the `RepeatDirection` enumeration: `Vertical` or `Horizontal`. The default is `Vertical`.

```
public virtual RepeatDirection RepeatDirection {get; set;}
```

RepeatLayout

This gets or sets whether the control is displayed in a table or in flow layout. It can take either of the values from the `RepeatLayout` enumeration: `Table` or `Flow`. The default is `Table`.

```
public virtual RepeatLayout RepeatLayout {get; set;}
```

SelectedItemTemplate

This provides the content and layout for the currently selected item in the `DataList` control. If this template is not defined, then the `ItemTemplate` will be applied instead.

```
public virtual ITemplate SelectedItemTemplate {get; set;}
```

SeparatorStyle

The `SeparatorStyle` property returns the style properties for the separator items in the `DataList` control. The style properties are returned as a `TableItemStyle` object. The default value is an empty `TableItemStyle` object meaning no style is defined.

```
public virtual TableItemStyle SeparatorStyle {get;}
```

SeparatorTemplate

This provides the content and layout for the separator between items in the `DataList` control. If this template is not defined, then no separator section will be displayed for the `DataList` control.

```
public virtual ITemplate SeparatorTemplate {get; set;}
```

DataList Class Protected Properties

The `DataList` class adds no new protected properties to those inherited from the `WebControl` class. See the `WebControl` class reference for a complete listing.

DataList Class Public Events

❑   `CancelCommand` – see `DataGrid` class reference for details.

❑   `DeleteCommand` – see `DataGrid` class reference for details.

❑   `EditCommand` – see `DataGrid` class reference for details.

❑   `ItemCommand` – see `DataGrid` class reference for details.

❑   `ItemCreated` – see `DataGrid` class reference for details.

❑   `ItemDataBound` – see `DataGrid` class reference for details.

❑   `UpdateCommand` – see `DataGrid` class reference for details.

Example: Binding to the DataList Control

The following example, `DataListUsage.aspx`, illustrates the `DataList` templates and binding data to `DataList`. We use a `DataList` to display the `Products` table from the Northwind. This example also shows how to include editing functionality. The user interface code is as follows:

```
<form id="FrmDataListUsage" method="post" runat="server">
  <h3>Binding and Editing records with DataList</h3>
  <asp:DataList id="DLstProducts" runat="server" CellPadding="2"
                CellSpacing="2">
    <HeaderTemplate>
      Product Details
    </HeaderTemplate>
    <AlternatingItemStyle BackColor="yellow"></AlternatingItemStyle>
    <ItemTemplate>
      Product ID:
      <%# DataBinder.Eval(Container.DataItem, "ProductID") %>
      <br>
      Product Name:
      <%# DataBinder.Eval(Container.DataItem, "ProductName") %>
      <br>
      Quantity Per Unit:
      <%# DataBinder.Eval(Container.DataItem, "QuantityPerUnit") %>
      <br>
      <asp:LinkButton id="BtnEdit" runat="server" Text="Edit"
```

```
        CommandName="Edit" />
    </ItemTemplate>
    <HeaderStyle BackColor="darksalmon"></HeaderStyle>
    <EditItemTemplate>
      Product ID:
      <asp:Label id=LblProductID Runat-"Server"
          Text='<%# DataBinder.Eval(Container.DataItem, "ProductID") %>'>
      </asp:Label><br>
      Product Name:
      <asp:TextBox id=TxtProductName Runat="server"
        Text='<%# DataBinder.Eval(Container.DataItem, "ProductName") %>'>
      </asp:TextBox><br>
      Quantity Per Unit:
      <asp:TextBox id=TxtQty runat="server"
     Text='<%# DataBinder.Eval(Container.DataItem, "QuantityPerUnit") %>'>
      </asp:TextBox>
      <br>
      <asp:LinkButton id="BtnUpdate" runat="server" Text="Update"
                    CommandName="Update" />
      <asp:LinkButton id="BtnCancel" runat="server" Text="Cancel"
                    CommandName="Cancel" />
    </EditItemTemplate>
  </asp:DataList>
</form>
```

The following code shows how to bind data to the DataList, and the various event handlers we need to code to enable editing functionality:

```
private void Page_Load(object sender, System.EventArgs e)
  {
    if(!Page.IsPostBack)
      BindDLstProducts();
  }

  private void BindDLstProducts()
  {
    // Create a SqlConnection and SqlDataAdapter object
    string ConnectionString =
            @"User ID=sa;Initial Catalog=Northwind;Data Source=(local);";
    SqlConnection cnn = new SqlConnection(ConnectionString);
    SqlDataAdapter da = new SqlDataAdapter("select * from products", cnn);

    // Create a dataset to store the Products data.
    DataSet ds = new DataSet();
    da.Fill(ds, "Products");
    // And then bind the Dataset with DataGrid

    DLstProducts.DataSource = ds;
    DLstProducts.DataMember = "Products";
    DLstProducts.DataBind();
  }
```

The following screenshot shows the `DataList` created:

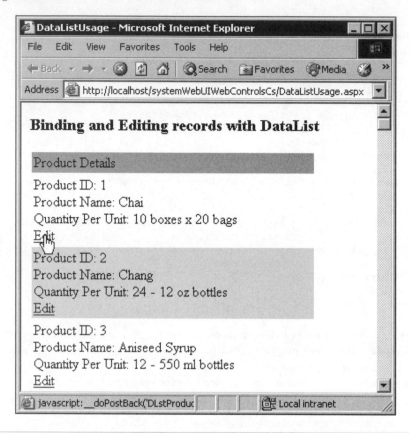

DropDownList Class

The `DropDownList` control allows the user to select a single item from a drop-down list. It occupies less space on the web page as compared to a list box. Items in the list can be added either at design time using the `<asp:ListItem>` element or at run-time by manipulating with the `ListItemCollection`, or the items can also be added by data-binding the `DropDownList` with the `DataSource`.

This class is inherited from the `System.Web.UI.WebControls.ListControl` class. It has the following syntax:

```
<asp:DropDownList id = "id_name"
                DataSource = "name of data source"
                DataTextField = "Data Source Field"
                DataValueField = "Data Source Field"
                AutoPostBack = "true | false"
                OnSelectedIndexChanged = "Method for selected ⌐
                                         index changed"
```

```
                    Runat = "server">
    <asp:ListItem text="content of ListItem" value="value of ListItem" />
  </asp:DropDownList>
```

DropDownList Class Public Methods

The `DropDownList` class adds no new public methods to those inherited from the `WebControl` class. See the `WebControl` class reference for a complete listing.

DropDownList Class Protected Methods

The `DropDownList` class adds no new protected methods to those inherited from the `WebControl` and `ListControl` classes. See those class references for a complete listing.

DropDownList Class Public Properties

❑ **SelectedIndex**

SelectedIndex

The `SelectedIndex` property gets or sets the index of the currently selected item in the `DropDownList` control. The index is zero-based. The default value is 0 indicating the first item in the list, resulting in an item always being selected in the list.

```
public override int SelectedIndex {get; set;}
```

Example: Creating Data-Bound DropDownList Control

The following code from `DropDownListUsage.aspx` shows how to create data-bound and simple drop-down lists. Here's the user interface:

```
<form id="FrmDropDownList" method="post" runat="server">
  Please Select Shipping Details:<br>
  Shipper:
  <asp:DropDownList id="DDLstShippers" Runat="server"
                    AutoPostBack="true"></asp:DropDownList>
  State:
  <asp:DropDownList id="DDLstState" runat="server">
    <asp:ListItem Text="MI"></asp:ListItem>
    <asp:ListItem Text="CA"></asp:ListItem>
    <asp:ListItem Text="FL"></asp:ListItem>
    <asp:ListItem Text="NY"></asp:ListItem>
    <asp:ListItem Text="OR"></asp:ListItem>
    <asp:ListItem Text="MA"></asp:ListItem>
    <asp:ListItem Text="IL"></asp:ListItem>
  </asp:DropDownList>
  <br>
  <asp:Button ID="BtnSubmit" runat="server" Text="Submit"></asp:Button>
  <hr>
  <asp:Label ID="LblShippers" Runat="server"></asp:Label>
  <asp:Label ID="LblState" Runat="server"></asp:Label><br>
</form>
```

The Shippers drop-down list is populated from the **Northwind** database in the `Page_Load` event. The code below also shows how to display the `SelectedItem` in the `DropDownList` in the `SelectionChanged` event handlers:

```
private void Page_Load(object sender, System.EventArgs e)
{
  if(!Page.IsPostBack)
  {
    //Add an Item programmatically to the State List
    DDLstState.Items.Add("IN");
    DDLstState.Items.Add("TN");

    // Create a SqlConnection and SqlDataAdapter object
    string ConnectionString =
            @"User ID=sa;Initial Catalog=Northwind;Data Source=(local);";
    SqlConnection cnn = new SqlConnection(ConnectionString);
    SqlDataAdapter da = new SqlDataAdapter("select * from Shippers",
                                                cnn);

    // Create a dataset to store the Shippers table data.
    DataSet ds  = new DataSet();
    da.Fill(ds, "Shippers");

    DDLstShippers.DataSource = ds;
    DDLstShippers.DataMember = "Shippers";
    DDLstShippers.DataTextField = "CompanyName";
    DDLstShippers.DataValueField = "ShipperID";
    DDLstShippers.DataBind();
  }
}

private void DDLstShippers_SelectedIndexChanged(object sender,
                                                System.EventArgs e)
{
  LblShippers.Text = "Shipper " + DDLstShippers.SelectedItem.Text
                  + " (" + DDLstShippers.SelectedItem.Value + ")";
}

private void DDLstState_SelectedIndexChanged(object sender,
                                                System.EventArgs e)
{
  LblState.Text = "State " + DDLstState.SelectedItem.Text
               + " (" + DDLstState.SelectedItem.Value + ")";
}
```

Here is a screenshot showing the output:

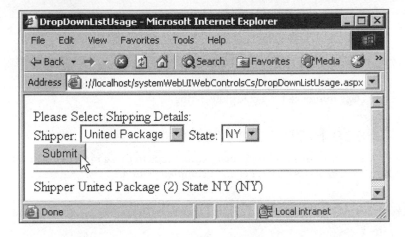

DropDownList Class Protected Properties

The DropDownList class adds no new protected properties to those inherited from the WebControl and ListControl classes. See those class references for a complete listing.

DropDownList Class Public Events

The DropDownList class adds no new public events to those inherited from the WebControl and ListControl classes. See those class references for a complete listing.

HyperLink Class

The HyperLink control displays a link on a web page that allows navigation to another page (URL). The link can either be an image or a text. The HyperLink control does not post the form to the server. It is inherited from the System.Web.UI.WebControls.WebControl class.

It corresponds to the HTML control <a> anchor element. It has the following syntax:

```
<asp:HyperLink id="id_name"
          NavigateUrl = "Url of target page"
          Text = "Visible Text for the HyperLink"
          ImageUrl = "Url of image"
          Target = "_blank | _parent | _self | _top"
          Runat = "server" />
```

or:

```
<asp:HyperLink id="id_name"
          NavigateUrl = "Url of target page"
          ImageUrl = "Url of image"
```

```
                  Target = "_blank | _parent | _self | _top"
                  Runat = "Server">
     Visible Text for the Hyperlink
  </asp:HyperLink>
```

HyperLink Class Public Methods

The HyperLink class adds no new public methods to those inherited from the WebControl class. See the WebControl class reference for a complete listing.

HyperLink Class Protected Methods

The DropDownList class adds no new protected methods to those inherited from the WebControl class. See the WebControl class reference for a complete listing.

HyperLink Class Public Properties

- ❑ **ImageUrl**
- ❑ **NavigateUrl**
- ❑ **Target**
- ❑ **Text**

ImageUrl

The ImageUrl property gets or sets the path of an image that is displayed on a web page as the HyperLink control. The default value is an empty string. When this property is set, the hyperlink control is displayed as the image specified.

```
    public virtual string ImageUrl {get; set;}
```

NavigateUrl

The NavigateUrl property gets or sets the URL that the user is transferred to when the HyperLink control is clicked. The default value is an empty string.

```
    public string NavigateUrl {get; set;}
```

Target

The Target property gets or sets the target window or frame to display the linked page when the control is clicked. The default value is an empty string. This property is case-insensitive and its value must begin with an alphabetic character (a-z) except for some special values that begin with the underscore symbol.

```
    public string Target {get; set;}
```

The following table summarizes the special values:

Value	Description
_blank	A new and unframed browser window
_parent	The immediate frameset parent in the same browser
_self	The current frame in the same browser window
_top	The full and unframed window in the same browser

If you don't set any values for the `Target` property, then by default it will display the content in the current frame in the same browser window. If you set any other values for the `Target` property, remember that it treats unknown parameters as the `_blank` parameter.

Text

The `Text` property gets or sets the text of the `HyperLink` control. If the `ImageUrl` and the `Text` property are both specified for a `HyperLink` control, then the `HyperLink` control is displayed as an image and the `Text` property acts as alternate text for the image. The alternate text for the image is displayed if the image is unavailable. This property also acts as a Tool Tip for the image if the browser supports ToolTip functionality. If the `ImageUrl` property is not set, then this property acts as caption text for the `HyperLink` control.

```
public virtual string Text {get; set;}
```

Example: Using the HyperLink Control

The following code from `HyperLinkUsage.aspx` shows how to set the `HyperLink` control as an image or text:

```
<form id="FrmHyperLink" method="post" runat="server">
  <asp:HyperLink ID="HLnkWrox" Runat="server" ImageUrl="wroxlogo.gif"
             NavigateUrl="http://www.wrox.com"
             Text="Click here to visit wrox.com"
             Target="_self">
  </asp:HyperLink>
  <br>
  <asp:HyperLink ID="HLnkWroxText" Runat="server"
             NavigateUrl="http://www.wrox.com"
             Text="Click here to visit wrox.com"
             Target="_self">
  </asp:HyperLink>
</form>
```

Unlike the majority of the Web controls, the `HyperLink` control doesn't raise a server-side event when the user clicks it, and simply performs the specified navigation directly.

Here is a screenshot of the output:

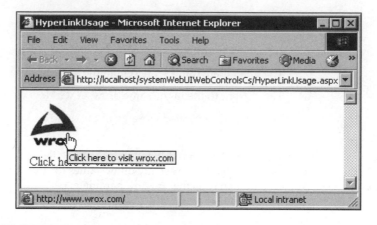

HyperLink Class Protected Properties

The HyperLink class adds no new protected properties to those inherited from the WebControl class. See the WebControl class reference for a complete listing.

HyperLink Class Public Events

The HyperLink class adds no new public events to those inherited from the WebControl class. See the WebControl class reference for a complete listing.

Image Class

The Image control displays an image on a web page or alternate text if the image is not available. It is inherited from the System.Web.UI.WebControls.WebControl class.

It is rendered as an <img> image element. It has the following syntax:

```
<asp:Image id="id_name"
           ImageUrl = "Url of image"
           AlternateText = "text of alert"
           ImageAlign = "alignment of image"
           Runat = "server" />
```

Image Class Public Methods

The Image class adds no new public methods to those inherited from the WebControl class. See the WebControl class reference for a complete listing.

Image Class Protected Methods

The Image class adds no new protected methods to those inherited from the WebControl class. See the WebControl class reference for a complete listing.

Image Class Public Properties

- ❑ **AlternateText**
- ❑ **ImageAlign**
- ❑ **ImageUrl**

AlternateText

The AlternateText property gets or sets the alternate text that is displayed in the Image control on a web page when the image is unavailable, the image is being downloaded, or if the browser doesn't support images. If a browser supports the Tool Tips feature, then the alternate text will also be displayed as a ToolTip when the cursor hovers over the image.

```
public virtual string AlternateText {get; set;}
```

ImageAlign

The ImageAlign property gets or sets the alignment of the image with reference to the other elements on the web page.

```
public virtual ImageAlign ImageAlign {get; set;}
```

The valid values for this property belong to the ImageAlign enumeration. An ArgumentException is thrown if this property is set with a value other than one of the ImageAlign values. The possible values of the ImageAlign enumeration are:

Alignment	Description
AbsBottom	In the same HTML line, the image will be aligned with the lower edge of the highest element
AbsMiddle	In the same HTML line, the image will be aligned with the middle of the highest element
Baseline	In the same HTML line, the lower edge of the image will be aligned with the bottom line of the first text in this line
Bottom	In the same HTML line, the lower edge of the image will be aligned with the bottom line of the first text in this line
Left	The image will be aligned with the left side of a web page in the next line rather than original line
Middle	In the same HTML line, the middle point of the image will be aligned with the bottom edge of the first line of text
NotSet	It sets no alignment (Default value of this property)

Alignment	Description
Right	The image will be aligned with the right side of a web page in the next line rather than original line
TextTop	In the same HTML line, the top side of the image will be aligned with the top edge of the highest text in this line
Top	In the same HTML line, the top side of the image will be aligned with the top edge of the highest element in this line

ImageUrl

The `ImageUrl` property gets or sets the URL of the image that is to be displayed by the control. The URL can be both absolute and relative.

```
public virtual string ImageUrl {get; set;}
```

The following code shows how to set the properties of an `Image` control:

```
<asp:Image ID="ImgWrox" Runat="server" ImageUrl="wroxlogo.gif"
           AlternateText="Logo of Wrox Press Ltd"
           ImageAlign="AbsBottom">
</asp:Image>
```

Image Class Protected Properties

The `Image` class adds no new protected properties to those inherited from the `WebControl` class. See the `WebControl` class reference for a complete listing.

Image Class Public Events

The `Image` class adds no new public events to those inherited from the `WebControl` class. See the `WebControl` class reference for a complete listing.

ImageButton Class

The `ImageButton` control enables you to click an image on a web page. The `ImageButton` web control submits the form to the server and it can raise an event that fires the appropriate event code in the server-side script. It is inherited from the `System.Web.UI.WebControls.Image` class. It behaves in the same way as a `Button` control.

It corresponds to the HTML control `<input type="image">`. It has the following syntax:

```
<asp:ImageButton id = "id_name"
                 ImageUrl = "URL of image"
                 CommandName = "Command name"
                 CommandArgument = "Command argument"
                 OnCommand = "Method name" | OnClick = "Method name"
                 Runat = "server" />
```

You can create either a Submit image button or a Command image button on a web page. When you don't specify a `CommandName` property, the image button is by default a Submit button. You can provide an event handler for the `Click` event to programmatically control the actions performed when the Submit image button is clicked.

An image button with a command name is called a Command image button. You can also provide additional information in the `CommandArgument` property for the image button. Furthermore, you can specify an event handler for the `Command` event that programmatically controls the action performed when the Command image button is clicked.

ImageButton Class Public Methods

The `ImageButton` class adds no new public methods to those inherited from the `WebControl` class. See the `WebControl` class reference for a complete listing.

ImageButton Class Protected Methods

- ❑ **OnClick**
- ❑ **OnCommand**

OnClick

The `OnClick` method will raise a `Click` event when a Submit image button is clicked. A Submit image button is one for which no `CommandName` or `CommandArgument` properties have been specified. This method notifies the server of the actions to be performed when the Submit button control is clicked and the form is submitted to the server. This method allows derived classes to handle the `Click` event without attaching to a delegate.

```
protected virtual void OnClick(ImageClickEventArgs e);
```

The parameter e represents an `ImageClickEventArgs` object that lets us know the exact coordinates where the image button was clicked, relative to the top-left corner of the image (0, 0).

OnCommand

The `Command` event is raised when a Command image button is clicked. A Command image button has the `CommandName` and `CommandArgument` properties specified. This method notifies the server of the actions to be performed when the Command image button control is clicked and the form is submitted to the server. This method allows derived classes to handle the `Command` event without attaching to a delegate.

```
protected virtual void OnCommand(CommandEventArgs e);
```

The parameter e receives information related to the event through the `CommandEventArgs` object. This object contains the `CommandName` and `CommandArgument` properties.

ImageButton Class Public Properties

- ❑ **CausesValidation**
- ❑ **CommandArgument**
- ❑ **CommandName**

CausesValidation

The `CausesValidation` property is used to specify whether validation should be performed when the `ImageButton` control is clicked. The validation is performed by the ASP.NET validation controls (if any) associated with the server controls in the page. This property therefore causes the validation controls to perform their validation test if set to `true`, and not if set to `false`. The default value is `true`. Sometimes it is necessary to submit the page without validation, like for example in the event of a Cancel or Reset button being clicked. This property when `true` may perform validations at both the client and server depending on capabilities of the browser and the setting of the `ClientTarget` attribute in the `Page` directive.

```
public bool CausesValidation {get; set;}
```

CommandArgument

The `CommandArgument` property gets or sets an argument for a Command Button. When you set the `CommandName` property indicating that the button is a Command image button, then this property provides the means for passing arguments to a `Command` event. The default value is an empty string. If this property is set, then it passes its value to the `Command` event when the image button is clicked.

```
public string CommandArgument {get; set;}
```

CommandName

The `CommandName` property gets or sets the command name associated with the `ImageButton` control. This value is passed to the `Command` event when the button is clicked. This command name can be used on the server to determine which image button control was triggered. The default value is an empty string.

```
public string CommandName {get; set;}
```

ImageButton Class Protected Properties

The `ImageButton` class adds no new protected properties to those inherited from the `WebControl` class. See the `WebControl` class reference for a complete listing.

ImageButton Class Public Events

- ❑ **Click**
- ❑ **Command**

368

Click

The Click event will occur when an image button control is clicked and the form is submitted to the server. The event is only raised for Submit buttons. A Submit button is a button control that does not have CommandName and CommandArgument properties specified for it.

```
public event ImageClickEventHandler Click;
```

The event handler receives information related to the event through the ImageClickEventArgs object, passed as its argument. This objects lets us know the exact coordinates where the image button was clicked, relative to the top-left corner of the image as (0, 0).

Command

The Command event will occur when an ImageButton control is clicked and the form is submitted to the server. The event is only raised for Command buttons. Command buttons have CommandName and CommandArgument properties specified.

```
public event CommandEventHandler Command;
```

The event handler receives information related to the event through the CommandEventArgs object, passed as its argument. This object contains the CommandName and CommandArgument properties to get the CommandName and CommandArgument property values.

Example: Using an ImageButton Control

The following code from ImageButtonUsage.aspx shows how to get the X and Y co-ordinates from the Click event of an ImageButton control:

```
<form id="FrmImageButtonUsage" method="post" runat="server">
  <asp:ImageButton ID="IBtnWrox" runat="server" ImageUrl="wrox.gif"
                   BorderStyle="Solid">
  </asp:ImageButton>
  <hr><asp:Label ID="LblMessage" runat="server"></asp:Label>
</form>
```

The BtnCommand_Command event handler code below shows how the X and Y properties can be accessed:

```
private void IBtnWrox_Click(object sender,
                           System.Web.UI.ImageClickEventArgs e)
{
  LblMessage.Text="You clicked at (" + e.X.ToString() + ","
                                    + e.Y.ToString() + ")";
}
```

The following screenshot shows the output when the image button is clicked:

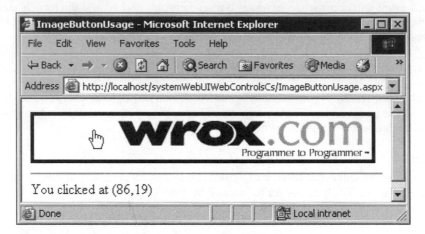

As you can see an image button can easily be substituted in the place of `Button` and `LinkButton` controls as it offers the same functionality.

Label Class

The `Label` control displays static text on a web page and allows you to manipulate it programmatically. It is inherited from the `System.Web.UI.WebControls.WebControl` class.

It is rendered as the HTML `<span>` element and has the following syntax:

```
<asp:Label id = "id_name"
          Text = "text of Label"
          runat = "server" />
```

or:

```
<asp:Label id = "id_name"
          runat = "server">
  Text of Label
</asp:Label>
```

Label Class Public Methods

The `Label` class adds no new public methods to those inherited from the `WebControl` class. See the `WebControl` class reference for a complete listing.

Label Class Protected Methods

The `Label` class adds no new protected methods to those inherited from the `WebControl` class. See the `WebControl` class reference for a complete listing.

Label Class Public Properties

❑ **Text**

Text

The `Text` property gets or sets the text content of a `Label` control. The `Label` control displays this text content when it is rendered in the web page. This property can contain plain text content or even HTML content. As always with other properties, the value of this property can be assigned declaratively or programmatically.

```
public virtual string Text {get; set;}
```

Example: Using a Label Control

The following code snippet from `LabelUsage.aspx` shows how to set the properties of a `Label` control:

```
<form id="FrmLabelUsage" method="post" runat="server">
  <asp:Label ID="LblText" Text="<B>Current DateTime: </b>"
             Runat="server">
  </asp:Label>
  <asp:Label ID="LblDateTime" Runat="server"></asp:Label>
</form>
```

The following code shows how to set the properties programmatically:

```
private void Page_Load(object sender, System.EventArgs e)
  {
    LblDateTime.Text = DateTime.Now.ToString();
  }
```

Here is a screenshot of the resulting output:

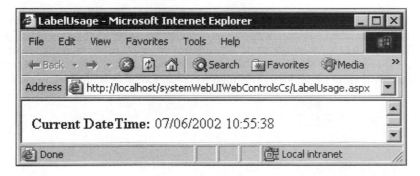

Label Class Protected Properties

The Label class adds no new protected properties to those inherited from the WebControl class. See the WebControl class reference for a complete listing.

Label Class Public Events

The Label class adds no new public events to those inherited from the WebControl class. See the WebControl class reference for a complete listing.

LinkButton Class

The LinkButton control has the appearance of a HyperLink but acts like a Button control. The LinkButton web control, unlike the HyperLink control, submits the form to the server and it can raise an event that fires the appropriate event code in our server-side script. It is inherited from the System.Web.UI.WebControls.WebControl class.

It is rendered as an <a> anchor element and has the following syntax:

```
<asp:LinkButton id = "id_name"
               Text = "Text of LinkButton"
               CommandName = "Command name parameter"
               CommandArgument = "Command argument parameter"
     OnCommand = "Method of LinkButton" | OnClick = "Method of LinkButton"
               Runat = "server" />
```

or:

```
<asp:LinkButton id="id_name"
               Command="Command name parameter"
               CommandArgument="Command argument parameter"
     OnCommand = "Method of LinkButton" | OnClick = "Method of LinkButton"
               Runat = "server" >
   Text of LinkButton
</asp:LinkButton>
```

The LinkButton control allows you to create either a Submit link button or a Command link button on a web page. By default, if you do not specify a CommandName property, the link button is a Submit link button. You can provide an event handler for the Click event to programmatically control the actions performed when such a Submit link button is clicked.

A link button with a command name is a Command link button. You can create Command buttons by specifying the CommandName property on a web page and programmatically determining which link button is clicked. You can also provide additional information by specifying a CommandArgument property for the link button. You can also add an event handler for the Command event to programmatically control the actions performed when the Command link button is clicked.

LinkButton Class Public Methods

The `LinkButton` class adds no new public methods to those inherited from the `WebControl` class. See the `WebControl` class reference for a complete listing.

LinkButton Class Protected Methods

❑ `OnClick`

❑ `OnCommand`

OnClick

The `OnClick` method will raise a Click event when a Submit link button is clicked. A Submit link button is one for which no `CommandName` or `CommandArgument` properties have been specified. This method notifies the server of the actions to be performed when the Submit link button control is clicked and the form is submitted to the server. This method allows derived classes to handle the `Click` event without attaching to a delegate.

```
protected virtual void OnClick(EventArgs e);
```

OnCommand

The `Command` event is raised when a Command link button is clicked. A Command link button must have `CommandName` and `CommandArgument` properties specified. This method notifies the server of the actions to be performed when the Command link button control is clicked and the form is submitted to the server. This method allows derived classes to handle the `Command` event without attaching to a delegate.

```
protected virtual void OnCommand(CommandEventArgs e);
```

The parameter e receives information related to the event through the `CommandEventArgs` object. This object contains the `CommandName` and `CommandArgument` properties' values.

LinkButton Class Public Properties

❑ `CausesValidation`

❑ `CommandArgument`

❑ `CommandName`

❑ `Text`

CausesValidation

The `CausesValidation` property is used to specify whether validation should be performed when the `LinkButton` control is clicked. The validation is performed by the ASP.NET validation controls (if any) associated with the server controls in the page. This property therefore causes the validation controls to perform their validation test if set to `true`, and not if set to `false`. The default value is `true`. Sometimes, it is necessary to submit the page without validation, like for example in the event of a Cancel or Reset button being clicked. This property, when `true`, may perform validations at both the client and the server depending on the capabilities of the browser and the setting of the `ClientTarget` attribute in the `Page` directive.

```
public bool CausesValidation {get; set;}
```

CommandArgument

The CommandArgument property gets or sets an argument for a Command LinkButton. When you set the CommandName property indicating that the link button is a Command button, then this property provides the means for passing arguments to a Command event. The default value is an empty string. If this property is set, then it passes its value to the Command event when the link button is clicked.

```
public string CommandArgument {get; set;}
```

CommandName

The CommandName property gets or sets the command name associated with the LinkButton control. This value is passed to the Command event when the button is clicked. This helps in creating multiple command buttons and then CommandName can be used on the server to determine which link button was triggered. The default value is an empty string. If this property is set, then it passes its value to the Command event when the link button is clicked.

```
public string CommandName {get; set;}
```

Text

The Text property gets or sets the caption text for the link button. The default value is an empty string.

```
public virtual string Text {get; set;}
```

LinkButton Class Protected Properties

The LinkButton class adds no new protected properties to those inherited from the WebControl class. See the WebControl class reference for a complete listing.

LinkButton Class Public Events

- ❑ **Click**
- ❑ **Command**

Click

The Click event will occur when a link button control is clicked and the form is submitted to the server. The event is raised for only Submit link buttons. A Submit link button is a link button control that does not have CommandName and CommandArgument properties specified for the link button control.

```
public event EventHandler Click;
```

The event handler receives information related to the event through the EventArgs object, passed as its argument.

Command

The Command event will occur when a LinkButton control is clicked and the form is submitted to the server. The event is raised for only Command link buttons. Command link buttons have CommandName and CommandArgument properties specified.

```
public event CommandEventHandler Command;
```

The event handler receives information related to the event through the CommandEventArgs object, passed as its argument. This object contains the CommandName and CommandArgument property values.

Example: Using Submit and Command LinkButton Controls

The following code example from LinkButtonUsage.aspx shows how to use Submit and Command link buttons. This example allows you to generate either five random numbers with a Command LinkButton or any amount of random numbers desired with a Submit LinkButton. The Command LinkButton also has its CausesValidation property set to false which results in no validation occurring when the LinkButton is clicked:

```
<form id="FrmLinkButtonUsage" method="post" runat="server">
  <h3>Generate Random Numbers</h3>
  <table>
    <tr>
      <td>How many:</td>
      <td>
      <asp:TextBox ID="TxtNumber" Runat="server"></asp:TextBox>
      <asp:RequiredFieldValidator ID="ReqValTxtNumber"
                                  Runat="server"
                                  ControlToValidate="TxtNumber"
                                  ErrorMessage="Please enter the number">
      </asp:RequiredFieldValidator></td>
    </tr>
    <tr>
      <td>
      <asp:LinkButton ID="LBtnSubmit" Text="Submit" Runat="server">
      </asp:LinkButton>
      </td>
      <td>
      <asp:LinkButton ID="LBtnCommand" CommandArgument="5"
                  CommandName="Random" runat="server"
                  CausesValidation="false"
                  Text="Generate 5 Random Numbers">
      </asp:LinkButton></td>
    </tr>
  </table>
  <p><span id="Message" runat="server"></span></p>
</form>
```

The `LBtnCommand_Command` event handler code below shows how the `CommandName` and `CommandArgument` properties can be accessed:

```csharp
private void LBtnSubmit_Click(object sender, System.EventArgs e)
{
  Message.InnerHtml="";
  GenerateRandomNumbers(Convert.ToInt32(TxtNumber.Text));
}

private void LBtnCommand_Command(object sender, CommandEventArgs e)
{
  Message.InnerHtml = e.CommandName + "Numbers:" + "<BR>";
  GenerateRandomNumbers(Convert.ToInt32(e.CommandArgument));
}

private void GenerateRandomNumbers(int numbersCount)
{
  // Generate Random Numbers
  Random rand = new Random();
  int counter;
  for(counter = 1; counter <= numbersCount; counter++)
    Message.InnerHtml += rand.Next() + "<BR>" ;
}
```

The following screenshot shows the output when the Submit link button is clicked:

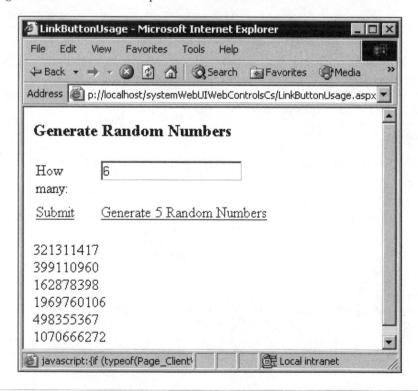

ListBox Class

The `ListBox` control represents a list of items in a list box. The space it occupies on screen depends on the setting of its `Rows` property. It allows the user to select multiple items in the list enabling multiple and single selections. Items in the list can be added either at design time using the `<asp:ListItem>` element or at run-time by manipulating with the `ListItemCollection`; or the items can also be added by data-binding the `ListBox` control with the `DataSource`.

This class is inherited from `System.Web.UI.WebControls.ListControl` class. It has the following syntax:

```
<asp:ListBox id = "id_name"
             DataSource = "name of data source"
             DataTextField = "DataSourceField"
             DataValueField = "DataSourceField"
             AutoPostBack = "true | false"
             Rows = "number of row"
             SelectionMode = "Single | Multiple"
             OnSelectedIndexChanged = "Method for selected index changed "
             Runat = "server">
    <asp:ListItem text="text of ListItem" value="value of ListItem" />
</asp:ListBox>
```

ListBox Class Public Methods

The `ListBox` class adds no new public methods to those inherited from the `WebControl` class. See the `WebControl` class reference for a complete listing.

ListBox Class Protected Methods

The `ListBox` class adds no new protected methods to those inherited from the `WebControl` class. See the `WebControl` class reference for a complete listing.

ListBox Class Public Properties

- ❑ **Rows**
- ❑ **SelectionMode**

Rows

The `Rows` property gets or sets the number of rows to display in the `ListBox` control on a web page. This property allows you to control the height of the `ListBox` control and to determine how many list items are visible in a `ListBox` at any one time. The value of this property must be between 1 and 2000 otherwise an `ArgumentOutOfRangeException` is thrown. The default value is 4.

```
public virtual int Rows {get; set;}
```

SelectionMode

The `SelectionMode` property assigns or determines the selection mode the `ListBox` control will accept. The `Selection` mode represents the number of items (single or multiple) that can be selected from the `ListBox`. It can take one of the values of the `ListSelectionMode` enumeration: either `Single` or `Multiple`. An `ArgumentException` is thrown if this property is set with a value other than those specified by the `ListSelectionMode` enumeration. The default value is `Single`.

```
public virtual ListSelectionMode SelectionMode {get; set;}
```

Example: Using a Multiple-Selection ListBox

In the following code from `ListBoxUsage.aspx`, we set up a multiple selection `ListBox` control that displays four rows on the web page. The user can press and hold down the *Shift* or *Ctrl* keys to make multiple selections. The user interface code is as follows:

```
<form id="FrmListBox" method="post" runat="server">
  How often do you take a vacation:<br>
  <asp:ListBox id="LBoxVacation" runat="server"
             SelectionMode="Single" Rows="2" AutoPostBack="true">
    <asp:ListItem value="Y">Yearly</asp:ListItem>
    <asp:ListItem value="H">Half Yearly</asp:ListItem>
    <asp:ListItem value="Q" Selected="true">Quarterly</asp:ListItem>
  </asp:ListBox><br>
  Select your favourite food category:<br>
  <asp:ListBox id="LBoxFoodCategory" Runat="server"
             SelectionMode="Multiple">
  </asp:ListBox>
  <br>
  <asp:Button ID="BtnSubmit" runat="server" Text="Submit"></asp:Button>
  <hr>
  <asp:Label ID="LblVacation" Runat="server"></asp:Label><br>
  <asp:Label ID="LblFoodCategory" Runat="server"></asp:Label>
</form>
```

The following code shows how the data-bound Food Category list gets populated from the Northwind database in the `Page_Load` event handler. It also shows the use of the `Items` property to display the selected items with the `SelectionChanged` event handlers. The values displayed are both the `Text` field and the `Value` field of the `ListItem` (you will need to modify the connection string to point to your server):

```
private void Page_Load(object sender, System.EventArgs e)
  {
    if(!Page.IsPostBack)
    {
      //Add an Item programmatically to the vacations List
      LBoxVacation.Items.Add(new ListItem("Monthly", "M"));
      LBoxVacation.Items.Add(new ListItem("Fortnight" , "F"));

      // Create a SqlConnection and SqlDataAdapter object
      string ConnectionString =
            @"User ID=sa;Initial Catalog=Northwind;Data Source=(local);";
SqlConnection cnn = new SqlConnection(ConnectionString);
```

```
        SqlDataAdapter da = new SqlDataAdapter(
                                    "select * from Categories", cnn);

    // Create a dataset to store the Category data.
    DataSet ds = new DataSet();
    da.Fill(ds, "Category");

    LBoxFoodCategory.DataSource = ds;
    LBoxFoodCategory.DataMember = "Category";
    LBoxFoodCategory.DataTextField = "CategoryName";
    LBoxFoodCategory.DataValueField = "CategoryID";
    LBoxFoodCategory.DataBind();
  }
}

private void LBoxVacation_SelectedIndexChanged(object sender,
                                             System.EventArgs e)
{
  LblVacation.Text = "You take a vacation "
                   +   LBoxVacation.SelectedItem.Text
                   + " (" + LBoxVacation.SelectedItem.Value + ") <br>";
}

private void LBoxFoodCategory_SelectedIndexChanged(object sender,
                                             System.EventArgs e)
{
  LblFoodCategory.Text = "Selected Food Category:" + "<br>";
  foreach(ListItem foodItem in LBoxFoodCategory.Items)
  {
    if(foodItem.Selected == true)
      LblFoodCategory.Text += foodItem.Text
                         + " (" + foodItem.Value + ") <br>" ;

  }
}
```

Here is a screenshot showing the output:

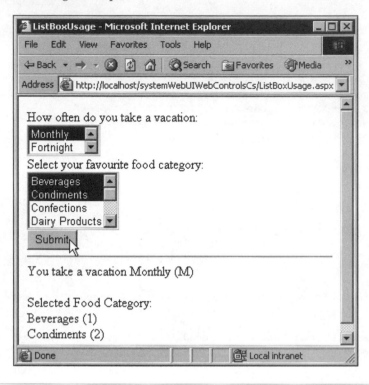

ListBox Class Protected Properties

The `ListBox` class adds no new protected properties to those inherited from the `WebControl` class. See the `WebControl` class reference for a complete listing.

ListBox Class Public Events

The `ListBox` class adds no new public events to those inherited from the `WebControl` class. See the `WebControl` class reference for a complete listing.

ListControl Class

The `MustInherit ListControl` class is a base class for the list type controls. This class is inherited from the `System.Web.UI.WebControls.WebControl` class. This class defines the properties, methods and events common to all inherited list controls like `CheckBoxList`, `DropDownList`, `ListBox`, and `RadioButtonList`. List controls are used to present a list of data to the user which the user can select from. This can be single as well as multiple selection. Different types of list controls represent data in different styles and enable different modes of selection (single/multiple).

ListControl Class Public Methods

The `ListControl` class adds no new public methods to those inherited from the `WebControl` class. See the `WebControl` class reference for a complete listing.

ListControl Class Protected Methods

❑ **`OnSelectedIndexChanged`**

OnSelectedIndexChanged

The `OnSelectedIndexChanged` method will raise the `SelectedIndexChanged` event when the selection in the list control is changed. If the `AutoPostBack` property of the checkbox is set to `true`, then the page is posted to the server, otherwise not. In the latter case, the `SelectedIndexChanged` event is raised whenever there is a change in the list control selection between posts to the server. The checkbox control must have `ViewState` enabled in order to be able to raise this event correctly. This method allows derived classes to handle the `SelectedIndexChanged` event directly without attaching to a delegate.

```
protected virtual void OnSelectedIndexChanged(EventArgs e);
```

The parameter e refers to an `EventArgs` object that contains the `SelectedIndexChanged` event data.

ListControl Class Public Properties

❑ **`AutoPostBack`**

❑ **`DataMember`**

❑ **`DataSource`**

❑ **`DataTextField`**

❑ **`DataTextFormatString`**

❑ **`DataValueField`**

❑ **`Items`**

❑ **`SelectedIndex`**

❑ **`SelectedItem`**

AutoPostBack

The `AutoPostBack` property gets or sets a value to determine whether the form should be posted back to the server automatically when the user changes the list selection. When set to `true`, the form which contains the list control is posted to the server automatically whenever there is a change in the list selection. The default value is `false` indicating that postback will not occur unless the page is posted back to the server by some other means (through the click of a button or another control having its `AutoPostBack` property set to `true`). The `AutoPostBack` property requires that client-side scripting is enabled. This property will not post the page to the server if the browser does not support JavaScript or if client-side scripting is disabled.

```
public virtual bool AutoPostBack {get; set;}
```

DataMember

The DataMember property indicates the data member of the data source to which the list control is bound. This property is very helpful when the DataSource has multiple sets of members to bind to. For example, a DataSet object can be a DataSource and a specific table in the DataSet can become the DataMember of the list control.

```
public virtual string DataMember {get; set;}
```

DataSource

The DataSource property gets or sets the data source to bind the list control to. The individual item elements in the list control will be filled with the data available in the DataSource. If the DataSource has multiple sets of members to bind to, then the DataMember property can be used to indicate the desired member name.

```
public virtual object DataSource {get; set;}
```

DataTextField

The DataTextField property gets or sets the field in the data source that provides the text for a list item element. The list option element maps to the ListItem object and this property maps to the ListItem.Text property. The default value is an empty string. A table in a DataSet may contain many columns. This property can be used to specify which column's values you want to be displayed in the list control.

```
public virtual string DataTextField {get; set;}
```

DataTextFormatString

The DataTextFormatString property gets or sets a format string that determines how to display the data that is bound to a control. The DataTextField will be formatted with this property and then displayed in the list control.

```
public virtual string DataTextFormatString {get; set;}
```

DataValueField

The DataValueField property gets or sets the field in the data source that provides the value for a list item element. The list item element maps to the ListItem object and this property maps to the ListItem.Value property. This property is not displayed in the list control but is stored as a value for the list item element behind the scenes. This property is very helpful when we want to show descriptive, user-friendly text to the user, but want to associate the text with a value which is programmatically very useful but can't be understood or displayed to the user. For example we might want to show the ProductName field in the list control on the web page but to work with the ProductID in the code; in this case the ProductID can be bound to the ListControl through this property. So when the user selects a particular product the associated ProductID can be found out very easily by querying the ListItem.Value property.

```
public virtual string DataValueField {get; set;}
```

Items

The Items property gets the collection of items within the list control. The list items are returned as a ListItemCollection object. The default value is an empty list. The ListItemCollection object can modify the list items of the list control allowing:

- ❑ Add – adds a new option item
- ❑ Clear – clears all option items
- ❑ Remove – deletes a selected option item
- ❑ Count – gets the total number of option items

```
public virtual ListItemCollection Items {get;}
```

SelectedIndex

The SelectedIndex property gets or sets the lowest ordinal index of the selected item in the list. If there aren't any items selected then the SelectedIndex returns –1, which is also the default value. An ArgumentOutOfRangeException is thrown if this property is assigned a value less than –1 or greater than or equal to the number of items in the list (the list is zero-based). If multiple items are selected, SelectedIndex holds the index of the first item selected in the list. You therefore need to iterate the Items collection and test whether the ListItem.Selected property is true to fetch the selected indexes.

```
public virtual int SelectedIndex {get; set;}
```

SelectedItem

The SelectedItem property gets the selected item in the list control. If there are no items selected then the SelectedItem returns null, else it returns a ListItem object representing the selected item. If multiple items are selected, SelectedItem holds the lowest (first) selected item in the list control. Hence you need to iterate the Items collection and test whether the ListItem.Selected property is true to fetch all the selected items.

```
public virtual ListItem SelectedItem {get;}
```

ListControl Class Protected Properties

The ListControl class adds no new protected properties to those inherited from the WebControl class. See the WebControl class reference for a complete listing.

ListControl Class Public Events

- ❑ **SelectedIndexChanged**

The `SelectedIndexChanged` event occurs whenever a selection in the list has been changed. If the `AutoPostBack` property is not set to `true`, this event will not immediately post back to the server. Rather this event will be raised if there is a change in the list control selection since the previous post to the server and when the data is posted to the server by some other means (through the click of a button or another control having its `AutoPostBack` property set to `true`). However, if the `AutoPostBack` property is set to `true` then whenever there is a change in the list selection, this event will be raised and the page will immediately be posted to the server. The list control must have `ViewState` enabled in order to be able to raise this event correctly.

```
public event EventHandler SelectedIndexChanged;
```

The event handler receives information related to the event through the `EventArgs` object, passed as its argument.

Literal Class

The `Literal` control displays static text on a web page and allows you to manipulate it programmatically. It is inherited from the `System.Web.UI.Control` class.

It has the following syntax:

```
<asp:Literal id = "id_name"
             Text="Text of Literal"
             Runat="server" />
```

or:

```
<asp:Literal id = "id_name"
             runat = "server">
   Text of Literal
</asp:Literal>
```

Unlike the `Label` web control, the `Literal` control does not allow you to apply styles to the text it contains, because text displayed by `Literal` controls only appears on a web page without any HTML code. For example, say you have the following code in a web page:

```
<asp:Literal id="Literal1"
             text="This is a Literal control"
             runat="Server" />
```

When you now open this web page with IE, you will find it contains no HTML code, only the text "This is a Literal control" in the HTML source. This is because `Literal` controls only provide plain, unadorned, text on a web page. This text will, however, inherit the style and formatting of its parent elements, according to the standard cascading rules of HTML. For instance, `Literal` controls can be used to place content in a table's cells where they inherit the styles of their parent cell.

Literal Class Public Methods

The Literal class adds no new public methods to those inherited from the WebControl class. See the WebControl class reference for a complete listing.

Literal Class Protected Methods

The Literal class adds no new protected methods to those inherited from the WebControl class. See the WebControl class reference for a complete listing.

Literal Class Public Properties

❏ **Text**

Text

The Text property gets or sets the text content of a Literal control. The Literal control displays this text content when it is rendered in the web page. As always with other properties, the value of this property can be assigned declaratively or programmatically.

```
public string Text {get; set;}
```

Example: Using a Literal Control

The following code snippet from LiterallUsage.aspx shows how to define a Literal control on your web page:

```
<form id="FrmLiteralUsage" method="post" runat="server">
  <asp:Literal ID="LitMessage" Runat="server"></asp:Literal>
  <h3><asp:Literal ID="LitH3Message" runat="Server"></asp:Literal></h3>
</form>
```

The following code shows how to set the properties of a Literal control programmatically:

```
private void Page_Load(object sender, System.EventArgs e)
  {
    LitMessage.Text = "I am a Simple Literal Control (styles "
                    + "cannot be applied to me individually)";
    LitH3Message.Text = "I am a Literal Control (inside "
                    + "a H3 tag). I have inherited the "
                    + "style and formatting of my parent H3 control";
  }
```

Here is a screenshot showing the output:

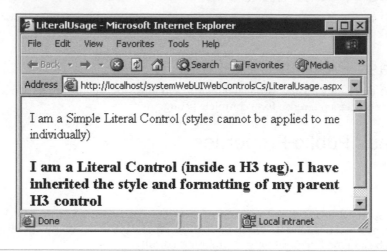

Literal Class Protected Properties

The Literal class adds no new protected properties to those inherited from the WebControl class. See the WebControl class reference for a complete listing.

Literal Class Public Events

The Literal class adds no new public events to those inherited from the WebControl class. See the WebControl class reference for a complete listing.

Panel Class

The Panel class acts as a container for other controls. The Panel class can be used to control the visibility of its child controls. It can also be used to load its child controls programmatically. It is inherited from the System.Web.UI.WebControls.WebControl class.

It is rendered as the HTML <div> element and has the following syntax:

```
<asp:Panel id = "id_name"
          BackImageUrl = "Url of background image"
          HorizontalAlign = "Center | Justify | Left | NotSet | Right"
          Wrap = "true | false"
          Runat = "server">
   Other controls
</asp:Panel>
```

Panel Class Public Methods

The `Panel` class adds no new public methods to those inherited from the `WebControl` class. See the `WebControl` class reference for a complete listing.

Panel Class Protected Methods

The `Panel` class adds no new protected methods to those inherited from the `WebControl` class. See the `WebControl` class reference for a complete listing.

Panel Class Public Properties

- ❑ **BackImageUrl**
- ❑ **HorizontalAlign**
- ❑ **Wrap**

BackImageUrl

The `BackImageUrl` property gets or sets the URL of the background image to be displayed behind the contents of the panel.

```
public virtual string BackImageUrl {get; set;}
```

HorizontalAlign

The `HorizontalAlign` property gets or sets the horizontal alignment of the contents of the `Panel` control with reference to its width. The possible values for this property are defined in the `HorizontalAlign` enumeration:

- ❑ `Center`
- ❑ `Justify`
- ❑ `NotSet` (Default value)
- ❑ `Left`
- ❑ `Right`

```
public virtual HorizontalAlign HorizontalAlign {get; set;}
```

Wrap

The `Wrap` property gets or sets a `Boolean` value that determines whether the contents of the `Panel` control wraps within its boundaries. `true` indicates that the contents will wrap within the panel and `false` otherwise. The default value is `true`.

```
public virtual bool Wrap {get; set;}
```

Example: Using a Panel Control

The following example from PanelUsage.aspx shows how to place content into a Panel control at design time and also at run-time. It also shows how the Panel control can be used to hide or display:

```
<form id="FrmPanelUsage" method="post" runat="server">
  <h3>Mode Of Communication</h3>
  <asp:CheckBox ID="ChkMail" Runat="server" Text="Postal Mail"
              AutoPostBack="true" TextAlign="Left" >
  </asp:CheckBox><br>
  <asp:CheckBox ID="ChkEmail" runat="server" Text="Electronic Mail"
              AutoPostBack="true" TextAlign="Left">
  </asp:CheckBox><br><br>
  <asp:Panel ID="PnlDetails" Runat="server" HorizontalAlign="Left"
          Wrap="false" Visible="false">
    Please enter the following details: <br>
  </asp:Panel>
</form>
```

The code below adds the labels and textboxes to get either the user's postal or email address, or both, depending on the user's choice as indicated by their input into the checkboxes:

```
private void ChkMode_CheckedChanged(object sender, EventArgs e)
  {
    if((ChkMail.Checked == true) || (ChkEmail.Checked == true))
      PnlDetails.Visible = true;
    else
      PnlDetails.Visible = false;

    if(ChkMail.Checked == true)
    {
      // Create controls programmatically and add to Panel control
      Label LblAddress = new Label();
      LblAddress.Text = "Postal Address";
      TextBox TxtAddress = new TextBox();
      TxtAddress.TextMode = TextBoxMode.MultiLine;
      TxtAddress.Rows = 4;
      TxtAddress.Columns = 35;
      PnlDetails.Controls.Add(LblAddress);
      PnlDetails.Controls.Add(TxtAddress);
      PnlDetails.Controls.Add(new LiteralControl("<BR>"));
    }
    if(ChkEmail.Checked == true)
    {
      // Create controls programmatically and add to Panel control
      Label LblEmailAddress = new Label();
      LblEmailAddress.Text = "Email Address";
      TextBox TxtEmailAddress = new TextBox();
      PnlDetails.Controls.Add(LblEmailAddress);
      PnlDetails.Controls.Add(TxtEmailAddress);
    }
  }
```

The following screenshot shows the output:

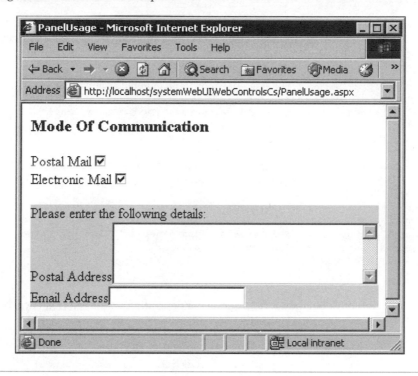

Panel Class Protected Properties

The Panel class adds no new protected properties to those inherited from the WebControl class. See the WebControl class reference for a complete listing.

Panel Class Public Events

The Panel class adds no new public events to those inherited from the WebControl class. See the WebControl class reference for a complete listing.

PlaceHolder Class

The PlaceHolder control reserves an area of a web page in which you may add, insert, and remove items programmatically via the Control.Controls collection of a PlaceHolder instance.

It is inherited from the System.Web.UI.Control class.

It has the following syntax:

```
<asp:PlaceHolder id="id_name"
            runat="server"/>
```

Example: Using the PlaceHolder Control

The following code shows how controls can be added to the `PlaceHolder` control. The `PlaceHolder` on its own does not have any formatting properties like the `Panel` control. The user interface code is as follows:

```
<form id="FrmPlaceHolderUsage" method="post" runat="server">
  <h3>Mode Of Communication</h3>
  <asp:CheckBox ID="ChkMail" Runat="server" Text="Postal Mail"
               AutoPostBack="true" TextAlign="Left">
  </asp:CheckBox>
  <br>
  <asp:CheckBox ID="ChkEmail" runat="server" Text="Electronic Mail"
               AutoPostBack="true" TextAlign="Left">
  </asp:CheckBox>
  <br>
  <br>
  <asp:PlaceHolder ID="PHldDetails" Runat="server" Visible="false">
    Please enter the following details: <br>
  </asp:PlaceHolder>
</form>
```

The code adds the control in the `Page_Load` event depending on the selected checkbox control:

```
private void Page_Load(object sender, System.EventArgs e)
  {
    if((ChkMail.Checked == true) || (ChkEmail.Checked == true))
      PHldDetails.Visible = true;
    else
      PHldDetails.Visible = false;
    if(ChkMail.Checked == true)
    {
      // Create controls programmatically and add to Panel control
      Label LblAddress = new Label();
      LblAddress.Text = "Postal Address";
      TextBox TxtAddress = new TextBox();
      TxtAddress.TextMode = TextBoxMode.MultiLine;
      TxtAddress.Rows = 4;
      TxtAddress.Columns = 35;
      PHldDetails.Controls.Add(LblAddress);
      PHldDetails.Controls.Add(TxtAddress);
      PHldDetails.Controls.Add(new LiteralControl("<BR>"));
    }
    if(ChkEmail.Checked == true)
    {
      // Create controls programmatically and add to Panel control
      Label LblEmailAddress = new Label();
      LblEmailAddress.Text = "Email Address";
      TextBox TxtEmailAddress = new TextBox();
      PHldDetails.Controls.Add(LblEmailAddress);
      PHldDetails.Controls.Add(TxtEmailAddress);
    }
```

The following screenshot shows the output when the Postal Mail checkbox is clicked:

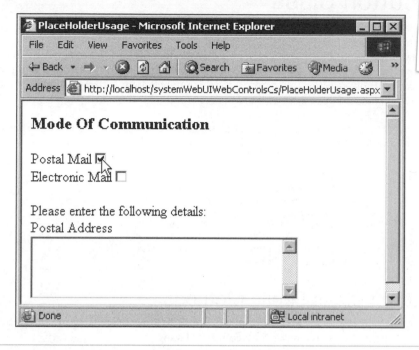

PlaceHolder Class Public Methods

The PlaceHolder class adds no new public methods to those inherited from the WebControl class. See the WebControl class reference for a complete listing.

PlaceHolder Class Protected Methods

The PlaceHolder class adds no new protected methods to those inherited from the WebControl class. See the WebControl class reference for a complete listing.

PlaceHolder Class Public Properties

The PlaceHolder class adds no new public properties to those inherited from the WebControl class. See the WebControl class reference for a complete listing.

PlaceHolder Class Protected Properties

The PlaceHolder class adds no new protected properties to those inherited from the WebControl class. See the WebControl class reference for a complete listing.

PlaceHolder Class Public Events

The PlaceHolder class adds no new public events to those inherited from the WebControl class. See the WebControl class reference for a complete listing.

RadioButton Class

The `RadioButton` control represents radio buttons on a web page, which allow the user to select one of a set of mutually exclusive choices. It is inherited from the `System.Web.UI.WebControls.CheckBox` class. The only difference between checkbox and radio button is that the radio button allows you to make only a single selection from a group of buttons. You cannot make multiple selections. The group to which they belong is represented by the `GroupName` property, which helps if there is more than one set of radio buttons on a page.

It corresponds to the `<input type="radio">` element of the HTML Controls. It has the following syntax:

```
<asp:RadioButton id = "id_name"
                 AutoPostBack = "true | false"
                 Checked = "true | false"
                 GroupName = "GroupName"
                 Text = "Text of RadioButton"
                 TextAlign = "Right | Left"
                 OnCheckedChanged = "Method name"
                 Runat = "server" />
```

RadioButton Class Public Methods

The `RadioButton` class adds no new public methods to those inherited from the `WebControl` class. See the `WebControl` class reference for a complete listing.

RadioButton Class Protected Methods

The `RadioButton` class adds no new protected methods to those inherited from the `WebControl` class. See the `WebControl` class reference for a complete listing.

RadioButton Class Public Properties

❑   **GroupName**

GroupName

The `GroupName` property gets or sets a group name for a set of inter-related radio buttons on a Web page. The default value is an empty string. When this property is set, only one radio button can be checked per group of `RadioButton` controls.

```
public virtual string GroupName {get; set;}
```

Example: Grouping RadioButton Controls

The following code example from `RadioButtonUsage.aspx` shows how to set radio buttons in a group so that only one can be selected:

```
<form id="FrmRadioButtonUsage" method="post" runat="server">
  How often do you take a holiday:
  <asp:RadioButton ID="RBtnMonthly" runat="server" Text="Monthly"
    GroupName="Holiday"></asp:RadioButton>
  <asp:RadioButton ID="RBtnQuarterly" runat="server" Text="Quarterly"
    GroupName="Holiday" Checked="true"></asp:RadioButton>
  <asp:RadioButton ID="RBtnHalfYearly" runat="server" Text="Half - Yearly"
    GroupName="Holiday"></asp:RadioButton>
  <asp:RadioButton ID="RBtnYearly" runat="server" Text="Yearly"
    GroupName="Holiday"></asp:RadioButton>
  <br><asp:Button ID="BtnSubmit" Runat="server" Text="Submit"></asp:Button>
  <hr><asp:Label ID="LblMessage" Runat="server"></asp:Label>
</form>
```

The event handler for the Submit button displays the selected option:

```
private void Page_Load(object sender, System.EventArgs e)
  {
    if(RBtnMonthly.Checked)
      LblMessage.Text="You Selected " + RBtnMonthly.Text;
    else if(RBtnQuarterly.Checked)
      LblMessage.Text="You Selected " + RBtnQuarterly.Text;
    else if(RBtnHalfYearly.Checked)
      LblMessage.Text="You Selected " + RBtnHalfYearly.Text;
    else if(RBtnYearly.Checked)
      LblMessage.Text="You Selected " + RBtnYearly.Text;

  }

  private void BtnSubmit_Click(object sender, System.EventArgs e)
  {
    if(RBtnMonthly.Checked)
      LblMessage.Text="You Selected " + RBtnMonthly.Text;
    else if(RBtnQuarterly.Checked)
      LblMessage.Text="You Selected " + RBtnQuarterly.Text;
    else if(RBtnHalfYearly.Checked)
      LblMessage.Text="You Selected " + RBtnHalfYearly.Text;
    else if(RBtnYearly.Checked)
      LblMessage.Text="You Selected " + RBtnYearly.Text;
  }
```

The following screenshot shows the output:

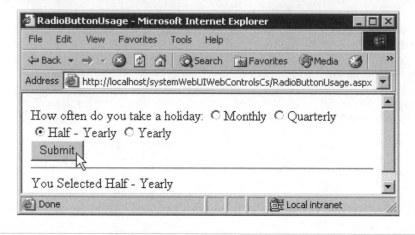

RadioButton Class Protected Properties

The RadioButton class adds no new protected properties to those inherited from the WebControl class. See the WebControl class reference for a complete listing.

RadioButton Class Public Events

The RadioButton class adds no new public events to those inherited from the WebControl and CheckBox classes. See the WebControl and CheckBox class references for a complete listing.

RadioButtonList Class

The RadioButtonList control represents a list of RadioButton controls. It allows the user to select only a single radio button from the list. Radio buttons in the list can be added either at design time using <asp:ListItem> element or at run-time by manipulating with the ListItemCollection, or the items can also be added by data-binding the RadioButtonList with the DataSource.

This class is inherited from the System.Web.UI.WebControls.ListControl class. It has the following syntax:

```
<asp:RadioButtonList id = "id_name"
                     AutoPostBack = "true | false"
                     CellPadding = "Pixels"
                     CellSpacing = "Pixels"
                     DataSource = "name of data source"
                     DataTextField = "Data Source Field"
                     DataValueField = "Data Source Field"
                     RepeatColumns = "Column Count"
                     RepeatDirection = "Vertical | Horizontal"
                     RepeatLayout = "Flow | Table"
                     TextAlign = "Right | Left"
                     OnSelectedIndexChanged = "Method of ˥
```

```
                                          SelectedIndexChanged"
                       Runat = "server">
    <asp:ListItem Text="text of ListItem" Value="value of ListItem" />
  </asp:RadioButtonList>
```

RadioButtonList Class Public Methods

The `RadioButtonList` class adds no new public methods to those inherited from the `WebControl` class. See the `WebControl` class reference for a complete listing.

RadioButtonList Class Protected Methods

The `RadioButtonList` class adds no new protected methods to those inherited from the `WebControl` and `ListControl` classes. See the `WebControl` and `ListControl` class references for a complete listing.

RadioButtonList Class Public Properties

- ❑ **CellPadding**
- ❑ **CellSpacing**
- ❑ **RepeatColumns**
- ❑ **RepeatDirection**
- ❑ **RepeatLayout**
- ❑ **TextAlign**

CellPadding

The `CellPadding` property gets or sets the width in pixels between the border and a radio button in the `RadioButtonList`. The default value is –1 indicating that the property is not set. The `CellPadding` is applied to all four sides of the radio button. This property only works when the `RepeatLayout` property is set to `Table`.

```
public virtual int CellPadding {get; set;}
```

CellSpacing

The `CellSpacing` property gets or sets the width in pixels between the individual radio buttons in the `RadioButtonList`. The default value is –1 indicating that the property is not set. The `CellSpacing` is applied both horizontally and vertically to individual radio buttons. This property only works when the `RepeatLayout` property is set to `Table`.

```
public virtual int CellSpacing {get; set;}
```

395

RepeatColumns

The RepeatColumns property gets or sets the number of columns used to display radio buttons in the RadioButtonList. The default value is 0 indicating that the property is not set. By default all radio buttons are rendered in a single column. An ArgumentOutOfRangeException is thrown if this property is set to a negative value.

```
public virtual int RepeatColumns {get; set;}
```

RepeatDirection

The RepeatDirection property gets or sets a value that indicates the layout of radio buttons in the RadioButtonList control. The radio buttons can be displayed vertically or horizontally. The valid values are from the RepeatDirection enumeration: either Vertical or Horizontal. The default value is Vertical. An ArgumentException is thrown if this property is set to a value other than one of the RepeatDirection enumeration values.

Vertical layout is as follows:

RadioButton 1	RadioButton 3
RadioButton 2	RadioButton 4

Horizontal layout is as follows:

RadioButton 1	RadioButton 2
RadioButton 3	RadioButton 4

```
public virtual RepeatDirection RepeatDirection {get; set;}
```

RepeatLayout

The RepeatLayout property gets or sets the layout of radio buttons in a RadioButtonList control. The valid values are from the RepeatLayout enumeration: either Flow or Table. The default value is Table, which ensures the radio buttons are displayed in a table structure. When this property is set to Flow, the output is displayed without a table structure. An ArgumentException is thrown if this property is set to a value other than one of the RepeatLayout enumeration values.

```
public virtual RepeatLayout RepeatLayout {get; set;}
```

TextAlign

The TextAlign property is used to get or set the alignment of the text label associated with the individual RadioButton control in the RadioButtonList. The valid values are Right and Left, specified by the TextAlign enumeration. An ArgumentException is thrown if the property is set to a value other than one of the values of the TextAlign enumeration. A value of Left means that the text of the associated radio button will be flush with the left-hand side of the control, while Right means that the text of the associated radio button appears flush with the right-hand side of the control. The default value is Right.

```
public virtual TextAlign TextAlign {get; set;}
```

Example: Using the RadioButtonList Control

The code from `RadioButtonListUsage.aspx` here illustrates the usage of most of the properties of the `RadioButtonList` control. The user interface code is as follows:

```
<form id="FrmRadioButtonList" method="post" runat="server">
  Please Select Shipping Details:
  <br>
  Packet Size:<br>
  <asp:RadioButtonList id="RBLstPacketSize" runat="server"
                       CellPadding="2" CellSpacing="2" RepeatColumns="2"
                       TextAlign="Left">
    <asp:ListItem Value="Small" Text="Small"></asp:ListItem>
    <asp:ListItem Value="Standard" Text="Standard"
                  Selected="true">
    </asp:ListItem>
    <asp:ListItem Value="Big" Text="Big"></asp:ListItem>
  </asp:RadioButtonList><br>
  Shipper:
  <asp:RadioButtonList id="RBLstShippers" Runat="server"
                       AutoPostBack="true" RepeatLayout="Flow"
                       RepeatDirection="Horizontal">
  </asp:RadioButtonList>
  <br>
  <asp:Button ID="BtnSubmit" runat="server" Text="Submit"></asp:Button>
  <hr>
  <asp:Label ID="LblPacketSize" Runat="server"></asp:Label><br>
  <asp:Label ID="LblShippers" Runat="server"></asp:Label>
</form>
```

Below we have the code for the `Page_Load` event where the databound Shippers `RadioButtonList` is populated from the Northwind database. It also shows the code for the `SelectedIndexChanged` event handler for the radio buttons that displays item that the user selects. You will need to change the connection string to point to your server:

```
private void Page_Load(object sender, System.EventArgs e)
{
  if(!Page.IsPostBack)
  {
    //Add an Item programmatically to the Packet Size List
    RBLstPacketSize.Items.Add(new ListItem("OverSize", "OverSize"));

    // Create a SqlConnection and SqlDataAdapter object
    string ConnectionString =
        @"User ID=sa;Initial Catalog=Northwind;Data Source=(local);";
    SqlConnection cnn = new SqlConnection(ConnectionString);
    SqlDataAdapter da = new SqlDataAdapter(
                                    "select * from Shippers", cnn);

    // Create a dataset to store the Shippers data.
    DataSet ds = new DataSet();
    da.Fill(ds, "Shippers");
```

```
        RBLstShippers.DataSource = ds;
        RBLstShippers.DataMember = "Shippers";
        RBLstShippers.DataTextField = "CompanyName";
        RBLstShippers.DataValueField = "ShipperID" ;
        RBLstShippers.DataBind();
    }
}

private void RBLstPacketSize_SelectedIndexChanged(object sender,
                                            System.EventArgs e)
{
  LblPacketSize.Text = "Packet Size is "
                    + RBLstPacketSize.SelectedItem.Text + " ("
                    + RBLstPacketSize.SelectedItem.Value + ")";
}

private void RBLstShippers_SelectedIndexChanged(object sender,
                                            System.EventArgs e)
{
  LblShippers.Text = "The Packet will be shipped via "
                    + RBLstShippers.SelectedItem.Text
                    + " (" + RBLstShippers.SelectedItem.Value + ")";
}
```

The following screenshot shows the output:

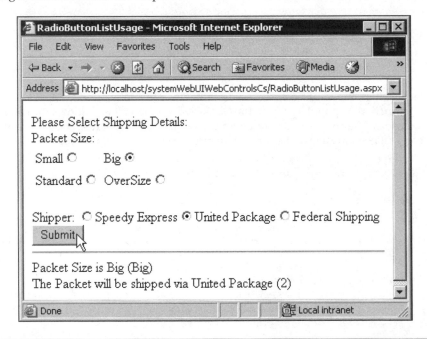

RadioButtonList Class Protected Properties

The `RadioButtonList` class adds no new protected properties to those inherited from the `WebControl` class. See the `WebControl` class reference for a complete listing.

RadioButtonList Class Public Events

The `RadioButtonList` class adds no new public events to those inherited from the `WebControl` and `ListControl` classes. See the `WebControl` and `ListControl` class references for a complete listing.

RangeValidator Class

The `RangeValidator` control is used to check whether an input control's value is within a specified range of values. When a web page is submitted some of the controls in the form may be required to have a certain range of values (for example, you might want the Quantity field to be greater than zero but less than 100 in an Order entry page). So to ensure valid data is sent to the server you need to validate the data before sending it to the server. The `RangeValidator` control, when associated with an input control, ensures that the associated control has a valid value eliminating the need to write validation logic to check for the data is within a specified range. This control performs range field validation on both the server and client side. However, validation at the client side depends on the capabilities of the user's browser and setting the `ClientTarget` attribute in the `Page` directive of the Web Form.

It can be used to check for a range of values against different data types like `Date`, `Currency`, `Double`, `Integer` or `String`. You can therefore check ranges for numbers, say 1 to 100, alphabetic characters, like A to F, and dates, such as 2001/5/1 to 2001/6/30.

Note that if the user is supposed to be obliged to enter a value for the input control, then a `RequiredFieldValidator` should be associated with the control as only this control checks whether the user has entered a value.

This class is inherited from the `System.Web.UI.WebControls.BaseCompareValidator` class. It has the following syntax:

```
<asp:RangeValidator id ="id_name"
                    ControlToValidate = "id name of the control which ⅂
                                        is validated"
                    MinimumValue = "The minimum value of the range"
                    MaximumValue = "The maximum value of the range"
                    Type = "type of the data"
                    ErrorMessage = "Error message"
                    Runat = server />
```

RangeValidator Class Public Methods

The `RangeValidator` class adds no new public methods to those inherited from the `WebControl` and `BaseValidator` classes. See the `WebControl` and `BaseValidator` class references for a complete listing.

RangeValidator Class Protected Methods

The `RangeValidator` class adds no new protected methods to those inherited from the `WebControl` and `BaseValidator` classes. See the `WebControl` and `BaseValidator` class references for a complete listing.

RangeValidator Class Public Properties

❑ **MaximumValue**

❑ **MinimumValue**

❑ **Type**

MaximumValue

The `MaximumValue` property gets or sets the upper value of the validation range. The maximum value is also included in the range. The default value is an empty string.

```
public string MaximumValue {get; set;}
```

MinimumValue

The `MinimumValue` property gets or sets the lower value of the validation range. The minimum value is also included in the range. The default value is an empty string.

```
public string MinimumValue {get; set;}
```

Type

The `Type` property specifies the data type to be used when comparing data. The `Type` property is inherited from the `BaseCompareValidator` class. The values to be compared are first converted to this data type and then the range check is performed. The valid data types are defined by the `ValidationDataType` enumeration. The default value is `String`. An `ArgumentException` is thrown if a value other than a `ValidatonDataType` enumeration values is assigned to this property. The following table lists the valid data types:

Type	Description
Currency	A currency data type
Date	A date data type
Double	A double precision floating point data type
Integer	A 32 bit signed integer data type
String	A string data type

```
public ValidationDataType Type {get; set;}
```

Example: Validating User Input Against a Range of Possible Values

The following example, `RangeValidatorUsage.aspx`, shows how to validate that a date is within a specified range:

```
<form id="FrmRangeValidatorUsage" method="post" runat="server">
  <h3>RangeValidator Example</h3>
  Input a date between May 1st,2002 and June 30th,2002:
  <br>
  <asp:textbox id="TxtDate" runat="server" />(Year/Month/Day)
  <asp:RangeValidator id="RagValTxtDate" runat="server"
                    controltovalidate="TxtDate"
                    MinimumValue="2002/5/1"
                    MaximumValue="2002/6/30"
                    Errormessage="The date entered is not in the ⌐
                    specified range." type="Date" />
  <br>
  <asp:button id="BtnValidate" text="Validate" runat="server" /><br>
  <asp:Label ID="LblMessage" Runat="server"></asp:Label>
</form>
```

The following screenshot shows the output showing the error message when the date entered was not within the specified range:

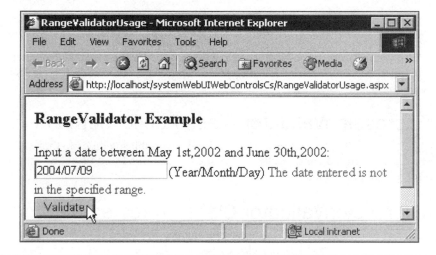

RangeValidator Class Protected Properties

The `RangeValidator` class adds no new protected properties to those inherited from the `WebControl` and `BaseValidator` classes. See the `WebControl` and `BaseValidator` class references for a complete listing.

RangeValidator Class Public Events

The RangeValidator class adds no new public events to those inherited from the WebControl class. See the WebControl class reference for a complete listing.

RegularExpressionValidator Class

The RegularExpressionValidator control is used to check whether the input control's value matches a pattern specified by the regular expression. When a web page is submitted some of the controls in the form may be required to have a value that matches a given pattern (for example, the zipcode field should contain five digits, or ensuring the format of an email address, phone number, or social security number). To ensure valid data is sent to the server you need to validate the data before sending it to the server. The RegularExpressionValidator control, when associated with an input control, ensures that the associated control has a valid value eliminating the need to write validation logic to check the data for a particular pattern. This control performs regular expression validation both at the server and client side. However, validation at the client side depends on the capabilities of the browser and setting the ClientTarget attribute in the Page directive of the Web Form.

This class is inherited from the System.Web.UI.WebControls.BaseValidator class. It has the following syntax:

```
<asp:RegularExpressionValidator id="id_name"
                        ControlToValidate = "id of control"
                        ValidationExpression = "expression"
                        ErrorMessage = "Error message"
                        Runat = "server" />
```

Note that if the user is supposed to be obliged to enter a value for the input control, then a RequiredFieldValidator should be associated with the control as only this control checks whether the user has actually entered a value.

RegularExpressionValidator Class Public Methods

The RegularExpressionValidator class adds no new public methods to those inherited from the WebControl and BaseValidator classes. See the WebControl and BaseValidator class references for a complete listing.

RegularExpressionValidator Class Protected Methods

The RegularExpressionValidator class adds no new protected methods to those inherited from the WebControl and BaseValidator classes. See the WebControl and BaseValidator class references for a complete listing.

RegularExpressionValidator Class Public Properties

❑ **ValidationExpression**

ValidationExpression

The `ValidationExpression` property gets or sets the regular expression that determines the pattern used to validate a field. This field specifies the pattern against which the validation is to be performed. If the associated input control's value matches the regular expression pattern specified by the validation expression then validation succeeds, otherwise it will fail.

The following table lists a few of the most common regular expression syntax rules:

Symbol	Description
*	Wildcard character representing zero or more unspecified characters. For example, `l*` would match love, lilo, la, l, and so on.
+	Must contain one or more occurrences of the preceding item. For example, `ha+` matches ha and haaaa, but not just h.
.	Matches any character except `\n`.
^	NOT operator. For example, `^a` means that a is not allowed.
?	Zero or one occurrences of the preceding item must be present. For example, `(good)?bye` matches bye or goodbye.
[abdj]	Allowed characters can be given inside square brackets. For example, `[abdj]` means only a, b, d, and j are allowed.
[^abj]	Only a, b, and j are not allowed.
x|y	x or y are allowed.
\w	Matches any word character. Same as `[a-zA-Z_0-9]`.
\s	Matches any whitespace character. Same as `[\f\n\r\t\v]`.
\S	Matches any non-whitespace character. Same as `[^\f\n\r\t\v]`.
\d	Any decimal digit. Same as `[0-9]`.
\D	Any non-digit. Same as `[^0-9]`.

```
public string ValidationExpression {get; set;}
```

Example: Validating User Input with a Regular Expression

The following code from `RegularExpressionValidatorUsage.aspx` shows how an email address entered by a user is tested against a regular expression:

```
<form id="FrmRegularExpressionValidator" method="post" runat="server">
<table>
  <tr>
    <td><asp:Label id="LblEmail" runat="server"
                   Text="Email Address"/>     </td>
    <td>
    <asp:TextBox id="TxtEmail" runat="server"></asp:TextBox>
      For example, someone@wrox.com
    <asp:requiredfieldvalidator id="ReqValTxtEmail" runat="server"
                                ControlToValidate="TxtEmail"
                                ErrorMessage="Please enter the Email "
                                             Address, it cannot be blank"
                                Display="dynamic">
      *
    </asp:requiredfieldvalidator>
    <asp:regularexpressionvalidator id="RegValTxtEmail" runat="server"
                                ControlToValidate="TxtEmail"
                                ErrorMessage="Please enter valid Email
                                              Address"
                                display="dynamic"
                                validationexpression=".*\S@.*\..*">
      *
    </asp:regularexpressionvalidator>
    </td>
  </tr>
</table>
<asp:Button ID="BtnValidate" Text="Validate"
            runat="server"></asp:Button><br>
<asp:Label ID="LblMessage" runat="server"></asp:Label>
<asp:ValidationSummary ID="VSumEmail"
                       Runat="server">
</asp:ValidationSummary>
</form>
```

The following screenshot shows the error message generated when the regular expression does not match the pattern we specified:

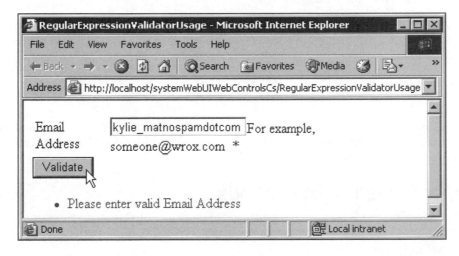

RegularExpressionValidator Class Protected Properties

The `RegularExpressionValidator` class adds no new protected properties to those inherited from the `WebControl` and `BaseValidator` classes. See the `WebControl` and `BaseValidator` class references for a complete listing.

RegularExpressionValidator Class Public Events

The `RegularExpressionValidator` class adds no new public events to those inherited from the `WebControl` class. See the `WebControl` class reference for a complete listing.

Repeater Class

The `Repeater` control has no built-in layout or style, so we must create it within some other HTML structure to provide formatting, such as within a table for instance. The `Repeater` control is much simpler than the `DataList` control. Basically, a `Repeater` control just displays data. It doesn't support editing, deleting, paging, or sorting features such as the `DataGrid` offers. It offers a straightforward mechanism for the display of data taken line by line from the data source.

This class is inherited from the `System.Web.UI.Control` class and has the following syntax:

```
<asp:Repeater id = "Repeater1"
          DataSource="name of data source"
          Runat = server>


  <HeaderTemplate>
    Header template HTML
  </HeaderTemplate>
  <ItemTemplate>
```

```
      Item template HTML
   </ItemTemplate>
   <AlternatingItemTemplate>
      Alternating item template HTML
   </AlternatingItemTemplate>
   <SeparatorTemplate>
      Separator template HTML
   </SeparatorTemplate>
   <FooterTemplate>
      Footer template HTML
   </FooterTemplate>
<asp:Repeater>
```

Note that some members of this class have the same functionality as their `DataGrid` and `DataList` equivalents, so those members are not explained again and you are referred to the `DataGrid` and `DataList` class references.

Repeater Class Public Methods

The `Repeater` class adds no new public methods to those inherited from the `WebControl` class. See the `WebControl` class reference for a complete listing.

Repeater Class Protected Methods

- ❑ `OnItemCommand` – see `DataGrid` class for details.
- ❑ `OnItemCreated` – see `DataGrid` class for details.
- ❑ `OnItemDataBound` – see `DataGrid` class for details.

Repeater Class Public Properties

- ❑ `AlternatingItemTemplate` – see `DataList` class for details.
- ❑ `DataMember` – see `DataGrid` class for details.
- ❑ `DataSource` – see `DataGrid` class for details.
- ❑ `FooterTemplate` – see `DataList` class for details.
- ❑ `HeaderTemplate` – see `DataList` class for details.
- ❑ **Items**
- ❑ `ItemTemplate` – see `DataList` class for details.
- ❑ `SeparatorTemplate` – see `DataList` class for details.

Items

The `Items` property returns a collection of the `RepeaterItem` objects that represent the individual data items in the `Repeater` control. The `Header`, `Footer` and `Separator` items are not included in the collection. The `RepeaterItemCollection` returned does not provide any methods to add or remove `RepeaterItem` objects. These objects are closely bound to `DataSource`.

```
public virtual RepeaterItemCollection Items {get;}
```

Repeater Class Protected Properties

The Repeater class adds no new protected properties to those inherited from the WebControl class. See the WebControl class reference for a complete listing.

Repeater Class Public Events

- ❑ ItemCommand – see DataGrid class for details.
- ❑ ItemCreated – see DataGrid class for details.
- ❑ ItemDatabound – see DataGrid class for details.

Example: Using a Repeater Control

Let's see some code from RepeaterUsage.aspx that illustrates the usage of the Repeater control. The code binds the Repeater control to the Products table of the Northwind database. The user interface code is as follows:

```
<form id="FrmRepeaterUsage" runat="Server">
  <h3>Binding records with Repeater</h3>
  <asp:Repeater id="RptProducts" runat="server">
    <HeaderTemplate>
      <table border="1">
      <tr bgcolor="LightBlue">
        <td>Product ID</td>
        <td>Product Name</td>
        <td>Quantity Per Unit</td>
      </tr>
    </HeaderTemplate>
    <ItemTemplate>
      <tr>
        <td>
          <%# DataBinder.Eval(Container.DataItem, "ProductID") %>
        </td>
        <td>
          <%# DataBinder.Eval(Container.DataItem, "ProductName") %>
        </td>
        <td>
          <%# DataBinder.Eval(Container.DataItem, "QuantityPerUnit") %>
        </td>
    </ItemTemplate>
    <FooterTemplate>
      </table>
    </FooterTemplate>
  </asp:Repeater>
</form>
```

The code below shows the databinding with the `Repeater` (again, you'll need to modify the connection string according to your settings):

```
private void Page_Load(object sender, System.EventArgs e)
{
  if(!Page.IsPostBack)
    BindRptProducts();
}

private void BindRptProducts()
{
  // Create a SqlConnection and SqlDataAdapter object
  string ConnectionString =
        @"User ID=sa;Initial Catalog=Northwind;Data Source=(local);";
  SqlConnection cnn = new SqlConnection(ConnectionString);
  SqlDataAdapter da = new SqlDataAdapter("select * from products", cnn);

  // Create a dataset to store the Products data.
  DataSet ds = new DataSet();
  da.Fill(ds, "Products");
  // And then bind the Dataset with DataGrid
  RptProducts.DataSource = ds;
  RptProducts.DataMember = "Products";
  RptProducts.DataBind();
}
```

Here is a screenshot showing the output:

RequiredFieldValidator Class

The `RequiredFieldValidator` control is used to check whether the input control has a value. You may require that when a web page is submitted some of the controls in the form have a value entered into them by the user. For example, you may require that the username field has a value in a registration form. The `RequiredFieldValidator` control, when associated with an input control, ensures that the associated control has a value eliminating the need to write validation logic to check for empty data fields. This validation control also takes care of trimming spaces and then performing the required field validation both at the server and client side. However, validation at the client side depends on the capabilities of the browser and setting of the `ClientTarget` attribute in the `Page` directive of the Web Form.

It inherits from the `System.Web.UI.WebControls.BaseValidator` and has the following syntax:

```
<asp:RequiredFieldValidator id="id_name"
                        ControlToValidate = "id of control to be
                                            validated"
                        InitialValue = "Initial value"
                        ErrorMessage = "Error message"
                        Runat = "server" />
```

RequiredFieldValidator Class Public Methods

The `RequiredFieldValidator` class adds no new public methods to those inherited from the `WebControl` and `BaseValidator` classes. See the `WebControl` and `BaseValidator` class references for a complete listing.

RequiredFieldValidator Class Protected Methods

The `RequiredFieldValidator` class adds no new protected methods to those inherited from the `WebControl` and `BaseValidator` classes. See the `WebControl` and `BaseValidator` class references for a complete listing.

RequiredFieldValidator Class Public Properties

❑ **InitialValue**

InitialValue

The `InitialValue` property gets or sets the initial value of the associated input control. It sets the initial value of the control to be validated that is specified by the `ControlToValidate` property. The default value is an empty string.

```
public string InitialValue {get; set;}
```

The following code from `RequiredFieldValidatorUsage.aspx` shows how to use a `RequiredFieldValidator`:

```
<form id="FrmRequiredFieldValidatorUsage" method="post" runat="server">
  <h3>Please Enter the following details</h3>
  <table>
    <tr>
      <td>Name</td>
      <td>
        <asp:TextBox ID="TxtName" Runat="server"></asp:TextBox>
        <asp:RequiredFieldValidator ID="ReqValTxtName"
                                    Runat="server" Text="*"
                                    ControlToValidate="TxtName"
                                    ErrorMessage="Please Enter your Name"
                                    ForeColor="Brown">
        </asp:RequiredFieldValidator>  </td>
    </tr>
    <tr>
      <td>Address1</td>
      <td>
        <asp:TextBox ID="TxtAddress1" Runat="server"></asp:TextBox>
        <asp:RequiredFieldValidator ID="ReqValTxtAddress1"
                                    Runat="server" Text="*"
                                    ControlToValidate="TxtAddress1"
                                    ErrorMessage="Please Enter your
                                                  Address1"
                                    ForeColor="Brown">
        </asp:RequiredFieldValidator>  </td>
    </tr>
    <tr>
      <td>Address2</td>
      <td>
        <asp:TextBox ID="TxtAddress2" Runat="server"></asp:TextBox>
      </td>
    </tr>
    <tr>
      <td>State</td>
      <td>
        <asp:DropDownList ID="DDLstState" Runat="server">
          <asp:ListItem></asp:ListItem>
          <asp:ListItem>MI</asp:ListItem>
          <asp:ListItem>CA</asp:ListItem>
        </asp:DropDownList>
        <asp:RequiredFieldValidator ID="ReqValDDLstState"
                                    Runat="server" Text="*"
                                    ControlToValidate="DDLstState"
                                    ErrorMessage="Please select your state"
                                    ForeColor="Brown">
        </asp:RequiredFieldValidator></td>
    </tr>
    <tr>
```

```
      <td><asp:Button ID="BtnSubmit" Runat="server"
                      Text="Submit">
      </asp:Button></td>
    </tr>
    <tr>
      <td colspan="2">
        <asp:ValidationSummary ID="VSumPage" runat="server"
                               ForeColor="Indigo" DisplayMode="List"
                               ShowSummary="true"
                               ShowMessageBox="true">
        </asp:ValidationSummary>
      </td>
    </tr>
    <tr>
      <td><asp:Label ID="LblMessage" Runat="server"></asp:Label></td>
    </tr>
  </table>
</form>
```

Here is the code for the `BtnSubmit_Click` event:

```
protected void BtnSubmit_Click(object sender, System.EventArgs e)
{
  if(Page.IsValid)
    LblMessage.Text = "Thanks for entering the details";
}
```

The following screenshot shows the error messages generated when required field validation fails:

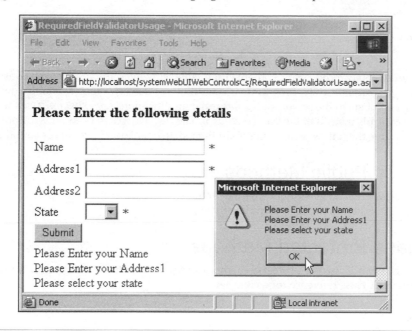

RequiredFieldValidator Class Protected Properties

The `RequiredFieldValidator` class adds no new protected properties to those inherited from the `WebControl` and `BaseValidator` classes. See the `WebControl` and `BaseValidator` class references for a complete listing.

RequiredFieldValidator Class Public Events

The `RequiredFieldValidator` class adds no new public events to those inherited from the `WebControl` class. See the `WebControl` class reference for a complete listing.

Table Class

The `Table` control allows you to build a table on a web page and set its properties. This helps you present data in tabular format. It is inherited from the `System.Web.UI.WebControls.WebControl` class.

It is rendered as `<table>` element and has the following syntax:

```
<asp:Table id = "id_name"
           BackImageUrl = "Url of background image"
           CellSpacing = "width of cell spacing"
           CellPadding = "width of cell padding"
           GridLines = "None | Horizontal | Vertical | Both"
           HorizontalAlign = "Center | Justify | Left | NotSet | Right"
           Runat = "server">
    <asp:TableRow>
      <asp:TableCell>
        Text ...
      </asp:TableCell>
    </asp:TableRow>
</asp:Table>
```

At design time, you can code static contents for a table. However, the `Table` web control can also be constructed programmatically. Programmatic additions or modifications to a table row or cell will not persist between posts to the server, so if substantial modifications are expected, use the `DataList` or `DataGrid` controls instead of the `Table` control. The `DataGrid` and `Datalist` controls have powerful features that allow them to maintain their state over successive server round trips.

Table Class Public Methods

The `Table` class adds no new public methods to those inherited from the `WebControl` class. See the `WebControl` class reference for a complete listing.

Table Class Protected Methods

The `Table` class adds no new protected methods to those inherited from the `WebControl` class. See the `WebControl` class reference for a complete listing.

Table Class Public Properties

- ❏ **BackImageUrl**
- ❏ **CellPadding**
- ❏ **CellSpacing**
- ❏ **GridLines**
- ❏ **HorizontalAlign**
- ❏ **Rows**

BackImageUrl

The BackImageUrl property gets or sets the URL of the background image to be displayed behind the contents of the table. If the image is smaller than the table, the image will be tiled for display.

```
public virtual string BackImageUrl {get; set;}
```

CellPadding

The CellPadding property gets or sets the width in pixels between the border of a cell and the contents of a cell in the Table control. The default value is –1 indicating that the property is not set. The CellPadding is applied to all four sides of the cell.

```
public virtual int CellPadding {get; set;}
```

CellSpacing

The CellSpacing property gets or sets the width in pixels between the individual cells in the table control. The default value is –1 meaning the property is not set. The CellSpacing is applied both horizontally and vertically to individual cells in the control.

```
public virtual int CellSpacing {get; set;}
```

Gridlines

The Gridlines property gets or sets the border between the cells of the Table control to be displayed. The valid values of this property belong to the GridLines enumeration:

- ❏ Horizontal – only horizontal grid lines appear
- ❏ Vertical – only vertical grid lines appear
- ❏ None (Default value of this property)
- ❏ Both

```
public virtual GridLines GridLines {get; set;}
```

HorizontalAlign

This property gets or sets the horizontal alignment of a control with respect to its container table control. The valid values of this property belong to the `HorizontalAlign` enumeration. They are:

- ❑ `Center`
- ❑ `Justify`
- ❑ `Left`
- ❑ `NotSet` (Default value for this property)
- ❑ `Right`

```
public virtual HorizontalAlign HorizontalAlign {get; set;}
```

Rows

The `Rows` property returns a `System.Web.UI.WebControls.TableRowCollection` object that contains all the rows in a table. An empty `TableRowCollection` is returned if no table row, `<tr>`, elements are contained within the table. With the help of the `TableRowCollection` class' properties and methods the rows and cells of a table can be added, updated or deleted.

```
public virtual TableRowCollection Rows {get;}
```

Example: Using the Table, TableRow, and TableCell Classes

The following code is taken from `TableUsage.aspx` and it shows the usage of `Table`, `TableRow` and `TableCell` class' properties. Here is the user interface code:

```
<form id="FrmTableUsage" method="post" runat="server">
  <asp:table id="TblMain" runat="server" width="300" height="100"
             cellspacing="1" cellpadding="2" bordercolor="#3d59ab"
             borderwidth="1">
    <asp:TableRow Runat="server" ID="Tablerow1">
      <asp:TableCell Runat="server" ID="Tablecell1">
        Rows:
      </asp:TableCell>
      <asp:TableCell Runat="server" ID="Tablecell2">
        <asp:TextBox id="TxtRow" runat="server" />
      </asp:TableCell>
    </asp:TableRow>
    <asp:TableRow Runat="server" ID="Tablerow2">
      <asp:TableCell Runat="server" ID="Tablecell3">
        Cells Per Row
      </asp:TableCell>
      <asp:TableCell Runat="server" ID="Tablecell4">
        <asp:TextBox id="TxtCell" runat="server" />
      </asp:TableCell>
    </asp:TableRow>
    <asp:TableRow id="TblRNew" runat="server">
      <asp:TableCell id="TblCNew" runat="server"
        ColumnSpan="2"></asp:TableCell>
```

```
    </asp:TableRow>
    </asp:table><br>
    <asp:Button id="BtnSubmit" Text="Submit" runat="server"></asp:Button>
</form>
```

The following code shows how the properties of these classes can be manipulated programmatically:

```
private void BtnSubmit_Click(object sender, System.EventArgs e)
  {
    Table TblNew = new Table();
    TableRow Row;
    TableCell Cell;

    int r,c;
    for(r = 1; r <= Convert.ToInt32(TxtRow.Text); r++)
    {
      Row = new TableRow();
      if(r % 2 == 0)
        Row.BackColor = Color.AliceBlue;
      for(c=1; c <= Convert.ToInt32(TxtCell.Text); c++)
      {
        Cell = new TableCell();
        Cell.Text = "<I>Cell (" + r +"," + c + ")<I>";
        Row.Cells.Add(Cell);
      }
      TblNew.GridLines= GridLines.Both;
      TblNew.BorderStyle=BorderStyle.Solid;
      TblNew.Rows.Add(Row);
      TblCNew.Controls.Add(TblNew);
    }
  }
```

The above code adds rows and cells to an empty table. Here is a screenshot showing the new table created:

Table Class Protected Properties

The `Table` class adds no new protected properties to those inherited from the `WebControl` class. See the `WebControl` class reference for a complete listing.

Table Class Public Events

The `Table` class adds no new public events to those inherited from the `WebControl` class. See the `WebControl` class reference for a complete listing.

TableCell Class

The `TableCell` control allows you to declare a table cell in a `Table` control. It is inherited from the `System.Web.UI.WebControls.WebControl` class. Please refer to the `Table` class reference for an example on the usage of this class.

It is rendered as a `<td>` element and has the following syntax:

```
<asp:TableCell id = "id_name"
               ColumnSpan = "number of columns"
               RowSpan = "number of rows"
               HorizontalAlign = "Center | Justify | Left | NotSet | Right"
               Text = "Content text"
               VerticalAlign = "Bottom | Middle | NotSet | Top"
               Wrap = "true | false"
               Runat = "server" />
```

or:

```
<asp:TableCell id = "id_name"
               ColumnSpan = "number of columns"
               RowSpan = "number of rows"
               HorizontalAlign = "Center | Justify | Left | NotSet | Right"
               VerticalAlign = "Bottom | Middle | NotSet | Top"
               Wrap="true | false"
               Runat = "server">
    Content text
</asp:TableCell>
```

TableCell Class Public Methods

The `TableCell` class adds no new public methods to those inherited from the `WebControl` class. See the `WebControl` class reference for a complete listing.

TableCell Class Protected Methods

The `TableCell` class adds no new protected methods to those inherited from the `WebControl` class. See the `WebControl` class reference for a complete listing.

TableCell Class Public Properties

- **ColumnSpan**
- **HorizontalAlign**
- **RowSpan**
- **Text**
- **VerticalAlign**
- **Wrap**

ColumnSpan

The ColumnSpan property returns or sets the number of columns occupied by a single table cell. The default value is 0 indicating that the property is not set. This property can be helpful in certain circumstances: for example, you may need to assign a heading that is common to two columns, so you can use the ColSpan=2 property to make that heading column span for two columns.

```
public virtual int ColumnSpan {get; set;}
```

HorizontalAlign

This property gets or sets the horizontal alignment of the contents of the cell with respect to the table cell control. The valid values of this property belong to the HorizontalAlign enumeration. They are:

- Center
- Justify
- Left
- NotSet (Default value for this property)
- Right

```
public virtual HorizontalAlign HorizontalAlign {get; set;}
```

RowSpan

The RowSpan property returns or sets the number of rows occupied by a single table cell. The default value is 0 indicating that it is not set. This property can be helpful in certain circumstances: for example, you may need to show some content that need more than a single row to display, so you can use the RowSpan property to make that cell span for two rows or more.

```
public virtual int RowSpan {get; set;}
```

Text

The Text property gets or sets the text that appears in the cell of a table. The default value is an empty string. The setting of the Text property clears the previously contained content in the table's cell.

```
public virtual string Text {get; set;}
```

VerticalAlign

The VerticalAlign property gets or sets the vertical alignment of the content in the cell of a table.

The valid values of this property are defined by the VerticalAlign enumeration:

- ❏ Bottom
- ❏ Middle
- ❏ NotSet (default value of this property)
- ❏ Top

```
public virtual VerticalAlign VerticalAlign {get; set;}
```

Wrap

The Wrap property gets or sets a value indicating whether the contents within a cell should be wrapped. Possible values are true and false. true allows for wrapping of the contents in the cell and is also the default value. false indicates that the value should not be wrapped, that it should not be automatically moved to the next line.

```
public virtual bool Wrap {get; set;}
```

TableCell Class Protected Properties

The TableCell class adds no new protected properties to those inherited from the WebControl class. See the WebControl class reference for a complete listing.

TableCell Class Public Events

The TableCell class adds no new public events to those inherited from the WebControl class. See the WebControl class reference for a complete listing.

TableRow Class

The TableRow control represents rows in a Table control. It is inherited from the System.Web.UI.WebControls.WebControl class. Please refer to the Table class reference for an example on the usage of this class.

It is rendered as `<tr>` element and has the following syntax:

```
<asp:TableRow id = "id_name"
              HorizontalAlign = "Center | Justify | Left | NotSet | Right"
              VerticalAlign = "Bottom | Middle | NotSet | Top"
              Runat = "server">

  <asp:TableCell>
    Content Text
  </asp:TableCell>

</asp:TableRow>
```

TableRow Class Public Methods

The `TableRow` class adds no new public methods to those inherited from the `WebControl` class. See the `WebControl` class reference for a complete listing.

TableRow Class Protected Methods

The `TableRow` class adds no new protected methods to those inherited from the `WebControl` class. See the `WebControl` class reference for a complete listing.

TableRow Class Public Properties

- ❏ **`Cells`**
- ❏ **`HorizontalAlign`**
- ❏ **`VerticalAlign`**

Cells

The `Cells` property returns a `System.Web.UI.WebControls.TableCellCollection` object that contains all of the cells in a table row. An empty `TableCellCollection` is returned if there are no `Cell` elements within the table row. Cells of a table row can be added, updated or deleted with the help of the `TableCellCollection` class' properties and methods.

```
public virtual TableCellCollection Cells {get;}
```

HorizontalAlign

This property gets or sets the horizontal alignment of the contents of the row with respect to the table row control. The valid values of this property belong to the `HorizontalAlign` enumeration. They are:

- ❏ `Center`
- ❏ `Justify`
- ❏ `Left`
- ❏ `NotSet` (Default value for this property)
- ❏ `Right`

```
public virtual HorizontalAlign HorizontalAlign {get; set;}
```

VerticalAlign

The `VerticalAlign` property gets or sets the vertical alignment of the content in a row of a table.

The valid values of this property are defined by the `VerticalAlign` enumeration:

- ❑   `Bottom`
- ❑   `Middle`
- ❑   `NotSet` (default value of this property)
- ❑   `Top`

```
public virtual VerticalAlign VerticalAlign {get; set;}
```

TableRow Class Protected Properties

The `TableRow` class adds no new protected properties to those inherited from the `WebControl` class. See the `WebControl` class reference for a complete listing.

TableRow Class Public Events

The `TableRow` class adds no new public events to those inherited from the `WebControl` class. See the `WebControl` class reference for a complete listing.

TextBox Class

The `TextBox` control displays a textbox on a web page ready for user input. However, it can also be used to display text that is read-only. The textbox can render three different forms of input controls. It can be rendered as the HTML `<input type=text>`, `<input type=password>` and `<textarea>`. The type of `TextBox` that is rendered depends on the setting of its `TextMode` property.

This class is inherited from the `System.Web.UI.WebControls.WebControl` class and has the following syntax:

```
<asp:TextBox id = "id_name"
            AutoPostBack = "true | false"
            Columns = "number of columns"
            MaxLength = "maximum characters in the textbox"
            Rows = "number of rows"
            Text = "content text"
            TextMode = "Singleline | Multiline | Password"
            Wrap = "true | false"
            OnTextChanged = "OnTextChangedMethod"
            Runat = "server"/>
```

TextBox Class Public Methods

The `TextBox` class adds no new public methods to those inherited from the `WebControl` class. See the `WebControl` class reference for a complete listing.

TextBox Class Protected Methods

❑ **OnTextChanged**

OnTextChanged

The `OnTextChanged` method will raise the `TextChanged` event when the content of the `TextBox` control is changed. If the `AutoPostBack` property of the `TextBox` is set to `true`, then the page is posted to the server, otherwise not. In the latter case, the `TextChanged` event is raised whenever there is a change in the state of the `TextBox` between posts to the server. The `TextBox` control must have viewstate enabled in order to be able to raise this event correctly. This method allows derived classes to handle the `TextChanged` event directly without attaching to a delegate.

```
protected virtual void OnTextChanged(EventArgs e);
```

The parameter e refers to an `EventArgs` object that contains the `TextChanged` event data.

TextBox Class Public Properties

❑ **AutoPostBack**

❑ **Columns**

❑ **MaxLength**

❑ **ReadOnly**

❑ **Rows**

❑ **Text**

❑ **TextMode**

❑ **Wrap**

AutoPostBack

The `AutoPostBack` property gets or sets a value to determine whether the state of the `TextBox` should be posted back to the server automatically when the `TextBox` is changed. When set to `true`, the form which contains the `TextBox` is posted to the server automatically whenever there is a change in the contents of the `TextBox`. The default value is `false` indicating that the postback will not occur unless the page is posted back to the server by some other means (the click of a button or another control having its `AutoPostBack` property set to `true`). The `AutoPostBack` property requires that client-side scripting is enabled. This property will not post the page to the server if the browser does not support JavaScript or if client-side scripting is disabled.

```
public virtual bool AutoPostBack {get; set;}
```

Columns

The `Columns` property indicates the width in characters of a `TextBox`. The default value is 0.

```
public virtual int Columns {get; set;}
```

MaxLength

The `MaxLength` property gets or sets the maximum number of characters that the user is allowed to type in the `TextBox` control. However, this property does not work if the `TextMode` is set to `MultiLine`.

```
public virtual int MaxLength {get; set;}
```

ReadOnly

The `ReadOnly` property indicates whether the contents of the `TextBox` control can be modified or not. The default value is `false` indicating that the contents of the `TextBox` can be modified. A value of `true` locks the `TextBox` so that the user can't input anything.

```
public virtual bool ReadOnly {get; set;}
```

Rows

The `Rows` property indicates the height in characters of a multiline `TextBox`. This property works if the `TextMode` property is set to `MultiLine`. The default value is 0.

```
public virtual int Rows {get; set;}
```

Text

The `Text` property gets or sets the text displayed in the `TextBox` control. The default value is an empty string.

```
public virtual string Text {get; set;}
```

TextMode

The `TextMode` property gets or sets the type of textbox that is to be displayed in the web page. The different types available are specified by the `TextBoxMode` enumeration. The default value is `SingleLine`. An `ArgumentException` is thrown if a value other than one defined by the `TextBoxMode` enumeration is set for this property. The possible values are:

- ❑ `SingleLine`
- ❑ `MultiLine`
- ❑ `Password`

```
public virtual TextBoxMode TextMode {get; set;}
```

Wrap

The `Wrap` property gets or sets a value indicating whether the content of the `TextBox` can wrap within the `TextBox`. It only works when the `TextMode` property is set to `MultiLine`. `true` indicates that content can be wrapped within the `TextBox`, `false` otherwise.

```
public virtual bool Wrap {get; set;}
```

TextBox Class Protected Properties

The `TextBox` class adds no new protected properties to those inherited from the `WebControl` class. See the `WebControl` class reference for a complete listing.

TextBox Class Public Events

❑ **TextChanged**

TextChanged

The `TextChanged` event occurs when the `Text` property (the contents of the `TextBox`) is changed. If the `AutoPostBack` property is not set to `true`, this event will not immediately post back to the server, rather this event will be raised whenever the data is posted to the server because of something else. In this case only if there is a change in the state of the textbox from the previous post to the server will this event be raised. However, if the `AutoPostBack` property is set to `true` then whenever there is a change in the `Text` property of the `TextBox` control, this event will be raised and the page will immediately be posted to the server. The `TextBox` control must have viewstate enabled in order to be able to raise this event correctly.

```
public event EventHandler TextChanged;
```

The event handler receives information related to the event through the `EventArgs` object, passed as its argument.

Example: Using a TextBox Control

We have already looked at the usage of `TextBox` controls many times in this book. The following code example, `TextBoxUsage.aspx`, shows usage of a `TextBox` control focusing on the `TextChanged` event and with the `AutoPostBack` property set to `true`. Here is the user interface code:

```
<form id="FrmTextBoxUsage" method="post" runat="server">
  <asp:textbox id="TxtMulti" accesskey="1" textmode="multiline" Rows="5"
          Columns="50" wrap="true" autopostback="true"
          runat="server" /><br><br>
  <asp:textbox id="TxtSingle" accesskey="2" autopostback="true"
          MaxLength="10"
    textmode="singleline" runat="server" />  <br>
  <span id="Message" runat="server"></span>
</form>
```

Here is the `TextChanged` event handler code:

```csharp
private void TxtMulti_TextChanged(object sender, System.EventArgs e)
{
  Message.InnerHtml = "<font color='red'>Multi line "
                      + "textbox has been changed.</font>";
  }

private void TxtSingle_TextChanged(object sender, System.EventArgs e)
{
  Message.InnerHtml = "<font color='blue'>Single line "
                      + "textbox has been changed.</font>";
}
```

The following screenshot shows the output. The `TextChanged` event triggers as soon as the text is changed and the `TextBox` control loses its focus because the `AutoPostBack` property is set to `true`:

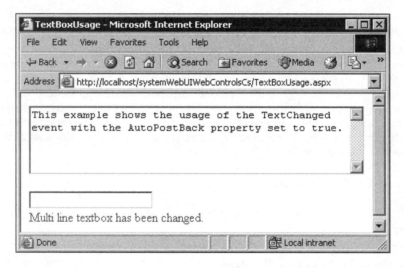

ValidationSummary Class

The `ValidationSummary` control displays a summary of all validation errors. It can display a summary in a web page or a message box or both. It shows the `ErrorMessage` property, or if that's not available the `Text` property of all validation controls whose validation fails. This control is very helpful as it can provide a great user interface to display all the error messages. Please refer to the `RequiredFieldValidator` class and other validator class reference for examples on using the `ValidationSummary` control.

This class is inherited from the `System.Web.UI.WebControls.WebControl` class. It has the following syntax:

```
<asp:ValidationSummary id = "id_name"
                  DisplayMode = "BulletList | List | SingleParagraph"
                  EnableClientScript = "true | false"
                  ShowSummary = "true | false"
                  ShowMessageBox = "true | false"
                  HeaderText = "TextToDisplayAsSummaryTitle"
                  Runat = "server" />
```

ValidationSummary Class Public Methods

The `ValidationSummary` class adds no new public methods to those inherited from the `WebControl` class. See the `WebControl` class reference for a complete listing.

ValidationSummary Class Protected Methods

The `ValidationSummary` class adds no new protected methods to those inherited from the `WebControl` class. See the `WebControl` class reference for a complete listing.

ValidationSummary Class Public Properties

- ❑ **DisplayMode**
- ❑ **EnableClientScript**
- ❑ **ForeColor**
- ❑ **HeaderText**
- ❑ **ShowMessageBox**
- ❑ **ShowSummary**

DisplayMode

The `DisplayMode` property gets or sets the display mode of the validation summary. The valid values are `BulletList`, `List`, and `SingleParagraph` as defined by the `ValidationSummaryDisplayMode` enumeration. The default value is `BulletList`.

```
public ValidationSummaryDisplayMode DisplayMode {get; set;}
```

EnableClientScript

The `EnableClientScript` property enables or disables client-side validation. The default value is `true` indicating that client-side validation is enabled; a value of `false` indicates client-side validation is disabled.

```
public bool EnableClientScript {get; set;}
```

ForeColor

The `ForeColor` property specifies the fore color of the message displayed by the validation summary control when validation fails. This property is overridden here. The default value is `Color.Red`. This property can be used to set any custom color using the `System.Drawing.Color` structure.

```
public override Color ForeColor {get; set;}
```

HeaderText

The `HeaderText` property gets or sets the header text that will display at the top of the summary.

```
public string HeaderText {get; set;}
```

ShowMessageBox

The `ShowMessageBox` property gets or sets a `Boolean` value indicating whether the validation summary should be displayed in a message box. The default is `false` indicating that the error messages of the validation summary will not be displayed in a message box.

```
public bool ShowMessageBox {get; set;}
```

ShowSummary

The `ShowSummary` property gets or sets a `Boolean` value indicating whether the validation summary is displayed inline in the control. The default is `true`.

```
public bool ShowSummary {get; set;}
```

ValidationSummary Class Protected Properties

The `ValidationSummary` class adds no new protected properties to those inherited from the `WebControl` class. See the `WebControl` class reference for a complete listing.

ValidationSummary Class Public Events

The `ValidationSummary` class adds no new public events to those inherited from the `WebControl` class. See the `WebControl` class reference for a complete listing.

WebControl Class

The `WebControl` class acts as a base class and provides the basic properties, methods, and events that are inherited by all ASP.NET web server controls. It inherits from the `System.Web.UI.Control` class.

WebControl Class Public Methods

- ❑ **ApplyStyle**
- ❑ **CopyBaseAttributes**
- ❑ DataBind – inherited from Control, see Chapter 2 for details.
- ❑ Dispose – inherited from Control, see Chapter 2 for details.
- ❑ Equals – inherited from Object, see Introduction for details.
- ❑ FindControl – inherited from Control, see Chapter 2 for details.
- ❑ GetHashCode – inherited from Object, see Introduction for details.
- ❑ GetType – inherited from Object, see Introduction for details.
- ❑ HasControls – inherited from Control, see Chapter 2 for details.
- ❑ **MergeStyle**
- ❑ **RenderBeginTag**
- ❑ RenderControl – inherited from Control, see Chapter 2 for details.
- ❑ **RenderEndTag**
- ❑ ResolveUrl – inherited from Control, see Chapter 2 for details.
- ❑ ToString – inherited from Object, see Introduction for details.

ApplyStyle

The ApplyStyle method applies a style to a web server control, overwriting any existing style that might be associated with that control. It copies non-blank elements of the Style object passed as its parameter and overwrites those existing style elements of the web server control.

```
public void ApplyStyle(Style s);
```

The parameter s specifies the Style object that needs to be applied to the web server control.

CopyBaseAttributes

The CopyBaseAttributes method is used to copy properties from one web control to another. This method copies the properties AccessKey, Attributes, Enabled, TabIndex and ToolTip (except those that are encapsulated by the Style object) from the source web control passed as its parameter to the control on which this method is called.

```
public void CopyBaseAttributes(WebControl controlSrc);
```

The parameter controlSrc specifies the source control from which the properties are to be copied.

MergeStyle

The MergeStyle method copies elements of the specified style to the web control. It copies only non-blank elements and while copying elements it does not overwrite any existing style elements of the control.

```
public void MergeStyle(Style s);
```

The parameter s represents the Style object whose elements need to be copied to the WebControl.

RenderBeginTag

The RenderBeginTag method is used to render the opening HTML tag to the output stream.

```
public virtual void RenderBeginTag(HtmlTextWriter writer);
```

The parameter writer is an HtmlTextWriter object and represents the output stream to render the contents on the client.

RenderEndTag

The RenderEndTag method is used to render the closing HTML tag to the output stream.

```
public virtual void RenderEndTag(HtmlTextWriter writer);
```

The parameter writer is an HtmlTextWriter object and represents the output stream to render the contents on the client.

WebControl Class Protected Methods

- ❏ **AddAttributesToRender**
- ❏ AddParsedSubObject – inherited from Control, see Chapter 2 for details.
- ❏ ClearChildViewState – inherited from Control, see Chapter 2 for details.
- ❏ CreateChildControls – inherited from Control, see Chapter 2 for details.
- ❏ CreateControlCollection – inherited from Control, see Chapter 2 for details.
- ❏ **CreateControlStyle**
- ❏ EnsureChildControls – inherited from Control, see Chapter 2 for details.
- ❏ Finalize – inherited from System.Object, see Introduction for details.
- ❏ IsLiteralContent – inherited from Control, see Chapter 2 for details.
- ❏ LoadViewState – (overridden) inherited from Control, see Chapter 2 for details.
- ❏ MapPathSecure – inherited from Control, see Chapter 2 for details.
- ❏ MemberwiseClone – inherited from System.Object, see Introduction for details.
- ❏ OnBubbleEvent – inherited from Control, see Chapter 2 for details.
- ❏ OnDataBinding – inherited from Control, see Chapter 2 for details.
- ❏ OnInit – inherited from Control, see Chapter 2 for details.
- ❏ OnLoad – inherited from Control, see Chapter 2 for details.
- ❏ OnPreRender – inherited from Control, see Chapter 2 for details.

- ❏ OnUnload – inherited from Control, see Chapter 2 for details.
- ❏ RaiseBubbleEvent – inherited from Control, see Chapter 2 for details.
- ❏ Render – (overridden) inherited from Control, see Chapter 2 for details.
- ❏ RenderChildren – inherited from Control, see Chapter 2 for details.
- ❏ RenderContents – (overridden) inherited from Control, see Chapter 2 for details.
- ❏ SaveViewState – (overridden) inherited from Control, see Chapter 2 for details.
- ❏ TrackViewState – (overridden) inherited from Control, see Chapter 2 for details.

AddAttributesToRender

The AddAttributesToRender method adds HTML attributes and styles that need to be rendered to the output stream.

```
protected virtual void AddAttributesToRender(HtmlTextWriter writer);
```

The parameter writer is an HtmlTextWriter object that represents the output stream.

CreateControlStyle

The CreateControlStyle method creates a Style object that is used internally by the WebControl class to work with the style related properties. It returns a System.Web.UI.WebControls.Style object.

```
protected virtual Style CreateControlStyle();
```

WebControl Class Public Properties

- ❏ **AccessKey**
- ❏ **Attributes**
- ❏ **BackColor**
- ❏ **BorderColor**
- ❏ **BorderStyle**
- ❏ **BorderWidth**
- ❏ ClientID – inherited from Control, see Chapter 2 for details.
- ❏ Controls – inherited from Control, see Chapter 2 for details.
- ❏ **ControlStyle**
- ❏ **ControlStyleCreated**
- ❏ **CssClass**
- ❏ **Enabled**
- ❏ EnableViewState – inherited from Control, see Chapter 2 for details.
- ❏ **Font**

- ❑ **ForeColor**

- ❑ **Height**

- ❑ ID – inherited from `Control`, see Chapter 2 for details.

- ❑ NamingContainer – inherited from `Control`, see Chapter 2 for details.

- ❑ Page – inherited from `Control`, see Chapter 2 for details.

- ❑ Parent – inherited from `Control`, see Chapter 2 for details.

- ❑ Site – inherited from `Control`, see Chapter 2 for details.

- ❑ **Style**

- ❑ **TabIndex**

- ❑ TemplateSourceDirectory – inherited from `Control`, see Chapter 2 for details.

- ❑ **ToolTip**

- ❑ UniqueID – inherited from `Control`, see Chapter 2 for details.

- ❑ Visible – inherited from `Control`, see Chapter 2 for details.

- ❑ **Width**

AccessKey

The `AccessKey` property gets or sets a keyboard shortcut key to quickly move focus to the web control. This property can be very useful, and makes Web Form pages resemble a Visual Basic application. The shortcut key, when pressed with the *Alt* key, will move the focus to the web control that has the key defined as the access key. This works only in Internet Explorer 4.0 or above.

```
public virtual string AccessKey {get; set;}
```

Attributes

The `Attributes` property gets all attribute name-value pairs expressed on a web control tag within an ASP.NET page. This property returns the name-value pairs as a `System.Web.UI.AttributeCollection` object. These attributes, the control's properties, are stored in the viewstate. The property is read-only, but the underlying `AttributeCollection` can be used to manipulate with the attributes. It can be used to get or set custom attributes where a control doesn't provide a specific property for a particular purpose.

```
public AttributeCollection Attributes {get;}
```

BackColor

The `BackColor` property specifies the background color of the web control. This property can be used to set any custom color using the `System.Drawing.Color` structure. The default value is `Color.Empty` indicating that the property is not set.

```
public virtual Color BackColor {get; set;}
```

BorderColor

The `BorderColor` property specifies the border color of the web control. This property can be used to set any custom color using the `System.Drawing.Color` structure. The default value is `Color.Empty` indicating that the property is not set.

```
public virtual Color BorderColor {get; set;}
```

BorderStyle

The `BorderStyle` property specifies the border style of the web control. This property can be used to set any border style using the `BorderStyle` enumeration values: `Dotted`, `Dashed`, `Double`, `Inset`, `NotSet`, `None`, `OutSet`, `Groove`, `Solid` and `Ridge`. The default value is `NotSet` indicating that the property is not set.

```
public virtual BorderStyle BorderStyle {get; set;}
```

BorderWidth

The `BorderWidth` property specifies the border width of the web control. This property can be used to set border width using the `Unit` structure. The default value is `Unit.Empty`, indicating that the property is not set.

```
public virtual Unit BorderWidth {get; set;}
```

ControlStyle

This property gets the style of a web control, and is primarily used by control developers.

```
public Style ControlStyle {get;}
```

ControlStyleCreated

The `ControlStyleCreated` property returns a `Boolean` value indicating whether a `Style` object has been created for the `ControlStyle` property, and is primarily used by control developers.

```
public bool ControlStyleCreated {get;}
```

CssClass

The `CssClass` property gets or sets a CSS class rendered by a web control. This property works for all browsers except browsers that do not support CSS. The default is `String.Empty`.

```
public virtual string CssClass {get; set;}
```

Enabled

The `Enabled` property gets or sets a `Boolean` value indicating whether a web control is enabled. The default value is `true` meaning the control is enabled for interaction; a value of `false` disables the web control.

```
public virtual bool Enabled {get; set;}
```

Font

The `Font` property gets the font information of a web control. The font information is returned as a `FontInfo` object. The `FontInfo` object has various properties available relating to the font, like `Bold`, `Italic`, `Name`, `Names`, `Strikeout`, `Underline`, `Overline`, and `Size`. All the properties work in all browsers except `Overline` which is not supported by earlier browsers.

```
public virtual FontInfo Font {get;}
```

ForeColor

The `ForeColor` property specifies a setting for the foreground color, typically the color of the text in the web control. This property can be used to set any custom color using the `System.Drawing.Color` structure. The default value is `Color.Empty` indicating that the property is not set.

```
public virtual Color ForeColor {get; set;}
```

Height

The `Height` property specifies the height of the web control. This property can be used to set height using the `Unit` structure. The default value is `Unit.Empty`.

```
public virtual Unit Height {get; set;}
```

Style

The `Style property` gets all cascading style sheet (CSS) properties that are applied to a specific web control in a web page. It gets all style sheet properties in a `CssStyleCollection` object.

```
public CssStyleCollection Style {get;}
```

TabIndex

The `TabIndex` property gets or sets the tab order of a web control. The default value is `0` indicating that the property is not set. An `ArgumentOutOfRangeException` is thrown if the tab index is not set within the range `-32768` to `32767`.

```
public virtual short TabIndex {get; set;}
```

ToolTip

The `ToolTip` property gets or sets the pop-up text displayed by a web control when the mouse cursor hovers over it. This property is designed to give a helpful description of the control. The default value is an empty string.

```
public virtual string ToolTip {get; set;}
```

Width

The `Width` property specifies the width of the web control. This property can be used to set width using the `Unit` structure. The default value is `Unit.Empty`. An `ArgumentException` is thrown if the property is set to a negative value.

```
public virtual Unit Width {get; set;}
```

WebControl Class Protected Properties

- ❑ `ChildControlsCreated` – inherited from `Control`, see Chapter 2 for details.
- ❑ `Context` – inherited from `Control`, see Chapter 2 for details.
- ❑ `Events` – inherited from `Control`, see Chapter 2 for details.
- ❑ `HasChildViewState` – inherited from `Control`, see Chapter 2 for details.
- ❑ `IsTrackingViewState` – inherited from `Control`, see Chapter 2 for details.
- ❑ **TagKey**
- ❑ **TagName**
- ❑ `ViewState` – inherited from `Control`, see Chapter 2 for details.
- ❑ `ViewStateIgnoresCase` – inherited from `Control`, see Chapter 2 for details.

TagKey

The `TagKey` property returns the `System.Web.UI.HtmlTextWriterTag` value that represents the web control. The `HtmlTextWriterTag` enumeration defines the `HTML` tags that are passed to an `HtmlTextWriter` or `Html32TextWriter` object output stream.

```
protected virtual HtmlTextWriterTag TagKey {get;}
```

TagName

The `TagName` property returns the name of the web control element.

```
protected virtual string TagName {get;}
```

WebControl Class Public Events

- ❑ `DataBinding` – inherited from `Control`, see Chapter 2 for details.
- ❑ `Disposed` – inherited from `Control`, see Chapter 2 for details.
- ❑ `Init` – inherited from `Control`, see Chapter 2 for details.
- ❑ `Load` – inherited from `Control`, see Chapter 2 for details.
- ❑ `PreRender` – inherited from `Control`, see Chapter 2 for details.
- ❑ `Unload` – inherited from `Control`, see Chapter 2 for details.

Xml Class

The `Xml` control displays on a web page a raw XML document or an XML document that has been formatted using an XSL stylesheet. There are three ways in which the XML document can be passed to the `Xml` control. You can pass the path of the document using the `DocumentSource` property, or a loaded `XmlDocument` object can be passed using the `Document` property, or finally a string representing the XML document content can be passed to the control using the `DocumentContent` property. The `Xml` control can display the formatted XML document using an XSLT stylesheet. The XSLT stylesheet is passed to the control in two ways. You can pass the path of the XSL document using the `TransformSource` property, or you can pass a loaded `XslTransform` object through the `Transform` property.

This class is inherited from the `System.Web.UI.Control` class. It has the following syntax:

```
<asp:Xml id = "id_name"
        Document = "loaded XmlDocument"
        DocumentContent = "String of XML"
        DocumentSource = "Path of XML Document"
        Transform = "loaded XslTransform (StyleSheet)"
        TransformSource = "Path of XSL Transform Document"
        Runat = "server">
```

Xml Class Public Methods

The `Xml` class adds no new public methods to those inherited from the `WebControl` class. See the `WebControl` class reference for a complete listing.

Xml Class Protected Methods

The `Xml` class adds no new protected methods to those inherited from the `WebControl` class. See the `WebControl` class reference for a complete listing.

Xml Class Public Properties

❑ **Document**

❑ **DocumentContent**

❑ **DocumentSource**

❑ **Transform**

❑ **TransformArgumentList**

❑ **TransformSource**

Document

The `Document` property gets or sets the `System.Xml.XmlDocument` object to display. This property is used to pass the XML document, if the document to be passed to the control is preloaded in the `XmlDocument` object.

```
public XmlDocument Document {get; set;}
```

DocumentContent

The `DocumentContent` property gets or sets a string that contains the XML document to display in the `Xml` control. This property is used to pass the XML document, if the document to be passed is contained in a string. Mostly this property is not set programmatically or at design time as an attribute to the control, rather this is usually set between the opening and closing tags of the `<asp:Xml>` control.

```
public string DocumentContent {get; set;}
```

DocumentSource

The `DocumentSource` property gets or sets the XML filename. This property is used to assign or return the path of the XML document to be displayed. The path can be relative or absolute. This property is used to pass the XML document, if the XML content is stored in an XML file.

```
public string DocumentSource {get; set;}
```

Transform

The `Transform` property gets or sets the `System.Xml.Xsl.XslTransform` object that represents the XSLT stylesheet to use to format the XML document before writing it to the output stream. This property is used if the XSLT stylesheet is already loaded into the `XslTransform` object.

```
public XslTransform Transform {get; set;}
```

TransformArgumentList

The `TransformArgumentList` property gets or sets the `System.Xml.Xsl.XsltArgumentList` object that contains a list of optional arguments passed to the stylesheet. These arguments are used when the stylesheet is used to convert the XML document.

```
public XsltArgumentList TransformArgumentList {get; set;}
```

TransformSource

The `TransformSource` property gets or sets the filename of an external XSL stylesheet to use for transforming the XML data. The path of the external stylesheet document can be relative or absolute.

```
public string TransformSource {get; set;}
```

Example: Passing XML into an Xml Control

The following example, `XmlUsage.aspx`, shows the two ways in which the document and XSLT stylesheet can be passed to the `Xml` Control. The user interface code is as follows:

```
<form id="FrmXmlUsage" method="post" runat="server">
  <table border=1>
    <tr>
      <td><asp:Xml id="XmlBookList" Runat="server"></asp:Xml></td>
      <td>
      <asp:Xml id="XmlBookListSource" Runat="server"
```

```
                    DocumentSource="booklist.xml"
                    TransformSource="booklist.xsl">
        </asp:Xml>
      </td>
    </tr>
  </table>
</form>
```

The following code shows how to set the `Document` and `Transform` properties:

```
private void Page_Load(object sender, System.EventArgs e)
{
  // Load the Xml Document
  XmlDocument bookXml  = new XmlDocument();
  bookXml.Load(Server.MapPath("booklist.xml"));

  // Load the Xsl Document
  XslTransform bookXsl = new XslTransform();
  bookXsl.Load(Server.MapPath("booklist.xsl"));

  XmlBookList.Document=bookXml;
  XmlBookList.Transform=bookXsl;
}
```

The following screenshot shows the same XML document being formatted and displayed but with the document and stylesheet being loaded in different ways:

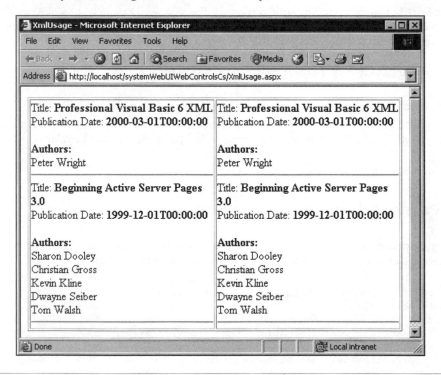

Xml Class Protected Properties

The Xml class adds no new protected properties to those inherited from the WebControl class. See the WebControl class reference for a complete listing.

Xml Class Public Events

The Xml class adds no new public events to those inherited from the WebControl class. See the WebControl class reference for a complete listing.

5

System.Web.UI.MobileControls

The Microsoft Mobile Internet Toolkit (or MMIT) is an extension to ASP.NET that supports the development of applications targeting a variety of mobile devices like cell phones, PDAs and smart pagers. This functionality is provided in the namespace `System.Web.UI.MobileControls`. The latest version of the Toolkit is available for download at http://msdn.microsoft.com/downloads/. The Toolkit provides the mobile controls assembly as well as design time support for Visual Studio .NET, although VS.NET is not required to develop mobile applications. The Mobile Controls seem to be truly an "add-on" from Microsoft's point of view as the `System.Web.UI.MobileControls` namespace is not part of the CLI class set and is documented independently.

Even though the mobile controls are documented independently they do integrate seamlessly with other user interface development in ASP.NET. This consistency stems from the fact that the `System.Web.UI.MobileControl` base class for mobile controls inherits from `System.Web.UI.Control`. In this sense a mobile control is fundamentally no different from any of the other controls provided for user interface development in ASP.NET. In fact, this commonality provides a great deal of programmatic consistency between UI development practices whether you are targeting a mobile user or an "immobile" one. (Most developers will typically be familiar with either the `System.Web.UI.HtmlControls` or `System.Web.UI.WebControls` namespaces before embarking on mobile development.)

The Mobile Internet Toolkit creates a single development framework for mobile applications. Given the variety of devices and technologies in the mobile platform universe, mobile controls have the remarkable ability to determine the client device at run time and then automatically adapt the rendered output to support the device. The degree of variation between clients is much greater than the "uplevel/downlevel" browser differences that must be addressed by the more typical Web and HTML controls. Mobile controls allow the developer to spend less development time thinking about the specific device being used, and more time on functionality and features.

Microsoft's mobile controls support an impressive but not exhaustive set of client devices and technologies. The vast majority of mobile devices on the market use some version of HTML, cHTML (Compact Hypertext Mark-up Language), or WML (Wireless Mark-up Language), all of which are supported by the MMIT. With perhaps the exception of cHTML, each of these has a wide variety of dialects and versions, so the mobile controls have device-specific filters to help render the appropriate version of the respective syntax depending on device.

Each mobile control has a set of device adapter classes that produce the output specific to one of these mark-up languages. There is sample device adapter source code available so that hardware manufacturers and developers can support new devices and customize output for particular devices. Although the MMIT is currently limited to HTML, cHTML and WML output, there is nothing to prevent new rendering syntaxes and devices from being supported as time goes on, due to the extensibility of the mobile control framework.

Example: helloWorld.aspx

Let's see a brief example of the MMIT in action. All of these examples are available in the `systemWebUIMobileControlExamples` folder of the code download, and are included in a VS.NET project of the same name for your convenience. Here is `helloWorld.aspx`:

```
<%@ Page Language="c#" AutoEventWireup="false"
        Codebehind="helloWorld.aspx.cs"
        Inherits="systemWebUIMobileControlExamples.helloWorld" %>
<%@ Register TagPrefix="mobile" Namespace="System.Web.UI.MobileControls"
            Assembly="System.Web.Mobile, Version=1.0.3300.0,
                    Culture=neutral, PublicKeyToken=b03f5f7f11d50a3a" %>
<meta name="GENERATOR" content="Microsoft Visual Studio.NET 7.0">
<meta name="CODE_LANGUAGE" content="C#">
<meta name="vs_targetSchema"
      content="http://schemas.microsoft.com/Mobile/Page">
<body Xmlns:mobile="http://schemas.microsoft.com/Mobile/WebForm">
  <mobile:Form id="Form1" runat="server">Hello World!</mobile:Form>
</body>
```

And here is the code-behind page, `helloWorld.aspx.cs`:

```
public class helloWorld : System.Web.UI.MobileControls.MobilePage
{
  protected System.Web.UI.MobileControls.Form Form1;

  private void Page_Load(object sender, System.EventArgs e)
  {
    // Put user code to initialize the page here
  }
}
```

When viewed in the Pocket Internet Explorer, generic OpenWave, and Nokia 7110 simulators the output looks like this:

The output is consistent even though the three devices depicted here use HTML and two variants of WML, respectively. You can download these simulators from these locations:

❑ Pocket PC 2002 SDK –
http://www.microsoft.com/mobile/developer/downloads/ppcsdk2002.asp

❑ OpenWave SDK WAP Edition 5.0 – http://developer.openwave.com/download/index.html

❑ Nokia 7110 – http://www.forum.nokia.com/wapforum/nokiasim_new.html

Note – in order to run the Pocket PC simulator you will also need to download and install the Embedded Visual Tools for VS.NET. This (312MB toolkit) can be downloaded from:

http://msdn.microsoft.com/vstudio/device/prodinfo.asp

Once the embedded development environment is up you "execute" an empty project which starts the emulator. You can then close down the development environment and the emulator stays running. The device emulator has its own IP address so if you're navigating to sample mobile pages on the same machine you'll need to give the URL the IP of your PC in order for Pocket IE to fetch the page.

The most important bits to notice at this point are that all mobile web pages inherit from `System.Web.UI.MobileControls.MobilePage`, which is the mobile equivalent of `Page` in normal ASP.NET development. Another important point is that the lifecycle of a mobile page differs slightly from that of the Web Forms page that it extends. When the request is first received, the headers of the device are examined to determine the capabilities of the requesting device. These capabilities are mapped in the server's `machine.config` file. Once the device type is determined the appropriate set of device adapters for control rendering is used. The following XML fragment from `machine.config` gives a sense of the properties associated with a device filter, in this case the Ericsson R380:

```
<!-- Ericsson -->
  <case
    match="R380 (?'browserMajorVersion'\w*)(?'browserMinorVersion'\.\w*) WAP1\.1">
    browser = "Ericsson"
    type = "Ericsson R380"
    version = ${browserMajorVersion}.${browserMinorVersion}
    majorVersion = ${browserMajorVersion}
    minorVersion = ${browserMinorVersion}
    preferredRenderingType = "wml11"
    preferredRenderingMime = "text/vnd.wap.wml"
    preferredImageMime = "image/vnd.wap.wbmp"
    inputType = "virtualKeyboard"
    canInitiateVoiceCall = "true"
    mobileDeviceManufacturer = "Ericsson"
    mobileDeviceModel = "R380"
    screenPixelsWidth = "310"
    screenPixelsHeight = "100"
    screenCharactersHeight = "7"
    screenBitDepth = "1"
    isColor = "false"
    maximumRenderedPageSize = "3000"
  </case>
```

To render a `Form` control for an HTML-capable device, the `HtmlFormAdapter` class will be used. If the device utilizes WML, `WmlFormAdapter` will be invoked instead, and so on. Just as in non-mobile controls, mobile controls are based on a class hierarchy that extends specificity of function down the hierarchy. Consider a mobile Calendar control. It has the following class definition:

```
public class System.Web.UI.MobileControls.Calendar :
              System.Web.UI.MobileControls.MobileControl,
              System.Web.UI.IPostBackEventHandler
```

So, the Calendar control inherits its base functionality from the `MobileControl` class and you use an instance of it to create a Calendar control in your mobile page. However, at run time the client device will be resolved and, in the case of a device that supports Compact HTML, a CHTML-specific adapter instance will be instantiated to support and "filter" the client rendering generated by the `Calendar` control.

The `ChtmlCalendarAdapter` class participates in the following hierarchy:

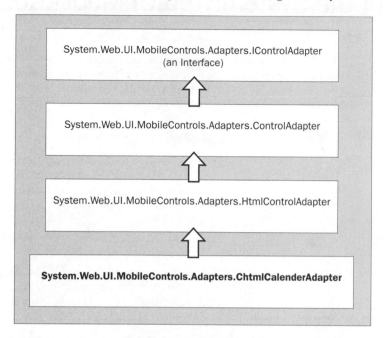

If the client device supported WAP/WML then a WML-specific adapter would be instantiated to support the Calendar control, and the adapter instance would participate in a hierarchy like this:

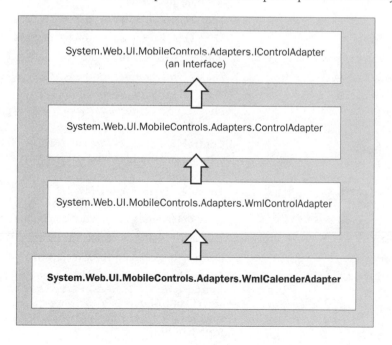

Classes of the System.Web.UI.MobileControl Namespace

The classes in the following table that are highlighted will be covered in depth in this chapter. We have chosen to cover these specific classes because the vast majority of these controls work in exactly the same way as their `System.Web.UI.WebControl` equivalents. We are therefore focussing our coverage on those classes that do not have counterparts in other namespaces.

Class	Description
AdRotator	The mobile version of the standard AdRotator control. Displays a randomly selected advertisement on the mobile page and is driven by the same XML configuration file as the `WebControls.AdRotator` class.
BaseValidator	Provides an abstract base class for all mobile control validation controls.
Calendar	The mobile version of the standard Calendar control. Provides a calendar display control that can render day, week and month views. Date selection is also provided.
ChtmlCalendarAdapter	The CHTML adapter for the `Calendar` class.
ChtmlCommandAdapter	The CHTML adapter for the Command control. (The `Command` class encapsulates "responsive" or interactive elements like buttons.)
ChtmlFormAdapter	The CHTML adapter for the `Form` class.
ChtmlLinkAdapter	The CHTML adapter for the `Link` class.
ChtmlMobileTextWriter	The CHTML version of the `MobileTextWriter` class.
ChtmlPageAdapter	The CHTML adapter for the `HTMLPageAdapter` class.
ChtmlPhoneCallAdapter	The CHTML adapter for a Phonecall control. A `Phonecall` control can dial a phone number on the device.
Command	**Control that encapsulates interactive UI elements like buttons and enables user-driven activation of ASP.NET event handlers.**
CompareValidator	The mobile equivalent of `System.Web.UI.WebControls.CompareValidator` class, determines value equivalency in form handling.
ControlAdapter	The base class from which all control adapters inherit.
ControlPager	Defines the page index for a control.
CustomValidator	This is the mobile equivalent of the ASP.NET `System.Web.UI.WebControls.CustomValidator` server control. It provides a base class from which you can create a control that provides custom validation for form handling.

Class	Description
`DeviceSpecific`	**Allows the choice between multiple content alternatives in the** `<DeviceSpecific>` **element of a declarative control specification. This and the other** `DeviceSpecific` **classes are used for rendering device-specific content within a control based on a set of filters.**
`DeviceSpecificChoice`	**Provides a single choice within a** `<DeviceSpecific><Choice/></DeviceSpecific>` **construct. Choices are evaluated in the sequence they appear within the** `<DeviceSpecific>` **element.**
`DeviceSpecificChoiceCollection`	An aggregation that represents the `DeviceSpecificChoice` elements in a `DeviceSpecific` property, this aggregation is typified by the `Choices` property of a `DeviceSpecific` instance.
`DeviceSpecificControlBuilder`	Created at run time and used to facilitate the parsing of a `DeviceSpecific` section within a control.
`ErrorFormatterPage`	Supports the internal page that handles run time exception information and error information rendering.
`FontInfo`	Provides access to all font-related style information about a mobile Web Forms control. The `FontInfo` class provides a subset of the functionality of the `System.Web.UI.WebControls.FontInfo` class.
`Form`	Acts as an aggregator for mobile controls. Unlike stardard ASP.NET pages, in mobile controls there can be multiple `Form` objects for a single page. This is to reduce total round trips to the server and support the "Deck and Card" model of WML.
`FormControlBuilder`	Supports the parsing required for Form controls.
`HtmlCalendarAdapter`	The HTML adapter for the `Calendar` class.
`HtmlCommandAdapter`	The HTML adapter for the `Command` class.
`HtmlControlAdapter`	The base class for all HTML adapter classes.
`HtmlFormAdapter`	The HTML adapter for the `Form` class.
`HtmlImageAdapter`	The HTML adapter for the `Image` class.
`HtmlLabelAdapter`	Provides a label adapter class for the HTML device adapter set.
`HtmlLinkAdapter`	The HTML adapter for the `Link` class.
`HtmlListAdapter`	The HTML adapter for the `List` class.
`HtmlLiteralTextAdapter`	The HTML adapter for the `LiteralText` class.
`HtmlMobileTextWriter`	The HTML version of the `MobileTextWriter` class.
`HtmlObjectListAdapter`	The HTML adapter for object lists.
`HtmlPageAdapter`	The HTML adapter for the `MobilePage` class

Class	Description
HtmlPanelAdapter	The HTML adapter for the Panel class.
HtmlPhoneCallAdapter	The HTML adapter for the PhoneCall class.
HtmlSelectionListAdapter	The HTML adapter for the SelectionList class.
HtmlTextBoxAdapter	The HTML adapter for the TextBox class.
HtmlTextViewAdapter	The HTML adapter for the TextView class.
HtmlValidationSummaryAdapter	The HTML adapter for the ValidationSummary class.
HtmlValidatorAdapter	The HTML adapter for validation control classes.
Image	Control that displays images in a Form.
ItemPager	Facilitates the pagination of a Form control. "Page"/Pagination handling is required in mobile devices due to limited screen sizes.
Label	Control that displays text labels in a Form.
Link	Control that defines a link to other mobile Form controls in a mobile page or to a URI like cnn.com.
List	Control that enables static, interactive list, or selection list generation and contains MobileListItem objects representing list elements.
ListCommandEventArgs	Encapsulates event arguments related to interactive or selection list events.
ListControlBuilder	Support parsing of the List and SelectionList controls.
ListDataBindEventArgs	Encapsulates event arguments related to an ItemDataBind event generated by a List control.
LiteralText	Represents instances of literal text in a Form. LiteralText objects are generated at run time to handle such text.
LoadItemsEventArgs	This object supports controls that customize pagination by detailing how many items should be loaded.
MobileCapabilities	**The extended mobile version of System.Web.HttpBrowserCapabilities class which provides details about the client device.**
MobileControl	**The base class for all mobile controls.**
MobileControlBuilder	Supports parsing of mobile controls.
MobileFormsAuthentication	While some devices/clients like Pocket Internet Explorer support cookies, all mobile apps by default are set to use "cookieless" session state management. Cookieless session management is handled by munging a session ID in all URLs passed between client and server. This class supports cookieless sessions by munging the session ID into URLs generated or referenced by mobile controls.
MobileListItem	An element within a mobile List control.
MobileListItemCollection	Provides a collection class for the List control.

Class	Description
MobilePage	The base class for all mobile web pages.
MobileTextWriter	The base class for mobile TextWriter objects.
MobileUserControl	The base class for customer mobile controls.
ObjectList	**A feature-enhanced list control that provides for multi-property support and automatic item details view generation.**
ObjectListCommand	The command object associated with an ObjectList control.
ObjectListCommandCollection	An aggregation or collection class representing the ObjectListCommands associated with an ObjectList control.
ObjectListCommandEventArgs	An EventArgs class derivative specific to the ObjectListCommand that details the ItemCommand event.
ObjectListControlBuilder	Supports parsing of ObjectList controls.
ObjectListDataBindEventArgs	An EventArgs class derivative that details the ItemDataBind event of an ObjectList control.
ObjectListField	A field or property of an ObjectList item. ObjectLists support multiple discrete values per item via this class.
ObjectListFieldCollection	The collection or aggregation class for ObjectListField objects.
ObjectListItem	A class representing a single list item within an ObjectList control.
ObjectListItemCollection	The collection or aggregation class for ObjectListItem objects.
ObjectListSelectEventArgs	An EventArgs class derivative that details the ItemSelect event of an ObjectList control.
ObjectListShowCommandsEventArgs	An EventArgs class derivative that details the ShowItemCommands event of an ObjectList control.
ObjectListTitleAttribute	A class representing the title or header of a field in an ObjectList control.
PagedControl	**An abstract base class to be used by custom controls that support custom pagination.**
PagerStyle	A derivative of the Style class that provides additional style capability for mobile controls that are participating in pagination.
Panel	A control subordinate to a Form control but capable of aggregating or grouping controls in its own right. Functionally similar to an HTML <div> element.
PanelControlBuilder	Supports parsing of Panel controls.

Class	Description
PhoneCall	A control that can render a phone number and, upon user selection, dial that phone number on devices equipped to make calls.
RangeValidator	The mobile equivalent of the `System.Web.UI.WebControls.RangeValidator` control, `RangeValidator` facilitates form validation, specifically that a value submitted by a user falls within a specified range.
RegularExpressionValidator	The mobile equivalent of the `System.Web.UI.WebControls.RegularExpressionValidator` class, the `RegularExpressionValidator` control is used in form validation. Specifically, it validates a value in another control against a regular expression provided in the `regular expression validation` control instance.
RequiredFieldValidator	The mobile equivalent of the `System.Web.UI.WebControls.RequiredFieldValidator` class, the `RequiredFieldValidator` is used in form validation. Specifically, it determines whether or not a user-generated value exists in a targeted control like a text box.
SelectionList	A control that renders a list wherein the list elements are selectable by a user.
Style	A base class that aggregates style properties shared by all mobile controls.
StyleSheet	A class that acts as a common style reference for one or more controls.
StyleSheetControlBuilder	Supports parsing for StyleSheet controls.
TemplateContainer	A class created at run time by mobile controls to contain template instances.
TextBox	A single-line text input user interface control class.
TextBoxControlBuilder	Supports the rendering of TextBox controls.
TextControl	The base class for text-based controls like TextBox, Label, Link and Command.
TextView	A control intended to display large amounts of text on a mobile page. TextView derives from the `PagedControl` base class and implicitly supports pagination when the `Paginate` property for the form or panel is set to `true`.
TextViewElement	A subordinate control that acts as a text element in a `TextView` instance. Text view elements are used by the pagination mechanism of `TextView` to break large text content across multiple screens of information.
UpWmlMobileTextWriter	The Openwave's UP browser WML adapter for the text writer adapter class.

Class	Description
UpWmlPageAdapter	The Openwave's UP browser WML adapter for the page adapter class.
ValidationSummary	A control that summarizes the errors generated by any validation controls in the form.
WmlCalendarAdapter	The WML adapter for the Calendar class.
WmlCommandAdapter	The WML adapter for the Command class.
WmlControlAdapter	The base adapter class for WML adapters.
WmlFormAdapter	The WML adapter for the Form class.
WmlImageAdapter	The WML adapter for the Image class.
WmlLabelAdapter	The WML adapter for the Label class.
WmlLinkAdapter	The WML adapter for the Link class.
WmlListAdapter	The WML adapter for the List class.
WmlLiteralTextAdapter	The WML adapter for the LiteralText class.
WmlMobileTextWriter	The WML version of the MobileTextWriter class.
WmlObjectListAdapter	The WML adapter for the ObjectList class.
WmlPageAdapter	The WML adapter for the MobilePage class.
WmlPanelAdapter	The WML adapter for the Panel class.
WmlPhoneCallAdapter	The WML adapter for the PhoneCall class.
WmlSelectionListAdapter	The WML adapter for the SelectionList class.
WmlTextBoxAdapter	The WML adapter for the TextBox class.
WmlTextViewAdapter	The WML adapter for the TextView class.
WmlValidationSummaryAdapter	The WML adapter for the ValidationSummary class.
WmlValidatorAdapter	The WML adapter for validation control classes.

> All Mobile Controls inherit from **System.Web.UI.Control**, so we are not going to
> waste your time by repeating the listing of all the members that are discussed in
> Chapter 2 for every control in this namespace. We will only give a full listing of all
> the new members that the Mobile controls add over and above those inherited from
> **Control**, and those members that are overridden.

Command Class

The Command class displays an interactive element in the user interface. It is essentially the mobile equivalent of a button control. Given the wide variety of input strategies in mobile devices a mobile-specific control was developed in order to abstract these different ways of inputting into one control. Command inherits from the TextControl base class and as such includes a Text property that is typically rendered within the "clickable" element of the control.

When a user invokes a command via whatever method is provided by the client device the OnItemCommand event is raised which passes a Command object to the event handler. The Command.ID property tells you the ID of the Command instance that raised the event. Using this property you could, for example, have a single OnItemCommand handle all command controls in a page.

Note: Microsoft warns against using non-standard characters in the URLs that are the hyperlink destination for your Command object because the HREF values are not "strictly validated". For example, spaces in a URL will probably result in the failure of some WML browsers to correctly resolve the URL.

Example: Command Event Handling

In this example we are going to show the Command control in action and handle its events. Consider the following mobile forms page, commandPage.aspx in the code download for this chapter:

```
<%@ Register TagPrefix="mobile" Namespace="System.Web.UI.MobileControls"
            Assembly="System.Web.Mobile, Version=1.0.3300.0,
                    Culture=neutral, PublicKeyToken=b03f5f7f11d50a3a" %>
<%@ Page Language="c#" AutoEventWireup="false"
        Codebehind="commandPage.aspx.cs"
        Inherits="systemWebUIMobileControlExamples.commandPage" %>
<meta name="GENERATOR" content="Microsoft Visual Studio.NET 7.0">
<meta name="CODE_LANGUAGE" content="C#">
<meta name="vs_targetSchema"
    content="http://schemas.microsoft.com/Mobile/Page">
<body Xmlns:mobile="http://schemas.microsoft.com/Mobile/WebForm">
  <mobile:Form id="Form1" runat="server">
    <mobile:TextView id="TextView1" runat="server">
      Do you like .NET?
    </mobile:TextView>
    <mobile:Command id="cmdYes" runat="server"
                    onItemCommand="cmd_OnItemCommand">
      Yes
    </mobile:Command>
    <mobile:Command id="cmdNo" runat="server"
                    onItemCommand="cmd_OnItemCommand">
      No
    </mobile:Command>
    <mobile:Label id="lblYes" runat="server" Visible="False">
      Bill is happy!
    </mobile:Label>
    <mobile:Label id="lblNo" runat="server" Visible="False">
      Scott is happy!
    </mobile:Label>
    <mobile:Label id="lblCmd" runat="server" Visible="False">
      Label
    </mobile:Label>
  </mobile:Form> 
</body>
```

A code behind as follows will render the selected command using run-time information passed in the event handler – a single event handler works for both commands:

```csharp
public class commandPage : System.Web.UI.MobileControls.MobilePage
  {
    protected System.Web.UI.MobileControls.Label lblCmd;
    protected System.Web.UI.MobileControls.Label lblNo;
    protected System.Web.UI.MobileControls.Label lblYes;
    protected System.Web.UI.MobileControls.Command cmdNo;
    protected System.Web.UI.MobileControls.Command cmdYes;
    protected System.Web.UI.MobileControls.TextView TextView1;
    protected System.Web.UI.MobileControls.Form Form1;
...

private void Page_Load(object sender, System.EventArgs e)
  {

    if( IsPostBack)
    {
      TextView1.Visible = false;
      cmdYes.Visible = false;
      cmdNo.Visible = false;
    }
    else
    {
      TextView1.Visible = true;
      cmdYes.Visible = true;
      cmdNo.Visible = true;
      lblYes.Visible = false;
      lblNo.Visible = false;
    }
  }

public void cmd_OnItemCommand( System.Object sender, CommandEventArgs e)
  {

    System.Web.UI.MobileControls.Command s =
            (System.Web.UI.MobileControls.Command)sender;

    if(s.ID =="cmdYes")
    {
      lblYes.Visible = true;
      lblCmd.Text = "Clicked:" + s.ID;
      lblCmd.Visible = true;
    }

    if (s.ID == "cmdNo")
    {
      lblNo.Visible = true;
      lblCmd.Text = "Clicked:" + s.ID;
      lblCmd.Visible = true;
    }
  }
}
```

The example is rendered as follows in the Nokia 7110 emulator:

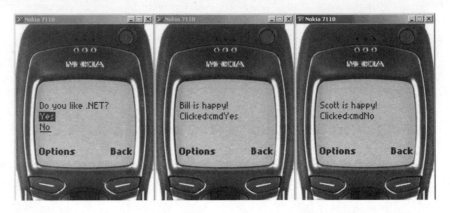

Command Public Methods

❑ `AddLinkedForms` – inherited from `MobileControl`, see `MobileControl` reference also in this chapter.

❑ `CreateDefaultTemplatedUI` – inherited from `MobileControl`, see `MobileControl` reference also in this chapter.

❑ `EnsureTemplatedUI` – inherited from `MobileControl`, see `MobileControl` reference also in this chapter.

❑ `GetTemplate` – inherited from `MobileControl`, see `MobileControl` reference also in this chapter.

❑ `IsVisibleOnPage` – inherited from `MobileControl`, see `MobileControl` reference also in this chapter.

❑ `PaginateRecursive` – inherited from `MobileControl`, see `MobileControl` reference also in this chapter.

❑ `RenderChildren`– inherited from `MobileControl`, see `MobileControl` reference also in this chapter.

❑ `ResolveFormReference` – inherited from `MobileControl`, see `MobileControl` reference also in this chapter.

Command Protected Methods

❑ `CreateStyle` – inherited from `MobileControl`, see `MobileControl` reference also in this chapter.

❑ `CreateTemplatedUI` – inherited from `MobileControl`, see `MobileControl` reference also in this chapter.

❑ `IsFormSubmitControl` – inherited from `MobileControl`, see `MobileControl` reference also in this chapter.

- ❑ LoadPrivateViewState – inherited from `MobileControl`, see `MobileControl` reference also in this chapter.

- ❑ **OnClick**

- ❑ **OnItemCommand**

- ❑ **OnPageChange**

- ❑ SavePrivateViewState – inherited from `MobileControl`, see `MobileControl` reference also in this chapter.

OnClick

The `OnClick` method is called when the user activates the control. If you are creating your own custom `Command` class you can override this to do any special handling.

```
protected virtual void OnClick(e)
```

OnItemCommand

The `OnItemCommand` method is called when the user activates a particular control, taking a `CommandEventArgs` object containing data about that event as input. By default, this method raises the `ItemCommand` event, although this behavior can be overriden to perform other tasks if required.

```
protected virtual void
        OnItemCommand(System.Web.UI.WebControls.CommandEventArgs e)
```

OnPageChange

The `OnPageChange` method is called when a new page has been navigated to by the user, taking an `EventArgs` as input and inheriting from `System.Web.UI.Control`.

```
protected virtual void OnPageChange(EventArgs e)
```

Command Public Properties

- ❑ `Adapter` – inherited from `MobileControl`, see `MobileControl` reference also in this chapter.

- ❑ `Alignment` – inherited from `MobileControl`, see `MobileControl` reference also in this chapter.

- ❑ `BackColor` – inherited from `MobileControl`, see `MobileControl` reference also in this chapter.

- ❑ `BreakAfter` – inherited from `MobileControl`, see `MobileControl` reference also in this chapter.

- ❑ **CausesValidation**

- ❑ **CommandArgument**

- ❑ **CommandName**

- ❑ CustomAttributes – inherited from MobileControl, see MobileControl reference also in this chapter.

- ❑ DeviceSpecific – inherited from MobileControl, see MobileControl reference also in this chapter.

- ❑ FirstPage – inherited from MobileControl, see MobileControl reference also in this chapter.

- ❑ Font – inherited from MobileControl, see MobileControl reference also in this chapter.

- ❑ ForeColor – inherited from MobileControl, see MobileControl reference also in this chapter.

- ❑ Form – inherited from MobileControl, see MobileControl reference also in this chapter.

- ❑ **Format**

- ❑ **ImageUrl**

- ❑ IsTemplated – inherited from MobileControl, see MobileControl reference also in this chapter.

- ❑ LastPage – inherited from MobileControl, see MobileControl reference also in ~ this chapter.

- ❑ MobilePage – inherited from MobileControl, see MobileControl reference also in this chapter.

- ❑ **SoftKeyLabel**

- ❑ StyleReference – inherited from MobileControl, see MobileControl reference also in this chapter.

- ❑ **Text**

- ❑ VisibleWeight – inherited from MobileControl, see MobileControl reference also in this chapter.

- ❑ Wrapping – inherited from MobileControl, see MobileControl reference also in this chapter.

CausesValidation

The CausesValidation property returns a Boolean value indicating if the specified command causes server-side validation to occur. The Command control is the only one that triggers validation by default and this property defaults to true. If you had a Command button that, say, caused additional data to render but didn't necessitate validation, you would set this value to false.

```
public virtual bool BreakAfter { get, set }
```

CommandArgument

Use this property to get or set an argument for a command in the `ItemCommand` event. It is set to an empty `String` by default.

```
public string CommandArgument { get, set }
```

CommandName

This property returns the name of the command that triggered the event.

```
public string CommandName { get }
```

Format

The `Format` property is of type `System.Web.UI.MobileControls.CommandFormat` and sets or gets an enumerated value that determines the format of the command. Command formats include:

❑   `CommandFormat.Button` (default) – the command looks like a button

❑   `CommandFormat.Link` – the command looks like a link

```
public System.Web.UI.MobileControls.CommandFormat Format { get,  set }
```

ImageUrl

The `ImageURL` property sets or gets the URL of an image that is used to represent the `Command` instance on devices that can support image rendering. The property is an empty `String` by default.

```
public string ImageUrl { get, set }
```

SoftKeyLabel

The `SoftKeyLabel` sets or gets a string that is the label for the control when a "softkey" is displayed. When combined with the `MaximumSoftKeyLabelLength` property of the `MobileCapabilities` instance, this property can be used to specify a softkey for the command that is descriptive but will also render appropriately in the target device. See `MobileCapabilities` class reference for additional details.

By default the `Text` property of the control acts as the softkey label when the `SoftKeyLabel` property is empty or fewer than nine characters.

```
public string SoftKeyLabel { get, set }
```

Text

The `Text` property is inherited from the `TextControl` base class. This allows the text of the Command button to be set declaratively.

```
public string Text {get,set}
```

Command Protected Properties

❑ `InnerText` – inherited from `MobileControl`, see `MobileControl` reference also in this chapter.

❑ `PaginateChildren` – inherited from `MobileControl`, see `MobileControl` reference also in this chapter.

Command Public Events

❑ `Click`

❑ `ItemCommand`

Click

The `Click` event is raised when the Command element is activated. The event is not bubbled up.

```
public event EventHandler Click
```

ItemCommand

The `ItemCommand` event is raised when the `Command` element is activated. The event is then cascaded to its parent, unlike the `Click` event.

```
public event CommandEventHandler ItemCommand
```

DeviceSpecific Class

The `DeviceSpecific` class provides a "construct" that lets the rendering process format content depending on device capabilities. Declaratively, `DeviceSpecific` is represented in a mobile page by a `<Mobile:DeviceSpecific>` element containing one or more `<Mobile:Choice>` elements. The `<Mobile:DeviceSpecific>` element is subordinate to some other control, and each `<Mobile:Choice>` element within it alters the parameters/properties of the parent control so that the parent will render appropriately on the client device. Naturally, you can also create `DeviceSpecific` instances and alter the properties of the declarative version of the control at run time, which is the purpose of this class.

Understanding Device-Specific Rendering

The ability to render content based on the specific capabilities of the requesting device is the central theme underlying the Mobile Internet Toolkit, and indeed to some extent ASP.NET in general. The flexibility provided by device-specific constructs allows an application to develop rich content while still using a single page to target a variety of devices with varying capabilities.

Example: Device-Specific Rendering

In the next example, deviceSpecificDemo.aspx, we will define filters to determine whether the requesting device prefers GIFs or WBMPs (wireless bitmap image format) for images and then render appropriately. First consider the following section from the Web.config file for our mobile application. (Note: the <deviceFilters> section was added automatically by Visual Studio .NET when we created a mobile project. If you aren't using Visual Studio you will need to add this section to your Web.config file.)

The <deviceFilters> section of your Web.config file provides the device capabilities class with easy-to-use "filters" to determine device capabilities. The Compare and Arguments properties of each filter are properties and values, respectively, of the MobileCapabilities instance associated with the mobile page. The DeviceSpecific class resolves the filter based on a behind-the-scenes check of the MobileCapabilities object associated with the page, but you can access this object programmatically as well, as we'll see in our code-behind file.

When a <choice> child element of a <deviceSpecific> is found that matches a filter in the web.config, the content of that element is used for the rendering, and other choices of that <deviceSpecific> element are skipped. Remember, the *first matching element* in the order they are declared is rendered and all other choice elements are ignored.

```
<deviceFilters>
  <filter name="isHTML32" compare="PreferredRenderingType"
          argument="html32" />
  <filter name="isWML11" compare="PreferredRenderingType"
          argument="wml11" />
  <filter name="isCHTML10" compare="PreferredRenderingType"
          argument="chtml10" />
  <filter name="isGoAmerica" compare="Browser" argument="Go.Web" />
  <filter name="isMME" compare="Browser"
          argument="Microsoft Mobile Explorer" />
  <filter name="isMyPalm" compare="Browser" argument="MyPalm" />
  <filter name="isPocketIE" compare="Browser" argument="Pocket IE" />
  <filter name="isUP3x" compare="Type" argument="Phone.com 3.x Browser" />
  <filter name="isUP4x" compare="Type" argument="Phone.com 4.x Browser" />
  <filter name="isEricssonR380" compare="Type" argument="Ericsson R380" />
  <filter name="isNokia7110" compare="Type" argument="Nokia 7110" />
  <filter name="prefersGIF" compare="PreferredImageMIME"
          argument="image/gif" />
  <filter name="prefersWBMP" compare="PreferredImageMIME"
          argument="image/vnd.wap.wbmp" />

  <filter name="supportsColor" compare="IsColor" argument="true" />
  <filter name="supportsCookies" compare="Cookies" argument="true" />
  <filter name="supportsJavaScript" compare="Javascript" argument="true" />
  <filter name="supportsVoiceCalls" compare="CanInitiateVoiceCall"
          argument="true" />
</deviceFilters>
```

The mobile page declaration for our `deviceSpecificDemo.aspx` example uses `<Choice>` elements that allow us to filter the different mobile devices as follows:

```
<%@ Register TagPrefix="mobile" Namespace="System.Web.UI.MobileControls"
             Assembly="System.Web.Mobile, Version=1.0.3300.0,
                       Culture=neutral, PublicKeyToken=b03f5f7f11d50a3a" %>
<%@ Page Language="c#" AutoEventWireup="false"
         Codebehind="deviceSpecificDemo.aspx.cs"
         Inherits="systemWebUIMobileControlExamples.deviceSpecificDemo" %>
<meta name="GENERATOR" content="Microsoft Visual Studio.NET 7.0">
<meta name="CODE_LANGUAGE" content="C#">
<meta name="vs_targetSchema"
     content="http://schemas.microsoft.com/Mobile/Page">
<body Xmlns:mobile="http://schemas.microsoft.com/Mobile/WebForm">
  <mobile:Form id="Form1" runat="server">
    <mobile:Image id="Image1" AlternateText="Gif Image"
                  ImageUrl="aspdotnet.gif" Runat="server">
    <mobile:DeviceSpecific id="DeviceSpecific1" Runat="server">
      <Choice Filter="prefersWBMP" ImageUrl="aspdotnet.wbmp"></Choice>
    </mobile:DeviceSpecific>
    </mobile:Image>
    <mobile:Label id="Label1" runat="server">Label</mobile:Label>
  </mobile:Form>
</body>
```

The code behind is as follows:

```
public class deviceSpecificDemo : System.Web.UI.MobileControls.MobilePage
{
  protected System.Web.UI.MobileControls.Label Label1;
  protected System.Web.UI.MobileControls.Image Image1;
  protected System.Web.UI.MobileControls.DeviceSpecific DeviceSpecific1;
  protected System.Web.UI.MobileControls.Form Form1;

  private void Page_Load(object sender, System.EventArgs e)
  {
    // Put user code to initialize the page here
    System.Web.Mobile.MobileCapabilities deviceCapabilites =
                  (System.Web.Mobile.MobileCapabilities)Request.Browser;
    Label1.Text = deviceCapabilites.PreferredImageMime.ToString();
  }
}
```

The filter ulitmately checks the `PreferredImageMime` defined in the `MobileCapabilities` class. For the choice to be rendered the `compare` attribute must correspond to a mobile capability found in the configuration *and* the argument needs to match for that capability.

Next, the `<deviceSpecific>` element must be inserted on our mobile page to indicate which `<Choice>` element applies for each possible filter result. In this example, the `<ImageUrl>` element is given, to provide the default when no filter is matched. The `<Choice>` elements are evaluated in order, and the first qualifying choice is selected. If no `filter` attribute is provided, and the choice is evaluated, it will always match. This provides a method for providing a default choice when no appropriate filter is found. The `<Choice>` element that is selected will override the `ImageURL` property of the containing `Image` control.

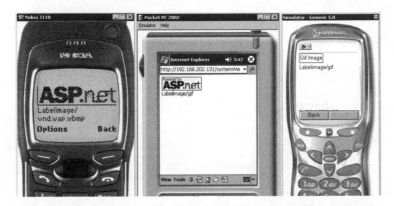

Note that the OpenWave device does not render the image and instead displays the alternate text. This is curious since the `MobileCapabilites` property returns that the device prefers GIF imagery. Regardless, this is an example of why you must *always* remember to include alternate text properties for *all* images you use in mobile applications because a great many mobile devices are still text only or may, like this simulator, decline to render the image even though mobile capabilities "promise" your image will get there.

DeviceSpecific Public Methods

The `DeviceSpecific` class adds no new public methods over those inherited from `System.Web.UI.Control`. See Chapter 2 for details.

DeviceSpecific Protected Methods

The `DeviceSpecific` class adds no new protected methods over those inherited from `System.Web.UI.Control`. See Chapter 2 for details.

DeviceSpecific Public Properties

- ❑ **Choices**
- ❑ **HasTemplates**
- ❑ **MobilePage**
- ❑ **Owner**
- ❑ **SelectedChoice**

Choices

The `Choices` property retrieves the Choice collection for the DeviceSpecific control. You can iterate through or select specific Choice instances using a numeric or string index.

```
public System.Web.UI.MobileControls.DeviceSpecificChoiceCollection
                                              Choices { get }
```

HasTemplates

The `HasTemplates` property returns a `Boolean` that specifies whether the device specific element has embedded templates within it.

```
public bool HasTemplates { get }
```

Consider the following fragment:

```
<DeviceSpecific>
  <Choice Filter="IsHtml">
    <HeaderTemplate>    </HeaderTemplate>
    <FooterTemplate>    </FooterTemplate>
    <ContentTemplate>
      <mobile:label runat=server Text="We like Real Html" />
    </ContentTemplate>
  </Choice>
  <Choice Filter="IsWml">
    <HeaderTemplate>    </HeaderTemplate>
</DeviceSpecific>
```

The `HasTemplates` property represented by this `DeviceSpecific` instance would return `true`.

MobilePage

The `MobilePage` property gets the `MobilePage` instance that contains the `DeviceSpecific` instance.

```
public System.Web.UI.MobileControls.MobilePage MobilePage { get }
```

Owner

The `Owner` property gets the `Form` instance that "owns" the `DeviceSpecific` instance. The owner property returns an `Object` value so you must cast the property to access the form properties and methods.

```
public object Owner { get, set }
```

SelectedChoice

The `SelectedChoice` property gets the currently selected `Choice` for the `DeviceSpecific` instance. If none are applicable it will return `null`. This property affords a more specific way to deal with filter and device-specifc handling by letting you programmatically respond to rendering once the Choice selection has been defined.

```
public System.Web.UI.MobileControls.DeviceSpecificChoice
                                       SelectedChoice { get }
```

DeviceSpecific Protected Properties

The `DeviceSpecific` class adds no new protected properties over those inherited from `System.Web.UI.Control`. See Chapter 2 for details.

DeviceSpecificChoice Class

The `DeviceSpecificChoice` class is the child class to `DeviceSpecific`, programmatically representing instances of `<Choice>` elements embedded within a `<DeviceSpecific>` construct. For more details on `DeviceSpecific` and device specific rendering see the `DeviceSpecific` reference earlier in this chapter.

DeviceSpecificChoice Public Methods

- ❑ `Equals` – inherited from `System.Object`, see Introduction for details.
- ❑ `GetType` – inherited from `System.Object`, see Introduction for details.
- ❑ `ToString` – inherited from `System.Object`, see Introduction for details.

DeviceSpecifcChoice Protected Methods

- ❑ `Finalize` – inherited from `System.Object`, see Introduction for details.
- ❑ `MemberwiseClone` – inherited from `System.Object`, see Introduction for details.

DeviceSpecificChoice Public Properties

- ❑ **Contents**
- ❑ **Filter**
- ❑ **HasTemplates**
- ❑ **Templates**

Contents

The `Contents` property gets the *overridden* properties defined for a `Choice` as an `IDictionary` object.

```
public IDictionary Contents {get}
```

Filter

The `Filter` property sets or gets the name of a device filter. It is important to remember that device filters are case sensitive and the default value is empty.

```
public string Filter { get, set }
```

Remember, if you are writing your own filters you must also remember that the *handler method* for the filter must conform to a specific format, where the function name matches the name in the `Filter` property, for example if the `Filter` property was called `SomeFilter` then the handler declared in your `Page` must take the format:

```
public bool SomeFilter(System.Web.Mobile.MobileCapabilities capabilities,
                       string optionalArgument)
{
  // your filter code here
}
```

When a `<Choice>` filter is processed, if a method that matches the `Filter` property as above isn't found in the page, then the `web.config` section is referenced by the runtime.

HasTemplates

The `HasTemplates` gets a `Boolean` indicating whether on not *this* `DeviceSpecificChoice` instance has templates defined within it.

```
public bool HasTemplates { get }
```

Templates

The `Templates` method returns an `IDictionary` instance containing the templates of a `DeviceSpecificChoice` instance. Remember to call `HasTemplates` prior to referencing elements within the `IDictionary` object or you may throw a runtime exception.

```
public IDictionary Templates { get }
```

MobileCapabilities Class

The `MobileCapabilities` class lets us determine an enormous number of device properties at run time. It can be used in place of or in addition to the declarative approach to device specific rendering provided by the `DeviceSpecific` construct. Developers interested in creating their own device adapter classes will want to fully explore and undertand the `MobileCapabilities` class since it is the foundation for device-specific run-time rendering.

`MobileCapabilities` inherits from `System.Web.HttpBrowserCapabilities`. See that namespace reference for additional details.

Example: Mobile Device Capabilities

The following example demonstrates how to access the MobileCapabilities object from your page. You may also find this handy because it renders the *entire* set of device properties on the targeted device in a paginated list.

The example page, deviceCapabilitiesPage.aspx, is declared as follows:

```
<%@ Register TagPrefix="mobile" Namespace="System.Web.UI.MobileControls"
            Assembly="System.Web.Mobile, Version=1.0.3300.0,
                    Culture=neutral, PublicKeyToken=b03f5f7f11d50a3a" %>
<%@ Page Language="c#" AutoEventWireup="false"
        Codebehind="deviceCapabilitiesPage.aspx.cs"
    Inherits="systemWebUIMobileControlExamples.deviceCapabilitiesPage" %>
<meta name="GENERATOR" content="Microsoft Visual Studio.NET 7.0">
<meta name="CODE_LANGUAGE" content="C#">
<meta name="vs_targetSchema"
    content="http://schemas.microsoft.com/Mobile/Page">
<body Xmlns:mobile="http://schemas.microsoft.com/Mobile/WebForm">
  <mobile:Form id="Form1" runat="server">
    <mobile:Label id="Label1" runat="server">
    Complete Capabilities Listing:
    </mobile:Label>
    <mobile:List id="List1" runat="server"></mobile:List>
    <mobile:DeviceSpecific id="DeviceSpecific1"
                        runat="server"></mobile:DeviceSpecific>
  </mobile:Form>
</body>
```

Below is the code-behind page, which we've abridged for clarity, although of course the full code is available in the code dowload:

```
public class deviceCapabilitiesPage :
                            System.Web.UI.MobileControls.MobilePage
{
  protected System.Web.UI.MobileControls.DeviceSpecific DeviceSpecific1;
  protected System.Web.UI.MobileControls.List List1;
  protected System.Web.UI.MobileControls.Label Label1;
  protected System.Web.UI.MobileControls.Form Form1;

  private void Page_Load(object sender, System.EventArgs e)
  {
    // Put user code to initialize the page here
    Form1.Paginate = true;

    List1.ItemsAsLinks = false;

    System.Web.Mobile.MobileCapabilities deviceCapabilities ;

    deviceCapabilities =
            (System.Web.Mobile.MobileCapabilities)Request.Browser;
```

463

```
      List1.Items.Add(new
          System.Web.UI.MobileControls.MobileListItem("ActiveXControls: "
          + deviceCapabilities.ActiveXControls.ToString()));
      List1.Items.Add(new
          System.Web.UI.MobileControls.MobileListItem("AOL: "
          + deviceCapabilities.AOL.ToString()));
      List1.Items.Add(new
          System.Web.UI.MobileControls.MobileListItem("BackgroundSounds: "
          + deviceCapabilities.BackgroundSounds.ToString()));

      List1.Items.Add(new
          System.Web.UI.MobileControls.MobileListItem("Win16: "
          + deviceCapabilities.Win16.ToString()));
      List1.Items.Add(new
          System.Web.UI.MobileControls.MobileListItem("Win32: "
          + deviceCapabilities.Win32.ToString()));
  }

  private void List1_ItemCommand(System.Object sender,
                  System.Web.UI.MobileControls.ListCommandEventArgs e)
  {
  }
}
```

This result in our sample devices is as follows:

MobileCapabilities Public Methods

- ❑ Equals – inherited from System.Object, see Introduction for details.
- ❑ GetHashCode – inherited from System.Object, see Introduction for details.
- ❑ GetType – inherited from System.Object, see Introduction for details.
- ❑ **HasCapability**
- ❑ ToString – inherited from System.Object, see Introduction for details.

HasCapability

The HasCapability method takes two strings as input and returns a Boolean value indicating whether the device has the capability referenced in the input strings. The input strings represent the capability name and an optional argument. Be careful to check your input here because if the capability parameter is not found by the runtime you will throw an exception.

```
public bool HasCapability(string capabilityName, string optionalArgument)
```

MobileCapabilities Protected Methods

- ❑ Finalize – inherited from System.Object, see Introduction for details.
- ❑ Init – inherited from System.Web.HttpCapabilitiesBase, see Chapter 1 for details.
- ❑ MemberwiseClone – inherited from System.Object, see Introduction for details.

MobileCapabilities Public Properties

- ❑ ActiveXControls – inherited from System.Web.HttpBrowserCapabilities, see Chapter 1 for details.
- ❑ AOL – inherited from System.Web.HttpBrowserCapabilities, see Chapter 1 for details.
- ❑ BackgroundSounds – inherited from System.Web.HttpBrowserCapabilities, see Chapter 1 for details.
- ❑ Beta – inherited from System.Web.HttpBrowserCapabilities, see Chapter 1 for details.
- ❑ Browser – inherited from System.Web.HttpBrowserCapabilities, see Chapter 1 for details.
- ❑ **CanCombineFormsInDeck**
- ❑ **CanInitiateVoiceCall**
- ❑ **CanRenderEmptySelects**
- ❑ **CanRenderInputAndSelectElementsTogether**
- ❑ **CanRenderMixedSelects**
- ❑ **CanRenderOneventAndPrevElementsTogether**
- ❑ **CanRenderPostBackCards**

- **CanRenderSetvarZeroWithMultiSelectionList**

- **CanSendMail**

- CDF – inherited from System.Web.HttpBrowserCapabilities, see Chapter 1 for details.

- ClrVersion – inherited from System.Web.HttpBrowserCapabilities, see Chapter 1 for details.

- Cookies – inherited from System.Web.HttpBrowserCapabilities, see Chapter 1 for details.

- Crawler – inherited from System.Web.HttpBrowserCapabilities, see Chapter 1 for details.

- EcmaScriptVersion – inherited from System.Web.HttpBrowserCapabilities, see Chapter 1 for details.

- Frames – inherited from System.Web.HttpBrowserCapabilities, see Chapter 1 for details.

- **GatewayMajorVersion**

- **GatewayMinorVersion**

- **GatewayVersion**

- **HasBackButton**

- **HidesRightAlignedMultiselectScrollbars**

- **InputType**

- **IsColor**

- **IsMobileDevice**

- **Item**

- JavaApplets – inherited from System.Web.HttpBrowserCapabilities, see Chapter 1 for details.

- JavaScript – inherited from System.Web.HttpBrowserCapabilities, see Chapter 1 for details.

- **MaximumRenderedPageSize**

- **MaximumSoftkeyLabelLength**

- **MobileDeviceManufacturer**

- **MobileDeviceModel**

- MSDomVersion – inherited from System.Web.HttpBrowserCapabilities, see Chapter 1 for details.

- **NumberOfSoftkeys**

- Platform – inherited from System.Web.HttpBrowserCapabilities, see Chapter 1 for details.

- **PreferredImageMime**

- **PreferredRenderingMime**

- ❑ PreferredRenderingType
- ❑ RendersBreakBeforeWmlSelectAndInput
- ❑ RendersBreaksAfterHtmlLists
- ❑ RendersBreaksAfterWmlAnchor
- ❑ RendersBreaksAfterWmlInput
- ❑ RendersWmlDoAcceptsInline
- ❑ RendersWmlSelectsAsMenuCards
- ❑ RequiresAttributeColonSubstitution
- ❑ RequiresContentTypeMetaTag
- ❑ RequiresHtmlAdaptiveErrorReporting
- ❑ RequiresNoBreakInFormatting
- ❑ RequiresOutputOptimization
- ❑ RequiresPhoneNumbersAsPlainText
- ❑ RequiresSpecialViewStateEncoding
- ❑ RequiresUniqueFilePathSuffix
- ❑ RequiresUniqueHtmlCheckboxNames
- ❑ RequiresUrlEncodedPostfieldValues
- ❑ ScreenBitDepth
- ❑ ScreenCharactersHeight
- ❑ ScreenCharactersWidth
- ❑ ScreenPixelsHeight
- ❑ ScreenPixelsWidth
- ❑ SupportsAccesskeyAttribute
- ❑ SupportsBodyColor
- ❑ SupportsBold
- ❑ SupportsCacheControlMetaTag
- ❑ SupportsCss
- ❑ SupportsDivAlign
- ❑ SupportsDivNoWrap
- ❑ SupportsFontColor
- ❑ SupportsFontName
- ❑ SupportsFontSize
- ❑ SupportsImageSubmit
- ❑ SupportsIModeSymbols
- ❑ SupportsInputIStyle

- ❑ **SupportsInputMode**

- ❑ **SupportsItalic**

- ❑ **SupportsJPhoneMultiMediaAttributes**

- ❑ **SupportsJPhoneSymbols**

- ❑ **SupportsQueryStringInFormAction**

- ❑ **SupportsSelectMultiple**

- ❑ **SupportsUncheck**

- ❑ `Tables` – inherited from `System.Web.HttpBrowserCapabilities`, see Chapter 1 for details.

- ❑ `TagWriter` – inherited from `System.Web.HttpBrowserCapabilities`, see Chapter 1 for details.

- ❑ `Type` – inherited from `System.Web.HttpBrowserCapabilities`, see Chapter 1 for details.

- ❑ `VBScript` – inherited from `System.Web.HttpBrowserCapabilities`, see Chapter 1 for details.

- ❑ `Version` – inherited from `System.Web.HttpBrowserCapabilities`, see Chapter 1 for details.

- ❑ `W3CDomVersion` – inherited from `System.Web.HttpBrowserCapabilities`, see Chapter 1 for details.

- ❑ `Win16` – inherited from `System.Web.HttpBrowserCapabilities`, see Chapter 1 for details.

- ❑ `Win32` – inherited from `System.Web.HttpBrowserCapabilities`, see Chapter 1 for details.

CanCombineFormsInDeck

The `CanCombineFormsInDeck` property gets a `Boolean` that defines whether the device can aggregate multiple forms in a deck as separate cards. The default is `true`.

```
public virtual bool CanCombineFormsInDeck { get }
```

CanInitiateVoiceCall

The `CanInitiateVoiceCall` property gets a `Boolean` value that defines whether the device can initiate a voice phone call. The default is `false`.

```
public virtual bool CanInitiateVoiceCall { get }
```

CanRenderEmptySelects

The `CanRenderEmptySelects` property gets a `Boolean` value that defines whether a device can handle `<Select>` elements that are empty. If `false` then the relevant markup won't be generated. The default is `true`.

```
public virtual bool CanRenderEmptySelects { get }
```

CanRenderInputAndSelectElementsTogether

The `CanRenderInputAndSelectElementsTogether` property gets a `Boolean` value that only applies to WML devices and specifies if the device can render `<Input>` and `<Select>` elements together.

```
public virtual bool CanRenderInputAndSelectElementsTogether { get }
```

CanRenderMixedSelects

The `CanRenderMixedSelects` property gets a `Boolean` value that only applies to WML devices and is `true` if the device supports `<select>` tags that have both `onpick` *and* `value` attributes specified in its list of `<options>`. The default value is `true`.

```
public virtual bool CanRenderMixedSelects { get }
```

CanRenderOneventAndPrevElementsTogether

The `CanRenderOneventAndPrevElementsTogether` property gets a `Boolean` value that is `true` if the device can handle a mix of `<Onevent>` and `<do type="prev" label="Back"></prev></do>` elements. The default value is `true`.

```
public virtual bool CanRenderOneventAndPrevElementsTogether { get }
```

CanRenderPostBackCards

The `CanRenderPostBackCards` property gets a `Boolean` value that only applies to WML devices and is `false` on devices that don't use postback cards. The default is `true`. Postback cards are consolidated versions of postback fields which are used to reduce the amount of WML that has to be sent between client and server. Hence setting this property to false will increase the amount of markup that is sent between client and server.

```
public bool CanRenderPostBackCards { get }
```

CanRenderSetvarZeroWithMultiSelectionList

The `CanRenderSetvarZeroWithMultiSelectionList` property gets a `Boolean` value that only applies to WML devices and is `true` if the device accepts `<setvar>` tags where the `value` attribute is zero. Default is `true`.

```
public virtual bool CanRenderSetvarZeroWithMultiSelectionList { get }
```

CanSendMail

The `CanSendMail` property gets a `Boolean` value that indicates whether the device can send e-mail via a `mailto` element. Use this property, for example, before you set a `Link` control to act as a `mailto` element. The default value is `true`.

```
public virtual bool CanSendMail { get }
```

GatewayMajorVersion

The `GatewayMajorVersion` property gets an integer value that represents the major version number of the wireless gateway used to access the server. The default value is `0`.

```
public virtual int GatewayMajorVersion { get }
```

GatewayMinorVersion

The `GatewayMinorVersion` property gets an integer value that represents the minor version number of the wireless gateway used to access the server. The default value is `0`.

```
public virtual int GatewayMinorVersion { get }
```

GatewayVersion

The `GatewayVersion` property gets a string value that represents the version of the wireless gateway used to access the server. The default value is `none`.

```
public virtual string GatewayVersion { get }
```

HasBackButton

The `HasBackButton` property gets a `Boolean` value that inidicates if the device has a dedicated "back" button. The default value is `true`.

```
public virtual bool HasBackButton { get }
```

HidesRightAlignedMultiselectScrollbars

The `HidesRightAlignedMultiselectScrollbars` property gets a `Boolean` value that is `true` if the scrollbar in a right-aligned `<select multiple>` element is obscured by the screen scrollbar. The default value is `false`.

```
public virtual bool HidesRightAlignedMultiselectScrollbars { get }
```

InputType

The `InputType` property gets a `String` value that specifies the input type of the device. The default value is `telephoneKeypad` but may also be `keyboard` or `virtualKeyboard`.

```
public virtual string InputType { get }
```

IsColor

The `IsColor` property gets a `Boolean` value that is `true` if the device displays colors. The default is `false`.

```
public virtual bool IsColor { get }
```

IsMobileDevice

The `IsMobileDevice` property gets a `Boolean` value that, not surprisingly, defaults to `true` for most mobile devices.

```
public virtual bool IsMobileDevice { get }
```

Item

The `Item` property is inherited from `HttpCapabilitiesBase` and returns a string and acts as the default "indexer" for the `MobileCapabilities` class. It lets you get a value for an arbitrary capability by providing the string name of the capability. Regardless of the real property value type this method of lookup will always return either a `String` or `null` if the capability is not found.

```
public string this[string key]
```

For example:

```
deviceCapabilities = (System.Web.Mobile.MobileCapabilities)Request.Browser;
string testCap;
testCap = deviceCapabilities("IsColor");
```

MaximumRenderedPageSize

The `MaximumRenderedPageSize` property returns an `Integer` that represents the maximum bytes in a page that the device can display. This value defaults to `2000`.

```
public virtual int MaximumRenderedPageSize { get }
```

MaximumSoftkeyLabelLength

The `MaximumSoftkeyLabelLength` property returns an `Integer` that represents the maximum length in bytes of a softkey label. The default value is 5.

```
public virtual int MaximumSoftkeyLabelLength { get }
```

MobileDeviceManufacturer

The `MaximumDeviceManufacturer` property returns a `String` with the name of the device manufacturer.

```
public virtual string MobileDeviceManufacturer { get }
```

MobileDeviceModel

The `MobileDeviceModel` property returns a `String` with the name of the device.

```
public virtual string MobileDeviceModel { get }
```

NumberOfSoftkeys

The `NumberOfSoftkeys` property returns an integer with the number of softkeys on the device. The default value is `0`.

```
public virtual int NumberOfSoftkeys { get }
```

PreferredImageMime

The `PreferredImageMime` property returns a `String` with the preferred image MIME type for the device. The default is `image/gif`.

```
public virtual string PreferredImageMime { get }
```

PreferredRenderingMime

The `PreferredRenderingMime` property returns a string with the preferred MIME type for markup rendering on the device. The default is `text/html`.

```
public virtual string PreferredImageMime { get }
```

PreferredRenderingType

The `PreferredRenderingType` property returns a `String` representing a generic name for the markup language preferred by the device. Possible values are `html32`, `wml11`, `wml12`, and `chtml10`. The default value is `html32`.

```
public virtual string PreferredRenderingType { get }
```

RendersBreakBeforeWmlSelectAndInput

The `RendersBreakBeforeWmlSelectAndInput` property gets a `Boolean` value that only applies to WML devices and is `true` if an extra break is inserted by the device when rendering a `<select>` or `<input>` tag. Default is `false`.

```
public virtual bool RendersBreakBeforeWmlSelectAndInput { get }
```

RendersBreaksAfterHtmlLists

The `RendersBreaksAfterHtmlLists` property gets a `Boolean` value that only applies to HTML devices and is `true` if the device automatically renders a break after HTML list tags. Default is `true`.

```
public virtual bool RendersBreaksAfterHtmlLists { get }
```

RendersBreaksAfterWmlAnchor

The `RendersBreaksAfterWmlAnchor` property gets a `Boolean` value that only applies to WML devices and is `true` if a standalone anchor tag is automatically followed by a break. Default is `false`.

```
public virtual bool RendersBreaksAfterWmlAnchor { get }
```

RendersBreaksAfterWmlInput

The `RendersBreaksAfterWmlInput` property gets a `Boolean` value that only applies to WML devices and is `true` if an input tag is automatically followed by a break. Default is `false`.

```
public virtual bool RendersBreaksAfterWmlInput { get }
```

RendersWmlDoAcceptsInline

The `RendersWmlDoAcceptsInline` property gets a `Boolean` value that only applies to WML devices and is `true` if a WML `<do>` element to accept a form is rendered inline as a button instead of rendering on a softkey. Default is `true`.

```
public virtual bool RendersWmlDoAcceptsInline { get }
```

RendersWmlSelectsAsMenuCards

The `RendersWmlSelectsAsMenuCards` property gets a `Boolean` value that only applies to WML devices and is `true` if instead of rendering `<select>` tags as a combo box they are rendered as menu cards. Default is `false`.

```
public virtual bool RendersWmlSelectsAsMenuCards { get }
```

RequiresAttributeColonSubstitution

The `RequiresAttributeColonSubstitution` property gets a `Boolean` value that is `true` if colons are not allowed in tag name attributes which would require substituting a different character upon rendering to the device. Default is `false`.

```
public virtual bool RequiresAttributeColonSubstitution{ get }
```

RequiresContentTypeMetaTag

The `RequiresContentTypeMetaTag` property gets a `Boolean` value that is `true` if the device requires the following meta tag be inserted into the rendered page header:

```
<meta http-equiv="Content-Type" content="MIMETYPE; charset=CHARSET">
```

MIMETYPE is the preferred rendering MIME type of the device and *CHARSET* is the character set to be used for encoding. This property reportedly is only required to support Pocket Internet Explorer but could be used to support any other device that requires this particular meta information to render properly. Default is `false`.

```
public virtual bool RequiresContentTypeMetaTag { get }
```

RequiresHtmlAdaptiveErrorReporting

The `RequiresHtmlAdaptiveErrorReporting` property gets a `Boolean` value that is `true` if the device, even if it supports HTML, will not render error reporting properly without the default error reporter first being adapted. Some devices, even if HTML-based, will not render the standard ASP.NET error page. Default is `false`.

```
public virtual bool RequiresHtmlAdaptiveErrorReporting { get }
```

RequiresNoBreakInFormatting

The `RequiresNoBreakInFormatting` property gets a `Boolean` value that is `true` if the device cannot accept formatting tags that contain `<br>` elements. Default is `false`.

```
public virtual bool RequiresNoBreakInFormatting { get }
```

RequiresOutputOptimization

The `RequiresOutputOptimization` property gets a `Boolean` value that is `true` if the device is particularly sensitive to total page size in terms of bytes. When `true`, for example for an i-Mode phone, device adapters can use this property to put extra effort into minimizing the quantity of resulting markup. Default is `false`.

```
public virtual bool RequiresOutputOptimization { get }
```

RequiresPhoneNumbersAsPlainText

The `RequiresOutputOptimization` property gets a `Boolean` value that is `true` if the device can only handle phone dialing when the phone number is provided as plain text. Naturally, this property does not apply to devices that can't make phone calls. Default is `false`.

```
public virtual bool RequiresPhoneNumbersAsPlainText { get }
```

RequiresSpecialViewStateEncoding

The `RequiresSpecialViewStateEncoding` property gets a `Boolean` value that is `true` if, due to particularities of this device, the view state information needs to be replaced by the adapter with non-alphabetical characters which do not need to be encoded for the HTTP request. This property is provided to support the writing of device adapters for devices or gateways that cannot transmit non-alphabetical characters correctly. Default is `false`.

```
public virtual bool RequiresSpecialViewStateEncoding { get }
```

RequiresUniqueFilePathSuffix

The `RequiresUniqueFilePathSuffix` property gets a `Boolean` value that is `true` if the device requires that a unique identifier be appended to the URL with each request so that gateways and devices that cache content will work properly during postback. This appended text takes the form of : `_ufps="<uniquefilepathsuffix>"`, where `uniquefilepathsuffix` is a number that changes after each request. Default is `false`.

```
public virtual bool RequiresUniqueFilePathSuffix { get }
```

RequiresUniqueHtmlCheckboxNames

The `RequiresUniqueHtmlCheckboxNames` property gets a `Boolean` value that is `true` if the device requires that all HTML `<input>` name values be unique. Default is `false`.

```
public virtual bool RequiresUniqueHtmlCheckboxNames { get }
```

RequiresUrlEncodedPostfieldValues

The `RequiresUrlEncodedPostfieldValues` property gets a `Boolean` value that is `true` if the device encodes text in the values submitted during postback. Default is `false`.

```
public virtual bool RequiresUrlEncodedPostfieldValues { get }
```

ScreenBitDepth

The `ScreenBitDepth` property gets an `Integer` value that indicates the bit depth (bits per pixel) of the display. Default is `1`.

```
public virtual int ScreenBitDepth { get }
```

ScreenCharactersHeight

The `ScreenCharactersHeight` property gets an `Integer` value that represents the approximate number of character lines of text that the display can render in one screen. Default is `6`.

```
public virtual int ScreenCharactersHeight { get }
```

ScreenCharactersWidth

The `ScreenCharactersWidth` property gets an `Integer` value that represents the approximate width of the screen in characters. Default is `12`.

```
public virtual int ScreenCharactersWidth { get }
```

ScreenPixelsHeight

The `ScreenPixelsHeight` property gets an `Integer` value that indicates the approximate height of the screen in pixels. Default is `72`.

```
public virtual int ScreenPixelsHeight { get }
```

ScreenPixelsWidth

The `ScreenPixelsWidth` property gets an `Integer` value that indicates the approximate width of the screen in pixels. Default is `96`.

```
public virtual int ScreenPixelsWidth { get }
```

SupportsAccesskeyAttribute

The `SupportsAccesskeyAttribute` property gets a `Boolean` value that is `true` if the device supports the `AccessKey` attribute for `<a>` and `<input>` tags. Most devices will not support this value, especially those with numeric keypads for input. Default is `false`.

```
public virtual bool SupportsAccesskeyAttribute{ get }
```

SupportsBodyColor

The SupportsBodyColor property gets a Boolean value that is true if the device supports the bgcolor property of the <body> tag. Default is true.

```
public virtual bool SupportsBodyColor { get }
```

SupportsBold

The SupportsBold property gets a Boolean value that is true if the device supports the <b> (bold) tag. Default is false.

```
public virtual bool SupportsBold { get }
```

SupportsCacheControlMetaTag

The SupportsCacheControlMetaTag property gets a Boolean value that is true if the device supports the meta tag Cache-Control: max-age-0. When the device doesn't support the meta tag, the querystring is appended with a unique value to ensure caching is avoided. Default is true.

```
public virtual bool SupportsCacheControlMetaTag { get }
```

SupportsCss

The SupportsCss property gets a Boolean value that is true if the device supports cascading style sheets for fonts. Default is false.

```
public virtual bool SupportsCss { get }
```

SupportsDivAlign

The SupportsDivAlign property gets a Boolean value that is true if the device supports aligning <DIV> elements with the align attribute. Default is true.

```
public virtual bool SupportsDivAlign { get }
```

SupportsDivNoWrap

The SupportsDivNoWrap property gets a Boolean value that is true if the device supports the nowrap attribute for <DIV> tags. Default is false.

```
public virtual bool SupportsDivNoWrap { get }
```

SupportsFontColor

The `SupportsFontColor` property gets a `Boolean` value that is `true` if the device supports the `color` attribute for `<font>` tags. Default is `true`.

```
public virtual bool SupportsFontColor { get }
```

SupportsFontName

The `SupportsFontName` property gets a `Boolean` value that is `true` if the device supports the `name` attribute for `<font>` tags. Default is `false`.

```
public virtual bool SupportsFontName { get }
```

SupportsFontSize

The `SupportsFontSize` property gets a `Boolean` value that is `true` if the device supports the `size` attribute for `<font>` tags. Default is `false`.

```
public virtual bool SupportsFontSize { get }
```

SupportsImageSubmit

The `SupportsImageSubmit` property gets a `Boolean` value that is `true` if the device can use images as submit elements. Default is `false`.

```
public virtual bool SupportsImageSubmit { get }
```

SupportsIModeSymbols

The `SupportsIModeSymbols` property gets a `Boolean` value that is `true` if the device can use i-mode specific picture symbol codes. See http://www.nttdocomo.com for details on i-mode. Default is `false`.

```
public virtual bool SupportsIModeSymbols { get }
```

SupportsInputIStyle

The `SupportsInputIStyle` property gets a `Boolean` value that is `true` if the device can use the `istyle` property of the `<input>` element to format the look of the input control. Default is `false`.

```
public virtual bool SupportsInputIStyle { get }
```

SupportsInputMode

The `SupportsInputMode` property gets a `Boolean` value that is `true` if the device can use the `attribute` property of the `<input>` element. Default is `false`.

```
public virtual bool SupportsInputMode { get }
```

SupportsItalic

The `SupportsItalic` property gets a `Boolean` value that is `true` if the device can use the `<i>` tag to render italics. Default is `false`.

```
public virtual bool SupportsItalic { get }
```

SupportsJPhoneMultiMediaAttributes

The `SupportsJPhoneMultiMediaAttributes` property gets a `Boolean` value that is `true` if the device supports the J-Phone HTML page definition language and the multimedia-related attributes `src`, `soundstart`, `loop`, `volume`, `vibration`, and `viblength`, for `<input>` and `<a>` tags. Default is `false`.

```
public virtual bool SupportsJPhoneMultiMediaAttributes { get }
```

SupportsJPhoneSymbols

The `SupportsJPhoneSymbols` property gets a `Boolean` value that is `true` if the device supports J-Phone HTML page definition language and J-Phone-specific picture symbols. Default is `false`.

```
public virtual bool SupportsJPhoneSymbols { get }
```

SupportsQueryStringInFormAction

The `SupportsQueryStringInFormAction` property gets a `Boolean` value that is `true` if the device supports putting a querystring in the `action` attribute of a `<form>` tag. If `false` then query string parameters will be put into hidden input fields for postback. Default is `true`.

```
public virtual bool SupportsQueryStringInFormAction{ get }
```

SupportsSelectMultiple

The `SupportsSelectMultiple` property gets a `Boolean` value that is `true` if the device supports more than one attribute being selected for HTML `<select>` tags. Default is `true`.

```
public virtual bool SupportsSelectMultiple{ get }
```

SupportsUncheck

The `SupportsUncheck` property gets a `Boolean` value that is `true` if the device will postback deselection from an HTML checkbox as form input. Default is `true`.

```
public virtual bool SupportsUncheck{ get }
```

MobileControl Class

All mobile controls inherit from the base `MobileControl` class, either directly, or indirectly by extending a class that in turn inherits from `MobileControl`. The `MobileControl` base class itself extends the `System.Web.UI.Control` class. Hence all mobile controls described here share the properties and methods that are defined by the `MobileControl` base class or the `Control` class depending on which has been overridden. Given that `System.Web.UI.Control` is literally the foundation for all ASP.NET controls you are strongly encouraged to review Chapter 2. Moreover, many mobile controls are essentially mobile equivalents to server controls provided by the `System.Web.UI.WebControls` namespace as covered in Chapter 4. Familiarity with Web controls will aid you in your understanding of mobile controls and vice versa.

Controls that inherit directly from the `MobileControl` class are:

- ❏ AdRotator
- ❏ Calendar
- ❏ Image
- ❏ Panel
- ❏ SelectionList
- ❏ StyleSheet
- ❏ TextView
- ❏ ValidationSummary

MobileControl Public Methods

- ❏ **AddLinkedForms**
- ❏ **CreateDefaultTemplatedUI**
- ❏ **EnsureTemplatedUI**
- ❏ **GetTemplate**
- ❏ **IsVisibleOnPage**
- ❏ **PaginateRecursive**
- ❏ **ResolveFormReference**

AddLinkedForms

The `AddLinkedForms` method takes an `IList` object as input that constitutes a list of `Form` objects linked to the current control. The `AddLinkedForms` method links the forms to the control. In the base implementation this method does nothing, but in the Link control, for example, this method is overridden to support user-driven navigation, without server participation, from one form to another form. Remember, unlike standard `.aspx` web pages, mobile web pages can, and typically do, have multiple Form controls rather than a single one.

```
public virtual void AddLinkedForms(System.Collections.IList linkedForms)
```

CreateDefaultTemplatedUI

The `CreateDefaultTemplateUI` method takes a `Boolean` value as input and has no return value. It is called to instantiate child templates. Device adapaters call this method to create the default template for the control. The `Boolean` parameter specifies whether the template instance requires data-binding to instantiate. Typically the value would be set to the value `true` for the first instance and then `false` as viewstate properties would be used to populate the control on subsequent postbacks.

```
public virtual void CreateDefaultTemplatedUI(bool doDataBind)
```

EnsureTemplatedUI

The `EnsureTemplatedUI` method can force the template elements of the control to be created, so that they can be accessed programmatically. It is not necessary to call this method during default page processing unless access to the template elements is required. It has a `void` return value. The `EnsureTemplatedUI` method is inherited from `System.Web.UI.Control`. See the `Control` class reference for details.

```
public virtual void EnsureTemplatedUI()
```

GetTemplate

The `GetTemplate` method returns an instance of the object contained by the control with a name matching the parameter. If the control is not templated or no match is found, `null` is returned. It takes the name of the template to retrieve as input.

```
public virtual System.Web.UI.ITemplate GetTemplate(string templateName)
```

IsVisibleOnPage

The `IsVisibleOnPage` method takes an integer as input and returns a `Boolean` indicating whether the control is visible on the page number referenced in the parameter. This method is used for pagination.

```
public bool IsVisibleOnPage(int pageNumber)
```

PaginateRecursive

The `PaginateRecursive` method takes a `System.Web.UI.MobileControls.ControlPager` as input. Mobile controls can be split across multiple pages of output, and this method paginates the control and all of its children. There is no return value

```
public virtual void
    PaginateRecursive(System.Web.UI.MobileControls.ControlPager pager)
```

ResolveFormReference

The `ResolveFormReference` method takes a string as input that constitutes the name of a form in the `#form` format. For example, if your have a link in the format `#someForm`, `ResolveFormReference` will return a reference to a form declared with the syntax `id=someForm`. If the form is not found the method returns `null`.

```
public form ResolveFormReference(string name)
```

MobileControl Protected Methods

- ❏ **CreateStyle**
- ❏ **CreateTemplatedUI**
- ❏ **IsFormSubmitControl**
- ❏ **LoadPrivateViewState**
- ❏ **SavePrivateViewState**

CreateStyle

The `CreateStyle` method is called by the runtime and returns the style object for a control. You can override this method if you intend to provide your own style class.

```
protected virtual Style CreateStyle()
```

CreateTemplatedUI

The `CreateTemplatedUI` method takes a `Boolean` as input. It creates a templated UI when called by the base class. Typically this method is called in the control adapter, then the control adapter either renders a device specific template or calls `CreateDefaultTemplatedUI` for the control as appropriate. See `CreateDefaultTemplatedUI` for additional details.

```
protected virtual void CreateTemplatedUI(bool doDataBind)
```

IsFormSubmitControl

The `IsFormSubmitControl` method returns a Boolean value to indicate whether the control is used to submit a form. If you were building a custom `Command` control you would override this method in your class definition as follows:

```
protected virtual bool IsFormSubmitControl()
{
  return true;
}
```

The method declaration for `IsFormSubmitControl` is:

```
protected virtual bool IsFormSubmitControl()
```

LoadPrivateViewState

The `LoadPrivateViewState` method takes an `Object` as input and loads the private view state. If you plan to override this method you must also override its companion, `SavePrivateViewState`.

```
protected virtual void LoadPrivateViewState(Object state)
```

The `SavePrivateViewState` method saves private view state changes that happened since the control was loaded. If there were no changes the method returns `null`. If you plan to store private view state info using this method you must also override its companion, `LoadPrivateViewState`.

```
protected virtual Object SavePrivateViewState()
```

MobileControl Public Properties

- ❏ `Adapter`
- ❏ `Alignment`
- ❏ `BackColor`
- ❏ `BreakAfter`
- ❏ `CustomAttributes`
- ❏ `DeviceSpecific`
- ❏ `FirstPage`
- ❏ `Font`
- ❏ `ForeColor`
- ❏ `Form`
- ❏ `IsTemplated`
- ❏ `LastPage`
- ❏ `MobilePage`
- ❏ `StyleReference`
- ❏ `VisibleWeight`
- ❏ `Wrapping`

Adapter

The `Adapter` property returns the device-specific adapter for the current control.

```
public System.Web.UI.MobileControls.IControlAdapter Adapter {get
```

Alignment

The `Aligment` property lets you set or determine the alignment for the style. If the client device doesn't support alignment this property may be ignored at render time. The `Alignment` property can be set to one of the following:

- ❏ `NotSet` – no alignment is set
- ❏ `Left` – aligns left
- ❏ `Center` – aligns center
- ❏ `Right` – aligns right

482

The default is NotSet.

```
public virtual System.Web.UI.MobileControls.Alignment Alignment {get, set}
```

BackColor

The BackColor property gets or sets the rendering background color for the control. The default value is Color.Empty. You should note that setting the BackColor property on a parent control does not mean that the child control inherits the same setting, and you will have to set it explicitly.

```
public virtual System.Drawing.Color BackColor {get, set}
```

BreakAfter

The BreakAfter property sets or gets a Boolean value indicating whether a logical break is required after the control has rendered. Depending on the markup language, a break may correspond to the end of a table, a paragraph, a div, or an explicit break tag. Default is true. Some controls may ignore this property if it doesn't make sense for them, an AdRotator for example. If a BreakAfter is set to true on a form, an exception will be thrown.

```
public virtual bool BreakAfter { get, set  }
```

CustomAttributes

The CustomAttributes property retrieves the System.Web.UI.StateBag object that details any custom attributes that have been defined for the control.

```
public virtual statebag CustomAttributes { get }
```

DeviceSpecific

The DeviceSpecific property resolves the device-specific construct for the control. If the control is not part of a device specific construct the property will be null.

```
public System.Web.UI.MobileControls.DeviceSpecific DeviceSpecific {get, set }
```

FirstPage

The FirstPage property indicates by an integer value the first rendered page of the form on which output of this control appears. When a form paginates, it splits up the children across multiple pages to better fit the capabilities of the requesting device. The FirstPage lets our control participate more intelligently in pagination by determining at run time where it will be rendered.

```
public int FirstPage {get, set }
```

Font

The `Font` property retrieves a `System.Web.UI.MobileControls.FontInfo` object. This `FontInfo` object can have one of the following properties: `Bold`, `Italic`, `Name`, and `Size`. This object gives more detailed information about the font settings for the control. Remember, if the requesting device does not support certain font elements, they will not be rendered for the device. For example, a grayscale display will not be able to take advantage of the `ForeColor` property of the `FontInfo` class, so that particular attribute will not be rendered for that device.

```
public virtual System.Web.UI.MobileControls.FontInfo Font {get }
```

ForeColor

The `ForeColor` property specifies the color used for the foreground where appropriate, typically corresponding to the text color for rendering a control. The default value is `Color.Empty`.

```
public virtual System.Drawing.Color ForeColor {get, set }
```

Example: Font Settings

In the following code we create a mobile page, `font.aspx`, with four labels. The first three have their font values set programmatically while the last label uses declarations in the page to set the formatting.

```
<%@ Page Language="c#" AutoEventWireup="false" Codebehind="font.aspx.cs"
        Inherits="systemWebUIMobileControlExamples.font" %>
<%@ Register TagPrefix="mobile" Namespace="System.Web.UI.MobileControls"
        Assembly="System.Web.Mobile, Version=1.0.3300.0,
        Culture=neutral, PublicKeyToken=b03f5f7f11d50a3a" %>
<meta name="GENERATOR" content="Microsoft Visual Studio.NET 7.0">
<meta name="CODE_LANGUAGE" content="C#">
<meta name="vs_targetSchema"
    content="http://schemas.microsoft.com/Mobile/Page">
<body Xmlns:mobile="http://schemas.microsoft.com/Mobile/WebForm">
  <mobile:Form id="Form1" runat="server">
    <mobile:Label id="Label1" runat="server">Bold Italic</mobile:Label>
    <mobile:Label id="Label2" runat="server">Large</mobile:Label>
    <mobile:Label id="Label3" runat="server">
    Small (&amp; Colorful?)
    </mobile:Label>
    <mobile:Label id="Label4" runat="server" Font-Bold="True"
                Font-Name="arial" >Declarative Formatting</mobile:Label>
  </mobile:Form>
</body>
```

The code behind for the page is as follows:

```
public class font : System.Web.UI.MobileControls.MobilePage
{
  protected System.Web.UI.MobileControls.Label Label4;
  protected System.Web.UI.MobileControls.Label Label3;
  protected System.Web.UI.MobileControls.Label Label2;
```

```
    protected System.Web.UI.MobileControls.Label Label1;
    protected System.Web.UI.MobileControls.Form Form1;

    private void Page_Load(object sender, System.EventArgs e)
    {
      // Put user code to initialize the page here
      Label1.Font.Bold =
              System.Web.UI.MobileControls.BooleanOption.True;
      Label1.Font.Italic =
              System.Web.UI.MobileControls.BooleanOption.True;
      Label2.Font.Size = System.Web.UI.MobileControls.FontSize.Large;
      Label3.Font.Size = System.Web.UI.MobileControls.FontSize.Small;
      Label3.ForeColor = Color.Red;
    }
  }
```

Using the above code as an example, only the Pocket PC device is able to render the red color on the final label because it is equipped with a color LCD. The Nokia device doesn't even render the Bold, Italic or Large font styles specified. You must always test your mobile applications on the broadest range of devices and never assume that any formatting you've selected will render to the client.

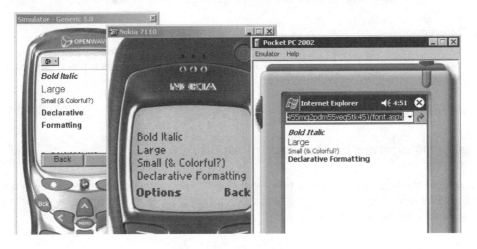

Form

The Form property retrieves the System.Web.UI.MobileControls.Form object that contains the control. Remember that mobile pages can have multiple Form objects so this method can be handy if you cannot know in advance to which Form the control will belong.

```
public System.Web.UI.MobileControls.Form Form {get }
```

IsTemplated

The `IsTemplated` property retrieves a `Boolean` indicating whether the control is part of a template construct where there is a `<DeviceSpecific>` element containing a `<Choice>` filter that is satisfied by the request. Refer to the section earlier in this chapter on *Understanding Device-Specific Rendering* for an explanation of templating.

```
public virtual bool IsTemplated { get }
```

LastPage

The `LastPage` property indicates the last rendered page of the form on which output of this control appears. It is the corollary method to `FirstPage`.

```
public int LastPage { get, set }
```

MobilePage

The `MobilePage` property retrieves the `MobilePage` object containing the control. It is of type `System.Web.UI.MobileControls.MobilePage`.

```
public System.Web.UI.MobileControls.MobilePage MobilePage { get }
```

StyleReference

The `StyleReference` property is a `String` that specifies the ID of the `Style` object associated with this control. The string must be the `Name` property of a `Style` object. This typically serves in the reuse of a set of style settings grouped together in an external stylesheet.

```
public virtual string StyleReference { get, set}
```

Example: Using the StyleReference Property

You can use the `StyleReference` property to bind a control to a different style at run time. Here we create a simple page, `simpleStyle.aspx`, that changes style each time a postback is invoked using the Command control.

```
<%@ Page Language="c#" AutoEventWireup="false"
        Codebehind="simpleStyle.aspx.cs"
        Inherits="systemWebUIMobileControlExamples.simpleStyle" %>
<%@ Register TagPrefix="mobile" Namespace="System.Web.UI.MobileControls"
        Assembly="System.Web.Mobile, Version=1.0.3300.0, Culture=neutral,
        PublicKeyToken=b03f5f7f11d50a3a" %>
<meta name="GENERATOR" content="Microsoft Visual Studio.NET 7.0">
<meta name="CODE_LANGUAGE" content="C#">
<meta name="vs_targetSchema"
        content="http://schemas.microsoft.com/Mobile/Page">
<body Xmlns:mobile="http://schemas.microsoft.com/Mobile/WebForm">
  <mobile:StyleSheet id="StyleSheet1" runat="server">
    <mobile:Style Font-Size="Normal" Font-Name="Arial" Font-Bold="True"
                  Font-Italic="False" ForeColor="Red" Wrapping="Wrap"
                  Alignment="Left" Name="Style1"></mobile:Style>
```

```
<mobile:Style Font-Size="Large" Font-Name="Arial" Font-Bold="False"
               Font-Italic="True" BackColor="LightGreen"
               ForeColor="Blue" Wrapping="NoWrap" Alignment="Right"
               Name="Style2"></mobile:Style>
</mobile:StyleSheet>
<mobile:Form id="Form1" runat="server" StyleReference="Style1">
  <mobile:Label id="Label1" runat="server">
    This text will render with two different styles.</mobile:Label>
  <mobile:Command id="Command1" runat="server">
    Change Style</mobile:Command>
</mobile:Form>
</body>
```

The code behind is as follows:

```
public class simpleStyle : System.Web.UI.MobileControls.MobilePage
{
  protected System.Web.UI.MobileControls.StyleSheet StyleSheet1;
  protected System.Web.UI.MobileControls.Command Command1;
  protected System.Web.UI.MobileControls.Label Label1;
  protected System.Web.UI.MobileControls.Form Form1;

  private void Page_Load(object sender, System.EventArgs e)
  {
    // Put user code to initialize the page here
    if( IsPostBack)
    {
      if (Form1.StyleReference == "Style1")
        Form1.StyleReference = "Style2";
      else
        Form1.StyleReference = "Style1";
    }
  }
}
```

The resulting output is highly dependent on the rendering capability of the target device. In fact, a better use of StyleReference is to create styles that target a particular device, use MobileCapabilities to determine the device, then set the style at run time. (See the MobileCapabilities reference earlier in this chapter for more details.) The results in our sample devices prove that while mobile controls may get the text to the device, the device may not do what we intend:

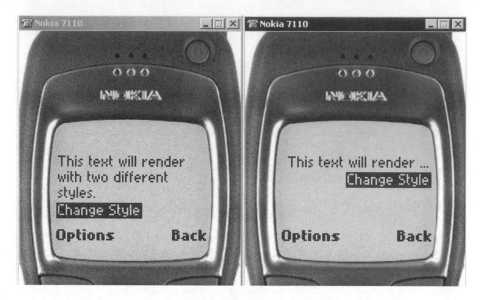

The Nokia gets the "align right" correct without any problem, but isn't sure how to render the text flush right.

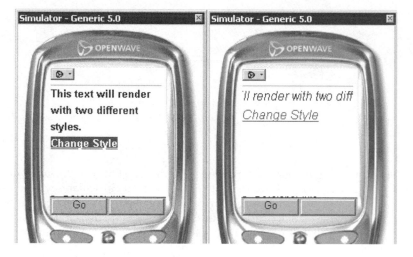

OpenWave decided to move the large text in Style2 "marquee" style across the screen to both make it flush right and be visible – a valiant effort to display the text. But it decided not to render the Command control flush right.

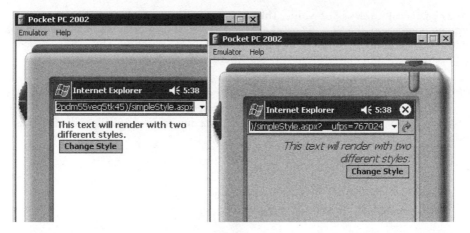

As usual, Pocket Internet Explorer with its big colourful screen and remarkably adept rendering engine did the best job. As of writing this, Microsoft is entering the mobile phone market with a "smart phone" version of Pocket PC that retains the big colourful screen.

VisibleWeight

The `VisibleWeight` property corresponds to an integer value associated with the control used for calculating pagination. If the return value is `-1`, it indicates that the default weighting should be used. Refer to the `machine.config` file on your machine for a listing of the default weights.

```
public virtual int VisibleWeight { get }
```

The following is an XML fragment from `machine.config` for the Nokia 7110 device.

```
<case match="Nokia7110/1.0 \((?'versionString'.*)\)">
      type = "Nokia 7110"
      version = ${versionString}
  <filter with="${versionString}"
      match="(?'browserMajorVersion'\w*)(?'browserMinorVersion'\.\w*).*">
    majorVersion = ${browserMajorVersion}
    minorVersion = ${browserMinorVersion}
  </filter>
    mobileDeviceModel = "7110"
    optimumPageWeight = "800"
    CharactersWidth="22"
    screenCharactersHeight="4"
    screenPixelsWidth="96"
    screenPixelsHeight="44"
</case>
```

Note the `optimumPageWeight` value. This value varies for every device. When a control is undergoing pagination, the `VisibleWeight` of the control's children is totaled and compared to the `optimumPageWeight` established for the device in the configuration. This determines how many pages the children should be rendered on and where the page breaks should occur.

Wrapping

The `Wrapping` property specifies the wrapping format for the output. As with the `Alignment` property, there may be no corresponding rendering if a device does not allow control over wrapping functionality. The wrapping modes enumerations are:

- ❑ `NotSet` – no size. (The default value.)
- ❑ `Wrap` – wrap to the next line.
- ❑ `NoWrap` – the text is not wrapped to the next line.

```
public virtual System.Web.UI.MobileControls.Wrapping Wrapping { get, set}
```

MobileControl Protected Properties

- ❑ **InnerText**
- ❑ **PaginateChildren**

InnerText

The `InnerText` returns a string constituting the text content of the control. Remember, this property may include text from child controls.

```
protected string InnerText { get, set }
```

PaginateChildren

The `PaginateChildren` property retrieves a `Boolean` indicating whether contained controls must be paginated. Pagination is the separation of controls onto multiple pages. This is done in order to make better use of the limited screen size of devices and to transmit smaller amounts of data where the download size of the device is limited.

```
protected virtual bool PaginateChildren {get, set}
```

MobileConrol Public Events

The `MobileControl` class adds no new public events over those inherited from `System.Web.UI.Control`. See Chapter 2 for details.

ObjectList Class

The `ObjectList` control extends the abstract `PagedControl` class. The `ObjectList` control provides much more flexibility than the `List` control in terms of rendering individual list items. Its main restriction is that is is limited to data-binding. This means that while you can add an item to a standard `List` control declaratively or programmatically, *you can only add an item to an ObjectList by calling its DataBind method and providing it with a datasource*. Despite this limitation an `ObjectList` is designed to list items that have multiple properties, whereas the single `Text` property of the `List` control limits its flexibility and utility. Moreover, items in an object list can fire a mixture of events, and even discrete items can fire events distinct from other items. This extensibility and flexibility makes the `ObjectList` a powerful control most akin to the `DataGrid` provided in the standard Web Controls set.

Example: Using the ObjectList Control

The following code demonstrates an `ObjectList` in action. First the page declaration, `ObjectListPage.aspx`:

```
<%@ Page Language="c#" CodeBehind="ObjectListPage.aspx.cs"
         Inherits="systemWebUIMobileControlExamples.ObjectListPage"
         AutoEventWireup="false" %>
<%@Register TagPrefix="Mobile" Namespace="System.Web.UI.MobileControls"
            Assembly="System.Web.Mobile" %>
<Mobile:Form runat="server" id="Form1">
  <Mobile:ObjectList id="developerList" runat="server"
                     LabelStyle-StyleReference="title"
                     CommandStyle-StyleReference="subcommand">
  </Mobile:ObjectList>
</Mobile:Form>
```

Then in the code behind we create a simple class that holds multiple properties for each instance. The `ObjectList` will *automatically render* the public properties of the custom class in a detailed view when we select the item from the list:

```
class Developer
{
  private string preferredLanguage ;
  private int phoneExtension ;
  private string devName ;

  public Developer(string devName,
                   string preferredLanguage, int phoneExtension)
  {
    this.devName = devName;
    this.preferredLanguage = preferredLanguage;
    this.phoneExtension = phoneExtension;
  }

  public string Language
  {
    get
```

```
      {
        return preferredLanguage;
      }
    }

    public int Extension
    {
      get
      {
        return phoneExtension;
      }
    }

    public string DeveloperName
    {
      // Retrieves the number data member.
      get
      {
        return devName;
      }
    }
  }

public class ObjectListPage : System.Web.UI.MobileControls.MobilePage
{
  protected System.Web.UI.MobileControls.ObjectList developerList;
  protected System.Web.UI.MobileControls.Form Form1;

  private void Page_Load(object sender, System.EventArgs e)
  {
    if( !IsPostBack)
    {
      // Put user code to initialize the page here

      //create an ArrayList of Developer objects
      ArrayList developers = new ArrayList();

      developers.Add(new Developer(  "Janell B.", "C++", 815));
      developers.Add(new Developer( "Jeff M.", "Fortran", 699));
      developers.Add(new Developer( "Joe C.", "JScript", 180));
      developers.Add(new Developer( "Wade R.", "C#", 549));

      //set DataSource and DataBind
      developerList.DataSource = developers;
      developerList.DataBind();
    }
  }
}
```

If you look carefully you'll see that there is no code detailing command handling to generate a detail view of the list item and render its properties, and so on. All the code exists in the sample simply to create a data source with multiple elements and properties. The only necessary call specific to the control is the call to DataBind. The rendered output produces two screens including the list and a list detail view:

ObjectList Public Methods

❑ AddLinkedForms – inherited from MobileControl, see MobileControl reference also in this chapter.

❑ CreateDefaultTemplatedUI – inherited from MobileControl, see MobileControl reference also in this chapter.

❑ **CreateTemplatedItemDetails**

❑ **CreateTemplatedItemsList**

❑ EnsureTemplatedUI – inherited from MobileControl, see MobileControl reference also in this chapter.

❑ GetTemplate – inherited from MobileControl, see MobileControl reference also in this chapter.

493

- ❏ `IsVisibleOnPage` – inherited from `MobileControl`, see `MobileControl` reference also in this chapter.

- ❏ `LoadPrivateViewState` – inherited from `MobileControl`, see `MobileControl` reference also in this chapter.

- ❏ **`OnItemSelect`**

- ❏ `OnLoadItems` – inherited from `PagedControl`, see `PagedControl` reference also in this chapter.

- ❏ `PaginateRecursive` – inherited from `MobileControl`, see `MobileControl` reference also in this chapter.

- ❏ **`PreShowItemCommands`**

- ❏ **`RaiseDefaultItemEvent`**

- ❏ `ResolveFormReference` – inherited from `MobileControl`, see `MobileControl` reference also in this chapter.

- ❏ `SavePrivateViewState` – inherited from `MobileControl`, see `MobileControl` reference also in this chapter.

CreateTemplatedItemDetails

When the details of a list item are to be displayed using templates, the control adapter calls `CreateTemplatedItemDetails`, passing a `Boolean` value to indicate the need for data-binding. The `Boolean` parameter is `true` when the instantiated template must data-bind and `false` when the data is to be drawn from the viewstate. The detail view of the currently selected list item is constructed according to the templates that match the requesting device.

```
public void CreateTemplatedItemDetails(bool doDataBind)
```

CreateTemplatedItemsList

The `CreateTemplatedItemsList` method takes a `Boolean` as input and is called by device adapters to build the `ObjectList` when the `ObjectList` is templated. The value returns `true` if the instantiated template list must data-bind and `false` when the data is to be drawn from the viewstate.

```
public void CreateTemplatedItemsList(bool doDataBind)
```

OnItemSelect

The `OnItemSelect` method takes an `ObjectListSelectEventArgs` as input and is called when a user selects an item in the list that raises the `ItemSelect` event.

```
protected virtual void OnItemSelect(ObjectListSelectEventArgs e)
```

PreShowItemCommands

The `PreShowItemCommand` method takes an `Integer` as input that represents an index to the affected list item. It's used by control adapters prior to displaying a particular item to call the events that may be triggered by `ShowItemCommands`. The `itemIndex` argument indicates which member of the `ObjectListItems` is being prepared.

```
public void PreShowItemCommands(int itemIndex)
```

RaiseDefaultItemEvent

The `RaiseDefaultItemEvent` method takes an `Integer` as input that represents an index to the list item for which the default event should be raised, and is called internally by the runtime but also can be used by custom device adapters. Control adapters can invoke this method specifying which item should have the default command handler invoked.

```
public void RaiseDefaultItemEvent(int itemIndex)
```

ObjectList Protected Methods

- ❑ **CreateAutoGeneratedFields**
- ❑ **CreateItem**
- ❑ **CreateItems**
- ❑ CreateStyle – inherited from `MobileControl`, see `MobileControl` reference also in this chapter.
- ❑ CreateTemplatedUI – inherited from `MobileControl`, see `MobileControl` reference also in this chapter.
- ❑ IsFormSubmitControl – inherited from `MobileControl`, see `MobileControl` reference also in this chapter.
- ❑ **OnItemCommand**
- ❑ **OnItemDataBind**
- ❑ **OnItemSelect**
- ❑ OnRender – inherited from `MobileControl`, see `MobileControl` reference also in this chapter.
- ❑ OnShowItemCommands – inherited from `MobileControl`, see `MobileControl` reference also in this chapter.

CreateAutoGeneratedFields

The `CreateAutoGeneratedFields` method automatically generates fields per the datasource provided as input.

```
protected void CreateAutoGeneratedFields(System.Collections.IEnumerable
                                         dataSource)
```

CreateItem

The `CreateItem` method binds the `dataItem` provided as input to a new list item that it creates. Inheriting classes can override the `CreateItemMethod` to customize the way items are created during data-binding.

```
protected virtual System.Web.UI.MobileControls.CreateItem(Object dataItem)
```

CreateItems

The `CreateItems` method binds the `dataSource` provided to an items collection that the method creates.

```
protected virtual void CreateItems(System.Collections.IEnumerable dataSource)
```

OnItemCommand

The `OnItemCommand` method takes an `ObjectListCommandEventArgs` and is called when an `ItemCommand` event is raised by user interaction with the command associated with a list item.

```
protected virtual void OnItemCommand(
            System.Web.UI.MobileControls.ObjectListCommandEventArgs e)
```

OnItemDataBind

The `OnItemDataBind` method takes an `ObjectListDataBindEventArgs` as input and handles data-binding events on a per item basis.

```
protected virtual void
OnItemDataBind(System.Web.UI.MobileControls.ObjectListDataBindEventArgs e)
```

OnItemSelect

The `OnItemSelect` method is called when the user selects an item, raising the `ItemSelect` event.

```
protected virtual void OnItemSelect(ObjectListSelectEventArgs e)
```

ObjectList Public Properties

- ❑ `Adapter` – inherited from `MobileControl`, see `MobileControl` reference also in this chapter.

- ❑ `Alignment` – inherited from `MobileControl`, see `MobileControl` reference also in this chapter.

- ❑ **`AllFields`**

- ❑ **`AutoGenerateFields`**

- ❑ `BackColor` – inherited from `MobileControl`, see `MobileControl` reference also in this chapter.

- ❑ **`BackCommandText`**

- ❏ BreakAfter – inherited from MobileControl, see MobileControl reference also in this chapter.

- ❏ **Commands**

- ❏ **CommandStyle**

- ❏ CustomAttributes – inherited from MobileControl, see MobileControl reference also in this chapter.

- ❏ **DataMember**

- ❏ **DataSource**

- ❏ **DefaultCommand**

- ❏ **Details**

- ❏ **DetailsCommandText**

- ❏ DeviceSpecific – inherited from MobileControl, see MobileControl reference also in this chapter.

- ❏ **Fields**

- ❏ FirstPage – inherited from MobileControl, see MobileControl reference also in this chapter.

- ❏ FirstVisibleItemIndex – inherited from PagedControl, see PagedControl reference also in this chapter.

- ❏ Font – inherited from MobileControl, see MobileControl reference also in this chapter.

- ❏ ForeColor – inherited from MobileControl, see MobileControl reference also in this chapter.

- ❏ Form – inherited from MobileControl, see MobileControl reference also in this chapter.

- ❏ **HasItemCommandHandler**

- ❏ InternalItemCount – inherited from MobileControl, see MobileControl reference also in this chapter.

- ❏ IsTemplated – inherited from MobileControl, see MobileControl reference also in this chapter.

- ❏ ItemCount – inherited from PagedControl, see PagedControl reference also in this chapter.

- ❏ **Items**

- ❏ ItemsPerPage – inherited from PagedControl, see PagedControl reference also in this chapter.

- ❏ **LabelField**

- ❏ **LabelFieldIndex**

- ❏ **LabelStyle**

- ❏ LastPage – inherited from MobileControl, see MobileControl reference also in this chapter.

- ❏ MobilePage – inherited from MobileControl, see MobileControl reference also in this chapter.
- ❏ **MoreText**
- ❏ **SelectedIndex**
- ❏ **Selection**
- ❏ **SelectMoreCommand**
- ❏ StyleReference – inherited from MobileControl, see MobileControl reference also in this chapter.
- ❏ **TableFieldIndices**
- ❏ **TableFields**
- ❏ **ViewMode**
- ❏ VisibleItemCount – inherited from PagedControl, see PagedControl reference also in this chapter.
- ❏ VisibleWeight – inherited from MobileControl, see MobileControl reference also in this chapter.
- ❏ Wrapping – inherited from MobileControl, see MobileControl reference also in this chapter.

AllFields

The AllFields property gets an IObjectListFieldCollection object constituting the fields of the ObjectList. Remember, this property is only available after data-binding has occurred and is read-only. It does not let you add or subtract fields.

```
public System.Web.UI.MobileControls.IObjectListFieldCollection
                                                AllFields { get }
```

AutoGenerateFields

The AutoGenerateFields property gets and sets a Boolean value specifying whether the fields for the ObjectList *must* be automatically generated from the provided dataset. If true, each public property of the dataset will be presented as a field. Default is true.

```
public bool AutoGenerateFields { get, set }
```

BackCommandText

The BackCommandText property gets and sets a String value for the "back" control rendered on item detail screens.

```
public bool AutoGenerateFields { get, set }
```

Commands

The `Commands` property gets an `ObjectListCommandCollection` constituting the commands associated with the `ObjectList` instance.

```
public virtual
   System.Web.UI.MobileControls.ObjectListCommandCollection Commands { get }
```

CommandStyle

The `CommandStyle` property gets or sets the `Style` instance to be associated with the `ObjectList`.

```
public style CommandStyle { get, set }
```

DataMember

The `DataMember` property gets or sets the data member that is the source for data within the dataset bound to the control. Default is an empty `String`.

```
public virtual string DataMember { get, set }
```

DataSource

The `DataSource` property gets or sets the datasource `Object` for the control. It should be set to an `IEnumerable` or `IListSource` type. If the `AutoGenerateFields` property is set to `true`, the members of the `IEnumerable` collection are created as fields for each `ObjectListItem`. If the `DataSource` implements `IListSource`, the data-binding operation looks to the types of the `DataSource` when generating `ObjectListItems`. Otherwise, the first item of the enumeration is used to determine the types of the `ObjectListItem` fields (using the field specified in the `DataMember` field of the `ObjectList`), so all elements of the `DataSource` enumeration must be of the same type. Default is `null`.

```
public virtual Object DataSource { get, set }
```

DefaultCommand

The `DefaultCommand` property sets or gets the name of the default command of the `ObjectList`. Default is an empty `String`.

```
public string DefaultCommand { get, set }
```

Details

The `Details` property gets a `Panel` instance that contains an `ObjectListItem` detail view. The view provided is device specific and details all public properties for the item as well as a "back" button to return to the list view.

```
public System.Web.UI.MobileControls.Panel Details { get }
```

DetailsCommandText

The `DetailsCommandText` property gets and sets a `String` value for the details command element generated in the list.

```
public string DetailsCommandText{ get, set }
```

Fields

The `Fields` property gets an `ObjectListFieldCollection` containing the fields associated with `ObjectListItems` in the control. The `ObjectListFieldCollection` instance has `Add`, `AddAt`, `Remove` and `RemoveAt` methods to let you work the fields programmatically.

```
public System.Web.UI.MobileControls.ObjectListFieldCollection Fields { get }
```

HasItemCommandHandler

The `HasItemCommandHandler` property gets a `Boolean` inidicating if the `ObjectList` has an `ItemCommandHandler`.

```
public bool HasItemCommandHandler { get }
```

Items

The `Items` property gets an `ObjectListItemCollection` constituting the items in the `ObjectList`. This collection cannot be modified by the `Items` property. Default is an empty collection.

```
public virtual System.Web.UI.MobileControls.ObjectListItemCollection
                                               Items { get }
```

LabelField

The `LabelField` property gets or sets the `String` value that identifies the label field for each item. The default is an empty `String`. When it is left empty, the first field of the `DataSource` is used as a label. When the `ObjectList` is rendered as a table, the `LabelField` is not used, as a more explicit delineation determined by the names of the individual fields of the `ObjectListItemCollection` is displayed. The `LabelField` will be overridden by the `<LabelTemplate>` element if present.

```
public string LabelField { get, set }
```

LabelFieldIndex

The `LabelFieldIndex` property gets an `Integer` indicating the current index within the `AllFields` collection that represents the label. See `LabelField` property for related details. Default is 0, in other words the first member.

```
public int LabelFieldIndex { get }
```

LabelStyle

The LabelStyle property gets or sets a Style instance that specifies the style for the header label.

```
public style LabelStyle { get, set }
```

MoreText

The MoreText property gets or sets the string value used as the "more" command on the details view page.

```
public string MoreText { get, set }
```

SelectedIndex

The SelectedIndex property is an Integer index indicating the currently selected ObjectListItem within the control.

```
public int SelectedIndex { get, set }
```

Selection

The Selection property returns the selected ObjectListItem. If no item is selected, this property will return null.

```
public ObjectListItem Selection { get }
```

SelectMoreCommand

This property allows you to assign text to a link basically that takes the place of the link in the listview of the objectList control. The more link is therefore rendered to provide a link from the listview to the detailsview. There are some specific rules for its use:

❑   It applies to HTML only

❑   You have to have a DefaultCommand property set

❑   There must be additional fields or commands to be rendered in the detailsview

```
public string SelectMoreCommand {get , set}
```

TableFieldIndices

The TableFieldIndices property is an Integer array representing the indices of the corresponding TableFields. This array corresponds to the indices of the AllFields collection to use when displaying the ObjectList as a table. If the TableFields property is empty this property is null. Default is null.

```
public int[] TableFieldIndices { get }
```

TableFields

The `TableFields` property is a string of semicolon-delimited identifiers where each value indicates the name or data field of the field that will be displayed. The default is an empty `String`.

```
public string TableFields { get, set }
```

ViewMode

The `ViewMode` property gets or sets an `ObjectListViewMode` enumerated value indicating the `ViewMode` of the `ObjectList` instance.

```
public ObjectListViewMode ViewMode { get, set }
```

The `ObjectListViewMode` enumeration supports the following values:

❑   `List` – this view displays each field of the item, including title and value. In HTML, this view is combined with the `Commands` view, with the commands appearing as hyperlinks below the details.

❑   `Commands` – the default view mode that typically includes the label fields of the items in the list.

❑   `Details` – on WML devices `Details` mode renders a menu with the `ObjectList` class' commands, and a menu item displaying the `Details` view. On HTML devices list and detail views are combined.

ObjectList Protected Properties

❑   `InnerText` – inherited from `MobileControl`, see `MobileControl` reference also in this chapter.

❑   `ItemWeight` – inherited from `PagedControl`, see `PagedControl` reference also in this chapter.

❑   `PaginateChildren` – inherited from `MobileControl`, see `MobileControl` reference also in this chapter.

ObjectList Public Events

❑   **ItemCommand**

❑   **ItemDatabind**

❑   **ItemSelect**

❑   **ShowItemCommands**

ItemCommand

The `ItemCommand` event is fired when a user selects an item's command control.

```
public event ObjectListCommandEventHandler ItemCommand
```

ItemDatabind

The `ItemDataBind` event is fired when an item participates in databinding.

```
public event ObjectListDataBindEventHandler ItemDataBind
```

ItemSelect

The `ItemSelect` event is fired when a list item is selected by a user.

```
public event ObjectListSelectEventHandler ItemSelect
```

ShowItemCommands

The `ShowItemCommands` event is fired prior to the rendering of a comand control for an item.

```
public event ObjectListShowCommandsEventHandler ShowItemCommands
```

PagedControl Class

`PagedControl` is the base class to be used for all controls that need to support pagination. Basically any control that might render large volumes of text should derive from `PagedControl`. `PagedControl` itself derives from `MobileControl` and provides a small number of methods and properties related to pagination. Most intrinsic mobile controls that might be required to support abundant text content also support pagination, including but not limited to: `List`, `LiteralText`, `ObjectList`, `TextView`, and so on.

Paginated Content

Due to the typically tiny screen sizes on mobile devices the Mobile Internet Toolkit provides pagination functionality to "break up" content for display across multiple pages. If the `Paginate` property is set to `true` for a `Panel`, it can have its contents split across multiple pages if needed. Since the `Form` class extends the `Panel` class, `Form` contents can also be paginated. By default, the `Paginate` property is `false`. Remember, when paginate is `true` for a parent `Form` instance, any `Panels` contained within the `Form` will still be rendered together on a single page where possible, unless the `Panel`'s `Paginate` property is also set to `true`.

Remember, if the requirement is to mark a group of controls on the page for pagination, set the `ControlToPaginate` property of the form to the ID of the pagination target. Any children of that control are then able to be broken across multiple pages. This is often used to split the contents of a single panel on a form.

Example: Custom Pagination

For our example, `PagedList.aspx`, we will render a long list of 100 items. The important thing to understand for custom pagination is that by using the `ItemIndex` property of the `LoadItemsEventArgument` we can keep track of where we are in our rendered list rendering between postbacks. This is very similar to paged recordsets in classic ADO. The list limit has been set declaratively in the `Mobile:List` control in the page.

The web page and list control are declared as follows:

```
<%@Register TagPrefix="Mobile" Namespace="System.Web.UI.MobileControls"
            Assembly="System.Web.Mobile" %>
<%@ Page Language="c#" CodeBehind="PagedList.aspx.cs"
        Inherits="systemWebUIMobileControlExamples.PagedList"
        AutoEventWireup="false" %>
</SCRIPT>
<mobile:Form runat="server" Paginate="true" id="Form1">
  <mobile:List id="MyList" runat="server" onLoadItems="MyList_OnLoadItems"
               ItemCount="100" itemsPerPage="5"></mobile:List>
</mobile:Form>
```

The code behind that has the event handler for the LoadItems event of the List control is:

```
public class PagedList : System.Web.UI.MobileControls.MobilePage
{
  protected System.Web.UI.MobileControls.List MyList;
  protected System.Web.UI.MobileControls.Form Form1;

  private void Page_Load(object sender, System.EventArgs e)
  {
    // Put user code to initialize the page here
  }

  public void MyList_OnLoadItems(object sender,
                      System.Web.UI.MobileControls.LoadItemsEventArgs e)
  {
    MyList.Items.Clear();

    //populate the list with the items requested
    int i ;

    // loop the list
    for (i = e.ItemIndex ; i< (e.ItemIndex + e.ItemCount)+1; i++)
    {
      if (i == e.ItemIndex)
        MyList.Items.Add(new
                         System.Web.UI.MobileControls.MobileListItem(
                         "Page Indexed to " + e.ItemIndex.ToString()));

      MyList.Items.Add(new System.Web.UI.MobileControls.MobileListItem(
                                          "#" + i.ToString()));
    }
  }
}
```

The result in our sample devices is as follows:

PagedControl Public Methods

- ❑ AddLinkedForms – inherited from MobileControl, see MobileControl reference also in this chapter.

- ❑ CreateDefaultTemplatedUI – inherited from MobileControl, see MobileControl reference also in this chapter.

- ❑ EnsureTemplatedUI – inherited from MobileControl, see MobileControl reference also in this chapter.

- ❑ GetTemplate – inherited from MobileControl, see MobileControl reference also in this chapter.

- ❑ IsVisibleOnPage – inherited from MobileControl, see MobileControl reference also in this chapter.

- ❑ PaginateRecursive – inherited from MobileControl, see MobileControl reference also in this chapter.

- ❑ ResolveFormReference – inherited from MobileControl, see MobileControl reference also in this chapter.

PagedControl Protected Methods

- ❑ CreateStyle – inherited from MobileControl, see MobileControl reference also in this chapter.

- ❑ CreateTemplatedUI – inherited from MobileControl, see MobileControl reference also in this chapter.

- ❑ IsFormSubmitControl – inherited from MobileControl, see MobileControl reference also in this chapter.

- ❑ LoadPrivateViewState – inherited from MobileControl, see MobileControl reference also in this chapter.

- ❑ OnRender – inherited from MobileControl, see MobileControl reference also in this chapter.

- ❑ SavePrivateViewState – inherited from MobileControl, see MobileControl reference also in this chapter.

PagedControl Public Properties

- ❑ Adapter – inherited from MobileControl, see MobileControl reference also in this chapter.

- ❑ Alignment – inherited from MobileControl, see MobileControl reference also in this chapter.

- ❑ BackColor – inherited from MobileControl, see MobileControl reference also in this chapter.

- ❑ BreakAfter – inherited from MobileControl, see MobileControl reference also in this chapter.

- ❑ CustomAttributes – inherited from MobileControl, see MobileControl reference also in this chapter.

- ❑ DeviceSpecific – inherited from MobileControl, see MobileControl reference also in this chapter.

- ❑ FirstPage – inherited from MobileControl, see MobileControl reference also in this chapter.

- ❑ **FirstVisibleItemIndex**

- ❑ Font – inherited from MobileControl, see MobileControl reference also in this chapter.

- ❑ ForeColor – inherited from MobileControl, see MobileControl reference also in this chapter.

- ❑ Form – inherited from MobileControl, see MobileControl reference also in this chapter.

- ❑ IsTemplated – inherited from MobileControl, see MobileControl reference also in this chapter.

- ❑ **ItemCount**

- ❑ **ItemsPerPage**

- ❑ LastPage – inherited from `MobileControl`, see `MobileControl` reference also in this chapter.

- ❑ MobilePage – inherited from `MobileControl`, see `MobileControl` reference also in this chapter.

- ❑ StyleReference – inherited from `MobileControl`, see `MobileControl` reference also in this chapter.

- ❑ **VisibleItemCount**

- ❑ VisibleWeight – inherited from `MobileControl`, see `MobileControl` reference also in this chapter.

- ❑ Wrapping – inherited from `MobileControl`, see `MobileControl` reference also in this chapter.

FirstVisibleItemIndex

The `FirstVisibleItem` gets the first item visible on the current form page.

```
public int FirstVisibleItemIndex { get }
```

ItemCount

The `ItemCount` property gets or sets an `Integer` value that is a metric of content "units" in the control such that this value indicates list item count for list controls but characters in the context of a `TextView` control.

```
public int ItemCount { get, set }
```

ItemsPerPage

The `ItemsPerPage` property gets or sets an `Integer` value that is a metric of content "units" displayed on a per page basis, such that the units may represent `ListItems` in a list control context and characters in a text control context.

```
public int ItemsPerPage { get, set }
```

VisibleItemCount

The `VisibleItemCount` property gets an `Integer` value signifying the number of items visible on the current page.

```
public int VisibleItemCount { get }
```

PagedControl Protected Properties

- ❑ InnerText – inherited from `MobileControl`, see `MobileControl` reference also in this chapter.

- ❑ **InternalItemCount**

- ❑ **ItemWeight**

❑   PaginateChildren – inherited from MobileControl, see MobileControl reference also
      in this chapter.

InternalItemCount

The InternalItemCount gets an Integer value of the number of control specific content units in
the current control instance.

```
protected abstract int internalItemCount { get }
```

ItemWeight

The ItemWeight gets an Integer value approximating the weight metric of a single unit in the
control. Inheriting classes must override this control.

```
public virtual int ItemWeight { get }
```

PagedControl Public Events

❑   **LoadItems**

LoadItems

The LoadItems event occurs when custom pagination of a control requires that more data be loaded.

```
public event LoadItemsEventHandler LoadItems
```

6

System.Web.Caching

"Caching" is the process of storing previously rendered or processed data in a quick, *efficiently* accessed location, with emphasis on efficiency. In ASP.NET, caching typically involves storing the HTTP responses that are rendered by .aspx pages and .ascx controls, so that rather than *executing* pages that we know will return identical results, we simply send the previously rendered *results* instead. The effect on the performance and scalability of your application can be dramatic – in some cases cached page "hits" can be over 30 times more efficient in terms of server resources and execution speed. While caching functionality could be achieved in classic ASP through custom code, caching is built into the ASP.NET framework and the functionality is provided in the System.Web.Caching namespace.

Naturally, caching isn't always appropriate, so a page or control must explicitly declare to the runtime that it requires run-time caching support. Moreover, the "return on investment" with caching depends entirely on two factors. First, for most applications, the cache hits *must return identical results* to an equivalent non-cached client request. This is axiomatic. The speed benefits of caching are moot if the cached data is outdated or inaccurate, so care must be taken to make sure that cached items are invalidated when the cached contents are no longer accurate within the requirements of the application. The second factor is that since caching itself involves some overhead, it is always the best practice when implementing caching to:

❑   Identify frequently accessed pages and controls that may benefit from caching

❑   Get baseline performance measurements without caching enabled

❑   Get comparable performance measurements (hits per minute, and so on) on the cache-enabled control or page

Regardless of which caching method you select you should always run performance tests to ensure that real benefits are being won in terms of processor time and memory allocation.

Classes of the System.Web.Caching Namespace

Class	Description
`Cache`	Implements all methods needed for adding, accessing, and removing cache items. Cannot be inherited.
`CacheDependency`	Tracks cache dependencies between an item in the cache and files, directories, keys to other items in the cache. It cannot be inherited.

ASP.NET provides two means of accessing caching functionality: **output caching** and **programmatic caching**. Both forms of caching exploit members of the `HttpCachePolicy` class instance, which is exposed for an individual response through the `Page.Response.Cache` property. Programmatic caching accesses the `Cache` property directly and can let you cache not only HTTP results but any object instance that may have been expensive to create, and provides a wide variety of means to invalidate the cached object. Output caching is limited to caching the HTTP results generated by a page or control and simply requires a page or control declaration. The declaration specifies that caching is required and specifies the conditions for the caching.

Output Caching

Basic "results" caching at the page or user control level is handled declaratively and is called **output caching**. What is actually stored in the cache is the HTTP response text, generated by the cache-enabled page – nothing more. It's important to remember that if a page includes images, those images are actually included via an HTML reference in the response. Images and any other content retrieved using separate HTTP requests are *not* stored in the output cache with the page. This is helpful because, in the case of images in particular, the browser itself often caches the content on the client side.

Output caching can be used for:

- ❑ Page output caching
- ❑ Partial Page or Fragment Caching (which caches user control output)
- ❑ Web Service caching

Each of these output caching types only requires that we mark the item as "cacheable". The system will then handle the management of our cached items.

Example: Basic Page Caching

Consider the following example, `outputCache.aspx`, that renders the current time:

```
<%@ Page language="c#" Codebehind="outputCache.aspx.cs"
        AutoEventWireup="false"
        Inherits="systemWebCachingCs.outputCache" %>
<%@ OutputCache Duration="10" VaryByParam="None"%>
<!DOCTYPE HTML PUBLIC "-//W3C//DTD HTML 4.0 Transitional//EN" >
<html>
  <head>
    <title>outputCache</title>
    <meta name="GENERATOR" Content="Microsoft Visual Studio 7.0">
    <meta name="CODE_LANGUAGE" Content="C#">
    <meta name="vs_defaultClientScript" content="JavaScript">
    <meta name="vs_targetSchema"
          content="http://schemas.microsoft.com/intellisense/ie5">
  </head>
  <body MS_POSITIONING="GridLayout">
    <form id="Form1" method="post" runat="server">
      <asp:Label id="Label1"
                 style="Z-INDEX: 101; LEFT: 34px; POSITION: absolute;
                        TOP: 32px" runat="server"></asp:Label>
    </form>
  </body>
</html>
```

To let the system know that we would like the results of this page to be cached, we just need to add a directive to the top of the page similar to the following:

```
<%@ OutputCache [List of Attributes] %>
```

The code-behind, `outputCache.aspx.cs`, simply sets the label text to the current time (the use of time in this example and others in this chapter is an easy way to demonstrate that cached results are being returned by the server):

```
public class outputCache : System.Web.UI.Page
{
  protected Label Label1;
  private void Page_Load(object sender, System.EventArgs e)
  {
    Label1.Text = DateTime.Now.ToString();
  }
}
```

The `OutputCache` directive in the `.aspx` page sets the cache duration (the time that the cached value is kept before being ejected) to 10 seconds, which is specified in the `Duration` attribute of the declaration. Since caching is enabled we will get the same results on our first hit after 10 seconds have elapsed, then the cache will be invalidated on the server and a new page will render when requested. The new page is, in turn, cached for 10 seconds, and so on. (To try this example you will need to hit the refresh key on your browser frequently to see the effect of caching.)

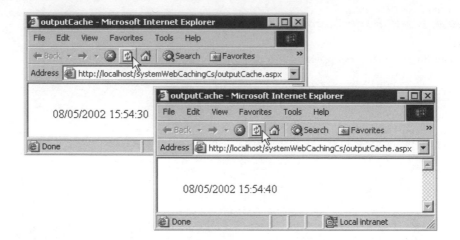

While this page simply renders the current time it could just as easily be one that runs a query on a database, returns a set of data, and fills a grid.

Declaring Output Caching

Output caching can be declared at the top of the page or control:

```
<%@ OutputCache [List of Attributes] %>
```

The declaration attributes that affect how caching works include the following:

Attribute	Required	Value(s)	Page	UserControl	Web Service
Duration	Yes for all	Number of seconds an item is considered valid and will remain in the cache	Y	Y	Y
Location	No	Specifies which cache-capable network applications involved in delivering the response can be used to cache the item	Y	N	N

Attribute	Required	Value(s)	Page	UserControl	Web Service
VaryByCustom	No	Determines whether different versions of an item will be cached depending on either the browser type or a custom string you specify	Y	Y	N
VaryByHeader	No	A determination is made on whether to cache an item based on the HTTP headers, either by the value of a single header or by multiple header values	Y	Y	N
VaryByParam	Yes for Control (unless you have a VaryByControl attribute specified) and Page caching	Makes a determination on whether to cache an item based on parameters passed to the request (typically as a form or on the query string)	Y	Y	N
VaryByControl	No	This parameter is only used for control-scoped caching. It is a semicolon-separated list of the fully qualified names of the public properties of the control. Each value associated at render/run time for the specified control property results in discrete cache instance for the control. (See *VaryByControl* section later in this chapter.)	N	Y	N

Page and Control Attributes

The following section examines in greater detail the OutputCache declaration attributes common to Page and Control attributes. The only attribute restricted for use to user controls is the VaryByControl attribute.

Duration Attribute

The `Duration` attribute is required for the `OutputCache` directive and specifies the amount of time in seconds that a page will remain in the cache. The first time a request is made for the page, the page is executed and the output is stored in the cache. When subsequent requests are received, the cache engine will check to see if a copy of the page output is in the cache. Independent of the number of requests that are received while the page is cached, once the specified duration of time has passed, the cache engine will automatically evict that item from the cache. Therefore, the next request received after the duration has expired will cause the page to be re-executed and the new result placed back in the cache for a new period of the specified duration.

There are two factors that can have an effect on how long an item remains in the cache regardless of the `Duration` value you specify. The first factor is system memory. When the web server that is hosting a particular ASP.NET application begins to run low on system memory, the cache engine will automatically begin selectively purging items from the cache to avoid it having an adverse effect on application performance. Items in the cache are assigned a **priority** that will affect the order in which items are removed. This is covered in more detail in the section on *Programmatic Caching*. The second factor that can override the `Duration` attribute you specify in the `OutputCache` directive is something called **Sliding Expiration**. The cache in ASP.NET is designed to store frequently used items and therefore includes this mechanism to avoid the cache growing too large with items that are accessed infrequently. The sliding expiration policy is set to five minutes by default and will cause an item to be evicted from the cache if it is not accessed within that period. Once again, this is regardless of the duration period you specify. However, unlike the `Duration`, this sliding expiration clock is reset each time the item in the cache is accessed. Also, it is possible to override this sliding expiration policy and we will discuss this in the section on *Programmatic Caching*.

The amount of overhead necessary to support these steps required by the caching process is very small but should be taken into consideration. Because every situation is different, the only truly accurate way to determine the effectiveness of caching for a particular page or the most appropriate duration value to use is through testing and performance monitoring.

Location Attribute

The `Location` attribute allows you to specify the "cacheability" of a page; it cannot be used for controls or Web Services. Setting this value results in the response header Cache Control being set for the page. The value is one of several in the `OutputCacheLocation` enumeration with a default value of `Any` and includes:

Member name	Description
`Any`	The output can be cached on any device in the HTTP chain capable of caching, from browser to server. The default.
`Client`	The output should be cached by the browser issuing the request.
`Downstream`	The output can be cached on any device in the HTTP chain capable of caching, from browser to proxy but *excluding the originating server*.
`None`	The output cache is disabled.
`Server`	The output should only be cached on the server which processed the request.

You might not want a logon page cached at all, for example, or if so only on the server. In contrast, less sensitive materials might be cached downstream or using the `Any` device value.

VaryByCustom Attribute

The `VaryByCustom` attribute is an extensible rather than "hard-wired" means of specifying the conditions that variegate cached content.

Curiously, the `VaryByCustom` attribute provides one "built-in" condition called "browser" which caches different views of a page depending on the browser version of the request. To vary by browser type, you specify `VaryByCustom="browser"`. The cache engine will then use the value of `request.Browser.Type` to determine whether a new item should be created in the cache. Only the browser's name and major version is used for this evaluation. Therefore, a different item will exist in the cache for IE 4 and IE 5 requests but not for IE 5 and IE 5.5 requests. This will happen automatically without writing any specific browser detection code in your ASP.NET pages. However, the real benefit of this capability is if you do write a page that will produce different output depending on the browser version. Then the cache engine will automatically cache this different output and deliver it to any future request made by a browser with the same name and major version. Otherwise, the same output will be cached twice with no added benefit.

To use your own custom string in the `VaryByCustom` attribute, you must override the `HttpApplication.GetVaryByCustomString` method in your application's `Global.asax` file. The code in this method will be used by the cache engine to determine whether a new item is added to the cache.

Example: Using a Custom String in the VaryByCustom Attribute

As an example, `VaryByCustom` would be useful for a site that provides different versions of a page depending on whether the browser supports client-side JavaScript. You could accomplish this using the `VaryByCustom` attribute within your `OutputCache` directive:

```
<%@ OutputCache Duration="10" VaryByParam="none"
                VaryByCustom="JavaScript"%>
```

You would then need to add your own custom logic to override the `GetVaryByCustomString` method in your application's `Global.asax` file. This will set the value for each of these name-value pairs to allow the cache engine to determine which versions of the output to cache and which to retrieve and return for future requests. The following is an example of what the code in your `Global.asax` file may look like:

```
public override string GetVaryByCustomString(HttpContext context,
                                             string arg)
{
  switch(arg)
  {
    case "JavaScript":
      return "JavaScript=" + context.Request.Browser.JavaScript.ToString();
    default:
      return "";
  }
}
```

The `case...default` clause that returns an empty string in this case simply represents the fact that no other strings are used in resolving the `VaryByCustom` attribute. This does not affect any other caching that may occur due to `VaryByParam` or `VaryByHeader` attributes.

517

The HTML for this, `outputCacheVaryByCustom.aspx`, is detailed below:

```
<%@ Page language="c#" Codebehind="outputCacheVaryByCustom.aspx.cs"
        AutoEventWireup="false"
        Inherits="systemWebCachingCs.outputCacheVaryByCustom" %>
<%@ OutputCache Duration="10" VaryByParam="none"
               VaryByCustom="JavaScript"%>
<!DOCTYPE HTML PUBLIC "-//W3C//DTD HTML 4.0 Transitional//EN" >
<html>
  <head>
    <title>outputCacheVaryByCustom</title>
    <meta name="GENERATOR" Content="Microsoft Visual Studio 7.0">
    <meta name="CODE_LANGUAGE" Content="C#">
    <meta name="vs_defaultClientScript" content="JavaScript">
    <meta name="vs_targetSchema"
          content="http://schemas.microsoft.com/intellisense/ie5">
  </head>
  <body MS_POSITIONING="GridLayout">
    <form id="Form1" method="post" runat="server">
      Hi!
      <asp:Label id="Label1"
                 style="Z-INDEX: 101; LEFT: 16px; POSITION: absolute;
                        TOP: 48px" runat="server"></asp:Label>
    </form>
  </body>
</html>
```

The code behind file, `outputCacheVaryByCustom.aspx.cs`, looks like this:

```
...

public class outputCacheVaryByCustom : System.Web.UI.Page
{
  protected Label Label1;
  private void Page_Load(object sender, System.EventArgs e)
  {
    Label1.Text = DateTime.Now.ToString();
  }
}
```

VaryByHeader Attribute

The attribute `VaryByHeader` operates in much the same way as the `VaryByParam` attribute. The only difference is that this attribute makes a determination of whether to add a separate item to the cache based on the HTTP header values instead of the query string and form values.

One example of where this capability can be useful is for web applications that provide a single page in more than one language. Browsers send an HTTP header that is named `Accept-Language`. This value is a code that identifies the preferred language for the browser. For example, `en-us` for English-US or `fr` for French. We can then modify our `OutputCache` directive to cache the different language versions of our page:

```
<%@ OutputCache Duration="10" VaryByParam="None"
                VaryByHeader="Accept-Language" %>
```

VaryByParam Attribute

Like `Duration`, `VaryByParam` is a required attribute for the `OutputCache` directive. The `VaryByParam` attribute allows you to control when these different views of a page are cached based on one or more query string or form parameters. In other words, postbacks of any kind that have a match in the specified parameter names are cached for the duration specified by the `Duration` attribute. Parameters that are listed for `VaryByParam` are not case-sensitive.

These are the possible values for `VaryByParam`:

Value	Description
None	Only GET requests with no query string values are cached. Any requests that include a GET or POST parameter will not result in a new item being added to the cache.
*	An item is created in the cache for each page requested with a different value in either the query string or the POST collection.
[Custom]	Allows you to list which GET or POST parameters will result in the output being cached. Multiple parameters are separated by semicolons.

If the results might vary based on any single form or querystring attribute being different then use the * value, otherwise you can reduce the number of cached instances by specifically listing those attributes which result in variegated output.

Example: Caching Using VaryByParam

To illustrate `VaryByParam`, we've created a simple postback scenario with a page, `outputCacheByParam.aspx`, which records its creation time. Instead of using the refresh button on your browser to see the effects of caching, you click the submit button repeatedly. Submissions within the cache duration window will result in identical results – we are simply getting a cached version of the postback results. Notice that we've specified a particular parameter in the `VaryByParam` attribute – * would also have worked.

```
<%@ Page language="c#" Codebehind="outputCacheByParam.aspx.cs"
         AutoEventWireup="false"
         Inherits="systemWebCachingCs.outputCacheByParam" %>
<%@ OutputCache Duration="10" VaryByParam="TextBox1"%>
<!DOCTYPE HTML PUBLIC "-//W3C//DTD HTML 4.0 Transitional//EN" >
<HTML>
  <HEAD>
    <title>outputCacheByParam</title>
    <meta name="GENERATOR" Content="Microsoft Visual Studio 7.0">
    <meta name="CODE_LANGUAGE" Content="C#">
    <meta name="vs_defaultClientScript" content="JavaScript">
    <meta name="vs_targetSchema"
          content="http://schemas.microsoft.com/intellisense/ie5">
```

```
    </HEAD>
      <body>
        <form id="Form1" method="post" runat="server">
          <P>
            <asp:TextBox id="TextBox1" runat="server"></asp:TextBox></P>
          <P>
            <asp:Button id="Button1" runat="server"
                        Text="Button"></asp:Button></P>
          <P>
            <asp:Label id="Label2" runat="server"></asp:Label></P>
          <P>
            <asp:Label id="Label1" runat="server"></asp:Label></P>
        </form>
      </body>
    </HTML>
```

The code behind, `outputCacheByParam.aspx.cs`, is as follows:

```
...

public class outputCacheByParam : System.Web.UI.Page
{
  protected System.Web.UI.WebControls.TextBox TextBox1;
  protected System.Web.UI.WebControls.Button Button1;
  protected System.Web.UI.WebControls.Label Label2;
  protected System.Web.UI.WebControls.Label Label1;

  private void Page_Load(object sender, System.EventArgs e)
  {
    if(IsPostBack)
    {
      Label2.Text = "Value submitted is: " + TextBox1.Text;
      Label1.Text = ("Page created at: " + DateTime.Now);
    }
  }
}
...
```

The output from this example is illustrated below:

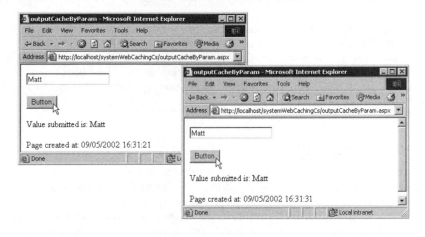

VaryByControl Attribute

Another attribute that becomes available when using an `OutputCache` directive in a user control is `VaryByControl`. Even though this attribute is restricted in use to User Controls, the other attributes previously defined are also available for the directive when used in the context of a control.

Example: Caching User Controls with VaryByControl

VaryByControl allows you to define a property in the User Control that you can then reference in the `VaryByControl` attribute to control what versions of the User Control are cached. For example, you could include code in a User Control similar to the following:

```
<%@ OutputCache Duration="10" VaryByControl="CategoryID" %>
<SCRIPT runat="server">
  public string CategoryID
  {
    get
    {
      return cmbCategoryID.Value;
    }
    set
    {
      cmbCategoryID.Value = CategoryID;
    }
  }
```

In this case, the property just represents the value of a `ComboBox` control on the User Control. This User Control could then just be dropped onto a parent page and the cache engine will use this property in much the same way as it uses parameters passed on the query string in the case of `VaryByParam`.

For example, if you have a user control that renders a drop-down list for choosing the category of books to display, you could use the value of the drop-down list to vary the output cache.

> There is one very important caveat to caching a User Control. Since the cached item represents the *end result* of the execution of the User Control, you cannot write any server-side code in the containing page that manipulates the User Control in any way. Essentially the control must be completely atomic at run time to successfully participate in caching. An error will occur if you try to interact programmatically with a cached control from the parent page.

Web Service Caching

In addition to page and control caching, ASP.NET provides the ability to cache the results of a Web Service method. This can be done simply by adding a further attribute to the definition of your publicly available Web Service method. This is possible since the output of a Web Service method that uses the default SOAP encoding, always has its results serialized into XML. The resulting XML is stored in the cache in the same way that the HTML from pages and controls is stored in the cache.

With Web Service Caching, the VaryBy*XXX* attributes listed for Page Output and Partial Page Caching do not apply. Web Service Caching behaves in a manner similar to VaryByParam="*". This makes sense since you can always attach additional parameters to a URL even if none are expected; however Web Service methods always explicitly specify what parameters are expected.

Example: Web Service Caching

Shown below is a simple Web Service class, webServiceCaching.asmx.cs, that exposes a single method returning the current time.

```
Using System.Web.Services;

...

[WebService(Namespace = "http://tempuri.org/")]
public class webServiceCaching : System.Web.Services.WebService
{
...

  [WebMethod(CacheDuration=10)]
  public string GetTime()
  {
    return DateTime.Now.ToString();
  }
}
```

The [WebMethod(CacheDuration=10)] declaration is all that is needed to invoke caching. If you bring up the system-provided test page and invoke this method, you should see something like the following display in your browser (your time will of course be different):

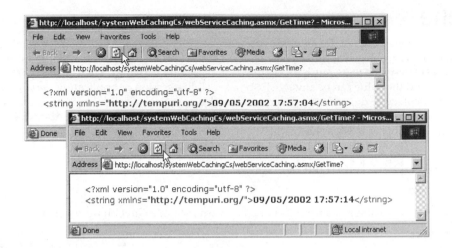

Just as with the examples using ASP.NET pages and User Controls, the value displayed for the time will not change no matter how many times you refresh the browser until the ten second duration we specified has expired.

Programmatic Caching

Programmatic caching goes beyond output caching by allowing us to retain specific objects in memory across HTTP requests. Since any variable in the .NET Runtime derives from Object you can cache any object at will.

Caching objects makes sense from a performance standpoint when the object is expensive to generate, frequently accessed, and generally static over a specific period of time. You can circumvent the guideline that the cached object be generally static over time by using caching dependency to intelligently invalidate cached items when other items upon which they depend change. (This is covered by example in the *CacheDependency* class reference.)

There are only two classes and one delegate contained within the System.Web.Caching namespace. These three items are listed in the table below and we continue by looking at each of these in turn.

Item	Type	Description
`Cache`	Class	Implements the cache for a web application.
`CacheDependency`	Class	Tracks cache dependencies, which can be files, directories, or keys to other objects in the cache.
`CacheItemRemoved Callback`	Delegate	Allows us to define a callback method that will be used to notify our application when an item is removed from the cache.

Cache

Cache implements all of the methods you will need for adding, accessing, and removing cache items. Cached items are stored at the application level. It's important to remember that items in the cache are really just key-value pairs much like application or session variables. The key is a string used to identify the item and the value can be any .NET Object. Unlike session or application variables, cached items can have a lifecycle dependent on time or other objects in your application. An instance of the Cache class is automatically created for you as an application-level variable in your ASP.NET application and is appropriately named "Cache".

Cache Public Methods

❑ **Add**

❑ Equals – inherited from System.Object, see Introduction for details.

❑ **Get**

❑ **GetEnumerator**

❑ GetHashCode – inherited from System.Object, see Introduction for details.

❑ GetType – inherited from System.Object, see Introduction for details.

❑ **Insert**

❑ **Remove**

❑ ToString – inherited from System.Object, see Introduction for details.

Add

The Add method takes a String, Object, CacheDependency, and DateTime as input and adds the specified item to the Cache object with dependencies, expiration and priority policies, and a delegate you can use to notify your application when the inserted item is removed from the Cache.

```
public object Add(string key,
                  object value,
                  CacheDependency dependencies,
                  DateTime absoluteExpiration,
                  TimeSpan slidingExpiration,
                  cacheItemPriority priority,
                  CacheItemRemovedCallBack);
```

Get

The Get method takes a String as input and provides an alternative way to retrieve items from the cache, which is in addition to using the Item property that will be described shortly.

```
public object Get(string key);
```

Remember, the return type of this method is Object. So, the example below shows how you might retrieve a DataView item that was previously added to the cache.

```
DataView Source;
Source = (DataView)Cache["MyData1"];
if(Source != null)
{
  MyDataGrid.DataSource = Source;
  MyDataGrid.DataBind();
}
```

It's worth noting that a type cast is used here to cast the cached item, which is of type Object, to the DataView type that we are expecting.

GetEnumerator

The GetEnumerator method gets an IDictionaryEnumerator that can be used to iterate through items in the cache.

```
public IDictionaryEnumerator GetEnumerator();
```

Insert

The Insert method enables one of four different versions of this method to insert an item into the cache. This allows us to add items to the cache without having to specify all of the parameters that are needed when using the Add method. The four different overloaded versions of this method are listed below:

```
public void Insert(string, object);

public void Insert(string, object, CacheDependency);

public void Insert(string, object, CacheDependency, DateTime,
                   TimeSpan);

public void Insert(string, object, CacheDependency, DateTime,
                   TimeSpan, CacheItemPriority, CacheItemRemovedCallback);
```

The simplest form of this method would simply insert an item into the cache and assign default values for all of the other parameters.

```
Cache.Insert("MyItemKey", MyItemValue);
```

On the other hand the most complex form of this method would look nearly identical to the Add method described earlier in this section. See the *Programmatic Caching of Objects with Expiration* example following the Cache class reference for more details and an example.

Remove

The Remove method takes for input a string that acts as a key index to a cached item. Typically items are automatically removed from the cache according to the information you provide regarding duration and dependencies. However, it is sometimes desirable to remove an item from the cache explicitly, perhaps when an authenticated user logs off and you want to remove any cached items pertaining to that user. This is done by using the Remove method of the Cache class. The Remove method takes only one parameter, which is the key of the item you wish to remove.

```
public object Remove(string key);
```

For example:

```
Cache.Remove("MyData1");
```

Cache Protected Methods

❑ Finalize – inherited from System.Object, see Introduction for details.

❑ MemberwiseClone – inherited from System.Object, see Introduction for details.

Cache Public Properties

❑ **Count**

❑ **Item**

Count

The Count property gets an integer indicating the number of items stored in the cache.

```
public int Count {get;}
```

Item

The Item property is the default property of the Cache class that can be used to retrieve items by specifying an item's key. This allows you to use the Cache object that is exposed to your application in much the same way as using the Application object in classic ASP. In other words, we can just reference our application's Cache instance followed by a key value in order to both retrieve and insert items into the cache as upcoming examples will show.

```
public object this[string key] {get; set;}
```

Notice that when retrieving items from the cache, this property returns a type of Object. So, for example, when retrieving a String item, you would want to call the ToString method to use the item.

```
string MyString;
myString = Cache["MyItem"].ToString();
```

The following code shows an example of inserting the value of a textbox into the cache:

```
Cache["UserName"] = txtName.Text;
```

Example: Programmatic Caching of Objects with Expiration

In this example, `developers.cs`, we create a class to act as a data source for a datagrid. If the data in this class instance were stable over time and expensive to create, it might be better to cache the object so any page could use it without creating an instance.

```
public class developer
{
  private string devName;
  private string preferredLanguage;
  private int phoneExtension;
  private string itemCreationTime;

  public developer(string devName, string preferredLanguage,
                   int phoneExtension, string itemCreationTime)
  {
    this.devName = devName;
    this.preferredLanguage = preferredLanguage;
    this.phoneExtension = phoneExtension;
    this.itemCreationTime = itemCreationTime;
  }

  public string Developer
  {
    get
    {
      return devName;
    }
  }

  public string Language
  {
    get
    {
      return preferredLanguage;
    }
  }

  public int Extension
  {
    get
    {
      return phoneExtension;
    }
  }

  public string objectCreationTime
  {
```

```
    get
      {
        return itemCreationTime;
      }
    }
}
```

Next we create a page with a datagrid, `programmaticCacheAdd.aspx`, and if the item already exists in the cache we bind the datagrid to the `Developer` class instance in the cache. Otherwise, we create an instance of the datasource (as an `ArrayList`), store it in the cache then databind and render.

Like output caching, we'll set an expiration time for the cached object of 10 seconds. When we refresh the page, the creation time property for each developer will update every 10 seconds as the old cached instance is removed from memory and a new instance is created upon page creation.

```
public class programmaticCacheAdd : System.Web.UI.Page
{
  protected Label Label1;
  protected Label Label2;
  protected DataGrid DataGrid1;

  private void Page_Load(object sender, System.EventArgs e)
  {
    //create an ArrayList of Developer objects
    if(Cache["developers"] == null)
    {
      ArrayList developers = new ArrayList();
      developers.Add(new systemWebCachingCs.developer("Janell B.",
        "C++", 815, DateTime.Now.ToString()));
      developers.Add(new systemWebCachingCs.developer("Jeff M.",
        "Fortran", 699, DateTime.Now.ToString()));
      developers.Add(new systemWebCachingCs.developer("Joe C.",
        "JScript", 180, DateTime.Now.ToString()));
      developers.Add(new systemWebCachingCs.developer("Wade R.",
        "C#", 549, DateTime.Now.ToString()));

      //set DataSource and DataBind
      //DataGrid1.
      DataGrid1.DataSource = developers;

      //Use insert so we can explicitly set the expiration time

      Cache.Insert("developers", developers, null,
                   DateTime.Now.AddSeconds(10), TimeSpan.Zero);
    }
    else
      DataGrid1.DataSource = Cache["developers"];

    DataGrid1.DataBind();

    //See the cache contents
    renderCache();
```

```
        Label2.Text = "Cache count is:" + Cache.Count.ToString();

        // Item property can be used implicitly or explicitly for
        // vb index references
        Cache["dog"] = 3;
        Cache["dog"] = 4;
    }

    private void renderCache()
    {
        // This sub loops through the cache dictionary

        // Declare variables.
        string dictName;

        // Display all the items stored in the ASP.NET cache.
        Label1.Text += "<b>The ASP.NET application cache contains:" +
          "</b><br/><table border=\"1\" >";

        Label1.Text += "<thead><th>Key</th><th>Value</th></thead>";

        // loop the cache dictionary and render a table of contents
        foreach(DictionaryEntry dictItem in Cache)
        {
            dictName = dictItem.Key.ToString();
            Label1.Text += "<tr><td>key=" + dictName + "</td><td>";
            Label1.Text += "value=" + Convert.ToString(dictItem.Value) +
              "</td></tr>";
        }
        Label1.Text += "</table>";

    }
}
```

This example demonstrates the two ways to reference items in the collection, using either the `Item` property or the implicit item reference. We also loop through the cache for good measure, revealing a large number of cache items that are instantiated and used by the runtime and use the `Cache.Count` property to reveal the cache item tally. If you refresh the page and look carefully through the list you will see the "dog" and "developers" objects we create in the page.

CacheDependency

The `CacheDependency` class is used to track dependencies between an item in the cache and files, directories, or keys to other items in the cache. You create and use an instance of `CacheDependency` as a parameter of the `Add` and `Insert` methods of the `Cache` class.

In all cases, whatever is identified as a dependency for a cached item will be monitored by the system. When a change is made to this file, directory, or other cached item, the system will automatically remove the dependent item from the cache.

CacheDependency Public Constructors

There are eight different constructors for this class.

- ❑ Creates a dependency with the file or directory specified.

  ```
  public CacheDependency(string);
  ```

- ❑ Creates a dependency between the item and an array of files or directories.

  ```
  public CacheDependency(string[]);
  ```

- ❑ Creates a dependency with the file or directory specified as a string and a datetime value that indicates when file change tracking is to begin.

  ```
  public CacheDependency(string, DateTime);
  ```

- ❑ Creates a dependency with an array of files or directories specified as a string array and a datetime value that specifies when tracking for changes in the dependents is to commence.

  ```
  public CacheDependency(string[], DateTime);
  ```

- ❑ Creates a dependency between the item and an array of files or directories and an array of cache keys.

  ```
  public CacheDependency(string[], string[]);
  ```

- ❑ Creates a dependency between the item and an array of files or directories and an array of cache keys and a cache dependency class instance.

  ```
  public CacheDependency(string[], string[], CacheDependency);
  ```

- ❑ Creates a dependency between the item and an array of files or directories and an array of cache keys and specifies when tracking for changes in the dependents is to commence.

  ```
  public CacheDependency(string[], string[],  DateTime);
  ```

- ❑ Creates a dependency between the item and an array of files or directories and an array of cache keys and a cache dependency class instance, as well as specifying when tracking for changes in the dependents is to commence.

  ```
  public CacheDependency(string[], string[], CacheDependency,
                         DateTime);
  ```

The wide variety of constructors reflects a highly flexible means of determining cache dependencies that includes files and directories, related cache items and other cache dependency instances as well as allowing you to set a start time for monitoring of changes.

The following example inserts a new item into the cache identified by the key CustomerData and which contains an object identified by the variable MyCustomerObject. In this case, we set this item's existence in the cache to be dependent on an XML file named cust.xml. Now, whenever a change is made to this XML file, our CustomerData item would automatically be evicted from the cache by ASP.NET.

```
Cache.Insert("CustomerData", MyCustomerObject, new
             CacheDependency(Server.MapPath("cust.xml")));
```

CacheDependency Public Methods

- ❑ **Dispose**
- ❑ `Equals` – inherited from `System.Object`, see Introduction for details.
- ❑ `GetHashCode` – inherited from `System.Object`, see Introduction for details.
- ❑ `GetType` – inherited from `System.Object`, see Introduction for details.
- ❑ `ToString` – inherited from `System.Object`, see Introduction for details.

Dispose

The `Dispose` method releases the resources associated with the `CacheDependency` instance.

```
public void Dispose();
```

CacheDependency Protected Methods

- ❑ `Finalize` – inherited from `System.Object`, see Introduction for details.
- ❑ `MemberwiseClone` – inherited from `System.Object`, see Introduction for details.

CacheDependency Public Properties

- ❑ **HasChanged**

HasChanged

The `HasChanged` property gets a `Boolean` that specifies whether the items tracked by the `CacheDependency` instance have changed. If the property returns `True` the `CacheDependency` has changed so the items currently in the `Cache` are invalid and hence you may need to recreate those items.

```
public bool HasChanged {get;}
```

CacheItemRemovedCallback Delegate

This `CachedItemRemovedCallback` delegate defines a callback method for notifying your application when an item is removed from the cache.

```
public delegate void CacheItemRemovedCallback(string key,
                                              object value,
                                              CacheItemRemovedReason reason);
```

To allow your application to be notified whenever an item is removed from the cache, you must create an event handler that has the same parameters as this delegate declaration. An example of such a method follows.

Example: Using the CacheItemRemovedCallback Delegate

The caching namespace provides a delegate so that your method can be invoked when the cached item is removed from the cache, `CacheItemRemovedCallback`. Typically you would use this delegate to create a common method for re-creating and refreshing the cached item.

The page declaration provides a single label control we will use to report the status and reason for the item being removed from the cache. The real meat is in the code behind, `cacheDependencyPage.aspx.cs`, which is as follows:

```
public class cacheDependencyPage : System.Web.UI.Page
{
  protected System.Web.UI.WebControls.Label Label1;
  private static CacheItemRemovedCallback onRemove;

  public void RemovedCallback(string k, object v, CacheItemRemovedReason r)
  {
    //Code to be executed when item is removed
    Label1.Text = "Item removed from cache because of '" +
                r.ToString() + "' and callback invoked";

  }

  private void Page_Load(object sender, System.EventArgs e)
  {

    string MyObject = "Hi there!";

    DateTime d = new DateTime();
    d.AddSeconds(30);
    TimeSpan t = new TimeSpan();

    onRemove = new CacheItemRemovedCallback(this.RemovedCallback);

    //Inserts the item into the cache
    Cache.Insert("MyItemKey", MyObject, null, d, t,
              CacheItemPriority.High, onRemove);

    Cache.Remove("MyItemKey");

    //Removes item from the cache which causes the callback to execute
    Cache.Remove("MyItemKey");
  }
}
```

The reason an item was removed from the cache is handed to our item removed handler and is delineated in the `CacheItemRemovedReason` enumeration, which is referenced hereafter. This is demonstrated in the resultant page, as shown in the screenshot below:

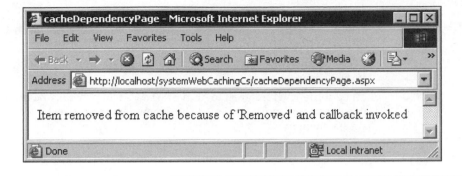

CacheItemRemovedReason Enumeration

`CacheItemRemovedReason` enumeration notifies your application when items are removed from the cache, and the reason why the item was removed.

- ❑ `DependencyChanged` – the item was removed because a file or key dependency changed.

- ❑ `Expired` – the item was removed because it expired.

- ❑ `Removed` – the item was explicitly removed using either the `Remove` or `Insert` method; the `Insert` method will cause an item to be removed if the key specified already exists in the cache.

- ❑ `Underused` – the item was removed because the sliding expiration was exceeded or the system needed to remove the item to free system memory.

CacheItemPriority Enumeration

`CacheItemPriority` enumeration allows you to assign items in your cache a value that will determine whether it is deleted before or after other items. If you wish for an item to be purged from the cache before others, you would assign it a lower priority value, though the default is `Normal`.

```
public enum CacheItemPriority
```

Possible values for this enumeration are:

Values	Description
NotRemovable	Those cached items with the NotRemovable value of enumeration will be excluded from removal when a system is seeking to remove items from memory.
Normal	Those items with a Normal priority level will be targeted for removal from the cache after those with Low or BelowNormal priority only.
Low	At this priority level, the cached item has the highest chance of being the first to be deleted when the server is seeking more memory.
High	Those items with High priority level are the most protected from deletion when the server is freeing system memory.

Table continued on following page

Values	Description
Default	The default priority value is Normal.
BelowNormal	Items assigned this value will usually be deleted before those with a Normal value.
AboveNormal	The priority level assigned to AboveNormal will generally be deleted after those assigned with a Normal value when the server is seeking to free system memory.

wrox

Programmer to Programmer™

7

System.Web.Configuration

The Web.config Configuration File

The web.config is an XML file that provides users with support for easily adding configurable properties to ASP.NET applications. Previously developers have used .ini files or registry keys to allow applications to store and retrieve values and settings without having to recompile the application. System.Web.Configuration provides a new and more powerful approach to maintaining application settings and preferences, using .config files to store items and a Configuration object to retrieve it.

ASP.NET has two types of configuration file, named the web.config file and the machine.config file. The web.config file primarily specifies settings to be used by the ASP.NET run-time in relation to a particular application including such things as debug tracing status, authentication, authorization and other details. A very common use of the web.config file is the storage of data access details like user names and passwords for accessing data sources. The configuration file can also contain application-specific name value pairs that can be used globally by the application by reference and then conveniently changed in a single location without requiring a developer to recompile or make code changes elsewhere. This capability is particularly important in high reliability/up-time web applications because it allows you to make changes at an application scope *without* shutting down the application.

The machine.config file is used to specify settings that apply to *all* ASP.NET applications on the server and there can be only one of these per server. The settings stored within this file are inherited by all of the ASP.NET applications. Therefore, if the machine.config file contained a setting specifying that session state is to be maintained, then that setting would apply to all ASP.NET applications on the server. However, if there was one application that was designed to be run without any session state being maintained, then that application could specify in its web.config file that no session state is to be kept, thus overriding the machine.config setting. This information would apply to this application only. Therefore individual applications can each have a web.config file and the settings in this file always override settings first specified in machine.config.

The relationship between `machine.config` files and `web.config` files is illustrated in the following diagram:

```
                    machine.config

        <appSettings>
                <add key=DatabaseServer value="MainSql">
                <add key=DatabaseDataSource
                value="Northwind"/>
                <add key=Login value=appUser/>
                <add key=PassWd value=appUser/>
        </appSettings>
```

```
  \wwwroot\Reports\web.config

<appSettings>
        <add key=DatabaseDataSource
        value="Reporting"/>
        <add key=Login value=reportUser/>
        <add key=PassWd value=reportUser/>
</appSettings>
```

```
  \wwwroot\management\web.config

<appSettings>
        <add key=DatabaseDataSource
        value="Personnel2/>
        <add key=Login value=adminUser/>
        <add key=PassWd value=adminUser/>
</appsettings>
```

In this example, all applications, other than those in the `Reports` and `Management` directories, will access the `Northwind` database with the login information provided in the `machine.config` file. However, the `Management` ASP.NET application will access the `Personnel` database using different login credentials. Also, the `Reports` ASP.NET application will access the `Reporting` database using another set of login credentials. It is important to note that the child applications need not define a setting for the `DatabaseServer` property, as they will inherit this from `machine.config`.

`Web.config` files are written in XML-based text and are formatted as below:

```
<configuration>
  <system.web>
    <sessionState timeout="10" />
  </system.web>
</configuration>
```

The code illustrated above will cause the ASP.NET application to timeout the `Session` after 10 minutes of inactivity, overriding the default of 20 minutes set in the server's `machine.config` file. The code is structured with the `<sessionState>` setting held within the `<system.web>` element, and the whole file wrapped within the `<configuration>` element. This example demonstrates just one of a large number of settings that can be defined within a `web.config` file to control web application behavior. Full details of the settings available to the `web.config` file are shown in the following sections.

> It is critical to remember, particularly for Visual Basic programmers, that XML syntax is case sensitive. Given the growing prevalence of XML and the popularity of case-sensitive languages such as C#, it is a good general practice to treat Visual Basic code as though it were case sensitive. In this way, Visual Basic programmers can work with XML with fewer unnecessary headaches!

538

<appSettings>

```
<appSettings>
  <add>
  <remove>
  <clear>
```

The `<appSettings>` section contains application-specific settings. Database connection information would typically be placed here. The section is composed of `<add>` tags, which add configuration settings as key-value pairs, as demonstrated below:

```
<appSettings>
  <add key="KeyName" value="KeyValue" />
</appSettings>
```

Additionally, the section supports `<remove>` and `<clear>` tags which remove and clear previously specified application settings, respectively.

Example: Using <appSettings>

Consider the following `<appSettings>` section in a `web.config` file:

```
<appSettings>
  <add key="theUsual" value="Hello World!" />
</appSettings>
```

The page code, `appSettingsDemo.aspx`, is as follows (remember that you will have to make the directory where this file and the `web.config` reside into a virtual application in IIS):

```
<%@ Page language="c#" Codebehind="appSettingsDemo.aspx.cs"
AutoEventWireup="false" Inherits="systemWebConfigurationCs.appSettingsDemo" %>
<!DOCTYPE HTML PUBLIC "-//W3C//DTD HTML 4.0 Transitional//EN" >
<HTML>
  <HEAD>
    <title>appSettingsDemo</title>
    <meta name="GENERATOR" Content="Microsoft Visual Studio 7.0">
    <meta name="CODE_LANGUAGE" Content="C#">
    <meta name="vs_defaultClientScript" content="JavaScript">
    <meta name="vs_targetSchema"
          content="http://schemas.microsoft.com/intellisense/ie5">
  </HEAD>
  <body>
    <form id="Form1" method="post" runat="server">
      <asp:Label id="Label1" runat="server"></asp:Label>
    </form>
  </body>
</HTML>
```

The code behind for this page, `appSettingsDemo.aspx.cs`, uses `ConfigurationSettings.AppSettings` to extract the value set in the `web.config` file for `appSettings`:

```
public class appSettingsDemo : System.Web.UI.Page
  {
     protected System.Web.UI.WebControls.Label Label1;

     private void Page_Load(object sender, System.EventArgs e)
     {
       Label1.Text = ConfigurationSettings.AppSettings["theUsual"];

       // If you remove the comment from the code
       // below the page will throw an exception because application
       // values are read only once the application is initialized

       //ConfigurationSettings.AppSettings["theUsual"] = "Other Text";
     }
       ...

  }
```

The output from this code, with the `ConfigurationSettings.AppSettings` line above (in bold) commented out would be as follows:

<authentication>

The <authentication> setting is written in the following format:

```
<authentication mode="Windows|Forms|Passport|None">
  <forms name="name"
         loginUrl="url"
         protection="All|None|Encryption|Validation"
         timeout="30" path="/" >
    <credentials passwordFormat="Clear|SHA1|MD5">
```

```
        <user name="username" password="password" />
      </credentials>
    </forms>
    <passport redirectUrl="internal"/>
  </authentication>
```

The `<authentication>` section specifies the application authentication mode. It supports four modes and various settings for each of these modes. The default mode is `Windows` but we can configure for other modes using the `mode` attribute of the `<authentication>` element. The required `mode` attribute specifies one of the following values:

❑ `Windows`
The application defaults to `Windows` authentication. It requires that the browser participates in `Windows` and IIS-base authentication using `Basic`, `Digest`, and `Integrated Windows Authentication`.

❑ `Forms`
If `mode` is set to `Forms`, we have a child element of `<authentication>` called `<forms>` that allows us to define behaviors for forms authentication.

❑ `Passport`
This `mode` is used if it is necessary for the application to be compatible with Microsoft Passport `authentication` and `authorization`.

❑ `None`
The application is set to anonymous user access.

Forms authentication allows us to use HTML forms to request credentials, and then issue an HTTP cookie that the requestor may use for identity on subsequent requests. ASP.NET provides the infrastructure to support this, but also gives us the flexibility to choose how we wish to validate credentials. For more information on authentication see Chapter 8.

The validation of credentials is completely up to us. Once the credentials are validated, we can then call some of the APIs provided by Forms authentication to issue an HTTP cookie to the requestor. On subsequent requests, the cookie is provided along with the request body, and ASP.NET can use the information in the cookie to recreate a valid identity.

`<authorization>`

The `<authorization>` section determines who is granted access to application resources. The `<authorization>` section includes `<allow>` and `<deny>` sub-tags that each support attributes where you may specify that you permit or deny by particular user, group, or verb. The default value for `<authorization>` gives access to all users:

```
<allow users="*" />
```

The verb attribute refers to the HTTP verb-type permitted access to the resource and can specify control over `post`, `get`, `head` and `debug` requests. The attributes must be provided as comma separated lists.

```
<authorization>
  <allow users="comma-separated list of users"
         roles="comma-separated list of roles"
         verbs="comma-separated list of verbs" />

  <deny users="comma-separated list of users"
        roles="comma-separated list of roles"
        verbs="comma-separated list of verbs" />
</authorization>
```

An example of this is demonstrated below:

```
<configuration>
  <system.web>
    <authentication mode="Forms">
      <forms name=".ASPXAUTH" loginUrl="login.aspx"
                  protection="all" timeout="30" path="/" >
      </forms>
    </authentication>
    <authorization>
      <allow users="Chris, Rob, Martin" roles="Administrator, Customer" />
      <allow verb="POST" users="Chris" />
      <deny users="?" roles="Blacklist" />
      <deny verb="POST" users="*" />
    </authorization>
  </system.web>
</configuration>
```

In the above configuration settings, we define `<authorization>` settings that allow the users `Chris`, `Rob` and `Martin`, as well as the roles of `Administrator` and `Customer`. We also allow `Chris` to use the `post` verb, but we explicitly declare that we have denied the `post` verb to everybody. This may seem contradictory but is possible because Chris has his `allow verb` above the `deny verb` and the higher `verb` in the configuration file takes precedence. In addition, all anonymous users (identified by `?`) and those on the `Blacklist` will not be granted access. For each `allow` and `deny` verb included in the `<authorization>` section, you will need to include a `users` or a `roles` attribute.

<browserCaps>

The `<browserCaps>` section is used to specify the browser capabilities. It contains a `<result>` tag that specifies the base `HttpBrowserCapabilities` class instance to be used to determine browser capabilities. Browser characteristics are defined using a filter system where `<use>` specifies the server variable to `<filter>` on and each `<case>` specifies particular capabilities or properties for the agent.

The `<browserCaps>` section can be useful in the event that the ASP.NET browser capabilities component is unable to determine any of the browser's capabilities. In those cases, the default value will be returned by the `HttpBrowserCapabilities` class.

```
<browserCaps>
  <result type="class" />
  <use var="HTTP_USER_AGENT" />
    browser=Unknown
```

```
      version=0.0
      majorver=0
      minorver=0
      frames=false
      tables=false
      <filter>
        <case match="Windows 98|Win98">
          platform=Win98
        </case>
        <case match="Windows NT|WinNT">
        platform=WinNT
      </case>
    </filter>
    <filter match="Unknown" with="%(browser)">
      <filter match="Win95" with="%(platform)">
      </filter>
    </filter>
  </browserCaps>
```

Example: Using <browserCaps>

Here is a simple example, browserCapsDemo.aspx.cs, where we are going to use the settings in
our web.config file as defaults if we can't determine at run time the capabilities of our
user's browser:

```
public class BrowserCapsDemo : System.Web.UI.Page
  {
    protected Label Label1;
    private void Page_Load(object sender, System.EventArgs e)
    {
      HttpBrowserCapabilities bc = Request.Browser;

      if(!bc.Frames)
        Label1.Text = "No Frames detected";
      else
        Label1.Text = "Frames support detected.";
    }
  ...
}
```

In the event that the browser's capabilities can't be determined by the application's
HttpBrowserCapabilities object, the value of the bc.Frames property would be determined
by what was the default setting in the configuration file.

The <browserCaps> section of the web.config file for this application is shown below:

```
<browserCaps>
  <result type="System.Web.HttpBrowserCapabilities" />
  <use var="HTTP_USER_AGENT" />
  browser="Unknown"
```

```
version=0.0
  majorver=0
  minorver=0
  frames=false
  tables=false
  <filter>
    <case match="Windows 95 | Win95">
      platform=Win95
    </case>
    <case match="Windows NT | WinNT">
      platform=WinNT
    </case>
  </filter>
</browserCaps>
```

As `frames` in the `web.config` file is set to `false`, the output from this code is as below :

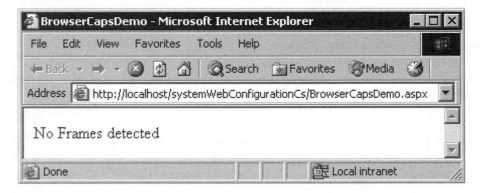

Alternatively, with `frames` in the `web.config` file set to `true`, the following page will be produced:

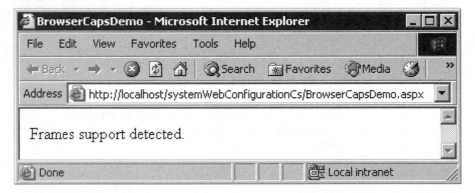

Although the application's `HttpBrowserCapabilities` object will usually be able to identify the browser, this could be an issue if a new browser is used, or if a request is made to the server from a browser that is not recognized, or not supported. In ASP.NET applications, the browser capabilities are exposed via the `Browser` property of the `Request` object.

<clientTarget>

The <clientTarget> section lets you add aliases for client agents to the internal collection used by the runtime to reference browser type, where <add> can add a new alias and <remove> and <clear> can remove individual aliases or clear the collection, respectively.

```
<clientTarget>
  <add alias="alias name to use"
       userAgent="identification of user agent" />
  <remove alias="alias name to remove" />
  <clear />
</clientTarget>
```

<compilation>

The <compilation> section is used to specify the compile options for ASP.NET applications. These options include specifying which compiler to use for specific file extensions, which assemblies to reference during compilation, and which namespaces to include at compilation time.

The example below lists the possible values for the various options within the <compilation> setting:

```
<compilation debug="true|false"
             batch="true|false"
             batchTimeout="number of seconds"
             defaultLanguage="language"
             explicit="true|false"
             maxBatchSize="maximim number of pages per
                          batched compilation"
             maxBatchGeneratedFileSize="maximum combined size (in KB)
                                       of the generated source file per
                                       batched compilation"
             numRecompilesBeforeAppRestart="number"
             strict="true|false"
             tempDirectory="directory under which the ASP.NET temporary
                           files are created" >
  <compilers>
    <compiler language="language"
              extension="ext"
              type=".NET Type"
              warningLevel="number"
              compilerOptions="options" />
  </compilers>

  <assemblies>
    <add assembly="assembly" />
    <remove assembly="assembly"  />
    <clear />
  </assemblies>
  <namespaces>
    <add namespace="System.Web" />
    <add namespace="System.Web.UI" />
    <add namespace="System.Web.UI.WebControls" />
    <add namespace="System.Web.UI.HtmlControls" />
  </namespaces>

</compilation>
```

The following example includes actual values against the tags:

```
<compilation defaultLanguage="VB"
             debug="false"
             numRecompilesBeforeAppRestart="15"
             explicit="true"
             strict="true"
             batch="false" >

  <compilers>
    <compiler language="VB;VBScript"
              extension=".cls"
              type="Microsoft.VB. VBCodeProvider,System" />
    <compiler language="C#;Csharp"
              extension=".cs"
              type="Microsoft.CSharp. CSharpCodeProvider,System" />
  </compilers>

  <assemblies>
    <add assembly="*" />
  </assemblies>

  <namespaces>
    <add namespace="System.Web" />
    <add namespace="System.Web.UI" />
    <add namespace="System.Web.UI.WebControls" />
    <add namespace="System.Web.UI.HtmlControls" />
  </namespaces>

</compilation>
```

<customErrors>

The `<customErrors>` section lets your application specify how run-time errors are rendered to the client. The required `mode` attribute specifies whether `customErrors` is `On`, `Off` or the default value of `RemoteOnly`. `On` means users receive a generic error message or are redirected to a custom error-handling page specified by the `defaultRedirect` attribute. `Off` means any user will get the full ASP.NET error handling output. `RemoteOnly` is good for developers because it shows remote users the custom page while `localhost` users (like developers) are given the gory details.

The `<error>` sub-tag lets you specify custom error pages for known server level errors by error codes like "500", "404", and so on.

```
<customErrors defaultRedirect="url"
              mode="On|Off|RemoteOnly">
  <error statusCode="statuscode"
         redirect="url"/>
</customErrors>
```

<globalization>

The <globalization> section is used to specify globalization options for the ASP.NET application. The requestEncoding, responseEncoding, and fileEncoding properties are used to specify which encoding method is to be used for processing requests, responses, and files handled by the ASP.NET application. These settings can be used to override a server's Regional Options settings for the Encoding method.

The Culture value is used to specify the CultureInfo object from which to retrieve culture-specific information. This information typically defines the proper formatting of dates and numbers, default languages, and country or region information. The Culture property is used to specify the culture used when handling requests to the web server. The uiCulture property is used to specify the culture used when executing locale-dependent resource searches.

```
<globalization requestEncoding="any valid encoding string"
               responseEncoding="any valid encoding string"
               fileEncoding="any valid encoding string"
               culture="any valid culture string"
               uiCulture="any valid culture string" />
```

The full list of cultures is extensive but listed below are some of the most commonly used.

CultureString	Country & Language
en-US	US– English
en-GB	Great Britain – English
De	German
de-DE	Germany – German
Fr	French
fr-CA	Canada – French
It	Italian
ru-RU	Russia – Russian
es-MX	Mexico – Spanish
zh-CHS	China – Chinese (Simplified)

Here is an example of a <globalization> section in which we specify the encoding method as "US ASCII" and the culture to be "US English".

```
<globalization
  requestEncoding="us-ascii"
  responseEncoding="ISO-8859-1"
  culture="en-US"
  uiCulture="en-US" />
```

Note: **The only property from the `<globalization>` section that has an easily identified impact on the resulting web pages is the `responseEncoding` property.** We can see the effect of this property's setting when examining the header of an ASP.NET page in the browser's View Source command. In the headers is a line specifying the content-type and charset. For many pages, the line appears like this:

```
<META HTTP-EQUIV="content-type" CONTENT="text/html; charset=ISO-8859-1">
```

It has a marked impact as it determines the character set to use in displaying the page.

<httpHandlers>

The `<httpHandlers>` section allows ASP.NET to configure request handlers. Request handlers specify which .dll or server components are to be handed inbound client requests based on the requested file type extension and the HTTP verb such as get and post. In classic ASP this was handled by IIS, via the MMC console, and as such was cumbersome when a multi-server application deployment needed to be updated because each machine had to be updated manually via MMC. By configuring request handlers in the configuration file, distribution and deployment are greatly simplified.

For example, to have any request for an .idq file passed to the Microsoft Index Server, you would configure the `<httpHandlers>` section as follows:

```
<httpHandlers>
  <add verb="verb list"
       path="path/wildcard"
       type="type,assemblyname"
       validate="true|false" />
  <remove verb="verb list"
          path="path/wildcard" />
  <clear />
</httpHandlers>
<httpHandlers>
  <add verb="GET, HEAD, POST"
       path="*.idq"
       type="idq,idq.dll" />
</httpHandlers>
```

In addition this section can also be used to *remove* handlers that were inherited from either the machine.config or the parent directory. If we wanted to remove the .idq handler, the section would appear like this:

```
<httpHandlers>
  <remove verb="GET, HEAD, POST"
          path="*.idq"  />
</httpHandlers>
```

As another option in the <httpHandlers> section, it is possible to remove all application <httpHandlers> mappings by using the <clear> tag:

```
<httpHandlers>
  <clear />
</httpHandlers>
```

Any of the settings in the <httpHandlers> section will apply not only to the existing directory, but to any directory below it as well. **Note: Any settings in the configuration files will override those from the Internet Services MMC, but will only apply to ASP.NET applications.**

<httpModules>

The <httpModules> section is used to determine which <httpModules> will be loaded with the ASP.NET application. <httpModules> are objects that are involved in each request to the server. These modules all expose events, which a developer can catch and process in the web application's global.asax.

```
<httpModules>
  <add type="classname,assemblyname" name="modulename" />
  <remove name="modulename" />
  <clear />
</httpModules>
```

The <httpModules> provided with ASP.NET are listed here, along with their function:

Member	Function
DefaultAuthenticationModule	Provides an Authentication object that can be used within the application
FileAuthorizationModule	Ensures that a user has the correct permissions to access the requested file
FormsAuthenticationModule	Provides the application with the ability to use FormsAuthentication
PassportAuthenticationModule	Provides wrapper functions for integrating PassportAuthentication into .NET applications
SessionStateModule	Provides the basic IIS session state object
UrlAuthorizationModule	Provides for authenticating access to a file or server resource via a URL
WindowsAuthenticationModule	Provides the application with the ability to use WindowsAuthentication

All `httpModules`, including those that are customized and extended, must implement the `iHttpModule interface`. Once a module is loaded with the application, the ASP.NET code can then make use of it. Since those familiar with classic ASP will be familiar with `Sessions`, we will look at the `SessionStateModule`. This module provides the application with the `Session` object. In order to be able to use `Session` objects, we must include the `SessionStateModule` in the application's configuration file. The syntax for this would be:

```
<httpModules>
  <add types="System.Web.State.SessionStateModule" name="Session">
</httpModules>
```

But, since session state is widely used in ASP.NET applications, the `machine.config` file already includes this module, so there is no need to declare it in `web.config`.

<httpRuntime>

The `<httpRuntime>` section lets you specify parameters that effect the runtime environment for page execution.

```
<httpRuntime useFullyQualifiedRedirectUrl="true|false"
             maxRequestLength="size in kbytes"
             executionTimeout="seconds"
             minFreeThreads="number of threads"
             minFreeLocalRequestFreeThreads="number of threads"
             appRequestQueueLimit="number of requests" />
```

The table below provides details on the values and purpose of the parameters used in `httpRuntime`:

Parameter	Function
`appRequestQueueLimit`	When amount of requests waiting in the queue exceed the limit specified in this attribute a "503 - Server Too Busy" error is generated. Requests are queued when there are not enough free threads to process the request.
`executionTimeout`	Specifies the timeout value in seconds for execution in ASP.NET pages.
`maxRequestLength`	Specifies the maximum file upload size.
`minFreeLocalRequestFreeThreads`	Sets the minimum number of free threads set aside for use by local requests.
`minFreeThreads`	Specifies the number of threads kept free by the runtime to handle execution of new requests.
`useFullyQualifiedRedirectUrl`	A `Boolean` value that specifies whether client-side redirect URLs are automatically formatted to be fully qualified or may be relative. `False` could yield a relative URL while `True` would force a fully qualified URL in all cases.

<identity>

The <identity> section of the configuration file can be used to specify which Windows user to impersonate when making requests from the operating system. The impersonate attribute determines whether client impersonation is used. If impersonate is set to true, ASP.NET will run under the identity provided by IIS. This would be whatever identity that IIS is configured to impersonate. However, if impersonate is set to false, which is the default value, then the web application executes with the permissions of the username and password values supplied.

```
<identity impersonate="true|false"
          userName="username"
          password="password"/>
```

If a web application should allow resource access based on the requesting user's own permissions, then the <identity> section would be:

```
<identity impersonate="True" />
```

Furthermore, any processes or resource requests executed by the web application would be run under the user account of the user that is requesting the page. Alternatively, to give all users the same access, then the <identity> section should look like this:

```
<identity
   impersonate="False"
   username="WebUser"
   password="WebPass"
/>
```

In controlling the identity of the impersonation account used by ASP.NET, we have control over what any particular user may or may not do. However, we also have to provide the impersonation account with the appropriate levels of access to be able to accomplish meaningful work in our system. Keep in mind that the user impersonated needs to have the necessary file access permissions, so that they are not too restricted, yet, it is also therefore necessary to ensure that you are not giving full access to everybody who may use your application. As a general rule, it is a good idea to explicitly grant access for exactly and only what is needed and, by default, grant access to nothing.

See Chapter 8 for more information about web security.

<machineKey>

ASP.NET uses a key to encrypt or hash some data so that the data is only accessible from the server that created the data. The <machineKey> section helps you specify how the server generates keys for encryption and decryption of forms authentication cookie data. Within this setting, there are three attributes: validationKey, decryptionKey and validation. Those operating across a network of web servers will want to specify a consistent value for validationKey and decryptionKey across servers rather then specify autogenerate, which is the default value. The validation attribute specifies the encryption method.

> It is important to remember that this section cannot be declared at the subdirectory level but is declared at the machine, site, or application levels.

```
<machineKey validationKey="autogenerate|value"
            decryptionKey="autogenerate|value"
            validation="SHA1|MD5|3DES" />
```

The attribute values for the `<machineKey>` element attributes are listed below:

Attribute Values	Function
`autogenerate`	Default value. A key that is randomly generated by ASP.NET and held in Local Security Authority.
`value`	A deliberately assigned value that overrides the `autogenerate` default. There are a number of security related restrictions attached to this value which dictate that the key must be at least 40 characters (20 bytes) and no more that 128 characters (64 bytes).
`MD5, SHA1, 3DES`	The three possible `validation` values that determine which encryption type ASP.NET will use are MD5, SHA1 and 3DES. The default is `SHA1`.

\<pages\>

The `<pages>` section is used to specify any page-specific settings. There are six different page attributes that can be specified in this section. The attributes are self-descriptive and analogous to the following declaration:

```
<%@ Page attribute="value" [attribute="value"…] %>
```

Remember, if you have created a common base class for all pages or controls in your application you can easily set pageBaseType or userControlBaseType to refer to this class.

```
<pages buffer="true|false"
       enableSessionState="true|false|ReadOnly"
       enableViewState="true|false"
       enableViewStateMac="true|false"
       autoEventWireup="true|false"
       smartNavigation="true|false"
       pageBaseType="typename, assembly"
       userControlBaseType="typename" />
```

\<processModel\>

The `username` and `password` settings found in `<processModel>` are used to control the user that the ASP.NET Worker process runs as. This section can be used to enable or disable the process model, specify the maximum number of requests that are to be queued before throwing a "`Server Too Busy`" error, and many other settings. The ASP.NET `<processModel>` section can be used to improve the scalability of an application, enable multiple processes for an application, and spread those processes across the CPUs in the web server.

```
<processModel  enable="true|false"
                timeout="mins"
                idleTimeout="mins"
                shutdownTimeout="hrs:mins:secs"
                requestLimit="num"
                requestQueueLimit="Infinite|num"
                restartQueueLimit="Infinite|num"
                memoryLimit="percent"
                cpuMask="num"
                webGarden="true|false"
                userName="username"
                password="password"
                logLevel="All|None|Errors"
                clientConnectedCheck="HH:MM:SS"
                comAuthenticationLevel="Default|None|Connect|Call|
                                        Pkt|PktIntegrity|PktPrivacy"
                comImpersonationLevel="Default|Anonymous|Identify|
                                        Impersonate|Delegate"
                maxWorkerThreads="num"
                maxIoThreads="num" />
```

The attributes and their functions are listed below:

Attribute	Function
Enable	True – enable process model. False – disable process model.
Timeout	Number of minutes until IIS replaces a current process with a new one.
idleTimeout	Number of minutes until IIS shuts down an idle process.
shutdownTimeout	Number of minutes that the process has to shut itself down; after this time, IIS will shut down the process.
requestLimit	Number of requests after which IIS will launch a new process and replace the existing one.
requestQueueLimit	Number of requests required in the queue before IIS will throw an Error 503, Server Too Busy.
memoryLimit	Maximum percentage of system memory that a process can use before IIS will launch a new process.
cpuMask	Determines which processors (on a multi-processor system) can be used for ASP.NET processes.
webGarden	True – Windows determines which CPU to use. False – the cpuMask attribute is used to determine which CPU to use.
Username	The username of an account under which the process will run.

Table continued on following page

Attribute	Function
`Password`	The password for the username.
`logLevel`	`All` – Logs all process events to event log. `None` – Logs no process events to event log. `Errors` – Log only unexpected errors to event log.
`clientConnectedCheck`	Specifies the time that ASP.NET will keep a request in the queue before checking that the client is still connected.
`comAuthenticationLevel`	`Default` – uses normal authentication. `None` – Specifies no authentication. `Connect` – only authenticates the client when the client establishes a relationship with server. `Call` – authenticates the client at the beginning of each remote procedure call. `Pkt` – authenticates that all data received from expected source `PktIntegrity` – authenticates and verifies transport integrity of data transferred between the client and the server `PktPrivacy` – authenticates all previous levels and encrypts the argument value of each remote procedure call.
`maxWorkerThreads`	Specifies maximum number of threads for a process on a per-CPU basis.
`maxIoThreads`	Specifies maximum number of IO related threads for a process on a per-CPU basis.

\<securityPolicy>

The `<securityPolicy>` section is used to specify code access security configuration files that should be used when our application is set to different trust levels. These policy files contain sets of restrictions and rules that are used when determining the trust under which each ASP.NET application on the server runs. As in the `<identity>` element, it is advisable to run with the minimum number of privileges required to guard against compromises in security.

```
<securityPolicy>
  <trustLevel name="value" policyFile="value" />
</securityPolicy>
```

The `<trustLevel>` tag has attributes that specify the name used in reference to the policy file. This section allows administrators to easily configure multiple servers with the same security settings. A `<trustLevel>` of `Full` means that security policy is not restricted; there is no `policyFile` associated with this level and it is always mapped to `internal`.

```
<securityPolicy>
  <trustLevel name="Full" policyFile="internal" />
</securityPolicy>
```

There are default .config files (in WINNT/Microsoft.NET/Framework/[version]/Config/) for high, low, and no trust, which can be used directly or adapted for specific access rights. The format for these settings are as follows:

```
<securityPolicy>
  <trustLevel name="High" policyFile="web_hightrust.config" />
  <trustLevel name="Low"  policyFile="web_lowtrust.config" />
  <trustLevel name="None" policyFile="web_notrust.config" />
</securityPolicy>
```

The overall purpose of having the `<securityPolicy>` element, rather than just the `<trust>` element, is to give us the ability to define our own trust levels, with their own .config files to set up the permissions granted in that trust level.

`<sessionState>`

The `<sessionState>` section specifies how the application manages session-scoped variables or state.

The mode attribute determines where and how the session state is maintained. The `Off` mode means that no session state is maintained. `Inproc` means that the session state is maintained by the local machine. The `StateServer` mode uses a different server to maintain session state, while `SqlServer` mode also uses a different server, but maintains the session state in a SQL database. The last two options are useful when using a web farm and you wish to maintain user's sessions across multiple servers.

```
<sessionState mode="Off|Inproc|StateServer|SQLServer"
              cookieless="true|false"
              timeout="number of minutes"
              stateConnectionString="tcpip=server:port"
              sqlConnectionString="sql connection string" />
```

For this tag, the `stateConnectionString` and `sqlConnectionString` attributes are mutually exclusive. Therefore, the `stateConnectionString` attribute is only applicable if the session mode is set to `StateServer`. To use this, the ASP.NET state service located in the `aspnet_estate.exe` file, needs to be running on the remote server used to store the session state information. To use the `sqlConnectionString` attribute (only applicable when the session mode is set to `SqlServer`), as with the `StateServer` mode, you will need to be working from the machine with the server that will store the session state information. In this case, this will be the machine with SQL Server on it. It is also necessary to run `InstallSqlState.sql` from this machine to create a database, named `ASPState`, to store the new procedures and `ASPStateTempApplications` and `ASPStateTempSessions` tables in the `TempDB` database. If the mode is set to `Inproc`, then neither the `stateConnectionString` nor the `sqlConnectionString` attributes are used.

Here is how you would configure a web site to maintain session state on the machine, enable the use of cookies, and set a 30 minute timeout for the session:

```
<sessionState mode="Inproc"
              cookieless="false"
              timeout="30" />
```

And, for a web farm environment, the session state would be configured to use a SQL server for maintaining state:

```
<sessionState mode="SQLServer"
              cookieless="false"
              sqlConnectionString="data source=StateServer;
                                   userid=userstate;
                                   password=userstate"
              timeout="30" />
```

<trace>

The `<trace>` section of the configuration file is used to enable debug or execution tracing for the web site, as well as to configure the output from the trace service. The `enabled` attribute determines whether tracing is enabled (`true`) or disabled (`false`) for the web application. The `requestLimit` attribute specifies the number of requests that are stored. Once the server has processed that number of trace requests, the oldest requests will be over-written on the server.

The `pageOutput` attribute determines whether the trace output is appended to the ASP.NET pages (`true`) or if the output is only available via the .NET `Trace` utility (`false`). The `traceMode` attribute is used to sort the trace results, either by time, or by user-defined categories. Finally, the `localOnly` attribute determines if the trace viewer is only available on the local server.

```
<trace enabled="true|false"
       requestLimit="integer"
       pageOutput="true|false"
       traceMode="SortByTime|sortByCategory"
       localOnly="true|false" />
```

To configure an ASP.NET application to append trace information to ASP.NET pages, the `web.config` would have a trace section like this:

```
<trace
  enabled="true"
  requestLimit="20"
  pageOutput="true"
  traceMode="SortByTime"
  localOnly="true" />
```

<trust>

The <trust> section specifies the application's trust level settings. The `level` attribute provides four values to scale trust from `Full` to `None`. The `originUrl` attribute can be specified to achieve a notional "host" as it relates to security. By specifying the application URL, the authorization of web requests, for example, can be expedited. See also the section on *<securityPolicy>* earlier in this chapter.

```
<trust level="Full|High|Low|None" originUrl="url" />
```

<webServices>

The <webServices> section affects the operation of Web Services hosted by the machine or application. It is unlikely that developers will need to make many changes to this section of the configuration files, though those wanting to extend SOAP will need to add extensions to their web.config files to utilize their amendments.

```
<webServices>
  <protocols>
    <add name="protocol name" />
  </protocols>
  <serviceDescriptionFormatExtensionTypes>
  </serviceDescriptionFormatExtensionTypes>
  <soapExtensionTypes>
    <add type="type" />
  </soapExtensionTypes>
  <soapExtensionReflectorTypes>
    <add type="type" />
  </soapExtensionReflectorTypes>
  <soapExtensionImporterTypes>
    <add type="type" />
  </soapExtensionImporterTypes>
  <wsdlHelpGenerator href="help generator file"/>
</webServices>
```

Element	Function
wsdlHelpGenerator	Allows you to define a custom Web Service Help page that is to be displayed to a browser when a browser navigates directly to an .asmx page.
soapExtensionImporterTypes	When a service description for a Web Service is accessed to create a proxy class, the associated configuration file defines the SOAP extensions to run.
soapExtensionReflectorTypes	This parameter defines the SOAP extensions to run when a service description is created for all Web Services within the configuration file.
soapExtensionTypes	Defines the SOAP extensions to run with all Web Services within the configuration file.
serviceDescriptionFormat ExtensionTypes	Defines the service description format extension to run within the configuration file.
protocols	Transmission protocols used by ASP.NET to decrypt data sent from client.

557

The <location> Tag

Although it is not a separate section, the <location> tag is an important tag for configuration files. This tag allows specification of different configurations within the same configuration file. For example, assume a web application has three subdirectories: HTML, WML, and HDML. In this case, it would be much easier to have a single web.config file that specified the properties for all of the directories. The <location> tag is what allows this to happen. In order to specify the configuration properties for multiple directories, it is necessary to contain the properties within <location> tags.

To specify different session and timeout details for each of these three directories you could create a web.config file like this:

```
<configuration>
  <system.web>
    <sessionState cookieless="false"/>
  </system.web>

  <location path="HDML">
    <system.web>
      <sessionState timeout="5"/>
      <httpHandlers>
        <add verb="*" path="*.hdml" type="web.Hdml"/>
      </httpHandlers>
    </system.web>
  </location>

  <location path="WML">
    <system.web>
      <sessionState timeout="2"/>
      <httpHandlers>
        <add verb="*" path="*.wml" type="web.Wml"/>
      </httpHandlers>
    </system.web>
  </location>

  <location path="HTML">
    <system.web>
      <sessionState timeout="30"/>
    </system.web>
  </location>

</configuration>
```

In this example, both the HDML and WML directories will have an httpHandler included so that the directories can correctly process HDML and WML files respectively. As a result of this configuration file, each of the directories has a different session timeout value as well so the server can adapt to the different conditions.

HttpCapabilitiesBase Class

While not directly related to the application and machine configuration details covered elsewhere in this chapter, the System.Web.Configuration.HttpCapabilitiesBase class is the base class from which the System.Web.HttpBrowserCapabilities class is derived. It provides some base functionality for reading capabilities information from configuration files. These capabilities only indicate what a client is capable of and not what it will actually support.

HttpCapabilitiesBase Public Methods

- ❏ Equals – inherited from System.Object, see Introduction for details.

- ❏ **GetConfigCapabilities**

- ❏ GetHashCode – inherited from System.Object, see Introduction for details.

- ❏ GetType – inherited from System.Object, see Introduction for details.

- ❏ ToString – inherited from System.Object, see Introduction for details.

GetConfigCapabilities

The GetConfigCapabilities method takes a string and HttpRequest as input. It returns the individual browser capabilities.

```
public static HttpCapabilitiesBase GetConfigCapabilities(
            string configKey, HttpRequest request);
```

HttpCapabilitiesBase Protected Methods

- ❏ Finalize – inherited from System.Object, see Introduction for details.

- ❏ MemberwiseClone – inherited from System.Object, see Introduction for details.

HttpCapabilitiesBase Public Properties

- ❏ **Item**

Item

The Item property gets the value of the specified Browser property.

```
public virtual string this[string key] {get;}
```

HttpConfigurationContext

The HttpConfigurationContext class provides context information to configuration section handlers in the form of a single significant property that returns the virtual path to the configuration file. Configuration section handlers define which code will process and handle configuration details specified in the web.config or machine.config file.

HttpConfigurationContext Public Methods

- ❏ Equals – inherited from System.Object, see Introduction for details.

- ❏ GetHashCode – inherited from System.Object, see Introduction for details.

- ❏ GetType – inherited from System.Object, see Introduction for details.

- ❏ ToString – inherited from System.Object, see Introduction for details.

HttpConfigurationContext Protected Methods

- ❏ Finalize – inherited from System.Object, see Introduction for details.
- ❏ MemberwiseClone – inherited from System.Object, see Introduction for details.

HttpConfigurationContext Public Properties

- ❏ **VirtualPath**

VirtualPath

The VirtualPath property gets the virtual path of the web.config file. A null reference is returned when referring to machine.config and an empty string is returned for the virtual root directory.

```
public string VirtualPath {get;}
```

System.Web.Security

Within this chapter, our primary interest is with the `System.Web.Security` namespace. However, we will also cover the `System.Security.Principal` namespace here as this also has considerable significance to ASP.NET security.

ASP.NET Security Overview

To understand how security works in ASP.NET, you need to understand its three key aspects:

❏ Authentication

❏ Authorization

❏ Impersonation

Authentication involves the vetting of a user's identity, using a username and a password pair known only to the user and the system. Authorization involves allowing or denying access to application resources, like specific web pages or directories, based on the identity of the user.

Impersonation describes the process by which a web page request is put into an alternative Windows user security context. All file and code execution requests in Windows, even those made via HTTP and IIS for a web page, must be made by a known user account. IIS generates an anonymous user account, typically IUSR_*machinename*, which acts as a proxy user account for anonymous user requests made over the Web. Impersonation, in other words, represents anonymous web requests using the credentials of a legitimate Windows user account.

There are three built-in security models in ASP.NET, including:

❏ Windows

❏ Forms

❏ Passport

Windows authentication uses integrated Windows authentication and ACL (Access Control List) authorization and is largely unchanged from the IIS/Windows security available under classic ASP. Forms authentication provides a convenient, highly extensible and often more web-friendly alternative to Windows security. Passport builds on Microsoft's Passport service, allowing your application to leverage a global database of users and user information. Of the three, most developers will likely find Forms security offers the most flexibility since the user account data store management is the most flexible and least centralized of the three. This is discussed further a little later in the chapter, under the section entitled *Windows-Based Security*.

Security Configuration Using Machine.Config and Web.Config

Regardless of the security model you select, they are all configurable using related settings/elements in the machine and web.config files. For more information on this, see Chapter 7, *System.Web.Configuration*. The machine.config and web.config sections related to security include:

- ❑ <authentication>
- ❑ <authorization>
- ❑ <identity>
- ❑ <securityPolicy>
- ❑ <trust>

The most commonly adjusted elements are <authentication> and <authorization>. Each of these elements are demonstrated below:

<authentication>

The <authentication> section specifies the default application authentication mode. The required mode attribute specifies one of the following default values:

```
<authentication mode="Windows|Forms|Passport|None">
  <forms name="name"
         loginUrl="url"
         protection="All|None|Encryption|Validation"
         timeout="30" path="/" >
    <credentials passwordFormat="Clear|SHA1|MD5">
      <user name="username" password="password" />
    </credentials>
  </forms>
  <passport redirectUrl="internal"/>
</authentication>
```

- ❑ Windows
  Application set to Windows authentication. Requires browser to be able to participate in Windows with IIS authentication. IIS Authentication performs this process using Basic, Digest or Integrated Windows authentication (Microsoft Windows NT LAN Manager (NTLM)/Kerberos). These forms of authentication are defined in *Implementing Windows Authentication*, later in the chapter.

- ❑ Form
  Application set to ASP.NET Forms forms-based authentication.

- ❑ Passport
  Application set to Microsoft Passport authentication.

- ❑ None
  Application set to anonymous user access.

The <forms> tag specifies forms-based authentication details, including optional user-name and password storage in the <credential> section. The <passport> section defines details if Microsoft Passport authentication is used.

<authorization>

The <authorization> section determines who is granted access to application resources. The <authorization> section includes <allow> and <deny> sub-tags that each support attributes to specify permit or deny by user, group or verb. The verb attribute refers to the HTTP verb-type permitted access to the resource and can specify control over POST, GET, HEAD and DEBUG requests. The attributes must be provided as comma separated lists.

```
<authorization>
  <allow users="comma-separated list of users"
         roles="comma-separated list of roles"
         verbs="comma-separated list of verbs" />

  <deny users="comma-separated list of users"
        roles="comma-separated list of roles"
        verbs="comma-separated list of verbs" />
</authorization>
```

<identity>

The <identity> section of the configuration file can be used to specify the user account under which the web application is run. The impersonate attribute determines whether client impersonation is used. If impersonate is set to false, then the web application executes with the permissions of the username and password values supplied.

```
<identity impersonate="true|false"
          userName="username"
          password="password"/>
```

If a web application should allow resource access based on the requesting user's own permissions, then the identity section would be:

```
<identity
  impersonate="true"
/>
```

Furthermore, any processes or resource requests executed by the web application would be run under the user account of the user that is requesting the page. Alternatively, to give all users the same access, then the <identity> section should look like this:

```
<identity
  impersonate="false"
  username="WebUser"
  password="WebPass"
/>
```

<securityPolicy>

The securityPolicy section is used to associate named security levels with specific policy files. These policy files contain sets of restrictions and rules that are used when determining what access ASP.NET code will have to other code as well as to the system's resources.

```
<securityPolicy>
  <trustLevel name="value" policyFile="value" />
</securityPolicy>
```

The trustLevel tag has attributes that specify the name used in reference to the policy file. This section allows administrators to easily configure multiple servers with the same security settings. Once the administrator or developer has created hightrust.config, lowtrust.config, and notrust.config files for the web servers, each web.config file would have this section in it:

```
<securityPolicy>
  <trustLevel name="High" policyFile="web_hightrust.config" />
  <trustLevel name="Low"  policyFile="web_lowtrust.config" />
  <trustLevel name="None" policyFile="web_notrust.config" />
</securityPolicy>
```

<trust>

The <trust> section specifies the application's trust level settings. The level attribute provides four values to scale trust from Full to None. The originUrl attribute can be specified to achieve a notional "host" as it relates to security. By specifying the application URL, the authorization of web requests, for example, can be expedited.

```
<trust level="Full|High|Low|None" originUrl="url" />
```

System.Security.Principal Namespace

This namespace contains classes that are important to the authentication framework in ASP.NET. Two of the classes (IPrincipal and IIdentity) are interfaces used by all three of the authentication providers. The third, WindowsIdentity, is used by Windows Authentication.

Once a user has been authenticated, the HttpContext object, which was discussed in Chapter 2, holds information about the current user in the form of a Principal object. In .NET, Principal represents the security context for the current user. Each Principal object implements the IPrincipal interface. This interface allows access to the user's identity, and to any groups to which the user belongs.

The following is a comprehensive list of classes provided in the System.Security.Principal namespace. Bold classes represent classes that are most frequently used and that are covered in this chapter.

Class	Description
GenericIdentity	An object representing a generic user.
GenericPrincipal	A class representing the current user.
WindowsIdentity	**A class representing the identity of the current Windows user.**
WindowsImpersonationContext	A class that holds the Windows user details before an impersonation operation is implemented.
WindowsPrincipal	**A class that verifies a Windows user's Windows group membership.**
IIdentity	**An object containing identity information on the user.**
IPrincipal	**An object containing the security context of the user.**

WindowsIdentity Class

The WindowsIdentity class implements the IIdentity and represents a user account in a Windows security context.

WindowsIdentity Class Public Methods

- ❑ Equals – inherited from System.Object, see Introduction for details.
- ❑ **GetAnonymous**
- ❑ **GetCurrent**
- ❑ GetHashCode – inherited from System.Object, see Introduction for details.
- ❑ GetType – inherited from System.Object, see Introduction for details.
- ❑ **Impersonate**

GetAnonymous

The GetAnonymous method returns a WindowsIdentity object instance that represents the anonymous user account on the system.

```
public static WindowsIdentity GetAnonymous();
```

GetCurrent

The GetCurrent method returns a WindowsIdentity that represents the user for whom the current code is executing.

```
public static WindowsIdentity GetCurrent();
```

Impersonate

The `Impersonate` method takes either no input or an integer representing a Windows account token as input. It sets the impersonation mode and account for the current process. By default, impersonation is turned off in ASP.NET. This means that even though a user is logged in using Windows Authentication, the current thread is not running under their security context in Windows. The default account that the ASP.NET framework runs under is the local System account. If the current user needs access to network resources, such as a Web Service that is protected by Windows Authentication, you can allow the current thread to start running under the `Identity` of the current user. The `Impersonate` method of the `WindowsIdentity` object allows the currently running code to run under the security context of the user it represents.

```
public virtual WindowsImpersonationContext Impersonate();
```

```
public static WindowsImpersonationContext Impersonate(IntPtr);
```

Example: Inline Impersonation

The following fragment uses the `Impersonate` method to dynamically change the identity under which the current code is executing, then reverts to the original account. In this case, the example assumes impersonation is disabled which means code is running as the `System` account. It then uses `Impersonate` to switch to the authenticated Windows user that logged in, then reverts back to the normal "system" mode.

```
WindowsImpersonationContext wicImpersContext =
                ((WindowsIdentity)Context.User.Identity).Impersonate();

Label1.Text = "This text written using " +
                            WindowsIdentity.GetCurrent().Name +
                            "'s account and privileges via impersonate.";

// Return to original identity context

wicImpersContext.Undo();
```

Here we create a `WindowsImpersonationContext` instance and impersonate by casting the `Context` property `User` as a `WindowsIdentity` instance. The impersonation `Context` instance preserves the user identity context under which the code was running prior to impersonation and lets us revert to that context when we've finished impersonating. Any code between here and `wicImpersContext.Undo` is run under the user's account privileges.

WindowsIdentity Protected Methods

- ❑ `Finalize` – inherited from `System.Object`, see Introduction for details.

- ❑ `MemberwiseClone` – inherited from `System.Object`, see Introduction for details.

WindowsIdentity Class Public Properties

- ❏ **AuthenticationType**
- ❏ **IsAnonymous**
- ❏ **IsAuthenticated**
- ❏ **IsGuest**
- ❏ **IsSystem**
- ❏ **Name**
- ❏ **Token**

AuthenticationType

The `AuthenticationType` property describes the authentication type, such as Basic authentication, NTLM, Kerberos, and Passport, which was used to authenticate the user.

```
public virtual string AuthenticationType {get;}
```

IsAnonymous

The `IsAnonymous` property is a `Boolean` that indicates whether Windows considers the account represented by the `WindowsIdentity` instance to be "anonymous".

```
public virtual bool IsAnonymous {get;}
```

IsAuthenticated

The `IsAuthenticated` property is a `Boolean` that indicates whether Windows authenticated the account for this `WindowsIdentity` instance.

```
public virtual bool IsAuthenticated {get;}
```

IsGuest

The `IsGuest` property is a `Boolean` that indicates whether Windows considers the account represented by the `WindowsIdentity` instance to be a "guest" account.

```
public virtual bool IsGuest {get;}
```

IsSystem

The `IsSystem` property is a `Boolean` that indicates whether Windows considers the account represented by the `WindowsIdentity` instance to be a "System" account. Remember, the System account cannot access resources outside the machine like remote Web Services. You could use this property to determine at run-time whether you need to switch to an impersonated context before accessing remote resources.

```
public virtual bool IsSystem {get;}
```

Name

The `Name` property is a string that represents the user name of the account represented by this `WindowsIdentity` instance.

```
public virtual string Name {get;}
```

Token

The `Token` property is an integer pointer that represents the Windows account token for the user represented by the `WindowsIdentity` instance. One of the overridden forms of the `Impersonate` method of `WindowsIdentity` takes a Windows account token as input. You can use this property to provide that method with a reference to the account you wish the code to execute under.

```
public virtual IntPtr Token {get;}
```

WindowsPrincipal Class

The `WindowsPrincipal` class is used in Windows Authentication to implement the `IPrincipal` interface. This object does not define any behavior beyond that interface. See the `IPrincipal` interface reference earlier in this chapter for additional details.

WindowsPrincipal Class Public Methods

- ❑ `Equals` – inherited from `System.Object`, see Introduction for details.
- ❑ `GetHashCode` – inherited from `System.Object`, see Introduction for details.
- ❑ `GetType` – inherited from `System.Object`, see Introduction for details.
- ❑ **`IsInRole`**
- ❑ `ToString` – inherited from `System.Object`, see Introduction for details.

IsInRole

The `IsInRole` method takes a string that is a role name as input and returns a `Boolean` indicating whether the user represented by this `Iprincipal` interface instance is a member of the role.

```
public virtual bool InInRole(int);
```

WindowsPrincipal Protected Methods

- ❑ `Finalize` – inherited from `System.Object`, see Introduction for details.
- ❑ `MemberwiseClone` – inherited from `System.Object`, see Introduction for details.

WindowsPrincipal Class Public Properties

❑ **Identity**

Identity

The `Identity` property is a `WindowsIdentity` instance that represents the user. See the `WindowsIdentity` class reference in this chapter for more details.

```
public virtual IIdentity Identity {get;}
```

IIdentity and IPrincipal Interfaces

The .NET framework and ASP.NET provide a number of classes in the `System.Security.Principal` namespace that implement authentication details common to `Windows`, `Forms` and `Passport` based security. Two interfaces, `IIdentity` and `IPrincipal`, are worth examining for a foundational understanding of security in ASP.NET as `Windows`, `Forms`, and `Passport` based security all provide classes that implement these interfaces.

IIdentity Interface

The `IIdentity` interface is returned by the `Context.Use.Identity` property and contains basic information about the user. Classes that implement the `IIdentity` interface and thus represent user identity in various run-time scenarios include:

❑ `System.Security.Principal.GenericIdentity`

❑ `System.Security.Principal.WindowsIdentity`

❑ `System.Web.FormsIdentity`

❑ `System.Web.PassportIdentity`

IIdentity Interface Public Properties

The interface's three public properties model the basic required information for representing identity in a .NET security context.

❑ **AuthenticationType**

❑ **IsAuthenticated**

❑ **Name**

AuthenticationType

The `AuthenticationType` property returns a string that specifically describes how the use was authenticated.

```
string AuthenticationType {get;}
```

IsAuthenticated

The `IsAuthenticated` property returns a `Boolean` value, indicating whether the user was authenticated.

```
bool IsAuthenticated {get;}
```

Name

The `Name` property is a string that represents the user name and is typically an empty string when the user has not been authenticated.

```
string Name {get;}
```

IPrincipal Interface

The `IPrincipal` interface is implemented by all ASP.NET authentication providers. It defines the basic set of properties and methods that a provider must implement to plugin to the authentication framework.

IPrincipal Interface Public Methods

❑ **`IsInRole`**

IsInRole

The `IsInRole` method takes a string that is a role name as input and returns a `Boolean` indicating whether the user represented by this `IPrincipal`-interfaced instance is a member of the role.

```
bool IsInRole(string role);
```

IPrincipal Interface Public Properties

❑ **`Identity`**

Identity

The `Identity` property returns an object that implements the `IIdentity` interface and allows access to the user's name and some information about their authentication status.

```
IIdentity Identity {get;}
```

Windows-Based Security

While inappropriate for many web-based applications due to the fact that user account management can be more difficult to manage, integrated Windows security is appropriate for intranets or other situations where having Windows store user account information is preferable. The Windows authentication provider allows you to restrict access to specific physical files and directories using ACL (Access Control List) Authorization. The main caveat of this approach is that it requires physical configuration changes to the server which can be tricky to manage in a single server environment and very difficult in a "web farm" scenario.

Despite the difficulties, Windows security does have advantages. The advantage of Windows over Forms authentication is that username and password information is automatically encrypted for safe transport over the public Internet because the browser (typically Microsoft's own Internet Explorer) actively participates in the authentication process. Forms authentication requires SSL encrypted pages to achieve the same effect. Moreover, Forms and Passport authentication have less granularity than Windows ACL security; the former two allow access control over directories but not as easily over individual files.

Implementing Windows Authentication

Implementing Windows Authentication is a two-step process. The first step is to make a modification to the web.config file. For example, this config file sets the authentication mode to Windows and denies anonymous access:

```
<configuration>
  <system.web>
    <authentication mode="Windows" />
        <identity impersonate="false" />
    <authorization>
        <!-- This following element denies anonymous access -->
        <deny users="?" />
    </authorization>
  </system.web>
</configuration>
```

By using the "?" wildcard in the deny field, this element is blocking all users from being authorized, meaning they will all be challenged to login. Of course, you can also remove access to the anonymous user through the IIS manager, but setting it in the web.config file makes a lot of sense, because it is much easier to deploy to a new server and copy to other servers. (See the <authorization> coverage earlier in the chapter for details.)

The second step is to make the necessary configuration changes to IIS. To enable Windows Authentication, IIS must be configured to allow Basic, Digest, or Integrated Windows Authentication (these are defined below), or any combination of them as appropriate. IIS can also be configured to authenticate users using certificates. Using Active Directory, certificates can be created that map to specific user accounts. If IIS is configured to authenticate users with certificates, the user's certificate takes the place of a login dialog.

There may be cases, however, when you allow access to portions of your web application to unauthenticated users. In this case, you will need to enable authorization of the anonymous user for those areas and force authentication for other areas. This is most easily done by placing the secure parts of the site in separate directories from the rest of the site. You can then create separate web.config files that contain the authorization specifications you require.

The IIS configuration screen for Directory Security allows you to choose an authentication type:

Anonymous Authentication

Anonymous Authentication is a method that, by default, allows IIS to map all incoming web requests to the identity of a single Windows domain account. As previously mentioned, when IIS is installed, it creates a new Windows account called IUSR_*machinename*. This account is the one that IIS uses to gain access to the requested web resources. This allows all requests to be handled without requiring the user to log on to the web server. Anonymous Authentication is used for web sites, or portions of web sites, that do not require user authentication.

Remember, if Anonymous Authentication is still enabled in IIS for the directory in which your application is based, IIS will attempt to authenticate the user using Anonymous Authentication first. If that fails, IIS will send a challenge response to the browser that will result in the user having to log in.

Basic Authentication

Basic Authentication is part of the HTTP 1.0 specification and most browsers have support for it. To log in to a web site running IIS using Basic Authentication, a user needs to supply their username and password. Here is a sample of the logon form used by a typical browser to handle Basic Authentication:

One weakness of Basic Authentication is that the username and password are sent over the network as plain text and can be easily harvested by hackers. If Basic Authentication is used together with HTTPS, however, the username and password are securely encrypted. Using HTTPS is truly the only secure way to use Basic Authentication.

Digest Authentication

Digest Authentication is a new standard that was proposed as part of the HTTP 1.1 specification. Digest Authentication is similar to, and has been proposed as a replacement for, Basic Authentication. In Digest Authentication, the username and password are passed through a hashing algorithm so that they are not sent as plain text over the network. The original username and password cannot be deciphered from the resulting hash.

Digest Authentication is only available to IIS if the web server is a domain controller. Currently, few browsers support Digest Authentication (IE 5 is included amongst these), but as it becomes more available, it will be a very viable option for authenticating users.

Integrated Windows Authentication

Integrated Windows Authentication has also been known as NTLM Authentication or Windows NT Challenge/Response. If a user has already logged into the same Windows domain as the web server, or one trusted by the web server, a hash of their login credentials can be automatically communicated to the server using a secure communication protocol.

ACL and Windows Authorization

ACL (Access Control List) authorization is built into the Windows server file system, commonly known as NTFS. Access can be explicitly granted to specific Windows users or Windows groups using the standard Windows server file access control dialogue through the Security sheet of the file, or the directory Property dialog presented by Windows Explorer. ACL authorization will fail for the anonymous user account if one of the following conditions is true:

- The anonymous account does not have read access to the file requested in the URL

- The anonymous account does not have rights to some other system resource needed to complete the current request

- Anonymous authentication is disabled for the current directory or virtual directory in IIS

If ACL authorization fails, IIS issues a challenge to the browser, which results in a login dialog being displayed to the user. This login dialog is only generated by browsers that support Windows Authentication, typically Internet Explorer. The user must then log in with an appropriate Windows Account that has sufficient access rights to complete the current request.

IIS is involved in the authentication process in Windows Authentication. When IIS receives a request that needs to be authenticated, it issues a challenge to the browser for authentication information. A login dialog is then presented to the user. Once the user's identity has been confirmed by the Windows Domain, the `WindowsAuthenticationModule` provider constructs `WindowsIdentity` and `WindowsPrincipal` instances, and attaches them to the current request. These objects will be discussed later in this chapter.

Impersonation in ASP.NET

For public web sites that do not require users to log in to Windows, IIS provides a guest account under which requests can be impersonated, commonly called the **Anonymous User**. When IIS is installed, it creates the account IUSR_*machinename* where *machinename* is the name of the computer at the time of installation.

Remember, unlike classic ASP, in ASP.NET impersonation is disabled by default and all requests in ASP.NET run under the identity of the **System** account. System is a special Windows account with virtually unlimited access to the resources on the local machine. This may be a security concern for some implementations, especially for an Internet Service Provider (ISP) that allows users to upload ASP.NET code to the server. In addition, the System account does not have access to network resources, such as file shares or printers on remote servers.

For situations when impersonation is required in ASP.NET, it can be enabled with the following code in your `web.config` file:

```
<system.web>
  <identity impersonate="true" userName="user" password="Password"/>
</system.web>
```

By setting impersonation to `true`, you can specify a particular Windows account and password that ASP.NET should use for impersonation. Another important tip is that impersonation can be changed at run time. You can switch the current account that code is running under by calling the `WindowsIdentity.Impersonate` method. See the `WindowsIdentity` class later for more details.

Forms-Based Security

Forms authentication is the most flexible of the built-in security models in ASP.NET due to the ability to store user credentials (typified by a user name and password) in any .NET accessible file or data-store. It provides implicit authentication methods for storing user information in the `<credentials>` section of the `machine.config` and `web.config` files. It also allows easy authentication against credentials stored in an XML file or database.

In order to implement Forms Authentication, the `<authentication>` section in `web.config` should be configured like this:

```
<authentication mode="Forms">
  <forms loginUrl="login.aspx"
         name="authCookie" />
</authentication>
```

See the `<authentication>` section earlier in the chapter for additional details.

Important Forms-Based Implementation Details

Authentication Cookie Name

You should be aware that if you are running forms authentication on a web host that is also running other web applications that you do not have control over, those applications could overwrite your cookie if they are using the same name, causing your user's authentication ticket to be invalidated. If you do not specify a name for the authentication cookie in the `web.config`, ASP.NET will use one with the default name of `.ASPXAUTH`.

Here is an example of how you would change the default cookie name by modifying the `web.config` file:

```
<authentication mode="Forms">
  <forms loginUrl="login.aspx"
         path="/mywebapplication"
         name="CookieName" />
</authentication>
```

Use of the CookiePath

The `CookiePath` property can be set in the `web.config`, as was shown in the previous example. If you are planning on using the path property to dictate where your cookies are stored, you should be aware that it can be prone to problems unless you are aware of the issues.

The cookie path property of an HTTP cookie is **case-sensitive**. This is part of the HTTP specification for cookies. If the case of the request path for a subsequent web request does not exactly match, the cookie will not be returned to your application. The following scenarios illustrate situations in which this may occur:

- ❑ The user clicks on a hyperlink in your application that invokes a page in your application. You have incorrectly specified the URL in the hyperlink, causing part of the URL path to differ in case from what you specified in your cookie path.

- ❑ The user comes into your application following a link from another web site or an e-mail that has an incorrect case specified in the URL.

- ❑ The user manually re-types part of the URL, causing the case of the page URL path to change.

While the `CookiePath` property is provided simply for the sake of completeness because it is part of the HTTP specification for a cookie, it is best to forget about it when working with cookies. If you do not specify the `CookiePath` attribute, the default path of "/" is used, which means that the cookie will be sent on every request to any URL on the host. The actual cookie will be sent to any application running under the same host name on the server. If you are sharing your web host with other web applications, cookies created with the default path will be sent to any request to any application on the server. An additional limitation on cookies is that a maximum of 20 cookies can be specified for any one host. Therefore, in a shared hosting environment, this is just one more thing that could cause forms authentication to go awry. (See Chapter 1 for more information on Cookies).

Spanning Multiple Servers

If you implement Forms Authentication across a web farm of servers or plan on passing encrypted Forms Authentication tickets (see the `FormsAuthenticationTicket` class for more details) between servers, the `<machinekey>` element in `web.config` must be synchronized properly so that all servers are using the same encryption key.

When Forms Authentication creates the cookie that stores the `FormsAuthenticationTicket`, it encrypts the data. The `<machinekey>` setting in `web.config` is merely a way to ensure that all of the servers that need to be able to decrypt this cookie are using the same encryption key.

Example: Forms-Based Authentication and Authorization

The following example demonstrates the Forms Authentication setup in configuration files and the flexibility of the authentication in terms of a user data-store. The application has a root directory and two sub-directories, `adminSecure` and `otherSecure`. There is a default page ("default.aspx") in each directory and a `web.config` file in each directory. The default page in each directory displays the current user's login details.

The `web.config` file in the root directory denies anonymous access and stores the credentials of two of the application users as follows:

```
<authentication mode="Forms" >
<forms
  name=".ExampleCookie"
  loginUrl="login.aspx"
  protection="All"
  timeout="80"
  path="/"
>
<credentials passwordFormat="Clear">
```

```
  <user name="Janell" password="password" />
    <user name="Sandy" password="password" />


  </credentials>

  </forms>
  </authentication>

  <!--    AUTHORIZATION
        This section sets the authorization policies of the application. You
        can allow or deny access to application resources by user or role.
        Wildcards: "*" mean everyone, "?" means anonymous (unauthenticated)
        users.
  -->
  <authorization>
    <deny users="?" /> <!-- Allow all users -->

      <!--   <allow      users="[comma separated list of users]"
                              roles="[comma_separated list of roles]"/>
            <deny       users="[comma_separated list of users]"
                              roles="[comma_separated list of roles]"/>
        -->
  </authorization>
```

The web.config files in the two sub directories restrict access to either Sandy or Janell for adminSecure and otherSecure, respectively, as follows:

```
<?xml version="1.0" encoding="utf-8" ?>
<configuration>

  <system.web>

    <authorization>
      <deny users="?" /> <!-- Allow all users -->
      <allow users="sandy" />
      <deny users="*" />
        <!--   <allow      users="[comma separated list of users]"
                            roles="[comma_separated list of roles]"/>
              <deny       users="[comma_separated list of users]"
                            roles="[comma_separated list of roles]"/>
        -->
    </authorization>


  </system.web>

</configuration>
```

And:

```xml
<?xml version="1.0" encoding="utf-8" ?>
<configuration>

  <system.web>

    <authorization>
      <deny users="?" /> <!-- Allow all users -->
      <allow users="janell" />
      <deny users="*" />
        <!-- <allow     users="[comma separated list of users]"
                         roles="[comma_separated list of roles]"/>
             <deny      users="[comma_separated list of users]"
                         roles="[comma_separated list of roles]"/>
        -->
    </authorization>


  </system.web>

</configuration>
```

When users launch the application they are automatically redirected to the login.aspx for authentication. Our example code behind file for the login page demonstrates authenticating a user-provided username and password against inline values, values stored in the <credentials> section of the web.config file and even values stored in a database.

The source for the login.aspx.cs code-behind is as follows:

```csharp
namespace systemWebSecurityFormExamplesCs
{
  /// <summary>
  /// Summary description for login.
  /// </summary>
  public class login : System.Web.UI.Page
  {
    protected System.Web.UI.WebControls.Label lblUserName;
    protected System.Web.UI.WebControls.TextBox txbUserName;
    protected System.Web.UI.WebControls.RequiredFieldValidator
                                        RequiredFieldValidator1;
    protected System.Web.UI.WebControls.Label lblPassword;
    protected System.Web.UI.WebControls.TextBox txbPassword;
    protected System.Web.UI.WebControls.RequiredFieldValidator
                                        RequiredFieldValidator2;
    protected System.Web.UI.WebControls.CheckBox chkPersistCookie;
    protected System.Web.UI.WebControls.Button Button1;
    protected System.Web.UI.WebControls.Label lblStatus;
    private string strConnect;
    private string strSelect;
    private SqlConnection objConnect;
```

```
private void Page_Load(object sender, System.EventArgs e)
{
  // Put user code to initialize the page here
}


...


private void Button1_Click(object sender, System.EventArgs e)
{
  // first validate the form
  if(Page.IsValid)
  {
    //''''''''''''''''''''''''''''''''''''''''''''
    //' First validate an "inline" user, in this case a "backdoor"
    if((txbUserName.Text == "secret") && (txbPassword.Text ==
                                          "backdoor"))
      System.Web.Security.FormsAuthentication.RedirectFromLoginPage
                  (txbUserName.Text, chkPersistCookie.Checked);
    else
      lblStatus.Text = "Username/password combination not found.";


    //Next validate against users in a database
    strConnect = "data source=(local);initial" +
                 "catalog=userStore;pwd=test;" +
                 "uid=test;";

    objConnect = new SqlConnection(strConnect);

    objConnect.Open();

    strSelect = "select * from users where username='" +
                txbUserName.Text + "' and password='" +
                txbPassword.Text + "'";

    SqlCommand objCommand = new SqlCommand(strSelect, objConnect);

    SqlDataReader objDataReader;

    objDataReader = objCommand.ExecuteReader();

    // if the reader has rows, we found our user
    if(objDataReader.Read())
    {
      // send user to default or requested page and make login
      // info persist as cookie if so directed
      System.Web.Security.FormsAuthentication.RedirectFromLoginPage
            (txbUserName.Text, chkPersistCookie.Checked);
    }
    else
      lblStatus.Text = "Username/password combination not found.";
```

```
     // Try to validate the user credentials against the
     //username/password pair stored in web.config
     if(System.Web.Security.FormsAuthentication.Authenticate
                        (txbUserName.Text, txbPassword.Text))
     {
       // send user to default or requested page and make login
       // info persist as cookie if so directed
       System.Web.Security.FormsAuthentication.RedirectFromLoginPage
                 (txbUserName.Text, chkPersistCookie.Checked);
     }
     else
       lblStatus.Text = "Username/password combination not found.";

   }

  }

 }
}
```

In the bold section above, we validate first against "inline" user credentials in the code, then against user values stored in a database table and finally against the user name values stored in the credentials section of the web.config file.

The output from running the login.aspx.cs file will be as follows:

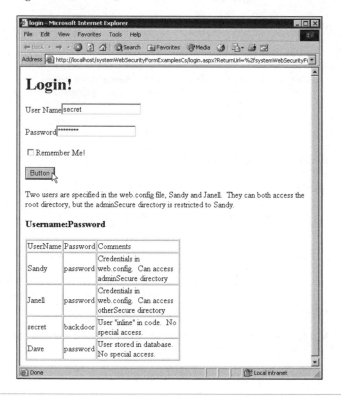

System.Web.Security Namespace

The following is a comprehensive list of classes provided in the `System.Web.Security` namespace. Bold classes represent classes that are most frequently used and that are covered in detail in this chapter.

Class	Description
DefaultAuthenticationEventArgs	A wrapper for the default authentication services.
DefaultAuthenticationModule	Determines that an authentication instance is present for the context.
FileAuthorizationModule	Resolves the NT permissions for remote users accessing files.
FormsAuthentication	**Supports authentication ticket use/manipulation.**
FormsAuthenticationEventArgs	Supports the `FormsAuthentication_OnAuthenticate` event.
FormsAuthenticationModule	Provides Forms Authentication support for ASP.NET by providing the `Authenticate` member that is the authentication event handler for Forms Authentication.
FormsAuthenticationTicket	**Represents and provides access to the authentication information generated during Forms Authentication that is stored in the authentication cookie.**
FormsIdentity	**The `IIdentity` representative for Forms Authentication.**
PassportAuthenticationEventArgs	Represents the event arguments passed to the `Authenticate` event by a `PassportAuthenticationModule`.
PassportAuthenticationModule	Provides Passport Authentication support for ASP.NET by providing the `Authenticate` member that is the authentication event handler for Passport Authentication.
PassportIdentity	**The `IIdentity` representative for Passport Authentication.**

Table continued on following page

Class	Description
UrlAuthorizationModule	URL-based authorization provider that allows or denies access to specified resources.
WindowsAuthenticationEventArgs	Represents event arguments passed to the Authenticate event by a WindowsAuthenticationModule.
WindowsAuthenticationModule	Provides Windows Authentication support for ASP.NET by providing the Authenticate member, which is the authentication event handler for Windows Authentication.

FormsAuthentication Class

The FormsAuthentication class consists entirely of shared helper methods for dealing with Forms Authentication in your application.

FormsAuthentication Class Public Methods

- ❑ **Authenticate**
- ❑ **Decrypt**
- ❑ **Encrypt**
- ❑ **GetAuthCookie**
- ❑ GetHashCode – inherited from System.Object, see Introduction for details.
- ❑ **GetRedirectUrl**
- ❑ **HashPasswordForStoringInConfigFile**
- ❑ **Initialize**
- ❑ **RedirectFromLoginPage**
- ❑ **RenewTicketifOld**
- ❑ **SetAuthCookie**
- ❑ **SignOut**
- ❑ ToString – inherited from System.Object, see Introduction for details.

Authenticate

The Authenticate method takes two strings as input, representing a user name and password. The FormsAuthentication class compares the user name against the user credentials stored in the <credentials> section of the web.config file and returns true if the user is valid, and false otherwise. As such, authenticate is only useful if your user data is stored in the web.config file. If the user data is stored elsewhere you must write your own authenticate routines to validate the credentials.

```
public static bool Authenticate(string name, string password);
```

Decrypt

The `Decrypt` method takes a string as input and returns a `FormsAuthenticationTicket` instance provided that the string input is the contents of an encrypted `FormsAuthenticationTicket` cookie. Normally you will never need to use this method, as the `FormsAuthenticationModule` class does this work for you. It is useful, however, to use the `Decrypt` and `Encrypt` methods if you need to pass the identity of the user securely to another server, such as another web server or a server at another tier in the application.

```
public static FormsAuthenticationTicket Decrypt(string encryptedTicket);
```

Encrypt

The `Encrypt` method takes a `FormsAuthenticationTicket` instance as input and returns an encrypted string appropriate for storage as a `FormsAuthentication` cookie. If you need more control over the cookie properties of the authentication ticket, this method can be used to get the cookie, modify it, and then send it to the user yourself.

```
public static string Encrypt(FormsAuthenticationTicket ticket);
```

GetAuthCookie

The `GetAuthCookie` method takes a string and a `Boolean` as input or a string, `Boolean` and string as input depending on the overloaded method you need. In both cases the method returns an `HttpCookie` instance. Normally, once you authenticate a user, you will call the `RedirectFromLoginPage` method. The `GetAuthCookie` method is only useful if you need to set some further properties on the cookie that `FormsAuthentication` could use to maintain the identity of the user that you have just authenticated.

```
public static HttpCookie GetAuthCookie(string, bool);
public static HttpCookie GetAuthCookie(string, bool, string);
```

GetRedirectUrl

The `GetRedirectUrl` method takes a string and a `Boolean` as input. This method returns a string that represents the URL that the user requested when they redirected to the login page due to lack of authenticated status. The URL of the originally requested page is passed to the login page via a querystring parameter. **Remember, this method is only valid if it is called from the login page specified in `web.config`.**

```
public static string GetRedirectUrl(string userName, bool
                                     createPersistentCookie);
```

HashPasswordForStoringInConfigFile

The `HashPasswordForStoringInConfigFile` method takes two strings as input representing a password to encrypt and the password encryption format. If you choose to store credentials in the `web.config` file and are adding users programmatically, it's a good practice to hash the passwords so that users with access to the `config` file can't easily steal user passwords.

```
public static string HashPasswordForStoringInConfigFile(string password,
                                            string passwordFormat);
```

Initialize

The `Initialize` method takes no input and initializes the `FormsAuthentication` instance by getting the configuration files, cookie values and encryption values for the application.

```
public static void Initialize();
```

RedirectFromLoginPage

The `RedirectFromLoginPage` takes a string and `Boolean` or a string, a `Boolean` and a string as input depending on the overloaded method required. If a user has been successfully authenticated by your application's custom code, you can call this method to redirect the user to the resource they initially requested, when they were prompted to log on.

The important thing to understand about this method is that, when called, the `FormsAuthentication` provider creates a `FormsAuthenticationTicket` object and stores it in a cookie. Subsequently, when a user hits any page in the application, the `FormsAuthentication` provider can verify that the user is authenticated.

```
public static void RedirectFromLoginPage(string, bool);
public static void RedirectFromLoginPage(string, bool, string);
```

> An important caveat is that after you have authenticated the user, your code is responsible for providing the unique username that will be stored in the `Context.User.Identity.Name` property. This username should be unique across all users of the application and has a limit of 32 characters.

RenewTicketIfOld

The `RenewTicketIfOld` method takes a `FormsAuthenticationTicket` as input and returns a `FormsAuthenticationTicket`, renewing the existing ticket. Normally, you do not have to call this method yourself as renewal and expiration are handled by Forms Authentication automatically, as needed. The default behavior is that the user's ticket will be renewed when it is about halfway towards its expiration. The default expiration, if not overridden in the `web.config`, is 30 minutes. You would normally only call this method if you want to override the Forms Authentication default behavior for renewing authentication tickets.

```
public static FormsAuthenticationTicket RenewTicketIfOld(
                                        FormsAuthenticationTicket tOld);
```

SetAuthCookie

The `SetAuthCookie` method takes a string and a `Boolean` or a string, a `Boolean` and a string as input. The method effectively authenticates the current user but, unlike `RedirectFromLoginPage`, does not redirect them to another page. The `FormsAuthentication` object creates the appropriate cookie to uniquely identify the user and sets it in the `Response.Cookies` collection. The parameters of this method and their usage are exactly same as for the `RedirectFromLoginPage` method.

Normally, once you authenticate a user, you will call the `RedirectFromLoginPage` method to send the user on their way. If you need more control over the chain of events that happens when a user is authenticated, such as sending them to a specific web page instead of the one they requested, the `SetAuthCookie` method can be used to authenticate the user and then manage the workflow yourself.

An example of this would be if you always wanted a user to go to a specific home page, rather than allowing them to go to any page they want when they first log in, you would use `SetAuthCookie` to log them in and then redirect them to your specific home page.

```
public static void SetAuthCookie(string, bool);
public static void SetAuthCookie(string, bool, string);
```

SignOut

The `SignOut` method takes no input. If you provide the option for a user to logout from within your application, you should call the `SignOut` method when the user chooses to leave. This method clears the Forms Authentication cookie and sets it to expire immediately. Once this method is called, the user will have to log in again if they attempt to access any resource for which authorization is required.

```
public static void SignOut();
```

FormsAuthentication Protected Methods

❑ `Finalize` – inherited from `System.Object`, see Introduction for details.

❑ `MemberwiseClone` – inherited from `System.Object`, see Introduction for details.

FormsAuthentication Class Public Properties

❑ **FormsCookieName**

❑ **FormsCookiePath**

FormsCookieName

The `FormsCookieName` property gets a string value that is the name of the cookie that Forms Authentication is using to store the user's authentication ticket representing their identity.

```
public static string FormsCookieName {get;}
```

FormsCookiePath

The `FormsCookiePath` property gets a string that is the path assigned to the current cookie used to maintain the user's identity.

```
public static string FormsCookiePath {get;}
```

FormsAuthenticationTicket Class

The FormsAuthenticationTicket class encapsulates the authentication cookie and authentication information for the current user.

FormsAuthenticationTicket Class Public Methods

- ❑ Equals – inherited from System.Object, see Introduction for details.
- ❑ GetHashCode – inherited from System.Object, see Introduction for details.
- ❑ GetType – inherited from System.Object, see Introduction for details.
- ❑ ToString – inherited from System.Object, see Introduction for details.

FormsAuthenticationTicket Protected Methods

- ❑ Finalize – inherited from System.Object, see Introduction for details.
- ❑ MemberwiseClone – inherited from System.Object, see Introduction for details.

FormsAuthenticationTicket Class Public Properties

- ❑ **CookiePath**
- ❑ **Expiration**
- ❑ **Expired**
- ❑ **IsPersistent**
- ❑ **IssueDate**
- ❑ **Name**
- ❑ **UserData**
- ❑ **Version**

CookiePath

The CookiePath property gets the path assigned to the authentication ticket cookie.

```
public string CookiePath {get;}
```

Expiration

The Expiration property gets the date and time when the authentication cookie expires.

```
public DateTime Expiration {get;}
```

Expired

The Expired property gets a Boolean indicating whether the authentication ticket has expired.

```
public bool Expired {get;}
```

IsPersistent

The `IsPersistent` property gets a `Boolean` indicating whether the cookie for the authentication ticket is a "persistent" rather than a session-termed cookie. Persistent cookies persist in the browser cache even after the browser is closed, allowing users to avoid the log in process if they revisit your application prior to the expiration date of the cookie.

```
public bool IsPersistent {get;}
```

IssueDate

The `IssueDate` property gets a date and time value indicating when the authentication cookie was issued.

```
public DateTime IssueDate {get;}
```

Name

The `Name` property gets a string value that is the user name of the authenticated user.

```
public string Name {get;}
```

UserData

The `UserData` property gets a string value that is an application-specified string specific to the user specified when the cookie was created. `UserData` is optional and will only have a value if your application populates the field upon user authentication.

```
public string UserData {get;}
```

Version

The `Version` property gets an integer value that currently defaults to "1" and that may be used in future versions of ASP.NET to differentiate cookie properties depending on the framework version that issued it.

```
public int Version {get;}
```

FormsIdentity Class

The `FormsIdentity` class provides the implementation of the `IIdentity` interface that is used when Forms Authentication is enabled. It also has a `Ticket` property that is used to gain access to the information stored in the authentication cookie for the currently logged in user.

FormsIdentity Class Public Methods

❑   `Equals` – inherited from `System.Object`, see Introduction for details.

❑   `GetHashCode` – inherited from `System.Object`, see Introduction for details.

❑   `GetType` – inherited from `System.Object`, see Introduction for details.

❑ ToString – inherited from `System.Object`, see Introduction for details.

FormsIdentity Protected Methods

❑ Finalize – inherited from `System.Object`, see Introduction for details.

❑ MemberwiseClone – inherited from `System.Object`, see Introduction for details.

FormsIdentity Class Public Properties

❑ **AuthenticationType**

❑ **IsAuthenticated**

❑ **Name**

❑ **Ticket**

AuthenticationType

The `AuthenticationType` property gets a string that describes the authentication type used to authenticate the `FormsIdentity` instance.

```
public string AuthenticationType {get;}
```

IsAuthenticated

The `IsAuthenticated` property gets a `Boolean` that specifies whether the user represented by this `FormsIdentity` instance has been authenticated.

```
public bool IsAuthenticated {get;}
```

Name

The `Name` property gets a string that represents the user name of the user represented by the `FormsIdentity` instance. If the name value is empty, there is a good chance the user has not been authenticated.

```
public string Name {get;}
```

Ticket

The `Ticket` property gets the `FormsAuthenticationTicket` instance for the current request.

```
public FormsAuthenticationTicket Ticket {get;}
```

Passport-Based Security

Microsoft's "Passport Service" provides solutions to some of the areas other forms of authentication fall down on. Examples of this would be if you want to establish a single-sign-on policy for several applications that are distributed across different servers and sites or if you wanted to enable a system where users can be authenticated using the same credentials across multiple sites that you don't provide yourself. (For example, you might want to build a solution where a user can log onto one of the well-known sites like Hotmail.com and then come to your sites and be automatically authenticated based on the logon credentials they provided when they logged onto Hotmail)

Passport authentication can be used to authenticate users on any passport-enabled site, anywhere on the Internet. When they log onto a participating site, their browser or user agent sends their credentials to the passport service, which authenticates them and places a secure cookie on their machine. Then, when they access another participating site, the browser presents this cookie to the passport service to prove that the user has already been authenticated. The passport service then indicates who that user is to the new site so they can be properly authorized - that is, the new site can check if this user has permission to access the resource they've requested.

So the power of the passport service is that a user can present the same credentials to any participating site, while only having to log in once during a session. When they close their browser, or indicate that they wish to log off, the cookie is destroyed. They must then log on again to re-access resources on any of the participating sites.

The ASP.NET framework provides classes that do the work of providing Passport authentication for your web site. The following sections will go through the methods and properties of the framework classes that implement integration with the Passport Service.

> *Please note that the following section is not intended to be exhaustive in its coverage of Passport Authentication. For more information on Passport implementation see our new title on security in ASP.NET, Professional ASP.NET Security also by Wrox Press (ISBN 1-861006-20-9).*

PassportIdentity Class

The `PassportIdentity` class contains a lot of behavior that is necessary to implement Passport authentication on your web site. For those of you who are familiar with the classic ASP Passport APIs, the `PassportIdentity` object implements most of the behavior of the COM `PassportManager` object.

PassportIdentity Class Public Methods

- ❑ `AuthURL`
- ❑ `AuthURL2`
- ❑ `Compress`
- ❑ `CryptIsValid`
- ❑ `CryptPutHost`
- ❑ `CryptPutSite`

- ❑ **Decompress**
- ❑ **Decrypt**
- ❑ **Encrypt**
- ❑ Equals – inherited from System.Object, see Introduction for details.
- ❑ **GetCurrentConfig**
- ❑ **GetDomainAttribute**
- ❑ **GetDomainFromMemberName**
- ❑ GetHashCode – inherited from System.Object, see Introduction for details.
- ❑ **GetIsAuthenticated**
- ❑ **GetLoginChallenge?**
- ❑ **GetOption**
- ❑ **GetProfileObject**
- ❑ GetType – inherited from System.Object, see Introduction for details.
- ❑ **HasFlag**
- ❑ **HasProfile**
- ❑ **HaveConsent**
- ❑ **LoginUser**
- ❑ **LogoTag**
- ❑ **LogoTag2**
- ❑ **SetOption**
- ❑ **SignOut**
- ❑ **Ticket**
- ❑ ToString – inherited from System.Object, see Introduction for details.

AuthURL

The AuthURL method has a variety of input signatures, as detailed below. It returns a URL that can be displayed as a hyperlink on a web page for a user who has not yet signed on, or whose authentication ticket has expired. Remember, this method should not be used to redirect the user directly as the LoginUser method handles this more efficiently.

```
public string AuthUrl();
public string AuthUrl(string, int, bool, string, int, string, int, bool);
public string AuthUrl(string, int, int, string, int, string, int, int);
```

AuthURL2

The AuthURL2 method has a variety of input signatures, shown below. It returns a URL that can be displayed as a hyperlink on a web page for a user who has not yet signed on, or whose authentication ticket has expired. Remember, this method should not be used to redirect the user directly as the LoginUser method handles this more efficiently.

```
public string AuthUrl2();

public string AuthUrl2(string, int, bool, string, int, string, int, bool);
public string AuthUrl2(string, int, int, string, int, string, int, int);
```

Compress

The Compress method takes a string as input and returns a compressed version of the string. The Compress method is only used in certain cases for Kids Passport implementations. It reduces the number of characters needed to send a URL string. It only supports low ASCII strings. The Decompress method must be used on the string to decode it.

```
public static string Compress( string strData);
```

CryptIsValid

The CryptIsValid method gets a Boolean value indicating if the Passport Manager is in a valid state for encryption. It can be called after the host name or site in Passport has been set, using the CryptPutHost or CryptPutSite methods. If Passport is configured correctly on the system, it will have a valid encryption key and this property will then return true; otherwise it returns false.

```
public static bool CryptIsValid();
```

CryptPutHost

The CryptPutHost method takes a string as input and returns an integer. It is used in Passport implementations running on machines with more than one host name running on them. For example, a single server could be hosting two separate DNS host names, such as www.foo.com and www.foobar.com. This method tells Passport to use the encryption key specified by the host name you pass to the method. Remember, the Passport framework automatically selects the appropriate authentication key, based on the host name it gets from the Request object. Overriding this behavior should only be done if you have a specific reason to do so.

```
public static int CryptPutHost(string strHost);
```

CryptPutSite

The CryptPutSite method takes a string as input and returns an integer representing the encryption/decryption key. It is used in conjunction with the CryptPutHost method to change the encryption key used by the Passport framework. Normally this is not necessary.

```
public static int CryptPutSite(string strSite);
```

Decompress

The Decompress method takes a string as input. This method is a shared function that decompresses data compressed using the Compress method. The Decompress method returns the string to its pre-compressed state.

```
public static string Decompress(string strData);
```

Decrypt

The `Decrypt` method takes a string as input. This method is a shared function that decrypts a string that was previously encrypted using the `Encrypt` method. The `Decrypt` method returns the string to its pre-encrypted state.

```
public static string Decrypt(string strData);
```

Encrypt

The `Encrypt` method takes a string as input. The returned string is an encrypted hash of the input string. The string can then be unencrypted using the `Decrypt` method. One use for this method would be to encrypt data that you wish to store in a user's cookie or pass on the query string to a page.

```
public static string Encrypt(string strData);
```

GetCurrentConfig

The `GetCurrentConfig` method takes a string as input. It returns an object representing the contents of a registry key under the `HKLM\SW\Microsoft\Passport` registry hive. The input string names the registry key to be returned.

```
public object GetCurrentConfig(string strAttribute);
```

GetDomainAttribute

The `GetDomainAttribute` method takes a string, an integer and another string as input. It returns a string about a Passport domain attribute. Some of the properties that are available are URLs to the Passport registration, profile editing, and privacy policy pages for the current Passport implementation. These properties are useful if you want to build links in your site to allow users to edit their Passport profile.

```
public string GetDomainAttribute(string strAttribute, int iLCID, string
                                                              strDomain);
```

GetDomainFromMemberName

The `GetDomainFromMemberName` method takes a string as input and returns the Passport domain name of the user name provided as input.

```
public string GetDomainFromMemberName(string strMemberName);
```

GetIsAuthenticated

The `GetIsAuthenticated` method is overloaded and has two different input signatures, defined below. `GetIsAuthenticated` returns `true` if the user currently has a valid Passport Authentication ticket. This method returns `false` if the user's login ticket has expired.

```
public bool GetIsAuthenticated(int, bool, bool);
public bool GetIsAuthenticated(int, int, int);
```

GetLoginChallenge

The `GetLoginChallenge` is overloaded and has two different input signatures defined below. It initiates the Passport login process by generating headers with either a 302 redirect URL or the initiation of a Passport-aware client authentication exchange.

```
public string GetLoginChallenge();
public string GetLoginChallenge(string, int, int, string, int, string,
                                                int, int, object);
```

GetOption

The `GetOption` method takes a string as input that represents a specific Passport logon option name and returns an object containing the option details for that name.

```
public object GetOption(string strOpt);
```

GetProfileObject

The `GetProfileObject` takes a string as input that specifies a Passport profile detail and returns an object containing that profile detail.

```
public object GetProfileObject(string strProfileName);
```

HasFlag

The `HasFlag` takes an integer acting as a flag mask as input and returns a `Boolean` `true` if the profile flag is `true` in the user's profile and `false` if it is `false`.

```
public bool HasFlag(int iFlagMask);
```

HasProfile

The `HasProfile` takes a string as input and returns whether a user has a profile. Please note that a user could have a valid Passport Identity, but not have a profile stored in the Passport system.

```
public bool HasProfile(string strProfile);
```

HaveConsent

The `HaveConsent` method takes two `Boolean`s as input and returns a `Boolean` indicating whether the user profile is operating in a full "have consent" context. This is typically used on sites or applications using Kids Passport service.

```
public bool HaveConsent(bool bNeedFullConsent, bool bNeedBirthdate);
```

LoginUser

The `LoginUser` method has a number of input signatures, specified below, and logs a user into Passport by generating headers with either a 302 redirect URL or the initiation of a Passport-aware client authentication.

```
public int LoginUser();
public int LoginUser(string, int, bool, string, int, string, int,
                                              bool, object);
public int LoginUser(string, int, int, string, int, string, int,
                                              int, object);
```

LogoTag

Note: The original `LogoTag` method has been deprecated. You should use `LogoTag2` for the same purpose.

LogoTag2

The `LogoTag2` method is overloaded and has a number of input signatures, defined below. It returns HTML that includes an image tag. The image will appropriately display "Sign In", if the user is not currently signed in, or "Sign Out" if the user is signed in. If the user clicks on the image, the appropriate hyperlink that is embedded into the HTML causes the user to go to the Passport login, or sign-out, screen. The image itself actually resides on a server controlled by the Passport system.

```
public string LogoTag2();
public string LogoTag2(string, int, bool, string, int, bool, string,
                                              int, bool);
public string LogoTag2(string, int, int, string, int, int, string,
                                              int, int);
```

LogoutURL

The `LogoutURL` method is overloaded and has a number of input signatures, defined below. It returns HTML that includes an image tag. The image tag provides a link that will log the user out of the Passport system.

```
public string LogoutURL();
public string LogoutURL(string, string, int, string, int);
```

SetOption

The `SetOption` method takes a string and object as input. The string value represents the Passport logon option name and the object represents the value to be set for that option.

```
public void SetOption( string strOpt, object vOpt);
```

SignOut

The `SignOut` method takes a string as input. The string value represents the URL to a `.gif` image that will be displayed when the user has signed out. Remember, `SignOut` signs the user out of *all* Passport network sites.

```
public static void SignOut(string strSignOutDotGifFileName);
```

Ticket

The `Ticket` method takes a string as input that represents the authentication ticket property specified in the string.

```
public object Ticket(string strAttribute);
```

PassportIdentity Protected Methods

❑   `Finalize` – inherited from `System.Object`, see Introduction for details.

❑   `MemberwiseClone` – inherited from `System.Object`, see Introduction for details.

PassportIdentity Class Public Properties

❑   `AuthenticationType`

❑   `Error`

❑   `GetFromNetworkServer`

❑   `HasSavedPassword`

❑   `HasTicket`

❑   `HexPUID`

❑   `IsAuthenticated`

❑   `Item`

❑   `Name`

❑   `TicketAge`

❑   `TimeSinceSignIn`

AuthenticationType

The `AuthenticationType` property gets a string detailing the authentication type for this `PassportIdentity` instance.

```
public string AuthenticationType {get;}
```

Error

The `Error` property gets an integer referencing an authentication error, if any, associated with this `PassportIdentity` instance.

```
public int Error {get;}
```

GetFromNetworkServer

The `GetFromNetworkServer` property returns a `Boolean` value. When a user logs in to a Passport server, they are redirected back to the web application. The `GetFromNetworkServer` property returns `true` if the user has just been redirected from logging in at a Passport network server.

```
public bool GetFromNetworkServer {get;}
```

HasSavedPassword

The `HasSavedPassword` property gets a `Boolean` value indicating whether their login information has been persisted to the client so that login happens automatically from session to session.

```
public bool HasSavedPassword {get;}
```

HasTicket

The `HasTicket` property gets a `Boolean` value indicating whether or not the query string has a Password ticket stored as a cookie.

```
public bool HasTicket {get;}
```

HexPUID

The `HexPUID` gets a string representing the Passport Unique Identifier in hexadecimal format.

```
public string HexPUID {get;}
```

IsAuthenticated

The `IsAuthenticated` gets a `Boolean` indicating the authentication status of the user.

```
public bool IsAuthenticated {get;}
```

Item

The `Item` property gets Passport profile values referenced by name.

```
public string this[string strProfileName] {get;}
```

Name

The `Name` property gets a string representing the name of the current user.

```
public string Name {get;}
```

TicketAge

The `TicketAge` property gets an integer value indicating the time (in seconds) since the authentication ticket was last refreshed.

```
public int TicketAge {get;}
```

TimeSinceSignIn

The `TimeSinceSignIn` property gets an integer value indicating the time (in seconds) since the user logged in to the service.

```
public int TimeSinceSignIn {get;}
```

9

System.Web.Services

Web Services are a new way of sharing information between computers using HTTP. The ability to create and consume Web Services, quickly and simply, is one of the evolutionary features of the .NET Framework. They can be made accessible from any point on an intranet or extranet, or over the Internet.

Not only are these services accessible over HTTP, but they also have the ability to describe themselves, what they offer, and how they can be accessed, using the emerging standards of UDDI and WSDL. Clients running on any system with support for HTTP communication can consume them, regardless of platform.

Web Services Overview

Understanding how to implement Web Services will be an important part of developing web applications in the near future. They bring a whole new suite of programming tools to classic ASP programmers, providing a mechanism for traditional enterprise programmers to expose their framework and business services in a brand new way.

The Web Services architecture will change the business model of many companies, as they will be able to easily connect to the internal systems of their suppliers, and offer direct connections for their customers to use. In the next phase of the Internet, a whole new group of client/server applications will be developed that will allow users to connect to business systems from a workstation on the Internet as seamlessly as if they were working on the local LAN.

What are Web Services?

The most basic definition of a Web Service is that it is **application logic accessible to programs via standard web protocols in a platform-independent way**. They are one way of invoking Remote Procedure Calls (RPC) over HTTP. The concept itself is nothing new, and has been implemented on network protocols many times over, using technologies like DCOM, RMI, CORBA, and EDI. What's different is that Web Services communicate using HTTP and XML, which are both industry standards.

Web Services overcome some of the limitations of previous technologies, including:

❑ **Platform interoperability** – Clients of Web Services do not have to be based upon any particular platform to consume the services. Platforms such as operating systems, programming languages, component specifications, or language frameworks, are irrelevant.

❑ **Proprietary protocols** – Web Services use the standard HTTP protocol to communicate. As such, they can easily reach through firewalls and allow communication between servers anywhere on the Internet.

It is important to understand that Web Services are more than just a single specification. They are a whole set of specifications that have been adopted by major companies such as Microsoft and IBM. These specifications will be described briefly in the section on *Key Web-Service Standards*.

Discovery and Description

Web Services are self-describing. They implement standards that allow application developers and integrators to easily find existing Web Services, discover their APIs, and build clients that can access them. The .NET Framework provides tools that can be leveraged to provide discovery and description information for the Web Services that you build.

Why Use Web Services?

There are many reasons why you may want to consider exposing Web Services using ASP.NET. We list some of the most salient points below:

Widely Accepted Standards

Web Services are based upon a set of standards that have already been adopted by a number of large software companies, and the World Wide Web Consortium (W3C). To review the latest standards affecting Web Services, go to http://www.w3.org/2002/ws/. Microsoft is seriously backing all of the latest Web Service standards, and a goldmine of developer documentation related to the subject can be found at http://msdn.microsoft.com/webservices/. A large number of tools for building Web Services have already been created, including Microsoft Visual Studio .NET, and more are being developed for other languages, such as Java and Perl.

Callable Even Through a Firewall

Communication between web clients and servers is not always smooth, often due to the settings of firewalls and proxy servers. Network administrators have very good reasons of security for not changing these settings. Nevertheless, Web Services can still expose middle-tier components as they are built on standard protocols, such as SOAP and HTTP, and they only transfer HTML and XML documents which easily pass through firewalls and proxy servers.

Cross Platform

Because Web Services are built on standard protocols, such as XML and HTTP, they are accessible from any language that can communicate over HTTP and can parse XML. A component built in Visual Basic .NET, C#, JavaScript, Perl, or Java can communicate with a component written in any other language and share data. This gives companies a new and exciting opportunity to **integrate with business partners, customers, and vendors, regardless of platform**. The servers, operating systems, and programming backgrounds of the development teams you are trying to integrate with are no longer a barrier.

Scalable

A Web Service can be deployed to run on a single web server and then later scaled across multiple servers without any changes to the application code. Better still, application updates can be made at any time without taking down the Web Service, or interrupting its servicing of clients.

Loosely Coupled

Because Web Services communicate using a message-based protocol, the service and client can evolve separately. As long as the public APIs of the Web Service do not change, recompiling one side or the other and adding functionality will not break existing installed applications.

Software as a Service

This point will perhaps be the hardest one for business managers to wrap their minds around. Building software that can be exposed to the Web allows for a whole new vertical industry that software companies can get involved in. Companies that have a valuable repository of data, information or functionality can expose it to the world using Web Services. Company-to-Company systems integration will become much more commonplace and will reach down to the level of the small business. One example of this would be a company that has a vast database of weather information. That company could expose this to the world via a Web Service. The information could then be accessed, for a fee, by media outlets such as web portals, newspapers, and other information providers. Prior to Web Services, information publishing to this broad a spectrum of customers and getting paid for it was difficult to achieve.

Reasons You May Not Want to Use Web Services

In order to balance the discussion, we'll also mention some reasons why Web Services may not be suitable for your project. They are, after all, not the answer to every application's needs.

Applications Communicating on the Same Machine or LAN

Web Services may not be well suited when different applications need to communicate with each other on the same machine or maybe even on a LAN. In this case, the performance overhead will make your application inefficient.

Remoting May Better Suit your Needs

Remoting is a feature of .NET that allows objects written in .NET languages to be hosted on a server application and accessed remotely from .NET clients. It is a very similar technology to Distributed COM (DCOM). If all of the following bullet points are true, you may be better off using .NET Remoting, instead of Web Services:

❑   All of the clients of your server application will be running the .NET platform

❑   You do not have a need for your server application to be accessible to the public on a variety of client platforms

❑   Performance is critical

❑   All of your components are on the same LAN, otherwise constant communication across firewalls becomes restrictive

This list is just a simple example; you should take the time to understand the Remoting and Web Services architectures if you are in the position of needing to make this kind of decision. A good place to find out more is in the book Professional ASP.NET Web Services, *ISBN 1-861005-458 (Wrox Press).*

Managing Access to the Web Service

Once you have published a Web Service on the Internet, it will be accessible to anyone. If it is important that only authorized users or applications have access to your Web Service, you'll have to create a way to manage access to it. This is quite easy to do with typical ASP.NET authentication and authorization mechanisms, and is mentioned here merely to remind you that it is an issue.

Key Web-Service Standards

As mentioned previously, Web Services are built upon a number of standards. The base standards of HTTP and XML are well known, and will not be covered in detail. We will look, instead, at some of the newer standards, specific to Web Services, in this section.

SOAP

The core specification for Web Service communication is **SOAP**, which stands for Simple Object Access Protocol. SOAP is a protocol for messaging between applications using XML. The SOAP standard specifies three different aspects of the messaging process:

❑ **Messaging Envelope** – defines an XML schema for common information that is part of every SOAP message. This information is typically referred to as an envelope because it contains addressing information and routing rules. The envelope contains a message that is being sent to, or from, the Web Service.

❑ **Encoding Rules** – defines how specific base data types (strings, numbers, dates, and so on) are encoded in XML.

❑ **Procedural conventions** – defines how an actual component method can be represented in a SOAP message packet.

A sample SOAP message, complete with HTTP Headers is shown below:

```
POST /ProgrammersReference/AddingMachine.asmx HTTP/1.1
Host: localhost
Content-Type: text/xml; charset=utf-8
Content-Length: nnnn
SOAPAction: "http://wrox.com/programmersreference/AddTwoNumbers"

<?xml version="1.0" encoding="utf-8"?>
<soap:Envelope xmlns:xsi="http://www.w3.org/2001/XMLSchema-instance"
               xmlns:xsd="http://www.w3.org/2001/XMLSchema"
               xmlns:soap="http://schemas.xmlsoap.org/soap/envelope/">
  <soap:Body>
    <AddTwoNumbers xmlns="http://wrox.com/programmersreference">
      <FirstNumber>10</FirstNumber>
      <SecondNumber>5</SecondNumber>
    </AddTwoNumbers>
  </soap:Body>
</soap:Envelope>
```

In the sample, you can see a `<soap:Envelope>` element. This is the root element of the XML document, and all other elements are nested inside it according to the rules of XML. Inside the root element we have a `<soap:Body>` element that acts as a container for the message sent to, or from, the Web Service. Within this container there is a nested group of elements defining the method call. If a Web Service returns an exception, the `Body` element will contain a `Fault` element describing the exception. The .NET Framework automatically handles the creation and processing of SOAP packets. More information can be found by reading the SOAP specification on the W3C's site at http://www.w3.org/TR/SOAP.

Data Types Supported in SOAP

In order to make cross-platform integration possible, SOAP defines a base set of data types that can be used in SOAP messaging. The data types are converted to the Web Services data type system, **XSD**. XSD defines certain basic standard data types and provides the ability to define custom types. (Using the base types will make for easier integration with other systems and platforms).

Here is a list of the primitive data types that can be exposed as parameters and return values for Web Methods. They are likely to be supported on most programming platforms:

Type	Description
Simple types	Here is a list of the .NET types that are mapped to the simple types defined in the SOAP specification: `String, Int64, UInt64, Int32, UInt32, Int16, UInt16, Byte, Boolean, Decimal, Double, Single, DateTime,` and `XMLQualifiedName`
Enumerations	Enumerations can be built using any of the simple types defined above, except for the `Boolean` type
Arrays	Arrays of the above types

For Web Service applications that will be serving .NET clients exclusively, you have a lot more flexibility to use richer data types. Here is a list of some of the more common types that are specific to .NET that you can also expose as parameters from a Web Service:

Type	Description
XmlNode	A fragment of an XML document.
Classes and Structs	Any class or struct. Only the public properties and methods will be marshaled across the wire. It is also important to note that the effect is to pass the class or struct **by value**, not by reference. To use remote classes or structs by reference, you must use .NET Remoting.
DataSet	The ADO.NET `DataSet`.
Arrays	Arrays of the above types.

WSDL

WSDL stands for Web Services Description Language. It is closely tied to SOAP and is a specification for describing Web Services to developers. WSDL is a schema for an XML document that defines, in detail, the methods that are available from a specific Web Service. It also defines the SOAP messages that must be created to communicate with each Web Method. A WSDL document is commonly referred to as a **WSDL contract** because it is a documented description of a Web Service that a developer can rely upon to be accurate enough to build client access code against. ASP.NET can automatically generate WSDL for any Web Service that you create. Web clients can use the `wsdl.exe` tool to generate a proxy class by passing it the service description of the Web Service. This proxy class can then be used by client code to access the Service. The great thing about the proxy class is that it enables us to reference a remote Web Service and use its functionality within our application as if the data it returns were generated locally.

Passing WSDL as the query parameter to the Web Service can access a service description of any .NET Web Service, such as the following for example:

```
http://localhost/WebService1/AddingMachine.asmx?wsdl
```

> ASP.NET Web Services take `.asmx` as their filename extension.

Here is an example piece of a WSDL contract that describes a Web Method that can add two numbers together to produce a result:

```xml
<?xml version="1.0" encoding="utf-8"?>
<definitions xmlns:s="http://www.w3.org/2001/XMLSchema">
  <service name="AddingService">
    <documentation>Adding Service Web Methods</documentation>
    <port name="AddingServiceHttpGet" binding="s0:AddingServiceHttpGet">
      <http:address
             location="http://localhost/WebService1/AddingMachine.asmx" />
    </port>
  </service>
</definitions>
```

This is just a small fragment of the entire contract that must be produced in order to fully document a Web Service. Because you are programming in ASP.NET, you may never have the need to fully understand the WSDL for your Web Service, because the .NET Framework provides numerous tools that harness the power of WSDL whilst abstracting the actual implementation from view. However, as with any technology, gaining an understating of the underlying ideas always makes you a more powerful programmer.

More information about WSDL can be found in the next chapter.

UDDI

UDDI (Universal Description, Discovery and Integration) is a specification to define a way of creating a registry of the Web Services available. This allows business to publish information about the Web Services that they are offering, and also search for providers of services that they need.

UDDI defines an XML schema for providing information about Web Services. It defines a SOAP API that the UDDI registry server must implement to allow for the publishing (and querying) of Web Services. More information about UDDI, including current UDDI registries, can be found at http://www.uddi.org. Microsoft is hosting one of the first UDDI registries available, at http://uddi.microsoft.com/.

The term "UDDI" is sometimes used to refer to the registry itself, rather than the specification.

DISCO

DISCO (which is shortened from the word "discovery") is a specification that allows an XML document to be created that can be queried for the locations of WSDL documents. The first part of the specification deals with how an application can go about finding and using documents describing Web Services. The second part defines an XML schema for documenting the locations of WSDL documents.

The .NET Framework ships with a tool, `Disco.exe`, which searches for .NET Web Services located on a machine. It returns a DISCO document containing the locations of the WSDL files for those services. For more information about the discovery of Web Services, see Chapter 11.

The System.Web.Services Namespace

`System.Web.Services` contains some of the most basic classes that are used to create a Web Service. It defines the basic attributes used to describe the behavior of the Web Methods and the basic description attributes of the Web Service. Here is a list of the classes available in the `System.Web.Services` namespace.

Class	Description
`WebMethodAttribute`	This class is a required attribute for any public method that you wish to expose as a Web Method.
`WebService`	This class acts as an optional base class to create a Web Service. When you inherit from this class, you have access to intrinsic ASP.NET objects.
`WebServiceAttribute`	This class is an optional attribute for any class that you wish to expose to the world as a Web Service. It provides additional information about the Web Service class like its name, description and namespace.
`WebServiceBindingAttribute`	This attribute can be applied to a class to declare that the class implements a binding defined in a WSDL contract.

WebMethodAttribute Class

The `WebMethodAttribute` class is a required attribute for any public method that you wish to expose to the world as a Web Method. Only methods that are declared public and contain `WebMethodAttribute` will be accessible to any remote web client. When the ASP.NET runtime sees this attribute on your method, it does the necessary work of generating WSDL for it and mapping appropriate SOAP messages to it. This attribute class is derived from the `System.Attribute` class and it cannot be further inherited. All of the properties of this attribute class are optional.

WebMethodAttribute Class Public Methods

- ❑ Equals – inherited from System.Object, see Introduction for details.
- ❑ **GetHashCode**
- ❑ GetType – inherited from System.Object, see Introduction for details.
- ❑ **IsDefaultAttribute**
- ❑ **Match**
- ❑ ToString – inherited from System.Object, see Introduction for details.

GetHashCode

The GetHashCode method returns the hash code for the current instance of the object. It is inherited from System.Attribute and is overridden here to return the hash code.

```
public override int GetHashCode();
```

IsDefaultAttribute

The IsDefaultAttribute method if overridden is used to indicate whether the values of the current instance are equal to the values of the default instance of the object. It is inherited from System.Attribute and is not overridden in the WebMethodAttribute class. As it is not overridden here, it always returns false irrespective of the current object holding default values or not.

```
public virtual bool IsDefaultAttribute();
```

Match

The Match method if overridden is used to compare current instance with another object. It is inherited from System.Attribute and is not overridden in the WebMethodAttribute class. As it is not overridden here, it returns the same value that the Equals method would return.

```
public virtual bool Match(object obj);
```

WebMethodAttribute Class Protected Methods

- ❑ Finalize – inherited from System.Object, see Introduction for details.
- ❑ MemberwiseClone – inherited from System.Object, see Introduction for details.

WebMethodAttribute Class Public Properties

- ❑ **BufferResponse**
- ❑ **CacheDuration**
- ❑ **Description**
- ❑ **EnableSession**

- ❏ **MessageName**

- ❏ **TransactionOption**

- ❏ `TypeId` – inherited from `System.Attribute`, not implemented in this class.

BufferResponse

If this property is set to `true` (the default), the SOAP layer will create the complete response SOAP packet in a memory buffer before sending it back to the client. If it is set to `false`, the SOAP packet is sent back to the client in pieces, as it is built on the server. Normally you'll want to leave this with the default value. However, if you anticipate that the Web Method will return a very large amount of data as its result, then setting the `BufferResponse` property to `false` will improve perceived performance by disabling buffering. You should also verify when all of the data has been received.

Here is an example that sets the `BufferResponse` property to `false` as the method returns a huge `DataSet` object:

```
[WebMethod(BufferResponse=False)]
public DataSet GetData()
{
  //We turned buffering off because we are going to return lots of data
  return db.HugeDataSet();
}
```

Note that if the `BufferResponse` property is set to `false`, SOAP extensions will be disabled for this method. See Chapter 11 for more information on SOAP extensions.

```
public bool BufferResponse {get; set;}
```

CacheDuration

Web Service output caching is a feature of ASP.NET that adds virtually automatic caching capability to methods exposed by your Web Service. If a Web Method is called more than once with the same parameters before the cached output expires, ASP.NET will return the cached output without calling your method again. The data that ASP.NET caches is the SOAP message packet that was generated as a response from the previous invocation of your Web Service. By default, the `CacheDuration` property is set to 0, which means that caching is disabled. If you set the `CacheDuration` property to a number greater than 0, then ASP.NET will cache the data for that many seconds.

Here's an example of how to set up output caching of a Web Method for 60 seconds:

```
[WebMethod(CacheDuration=60)]
string GetTaskList(string GroupID)
{
  return db.getTaskList(GroupID);
}
```

A cached copy of the data will be maintained for each distinct set of parameters that are passed to the Web Method. If your Web Method will return large amounts of data and has a large number of different parameter combinations that it will be called with, caching the data may not be the right choice.

Caching frequently used pieces of data for even short periods of time can dramatically increase the potential scalability of your web application. You should weigh up the benefits against the amount of server resources you could be tying up to maintain the caches.

```
public int CacheDuration {get; set;}
```

Description

The Description property contains the string (default is String.Empty) description of the Web Method. This property is very helpful as its value is displayed in the browser when the Web Service test page is viewed in a browser. Also, this property comes in the service description document of the Web Service in the documentation element. You can help other developers understand your code by giving a brief description identifying the purpose of the method.

```
public string Description {get; set;}
```

Example: Describing Your Web Service

In this example we are going to create a simple Web service which returns the current date and time and describe it as such using the Description property. Here is the Web Service code, DateTime.asmx.cs in the code download for this chapter:

```
using System.Web.Services;

[WebService (Namespace="http://wrox.system.web.services")]
public class DateTime : System.Web.Services.WebService

...

  [WebMethod(Description="This method returns the current date and time.")]
  public string GetDateTime()
  {
    return System.DateTime.Now.ToString();
  }
```

Below-left is the output we get if we browse to the Web Service test page, DateTime.asmx, and below-right is the output of the Web Service if we invoke it from the default test page:

Furthermore here is an extract of the output if we append `?WSDL` to the query string (or click the Service Description link in the test page) in order to make the ASP.NET runtime generate a WSDL contract for our Web Service:

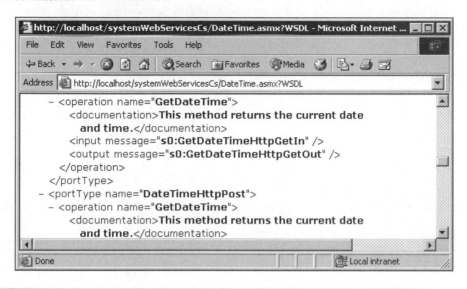

EnableSession

This property enables use of the `Session` object in a Web Method, if set to `true`. By default it is set to `false`. A Web Service can only maintain a `Session` object through the use of cookies. If the `<sessionState>` section of the `web.config` is set as `cookieless="true"`, then the Web Method will not be able to maintain a `Session` state for the Web Method. Web Service clients that do not properly handle cookies will not have any state maintained for them in their `Session` objects on the server between Web Service requests, regardless of whether this property is set to `true` or `false`.

If this property is set to `true` and the Web Service class inherits from `System.Web.Services.WebService`, then the session state collection can be accessed using the `WebService.Session` property. If the Web Service does not inherit from the `WebService` class, session state can be accessed through the `HttpContext.Current.Session` property.

Note that setting this property to `true` may increase performance overhead.

```
public bool EnableSession {get; set;}
```

The following example, `HitCounter.asmx` in the code download for this chapter, shows how to enable session state for your Web Service. Here is the code-behind for the Service, `HitCounter.asmx.cs`:

```
using System.Web.Services;

[WebService(Namespace="http://wrox.system.web.services")]
public class HitCounter : System.Web.Services.WebService

...

  [WebMethod(EnableSession=true)]
  public string UpdateHitCounter()
  {
    // Initialize Session HitCounter to 1 if it is null
    if(Session["HitCounter"] == null)
      Session["HitCounter"] = 1;
    // Increment HitCounter's value by 1
    else
      Session["HitCounter"] = (int)(Session["HitCounter"]) + 1;
    return "Total Hits: " + Session["HitCounter"].ToString();
  }
```

When you test this Web Service a couple of times you can see that the hit counter increases with each new request:

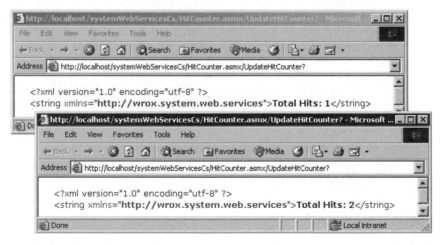

If you were to call this Web Method from an `.aspx` page, the web page will need to pass the Session information to the Web Method. This can be done in an `.aspx` page by creating a cookie container object and associating it with the Web Service object. Here is the piece of code that will be able to maintain session while calling a Web Method:

```
MyService  ms = new MyService();
ms.CookieContainer = new CookieContainer();
Label1.Text = ms.UpdateHitCounter();
Label2.Text = ms.UpdateHitCounter();
```

MessageName

The name that SOAP uses by default to identify your Web Method is derived from the actual method name defined in the Web Service class. This behavior can be overridden by the use of the `MessageName` property.

This property is typically used to expose Web Methods that have several overloaded versions, as SOAP does not support overloading. If your Web Service class has overloaded versions of the same method, they must be distinguished from each other by having a unique SOAP message name. Otherwise compilation errors will occur telling the user to specify unique names for methods using the `MessageName` property. If the `MessageName` property is assigned then the `name` attribute of the input and output elements of the `operation` element in the WSDL document describing the service will contain the value of the `MessageName` property.

Here is an example of an overloaded method. That is, the same name is used for two different methods, and the methods only vary by the data types of their parameters. In order for them to be exposed over SOAP as Web Methods, they must have a unique SOAP message name, and the client must reference the `MessageName` to get the correct overloaded method:

```
[WebMethod]
public string GetCustomerName(Guid CustomerID)
{
  return db.GetCustomerName(CustomerID);
}

[WebMethod(MessageName="GetCustomerByID")]
public string GetCustomerName(int CustomerID)
{
  return db.GetCustomerName(CustomerID);
}
```

The syntax for this property is as follows:

```
public string MessageName {get; set;}
```

TransactionOption

This property sets the transactional behavior for the Web Method. Enabling transactional support in a Web Method means that it can participate as the root object in a COM+ (MTS) transaction.

Web Methods in ASP.NET currently do not support sharing transactions with the application that is calling them. A Web Service is transactional only if it is the root object that started the transaction. In other words, if a Web Method begins a transaction and then calls another Web Method that requires a transaction, the two Web Services cannot mutually share the same transaction. Each Web Method participates solely in the context of its own transaction. This could change with future versions of ASP.NET as Web Service technology becomes more mature.

The `TransactionOption` property may be set with any of the values from the `TransactionOption` enumeration, which is shown below. By default, this property is set to `TransactionOption.Disabled`.

Note that this enumeration is from the `System.EnterpriseServices` namespace.

Enumeration Name	Description
Disabled	The Web Method will be run without any transaction in place.
NotSupported	Run this component outside the context of a transaction. For a Web Method, this setting is effectively the same as `Disabled`.
Required	If a transaction is already in place, share in it. If not, create a new transaction. For a Web Method, this is always the same as `RequiresNew`.
RequiresNew	Always create a new transaction for this component.
Supported	If a transaction is already in place, share in it. Because Web Methods do not share in transactions, this setting is effectively the same as `Disabled`.

Here is an example usage of a Web Method with transaction support enabled:

```
[WebMethod(TransactionOption=TransactionOption.RequiresNew)]
public void SaveCustomer()
{
  // run the save customer logic here within the scope of the transaction
}
```

The transaction is automatically committed unless an exception occurs in the Web Method. However, a transaction can be forcefully aborted by calling the `SetAbort` method of the `System.EnterpriseServices.ContextUtil` class.

```
public TransactionOption TransactionOption {get; set;}
```

WebService Class

`WebService` is a class that can be inherited to create a Web Service in ASP.NET. This class is derived from the `System.ComponentModel.MarshalByValueComponent` class. When you inherit from this class you get immediate access to the ASP.NET intrinsic objects like `Application`, `Session`, `Server`, `User`, `Context`. You should be aware that these objects are the same ones used in ASP.NET Web Form applications. In fact, the `Session` and `Application` objects are shared between Web Services and Web Forms if they are running within the same application scope in Internet Information Server (IIS).

Example: Web Service Classes

Here is an example of a Web Service class derived from WebService (MyWebService.asmx.cs in the code download):

```
using System.Web.Services;

[WebService(Namespace="http://wrox.system.web.services")]
public class MyWebService : System.Web.Services.WebService

...

[WebMethod]
public string ShowHostAddress()
{
  // Get the UserHostAddress through the
  //Context.Request.UserHostAddress property
  return Context.Request.UserHostAddress;
}
```

Note that this Web Method uses the Context intrinsic property, which is derived from WebService. The example then accesses the UserHostAddress property of HttpRequest class through the Context property. Properties of WebService class are discussed in detail later in this section.

The main advantage of inheriting from WebService is the intrinsic access to the Application, Context, Server, Session, and User objects. Because multiple-inheritance is not supported in .NET, there may be a case where you would like your class to inherit from some other class instead of WebService. Even if your class is not inherited from WebService, the intrinsic objects can still be accessed through the shared Current property of the HttpContext object of the current request. The HttpContext class provides access to other objects as well like Cache, Request, Response and so on.

Here, the previous example is changed to provide access to the Context object via the HttpContext.Current property. Note that the Web Service also does not inherit from the WebService class. This code is from MyWebService2.asmx.cs:

```
using System.Web.Services;
using System.Web;

[WebService(Namespace="http://wrox.System.Web.Services")]
public class MyWebService2
{

  [WebMethod]
  public string ShowHostAddress()
  {
    // Get the user host address through
    // HttpContext.Current.Request.UserHostAddress
```

```
    return HttpContext.Current.Request.UserHostAddress;
    }
}
```

Both of these Web Service classes give the same output:

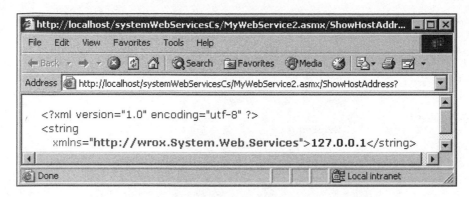

Note that if a Web Service method applies RPC formatting via
SoapRpcMethodAttribute or Document formatting via
SoapDocumentMethodAttribute and sets the OneWay property of these classes
to true then the Web Method will not be able to have a reference to Context and
other intrinsic objects (Application, Server, Session, User) in any way.

WebService Class Public Methods

❑ **Dispose**

❑ Equals – inherited from System.Object, see Introduction for details.

❑ GetHashCode

❑ **GetService**

❑ GetType – inherited from System.Object, see Introduction for details.

❑ ToString – inherited from System.Object, see Introduction for details.

Dispose

The Dispose method releases all the resources used by MarshalByValueComponent. It is inherited
from the System.ComponentModel.MarshalByValueComponent class.

```
public void Dispose();
```

GetHashCode

The GetHashCode method returns the hash code for the current instance of the object. It is inherited
from System.Attribute.

```
public virtual int GetHashCode();
```

GetService

The GetService method returns the implementer of the IServiceProvider interface. It is inherited from the System.ComponentModel.MarshalByValueComponent class, and takes the type of service you want as input.

```
public virtual object GetService(Type service);
```

WebService Class Protected Methods

❑ **Dispose**

❑ Finalize – inherited from System.Object, see Introduction for details.

❑ MemberwiseClone – inherited from System.Object, see Introduction for details.

Dispose

This Dispose method releases all the unmanaged resources used by MarshalByValueComponent. It also releases the managed resources based on the Boolean value passed as the parameter. It is inherited from the System.ComponentModel.MarshalByValueComponent class.

```
protected virtual void Dispose(bool);
```

Passing in the parameter true indicates that the managed resources should also be released, and not if false. This method is called by the Finalize method discussed below, with false as the parameter value. The public Dispose method discussed above also calls this method with the parameter value set to true.

WebService Class Public Properties

❑ **Application**

❑ **Container**

❑ **Context**

❑ **DesignMode**

❑ **Server**

❑ **Session**

❑ **Site**

❑ **User**

Application

The Application property returns an HttpApplicationState object. This object is similar to the Application object in classic ASP.

Here is an example of using the `Application` property:

```
[WebMethod]
public string GetConnectionString()
{
  // This code will only work if we have previously stored
  // the connection string in the Application object
  return Application["ConnectStr"].ToString();
}
```

The syntax for this property is as follows:

```
public HttpApplicationState Application {get;}
```

Container

This property returns the container of the component (the implementer of the `IContainer` interface).
It is inherited from the `System.ComponentModel.MarshalByValueComponent` class. This
property returns `null` if the component does not have a site. `Site` is used to bind a `Component` to a
`Container`.

```
public virtual IContainer  Container {get;}
```

Context

The `Context` property returns the `HttpContext` object for the current request. The `HttpContext`
class contains accessors for all of the normal objects you would use to retrieve the state of the current
request, including the `Session`, `Request`, `Response`, `Application`, `Server`, and `User` objects.
Here is an example of getting the `Items` property of the `HttpContext` object:

```
// This code will only work if we have previously stored
// ItemKey in the Context object
string aContextItem  = Context.Items["ItemKey"].ToString();
```

The syntax for this property is as follows:

```
public HttpContext Context {get;}
```

DesignMode

This property indicates whether the container is in design mode. It is inherited from
`System.ComponentModel.MarshalByValueComponent` class. This property returns `false` if the
component does not have a site or is not in design mode.

```
public virtual bool DesignMode {get;}
```

Server

The `Server` property returns the current `HttpServerUtility` object. The `HttpServerUtility` object is similar to the `Server` object in classic ASP.

```
public HttpServerUtility Server {get;}
```

Session

The `Session` property returns an `HttpSessionState` object. This object stores state for the current user between requests. The `Session` object is turned off by default in a Web Service. In order to enable it, you will need to set the `EnableSession` property on the `WebMethod` attribute to `true`. See the `WebMethodAttribute` class reference earlier in this chapter for more details.

Typically the `Session` object is not used in Web Services, as they are best designed to run in a stateless manner. In other words, each request will have all of the information the server needs to process the information and return a response. The server should not need to persist any information about the client in between requests. In some cases, however, session state within a Web Service may be a necessary and an important part of the design.

> Note that the use of session state requires that the client application be able to process and return cookies for each subsequent request.

```
public HttpSessionState Session {get;}
```

Site

This property returns the site of the component (implementer of the `ISite` interface) indicating that a component is to be added to the container. It is inherited from the `System.ComponentModel.MarshalByValueComponent` class. This property returns `null` if the component has not been added to the container, or is being removed from the container. Nevertheless this property does not remove a component from a container.

```
public virtual ISite Site {get; set;}
```

User

If user authentication has been enabled for the current Web Service, the `User` property will contain an object that implements the `IPrincipal` interface and represents the identity of the current user. See Chapter 8 for more details on user authentication. Here is an example of retrieving the current user's name.

```
string aName = User.Identity.Name;
```

The syntax for this property is as follows:

```
public IPrincipal User {get;}
```

WebService Class Protected Properties

❏ **Events**

Events

This property returns an `EventHandlerList` object representing all the event handlers attached to this component. If there are any event handlers associated with the component, they will be accessible through the `EventHandlerList` object. You can call various methods of the `EventHandlerList` object on the return value. It is inherited from the `System.ComponentModel.MarshalByValueComponent` class.

```
protected EventHandlerList Events {get;}
```

WebService Class Public Events

❏ **Disposed**

Disposed

The `Disposed` event can be used to add an event handler. This event handler is invoked whenever the `Disposed` event occurs. It is inherited from the `System.ComponentModel.MarshalByValueComponent` class.

```
public Event EventHandler Disposed;
```

WebServiceAttribute Class

The `WebServiceAttribute` class is an optional attribute for any class that you wish to expose to the world as a Web Service. It provides additional information about the Web Service class including the custom name, description of the Web Service and most importantly the namespace to which the Web Service belongs. It is good programming practice to specify all three of these properties when your Web Service is ready to be exposed to the outside world. They provide great information about the Web Service to web clients who may want to consume it. This attribute class is derived from the `System.Attribute` class and it cannot be further inherited. All of the properties of this attribute class are optional. These properties can partially change the SOAP and WSDL that is automatically generated for your code by ASP.NET at run time. The methods discussed below will not be of much significance to programmers as this class is basically used to set the behavior of the Web Method through its properties.

WebServiceAttribute Public Methods

❏ `Equals` – inherited from `System.Object`, see Introduction for details.

❏ **GetHashCode**

❏ `GetType` – inherited from `System.Object`, see Introduction for details.

❏ **IsDefaultAttribute**

❏ **Match**

❏ `ToString` – inherited from `System.Object`, see Introduction for details.

GetHashCode

The GetHashCode method returns the hash code for the current instance of the object. It is inherited from System.Attribute and is overridden here to return the hash code.

```
public override int GetHashCode();
```

IsDefaultAttribute

The IsDefaultAttribute method if overridden is used to indicate whether the values of the current instance are equal to the values of the default instance of the object. It is inherited from System.Attribute and is not overridden in the WebServiceAttribute class. As it is not overridden here, it always returns false irrespective of whether or not the current object is holding default values.

```
public virtual bool IsDefaultAttribute();
```

Match

The Match method if overridden is used to compare the current instance with another object. It is inherited from System.Attribute and is not overridden in the WebServiceAttribute class. As it is not overridden here, it returns the same value that the Equals method would return.

```
public virtual bool Match(object obj);
```

WebServiceAttribute Class Protected Methods

- ❑ Finalize – inherited from System.Object, see Introduction for details.
- ❑ MemberwiseClone – inherited from System.Object, see Introduction for details.

WebServiceAttribute Class Public Properties

- ❑ **Description**
- ❑ **Name**
- ❑ **Namespace**
- ❑ TypeId – inherited from System.Attribute, not implemented in this class.

Description

The Description property of the WebServiceAttribute can be set on your class to briefly describe your Web Service to consumers of your class. The WSDL that is generated will contain this description in a new element documentation added to the service element. The default ASP.NET Web Service description page for your Web Service also displays the description right after the header of the page. It is very similar to its WebMethodAttribute counterpart except its purpose is to explain the Service in general rather than a particular Web Method.

```
public string Description {get; set;}
```

Name

The `Name` property is used to assign a custom name to the Web Service. By default this property holds the name of the Web Service class. The ASP.NET Web Service description page for your Web Service also displays the Web Service name as the header of the page.

```
public string Name {get; set;}
```

Namespace

The `Namespace` property is probably the most important attribute to use. It defines a unique URI that defines the XML namespace that will be applied to the specific XML elements in SOAP messages sent to, and from, your Web Service. Your namespace is what sets your Web Service apart from all other Web Services in the world. Other Web Services could have the same method names as yours, but if your namespace is unique, there is no ambiguity about which Web Service belongs to you. Typically, businesses that already have a unique domain name for their web site will use it for part of the namespace for their Web Services.

```
public string Namespace {get; set;}
```

Example: Using Web Service Attributes

In this example we are going to use the properties we have been discussing from the `WebServiceAttribute` class to distinguish our simple Web Service. Here is the code-behind for our service, `PersonalizedService.asmx.cs`:

```
using System.Web.Services;

[WebService(Name="My Very Own Personalized Web Service",
Description="This is a Hello World service for illustration purposes",
Namespace="http://www.wrox.com/System.Web.Services")]
public class PersonalizedService : System.Web.Services.WebService
{
...

  [WebMethod]
  public string HelloWorld()
  {
    return "Hello World";
  }
}
```

As you can see if we open up the test page for this service, and if we look at the WSDL contract by clicking the Service Description link, adding these attributes has given our simple Web Service a much more descriptive interface:

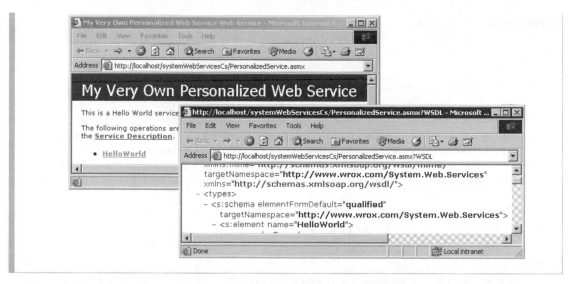

WebServiceBindingAttribute Class

The binding defines a set of operations provided by your Web Service; you can think of this as a template or an interface. Here each operation is nothing but a Web Method. This attribute can be applied to a class to declare that the class implements a binding defined in a WSDL contract. If you wish to implement multiple bindings, you can include numerous `WebServiceBindingAttributes` in the Web Service class declaration. This attribute class is derived from the `System.Attribute` class and it cannot be further inherited. The `WebServiceBindingAttribute` simply describes the details of one or more bindings that are described elsewhere in addition to their own default bindings. For more information on bindings, see Chapter 10.

As Web Services evolve, the ability to be able to bind to a particular set of operations will become crucial to allow Web Services to seamlessly interact with one another. It is likely that standards bodies will define particular bindings for common types of Web Services that Web Service developers can then build to.

Note that if you have applied a `WebServiceBindingAttribute` attribute to your Web Service, the individual methods that implement the binding interface must also be marked with a `SoapDocumentMethodAttribute` or a `SoapRpcMethodAttribute`. These attributes map the specific Web Methods to the associated binding that they are implementing. See Chapter 11 for more details on these attributes.

WebServiceBindingAttribute Class Public Methods

- ❑ Equals – inherited from `System.Object`, see Introduction for details.
- ❑ **GetHashCode**
- ❑ GetType – inherited from `System.Object`, see Introduction for details.
- ❑ **IsDefaultAttribute**
- ❑ **Match**
- ❑ ToString – inherited from `System.Object`, see Introduction for details.

GetHashCode

The `GetHashCode` method returns the hash code for the current instance of the object. It is inherited from `System.Attribute` and is overridden here to return the hash code.

```
public override int GetHashCode();
```

IsDefaultAttribute

The `IsDefaultAttribute` method if overridden is used to indicate whether the values of the current instance are equal to the values of the default instance of the object. It is inherited from `System.Attribute` and is not overridden in the `WebServiceAttribute` class. As it is not overridden here, it always returns `false` irrespective of whether or not the current object is holding default values.

```
public virtual bool IsDefaultAttribute();
```

Match

The `Match` method if overridden is used to compare the current instance with another object. It is inherited from `System.Attribute` and is not overridden in the `WebServiceAttribute` class. As it is not overridden here, it returns the same value that the `Equals` method would return.

```
public virtual bool Match(object obj);
```

WebServiceBindingAttribute Class Protected Methods

- ❑ `Finalize` – inherited from `System.Object`, see Introduction for details.

- ❑ `MemberwiseClone` – inherited from `System.Object`, see Introduction for details.

WebServiceBindingAttribute Class Public Properties

- ❑ **Location**
- ❑ **Name**
- ❑ **Namespace**
- ❑ `TypeId` – inherited from `System.Attribute`, not implemented in this class.

Location

The `Location` property specifies the URL to the WSDL contract that this Web Service is bound to. The default value is the URL of the Web Service that this attribute is applied to.

```
public string Location {get; set;}
```

Name

The Name property defines a unique name that distinguishes this binding from all other bindings. The default value is the name of the class with the word SOAP appended to it.

```
public string Name {get; set;}
```

Namespace

The Namespace property sets the namespace that is associated with the particular binding.

```
public string Namespace {get; set;}
```

10

System.Web.Services.Description

Web Services provide the functionality of components over the Web. They are accessed using standard web protocols and offer a new way of allowing for the communication and sharing of data. Web Services can be created in any language and can be consumed by remote clients written in any language, any component model and any platform that supports the movement of SOAP (Simple Object Access Protocol) packets over HTTP or SMTP. Since Web Services can be consumed by a large community of web clients, the clients should be made aware of the Web Service location, its web methods, methods parameters and return values by means of a formal definition. This is achieved via a number of services established to directly address this need. The need for a formal standardized definition is addressed using Web Service Description Language (WSDL). This is a type of grammar based on XML that provides a standard way of describing Web Services. WSDL is an industry-wide specification that all SOAP servers and clients adhere to. These WSDL services can be located using DISCO (Discovery of Web Services) which not only offers information on where to find Web Services but also on their functionality and how to interact with them. In addition, there is the Universal Description, Discovery, and Integration project (UDDI), which is a database of information that enables developers to advertise their Web Services and for consumers to locate those that they are interested in.

The System.Web.Services.Description namespace contains a hierarchy of object-oriented classes and collections that allow you to interrogate WSDL files. The information contained in a WSDL schema definition is used to construct a SOAP request message that can be sent to an ASP.NET Web Service; the schema structure adhered to by ASP.NET follows the standards defined by the World-Wide Web Consortium (W3C) document at http://www.w3.org/TR/wsdl; the v1.1 WSDL draft specification. The Web Service request handler then interprets the SOAP request, calls the specific method in the Web Service by passing required arguments to it and creates a SOAP response to be returned back to the calling client.

Displaying a WSDL File

To display the WSDL file for any ASP.NET Web Service you simply need to point your web browser to the Web Service URL and just append the text "?wsdl" at the end:

http://localhost/systemWebServicesDescription/SimpleCalculator/SimpleCalculator.asmx**?wsdl**

Browse to the above URL, including the `?wsdl` query string parameter and the WSDL file will now be displayed describing the location and structure of the Web Service. Although the output from the WSDL is vast, the example below illustrates the type of content to be found in here:

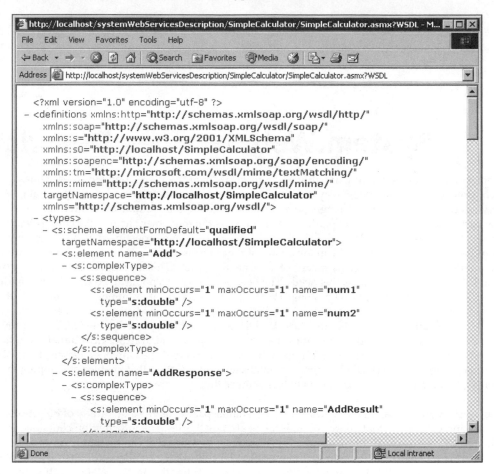

The WSDL page can also be viewed by clicking on the Service Description link in the Web Service Help Page. This link actually does a HTTP GET query for Web Service with a WSDL parameter.

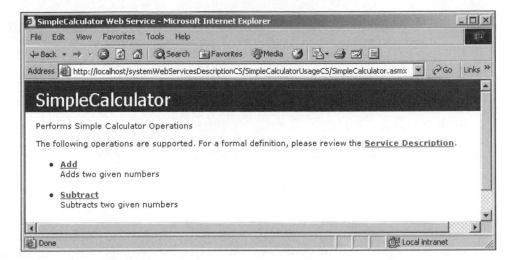

Note that the above method displays a WSDL schema file for an ASP.NET Web Service. For those Web Services that are not ASP.NET applications, their respective Web Service providers will supply you with the location of the WSDL file.

Using WSDL Schema

Usually the schema definition will be required by the client to invoke a Web Service, but in some cases where an ASP.NET server is using another server's Web Service to pass on processing, it may also be helpful to use the Description namespace on the server as well.

There is usually a little confusion about what the Description namespace can be used for, so an explanation using two scenarios will allow you to get a better grasp as to how this namespace can significantly help cure what are two very common problems in any software development team today: versioning and naming conventions.

Scenario 1: Version Control

Say you wanted to implement versioning and, as part of your versioning control management, you set the target Namespace you wanted to use for the entire WSDL schema to include the name of the Web Service plus the version number as CalculatorWebService_v102.

Setting the name for the Web Service on an ASP.NET server is done as follows:

```
[WebService (Namespace="Calculator_v102")]
public class SimpleCalculator : System.Web.Services.WebService
{
  [WebMethod (Description="Adds two given numbers")]
  public double Add(double num1, double num2)
  {
    return num1+num2;
```

```
      }
   }
```

The client can now read the `Namespace` for the schema by placing the following code wherever they require version checking:

```
String supportedVersion = "SimpleCalculator_v101";
XmlReader reader = new
XmlTextReader("http://localhost/Calculator/Calculator.asmx?wsdl");
ServiceDescription sdDescription = ServiceDescription.Read(reader);

if(sdDescription.Namespace == supportedVersion)
  Response.Write("This version IS supported");
else
  Response.Write("This version IS NOT supported");
```

As can be seen, this value-added information for a WSDL definition enables you to programmatically determine business flow, and produce specialist SOAP interpretation and response routines.

Scenario 2: Naming Convention

In this scenario you have a strict naming convention within your organization for Web Services that states that all string variables must start with "`str`" and all other variables (independent of their type) must start with "`var`". Using the following code you can check through large quantities of Web Service schemas quickly looking for inconsistencies within your WSDL definitions:

```
foreach(Message message in sDescription.Messages)
{
  foreach(MessagePart part in message.Parts)
  {
    if((part.Type.Name!="string") & (!part.Name.StartsWith("str")))
      //Raise an error or log an error
    else if(!part.Name.StartsWith("var"))
      // Raise an error or log an error
  }
}
```

WSDL Schema Definition

Before we attempt to describe the `Description` namespace we will discuss the hierarchy of WSDL/XML schema definitions.

Below we have outlined each of the classes within the `Description` namespace along with their related `<element>` names:

❑ '*' denotes 0 or more entries allowed using a collection class

❑ '?' denotes 0 or 1 entry only allowed using a collection class

WSDL Section	Classes and Elements
Interface	**Types** (`<types>` element) * **Message** (`<message>` element) * MessagePart (`<part>` element) * **PortType** (`<porttype>` element) * Operation (`<operation>` element) * InputMessage (`<input>` element) ? OutputMessage (`<output>` element) ? FaultMessage (`<fault>` element) *
Binding	**Binding** (`<binding>` element) * OperationBinding (`<operation>` element) * InputBinding (`<input>` element) ? OutputBinding (`<output>` element) ? FaultBinding (`<fault>` element) *
Communication	**Service** (`<service>` element) * **Port** (`<port>` element) *

This table should serve as a reference as to which XML element these classes are associated with. They are all covered in more detail later in the chapter.

To see how the hierarchy of the Description namespace correlates to a WSDL schema, you can view the WSDL within the SimpleCalculatorUsage project. The full version of this can be accessed using either of the methods detailed above in the SimpleCalculator.asmx?wsdl example or by simply looking at the SimpleCalculator.wsdl file in the code download. Sections of this WSDL will be shown throughout the rest of this chapter to highlight particular topics.

WSDL Sections

The ServiceDescription class has many child collections and classes that map directly to WSDL elements. By instantiating the ServiceDescription class you are effectively mapping every element of a given WSDL schema to your class or property. However, the bulk of the namespace's functionality lies within the six classes, which are in bold font in the above table. These classes represent the principal areas of a WSDL file, and each provides information relating to a particular aspect of a Web Service's functionality.

A WSDL file is split, not just by the XML tags within it, but also into definitive business sections. Each of these sections is self-describing, with regard to how one area of its internal structure can reference other internal areas. The three primary sections of a WSDL file are listed next.

The Interface Section

This section of a WSDL document defines the methods, arguments, and namespaces available for this Web Service on a remote SOAP server. It defines the format for SOAP Requests, Responses, Faults, and Data Types.

The main classes for handling the data contained in this section are:

❑   Messages (class correlates to the <message> element)

❑   Types (class correlates to the <types> element)

❑   PortTypes (class correlates to the <porttype> element)

The Communication Section

This section defines the supported communication methods for transferring a request to a server, such as HTTP GET, HTTP POST, and SOAP. This information is linked to an associated interface and protocol using a Binding namespace.

The main classes that fall into this section are:

❑   Services (class correlates to the <service> element)

❑   Ports (class correlates to the <port> element)

The Binding Section

The binding section associates definitions given in the Communication section with definitions in the Interface section using the <binding> element.

The class in the Description namespace that deals with this section is:

❑   Bindings (class correlates to the <binding> element)

Extensibility

This is a commonly used term within WSDL creation to denote the ability to enhance the basic function of WSDL key elements, without changing the fundamental structure of the WSDL schema format.

Some situations where extensibility can be useful include:

❑   Extending style definitions (for example, Remote Procedure Calls (RPC) and Document)

❑   Specifying a location address for a port

❑   Providing Multipurpose Internet Mail Extensions (MIME) information for file attachments

❑   Providing message definitions

Extensions of these elements are defined using existing XML elements, such as <soap:binding>, which can be easily read and understood by a compliant WSDL reader, like ASP.NET.

Even though extensibility may seem, at first glance, like an issue for advanced users only, it does in fact include certain WSDL elements, which if not available would mean that the WSDL schema definition could not be read. Therefore you need to be aware that extensibility refers to mandatory XML elements of a WSDL file, as well as optional, and possibly more advanced, elements.

Extensibility elements must use a unique namespace within the WSDL schema in which they are defined.

How Do Extensibility Classes Work?

Extensibility can be simply described by stating that if you add an extensibility class to a class with extensions capability (`Extensions` property), you extend the features of that class. Therefore if you add an `HttpBinding` class to a `Binding` class you are in the initial stages of indicating that you want this `Binding` class to support `HttpBinding`. This alteration is then reflected in the WSDL schema when written out to a file.

Using extensibility provides the flexibility to define a set of messages and protocols that represent the business logic once, and then reuse the same set of business logic multiple times with varying protocols. The WSDL 1.1 specification comes with SOAP, HTTP GET/POST, and MIME extensions layered on top of the base specification, although there is nothing to prevent the specification from being extended to support other protocols.

The following classes are all the extensibility classes that are supported within ASP.NET and can serve to extend functionality:

Extensibility Classes

- ❏ HttpAddressBinding
- ❏ HttpBinding
- ❏ HttpOperationBinding
- ❏ HttpUrlEncodedBinding
- ❏ HttpReplacementBinding
- ❏ MimeMultipartRelatedBinding
- ❏ MimePart
- ❏ MimeTextBinding
- ❏ MimeXmlBinding
- ❏ MimeContentBinding
- ❏ SoapAddressBinding
- ❏ SoapBinding
- ❏ SoapBodyBinding
- ❏ SoapFaultBinding
- ❏ SoapHeaderBinding
- ❏ SoapHeaderFaultBinding
- ❏ SoapOperationBinding

Within the following list are the classes within the `Description` namespace that have an `Extensions` property:

Classes with Extensions Property

❑ `Binding`

❑ `FaultBinding`

❑ `InputBinding`

❑ `MimePart`

❑ `OperationBinding`

❑ `OutputBinding`

❑ `Port`

❑ `Service`

❑ `ServiceDescription`

❑ `Types`

> *Note that even though you have amended the schema this does not mean that your Web Service actually supports this functionality.*

System.Web.Services.Description Namespace

The `System.Web.Services.Description` namespace contains classes that help to describe the Web Services using the Web Service Description Language (WSDL). They help Web Services to describe location, web methods, method parameters and method return values. They also help in specifying the protocols that can be used to invoke the Web Services.

Here is a list of the classes available in the `System.Web.Services.Description` namespace. The classes that are shaded below will be discussed in further detail throughout the chapter.

Class	Description
`Binding`	**`Binding` class contains concrete definitions binding the different sections of the schema into a single WSDL schema. This class joins the protocols section to the messages section, introducing information on the format of the structure of the WSDL schema, for example RPC or Document binding styles.**
`BindingCollection`	`BindingCollection` class is a collection of `Binding` objects.

Class	Description
DocumentableItem	DocumentableItem class acts as an abstract base class for a number of other classes in the System.Web.Services.Description namespace. It provides the documentation for a particular WSDL. It has one property, Documentation (read/write), which is inherited by all classes that use it as their base class.
FaultBinding	Specifies the format for any error messages that may be generated by the Web Service interaction.
FaultBindingCollection	FaultBindingCollection class is a collection of FaultBinding objects.
HttpAddressBinding	Usually used to extend or enhance the WSDL schema to deal with a specific protocol or message format, where the binding uses the HTTP protocol. The address binding of the Location property supplies an Internet address for the port. Definition maps to an <http> element within the <binding> element of a WSDL schema that supports this protocol.
HttpBinding	Used to extend or enhance the WSDL schema for a specific protocol or message format. If this definition is available it defines that the binding uses the HTTP protocol format.
HttpOperationBinding	Used to extend or enhance the WSDL schema for a specific protocol or message format. HTTPOperationBinding links data formats and messages supported by the Web Service.
HttpUrlEncodedBinding	Indicates that the parameters may be transferred to the server using standard URL encoding techniques, for instance appending the values of the MessageParts (arguments) to a URL (as in: www.somedomain.org?name1=value&name2=value).
HttpUrlReplacementBinding	Indicates that all the message parts (arguments) are encoded into the HTTP request using a replacement algorithm.
Import	The Import class indicates the location of an importable WSDL sub-document, that is, an external XML file to insert into the main document.
ImportCollection	ImportCollection represents a collection of Import objects.
InputBinding	Provides details on rules and structure for data formats and protocol needed for input messages. Operation binding names are not required to be unique, and so the InputBinding class defines a unique name attribute to correctly identify request methods. This class resides within the OperationBinding class.
Message	This class represents a single input, output, or fault message.

Class	Description
MessageBinding	MessageBinding is an abstract base class for a number of other classes within the System.Web.Services.Description namespace. It details how content is mapped into set format. It cannot be instantiated directly. Its properties are inherited by all classes that use it as their base class.
MessageCollection	MessageCollection represents a collection of Message objects
MessagePart	**This class identifies the arguments to a single input, output or fault message. It cannot be inherited.**
MessagePartCollection	MessagePartCollection represents a collection of MessagePart objects
MimeContentBinding	To avoid having to define a new element for similar MIME formats, the optional element mime:content may be used to indicate there is no special feature of the format other than its MIME type string.
MimeMultipartRelatedBinding	This class groups together multiple MIME content binding classes into one abstract set of MIME parts.
MimePart	This class contains one or more MimeContentBinding extensibility classes.
MimePartCollection	MimePartCollection class represents a collection of objects of MimePart class.
MimeTextBinding	MimeTextBinding adds extensibility to the InputBinding, OutputBinding and MimePart objects. This class specifies the collection of MIME text pattern to search for in HTTP transmission.
MimeTextMatch	Represents the MIME text pattern for which HTTP transmission is searched.
MimeTextMatchCollection	This class provides a collection of MimeTextMatch instances.
MimeXmlBinding	This allows non-SOAP XML-structured data to be sent or received as attachments to standard messages.
Operation	**The Operation class defines the structure of a function provided by a communication end-point such as an ASP.NET server.**
OperationBinding	**The OperationBinding class controls the binding of the messages section of the WSDL schema to the protocols section of the WSDL schema along with identifying the message formats to be used, for example RPC or document.**
OperationBindingCollection	This class provides a collection of OperationBinding objects.
OperationCollection	This class provides a collection of Operation objects.

Class	Description
OperationFault	The **OperationFault** class defines the format and structure for Fault messages returned by a specific service identified in the WSDL schema.
OperationFaultCollection	This class provides a collection of OperationFault objects.
OperationInput	The **OperationInput** class defines the format and structure for Request messages returned by a specific service identified in the WSDL schema.
OperationMessage	The OperationMessage class is an abstract base class for a number of other classes within the System.Web.Services.Description namespace. It cannot be instantiated directly.
OperationMessageCollection	This class provides a collection of OperationMessageCollection objects.
OperationOutput	The **OperationOutput** class defines the format and structure for Response messages returned by a specific service identified within the WSDL schema.
OutputBinding	OutputBinding details how content is mapped into set format. Operation binding names are not required to be unique, and so the OutputBinding class defines a unique name attribute to correctly identify request methods. This class resides within the OperationBinding class.
Port	The **Port** class defines a specific communication endpoint (commonly known as an address) for calling remote methods of the current service.
PortCollection	This class provides a collection of Port objects.
PortType	The **PortType** class connects binding information to the **Interface** section of the current WSDL definition. The name of the class, taken from the **name** attribute of the WSDL **<portType>** element, references an element in the **Binding** section.
PortTypeCollection	This class provides a collection of PortType objects.
Service	Groups together all the ports related to the current WSDL schema definition.
ServiceCollection	This class provides a collection of Service objects.
ServiceDescription	The **ServiceDescription** class is the root class for the entire WSDL file structure. It enables the development of WSDL files for use with an XML Web Service. If you use the **Read** method within this class you can read in any valid WSDL file.
ServiceDescriptionBase Collection	This is an abstract class that provides a base class for strongly typed collections in the System.Web.Services.Description namespace.

Class	Description
ServiceDescription Collection	This `ServiceDescription` collection allows you to add multiple WSDL schemas (`ServiceDescription` objects) into a single collection. You can then use the methods of the collection to retrieve, search or manipulate a `ServiceDescription` (single WSDL schema) object.
ServiceDescription FormatExtension	`ServiceDescriptionFormatExtension` acts as an abstract base class for a number of other classes within the `System.Web.Services.Description` namespace. It cannot be instantiated directly.
ServiceDescription FormatExtensionCollection	This class provides a collection of `ServiceDescriptionFormatExtension` objects.
ServiceDescriptionImporter	This class allows the developer to create client proxy classes for WSDL schemas.
ServiceDescriptionReflector	This class lets you access the types supported by an XML Web service. You can use this to dynamically create, invoke and view a type.
SoapAddressBinding	This is the SOAP address binding used to give a port an address.
SoapBinding	The purpose of the SOAP binding element is to signify that the message is based on the SOAP format of Envelope, Header, and Body.
SoapBodyBinding	This class represents an extensibility element added to `InputBinding` and `OutputBinding` class within the SOAP body element.
SoapFaultBinding	Defines the protocol and contents of SOAP Fault messages.
SoapHeaderBinding	This class represents an extensibility element added to `InputBinding` and `OutputBinding` class within the SOAP header element.
SoapHeaderFaultBinding	If the SOAP header itself produces an error, the SOAP standard states that such errors must be notified and returned in headers. This class allows such header error messages to be defined.
SoapOperationBinding	This class specifies the Request protocols supported by the ASP.NET server or other SOAP-compliant end-point.
SoapTransportImporter	This abstract class serves as a base class to create user-defined classes that import SOAP transmission protocol into XML Web service.
Types	**Types allow you to create user-defined types for particular message or operation requirements.**

Binding Class

The `Binding` class forms the basis of the mechanism that binds together messages and communication end-points, at the same time assigning a transmission protocol. This class is derived from `System.Web.Services.Description.DocumentableItem` class and it cannot be further inherited.

This class contains set definitions binding the different sections of the schema into a single WSDL schema. The `Binding` class joins the protocols section to the messages section, introducing information on the format of the structure of the WSDL schema, for example RPC or Document binding styles.

Binding helps us identify the actual protocol used to invoke the Web Service operation. It also contains the actual format of input and output messages of the related operation. You cannot directly specify any address or transmission information within this class.

The following XML extract, from the `SimpleCalculator.wsdl` example, picks out the XML elements that are used to instantiate the `Binding`, `Operation`, and other child classes within this section:

```xml
<binding name="SimpleCalculatorHttpPost"
        type="s0:SimpleCalculatorHttpPost">
  <http:binding verb="POST" />
  <operation name="Add">
    <http:operation location="/Add" />
    <input>
      <mime:content type="application/x-www-form-urlencoded" />
    </input>
    <output>
      <mime:mimeXml part="Body" />
    </output>
  </operation>
  <operation name="Subtract">
    <http:operation location="/Subtract" />
    <input>
      <mime:content type="application/x-www-form-urlencoded" />
    </input>
    <output>
      <mime:mimeXml part="Body" />
    </output>
  </operation>
</binding>
```

Binding Class Public Methods

- ❑ `Equals` – inherited from `System.Object`, see Introduction for details.
- ❑ `GetHashCode` – inherited from `System.Object`, see Introduction for details.
- ❑ `GetType` – inherited from `System.Object`, see Introduction for details.
- ❑ `ToString` – inherited from `System.Object`, see Introduction for details.

Binding Class Protected Methods

❏ `Finalize` – inherited from `System.Object`, see Introduction for details.

❏ `MemberwiseClone` – inherited from `System.Object`, see Introduction for details.

Binding Class Public Properties

❏ **Documentation**

❏ **Extensions**

❏ **Name**

❏ **Operations**

❏ **ServiceDescription**

❏ **Type**

Documentation

The property `Documentation` is inherited from `System.Web.Services.DocumentableItem` and is used to assign or return text documentation for a particular `Binding` object. See `DocumentableItem` class reference in this chapter for detailed explanation.

```
public string Documentation {get; set;}
```

The WSDL format was designed to allow additions peculiar to a specific protocol or message format by the use of extensibility elements. These allow enhancements to be made available without changing the underlying WSDL standard.

Extensions

This property represents the collection of extension elements within the current `<binding>`. It allows for the extension of the basic abilities of the `Binding` class and returns a collection of extensibility elements as a `ServiceDescriptionFormatExtensionCollection` object (part of the `Description` namespace). For more information, refer to the *Extensibility* discussion at the beginning of this chapter.

```
public ServiceDescriptionFormatExtensionCollection Extensions {get;}
```

Here is a code snippet that extracts the `Extensions` of the `Binding` class and then individually displays the extension object's name and whether it is required or not:

```
foreach(ServiceDescriptionFormatExtension extension in binding.Extensions)
{
   sbText.AppendFormat("Extensibility Class: {0}, " +
                    "Required for Binding: {1}",
                    extension.ToString(),
                    extension.Required);
}
```

The WSDL format was designed to allow additions peculiar to a specific protocol or message format by the use of extensibility elements. These allow enhancements to be made available without changing the underlying WSDL standard.

Name

The `Name` property is used to assign or return the name of the `Binding` instance. It maps to the `Name` attribute from the `<binding>` element in the WSDL schema. It returns or sets a `String` object and if the `Name` attribute is not specified, then its value is an empty `String`. However, if the `Name` attribute is specified in the `<binding>` element, then the `Name` property should be unique within all the `Binding` section, this means that every `<binding>` element should have a unique `Name` attribute.

```
public string Name {get; set;}
```

The following code shows you how to use the `Name` property in conjunction with the `BindingsCollection` to iterate through all the bindings defined by a schema:

```
foreach(Binding binding in sdBinding.Bindings)
  {
    sbText.AppendFormat("Name: {0}, Type: {1}",
                          binding.Name, binding.Type);
  }
```

Operations

An `Operation` defines the valid protocols for messages between client and server during the execution of a remote Web Service. This property exposes an `OperationBindingCollection` object that contains the information extracted from the `<operation>` elements of the `<binding>` element's current WSDL definition. In its simplest form, a single `<operation>` element represents a basic web method for that binding instance.

```
public OperationBindingCollection Operations {get;}
```

This code displays the entire `<operation>` element name attribute within a `Binding` object:

```
foreach(OperationBinding opBinding in binding.Operations)
  {
    sbText.AppendFormat("Operation: {0}", opBinding.Name);
  }
```

ServiceDescription

`ServiceDescription` property allows access to the parent `ServiceDescription` class. The `ServiceDescription` class is the main class that contains the WSDL schema. It returns a `System.Web.Services.Description.ServiceDescription` object.

```
public ServiceDescription ServiceDescription {get;}
```

The following code displays the `TargetNamespace` property of the returned `ServiceDescription` object:

```
sbText.AppendFormat("Service Description: {0}",
        binding.ServiceDescription.TargetNamespace);
```

Type

This property represents the namespace-qualified, local name of the `PortType` linked with the binding element. This property can be used to set or retrieve the value linking to the `<portType>` element.

It returns an `XmlQualifiedName` object in the format of `namespace:name` of the `<portType>` element. This property maps to the `Type` attribute of the `<binding>` element.

The following code snippet displays the `Type` property of the `Binding` object:

```
sbText.AppendFormat("Name: {0}, Type: {1} ",
                    binding.Name, binding.Type);
```

Example: BindingUsage

Here is an example showing usage of all the properties of `Binding` class. You can find the complete code in `BindingUsage.aspx.cs` in the code download:

```
StringBuilder sbText = new StringBuilder();
String fileName=Request.PhysicalApplicationPath + "SimpleCalculator.wsdl";
ServiceDescription sdBinding = ServiceDescription.Read(fileName);

// Display the Name property of each Binding in the WSDL Document
sbText.Append("The Binding defined in the WSDL Document are:");
sbText.Append("<br>");

foreach(Binding binding in sdBinding.Bindings)
{
  sbText.AppendFormat("Name: {0}, Type: {1} ",binding.Name, binding.Type);
  sbText.Append("<br>");

  sbText.AppendFormat("Service Description: {0}",
                      binding.ServiceDescription.TargetNamespace);
  sbText.Append("<br>");

  foreach(ServiceDescriptionFormatExtension extension in
          binding.Extensions)
  {
    sbText.AppendFormat("Extensibility Class: {0}, Required: {1}",
                        extension.ToString(), extension.Required);
    sbText.Append("<br>");
  }

  foreach(OperationBinding opBinding in binding.Operations)
  {
    sbText.AppendFormat("Operation: {0}", opBinding.Name);
    sbText.Append("<br>");
  }
}
```

```
        LblBinding.Text=sbText.ToString();
```

The output from `BindingUsage.aspx.cs` is as follows:

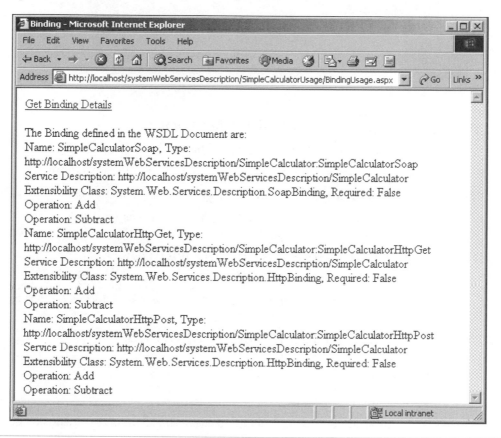

DocumentableItem Class

`DocumentableItem` acts as an abstract base class for a number of other classes in the `System.Web.Services.Description` namespace. The class is derived from `System.Object` and it cannot be instantiated directly. The `DocumentableItem` class consists of a single property `Documentation` that is used to describe the text documentation for one of its derived class instance.

The classes inherited from `DocumentableItem` in the `System.Web.Services.Description` namespace are:

❑ Binding

❑ Import

❑ Message

❑ MessagePart

- ❑ Operation
- ❑ OperationBinding
- ❑ OperationMessage
- ❑ Port
- ❑ PortType
- ❑ Service
- ❑ Types

DocumentableItem Class Public Methods

- ❑ Equals – inherited from `System.Object`, see Introduction for details.
- ❑ GetHashCode – inherited from `System.Object`, see Introduction for details.
- ❑ GetType – inherited from `System.Object`, see Introduction for details.
- ❑ ToString – inherited from `System.Object`, see Introduction for details.

DocumentableItem Class Protected Methods

- ❑ Finalize – inherited from `System.Object`, see Introduction for details.
- ❑ MemberwiseClone – inherited from `System.Object`, see Introduction for details.

DocumentableItem Class Public Properties

- ❑ **Documentation**

Documentation

The `Documentation` property is a single property exposed by the `DocumentableItem` class that is inherited by all its derived classes. It assigns or interrogates a single line of documentation given for a particular inherited class instance.

```
public string Documentation {get; set;}
```

Documentation can be identified in the WSDL schema by the `<documentation>` element added to one of its derived class instance. It returns the value of the `<documentation>` element when the text description is added with the `<documentation>` element in the WSDL. If the text description is not added, then by default it represents an empty string.

Example: Documentation

Here is an example that displays the Documentation property of some of the derived classes of the DocumentableItem like the Service, PortType and Operation. You can find the complete code in Documentation.aspx.cs file in the code download:

```
StringBuilder sbText = new StringBuilder();
String fileName=Request.PhysicalApplicationPath + "SimpleCalculator.wsdl";
ServiceDescription sdDocumentation = ServiceDescription.Read(fileName);

// Display the Documentation property of each Service in the WSDL Document
foreach(Service service in sdDocumentation.Services)
{
  sbText.AppendFormat("Service : {0}, Documentation : {1}",service.Name ,
                      service.Documentation);
  sbText.Append("<br>");
}
//Display the Documentation property of each PortType in the WSDL Document
foreach(PortType portType in sdDocumentation.PortTypes)
{
  sbText.AppendFormat("PortType : {0}, Documentation : {1}",
                      portType.Name,portType.Documentation);
  sbText.Append("<br>");
  //Display the Documentation property of each Operation in PortType
  //element
  foreach(Operation operation in portType.Operations)
  {
    sbText.Append("    ");
    sbText.AppendFormat("Operation : {0}, Documentation : {1}",
                        operation.Name,operation.Documentation);
    sbText.Append("<br>");
  }
}
LblDocumentation.Text = sbText.ToString();
```

This will result in the following form:

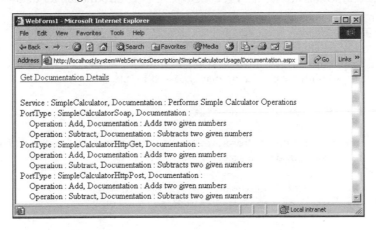

Message Class

This class represents a single input, output, or fault message passed by an XML Web service. This class is derived from the `System.Web.Services.Description.DocumentableItem` class and it cannot be further inherited. A message refers to a single SOAP transaction; it requires particular arguments and data type definitions, and these are specified in corresponding `<message>` elements of a WSDL file. SOAP messages are either a request to a Web Service to perform a particular task, or a response from a Web Service to a previous request.

The WSDL schema extract below shows two `<message>` elements. This message contains procedure-oriented information and hence provide information about its parameters, return values and their type.

```
<message name="AddHttpGetIn">
  <part name="num1" type="s:string" />
  <part name="num2" type="s:string" />
</message>

<message name="AddHttpGetOut">
  <part name="Body" element="s0:double" />
</message>
```

The `Message` class is contained within a `MessageCollection` and can be interrogated by the `Item` property and an appropriate index.

Message Class Public Methods

❑ `Equals` – inherited from `System.Object`, see Introduction for details.

❑ **FindPartByName**

❑ **FindPartsByName**

❑ `GetHashCode` – inherited from `System.Object`, see Introduction for details.

❑ `GetType` – inherited from `System.Object`, see Introduction for details.

❑ `ToString` – inherited from `System.Object`, see Introduction for details.

FindPartByName

The `FindPartByName` method returns a `MessagePart` object and accepts a `MessagePart` name string object as its parameters. The method searches the `MessagePartCollection` to find a `MessagePart` object with the part name that is passed to it.

```
public MessagePart FindPartByName(String);
```

Here is an example that searches for `MessagePart` with "parameters" as its part name. Complete code is available in the `MessageUsage.aspx.cs` file:

```
Message message = sdMessage.Messages["AddSoapIn"];
MessagePart mpart = message.FindPartByName("parameters");
```

Note if a MessagePart *object with a passed part name is not found, like* parameters *in this example, then an* ArgumentException *is thrown.*

FindPartsByName

The FindPartsByName method returns a MessagePart array object and accepts a string array containing MessagePart names as its parameters. The method searches the MessagePartCollection to find all MessagePart objects containing the part names in the array.

```
public MessagePart[] FindPartsByName(String[]);
```

Here is an example that searches for MessagePart with string array containing num1 and num2 part names. Complete code is available in the MessageUsage.aspx.cs file:

```
String[] partnames={"num1", "num2"};
Message message = sdMessage.Messages["AddHttpGetIn"];
MessagePart[] parts = message.FindPartsByName(partnames);
```

Note if a MessagePart *object with the passed part name in the array is not found, like num1 or num2 in the example, then an* ArgumentException *is thrown.*

Message Class Protected Methods

❑ Finalize – inherited from System.Object, see Introduction for details.

❑ MemberwiseClone – inherited from System.Object, see Introduction for details.

Message Class Public Properties

❑ **Documentation**

❑ **Name**

❑ **Parts**

❑ **ServiceDescription**

Documentation

The Documentation property is inherited from System.Web.Services.DocumentableItem and is used to assign or return text documentation for a particular Message object. See DocumentableItem class reference in this chapter for detailed explanation.

```
public string Documentation {get; set;}
```

Here is the Documentation property in action:

```
sbText.AppendFormat("Message : {0}, Documentation : {1}",
                    message.Name ,message.Documentation);
```

Name

The `Name` property is used to assign or return the name of the `Message` instance. It maps to the `Name` attribute from the `<message>` element in the WSDL schema. This naming convention is followed throughout the `System.Web.Services.Description` namespace and is very handy when correlating the property name of a class with its corresponding WSDL attribute or element. It returns or sets a `String` object, if the `Name` attribute is not specified, then its value is an empty string. However, if the `Name` attribute is specified in the `<message>` element, then the `Name` property should be unique within the entire `Message` section, which in turn means that every `<message>` element should have a unique name attribute.

```
public string Name {get; set;}
```

The following code shows you how to use the `Name` property in conjunction with the `MessageCollection` object to iterate through all the messages defined by a schema:

```
foreach(Message message in sdMessage.Messages)
  {
    sbText.AppendFormat("Message : {0}, " +
                        "Documentation : {1}",
                        message.Name,
                        message.Documentation);
  }
```

Parts

Each `<message>` element in a WSDL file contains a set of child `<part>` elements describing each argument sent to, or received from, a web method. Each message can contain any number of arguments. Every item in this collection is an argument for a message.

Therefore this property returns `MessagePartCollection` objects that contain all the `MessagePart` objects.

```
public MessagePartCollection Parts {get;}
```

Here is a code snippet that iterates through `MessagePartCollection` and displays the part name and element:

```
foreach(MessagePart part in message.Parts)
{
  sbText.AppendFormat("Part Name: {0}, Part Element: {1}",
                      part.Name, part.Element);
}
```

ServiceDescription

`ServiceDescription` property allows access to the parent `ServiceDescription` class. The `ServiceDescription` class is the main class that contains the WSDL schema. It returns a `System.Web.Services.Description.ServiceDescription` object.

```
public ServiceDescription ServiceDescription {get;}
```

The following code displays the `TargetNamespace` property of the returned `ServiceDescription` object:

```
sbText.AppendFormat("Service Description: {0}",
                    message.ServiceDescription.TargetNamespace);
```

Example : MessageUsage

Here is an example showing usage of all the properties of `Message` class. You can find the complete code in `MessageUsage.aspx.cs` in the code download:

```
StringBuilder sbText = new StringBuilder();
String fileName=Request.PhysicalApplicationPath + "SimpleCalculator.wsdl";
ServiceDescription sdMessage = ServiceDescription.Read(fileName);

//Display properties of message objects in the WSDL document
foreach(Message message in sdMessage.Messages)
{
  sbText.AppendFormat("Message : {0}, Documentation : {1}",
                      message.Name ,message.Documentation);
  sbText.Append("<br>");
  sbText.AppendFormat("Service Description: {0}",
                      message.ServiceDescription.TargetNamespace);
  sbText.Append("<br>");
  //Display each MessagePart object in the message object
  foreach(MessagePart part in message.Parts)
  {
    sbText.AppendFormat("Part Name: {0}, Part Element: {1}",
                        part.Name, part.Element);
    sbText.Append("<br>");
    sbText.AppendFormat("Part Type Name: {0}," +
                        "Part Type Namespace: {1}",
                        part.Type.Name, part.Type.Namespace);
    sbText.Append("<br>");
    sbText.AppendFormat("Part Documentation: {0}," +
                        "Part Message Name: {1}",
                        part.Documentation, part.Message.Name);
    sbText.Append("<br>");
  }

  sbText.Append("<br>");
}
LblMessage.Text = sbText.ToString();
```

Below is the top half of the output from this code, and therefore some of the Get Message Details segment of the output is omitted in this screenshot:

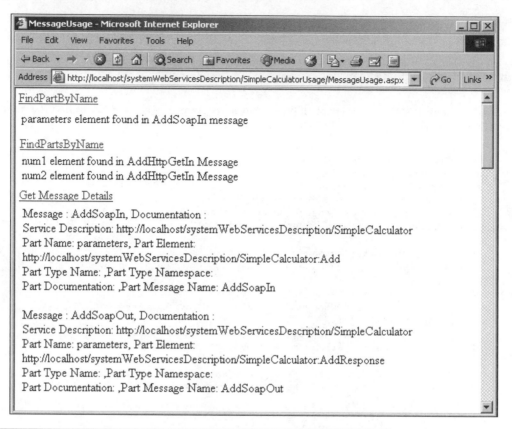

MessagePart Class

This class identifies the arguments to a single input, output or fault message. This class is derived from the `System.Web.Services.Description.DocumentableItem` class and it cannot be further inherited.

The `MessagePart` class defines the structure for the interface that the message requires, along with the data types, more commonly referred to as method arguments, that it accepts.

The following extract is taken from our example file, `SimpleCalculator.wsdl`. It shows two of the elements that are consumed by the `MessagePart` class:

```
<part name="num1" type="s:string" />
<part name="num2" type="s:string" />
```

MessagePart Class Public Methods

- ❏ `Equals` – inherited from `System.Object`, see Introduction for details.
- ❏ `GetHashCode` – inherited from `System.Object`, see Introduction for details.
- ❏ `GetType` – inherited from `System.Object`, see Introduction for details.
- ❏ `ToString` – inherited from `System.Object`, see Introduction for details.

MessagePart Class Protected Methods

- ❏ `Finalize` – inherited from `System.Object`, see Introduction for details.
- ❏ `MemberwiseClone` – inherited from `System.Object`, see Introduction for details.

MessagePart Class Public Properties

- ❏ **Documentation**
- ❏ **Element**
- ❏ **Message**
- ❏ **Name**
- ❏ **Type**

Documentation

The property `Documentation` is inherited from `System.Web.Services.DocumentableItem` and is used to assign or return text documentation for a particular `MessagePart` object. See `DocumentableItem` class reference in this chapter for detailed explanation.

```
public string Documentation {get; set;}
```

Here is an example of the `Documentation` property in action:

```
sbText.AppendFormat("Part Documentation: {0}," +
                    "Part Message Name: {1}",
                    part.Documentation,
                    part.Message.Name);
```

Element

The `Element` property provides access to the data type information specified by the `Element` attribute of a message's `<part>` elements (in other words the types of its method arguments). This property returns an `XmlQualifiedName` object that can be interrogated to provide a namespace value, which allows access to the defined type for this message part.

```
public XmlQualifiedName Element {get; set;}
```

Here is a code snippet that displays the `MessagePart Element` property in namespace qualified way:

```
foreach(MessagePart part in message.Parts)
{
  sbText.AppendFormat("Part Name: {0}, Part Element: {1}",
                       part.Name, part.Element);
}
```

Message

It allows access to the parent `Message` class, the `<message>` element of the WSDL schema. It returns a `System.Web.Services.Description.Message` object.

```
public Message Message {get;}
```

Here is a code snippet that displays the name of the parent `Message` of the part object:

```
sbText.AppendFormat("Part Documentation: {0}, " +
                     "Part Message Name: {1}",
                      part.Documentation, part.Message.Name);
```

Name

The `Name` property is used to assign or return the name of the `MessagePart` instance. It maps to the `Name` attribute from the `<part>` element in the WSDL schema. It returns or assigns a `String` object and, if the `Name` attribute is not specified, then its value is an empty string. However, if the `Name` attribute is specified in the `<part>` element, then the `Name` property should be unique within the parent `Message` class, meaning that every `<part>` element within `<message>` should have a unique name attribute. It is more commonly known as the method argument name.

```
public string Name {get; set;}
```

The following code shows you how to use the `Name` property in conjunction with the `MessagePartCollection` object to iterate through all the messages defined by a schema:

```
foreach(MessagePart part in message.Parts)
{
  sbText.AppendFormat("Part Name: {0}, Part Element: {1}",
                       part.Name, part.Element);
}
```

Type

The `Type` property refers to the WSDL complex data type definitions. The property is used instead of the `MessagePart.Element` property to obtain the data type for any specific message part; this is because the `MessagePart.Element` contains an XML namespace that has to be deconstructed. The `Type` property however just contains the data type information. It returns an `XmlQualifiedName` object that can be interrogated to return a deconstructed namespace for the defined type. It maps to the type attribute of the WSDL `<part>` element.

```
public XmlQualifiedName Type {get; set;}
```

Here is a usage of `Type` property of the `MessagePart` class that displays the `Type`'s `Name` and the `Type`'s namespace individually:

```
sbText.AppendFormat("Part Type Name: {0}, " +
                    "Part Type Namespace: {1}",
                    part.Type.Name, part.Type.Namespace);
```

You can extend the data types available by allocating a unique namespace, and then inserting a reference to the data type definition's location in the WSDL header. If an alternative data type definition is used, its namespace must be unique within this schema, see the `Types` class reference for more details.

Example: Using the MessagePart Class

Here is an example showing usage of all the properties of the `MessagePart` class. You can find the complete code in the `MessageUsage.aspx.cs` file in the code download, with the output of this file demonstrated in the `MessageUsage` example.

```
foreach(MessagePart part in message.Parts)
{
  sbText.AppendFormat("Part Name: {0}, Part Element: {1}",
                      part.Name, part.Element);
  sbText.Append("<br>");
  sbText.AppendFormat("Part Type Name: {0}," +
                      "Part Type Namespace: {1}",
                      part.Type.Name, part.Type.Namespace);
  sbText.Append("<br>");
  sbText.AppendFormat("Part Documentation: {0}," +
                      "Part Message Name: {1}",
                      part.Documentation, part.Message.Name);
  sbText.Append("<br>");
}
```

Operation Class

The `Operation` class defines the structure of an action provided by a communication end-point such as an ASP.NET server. An operation contains an input, output and fault messages. This class maps to the `<operation>` element in the `<portType>` definition. This class is derived from the `System.Web.Services.Description.DocumentableItem` class and it cannot be further inherited.

The following extract shows the `<operation>` element within our example WSDL schema:

```
<portType name="SimpleCalculatorSoap">
  <operation name="Add">
    <documentation>Adds two given numbers</documentation>
    <input message="s0:AddSoapIn" />
```

```
      <output message="s0:AddSoapOut" />
    </operation>
    <operation name="Subtract">
      <documentation>Subtracts two given numbers</documentation>
      <input message="s0:SubtractSoapIn" />
      <output message="s0:SubtractSoapOut" />
    </operation>
  </portType>
```

Operation Class Public Methods

❏ Equals – inherited from System.Object, see Introduction for details.

❏ GetHashCode – inherited from System.Object, see Introduction for details.

❏ GetType – inherited from System.Object, see Introduction for details.

❏ **IsBoundBy**

❏ ToString – inherited from System.Object, see Introduction for details.

IsBoundBy

This method returns true or false indicating whether the OperationBinding object passed as a parameter to this method is used in this Operation object or not. The method requires an OperationBinding object.

```
    public bool IsBoundBy(OperationBinding);
```

Operation Class Protected Methods

❏ Finalize – inherited from System.Object, see Introduction for details.

❏ MemberwiseClone – inherited from System.Object, see Introduction for details.

Operation Class Public Properties

❏ **Documentation**

❏ **Faults**

❏ **Messages**

❏ **Name**

❏ **ParameterOrder**

❏ **ParameterOrderString**

❏ **PortType**

Documentation

The property Documentation is inherited from System.Web.Services.DocumentableItem and is used to assign or return text documentation for a particular Operation object. See DocumentableItem class reference in this chapter for detailed explanation.

```
public string Documentation {get; set;}
```

Here is a usage of Documentation property:

```
sbText.AppendFormat("Operation : {0}, Documentation : {1}",
                    operation.Name, operation.Documentation);
```

Faults

This property allows access to the collection of fault messages assigned to an operation using the <fault> element in the WSDL schema. Multiple fault messages can be defined to return information appropriate to the actual fault that occurred. It returns an OperationFaultCollection object. Once again, this is read-only although you are able to alter the underlying collection items.

```
public OperationFaultCollection Faults {get;}
```

This code displays the fault messages if any assigned to the Operation object:

```
//Display each fault objects in the operation object

foreach(OperationFault fault in operation.Faults)
  sbText.AppendFormat("Fault Message: {0}, " +
                      "Fault Documentation: {1}",
                      fault.Message, fault.Documentation);
```

Messages

This property allows access to the collection of messages for this instance of the Operation class. As any <operation> element may have no more than one <input> and one <output> class, there will only ever be a maximum of two items in this OperationMessageCollection. The properties Input and Output of the OperationMessageCollection allow access to the OperationInput and OperationOutput classes. This property is read-only property, but you can alter the underlying collection of Messages (excluding Faults) assigned to this operation.

```
public OperationMessageCollection Messages {get;}
```

This code displays the input and output messages assigned to the Operation object:

```
OperationInput input= operation.Messages.Input;
sbText.AppendFormat("Input Message: {0}, Message Documentation: {0}",
                    input.Message, input.Documentation);

OperationOutput output= operation.Messages.Output;
sbText.AppendFormat("Output Message: {0}, Message Documentation: {0}",
                    output.Message, output.Documentation);
```

Name

The Name property identifies this current instance of the Operation class, and need not be unique for all operations within the WSDL definition. If not set, this property returns an empty string. It maps to the name attribute of the WSDL <operation> element.

```
public string Name {get; set;}
```

Here is a usage of the `Name` property:

```
sbText.AppendFormat("Operation : {0}, Documentation : {1}",
                    operation.Name ,operation.Documentation);
```

ParameterOrder

This property allows access to an array of string values that have already been identified and extracted from the `ParameterOrderString` property. This property is only required if you are using an RPC binding style, as this style actually includes the requirement for a `ParameterOrder`.

```
public string[] ParameterOrder {get; set;}
```

Here is a usage of `ParameterOrder` property:

```
string[] parameters = operation.ParameterOrder;
  if(parameters != null)
  {
    sbText.Append("Parameter Order:");
    foreach (string parameter in parameters)
    sbText.AppendFormat("{0}", parameter);
  }
```

ParameterOrderString

Operations do not specify by default whether they use RPC-like bindings (an RPC binding is a style/format for binding together the WSDL schema). This property therefore allows you to assign the original RPC function signature to the `ParameterOrder` attribute within the operation element. The property contains a list of parameter names separated by a single space for SOAP Request-Response or Solicit-Response operations. When validating this property, you should note that it must adhere to the following rules:

❑ The part name order mirrors the order of the parameters in the RPC signature

❑ The **return** value part is not present in the list

❑ If a part name appears in both the input and output message, it is an **in/out** parameter

❑ If a part name appears in only the input message, it is an **in** parameter

❑ If a part name appears in only the output message, it is an **out** parameter

This property may be ignored if you are not concerned with RPC signatures.

```
public string ParameterOrderString {get; set;}
```

Here is a usage of `ParameterOrderString` property:

```
sbText.AppendFormat("Parameter Order String: {0}",
                    operation.ParameterOrderString);
```

PortType

This property returns a `PortType` object of which this `Operation` element is a member. In effect, this allows you to determine the parent `<portType>` element of the corresponding `<operation>` element in the WSDL schema.

```
public PortType PortType {get;}
```

Here is a code snippet that displays the `Name` property of the `PortType` object to which the `Operation` object belongs:

```
sbText.AppendFormat("Port Type Name: {0}",
                    operation.PortType.Name);
```

Example: Operation Class

Here is an example showing usage of all the properties of `Operation` class. You can find the complete code in `OperationUsage.aspx.cs` in the code download:

```
StringBuilder sbText = new StringBuilder();
String fileName=Request.PhysicalApplicationPath + "SimpleCalculator.wsdl";
ServiceDescription sdOperation = ServiceDescription.Read(fileName);

//Display properties of operation objects in the WSDL document
foreach(Operation operation in
        sdOperation.PortTypes["SimpleCalculatorSoap"].Operations)
{
  sbText.AppendFormat("Operation : {0}, Documentation : {1}",
                      operation.Name ,operation.Documentation);
  sbText.Append("<br>");
  sbText.AppendFormat("Port Type Name: {0}",
                      operation.PortType.Name);
  sbText.Append("<br>");

  sbText.AppendFormat("Parameter Order String: {0}",
                      operation.ParameterOrderString);
  sbText.Append("<br>");

  String[] parameters = operation.ParameterOrder;
  if(parameters != null)
  {
    sbText.Append("Paremter Order:");
    foreach (string parameter in parameters)
      sbText.AppendFormat("{0}", parameter);
  }
```

```
        //Display each messages in the operation object

        OperationInput input= operation.Messages.Input;
        sbText.AppendFormat("Input Message: {0}," +
                        "Message Documentation: {0}",
                        input.Message, input.Documentation);
        sbText.Append("<br>");
        sbText.AppendFormat("Input Name: {0}, Operation Name: {1}",
                        input.Name, input.Operation.Name);
        sbText.Append("<br>");

        OperationOutput output= operation.Messages.Output;
        sbText.AppendFormat("Output Message: {0}," +
                        "Message Documentation: {0}",
                        output.Message, output.Documentation);
        sbText.Append("<br>");
        sbText.AppendFormat("Output Name: {0}, Operation Name: {1}",
                        output.Name, output.Operation.Name);
        sbText.Append("<br>");

        //Display each fault objects in the operation object
        foreach(OperationFault fault in operation.Faults)
        {
        sbText.AppendFormat("Fault Message: {0}," +
                        "Fault Documentation: {1}",
                        fault.Message, fault.Documentation);
        sbText.Append("<br>");
        sbText.AppendFormat("Name: {0}, Operation Name: {1}",
                        fault.Name, fault.Operation.Name);
        sbText.Append("<br>");
}
```

The output from this code should be as illustrated below:

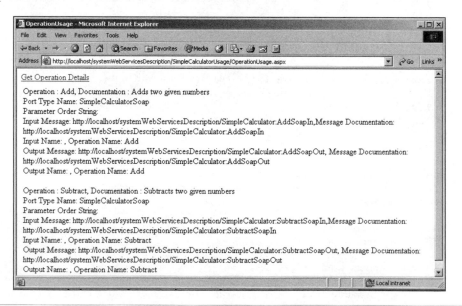

OperationBinding Class

The `OperationBinding` class, a child of the `Binding` class, defines the protocol to use for a particular operation, such as SOAP, using extensibility. The `OperationBinding` class controls the binding of the messages section of the WSDL schema to the protocols section of the WSDL schema along with identifying the message formats to be used, for example RPC or document.

This class is derived from `System.Web.Services.Description.DocumentableItem` class and it cannot be further inherited. It maps to the `<operation>` element enclosed in the `<binding>` element.

The following extract shows the `<operation>` element within our example WSDL schema:

```
<binding name="SimpleCalculatorSoap" type="s0:SimpleCalculatorSoap">
  <soap:binding transport="http://schemas.xmlsoap.org/soap/http"
              style="document" />
  <operation name="Add">
    <soap:operation soapAction="http://localhost/SimpleCalculator/Add"
                  style="document" />
    <input>
      <soap:body use="literal" />
    </input>
    <output>
      <soap:body use="literal" />
    </output>
  </operation>
</binding>
```

OperationBinding Class Public Methods

- ❑ `Equals` – inherited from `System.Object`, see Introduction for details.

- ❑ `GetHashCode` – inherited from `System.Object`, see Introduction for details.

- ❑ `GetType` – inherited from `System.Object`, see Introduction for details.

- ❑ `ToString` – inherited from `System.Object`, see Introduction for details.

Operation Class Protected Methods

- ❑ `Finalize` – inherited from `System.Object`, see Introduction for details.

- ❑ `MemberwiseClone` – inherited from `System.Object`, see Introduction for details.

OperationBinding Class Public Properties

- ❑ **Binding**
- ❑ **Documentation**
- ❑ **Extensions**
- ❑ **Faults**

- ❑ **Input**
- ❑ **Name**
- ❑ **Output**

Binding

This property returns a `Binding` object of which the `Operation` element is a member. In effect, this allows you to determine the parent `<binding>` element of the corresponding `<operation>` element in the WSDL schema.

```
public Binding Binding {get;}
```

Here is a code example that displays the `Name` property of the `Binding` object to which the `Operation` object belongs:

```
sbText.AppendFormat("Binding Name: {0}", operationBinding.Binding.Name);
```

Documentation

The property `Documentation` is inherited from `System.Web.Services.DocumentableItem` and is used to assign or return text documentation for a particular `OperationBinding` object. See `DocumentableItem` class reference in this chapter for detailed explanation.

```
public string Documentation {get; set;}
```

Here is a usage of the `Documentation` property:

```
sbText.AppendFormat("OperationBinding : {0},
                     Documentation : {1}",
                     operationBinding.Name,
                     operationBinding.Documentation);
```

Extensions

This property represents the collection of extension elements within the current `<operation>` element in the `<binding>` element. It allows for extension of the basic abilities of the `OperationBinding` class. The WSDL format was designed to allow additions peculiar to a specific protocol or message format by the use of extensibility elements. These allow enhancements to be made available without changing the underlying WSDL standard. It returns a collection of extensibility elements as a `System.Web.Services.Description.ServiceDescriptionFormatExtensionsCollection` object. Also refer to the *Extensibility* discussion at the beginning of this chapter.

```
public ServiceDescriptionFormatExtensionCollection Extensions {get;}
```

Here is a code snippet that extracts the `Extensions` of the `OperationBinding` class and then individually display the extension object's name and whether it is required or not:

```
foreach(ServiceDescriptionFormatExtension extension in
                    operationBinding.Extensions)
  sbText.AppendFormat("Extensibility Class: {0}," +
                    " Required: {1}",
                    extension.ToString(),
                    extension.Required);
```

Faults

This property allows access to the collection of fault messages assigned to an operation during binding using the <fault> element in the WSDL schema. Multiple fault messages can be defined to return information appropriate to the actual fault that occurred. It returns a FaultBindingCollection object. Once again, this is read-only although you are able to alter the underlying collection items.

```
public FaultBindingCollection Faults {get;}
```

This code displays the fault messages if any have been assigned to the OperationBinding object:

```
//Display each fault objects in the operation element in binding object
foreach(FaultBinding fault in operationBinding.Faults)
  sbText.AppendFormat("Fault Name: {0}, " +
                    "Fault Documentation: {1}",
                    fault.Name, fault.Documentation);
```

Input

This property returns the input message assigned to this operation binding. It maps to the <input> element inside the operation <binding> element of the WSDL schema. It returns an InputBinding object associated with the current OperationBinding object.

```
public InputBinding Input {get; set;}
```

This code displays the input message name, if any, assigned to the <input> element:

```
sbText.AppendFormat("Input Name: {0}, Output Name: {1}",
                    operationBinding.Input.Name ,
                    operationBinding.Output.Name);
```

Name

The Name property identifies this current instance of the OperationBinding class, and need not be unique for all operations within the WSDL definition. If not set, this property returns an empty string. It maps to the name attribute of the WSDL <operation> element in the <binding> element.

```
public string Name {get; set;}
```

Here is a usage of the `Name` property:

```
sbText.AppendFormat("OperationBinding : {0}," +
                    "Documentation : {1}",
                    operationBinding.Name,
                    operationBinding.Documentation);
```

Output

This property returns the output message assigned to this operation binding. It maps to the `<output>` element inside the operation `<binding>` element of the WSDL schema. It returns an `OutputBinding` object associated with the current `OperationBinding` object.

```
public OutputBinding Output {get; set}
```

This code displays the input message name if any is assigned to the `<output>` element:

```
sbText.AppendFormat("Input Name: {0}, Output Name: {1}",
                    operationBinding.Input.Name ,
                    operationBinding.Output.Name);
```

Example OperationBinding Class:

Here is an example showing usage of all the properties of `OperationBinding` class. You can find the complete code in the `OperationBindingUsage.aspx.cs` file in the code download:

```
StringBuilder sbText = new StringBuilder();
String fileName=Request.PhysicalApplicationPath + "SimpleCalculator.wsdl";
ServiceDescription sdOperationBinding = ServiceDescription.Read(fileName);

//Display properties of operationBinding objects in the WSDL document

foreach(OperationBinding operationBinding in
        sdOperationBinding.Bindings ["SimpleCalculatorSoap"].Operations)
{
  sbText.AppendFormat("OperationBinding : {0}," +
                      "Documentation : {1}", operationBinding.Name,
                      operationBinding.Documentation);
  sbText.Append("<br>");
  sbText.AppendFormat("Binding Name: {0}",
                      operationBinding.Binding.Name);
  sbText.Append("<br>");

  sbText.AppendFormat("Input Name: {0}, Output Name: {1}",
                      operationBinding.Input.Name,
                      operationBinding.Output.Name);
  sbText.Append("<br>");

  //Display each fault object in the operationBinding object
```

```
foreach(FaultBinding fault in operationBinding.Faults)
  {
    sbText.AppendFormat("Fault Name: {0}, Fault Documentation: {1}",
                        fault.Name, fault.Documentation);
    sbText.Append("<br>");
  }

    foreach(ServiceDescriptionFormatExtension extension in
                            operationBinding.Extensions)
    {
      sbText.AppendFormat("Extensibility Class: {0}, Required: {1}",
                          extension.ToString(), extension.Required);
      sbText.Append("<br>");
    }
    sbText.Append("<br>");
}
```

This code will produce the following .aspx page;

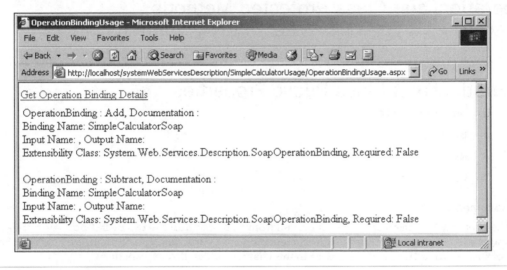

OperationFault Class

The OperationFault class defines the format and structure for error messages returned by a specific service identified within the WSDL schema. This class is derived from the OperationMessage class and cannot be further inherited.

The following snippet describes the <fault> elements of an <operation> element:

```
<operation ...>
 <input ...>
 <output ...>
   <fault name="FaultWarning" message="tns:AddFaultWarn"/>
   <fault name="FaultCritical" message="tns:AddFaultCrit">
```

```
  <documentation>
    'Special fault message
  </documentation>
  </fault>
</operation>
```

The OperationFault class defines the format and structure for fault messages returned by a specific service identified in the WSDL schema.

OperationFault Class Public Methods

❑   Equals – inherited from System.Object, see Introduction for details.

❑   GetHashCode – inherited from System.Object, see Introduction for details.

❑   GetType – inherited from System.Object, see Introduction for details.

❑   ToString – inherited from System.Object, see Introduction for details.

OperationFault Class Protected Methods

❑   Finalize – inherited from System.Object, see Introduction for details.

❑   MemberwiseClone – inherited from System.Object, see Introduction for details.

OperationFault Class Public Properties

❑   **Documentation**

❑   **Message**

❑   **Name**

❑   **Operation**

Documentation

The property Documentation is inherited from System.Web.Services.DocumentableItem and is used to assign or return text documentation for a particular OperationFault object. See DocumentableItem class reference in this chapter for detailed explanation.

```
public string Documentation {get; set;}
```

Here is a usage of Documentation property:

```
sbText.AppendFormat("Fault Message: {0}, " +
                    "Message Documentation: {0}",
                    fault.Message, fault.Documentation);
```

Message

This property returns the value of the `Message` attribute of the `<operation>`'s child `<fault>` element. This will include data type information as well as a name binding to the appropriate `<message>` element (which specifies the format for the Request message). It returns or assigns an `XmlQualifiedName` object. It maps to the `Message` attribute of the `<fault>` element and is inherited from `OperationMessage`.

```
public XmlQualifiedName Message {get; set;}
```

Here the following code snippet displays the message attribute if any is assigned to the `<fault>` element:

```
sbText.AppendFormat("Fault Message: {0}, " +
                    "Message Documentation: {0}",
                    fault.Message, fault.Documentation);
```

Name

This property returns the name attribute of the `<fault>` element for an operation. It is inherited from `OperationMessage`. The `Name` attribute is an optional attribute: if not supplied, this property returns an empty string.

```
public string Name {get; set;}
```

Here is a usage of `Name` property:

```
sbText.AppendFormat("Fault Name: {0}, Operation Name: {1}",
                    fault.Name, fault.Operation.Name);
```

Operation

It returns and allows access to the parent `Operation` class derived from the `<operation>` element of the WSDL schema. It is inherited from `OperationMessage`.

```
public Operation Operation {get;}
```

The following code snippet displays the `Name` property of the parent `Operation` object:

```
sbText.AppendFormat("Fault Name: {0}, Operation Name: {1}",
                    fault.Name, fault.Operation.Name);
```

Here is an example showing usage of all the properties of `OperationFault` class. You can find the complete code in `OperationUsage.aspx.cs` file in the code download:

```
foreach(OperationFault fault in operation.Faults)
{
  sbText.AppendFormat("Fault Message: {0}," +
                      "Fault Documentation: {1}",
                      fault.Message, fault.Documentation);
  sbText.Append("<br>");
  sbText.AppendFormat("Name: {0}, Operation Name: {1}",
                      fault.Name, fault.Operation.Name);
  sbText.Append("<br>");
}
```

OperationInput Class

The `OperationInput` class defines the format and structure for Request messages returned by a specific service described in a WSDL file. It is derived from `OperationMessage` class and cannot be further inherited.

The following code, taken from our WSDL example, shows the portion of the `Interface` section associated with the `OperationInput` class:

```
<portType name="SimpleCalculatorSoap">
  <operation name="Add">
    <documentation>Adds two given numbers</documentation>
    <input message="s0:AddSoapIn" />
    <output message="s0:AddSoapOut" />
  </operation>
</portType>
```

OperationInput Class Public Methods

- ❑ `Equals` – inherited from `System.Object`, see Introduction for details.

- ❑ `GetHashCode` – inherited from `System.Object`, see Introduction for details.

- ❑ `GetType` – inherited from `System.Object`, see Introduction for details.

- ❑ `ToString` – inherited from `System.Object`, see Introduction for details.

OperationInput Protected Methods

- ❑ Finalize – inherited from System.Object, see Introduction for details.
- ❑ MemberwiseClone – inherited from System.Object, see Introduction for details.

OperationInput Class Public Properties

- ❑ **Documentation**
- ❑ **Message**
- ❑ **Name**
- ❑ **Operation**

Documentation

The property Documentation is inherited from System.Web.Services.DocumentableItem and is used to assign or return text documentation for a particular OperationInput object. See DocumentableItem class reference in this chapter for detailed explanation.

```
public string Documentation {get; set;}
```

Here is a usage of Documentation property:

```
sbText.AppendFormat("Input Message: {0}, " +
                    "Message Documentation: {0}",
                    input.Message, input.Documentation);
```

Message

This property returns the value of the Message attribute of the <operation>'s child <input> element. This will include data type information as well as a name binding to the appropriate <message> element (which specifies the format for the Request message). It returns or assigns an XmlQualifiedName object. It maps to the message attribute of the <input> element. It is inherited from OperationMessage.

```
public XmlQualifiedName Message {get; set;}
```

Here the following code snippet displays the message attribute if any is assigned to the <input> element:

```
sbText.AppendFormat("Input Message: {0}, " +
                    "Message Documentation: {0}",
                    input.Message, input.Documentation);
```

Name

This property returns the Name attribute of the <input> element for an operation. The Name attribute is an optional attribute: if not supplied, this property returns an empty string. It is inherited from OperationMessage.

```
public string Name {get; set;}
```

Here is a usage of the `Name` property:

```
sbText.AppendFormat("Input Name: {0}, Operation Name: {1}",
                    input.Name, input.Operation.Name);
```

Operation

`Operation` returns and allows access to the parent `Operation` class derived from the `<operation>` element of the WSDL schema. It is inherited from `OperationMessage`.

```
public Operation Operation {get;}
```

The following code example displays the `Name` property of the parent `Operation` object:

```
sbText.AppendFormat("Input Name: {0}, Operation Name: {1}",
                    input.Name, input.Operation.Name);
```

Example: Using the OperationInput Class

Here is an example showing usage of all the properties of the `OperationInput` class. You can find the complete code in `OperationUsage.aspx.cs` file in the code download:

```
OperationInput input= operation.Messages.Input;
sbText.AppendFormat("Input Message: {0}," +
                    "Message Documentation: {0}",
                    input.Message, input.Documentation);
sbText.Append("<br>");
sbText.AppendFormat("Input Name: {0}, Operation Name: {1}",
                    input.Name, input.Operation.Name);
```

OperationOutput Class

The `OperationOutput` class defines the format and structure for Response messages returned by a specific service identified by the WSDL document. This class is derived from the `OperationMessage` class and cannot be inherited.

The following snippet taken from the WSDL example shows the portion of the `Interface` section associated with the `OperationOutput` class:

```
<portType name="SimpleCalculatorSoap">
  <operation name="Add">
    <documentation>Adds two given numbers</documentation>
    <input message="s0:AddSoapIn" />
    <output message="s0:AddSoapOut" />
  </operation>
</portType>
```

OperationOutput Class Public Methods

❑ Equals – inherited from System.Object, see Introduction for details.

❑ GetHashCode – inherited from System.Object, see Introduction for details.

❑ GetType – inherited from System.Object, see Introduction for details.

❑ ToString – inherited from System.Object, see Introduction for details.

OperationOutput Class Protected Methods

❑ Finalize – inherited from System.Object, see Introduction for details.

❑ MemberwiseClone – inherited from System.Object, see Introduction for details.

OperationOutput Class Public Properties

❑ **Documentation**

❑ **Message**

❑ **Name**

❑ **Operation**

Documentation

The property Documentation is inherited from System.Web.Services.DocumentableItem and is used to assign or return text documentation for a particular OperationOutput object. See the DocumentableItem class reference in this chapter for detailed explanation.

```
public string Documentation {get; set;}
```

Here is a usage of Documentation property:

```
sbText.AppendFormat("Output Message: {0}, " +
                    "Message Documentation: {0}",
                    output.Message, output.Documentation);
```

Message

This property returns the value of the message attribute of the <operation>'s child <output> element. This will include data type information as well as a name binding to the appropriate <message> element (which specifies the format for the Request message). It returns or assigns an XmlQualifiedName object. It maps to the message attribute of the <output> element. It is inherited from OperationMessage.

```
public XmlQualifiedName Message {get; set;}
```

Here the following code snippet displays the Message attribute if any is assigned to the <output> element:

```
sbText.AppendFormat("Output Message: {0}, " +
                    "Message Documentation: {0}",
                    output.Message, output.Documentation);
```

Name

This property returns the `Name` attribute of the `<output>` element for an operation. The `Name` attribute is an optional attribute: if not supplied, this property returns an empty string. It is inherited from `OperationMessage`.

```
public string Name {get; set;}
```

Here is a usage of `Name` property:

```
sbText.AppendFormat("Name: {0}, Binding: {1} ",
                    port.Name, port.Binding);
```

Operation

It returns and allows access to the parent `Operation` class derived from the `<operation>` element of the WSDL schema. It is inherited from `OperationMessage`.

```
public Operation Operation {get;}
```

The following code snippet displays the `Name` property of the parent `Operation` object:

```
sbText.AppendFormat("Output Name: {0}, Operation Name: {1}",
                    Output.Name, Output.Operation.Name);
```

Example: Using the OperationOutput Class

Here is an example showing usage of all the properties of `OperationOutput` class. You can find the complete code in `OperationUsage.aspx.cs` file in the code download:

```
OperationOutput output= operation.Messages.Output;
sbText.AppendFormat("Output Message: {0}," +
                    "Message Documentation: {0}",
                    output.Message, output.Documentation);
sbText.Append("<br>");
sbText.AppendFormat("Output Name: {0}, Operation Name: {1}",
                    output.Name, output.Operation.Name);
```

Port Class

The `Port` class defines a specific single communication end-point (commonly known as an address) for calling remote methods of the current service. This class is derived from `System.Web.Services.Description.DocumentableItem` class and it cannot be further inherited.

The Port class maps to the <port> element contained in the <service> element. It specifies a single address for Binding. Binding gets the operation and message details for the port with the help of PortType.

Here is a segment of WSDL that shows Port element inside the Service element:

```
<service name="SimpleCalculator">
  <documentation>Performs Simple Calculator Operations</documentation>
  <port name="SimpleCalculatorSoap" binding="s0:SimpleCalculatorSoap">
    <soap:address location=
              "http://localhost/SimpleCalculator/SimpleCalculator.asmx" />
  </port>
</service>
```

A Port will not specify more than one address and will not specify any binding information other than the address information.

Port Class Public Methods

❑ Equals – inherited from System.Object, see Introduction for details.

❑ GetHashCode – inherited from System.Object, see Introduction for details.

❑ GetType – inherited from System.Object, see Introduction for details.

❑ ToString – inherited from System.Object, see Introduction for details.

Port Class Protected Methods

❑ Finalize – inherited from System.Object, see Introduction for details.

❑ MemberwiseClone – inherited from System.Object, see Introduction for details.

Port Class Public Properties

❑ **Binding**

❑ **Documentation**

❑ **Extensions**

❑ **Name**

❑ **Service**

Binding

In WSDL, <port> elements are associated with the operations that the end-point supports through the binding attribute of the <port>, the binding attribute links to <binding> element in the WSDL document. Binding objects are the underlying mechanism that collates messages, communications, and protocols to form a coherent WSDL schema. The Port.Binding property returns the value of this binding attribute. It returns an XmlQualifiedName object with namespace and local name.

```
public XmlQualifiedName Binding {get; set;}
```

Here is a code snippet displaying the `Binding` qualified name of a `Port`:

```
sbText.AppendFormat("Name: {0}, Binding: {1} ",
                    port.Name, port.Binding);
```

Documentation

The property `Documentation` is inherited from `System.Web.Services.DocumentableItem` and is used to assign or return text documentation for a particular `Port` object. See `DocumentableItem` class reference in this chapter for detailed explanation.

```
public string Documentation {get; set;}
```

Here is a usage of `Documentation` property:

```
sbText.AppendFormat("Service: {0}, Documentation: {1} ",
                    port.Service.Name, port.Documentation);
```

Extensions

The WSDL format was designed to allow additions peculiar to a specific protocol or message format by the use of extensibility elements. These allow enhancements to be made available without changing the underlying WSDL standard. Also refer to the *Extensibility* discussion at the beginning of this chapter.

This property represents the collection of extension elements within the current `<port>`. These elements can extend the capability of the `Port` by adding support for additional messaging formats for SOAP messages. It returns a collection of extensibility elements as a `System.Web.Services.Description.` `ServiceDescriptionFormatExtensionsCollection` object.

```
public ServiceDescriptionFormatExtensionCollection Extensions {get;}
```

Here is a code snippet that extracts the `Extensions` of the `Port` class and then individually display the `Extension` object's name and whether it is required or not:

```
foreach(ServiceDescriptionFormatExtension extension in port.Extensions)
{
  sbText.AppendFormat("Extensibility Class: {0}, "
                      Required: {1}",
                      extension.ToString(),
                      extension.Required);
```

Name

This is the name given to the `Port` class, taken from the name of the `<port>` element in the WSDL file. It returns or assigns a `String` object, if the `name` attribute is not specified, then its value is an empty string. However, if the `name` attribute is specified in the `<port>` element, then the `Name` property should be unique within the `Port` section, this means that every `<port>` element should have a unique `name` attribute.

```
public string Name {get; set;}
```

Here is a usage of Name property:

```
sbText.AppendFormat("Name: {0}, Binding: {1} ",
                    port.Name, port.Binding);
```

Service

This property returns the Service object of which this Port instance is a member. The returned object represents the parent <service> element of the <port> mapped by the given instance of the Port class. It returns a System.Web.Services.Description.Service object.

```
public Service Service {get;}
```

Here is a piece of code that displays the name of the Service to which port belongs:

```
sbText.AppendFormat("Service: {0}, Documentation: {1} ",
                    port.Service.Name, port.Documentation);
```

Example: Using the Port Class

Here is an example showing usage of all the properties of Port class. You can find the complete code in PortUsage.aspx.cs file in the code download:

```
StringBuilder sbText = new StringBuilder();
String fileName=Request.PhysicalApplicationPath +
                "SimpleCalculator.wsdl";
ServiceDescription sdPort = ServiceDescription.Read(fileName);

sbText.Append("The Ports defined in the WSDL Document are:");
sbText.Append("<br>");

foreach(Port port in sdPort.Services ["SimpleCalculator"].Ports)
{
  // Display the Name property and Binding.Name of each
  // Port in the WSDL Document
  sbText.AppendFormat("Name: {0}, Binding: {1} ",port.Name,
                      port.Binding);
  sbText.Append("<br>");

  sbText.AppendFormat("Service: {0}, Documentation: {1} ",
                      port.Service.Name, port.Documentation);
  sbText.Append("<br>");

  foreach(ServiceDescriptionFormatExtension extension in
          port.Extensions)
  {
    sbText.AppendFormat("Extensibility Class: {0}," +
                        "Required: {1}",
                        extension.ToString(),
```

```
        extension.Required);
        sbText.Append("<br>");
    }
    sbText.Append("<br>");
}
LblPort.Text=sbText.ToString();
```

This code will produce the following output:

PortType Class

The PortType class groups operations under a single port type name. With this in place, operations (an operation is a single entity that brings together the `<output>`, `<input>`, and `<fault>` messages into one coherent area) can define valid message groups associated with a specific operation. The PortType class maps to the `<portType>` element contained in the WSDL schema. It contains `<operation>` element that are linked to web methods.

```xml
<portType name="SimpleCalculatorSoap">
  <operation name="Add">
    <documentation>Adds two given numbers</documentation>
    <input message="s0:AddSoapIn" />
    <output message="s0:AddSoapOut" />
  </operation>
  <operation name="Subtract">
    <documentation>Subtracts two given numbers</documentation>
    <input message="s0:SubtractSoapIn" />
    <output message="s0:SubtractSoapOut" />
  </operation>
</portType>
```

The <portType> element's name attribute is used as the unique name to link to the binding section. See the Binding class reference for details on how the <portType> element name is linked to the <binding> element.

The PortType class connects binding information to the Interface section of the current WSDL definition. The name of the class, taken from the name attribute of the WSDL <portType> element, references an element in the Binding section.

An abstract combination of operations and messages forms a single WSDL <portType> element for a particular function of a Web Service. This element dictates the message format and other conditions that apply when communicating with a SOAP end-point.

There are four primary interaction modes that can apply to a particular PortType, which are defined by using a combination of alternative messages:

- **One Way message**
  Transfer a message to a SOAP server, no reply expected
  <input> element only

- **Request/Response message**
  Transfer a message to a SOAP server and receive back a reply
  <output> and <input> elements

- **Solicit Response message**
  SOAP Server sends the client a message, a reply is expected in return
  <output> and <input> elements, but server initiates call

- **Notification message**
  SOAP Server notifies the client, no reply expected
  <output> element only

PortType Class Public Methods

- Equals – inherited from System.Object, see Introduction for details.
- GetHashCode – inherited from System.Object, see Introduction for details.
- GetType – inherited from System.Object, see Introduction for details.
- ToString – inherited from System.Object, see Introduction for details.

PortType Class Protected Methods

- Finalize – inherited from System.Object, see Introduction for details.
- MemberwiseClone – inherited from System.Object, see Introduction for details.

PortType Class Public Properties

- **Documentation**
- **Name**
- **Operations**
- **ServiceDescription**

Documentation

The property `Documentation` is inherited from `System.Web.Services.DocumentableItem` and is used to assign or return text documentation for a particular `Port` object. See `DocumentableItem` class reference in this chapter for detailed explanation.

```
public string Documentation {get; set;}
```

Here is a usage of `Documentation` property:

```
sbText.AppendFormat("Name: {0}, Documentation: {1} ",
                    portType.Name, portType.Documentation);
```

Name

This property holds the name assigned to the `PortType` class, taken from the name of the `<portType>` element in the WSDL file. It returns or assigns a string object, if the name attribute is not specified, then its value is an empty string. However, if the name attribute is specified in the `<portType>` element, then the `Name` property should be unique within the `PortType` section in the WSDL schema, this means that every `<port>` element should have a unique name attribute.

```
public string Name {get; set;}
```

Here is a usage of `Name` property:

```
sbText.AppendFormat("Name: {0}, Documentation: {1} ",
                    portType.Name, portType.Documentation);
```

Operations

This property provides access to the `<operation>` elements contained by the `<portType>` element of the WSDL schema. An operation contains the input and output messages needed between client and server during execution of a remote Web Service. A single `<operation>` element represents a basic web method and its input, output, and fault message formats.

```
public OperationCollection Operations {get;}
```

This code displays the entire `<operation>` element name attribute within a `PortType` object:

```
foreach(Operation operation in portType.Operations)
{
  sbText.AppendFormat("Operation Name: {0}",
                      operation.Name);
}
```

Although this is a read-only property, you may alter the underlying collection items.

ServiceDescription

ServiceDescription property allows access to the parent ServiceDescription class. The ServiceDescription class is the main class that contains the WSDL schema. It returns a System.Web.Services.Description.ServiceDescription object.

```
public ServiceDescription ServiceDescription {get:}
```

The following code displays the TargetNamespace property of the returned ServiceDescription object:

```
sbText.AppendFormat("Service Description: {0}, ",
            portType.ServiceDescription.TargetNamespace);
```

Example Using the PortType Class:

Here is an example showing usage of all the properties of PortType class. You can find the complete code in PortTypeUsage.aspx.cs file in the code download:

```
StringBuilder sbText = new StringBuilder();
String fileName=Request.PhysicalApplicationPath + "SimpleCalculator.wsdl";
ServiceDescription sdPortType = ServiceDescription.Read(fileName);

sbText.Append("The Port Types defined in the WSDL" +
              " Document are:");
sbText.Append("<br>");

foreach(PortType portType in sdPortType.PortTypes)
{
  // Display the Name and Documentation property of each
  // PortType in the WSDL Document
  sbText.AppendFormat("Name: {0}, Documentation: {1}", +
                      portType.Name,
                      portType.Documentation);
  sbText.Append("<br>");

  sbText.AppendFormat("Service Description: {0} ",
                      portType.ServiceDescription.TargetNamespace);
  sbText.Append("<br>");
  // Display operation name of each operation in the Port
  //object
  foreach(Operation operation in portType.Operations)
  {
    sbText.AppendFormat("Operation Name: {0}",operation.Name);
    sbText.Append("<br>");
  }
  sbText.Append("<br>");
}
LblPortType.Text=sbText.ToString();
```

This will produce the following output:

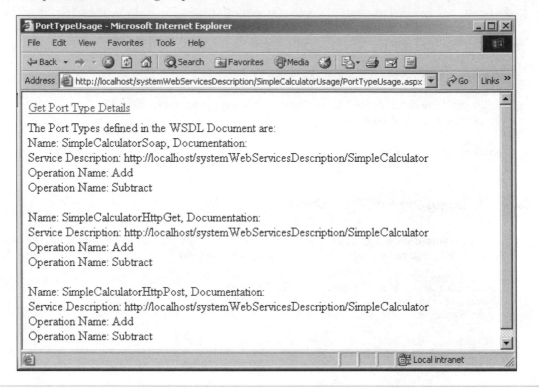

Service Class

The `Service` class defines multiple communication end-points for handling remote method calls within the current service. The class is described in WSDL documents using the `<service>` element. It groups together all the ports related to the current WSDL schema definition. This class is derived from the `System.Web.Services.Description.DocumentableItem` class and it cannot be further inherited.

The following snippet, taken from our WSDL example, shows the section associated with the `Service` class:

```
<service name="SimpleCalculator">
  <documentation>Performs Simple Calculator Operations</documentation>
  <port name="SimpleCalculatorSoap" binding="s0:SimpleCalculatorSoap">
    <soap:address
      location="http://localhost/SimpleCalculator/SimpleCalculator.asmx" />
  </port>
  <port name="SimpleCalculatorHttpGet"
        binding="s0:SimpleCalculatorHttpGet">
   <http:address
     location="http://localhost/SimpleCalculator/SimpleCalculator.asmx" />
```

```
      </port>
      <port name="SimpleCalculatorHttpPost"
            binding="s0:SimpleCalculatorHttpPost">
        <http:address
            location="http://localhost/SimpleCalculator/SimpleCalculator.asmx" />
      </port>
    </service>
```

`Services` group together sets of related ports. `Ports` provide alternative communication methods for a service, allowing the developer to choose which communication method to use to transfer messages to the SOAP server.

Service Class Public Methods

❑   `Equals` – inherited from `System.Object`, see Introduction for details.

❑   `GetHashCode` – inherited from `System.Object`, see Introduction for details.

❑   `GetType` – inherited from `System.Object`, see Introduction for details.

❑   `ToString` – inherited from `System.Object`, see Introduction for details.

Service Class Protected Methods

❑   `Finalize` – inherited from `System.Object`, see Introduction for details.

❑   `MemberwiseClone` – inherited from `System.Object`, see Introduction for details.

Service Class Public Properties

❑   **Documentation**

❑   **Extensions**

❑   **Name**

❑   **Ports**

❑   **ServiceDescription**

Documentation

The property `Documentation` is inherited from `System.Web.Services.DocumentableItem` and is used to assign or return text documentation for a particular `Service` object. See `DocumentableItem` class reference in this chapter for detailed explanation.

```
public string Documentation {get; set;}
```

Here is a usage of `Documentation` property:

```
sbText.AppendFormat("Name: {0}, Documentation: {1}",
                    service.Name, service.Documentation);
```

Extensions

This property represents the collection of extension elements within the current `<service>`. These elements can extend the capability of the `Service` adding support for additional messaging formats for SOAP messages. It returns a collection of extensibility elements as a `System.Web.Services.Description.ServiceDescriptionFormatExtensionsCollection` object. Also refer to the *Extensibility* discussion at the beginning of this chapter.

```
public ServiceDescriptionFormatExtensionCollection
                            Extensions {get;}
```

Here is a code snippet that extracts the `Extensions` of the `Service` class and then individually displays the `Extension` object's name and whether it is required or not:

```
foreach(ServiceDescriptionFormatExtension extension in
        service.Extensions)
  sbText.AppendFormat("Extensibility Class: {0}," +
                      " Required: {1}",
                      extension.ToString(),
                      extension.Required);
```

Name

This is the name given to the `Service` object, taken from the name of the `<service>` element in the WSDL file. It returns or assigns a `String` object; if the name attribute is not specified, then its value is an empty string. However, if the `name` attribute is specified in the `<port>` element, then the `Name` property should be unique within the `Port` section, this means that every `<port>` element should have a unique `name` attribute.

```
public string Name {get; set;}
```

Here is a usage of `Name` property:

```
sbText.AppendFormat("Name: {0}, Documentation: {1}",
                    service.Name, service.Documentation);
```

Ports

This property represents a collection containing all the ports available for the current Web Service. This property provides access to the `<port>` elements contained by the `<service>` element of the WSDL schema. Each port holds the address of one communication end-point.

```
public PortCollection Ports {get;}
```

Here is an example iterating through the `PortCollection` returned by the `Ports` property:

```
// Display port name of each port in the Service object
foreach(Port port in service.Ports)
  sbText.AppendFormat("Port Name: {0}", port.Name);
```

This is a read-only property, but you may change the underlying collection items.

ServiceDescription

ServiceDescription property allows access to the parent ServiceDescription class. The ServiceDescription class is the main class that contains the WSDL schema. It returns a System.Web.Services.Description.ServiceDescription object.

```
public ServiceDescription ServiceDescription{get;}
```

The following code displays the TargetNamespace property of the returned ServiceDescription object:

```
sbText.AppendFormat("Service Description " +
                    "Target Namespace: {0}",
                    service.ServiceDescription.TargetNamespace);
```

Example: Using the Service Class

Here is an example showing usage of all the properties of Service class. You can find the complete code in ServiceUsage.aspx.cs file in the code download:

```
StringBuilder sbText = new StringBuilder();
String fileName=Request.PhysicalApplicationPath +
                "SimpleCalculator.wsdl";
ServiceDescription sdService = ServiceDescription.Read(fileName);

sbText.Append("The Services defined in the WSDL Document" +
              " are:");
sbText.Append("<br>");

foreach(Service service in sdService.Services)
{
  // Display the Name and Documentation property of each
  // Service in the WSDL Document
  sbText.AppendFormat("Name: {0}, Documentation: {1}", +
                      service.Name, service.Documentation);
  sbText.Append("<br>");

  sbText.AppendFormat("Service Description Target " +
                      "Namespace: {0}",
                      service.ServiceDescription.TargetNamespace);
  sbText.Append("<br>");

  // Display port name of each port in the Service object

  foreach(Port port in service.Ports)
  {
    sbText.AppendFormat("Port Name: {0}", port.Name);
    sbText.Append("<br>");
  }
  // Display the Extensibility classes
```

```
    foreach(ServiceDescriptionFormatExtension extension in
            service.Extensions)
    {
        sbText.AppendFormat("Extensibility Class: {0}, " +
                            "Required: {1}",
                            extension.ToString(),
                            extension.Required);
        sbText.Append("<br>");
    }
    sbText.Append("<br>");
}
LblService.Text=sbText.ToString();
```

This will produce the following output;

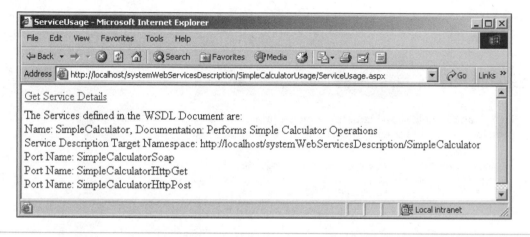

ServiceDescription Class

The ServiceDescription class is the root class containing the Web Service definition in its entirety. Using ServiceDescription, you can import the WSDL schema definitions from an external WSDL schema file.

The ServiceDescription class is the root class for the entire WSDL file structure with namespaces, elements and attributes. This class maps to the <definitions> root element of the WSDL schema file. This class in inherited from System.Web.Services.Description.DocumentableItem class and it cannot be further inherited.

ServiceDescription Class Public Methods

❑ **CanRead**

❑ Equals – inherited from System.Object, see Introduction for details.

❑ GetHashCode – inherited from System.Object, see Introduction for details.

❑ GetType – inherited from System.Object, see Introduction for details.

❑ **Read**

❑ ToString – inherited from System.Object, see Introduction for details.

❑ **Write**

CanRead

`CanRead` is a static method that helps to determine whether a document conforms to the WSDL specification by loading it into an `XmlReader` object (a class for reading generic XML files) and subsequently using the `CanRead` method. The method returns `true` if the file is of the correct structure and can be read. The method should be referenced by `ServiceDescription` class name.

```
public static bool CanRead(XmlReader reader);
```

The `CanRead` method needs an `XmlReader` object containing the WSDL schema. It is always a good practice to call `CanRead` method before loading the `ServiceDescription` object.

Following is some example code for loading a WSDL file, verifying that it can be read and is a valid WSDL schema file:

```
StringBuilder sbText = new StringBuilder();
String fileName=Request.PhysicalApplicationPath + "SimpleCalculator.wsdl";
            XmlReader reader = new XmlTextReader(fileName);

if(ServiceDescription.CanRead(reader))
{
  LblCanRead.Text = fileName + "contains valid WSDL schema";
}
else
{
  LblCanRead.Text = fileName + "contains invalid WSDL schema";
}
```

> *The `XmlTextReader` constructor can also take a URI for loading, for example,*
> `http://localhost/SimpleCalculator/SimpleCalculator.asmx?wsdl`*.*

Read

This method populates the `ServiceDescription` class. The method is overloaded. You can use any one of the following four argument types to populate this class.

The first overload requires a `Stream` pointing to WSDL file:
```
public static ServiceDescription Read(Stream);
```

The second overload requires a `String` denoting a WSDL file:
```
public static ServiceDescription Read(String);
```

The third overload requires an `XmlReader` object associated with a WSDL file:
```
public static ServiceDescription Read(XmlReader);
```

The last overload requires a `TextReader` object associated with a WSDL file:
```
public static ServiceDescription Read(TextReader);
```

The following code shows how you could populate a `ServiceDescription` object by passing in the filename of a valid local WSDL document as a string argument:

```
StringBuilder sbText = new StringBuilder();
String fileName=Request.PhysicalApplicationPath + "SimpleCalculator.wsdl";
ServiceDescription sDescription = ServiceDescription.Read(fileName);
```

Note that the above method cannot be called with the http *parameter, as we displayed the WSDL.
URI formats are not allowed as parameters.*

This code assumes that you have a valid WSDL schema on your C:drive and then uses it to instantiate
and populate the ServiceDescription class. After this you can use the collections and objects
contained within this class to interrogate any part of the WSDL schema definition.

The ServiceDescription class forms the basic building block for a WSDL schema, allowing you to
read in, and subsequently interrogate, each of the schema's collections and associated objects.

Write

Writes the currently loaded ServiceDescription object containing WSDL schema into an output
File, Stream, XmlWriter or TextWriter object. After you have read in a valid WSDL file you may
want to manipulate its values. For example, the following code shows you how to change the
TargetNamespace property:

```
os.TargetNamespace = http://www.salcentral.com/wrox/tnspace.xml
```

Once you have altered your schema, you can save it using one of the following methods:

The first overload requires a stream pointing to WSDL file:

```
public void Write(string);
```

The second overload requires a string denoting a WSDL file:

```
public void Write(Stream);
```

The third overload requires an XmlReader object associated with a WSDL file:

```
public void Write(XmlReader);
```

The last overload requires a TextReader object associated with a WSDL file:

```
public void Write(TxtReader);
```

In the following example we alter our WSDL schema file and save it to a local file on our hard drive by
using the following code:

```
ServiceDescription os;
os = ServiceDescription.Read(@"c:\Calculator.wsdl");
os.TargetNamespace = "http://www.salcentral.com/wrox/tnspace.xml";
os.Write("C:\test.wsdl");
```

ServiceDescription Class Protected Methods

- ❑ `Finalize` – inherited from `System.Object`, see Introduction for details.

- ❑ `MemberwiseClone` – inherited from `System.Object`, see Introduction for details.

ServiceDescription Class Public Properties

- ❑ **Bindings**

- ❑ **Documentation**

- ❑ **Extensions**

- ❑ **Imports**

- ❑ **Messages**

- ❑ **Name**

- ❑ **PortTypes**

- ❑ **RetrievalUrl**

- ❑ **ServiceDescriptions**

- ❑ **Services**

- ❑ **TargetNamespace**

- ❑ **Types**

Bindings

This property returns a `BindingCollection` class object containing the collection of `<binding>` elements extracted from the `ServiceDescription`. This `Binding` class describes associations between the messages defined by the WSDL and the communication end-point.

This collection is read-only, meaning that you cannot assign a `BindingCollection` object directly, once it has be instantiated by reading in a WSDL schema; however, you alter the underlying collection items.

```
public BindingCollection Bindings {get;}
```

Here is an example displaying the Name and Type property of each Binding in the `ServiceDescription`:

```
// Display the Name and Type property of each Binding in the // Service
Description
foreach(Binding binding in sDescription.Bindings)
  sbText.AppendFormat("Binding Name: {0}, Type: {1} ",
                      binding.Name, binding.Type);
```

Documentation

The property `Documentation` is inherited from `System.Web.Services.DocumentableItem` and is used to assign or return text documentation for a particular `ServiceDescription` object. See `DocumentableItem` class reference in this chapter for detailed explanation.

```
public string Documentation {get; set;}
```

Here is a usage of `Documentation` property:

```
sbText.AppendFormat("Service Description Name: {0}," +
                    " Documentation: {1}" ,
                    sDescription.Name,
                    sDescription.Documentation);
```

Extensions

This property represents the collection of `Extension` elements within the current `ServiceDescription` object. These elements can extend the capability of the `Service` adding support for additional messaging formats for SOAP messages. It returns a collection of extensibility elements as a `System.Web.Services.Description.ServiceDescriptionFormatExtensionsCollection` object. Also refer to the *Extensibility* discussion at the beginning of this chapter.

```
public ServiceDescriptionFormatExtensionCollection Extensions {get;}
```

Here is a code snippet that extracts the `Extensions` of the `ServiceDescription` class and then individually displays the `Extension` object's name and whether it is required or not:

```
// Display the Extensibility class name and whether required
// of each Extension in the Service Description
foreach(ServiceDescriptionFormatExtension extension in
        sDescription.Extensions)
  sbText.AppendFormat("Extensibility Class: {0}, " +
                      "Required: {1}",
                      extension.ToString(),
                      extension.Required);
```

It's worth noting that although extensibility properties can be found throughout a WSDL document, they represent unique features that are only related to the specific WSDL area to which they have been bound.

This collection is read-only, meaning that you cannot assign an `Extensions` collection object directly to it, once it has be instantiated by reading in a WSDL schema; however, you are able to alter the underlying collection items.

Imports

WSDL allows for the definition of portions of its structure inside separate XML files external to the main WSDL document. Such external XML files are referenced by a WSDL document by means of an `<import>` element. The external XML is inserted into the WSDL document at the exact position of the import statement. The `Imports` property contains information about all `<import>` elements in a WSDL file as an `ImportCollection` object.

```
public ImportCollection Imports {get;}
```

You can extract the data from another XML file by adding an import element:

```
<import ref="http://www.salcentral.com/wrox/import.xml"/>
```

This property is read-only although you may alter the underlying collection items.
The following code snippet displays the `Namespace` and `Location` properties of each `Import` object in the `ServiceDescription`:

```
// Display the Namespace and Location property of each
// Import in the Service Description
foreach(Import import in sDescription.Imports)
  sbText.AppendFormat("Import Namespace: {0}, Location: {1}",
                      import.Namespace, import.Location);
```

Messages

The `<message>` elements in a WSDL file provide definitions of the arguments and method name for either the Request or the Response message, through sub-elements of the `<part>` elements in the WSDL schema. The `Messages` property contains collection information about all such `<message>` elements defined within the WSDL schema. It returns a `MessageCollection` object that is, again read-only, although you may alter the underlying collection items.

```
public MessageCollection Messages {get;}
```

Here is a piece of code that displays the `Name` and `Documentation` property of each `Message` object in the `ServiceDescription`:

```
// Display the Name and Documentation property of each
// Message in the Service Description
foreach(Message message in sDescription.Messages)
  sbText.AppendFormat("Message Name: {0}, " +
                      "Documentation : {1}",
                      message.Name, message.Documentation);
```

Name

This is the name given to the `ServiceDescription` class object, taken from the name of the `<definitions>` element in the WSDL file. It returns or assigns a string object, if not assigned then returns an empty string.

```
public string Name {get; set;}
```

Here is a usage of `Name` property:

```
sbText.AppendFormat("Service Description Name: {0}," +
                    "Documentation: {1}" ,
                    sDescription.Name,
                    sDescription.Documentation);
```

PortTypes

This property represents an abstract collection of messages and operations defined in the `<portType>` element. It is used to link the bindings section of the WSDL schema to the messages section of the WSDL schema. It returns a `PortTypeCollection` object.

```
public PortTypeCollection PortTypes {get;}
```

The following code snippet displays the details of the `PortTypes` in a particular WSDL file:

```
// Display the Name and Documentation property of each
// PortType in the WSDL Document
foreach(PortType portType in sDescription.PortTypes)
  sbText.AppendFormat("PortType Name: {0}, " +
                      "Documentation: {1}",
                      portType.Name,
                      portType.Documentation);
```

RetrievalUrl

This property returns or assigns the URL of the Web Service in which `ServiceDescription` object belongs to. By default it returns an empty string.

```
public string RetrievalUrl {get; set;}
```

Here is a usage of `RetrievalUrl` property

```
sbText.AppendFormat("Target Namespace: {0}, " +
                    "Retrieval Url: {1}",
                    sDescription.TargetNamespace,
                    sDescription.RetrievalUrl);
```

ServiceDescriptions

The `ServiceDescriptions` property makes available the parent collection that contains this instance of `ServiceDescription`, if the current `ServiceDescription` is attached to a collection. If this instance has no parent collection, then a `NullReferenceException` occurs.

This property allows for the collation of multiple schemas into a single business solution comprising a collection of various Web Services. Each schema added to the `ServiceDescriptions` collection must have its own unique `TargetNamespace`.

```
public ServiceDescriptionCollection ServiceDescriptions {get;}
```

The following code displays the `Count` property of `ServiceDescriptionCollection` of which the `ServiceDescription` is a member:

```
// Display the Count property of
// ServiceDescriptionCollection of which the Service
// Description is a member ServiceDescriptionCollection
sdCollection = sDescription.ServiceDescriptions;
if(sdCollection != null)
  sbText.AppendFormat("The number of Service Description " +
                     " in the WSDL document are {0}",
                     sdCollection.Count.ToString());
```

Services

`Services` group together a set of related ports defined in the WSDL schema. A port is the destination and transport protocol to use when transferring messages to a SOAP-compliant server. This property returns a collection of `ServiceCollection` objects. This collection allows you to interact with services and their associated ports for a specific Web Service.

```
public ServiceCollection Services {get;}
```

The following code snippet displays the `Name` and `Documentation` property of each `Service` object in the WSDL Schema:

```
// Display the Name and Documentation property of each
// Service in the WSDL Document
foreach(Service service in sDescription.Services)
  sbText.AppendFormat(" Service Name: {0}, " +
                      "Documentation: {1}",
                      service.Name, service.Documentation);
```

TargetNamespace

This specifies the namespace taken from the `<definitions>` element's `TargetNamespace` attribute in the WSDL header. This is the Internet or intranet location of the current WSDL file. This property returns or assigns a `String` object to the `TargetNamespace` attribute of the `definitions` element.

```
public string TargetNamespace {get; set;}
```

Here is a usage of `TargetNamespace` property:

```
sbText.AppendFormat("Target Namespace: {0}, " +
                    "Retrieval Url: {1}",
                    sDescription.TargetNamespace,
                    sDescription.RetrievalUrl);
```

Types

It is possible to create your own data types tailored for specific messages and requirements in the `<types>` section of WSDL schema. For example, when transmitting a customer's name and address, you could define a single complex data type to contain both name and address. The `Types` collection allows you to iterate through all user-defined types given in the current WSDL document.

Another read-only property that does not allow you to assign a new collection, it does, however, allow the underlying collection items to be altered.

`Types` allow you to create data type definitions for particular message or operation requirements. For example, you can define a `Type` reflecting an internal structure of the Web Service application, such as a customer record.

```
public Types Types {get; set;}
```

The following code displays the `Documentation` property of `Types` object in the WSDL Schema:

```
// Display the Documentation property of Types object in the
// WSDL Document
sbText.AppendFormat("Types Documentation: {0} ",
                    sDescription.Types.Documentation);
```

ServiceDescription Class Public Fields

❑ **Namespace**

Namespace

This constant field identifies the XML namespace for the `ServiceDescription` class. The WSDL namespace used for this is http://schemas.xmlsoap.org/wsdl/. This description is similar to a constant that defines a data type, for example, the word "string" defines a string variable. In this instance the above namespace identifies that this WSDL schema construct adheres to the WSDL definition.

```
public const string Namespace
```

It returns a `String` object and should be referenced using the `ServiceDescription` class name.

Here is some code that calls this `Namespace` field:

```
sbText.AppendFormat("Namespace: {0}" ,
                    ServiceDescription.Namespace);
```

Example: Using the ServiceDescription Class

Here is an example showing usage of all the properties of `ServiceDescription` class. You can find the complete code in `ServiceDescriptionUsage.aspx.cs` file in the code download:

```
{
  StringBuilder sbText = new StringBuilder();
  String fileName=Request.PhysicalApplicationPath +
                  "SimpleCalculator.wsdl";
  XmlReader reader = new XmlTextReader(fileName);

  if(ServiceDescription.CanRead(reader))
  {
    LblCanRead.Text = fileName + " contains valid WSDL" +
```

```
      " schema";
    }
    else
    {
      LblCanRead.Text = fileName + " contains invalid WSDL" +
                                   " schema";
    }
  }

  private void LBtnSDescription_Click(object sender,
                                      System.EventArgs e)
  {
    StringBuilder sbText = new StringBuilder();
    String fileName=Request.PhysicalApplicationPath +
                    "SimpleCalculator.wsdl";
    ServiceDescription sDescription =
                    ServiceDescription.Read(fileName);

    sbText.Append("The complete ServiceDescription defined " +
                  "in the WSDL Document is:");
    sbText.Append("<br>");

    // Display the Name,Documentation, Target Namespace and
    // RetrievalUrl property of ServiceDescription
    sbText.AppendFormat("Service Description Name: {0}," +
                        " Documentation: {1}" ,
                        sDescription.Name,
                        sDescription.Documentation);
    sbText.Append("<br>");
    sbText.AppendFormat("Namespace: {0}" ,
                        ServiceDescription.Namespace);
    sbText.Append("<br>");
    sbText.AppendFormat("Target Namespace: {0}, " +
                        "Retrieval Url: {1}" ,
                        sDescription.TargetNamespace,
                        sDescription.RetrievalUrl);
    sbText.Append("<br>");

    // Display the Name and Type property of each Binding in
    // the Service Description
    foreach(Binding binding in sDescription.Bindings)
    {
      sbText.AppendFormat("Binding Name: {0}, Type: {1}"
                          ,binding.Name, binding.Type);
      sbText.Append("<br>");
    }

    // Display the Extensibility class name and whether
    // required of each Extension in the Service Decription
    foreach(ServiceDescriptionFormatExtension extension in
            sDescription.Extensions)
    {
      sbText.AppendFormat("Extensibility Class: {0}, " +
                          "Required: {1}",extension.ToString(),
```

```
                              extension.Required);
   sbText.Append("<br>");
}


// Display the Namespace and Location property of each
// Import in the Service Description
foreach(Import import in sDescription.Imports)
{
sbText.AppendFormat("Import Namespace: {0}, " +
                     "Location: {1} ",import.Namespace,
                      import.Location);
sbText.Append("<br>");
}

// Display the Name and Documentation property of each
// Message in the Service Description
foreach(Message message in sDescription.Messages)
{
  sbText.AppendFormat("Message Name: {0}, " +
                       "Documentation : {1}",
                        message.Name,
                        message.Documentation);
  sbText.Append("<br>");
}


// Display the Name and Documentation property of each
// PortType in the WSDL Document
foreach(PortType portType in sDescription.PortTypes)
{
  sbText.AppendFormat("PortType Name: {0}, " +
                       "Documentation: {1} ",portType.Name,
                        portType.Documentation);
  sbText.Append("<br>");
}


// Display the Count property of
// ServiceDescriptionCollection of which the Service
// Description is a member
ServiceDescriptionCollection sdCollection =
                     sDescription.ServiceDescriptions;
if(sdCollection != null)
{
  sbText.AppendFormat("The number of Service " +
                       "Description in the WSDL document" +
                       "are {0}",
                        sdCollection.Count.ToString());
  sbText.Append("<br>");
}

// Display the Name and Documentation property of each
// Service in the WSDL Document
foreach(Service service in sDescription.Services)
{
```

```
        sbText.AppendFormat(" Service Name: {0}, " +
                            "Documentation: {1} ",service.Name,
                            service.Documentation);
        sbText.Append("<br>");
    }

    // Display the Documentation property of Types object in
    // the WSDL Document
    sbText.AppendFormat("Types Documentation: {0} ",
                        sDescription.Types.Documentation);

    LblSDescription.Text=sbText.ToString();
}
```

The example below includes much of the output this code should produce:

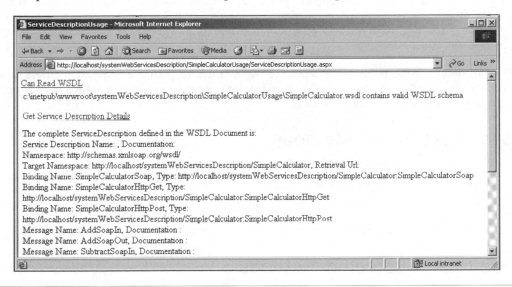

Types Class

The Types class allows you to iterate through all types defined by the currently applicable WSDL definition. These data types conform to standard XML notation. The following XML extract shows the <types> element of our example WSDL schema. This XML information is consumed by the Types class, and in turn the Schemas collection class instantiated inside it:

```
<types>
  <s:schema elementFormDefault="qualified"
            targetNamespace="http://localhost/SimpleCalculator">
    <s:element name="Add">
      <s:complexType>
        <s:sequence>
          <s:element minOccurs="1" maxOccurs="1" name="num1"
                     type="s:double" />
```

```
            <s:element minOccurs="1" maxOccurs="1" name="num2"
                       type="s:double" />
         </s:sequence>
       </s:complexType>
     </s:element>
   </schema>
 </types>
```

Our example defines a complex type that comprises the two double values `num1` and `num2` that may be passed as a single unit to our remote Web Service.

The `Types` class exposes such complex types through the `XMLSchema` object contained in the `Types` collection.

`Types` allow you to create user-defined types for a particular message or operation requirement. They are XML structures that define a custom data type for use within a particular context. They are helpful for defining data types that can be used within messages for transferring structured data sets or unique language-dependent data types.

The data definition can be anything from a high-level structure, such as a name and address record, to low-level redefinitions of a basic data type, such as long, integer, and string, to suit a particular requirement of a given message interface.

Types Class Public Methods

❑ `Equals` – inherited from `System.Object`, see Introduction for details.

❑ `GetHashCode` – inherited from `System.Object`, see Introduction for details.

❑ `GetType` – inherited from `System.Object`, see Introduction for details.

❑ `ToString` – inherited from `System.Object`, see Introduction for details.

Types Class Protected Methods

❑ `Finalize` – inherited from `System.Object`, see Introduction for details.

❑ `MemberwiseClone` – inherited from `System.Object`, see Introduction for details.

Types Class Public Properties

❑ **Documentation**

❑ **Extensions**

❑ **Schemas**

Documentation

The property `Documentation` is inherited from `System.Web.Services.DocumentableItem` and is used to assign or return text documentation for a particular `Types` object. See `DocumentableItem` class reference in this chapter for detailed explanation.

```
public string Documentation {get; set;}
```

Here is a usage of `Documentation` property:

```
sbText.AppendFormat("Types Documentation: {0} ",
                     types.Documentation);
```

Extensions

This property represents the collection of extension elements within the current `<types>`. These elements can extend the capability of the `Types` adding support for additional messaging formats for SOAP messages. It allows for extension of the basic functionality of the `Types` class. It returns a collection of extensibility elements as a `System.Web.Services.Description.`↲ `ServiceDescriptionFormatExtensionsCollection` object.

```
public ServiceDescriptionFormatExtensionCollection Extensions {get;}
```

Here is a code snippet that extracts the `Extensions` of the `Service` class and then individually displays the `Extension` object's name and whether it is required or not:

```
foreach(ServiceDescriptionFormatExtension extension in types.Extensions)
   sbText.AppendFormat("Extensibility Class: {0}," +
                        "Required: {1}", extension.ToString(),
                        extension.Required);
```

Schemas

This property returns a collection of XML Schema data type definitions for objects within the current WSDL schema. It returns an object of type `XmlSchemas` collection. The default implementation of `Types` returns an empty collection of schema.

```
public XmlSchemas Schemas {get;}
```

Example: Using the Types Class

Here is an example showing usage of all the properties of `Types` class. You can find the complete code in the `TypesUsage.aspx.cs` file in the code download:

```
StringBuilder sbText = new StringBuilder();
String fileName=Request.PhysicalApplicationPath +
               "SimpleCalculator.wsdl";
ServiceDescription sdTypes = ServiceDescription.Read(fileName);

Types types = sdTypes.Types;

// Display the Documentation property of Types object in
// the WSDL Document
sbText.AppendFormat("Types Documentation: {0} ",
                     types.Documentation);
```

```
sbText.Append("<br>");
sbText.AppendFormat("Schemas: {0} ",
                    types.Schemas.ToString());

// Display the Extensibility classes
foreach(ServiceDescriptionFormatExtension extension in types.Extensions)
{
  sbText.AppendFormat("Extensibility Class: {0}, " +
                      "Required: {1}",
                      extension.ToString(),
                      extension.Required);
  sbText.Append("<br>");
}

LblTypes.Text=sbText.ToString();
```

The output for this code is shown below;

System.Web.Services.Description Enumerations

OperationFlow

This defines the values that indicate the direction of communication between a client and a Web Service. It is used by the
`System.Web.Services.Description.OperationMessageCollection.Flow` property.

Member Name	Description	Value
None	Indicates that the Web Service end-point receives and makes no communication	0
OneWay	Indicates that the Web Service receives messages but is not expected to respond	1

Member Name	Description	Value
`Notification`	Indicates that an end-point sends messages without a Request being issued	2
`RequestResponse`	Indicates that the Web Service receives Request messages, and returns Response messages	3
`SolicitResponse`	(Default) Indicates that an end-point sends a message, and expects a reply by the client	4

ServiceDescriptionImportStyle

This defines the point at which the XML parser should import an XML file defined by the `<import>` element of the current WSDL definition.

If this is specified as `Server` then when the client attempts to read the WSDL schema, the import XML file will be imported and embedded directly into the schema file at the location where the import element is situated. Therefore the client will simply see a single and completed WSDL file. If, however, it is set to client the client must import the XML file itself.

It is used by the `System.Web.Services.Description.ServiceDescriptionImporter.Style` property.

Member Name	Description	Value
`Client`	(Default) Indicates that the XML file should be imported by a client-based XML parser	0
`Server`	Indicates that the XML file should be imported before it reaches the client by a server-based XML parser	1

ServiceDescriptionImportWarnings

This is the return warning indication produced when attempting to import an XML file into the current WSDL schema definition, by either a client- or server-based XML parser.

This enumeration is returned by the `System.Web.Services.Description.ServiceDescriptionImporter.Import` method.

Member Name	Value	Description
`NoCodeGenerated`	1	The `Import` method didn't create a proxy class.
`OptionalExtensionsIgnored`	2	The proxy class created by the `Import` method doesn't include any methods.

Member Name	Value	Description
RequiredExtensionsIgnored	4	At least one optional `ServiceDescriptionFormatExtension` for the `ServiceDescription` to be imported has been ignored.
UnsupportedOperationsIgnored	8	At least one necessary `ServiceDescriptionFormatExtension` for the `ServiceDescription` to be imported has been ignored.
UnsupportedBindingsIgnored	16	At least one `Binding` for the `ServiceDescription` to be imported is of an unsupported type and has been ignored.
NoMethodsGenerated	32	At least one `Operation` for the `ServiceDescription` to be imported is of an unsupported type and has been ignored.

SoapBindingStyle

This indicates an appropriate programming model that can potentially affect the structure of the SOAP message body. It should be noted that RPC and Document binding styles simply indicate that schema definitions use different methods of structuring elements, most noticeably in the case of comparing these two methods with the definition of the messages and its arguments.

It is used by the `System.Web.Services.Description.SoapBinding.Style` property.

Member Name	Description	Value
Default	(Default) The default for this enumeration is `Document`	0
Document	Indicates that the operation involves document-oriented messages (messages contain documents)	1
Rpc	Indicates that the operation involves RPC-oriented messages (messages contain parameters, and return values)	2

SoapBindingUse

The `SoapBindingUse` enumeration specifies the parameter encoding styles available to an ASP.NET Web Service.

It is used by the following properties in the `System.Web.Services.Description` namespace:

- ❑ `SoapBodyBinding.Use`
- ❑ `SoapFaultBinding.Use`
- ❑ `SoapHeaderBinding.Use`
- ❑ `SoapHeaderFaultBinding.Use`

Member Name	Description	Value
`Default`	An empty string value for the corresponding XML `use` attribute	0
`Encoded`	Identifies that the values are encoded as specified by the `encodingStyle` attribute. (To encode text means to translate it from one character set to another.)	1
`Literal`	Identifies that the class's values are explicitly stated by an XML Schema definition associated by either the `element` or the `type` attribute. This also refers to the fact that the value is non-encoded, in other words it is held in its original form.	2

11

System.Web.Services.Protocols

The `System.Web.Services.Protocols` namespace controls the main connectivity between Web Service clients and servers. It is used by .NET Web Service clients, and ASP.NET Web Services, to manipulate service requests and responses, such as SOAP messages (Simple Object Access Protocol), and in turn to allow the processing of Web Service functionality.

The `System.Web.Services.Protocols` namespace groups together the classes that handle the communication of the basic types of Web Service messages required by all Web Service applications and SOAP-compliant servers:

❑ **Request** – transmitted by the client to the server

❑ **Response** – returned by the server to the client

❑ **Fault messages** – returned by the server in the event of an error

In addition to dealing with communication classes, this namespace also controls the construction (also known as **serialization**) and interpretation (also known as **de-serialization**) of SOAP messages according to the currently supported SOAP standard. This allows us to produce advanced customized SOAP messages; for example adding compression, encryption, or even a header section that contains logon details and/or transaction information.

This namespace is particularly useful in a number of situations:

❑ **Interrogation** – to interrogate the current Web Service session to find information about the transfer protocol. This allows you to programmatically determine which communication technique (SOAP, HTTP-GET, or HTTP-POST) to use or even change the values to send to the ASP.NET server at run time: encrypting or compressing your SOAP message, for example.

❑ **XML Element Control** – to change XML elements within the SOAP message. The namespace grants you fine-grained control over SOAP messages, such as adding headers, performing user validation, and assigning specialist XML namespaces.

❑ **Proxy Class Wrapper** – to create your own client communication proxy class wrapper that encapsulates available communication calls to the remote ASP.NET server, and to allow you to control the sending of SOAP requests at a very low level, for example adding a validation username and password that gives access to a specific Web Service.

❑ **Customize Proxy Class Wrapper** – to customize a client proxy class or Web Service method using attributes. This allows you to introduce specific extensions to fulfill your own particular requirements not catered for by the default Web Service settings. For example, by changing the default SOAP action for a Web Method you can effectively tell the SOAP server to redirect your message to another SOAP server instead of processing it.

We will start this chapter with a general discussion of the various communication protocols that are used with Web Services, and we will then move on to discuss in depth some of the most important classes in the namespace.

Communication Protocols

.NET supports three basic communication protocols for Web Services. The protocol has to be able to encode parameters for a Web Service request, and encode the return value from a Web Service. All of .NET's Web Service protocols are layered over the standard Web protocols.

❑ **SOAP** – transfer messages with HTTP and SOAP wrappers using form post. This is the typical and default SOAP communication method.

❑ **HTTP GET** – transfer messages using HTTP GET with URL defined parameters. In this instance, a complete SOAP message is not created.

❑ **HTTP POST** – transfer messages using HTTP form post. In this instance a complete SOAP message is not created.

The basic SOAP specification as defined by W3C does not require the use of any particular mode of communication, and you are free to transfer SOAP messages over HTTP, COM, COM+, CORBA, and SMTP. The definition of which communication techniques are available for any Web Service is specified by the `<service>` element within the corresponding WSDL (Web Service Definition Language) file. This WSDL file defines the structure of the Web Services available along with the supported communication techniques.

When ASP.NET transmits SOAP messages between a client and a server, it first interrogates the communication information contained by this `<service>` element to ensure that the technique you wish to use is supported. Secondly, once ASP.NET finds a communication technique it understands (SOAP, HTTP-GET, or HTTP-POST) the information contained within that element provides the end-point server information required to pinpoint the location of the SOAP-compliant server address and port. This may be an ASP.NET server or it may be in fact another server that supports SOAP standards for running remote Web Services.

Supported Communication Techniques

The `System.Web.Services.Protocols` namespace supports three communication techniques for transferring the three varieties of SOAP message between client and the Web Service server: SOAP, HTTP-GET, and HTTP-POST.

SOAP

The most common communication technique, SOAP, uses the TCP/IP transport to send a SOAP request inside standard HTTP formatted text. The example below shows its two distinct sections:

Member Name	Text Sent to Server

HTTP Header	```POST /Service1.asmx HTTP/1.1```
	```Host: localhost```
	```Content-Type: text/xml; charset=utf-8```
	```Content-Length: length```
	```SOAPAction: "http://tempuri.org/HelloWorld"```

HTTP Body	```<?xml version="1.0" encoding="utf-8"?>```
	```<soap:Envelope```
	```xmlns:xsi="http://www.w3.org/2001/XMLSchema-```
	```instance"```
	```xmlns:xsd="http://www.w3.org/2001/XMLSchema"```
	```xmlns:soap="http://schemas.xmlsoap.org/soap/```
	``` envelope/" >```
	```<soap:Body>```
	``` <HelloWorld xmlns="http://tempuri.org/">```
	``` <Arg1>Hello</Arg1>```
	``` <Arg2>World</Arg2>```
	``` </HelloWorld>```
	``` </soap:Body>""```
	```</soap:Envelope>```

❑ HTTP Header – this section contains the standard HTTP header information that you would normally find in any HTTP request, for example, when you want to display a page on a web site. However, one important key is added: the SOAPAction key is added to SOAP requests and indicates the intended recipient for this SOAP message. This can allow us to pass a request to one server but indicate that we wish it to be redirected to another server for processing (this is covered in more detail later in this chapter). SOAPAction is ignored if used for sending a SOAP response back to a client.

❑ HTTP Body – contains a valid message that conforms to the supported SOAP specification. In the above example we show the SOAP message we could expect from the HelloWorld example that VS.NET creates when you start a new Web Service project. When we actually run this HelloWorld Web Service for the first time from a client this is the actual message that is sent to the ASP.NET server.

The above template is followed for every SOAP communication transfer, although naturally the content will reflect the actual Web Service you are calling.

The SoapHttpClientProtocol class is the highest-level class that controls this SOAP communication technique. This is the default class employed by the proxy class created from the Web Service schema using the wsdl.exe command-line tool included with the .NET SDK.

HTTP GET

HTTP GET describes a technique for passing data to an ASP.NET server by appending information to the server's URL. Arguments are passed to the server by using name-value pairs, as shown in the following example:

```
http://www.WSserver.com/Service1.asmx/HelloWorld?Arg1=Hello&Arg2=World
```

This URL is composed of protocol (`http://`), name of the web server (`www.WSserver.com/`) followed by the name of the Web Service (`Service1.asmx`), and the web method name (`HelloWorld`). A "?" character denotes the start of the list of passed parameters, known as the **querystring**. The name of each parameter is followed by the value of that parameter, separated by the "=" sign. The ampersand character (`&`) marks the start of additional name-value pairs.

The above address line can be typed in the address bar of any web browser as if you were browsing to a specific page on the Internet. Instead of displaying an HTML page however, this process now runs a specific ASP.NET Web Service with the arguments specified and returns and displays an XML formatted string.

The `HttpGetClientProtocol` class is the highest-level class that controls the HTTP-GET communication technique. The `HttpGetClientProtocol` class simulates a URL GET by constructing a valid HTTP-GET header and sending it down to the relevant ASP.NET server. In the case of HTTP GET, unlike the SOAP communication technique, a SOAP message is *not* created. The values for the method name and argument are sent down to the SOAP server using URL parameter passing.

Member Name	Text Sent to Server
HTTP Header	GET /Service1.asmx/Helloworld?Arg1=Hello&Arg2=World HTTP/1.1 Host: localhost

❑ HTTP Header – the above HTTP header is sent to the ASP.NET server. The header has no special keys or tags and in its simplest form can be reproduced by simply typing the address and name-value pairs for arguments into any browser capable of displaying an HTML file on the Internet.

> The HTTP-GET communication technique is simply used for running a Web Service, rather than an actual implementation of the SOAP messaging standard. Its primary significance would be for testing a response from an already created ASP.NET Web Service.

Note that there is a 2,048 character limit on sending characters on an Internet Explorer URL address line. This limit varies depending on your browser, but it must be noted that the limitation exists and that transfer errors may occur when sending large quantities of information to the Web Service in this way. Passing the arguments as part of a query string also exposes the information; you would certainly not like sensitive information like passwords or a credit card number to appear as part of the URL in a web browser and also for it to be stored in the browser's history. In that case you would like to use one of the two other communication protocols described here.

HTTP POST

The HTTP-POST method of communication is similar to HTTP GET, except that parameter name-value pairs are transmitted as part of the actual body of the HTTP request, rather than appended to the URL request line.

Member Name	Text Sent to Server
HTTP Header	POST /Service1.asmx HTTP/1.1 Host: localhost Content-Type: text/xml; charset=utf-8 Content-Length: length
HTTP Body	Arg1=Hello Arg2=World

❑ HTTP Header – The above HTTP header is sent to any SOAP server that understands HTTP-POST requests. It uses standard form post techniques and in its simplest form can be created using a web page with a form and suitably named fields.

❑ HTTP Body – The arguments for the web method are encapsulated using the standard HTML form post techniques.

The ASP.NET server receives form post fields representing name-value pairs for the parameters in question, which are then used as arguments for the requested Web Service. As with HTTP GET, this method is simply a technique for running a Web Service, rather than an actual implementation of the SOAP messaging standard.

The `HttpPostClientProtocol` class is the highest-level class that controls the HTTP-POST communication technique. The `HttpPostClientProtocol` class simulates a form post by constructing a valid HTTP-POST header and HTTP body and sending them down to the relevant ASP.NET server.

> One potential benefit of the HTTP-POST communication technique is that you can create your own form within a web site, which, as long as it has the correct named arguments, can actually run a remote Web Service. Its flaw, however, is that it must then be able to capture and respond to an XML-formatted response.

This technique gives this method of transfer an unlimited size. However, in reality the inherent limitations of traffic information on the Internet restrict size. HTTP-POST also allows you to encrypt information using SSL; it's therefore a good choice as opposed to HTTP-GET for transferring sensitive information between client and server.

Asynchronous Communication

The default method of communicating with a remote server relies on the `Invoke` method of the `SoapHttpClientProtocol`, `HttpPostClientProtocol`, and `HttpGetClientProtocol` classes. When called, this method initiates a data exchange, and does not terminate until the response has been fully received. This is known as **synchronous** communication, meaning the client has to wait for the end of the transfer before it is able to start processing any other tasks.

However, in some cases, it will be appropriate to select **asynchronous** communication, which is achieved with the `BeginInvoke` and `EndInvoke` method calls. Asynchronous communication allows the client to continue processing independently of the call to the Web Service while waiting for responses to SOAP messages to be received from the ASP.NET server. The client handles this communication technique by using the `BeginInvoke` and `EndInvoke` methods from within a proxy class. We'll see how to create this proxy class shortly.

Within this proxy class you will now notice sets of corresponding methods that are named `BeginXXX` and `EndXXX`, where *XXX* is the name of the original method. For example, in the `SimpleCalc` Web Service we have used in the previous two chapters you would have a `BeginAdd` and an `EndAdd` method, which allow the Web Service to be called asynchronously.

When you use the `BeginAdd` method to invoke the Web Service asynchronously you also pass in a delegate or callback object. This object has been created within your client, and, once the Web Service has completed, the proxy class runs your callback object, and you then use the `EndAdd` method to retrieve the values returned from the remote Web Service.

Example: Calling a Web Service Asynchronously

Below is some client code, from `IsbnQueryHttpGet.aspx.cs` in the code download for this chapter, that calls the `GetPrice` web method of our `IsbnQuery` Web Service that we will see later in the chapter using asynchronous calls. This is a **non-callback asynchronous** example; instead it uses a process that waits for the `AsyncResult` object to complete its task:

```
{
    //Create a proxy class object
    IsbnQuery Isbn = new IsbnQuery();
    IAsyncResult asResult;

    // Call the web method BeginGetPrice of IsbnQuery to
    // start Asynchronous communication
    asResult = Isbn.BeginGetPrice(TxtIsbn.Text, null, null);

    //Insert code for extra processing here
    asResult.AsyncWaitHandle.WaitOne();

    // Call the web method EndGetPrice of IsbnQuery
    // to end Asynchronous communication
    LblPrice.Text = "Price is " + Isbn.EndGetPrice(asResult).ToString();
```

The above code, although it's practical and shows how you can go back and test an `AsyncResult` object to see if it has completed processing, is not a true asynchronous event as it does not complete unattended. Therefore we can also use a callback method, which is called once the asynchronous event has completed.

Below is an example of a **callback asynchronous** event:

```
    IsbnQuery AIsbn = new IsbnQuery();
    IAsyncResult asAResult;
    AsyncCallback asACallback;
```

```
public void  RunAsynchronousEvent()
{
  //Create AysncCallback object
  asACallBack = new AsyncCallback(CallB);

  // Call the web method BeginGetPrice of IsbnQuery
  asAResult = AIsbn.BeginGetPrice(TxtIsbn.Text, asACallback, null);
}

public void CallB(IAsyncResult asResult)
{
  // Call the web method EndGetPrice of IsbnQuery to end
  // Asynchronous communication
  LblPrice.Text = "Price is " + AIsbn.EndGetPrice(asResult).ToString();
}
```

As can be seen it only differs from the previous example code by the inclusion of the passing in of an address pointer to a specific method. This method is then called once the asynchronous event has completed its task.

The Client Proxy Class

The .NET SDK comes complete with a command-line utility called WSDL.exe, which can automatically generate a proxy class wrapper for a remote Web Service from the WSDL schema file describing a Web Service. This utility simply reads the WSDL schema and creates a framework class that neatly controls all communication with the remote server and also supplies you with a ready-made interface containing methods that match those described in the WSDL schema document.

The WSDL.exe utility is run from the command line, with a command similar to the following:

```
wsdl /l:cs http://localhost/IsbnQuery/IsbnQuery.asmx?wsdl
```

The first parameter (/l:cs, the default) signifies the language you want to create in; other available options are VB (/l:vb) or JScript (/l:js). The other argument is the full URL location of the WSDL schema you want to create a proxy class for.

> The proxy class you generate using the WSDL.exe command-line utility must be written in the same language as you have created your project with.

You can then access this class's functionality and subsequently call the Web Service by using one of two techniques:

❑ Adding this proxy class directly into your client project as a new class and then instantiating it

❑ Compiling the class within a new client project and adding its reference into your project

One interesting thing about this class is that, by default, it utilizes the `SoapHttpClientProtocol` class to communicate with the remote SOAP server. This means you can now use it as a template to amend certain definitions such as adding headers, or changing the character encoding, all from the client's proxy class.

If you look at a proxy class in more detail, you will see that it inherits the `SoapHttpClientProtocol` class. This inherited class and the other communication classes, `HttpGetClientProtocol` and `HttpPostClientProtocol`, have the same template for the methods that are available in each class. Therefore if you wish your proxy to communicate with the ASP.NET server using HTTP GET instead of SOAP (a reason to do this would be for example to reduce traffic in data-traffic-critical situation), you merely need to change the class declaration to inherit from `HttpGetClientProtocol` instead, then amend the `Invoke` method used within the proxy class to include the destination URL.

Web Service Discovery

Web Service Discovery is the process of locating and interrogating Web Service definitions, which is a preliminary step for accessing a Web Service. It is through this discovery process that Web Service clients learn that a Web Service exists, what its capabilities are, and how to properly interact with it. The term "Web Service Discovery" is often referred to as simply **DISCO**.

The term is not restricted to ASP.NET and the Discovery standard has been publicized on the Internet to allow others to adopt it. There are currently, however, only two industry adoptions of this standard: UDDI and Salcentral. The UDDI (Universal Description, Discovery and Integration) service is the industry-recognized directory service supported by major XML vendors including Microsoft, IBM, and Ariba. The second service, **www.salcentral.com**, is a widely used Web Services search engine that creates DISCO (DISCOvery) files dynamically. As the Web Services industry starts to mature we would expect to see more services appearing.

The DISCO standard is based around a strictly defined, XML-structured file with a `.disco` extension that is available for Web Service clients to read to ascertain what Web Services are available. In the case of ASP.NET this file is created at run time by the `.asmx` file for a specific Web Service project. However, this is not a requirement and in fact you can create your own `.disco` file independently of the `.asmx` file that can be placed on IIS or another Internet server. It is not compulsory to create a discovery file for each Web Service, as you may simply want your Web Service to be for your organization's own internal use. In that particular case you can simply supply the location of the WSDL schema to people in your organization that will use it.

This XML `.disco` file uses its own internal attributes and elements to supply a Web Service client with information as to the location of Web Services that may be available on your server. An example of an XML structured `.disco` file is shown below:

```xml
<?xml version="1.0" encoding="utf-8"?>
<discovery xmlns="http://schemas.xmlsoap.org/disco/">
  <contractRef ref="http://localhost/webservice1/service1.asmx?wsdl"
               docRef="http://localhost/webservice1/service1.asmx"
               xmlns="http://schemas.xmlsoap.org/disco/scl/" />
  <soap address="http://localhost/webservice1/service1.asmx"
        xmlns:q1="http://tempuri.org/" binding="q1:Service1Soap"
        xmlns="http://schemas.xmlsoap.org/disco/soap/" />
</discovery>
```

This simple XML file can be viewed and interrogated to identify the location of the WSDL schema files. These WSDL files describe the methods and arguments that a specific Web Service has available for a remote Web Service client to consume.

There is usually one `.disco` file for every ASP.NET Web Service `.asmx` file. However, `.disco` files can in fact point to other `.disco` files to allow for multiple Web Service promotion. The location of this `.disco` file can be publicly advertised to a dynamic search engine (UDDI), or specialist environment (www.salcentral.com) that can openly use it to advertise the location of your Web Service. It can also be used within the 'Add Web Reference' menu option in Visual Studio .NET to allow others to add your Web Services directly into their project.

Whenever you request a Web Service, ASP.NET dynamically generates a discovery file. The creation of a Web Service does not require the creation of a `.disco` file, so when consuming other organization's Web Services that have not been written in ASP.NET, it will most likely not be available. This does not mean that the creation of `.disco` files is peculiar to ASP.NET. It does, however, mean that ASP.NET is currently the only large-scale product that supports `.disco` files.

Displaying a Disco File

The discovery of Web Services is accomplished by making available to interested parties an XML file that adheres to the DISCO standard (more about the details of this standard later). To display the `.disco` file for your ASP.NET Web Service you simply need to append the string `?disco` to the end of the URL of your Web Service in the address line of your browser.

The `.disco` file does not need to reside on the server where the Web Service is located; you can in fact create your own `.disco` file and place it on any Internet server. ASP.NET however generates the `.disco` file dynamically when you run the `.asmx` file, therefore by default it is always situated in the same location as the `.asmx` file.

Customization of the ASP.NET Server

In ASP.NET, you can fine-tune or generally customize the format of SOAP messages using an attribute-based mechanism that is built into .NET. It provides sophisticated techniques allowing you to control SOAP constructs at a low level of detail, enabling the implementation of advanced features such as specialist encoding, transaction processing, compression, and more.

The `System.Web.Services.Protocols` namespace contains a number of classes for altering the defaults set by the WSDL schema for a Web Service by providing values to override specific attributes from the WSDL file on the server. These attributes can either be assigned directly to the definition of the Web Service at design time or in the proxy class at the client in the same manner.

An example of method customization on an ASP.NET server is shown below:

```
[SoapDocumentMethodAttribute(RequestNamespace="http://www.wrox.com",
    ResponseNamespace="http://www.wrox.com")] public string HelloWorld()
```

The above example would be used within the `.asmx` Web Service file, prefixing whichever Web Service method you wished to customize. The example used actually changes the `Request` namespace and `Response` namespace within the SOAP message. This recommended alteration is required to change the default temporary name space from `http://tempuri.org/` to a recognizable namespace that uniquely identifies your Web Service.

You would want to change the namespace to make sure that when a SOAP request (or multiple SOAP requests) arrive from a client you can match up each specific SOAP request with a specific Web Service method.

When attribute customization is performed on the ASP.NET server, the alterations actually change the WSDL definition file created during the Web Service build process. This alteration can then be read and acted upon by any SOAP-compliant client. Not all attribute customizations are fed into the WSDL schema, however; for example headers.

The classes from the `System.Web.Services` namespace that can perform this attribute customization at Web Service method level are:

- ❑ `SoapDocumentMethodAttribute`
- ❑ `SoapRpcMethodAttribute`
- ❑ `HttpMethodAttribute`
- ❑ `SoapHeaderAttribute`
- ❑ `WebServiceBindingAttribute`

In addition, you can similarly fine-tune the WSDL schema at class level by means of the following:

- ❑ `SoapRpcServiceAttribute`
- ❑ `SoapDocumentServiceAttribute`

An example of class customization for an ASP.NET server is shown below:

```
<[SoapDocumentServiceAttribute(Use = SoapBindingUse.Literal)]
    public class SoapDocumentServiceSample
```

The above example changes the encoding style for a class. The encoding style defines how to describe data types within an XML document.

Customization of the ASP.NET Client

By generating a proxy class using the `WSDL.exe` utility provided with the .NET SDK, you are able to customize each method contained within the proxy class to introduce alternative features. This allows you to perform advanced client tasks such as data compression, transaction processing, and so on.

Below are the customization classes applicable to proxy classes at Web Service method level:

- ❑ SoapRpcMethodAttribute
- ❑ SoapDocumentMethodAttribute
- ❑ HttpMethodAttribute
- ❑ SoapHeaderAttribute
- ❑ WebServiceBindingAttribute (System.Web.Services namespace)

Each of the above classes can be used to customize a proxy class. An example of proxy Web Service customization would be:

```
public UserName [System.Web.Services.Protocols.HttpMethodAttribute(
  GetType(System.Web.Services.Protocols.XmlReturnReader),
  GetType(System.Web.Services.Protocols.HtmlFormParameterWriter))]
  GetUserName()
{
  return (UserName) this.Invoke("GetUserName", this.Url + "/GetUserName",
  new object[0])
}
```

The above customization defines the return message type (XmlReturnReader) and transport technique (HtmlFormParameterWriter) for transferring messages. For example, using the term XmlReturnReader sets the method to expect an XML formatted message in response to the Invoke command, and the term HtmlFormParameterWriter identifies that the Invoke command will use the HTTP-POST protocol to send the request to the server. We can further alter this attribute by invoking the server Web Service using HTTP GET. To do this we simply change the above parameter to UrlParameterWriter.

As well as customizing a method within a proxy class you can use the following attribute classes to customize all Web Services within the current proxy. Therefore, unless these values are overridden by another assignment to each specific Web Service, every Web Service adopts the attributes of the class.

The following can perform customization for proxy classes at class level:

- ❑ SoapRpcServiceAttribute
- ❑ SoapDocumentServiceAttribute

In most circumstances though, Web Service method and class customization within a client proxy class should not be necessary, and in any case it is preferable to do this by modifying the Web Service definition on the server. However in certain circumstances, such as creating headers for transaction control (as headers are not defined within the WSDL specification and so do not filter up to the client), it is preferable to create a client proxy class and use attribute classes to add header information. Adding header information to a SOAP request and SOAP response is covered later within this chapter.

SoapMessageStage Process Trapping

When the ASP.NET client and ASP.NET server create and send SOAP messages, they both go through a series of common stages/events that can be captured by creating a specific framework of methods. This framework traps each stage of the lifecycle of the SOAP message transfer and allows you to programmatically react and perform specialist and advanced features, including, but not limited to:

❑ Logging the SOAP request or SOAP response. By trapping the transfer of a SOAP message after it has been created and before it has been transferred to either the client or the server, you can simply read it and store the message in a database. That way you can store the exact SOAP message you send or receive for your own organization's analysis or security purposes.

❑ Adding authority information to a header for security checking.

❑ Adding encryption to your SOAP message. This allows you to trap the message and perform encryption on the entire SOAP request or SOAP response, to make sure that the SOAP message remains unreadable during transfer.

❑ Adding compression to your SOAP message. One concern about SOAP messages is the amount of text that needs to be transferred. This allows you to compress your SOAP message before it is sent to the Client or Server.

During this event trapping you are supplied with the `SoapClientMessage` or `SoapServerMessage` object that allows you to query or amend the current SOAP message.

Example: Trapping Events

By default event trapping is turned off, and to turn it on, you need to ensure the appropriate code is inserted into either your Web Service file, or your client proxy class. The example below shows the template for introducing trappable events within a `HelloWorld` function on an ASP.NET server. You can find this code in `Service1.asmx` in the **HelloWorld** project in the code download:

```
using System;
using System.Collections;
using System.ComponentModel;
using System.Data;
using System.Diagnostics;
using System.Web;
using System.Web.Services;
using System.Reflection;
using System.Web.Services.Protocols;
using System.IO;

namespace HelloWorld
{
    /// <summary>
    /// Summary description for Service1.
    /// </summary>
    public class Service1 : System.Web.Services.WebService
    {
        public Service1()
        {
            //CODEGEN: This call is required by the ASP.NET Web Services Designer
            InitializeComponent();
```

```csharp
      }

    // WEB SERVICE EXAMPLE
    // The HelloWorld() example service returns the string Hello World
    // To build, uncomment the following lines then save and
    // build the project
    // To test this web service, press F5

    [WebMethod]
    public string HelloWorld()
    {
      return "Hello World";
    }
}

// This class is a required class for the trace extension to work
// it defines the binding between the actual class that reacts to the
// events and the HelloWorld Web Service
[AttributeUsage(AttributeTargets.Method)]
public class TraceExtensionAttribute : SoapExtensionAttribute
{
  private int m_Priority;

  public override Type ExtensionType
  {
    get
    {

      // The following line binds your named class
      // to the trace extension event
      return typeof(TraceExtension1);
    }
  }

  public override int Priority
  {
    get
    {
      return m_Priority;
    }
    set
    {
      m_Priority = value;
    }
  }
}

// The following class allows you to develop a method to handle
// the events being raised from the trace extension
public class TraceExtension1 :
                          System.Web.Services.Protocols.SoapExtension
{
  string sLogFile;
```

713

```csharp
public override object GetInitializer(LogicalMethodInfo MethodInfo,
                                      SoapExtensionAttribute attribute)
{
    // Place any initialization data that can
    // be cached ready for initialization
}

public override object GetInitializer(Type type)
{

}

public override void Initialize(object initializer)
{
    // Initialize any local variables
    sLogFile = @"c:\wroxlog.txt";
}

public override void ProcessMessage(SoapMessage message)
{
    StreamWriter swLog;
    swLog = new StreamWriter(sLogFile, true);
    switch(message.Stage)
    {
        case SoapMessageStage.BeforeSerialize:
            swLog.WriteLine(DateTime.Now + "-BeforeSerialize stage");
            break;
        case SoapMessageStage.AfterSerialize:
            swLog.WriteLine(DateTime.Now + "-AfterSerialize stage");
            break;
        case SoapMessageStage.BeforeDeserialize:
            swLog.WriteLine(DateTime.Now + "-BeforeDeserialize stage");
            break;
        case SoapMessageStage.AfterDeserialize:
            swLog.WriteLine(DateTime.Now + "-AfterDeserialize stage");
            break;
        default:
            swLog.WriteLine(DateTime.Now + "-Invalid stage");
            break;
    }
    swLog.Close();
}
}
}
```

The above example is created within the Web Service file and shows how you can trap events in the stages of a SOAP message. It writes a single line of code to a log file so that you can see the order in which events are performed. Note, if you intend to use the above example code make sure that the log file does not overwrite an existing file on your C: drive.

This example code is a template for handling trace extension events and is used as the container for your code to allow you to interrogate or manipulate a SOAP message at predetermined stages of its creation. As you can see, the single parameter that is passed in is of the type SoapMessage within the ProcessMessage subroutine. This method in fact receives either a SoapServerMessage or a SoapClientMessage depending on whether you have placed your code on the server or on the client.

> For trace extension event trapping to work on the client you must first create a proxy class for a specific WSDL Web Service schema using the `WSDL.exe` command-line utility.

System.Web.Services.Protocols Namespace

The `System.Web.Services.Protocols` namespace covers all the classes that define the data transmission protocol between ASP.NET Web Services and Web Service clients. The following table gives you a brief overview of these classes. All classes that are highlighted in this table are also discussed in detail following this table in alphabetical order.

Class	Description
HttpGetClientProtocol	This defines the mechanisms for requests to the server using HTTP GET. It acts as a base class for client proxies that consume the Web Service using the HTTP-GET protocol.
HttpMethodAttribute	This class defines the method for serializing and de-serializing SOAP messages for the client and/or the ASP.NET server.
HttpPostClientProtocol	This class is used to define the mechanisms for sending SOAP requests to the server using HTTP POST. It acts as a base class for client proxies that consume the Web Service using the HTTP-POST protocol.
HttpSimpleClientProtocol	The `HttpSimpleClientProtocol` class acts as an abstract base class for other classes within the `System.Web.Services.Protocols` namespace that communicate with the Web Service using HTTP-GET or HTTP-POST protocols.
HttpWebClientProtocol	The `HttpWebClientProtocol` class acts as an abstract base class for other classes within the `System.Web.Services.Protocols` namespace that communicate with Web Services using any form of HTTP protocol.
LogicalMethodInfo	This class exposes information about a Web Service using attributes and other metadata. This information is then interrogated by the SOAP extensions to find the behavior of a Web Service. This is a sealed class and therefore cannot be inherited from.
MatchAttribute	This class is mostly used with Web Services that do HTML parsing to generate information. This class stores the attributes or properties of a match during the text pattern matching operation commonly performed during HTML parsing. This is a sealed class and cannot be inherited from.

Table continued on following page

Class	Description
SoapClientMessage	The SoapClientMessage class contains the SOAP Request and may be interrogated either by the client application or by the Web Service on the server. You can interrogate this class during the SoapMessageStage event.
SoapDocumentMethodAttribute	This class alters the structure of the generated WSDL schema created during the build process for an ASP.NET Web Service project. It consequently affects the SOAP message structure and format used, as this structure adheres to the rules set out by the WSDL schema.
SoapDocumentServiceAttribute	This class is used to customize SOAP Requests or SOAP Responses for a particular Web Service. Any changes made using this class will be reflected in the WSDL schema definition file produced by **WSDL.exe**. Unlike the **SoapDocumentMethodAttribute** class, these values are set at service level using a service-level attribute. This class cannot be used at method level.
SoapException	When an error occurs during the execution of a Web Service over SOAP, the SoapException class can provide the associated error information. This class is populated by the server when returning a SOAP Fault.
SoapExtension	SOAP extensions give you the ability to utilize facilities of the basic ASP.NET framework by providing a means of accessing the underlying engine that processes events, allowing you to modify or inspect a SOAP message at a particular stage in its processing.
SoapExtensionAttribute	This class lets you assign a **SoapExtensionAttribute** to a specific Web Service. This enables the **SoapMessageStage** events to work.
SoapHeader	The **SoapHeader** class allows you to pass extra information to the Web Service not directly related to the SOAP message parameters. This allows for performing specialist tasks such as user authorization, or defining particular transaction requirements.
SoapHeaderAttribute	This class can customize a client proxy class or a Web Service method by creating SOAP headers that can be transferred as part of the SOAP request or SOAP response. This class cannot be inherited.
SoapHeaderCollection	This class is a Collection class for instances of the SoapHeader class.
SoapHeaderException	This class is used for exceptions thrown when a Web Service method is called over SOAP, and an error occurs during the processing of the SOAP header.

Class	Description
SoapHttpClientProtocol	This class defines the means for sending SOAP requests to the server using the SOAP communication technique. It sits at the bottom of a hierarchy of inherited classes, each of which is responsible for a specific process within the transport mechanism.
SoapMessage	SoapMessage is as an abstract base class for a number of other classes within the System.Web.Services.Protocols namespace, and may not be instantiated directly. It represents the contents of a SOAP message at a particular stage in its processing.
SoapRpcMethodAttribute	This class allows you to alter the style in which a SOAP Request or Response encodes and formats parameters. This class defines the requirement to use RPC methods to encode a message. RPC style refers to encoding the Web Service method according to the SOAP specification for using SOAP for RPC, otherwise known as Section 7 of the SOAP specification.
SoapRpcServiceAttribute	This class allows you to set the encoding method to RPC for all Web Service methods within a specific class.
SoapServerMessage	This class is used during a SoapMessageStage event to interrogate the Web Service call during each of its processing stages.
SoapUnknownHeader	This class allows you to interrogate headers that were transferred as part of the SOAP message, but whose structure was not known by the client or Web Service.
WebClientAsyncResult	This allows Web services proxies to implement asynchronous processing. When you initiate an asynchronous operation using Begin*XXX* method (where *XXX* is the name of your method), a WebClientAsyncResult object is returned. This objects needs to be passed to a corresponding End*XXX* method to end the asynchronous processing.
WebClientProtocol	The WebClientProtocol class acts as an abstract base class for other classes within the System.Web.Services.Protocols namespace that communicate with Web Services using any supported protocol.

HttpGetClientProtocol Class

This class defines the mechanisms for calling Web Services using the HTTP-GET protocol. An HTTP-GET communication allows the transfer of name-value pairs as arguments within the Internet URL and simulates a typical GET-HTTP page request.

This class can customize a Web Service method by using attributes assigned to either the Web Service method or to a client proxy class. The client proxy class should inherit from `HttpGetClientProtocol` in order to call the web method in the Web Service using the HTTP-GET protocol. The `WSDL.exe` tool of the .NET Framework can help in the automatic creation of such a client proxy class by passing the WSDL reference of the Web Service and setting the protocol switch to the desired protocol. Below is a sample command which would create such a proxy:

```
wsdl /protocol:HttpGet /l:cs ⌐
http://localhost/systemWebServicesProtocols/IsbnQuery/IsbnQuery.asmx?wsdl
```

You can see such a proxy in action in the IsbnQueryHttpGet project in the code download.

HttpGetClientProtocol Class Public Methods

- ❑ **Abort**
- ❑ **CreateObjRef**
- ❑ **Dispose**
- ❑ `Equals` – inherited from `System.Object`, see Introduction for details
- ❑ `GetHashCode` – inherited from `System.Object`, see Introduction for details
- ❑ **GetLifeTimeService**
- ❑ `GetType` – inherited from `System.Object`, see Introduction for details
- ❑ **InitializeLifeTimeService**
- ❑ `ToString` – inherited from `System.Object`, see Introduction for details

Abort

The `Abort` method stops any currently executing synchronous request from the client. This method is helpful when you start a long-running web method synchronously on the server, such as creating a report for annual sales analysis. If it seems to be taking too long, since the call may block the thread, you can stop it from running by executing this `Abort` command with a separate thread, for example, by attaching the abort to a button on your client form and calling the `Abort` method as a click event of the button. A `WebException` is thrown when an `Abort` method is called and its `Status` property will have the value `WebExceptionStatus.RequestCancelled`. It is inherited from the `System.Web.Services.Protocols.WebClientProtocol` class.

```
public virtual void Abort();
```

CreateObjRef

This method is used to create an object that contains information on how to generate a proxy. This proxy will be used for communicating with remote objects. The parameter passed to this method is the `Type` that the return object would refer to. The method throws a `RemotingException` if the object created is not valid for remote communication. It is inherited from `System.MarshalByRefObject`.

```
public virtual ObjRef CreateObjRef(Type);
```

Dispose

The `Dispose` method flags up the resources that are to be liberated by the non-deterministic garbage collection system. It is inherited from the `System.ComponentModel.Component class`.

```
public void Dispose();
```

GetLifeTimeService

This method gets the lifetime service object of the current instance as an `ILease` object. This object is used to control the lifetime of a remote object. In the case of high-traffic web site, the automatic garbage collection won't scale well. You can instead use the `LifeTimeServices` object to specify the lease time for your remote object. The remote object will be removed when the lease expires; this way you can have fine control over your remote object's lifetime. This method is inherited from the `System.MarshalByRefObject` class.

```
public object GetLifeTimeService();
```

InitializeLifeTimeService

This method gets the lifetime service object of the current instance as an object of `ILease` type. If no object already exists for this instance then it will return a new instance of `ILease` type that is initialized with the value of the `LifeTimeServices.LeaseManagerPollTime` property. This object is used to control the lifetime of a remote object. In the case of a high-traffic web site, the automatic garbage collection won't scale well. You can instead use this `LifeTimeServices` object to specify the lease time for your remote object. The remote object will be removed when the lease expires, this way you can have fine control over your remote object's lifetime. The default value of the `LifeTimeServices.LeaseManagerPollTime` property is 10 seconds, which means that leases are inspected and cleaned every 10 seconds. This method is inherited from the `System.MarshalByRefObject` class.

```
public virtual object InitializeLifeTimeService();
```

HttpGetClientProtocol Class Protected Methods

❑ `BeginInvoke`

❑ `Dispose`

❑ `EndInvoke`

❑ `Finalize` – inherited from `System.Object`, see Introduction for details

❑ `GetService`

❑ `GetWebRequest`

❑ `GetWebResponse`

❑ `Invoke`

❑ `MemberWiseClone` – inherited from `System.Object`, see Introduction for details

BeginInvoke

The `BeginInvoke` method starts an asynchronous communication link to a remote Web Service.

```
protected IAsyncResult BeginInvoke(methodName, requestUrl,
                                   parameters, callback, asyncState);
```

The `methodName` parameter specifies a `String` object referring to the web method name expected to run asynchronously. The `requestUrl` parameter, a `String`, specifies the Internet location of the destination Web Service listener. The `parameters` parameter specifies an array of `Objects` containing the parameters to be passed to the web method. The order of values in the array must correspond exactly to the order of the parameters that the web method is expecting. The `callback` parameter specifies an `Object` containing the method/delegate to call on the client once the event for completion of the asynchronous message is performed. If `callback` is nothing then no process is called on completion of the Web Service. The `asyncState` parameter specifies a parameter type container object for holding useful information about the client responsible for using this asynchronous request.

An `AsyncResult` object is returned that can be used within your code while the asynchronous communication continues. This object can be used to retain any state values you wish to retrieve at the end of the asynchronous communication process. Once the Web Service completes its processing the `AsyncResult` object is passed back into the `EndInvoke` method to obtain the return values. Typically, you would not call the `BeginInvoke` method directly, unless you were building your own proxy class for a Web Service. The method throws an `Exception` if the request reached the server machine, but failed to process successfully.

The following code shows the call to `BeginInvoke` that is located in the `BeginGetPrice` method in the class proxy from the IsbnQueryHttpGet example project in the code download:

```
return this.BeginInvoke("GetPrice", (this.Url + "/GetPrice"), new object[] {
                        Isbn}, callback, asyncState);
```

Dispose

This `Dispose` method flags all unmanaged resources used as being ready for cleanup by the garbage collector. It also releases managed resources based on the `Boolean` value passed as the parameter. It is inherited from the `System.ComponentModel.Component class`.

```
protected virtual void Dispose(bool);
```

Passing in the parameter `true` indicates that the managed resources should also be released and `false` if they should not. This method is called by the `Finalize` method, with `false` as the parameter value. The public `Dispose` method discussed above also calls this method with the parameter value set to `true`.

EndInvoke

This method is called to complete the asynchronous invocation of a Web Service method. This method will be called on completion of the Web Service call to the server by the method identified as the callback delegate in the `BeginInvoke` method or simply from the client code.

```
protected object EndInvoke(asyncResult);
```

The parameter `asyncResult` specifies the `AsyncResult` object instantiated by the `BeginInvoke` method that initiated this Web Service request. An `ArgumentException` is thrown when the `AsyncResult` parameter does not match the one created by `BeginInvoke`.

An array of objects is returned that matches the return values produced by the Web Service in question. It also includes any "by reference" or "out" arguments. This is functionally similar to returning multiple return values from the same method.

The following code shows the call to `EndInvoke` method that is located in the `EndGetPrice` method in the class proxy from the IsbnQueryHttpGet example project in the code download:

```
return ((System.Double)(this.EndInvoke(asyncResult)));
```

GetService

The `GetService` method returns an object that represents a service provided by the `Component`. It returns `null` if the object does not provide the specified service. It is inherited from `System.ComponentModel.Component` class.

```
protected virtual object GetService(service);
```

GetWebRequest

The method returns a `WebRequest` instance for the specified URI. This method overrides the default `WebRequest` specified by `System.Web.Services.Protocols.HttpWebClientProtocol`. The new instance of the `WebRequest` class can then be used to further customize by adding additional values as a custom header to the `Request` object.

```
protected override WebRequest GetWebRequest(uri);
```

The parameter `uri` specifies a valid and existing URI for which to create a `WebRequest` object. If the `uri` parameter passed is `null` then an `InvalidOperationException` occurs. This method returns a `System.Net.WebRequest` object.

GetWebResponse

This method is inherited from the `System.Web.Services.Protocols.HttpWebClientProtocol` class and is overridden here. This method returns a `System.Net.WebResponse` object for a `System.Net.WebRequest` object passed to it as its parameter.

This method has two overloads basically to get `WebResponse` objects both for synchronous and asynchronous web method calls. Let's see them one by one:

The following method is only valid for **synchronous** communication:

```
protected override WebResponse GetWebResponse(request);
```

The parameter `request` refers to the `WebRequest` object associated with this connection to the server. The `WebResponse` object returned can be interrogated to determine the values returned by the server. You can use instances of this class to perform customization such as adding headers.

The following method is only valid for **asynchronous** communication.

```
protected override WebResponse GetWebResponse(request, result);
```

The parameter `request` refers to the `WebRequest` object associated with this connection to the server. The parameter `result` specifies the `AsyncResult` object that was instantiated by the `BeginInvoke` method. Again, a `WebResponse` object is returned, which can be interrogated to find out the return values for the Web Service call.

Invoke

This method initiates synchronous communication with a web method. You should use it instead of its asynchronous counterparts `BeginInvoke` and `EndInvoke` if you want to use synchronous communication, meaning that the client must wait for a response before continuing.

```
protected object Invoke(methodName, requestUrl, parameters);
```

The parameter `methodName` specifies a `String` containing the name of the method you are attempting to run synchronously on the Web Service. The `requestUrl` parameter, a `String`, specifies the Internet location of the destination Web Service listener. The parameter `parameters` specifies an array of `Objects` containing the parameters to pass to the web method. The order of values in the array must correspond to the exact order of the parameters expected by the Web Service. An `Exception` occurs if the request reached the server machine, but was not processed successfully.

An array of `Objects` containing the return values and the "by reference" or "out" parameters from the web method is returned.

The following code shows the call to the `Invoke` method that is located in the `GetPrice` method in the class proxy in the IsbnQueryHttpGet example project in the code download:

```
return ((System.Double)(this.Invoke("GetPrice", (this.Url + "/GetPrice"),
                                    new object[] {Isbn})));
```

HttpGetClientProtocol Class Public Properties

- ❑ **AllowAutoRedirect**
- ❑ **ClientCertificates**
- ❑ **ConnectionGroupName**
- ❑ **Container**
- ❑ **CookieContainer**
- ❑ **Credentials**
- ❑ **PreAuthenticate**
- ❑ **Proxy**

722

- ❑ **RequestEncoding**
- ❑ **Site**
- ❑ **Timeout**
- ❑ **Url**
- ❑ **UserAgent**

AllowAutoRedirect

This property helps you in either allowing or preventing automatic redirection of the client proxy to the server redirects by setting it to `true` or `false` respectively. This property is inherited from `System.Web.Services.Protocols.HttpWebClientProtocol` and returns or assigns a `Boolean` object.

For security reasons, when the client proxy needs to send sensitive data like the authentication information or financial information, then this property can be set to `false`, which will not allow the server to redirect the client. If a redirection is attempted when this property is set to `false`, a `WebException` is thrown. The `Response` object will contain `StatusCode` and `Headers` properties which will show the location where redirection was attempted and the HTTP status code of redirection (301, 302, or 307).

```
public bool AllowAutoRedirect {get; set;}
```

ClientCertificates

Certificates are digital documents that allocate unique public keys to identify an individual or other entity. They allow verification by ensuring that a public key does in fact belong to a given individual.

This property returns the collection of valid certificates for the current communication session by returning an `X509CertificateCollection` object. This property allows you to add client certificates to this collection object, which can be used to verify the identity of the client. These client certificates can be then used by the Web Service to authenticate the client proxy. It is inherited from `System.Web.Services.Protocols.HttpWebClientProtocol`.

```
public X509CertificateCollection ClientCertificate {get;}
```

ConnectionGroupName

This property enables you to associate a request with a specific and unique group name within your application session. This can be useful when your application makes requests to a server regarding different users, such as a web site that retrieves customer information from a database server.

Under normal circumstances, when a connection is opened to a .NET server, the connection pooling mechanism built into .NET kicks in. This is designed to save network latency by reusing already established connections rather than creating new ones. Problems can occur, however, if the connection requires a secure connection, and a user-specific authentication occurred between the client and the server. This creates a gray area when you then try to reuse a pooled secure connection for a non-secure user. By using `ConnectionGroupName` when establishing the connection, you create a new connection that is unique to that user, and will not be pooled for reuse by any other user.

Note that each connection group creates an additional connection with the associated server. This may not be the same server for all connection groups. If many connection groups are used then this may result in exceeding the `ServicePoint.ConnectionLimit` (that specifies the maximum allowed) for that server.

This property is inherited from the `System.Web.Services.Protocols.WebClientProtocol` class.

```
public string ConnectionGroupName {get; set;}
```

Container

This property returns the `IContainer` object encapsulated in the component. This property returns `null` if the component is not encapsulated in the `Component`. It is inherited from the `System.ComponentModel.Component` class.

```
public IContainer Container {get;}
```

CookieContainer

The client proxy uses this property to get or set the cookies collection associated with the request. Cookies in Web Services can be used in a similar fashion to how cookies are used within web sites: to allow for the automatic retrieval of relevant data that can be stored on the client computer instead of the server. Note that this method of storing stateful data relies on many things, such as the client having cookies turned on, the client being able to understand cookies (non-cookie systems include most PDAs and WAP devices). It also invokes an additional round trip to retrieve cookie information that may significantly lengthen the time required to run that Web Service.

If a Web Service supports session state, then a cookie is sent to the client in the response header to identify the session of the Web Service client. This property is inherited from the `System.Web.Services.Protocols.HttpWebClientProtocol` class.

```
public CookieContainer Container {get; set;}
```

Credentials

This property contains authentication information to identify the client for a request. When using the `Credentials` property, a Web Service client must instantiate the `NetworkCredential` class, and then set the client credentials according to the authentication mechanism employed. This information will then be used to authenticate your connection to an ASP.NET server or any server supporting basic, digest, NTLM, or Kerberos authentication mechanisms.

Credential authentication is possibly the most important authentication technique available. It allows us to use the existing methods of username and password authority, which have over past years been tried and tested. Though some are not encrypted, such as basic authentication, with the addition of SSL connections this becomes a significant security boost for transferring messages between client and server.

This property is inherited from the `System.Web.Services.Protocols.WebClientProtocol` class.

```
public ICredentials Credentials {get; set;}
```

PreAuthenticate

When using the `Credentials` property and connecting to the ASP.NET server, the default behavior, this property being `false`, is to send authentication information to the server only if that server has previously returned a 401 HTTP access denied error to the client after the first request. This happens when anonymous access to the Web Service is not allowed and the server requires authentication information. However, by setting the `PreAuthenticate` property to `true`, you can send authentication information in a `WWW-authenticate` HTTP header with the request. This will save any latency arising from the additional roundtrip caused from the server having to request authentication information additionally. It is inherited from the `System.Web.Services.Protocols.WebClientProtocol` class.

```
public bool PreAuthenticate {get; set;}
```

Proxy

If your local network setup requires that you process requests through a firewall, then you need to use this property to configure firewall authentication information. This can be used to bypass the default proxy settings for your machine.

This property allows you to assign and interrogate the proxy settings. It contains information like URL, port, username, password, and so on, necessary to connect to the proxy server. To pass in authentication information you must create credentials and assign them to the proxy class, before assigning the proxy class to your instantiated class. It returns a `WebProxy` class object implementing the `IWebProxy` interface. It is inherited from the `System.Web.Services.Protocols.HttpWebClientProtocol` class.

```
public IWebProxy Proxy {get; set;}
```

Example: Calling Web Services Through a Firewall

This property can be used within the Web Service's proxy class. Below we have some example code that shows how the proxy class can be altered to allow proxy connections:

```
public double GetPrice(string Isbn As String)
    [System.Xml.Serialization.XmlRootAttribute("double",
    [Namespace]="http://localhost/IsbnQuery/", IsNullable=false)]
{
  //Create a proxy object with your details
  WebProxy proxyObject = new WebProxy("yourproxyservername", 80);

  //Assign the object to the proxy property
  this.Proxy = proxyObject;
  return ((System.Double)(this.Invoke("GetPrice",
                    (this.Url + "/GetPrice"), new object[] {Isbn})));
}
```

As well as using it from within the proxy class you can also use it within the client code, for example:

```
private void BtnProxy_Click(object sender,
                            System.EventArgs e)
{

  IsbnQuery Isbn = new IsbnQuery();

  //Create a proxy object with your details
  WebProxy proxyObject = new WebProxy("yourproxyservername", 80);

  //Assign the object to the proxy property
  Isbn.Proxy=proxyObject;

  LblPrice.Text = Isbn.GetPrice(TxtIsbn.Text);
}
```

RequestEncoding

This property allows you to get and set the character encoding method to be used for serializing request messages. The default value is the default encoding value of the transport protocol. You must use and populate the `Encoding` class appropriately, and pass it into this property. The response returned by the ASP.NET server will then reflect the encoding method given by `RequestEncoding`. It is inherited from the `System.Web.Services.Protocols.WebClientProtocol` class.

Valid encoding types are:

- ❑ ASCIIEncoding
- ❑ UnicodeEncoding
- ❑ UTF7Encoding
- ❑ UTF8Encoding

```
public Encoding RequestEncoding {get; set;}
```

Site

This property returns the site of the component (implementer of the `ISite` interface) indicating that a component is to be added to the container. It is inherited from the `System.ComponentModel.Component` class. This property returns `null` if the component has not been added to the container, or is being removed from the container, or is not associated with `ISite`.

```
public virtual ISite Site {get; set;}
```

Timeout

This property denotes the time period in milliseconds that the Web Service client proxy waits for a synchronous web request to complete before the request is timed out or aborted. The default period is 100,000 milliseconds or one minute and 40 seconds. Setting it to –1 sets this property to `Timeout.Infinity`, which means that the request doesn't time out at all, waiting indefinitely at the client proxy side. It is inherited from the `System.Web.Services.Protocols.WebClientProtocol` class.

```
public int TimeOut {get; set;}
```

Url

This contains the base or listener URL of the Web Service the client is requesting. You can use this property to specify an alternative Web Service listener, for example to redirect the request to an alternative mirrored server in the event of failure on the main server. It is inherited from `System.Web.Services.Protocols.WebClientProtocol`.

```
public string Url {get; set;}
```

This property includes a definitive URL address location, as well as a port number when relevant.

UserAgent

This property is used to return or assign the value of the user agent header sent with each request to the server. The user agent is a value in the `HTTP` header that identifies the client. By default, this is `MS Web Services Client Protocol x.x.xxxx.x`, where `x.x.xxxx.x` is the version of the Common Language Runtime. You can change it to uniquely identify your client either by type or even by location, for example `"dotNET client in New York"`. It is inherited from the `System.Web.Services.Protocols.HttpWebClientProtocol` class.

```
public string UserAgent {get; set;}
```

HttpGetClientProtocol Class Protected Properties

- ❑ **DesignMode**
- ❑ **Events**

DesignMode

This property indicates whether the container is in design mode. It is inherited from the `System.ComponentModel.Component` class.

```
protected bool DesignMode {get;}
```

Events

This property returns an `EventHandlerList` object representing all the event handlers attached to this component. If there are any event handlers associated with the component, they will be accessible through the `EventHandlerList` object. You can call various methods of the `EventHandlerList` object on the return value. It is inherited from the `System.ComponentModel.Component` class.

```
protected EventHandlerList Events {get;}
```

HttpGetClientProtocol Class Public Events

❑ **Disposed**

Disposed

The `Disposed` event can be used to add an event handler. This event handler is invoked whenever the `Disposed` event on the proxy occurs. It is inherited from the `System.ComponentModel.Component` class.

```
public event EventHandler Disposed;
```

HttpMethodAttribute Class

This class allows you to customize, by defining the Web Service method, a Web Service client that receives and sends HTTP-GET or HTTP-POST requests. This class defines the way in which the parameters are serialized and then passed to the Web Service methods and how the response is de-serialized when it is returned from the Web Service.

Serialization refers to the process of converting the current state of an object to a stream that can be processed or stored independently of the original object as a string variable. Once this object needs to be restored, the stream can be de-serialized to re-create the original state of the object.

Serialization and de-serialization are performed by different classes, and can be in various formats, such as a single text line, an XML string, or comma separated values. In the context of the `System.Web.Services.Protocols` namespace, the `HttpMethodAttribute` class handles serialization to and de-serialization from an XML string to be sent within an HTTP message. Even though the serialization method can be changed, it is worth remembering that in practice, because HTTP messages and ASP.NET only understand certain `ParameterFormat` and `ReturnFormatter` values, you are constrained by these requirements for HTTP Requests and Responses.

HttpMethodAttribute Class Public Methods

❑ `Equals` – inherited from `System.Object`, see Introduction for details

❑ **GetHashCode**

❑ `GetType` – inherited from `System.Object`, see Introduction for details

❑ **IsDefaultAttribute**

❑ **Match**

❑ `ToString` – inherited from `System.Object`, see Introduction for details

GetHashCode

The `GetHashCode` method returns the hash code for the current instance of the object. It is inherited from `System.Attribute`.

```
public override int GetHashCode();
```

IsDefaultAttribute

The `IsDefaultAttribute` method if overridden is used to indicate whether the values of the current instance are equal to the values of the default instance of the object. It is inherited from `System.Attribute` and is not overridden in this class. As it is not overridden here, it always returns `false` irrespective of whether the current object holds default values or not.

```
public virtual bool IsDefaultAttribute();
```

Match

The `Match` method if overridden is used to compare the current instance with another object. It is inherited from `System.Attribute` and is not overridden in this class. As it is not overridden here, it returns the same value as the `Equals` method would return.

```
public virtual bool Match(object obj);
```

HttpMethodAttribute Class Protected Methods

- ❑ `Finalize` – inherited from `System.Object`, see Introduction for details
- ❑ `MemberwiseClone` – inherited from `System.Object`, see Introduction for details

HttpMethodAttribute Class Public Properties

- ❑ **ParameterFormatter**
- ❑ **ReturnFormatter**
- ❑ `TypeId` – inherited from `System.Attribute`, not implemented in this class

ParameterFormatter

`ParameterFormatter` is used for serializing the parameters sent from ASP.NET client to a Web Service. If a client invokes a Web Service using HTTP GET or HTTP POST, then this property must be set to `XmlReturnReader`.

```
public Type ParameterFormatter {get; set;}
```

ReturnFormatter

This property is used for deserializing the XML response received from a Web Service method. When a proxy client invokes a Web Service method using HTTP GET, this property must be set to `UrlParameterWriter`. When a proxy client invokes a Web Service method using HTTP POST this property must be set to `HtmlFormParameterWriter` (the default).

This value is set by default within the proxy client but can be changed to alter the characteristics of the web request. In the below example usage, setting the value to `UrlParameter` means that the message will be sent as part of a URL address line. Setting the value to `HtmlFormParameterWriter` means the message will be sent in the main body of the HTML request using a form post.

```
public Type ReturnFormatter {get; set;}
```

The following example shows how you set both the `ParameterFormatter` and the `ReturnFormatter` within a proxy client class using the `HttpMethodAttribute`:

```
[System.Diagnostics.DebuggerStepThroughAttribute(),
    System.Web.Services.Protocols.HttpMethodAttribute
    GetType(System.Web.Services.Protocols.XmlReturnReader),
    GetType(System.Web.Services.Protocols.UrlParameterWriter))]
public double GetPrice(string Isbn)
    [System.Xml.Serialization.XmlRootAttribute("double",
    [Namespace]="http://localhost/IsbnQuery/", IsNullable=false)]
{
  return ((System.Double)(this.Invoke("GetPrice",
                         (this.Url + "/GetPrice"), new object[] {Isbn})));
}
```

HttpPostClientProtocol Class

This class defines the mechanisms for calling Web Services using the HTTP-POST protocol. The HTTP-POST method of communication is similar to HTTP GET, except that parameter name-value pairs are transmitted as part of the actual body of the HTTP request, rather than being appended to the URL request line.

This class can customize a Web Service method by using attributes assigned to either the Web Service method or to a client proxy class. The client proxy class should inherit from `HttpPostClientProtocol` to call the web method in the Web Service using the HTTP POST protocol. The `WSDL.exe` .NET Framework tool can create a client proxy class by passing in the reference to the Web Service and setting the protocol switch to the desired protocol. This is shown in the following example:

```
wsdl /protocol:HttpPost /l:cs ⌐
http://localhost/systemWebServicesProtocols/IsbnQuery/IsbnQuery.asmx?wsdl
```

HttpPostClientProtocol Class Public Methods

The `HttpPostClientProtocol` class offers the same public methods as the `HttpGetClientProtocol` class explained earlier in this chapter. The only difference is the communication protocol in question here is HTTP POST instead of HTTP GET. See *HttpGetClientProtocol Class Public Methods* for detailed explanation.

HttpPostClientProtocol Class Protected Methods

The HttpPostClientProtocol class offers the same protected methods as the HttpGetClientProtocol class explained earlier in this chapter. The only difference is the communication protocol in question here is HTTP POST instead of HTTP GET. See *HttpGetClientProtocol Class Protected Methods* for detailed explanation.

HttpPostClientProtocol Class Public Properties

The HttpPostClientProtocol class offers the same public properties as the HttpGetClientProtocol class explained earlier in this chapter. The only difference is the communication protocol in question here is HTTP POST instead of HTTP GET. See *HttpGetClientProtocol Class Public Properties* for detailed explanation.

HttpPostClientProtocol Class Protected Properties

The HttpPostClientProtocol class offers the same protected properties as the HttpGetClientProtocol class explained earlier in this chapter. The only difference is the communication protocol in question here is HTTP POST instead of HTTP GET. See *HttpGetClientProtocol Class Protected Properties* for detailed explanation.

HttpPostClientProtocol Class Public Events

The HttpPostClientProtocol class offers the same public events as the HttpGetClientProtocol class explained earlier in this chapter. The only difference is the communication protocol in question here is HTTP POST instead of HTTP GET. See *HttpGetClientProtocol Class Public Events* for detailed explanation.

SoapDocumentMethodAttribute Class

The SoapDocumentMethodAttribute when applied to any web method changes the web method's default encoding to Document style for request and response messages. The messages should be in the format dictated by an XSD schema. Document encoding formats the Body element as a series of message parts under it.

You can use this attribute to override the default encoding, if any, applied to a Web Service. A web method can have only one of the following attributes applied: either SoapDocumentMethodAttribute or SoapRpcMethodAttribute.

It is inherited from System.Attribute and it cannot be further inherited.

SoapDocumentMethodAttribute Class Public Methods

- ❏ Equals – inherited from System.Object, see Introduction for details
- ❏ **GetHashCode**
- ❏ GetType – inherited from System.Object, see Introduction for details

- ❑ **IsDefaultAttribute**
- ❑ **Match**
- ❑ `ToString` – inherited from `System.Object`, see Introduction for details

GetHashCode

The `GetHashCode` method returns the hash code for the current instance of the object. It is inherited from `System.Attribute`.

```
public override int GetHashCode();
```

IsDefaultAttribute

The `IsDefaultAttribute` method if overridden is used to indicate whether the values of the current instance are equal to the values of the default instance of the object. It is inherited from `System.Attribute` and is not overridden in this class. As it is not overridden here, it always returns `false` irrespective of whether the current object holds default values or not.

```
public virtual bool IsDefaultAttribute();
```

Match

The `Match` method if overridden is used to compare the current instance with another object. It is inherited from `System.Attribute` and is not overridden in this class. As it is not overridden here, it returns the same value as the `Equals` method would return.

```
public virtual bool Match(object obj);
```

SoapDocumentMethodAttribute Class Protected Methods

- ❑ `Finalize` – inherited from `System.Object`, see Introduction for details
- ❑ `MemberwiseClone` – inherited from `System.Object`, see Introduction for details

SoapDocumentMethodAttribute Class Public Properties

- ❑ **Action**
- ❑ **Binding**
- ❑ **OneWay**
- ❑ **ParameterStyle**
- ❑ **RequestElementName**
- ❑ **RequestNamespace**
- ❑ **ResponseElementName**
- ❑ **ResponseNamespace**
- ❑ `TypeId` – inherited from `System.Attribute`, not implemented in this class
- ❑ **Use**

732

Action

The `Action` property can be used to get or set the SOAP `Action` header for the message. The SOAP `Action` specifies a `String` object representing a URI that indicates the intended business processing end point for the SOAP request. It can be used to indicate to the SOAP server that this message must be passed to another server or it can simply indicate that the next server receiving this SOAP message should process it.

SOAP places no restrictions on the format or specificity of the URI, and doesn't even require that it be resolvable. This property is used during SOAP, HTTP-GET, and HTTP-POST transfers, and is placed inside the HTML wrapper's header, not within the SOAP message.

```
public string Action {get; set;}
```

Binding

This property represents or assigns the `Binding` that links the Web Method with the assigned binding. The binding is assigned using `WebServiceBindingAttribute` customization. This will allow you to alter the binding and introduce advanced features such as describing a new communication end point that is not described in the WSDL schema.

This property identifies the binding a Web Service method implements during an operation. The `Binding`, as its name suggests, forms the namespace or interface that brings together different items within the WSDL schema to form a complete set of operations.

A `Binding` is an XML definition for attaching Web Services to a known end-point or communication technique. This property can be used to create a new `Binding` for a Web Service that was not included within the original WSDL schema definition.

When assigning a `Binding` name you must first of all create a new binding XML construct using the `WebServiceBinding` attribute at class level. This will create the XML within the WSDL schema; you can then use this binding construct by simply assigning its name to the Web Service with the `Binding` property (see Chapter 9 for more details on binding).

```
public string Binding {get; set;}
```

OneWay

This property indicates whether the Web Service client will receive a response back from the web server or not when calling a web method. It assigns or returns a `Boolean` object. When this property is set to `true`, then the client need not wait for the server to finish executing the method, as it does not want to receive a response back from the server. However, the client still needs to know that the server has started executing its request, and this is indicated when the client receives the HTTP 202 status code. The server sends this message after it de-serializes the message request and is starting working on the request. Web methods with the `OneWay` property set to `true` do not have access to the intrinsic objects like `Context`, `Application`, `Session`, `Cache`, `User`, and so on.

This property can only be set to `true` for subroutine procedures as they do not return a result to the client. This property is useful for instructing the server to initiate a task where the result is not required or there is no result.

One potential use of one-way methods is to create an asynchronous message queuing system, where you create methods that do not return SOAP messages, but simply process requests. After you have asked for a Web Service to run, you can send another SOAP message to the server to find out the status of the previous Web Service. All state, however, will be controlled within the server using database activity.

```
public bool OneWay {get; set;}
```

ParameterStyle

This property indicates the position within the message where the SOAP parameters are to be placed during SOAP request or response. This position can return or assign the members of the `System.Web.Services.Protocols.SoapParameterStyle` enumeration: either `Bare`, `Default`, or `Wrapped`.

If you select a `SoapParameterStyle` of `Bare`, the method parameters are not wrapped by any container element, instead they appear directly beneath the body element of the SOAP request. The default for this property is `Wrapped`, if a default is not specified by the `SoapDocumentServiceAttribute` for the Web Service. `Wrapped` means that the parameters are wrapped within a container element, which is in turn held inside the SOAP body element.

If the `ParameterStyle` property is `Bare`, then the properties `RequestElementName` and `ResponseElementName` will be ignored.

See the `SoapParameterStyle` enumeration section in this chapter for further explanation.

```
public SoapParameterStyle ParameterStyle {get; set;}
```

RequestElementName

When `ParameterStyle` is `Wrapped`, this property can be used to get or set the element name used for the element wrapper around the parameters of the **SOAP Request**. The default value is the name of the Web Service method being called. It assigns or returns a `String` object. If the `ParameterStyle` is `Bare`, then this property will be ignored.

```
public string RequestElementName {get; set;}
```

RequestNamespace

Each SOAP request has an XML namespace associated with it. The default namespace for all .NET Web Services is `http://tempuri.org/`. This property allows you to declare an alternative namespace for a web method's SOAP request. It assigns or returns a `String` object.

```
public string RequestNamespace {get; set;}
```

ResponseElementName

As you may have guessed, this property serves the same purpose as `RequestElementName`, except that it defines parameter names for the **SOAP Response**. So, for a `ParameterStyle` of `Wrapped`, this property defines the element wrapper to use for the parameters of the SOAP Response. Again, the default value is the name of the Web Service method used. It assigns or returns a `String` object. If the `ParameterStyle` is `Bare`, then this property will be ignored.

```
public string ResponseElementName {get; set;}
```

ResponseNamespace

This property mirrors the `RequestNamespace` property for the SOAP Response. Again, the default namespace for the response is `http://tempuri.org/`. This property lets you specify a different namespace for a web method's SOAP response. It assigns or returns a `String` object.

It should be noted that the `ResponseNamespace` does not have to be different from the `RequestNamespace`. Namespaces are simply used to identify a particular SOAP message to a Web Service (if on the server) or match a request with a response message (if on the client).

```
public string ResponseNamespace {get; set;}
```

Use

This property gets or sets the parameter encoding that applies to a Web Service method within the XML portion of a SOAP message using the `System.Web.Services.Description.SoapBindingUse` enumeration.

There are two styles of parameter encoding styles: `Literal` and `Encoded`. The default is `Literal`. `Literal` identifies that the class's values are explicitly stated by an XML Schema definition associated with either the `element` or the `type` attribute. The parameters are held in their original form. `Encoded` implies that the values are encoded as specified by the `encodingStyle` attribute in the `<soap:Body>` element. See `SoapBindingUse` enumeration in Chapter 10 for further explanation.

```
public SoapBindingUse Use {get; set;}
```

Example: Using SoapDocumentMethodAttribute's Properties

The following code is taken from `SoapDocumentMethodAttributeUsage`, an ASP.NET Web Service project in the code download for this chapter, detailing how you can set some of the properties of this class that will override the default definitions during building the WSDL file:

```
[WebMethod(), SoapDocumentMethod(RequestElementName="IsbnQueryGetPrice",
        RequestNamespace="http://localhost/┐
        SoapDocumentMethodAttributeUsage/IsbnQuery",
        ResponseElementName="IsbnQueryGetPriceResponse",
        ResponseNamespace="http://localhost/┐
        SoapDocumentMethodAttributeUsage/IsbnQuery",
        Use=SoapBindingUse.Encoded,
        Action="http://localhost/┐
        SoapDocumentMethodAttributeUsage/GetPrice")]
```

```
public double GetPrice(string Isbn)
```

Here is a screenshot showing that the `RequestElementName`, `ResponseElementName`, and a few other properties have been changed in the WSDL file:

SoapDocumentServiceAttribute Class

This class is used to customize SOAP Requests or SOAP Responses for a particular Web Service. Any changes made using this class will be reflected in the WSDL schema definition file produced by `WSDL.exe`. Unlike the `SoapDocumentMethodAttribute` class, these values are set at service level using a service-level attribute. This attribute sets the default encoding style for all the web methods in the Web Service. The web methods can override the default behavior set by this attribute if need be using `SoapDocumentMethodAttribute` or `SoapRpcMethodAttribute`.

It is inherited from `System.Attribute` and it cannot be further inherited.

SoapDocumentServiceAttribute Class Public Methods

- ❑ `Equals` – inherited from `System.Object`, see Introduction for details
- ❑ `GetHashCode` – inherited from `System.Object`, see Introduction for details
- ❑ `GetType` – inherited from `System.Object`, see Introduction for details
- ❑ **`IsDefaultAttribute`**
- ❑ **`Match`**
- ❑ `ToString` – inherited from `System.Object`, see Introduction for details

IsDefaultAttribute

The `IsDefaultAttribute` method if overridden is used to indicate whether the values of the current instance are equal to the values of the default instance of the object. It is inherited from `System.Attribute` and is not overridden in this class. As it is not overridden here, it always returns `false` irrespective of whether the current object holds default values or not.

```
public virtual bool IsDefaultAttribute();
```

Match

The `Match` method if overridden is used to compare the current instance with another object. It is inherited from `System.Attribute` and is not overridden in this class. As it is not overridden here, it returns the same value as the `Equals` method would return. If it had been overridden, then it could have been used to compare different flag sets too.

```
public virtual bool Match(object obj);
```

SoapDocumentServiceAttribute Class Protected Methods

❑ `Finalize` – inherited from `System.Object`, see Introduction for details

❑ `MemberwiseClone` – inherited from `System.Object`, see Introduction for details

SoapDocumentServiceAttribute Class Public Properties

❑ **ParameterStyle**

❑ **RoutingStyle**

❑ `TypeId` – inherited from `System.Attribute`, not implemented in this class

❑ **Use**

ParameterStyle

This property indicates the default position within the message where the SOAP parameters are to be placed during SOAP request or response. This position can return or assign the members of the `System.Web.Services.Protocols.SoapParameterStyle` enumeration: either `Bare`, `Default`, or `Wrapped`.

If you select a `SoapParameterStyle` of `Bare`, the method parameters are not wrapped by any container element, instead they appear directly beneath the body element of the SOAP request. If this property is set to `Wrapped` then the parameters are wrapped within a container element, which is in turn held inside the SOAP body element. The parent element will have the same name as the web method. If no value is specified for this property, then the default value will be `Wrapped`. The value of this property is the default value for all the web methods' `ParameterStyle` in the Web Service.

See the `SoapParameterStyle` enumeration section in this chapter for further explanation.

```
public SoapParameterStyle ParameterStyle {get; set}
```

RoutingStyle

This property gets or sets how SOAP messages are routed, specifying whether the SOAPAction Header should be populated or not. It assigns a routing style as one of the two values of the enumeration System.Web.Services.Protocols.SoapServiceRoutingStyle: either RequestElement or SoapAction.

The default is SoapAction, which means the message is routed on the basis of the SOAPAction Header. When it is set to RequestElement, the message is routed on the basis of the first child element of the <Body> element and the SOAPAction Header can be left blank.

See the SoapServiceRoutingStyle enumeration section in this chapter for further explanation.

```
public SoapServiceRoutingStyle RoutingStyle {get; set;}
```

Use

This property gets or sets the default parameter encoding that applies to a Web Service within the XML portion of a SOAP message using the System.Web.Services.Description.SoapBindingUse enumeration.

There are two styles of parameter encoding: Literal and Encoded. The default is Literal. Literal identifies that the class's values are explicitly stated by an XML Schema definition associated with either the element or the type attribute. The parameters are held in their original form. Encoded implies that the values are encoded as specified by the encodingStyle attribute in the <soap:Body> element.

See the SoapBindingUse enumeration in Chapter 10 for further explanation.

```
public SoapBindingUse Use {get; set;}
```

Example: Using the SoapDocumentServiceAttributeUsage Class

The following code is taken from SoapDocumentServiceAttributeUsage, an ASP.NET Web Service project, detailing how you can set some of the properties of this class that will override the default definitions during the building of the WSDL file for all web methods in a Web Service:

```
[WebService(
    Namespace="http://localhost/SoapDocumentServiceAttributeUsage/"),
    SoapDocumentService(
    ParameterStyle=SoapParameterStyle.Bare,
    RoutingStyle=SoapServiceRoutingStyle.RequestElement,
    Use=SoapBindingUse.Literal)]
    public class SoapDocumentServiceAttributeUsage :
                                        System.Web.Services.WebService
```

On the top is a screenshot showing the effect of setting the `ParameterStyle` to `Wrapped` in the WSDL file, as compared to a `ParameterStyle` of `Bare` on the bottom:

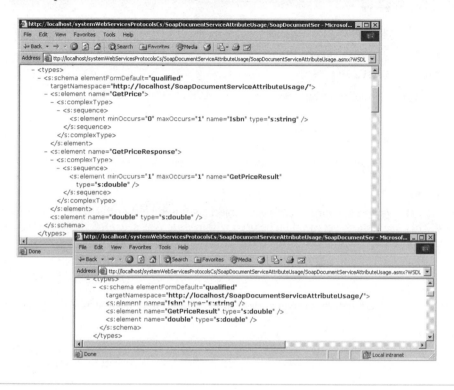

SoapExtension Class

SOAP extensions give you the ability to extend the facilities of the basic ASP.NET framework by providing a means of accessing the underlying engine that processes events.

The class does this by allowing you to trap any of the four stages/events in the lifecycle of a SOAP message so that you may process through your own handler whenever one of these events is caught. These stages are:

❑ BeforeSerialize

❑ AfterSerialize

❑ BeforeDeserialize

❑ AfterDeserialize

Your code can then react to each event by firing a user-defined handler to change the SOAP message or environment to suit your particular needs.

SoapExtension Class Public Methods

- ❏ **ChainStream**
- ❏ Equals – inherited from System.Object, see Introduction for details
- ❏ GetHashCode – inherited from System.Object, see Introduction for details
- ❏ **GetInitializer**
- ❏ GetType – inherited from System.Object, see Introduction for details
- ❏ **Initialize**
- ❏ **ProcessMessage**
- ❏ ToString – inherited from System.Object, see Introduction for details

ChainStream

This method allows you to capture a Stream object containing either the SOAP Request or SOAP Response. This Stream object can then be used within *SoapMessageStage* to manipulate the SOAP message, for example to apply compression or encryption.

```
public virtual Stream ChainStream(stream);
```

The parameter stream specifies the memory buffer containing either the SOAP request or the SOAP response.

Note that the Stream object attached to the message during *SoapMessageStage* is read-only, so if you wish to amend the SOAP message, you must use the Stream object passed by the ChainStream method.

GetInitializer

This method is used to perform initialization of data specific to the Web Service method. This method is overloaded and can initialize the data of the Web Service as a whole or by each individual web method. Let's see them one by one:

```
public abstract object GetInitializer(serviceType);
```

The parameter serviceType refers to the XML Web Service class to which the SOAP extension is applied. This method allows the SOAP extension to initialize data specific to the Web Service at a one-time performance cost.

```
public abstract object GetInitializer(methodInfo, attribute);
```

The parameter methodInfo is a LogicalMethodInfo object specifying the web method to be initialized. The parameter attribute is the SoapExtensionAttribute applied to the web method.

These methods can provide perfomance enhancement by specifying how data is to be cached during the processing of a SoapExtension.

Initialize

This method when overridden can be used to initialize a `SoapExtension` using the data cached during a previous `GetInitializer` method call.

```
public abstract void Intialize(intializer);
```

The parameter `intializer` is the object returned by the `GetInitializer` method call, a reference to the object initialized.

ProcessMessage

This method if overridden is called to process the `SoapExtension` at any particular `SoapMessageState`. This method forms the heart of the entire `SoapExtension`, allowing you to assign code to react to the various events that are triggered during the processing of a SOAP message.

```
public abstract void ProcessMessage(message);
```

SoapExtension Class Protected Methods

❑   `Finalize` – inherited from `System.Object`, see Introduction for details

❑   `MemberwiseClone` – inherited from `System.Object`, see Introduction for details

SoapExtensionAttribute Class

This class lets you assign a `SoapExtensionAttribute` to a specific Web Service. This enables the `SoapMessageStage` events to work.

SoapExtensionAttribute Class Public Methods

❑   `Equals` – inherited from `System.Object`, see Introduction for details

❑   `GetHashCode` – inherited from `System.Object`, see Introduction for details

❑   `GetType` – inherited from `System.Object`, see Introduction for details

❑   **`IsDefaultAttribute`**

❑   **`Match`**

❑   `ToString` – inherited from `System.Object`, see Introduction for details

IsDefaultAttribute

The `IsDefaultAttribute` method, if overridden, is used to indicate whether the values of the current instance are equal to the values of the default instance of the object. It is inherited from `System.Attribute` and is not overridden in this class. As it is not overridden here, it always returns `false` irrespective of whether the current object holds default values or not.

```
public virtual bool IsDefaultAttribute();
```

Match

The `Match` method if overridden is used to compare the current instance with another object. It is inherited from `System.Attribute` and is not overridden in this class. As it is not overridden here, it returns the same value as the `Equals` method would return.

```
public virtual bool Match(object obj)
```

SoapExtensionAttribute Class Protected Methods

❑ `Finalize` – inherited from `System.Object`, see Introduction for details

❑ `MemberwiseClone` – inherited from `System.Object`, see Introduction for details

SoapExtensionAttribute Class Public Properties

❑ **ExtensionType**

❑ **Priority**

❑ `TypeId` – inherited from `System.Attribute`, not implemented here

ExtensionType

This property returns the `Type` object of the `SoapExtension` class. Classes that derive from `SoapExtensionAttribute` must override this property. The ASP.NET runtime accesses this property to locate the `SoapExtension` class.

```
public abstract Type Priority {get;}
```

Priority

This property indicates the `SoapExtensionAttribute` with which the SOAP Extension will be executed over other SOAP extensions. The `Priority` class must override this property.

```
public abstract int ExtensionType {get; set;}
```

SoapHeader Class

The `SoapHeader` class allows you to pass extra information to the Web Service not directly related to the SOAP message parameters. This allows for performing specialist tasks such as user authorization, or defining particular transaction requirements.

SoapHeader Class Public Methods

❑ `Equals` – inherited from `System.Object`, see Introduction for details

❑ `GetHashCode` – inherited from `System.Object`, see Introduction for details

❑ `GetType` – inherited from `System.Object`, see Introduction for details

❑ `ToString` – inherited from `System.Object`, see Introduction for details

SoapHeader Class Protected Methods

❏ `Finalize` – inherited from `System.Object`, see Introduction for details

❏ `MemberwiseClone` – inherited from `System.Object`, see Introduction for details

SoapHeader Class Public Properties

❏ **Actor**

❏ **DidUnderstand**

❏ **EncodedMustUnderstand**

❏ **MustUnderstand**

Actor

This property is used to return or assign the recipient of the SOAP header. If the recipient is the current Web Service but the message needs to be passed on to the next server then the header specific to the current Web Service should be stripped out. Also if the intended recipient is not the current Web Service server then the header should be ignored.

```
public string Actor {get; set;}
```

DidUnderstand

This property is used to indicate whether the SOAP header was properly understood or not by the recipient. It returns or assigns a Boolean object. If this property is set to `true`, then that means the recipient properly understood the SOAP header. If its value is `false`, it means the recipient could not process the header successfully.

```
public bool DidUnderstand {get; set;}
```

EncodedMustUnderstand

This property indicates that a header that has a `MustUnderstand` property equals to `true`, must be encoded, and also must be understood by the recipient. If the property value is set to `true`, then it also sets the value of the `MustUnderstand` property to `true`. The default value is 0 that meaning `false`; `true` is 1, although you can also use `true` and `false`. An `ArgumentException` is thrown if a value other than the above-mentioned four values is assigned to this property.

```
public bool EncodedMustUnderstand {get; set;}
```

MustUnderstand

This property is used to indicate whether the sender of the `SoapHeader` intends the recipient to understand the header or not. If this property is set to `true`, the intended recipient must understand this header. If it does not understand, it *must* throw a `SoapException`. The default value is `false`.

```
public bool MustUnderstand {get; set;}
```

SoapHeaderAttribute Class

This class can customize a client proxy class or a Web Service method by creating SOAP headers that can be transferred as part of the SOAP request or SOAP response. It is inherited from `System.Attribute` and cannot be further inherited.

As we saw in our more detailed examination previously, this class allows the customization of a Web Service by adding SOAP header information. The attribute is applied to the Web Service at design time, and is reflected in the actual WSDL schema file created. This class cannot be inherited.

A SOAP header is an XML structure that can be placed within a SOAP message to send additional information down to the server that is not included in the arguments to the Web Service. It usually defines environment variables that can be acted upon, for example advising the server that you want this SOAP request to be included within a transaction, or passing down a security username and password for authorization. A SOAP header within a SOAP message looks like this:

```
<?xml version="1.0" encoding="utf-8"?>
<soap:Envelope xmlns:xsi="http://www.w3.org/2001/XMLSchema-instance"
               xmlns:xsd="http://www.w3.org/2001/XMLSchema"
               xmlns:soap="http://schemas.xmlsoap.org/soap/envelope/" >
  <soap:Header>
    <MyHeader xmlns="http://www.contoso.com">
      <Username>Admin</Username>
      <Password>MyPassword</Password>
    </MyHeader>
  </soap:Header>
  <soap:Body>
    <HelloWorld xmlns="http://tempuri.org/">
      <Argument1>Hello</Argument1>
    </HelloWorld>
  </soap:Body>
</soap:Envelope>
```

Example: Defining a SOAP Header and Sending it to a SOAP Server

The following example outlines a step-by-step approach for defining a client SOAP header and sending it to a SOAP server.

Client Code for Sending a SOAP Header

The following code, `Service1.cs`, reflects example code required for a `HelloWorld` proxy class created using the `WSDL.exe` command, which you can find in the **SoapHeader** project in the code download:

```
using System.Diagnostics;
using System.Xml.Serialization;
using System;
using System.Web.Services.Protocols;
using System.ComponentModel;
using System.Web.Services;
```

```
/// <remarks/>
[System.Diagnostics.DebuggerStepThroughAttribute()]
[System.ComponentModel.DesignerCategoryAttribute("code")]
[System.Web.Services.WebServiceBindingAttribute(Name="Service1Soap",
Namespace="http://tempuri.org/")]
public class Service1 :
                System.Web.Services.Protocols.SoapHttpClientProtocol {

  //This defines the structure of a simple SOAP header
  //this SOAP header allows you to pass down two values to the server.
  public class MyHeader : System.Web.Services.Protocols.SoapHeader
  {
    public string MyValue;
    public int MyNumber;
  }

  //This defines a specific instance of the header
  //it also defines the variable name to use within
  //the SOAP header attribute.
  public MyHeader MyHeaderValue;

  /// <remarks/>
  public Service1() {
    this.Url =
              "http://localhost/systemwebservicesprotocols/↴
              soapheaderserver/service1.asmx";
    MyHeaderValue = new MyHeader();
  }

  /// <remarks/>
  [System.Web.Services.Protocols.SoapHeaderAttribute("MyHeaderValue",
  Direction=System.Web.Services.Protocols.SoapHeaderDirection.InOut)]
  [System.Web.Services.Protocols.SoapDocumentMethodAttribute(
  "http://tempuri.org/HelloWorld", RequestNamespace="http://tempuri.org/",
  ResponseNamespace="http://tempuri.org/",
  Use=System.Web.Services.Description.SoapBindingUse.Literal,
  ParameterStyle=System.Web.Services.Protocols.SoapParameterStyle.Wrapped)]
  public string HelloWorld() {
    object[] results = this.Invoke("HelloWorld", new object[0]);
    return ((string)(results[0]));
  }

  /// <remarks/>
  public System.IAsyncResult BeginHelloWorld(System.AsyncCallback callback,
                                             object asyncState) {
    return this.BeginInvoke("HelloWorld", new object[0], callback,
                            asyncState);
  }

  /// <remarks/>
  public string EndHelloWorld(System.IAsyncResult asyncResult) {
    object[] results = this.EndInvoke(asyncResult);
    return ((string)(results[0]));
```

```
    }
}

/// <remarks/>
[System.Xml.Serialization.XmlTypeAttribute(
                          Namespace="http://tempuri.org/")]
[System.Xml.Serialization.XmlRootAttribute(Namespace="http://tempuri.org/",
                                           IsNullable=false)]
public class MyHeader : System.Web.Services.Protocols.SoapHeader {

  /// <remarks/>
  public string MyValue;

  /// <remarks/>
  public int MyNumber;
}
```

First off we define the class structure for the header, inserting the values that we wish to send to the SOAP server. As can be seen, the `MyValue` and `MyNumber` entries are the actual values that will be sent to the SOAP server:

```
public class MyHeader : System.Web.Services.Protocols.SoapHeader
{
  public string MyValue;
  public int MyNumber;
}
```

It's worth noting that to declare this header you can also create another project with a public class and then simply reference that instead of declaring it locally. This gives the added advantage of having the ability to share the same class within the ASP.NET server, guaranteeing that you conform to the same header structure. The above definition is not restricted to simple variable definitions; you may also use get and set definitions within your code.

You must then declare a local `MyHeader` variable within your proxy to contain the header values:

```
public MyHeader MyHeaderValue;
```

Now to complete the client end, you must make sure that the `SoapHeaderAttribute` class is used to add the SOAP header to the outbound SOAP request.

```
[System.Web.Services.Protocols.SoapHeaderAttribute("MyHeaderValue",
Direction=System.Web.Services.Protocols.SoapHeaderDirection.InOut)]
[System.Web.Services.Protocols.SoapDocumentMethodAttribute(
  "http://tempuri.org/HelloWorld",
  RequestNamespace="http://tempuri.org/",
  ResponseNamespace="http://tempuri.org/",
  Use=System.Web.Services.Description.SoapBindingUse.Literal,
  ParameterStyle=System.Web.Services.Protocols.SoapParameterStyle.Wrapped)]
public string HelloWorld() {
  object[] results = this.Invoke("HelloWorld", new object[0]);
  return ((string)(results[0]));
```

Please note that you can assign values to the SOAP header internally within this proxy class. However, you can also assign values to the SOAP header outside the proxy class from the client code. The following example shows code that can be used anywhere within your client application as long as the proxy class you created with the WSDL.exe tool has been attached to your project:

```
Service1 oWS = new Service1();

oWS.MyHeaderValue.MyValue = "Hello to you";
oWS.MyHeaderValue.MyNumber = 42;
lblResult.Text = oWS.HelloWorld();
```

Server Code for Receiving a SOAP Header

Now that you have prepared the client to send a SOAP header to the server, you must also prepare the ASP.NET Web Service to receive the SOAP header and automatically assign it to a local variable, which can then be interrogated or changed.

If the SOAP header was created as an InOut, you can also use this local variable to return values to the client. Reasons you would want to return values to the client include (but are not limited to) for returning the successful outcome of any transaction processing or returning the last date logged on for the username and password you passed to the server.

```
public class Service1 : System.Web.Services.WebService
{
  public class MyHeader : System.Web.Services.Protocols.SoapHeader
  {
    public string MyValue;
    public int MyNumber;
  }

  public MyHeader hName;

  public Service1() : base()
  {
    //CODEGEN: This call is required by the ASP.NET Web Services Designer
    InitializeComponent();
  }

  [WebMethod(), SoapHeader("hName", Direction=SoapHeaderDirection.InOut)]
  public string HelloWorld()
  {
    return "This is what you sent me - MyValue = " +
                hName.MyValue + " and MyNumber = " + hName.MyNumber;
  }
}
```

First off we declare the local header variable, this time omitting the New keyword, as this variable will be instantiated when receiving the SOAP request:

```
public MyHeader hName;
```

Then within the web method attribute area, we assign the SOAP header to the method. Because this is assigned to a web method this now means that the web method is ready to accept a SOAP header from the client and assign it to a local variable.

```
SoapHeader("hName", Direction=SoapHeaderDirection.InOut)
```

That's it. You can now run your project and pass values into the Web Service using this SOAP header.

SoapHeaderAttribute Class Public Methods

- ❏ Equals – inherited from System.Object, see Introduction for details
- ❏ **GetHashCode**
- ❏ GetType – inherited from System.Object, see Introduction for details
- ❏ **IsDefaultAttribute**
- ❏ **Match**
- ❏ ToString – inherited from System.Object, see Introduction for details

GetHashCode

The GetHashCode method returns the hash code for the current instance of the object. It is inherited from System.Attribute.

```
public override int GetHashCode();
```

IsDefaultAttribute

The `IsDefaultAttribute` method if overridden is used to indicate whether the values of the current instance are equal to the values of the default instance of the object. It is inherited from `System.Attribute` and is not overridden in this class. As it is not overridden here, it always returns `false` irrespective of the current object holding default values or not.

```
public virtual bool IsDefaultAttribute();
```

Match

The `Match` method if overridden is used to compare the current instance with another object. It is inherited from `System.Attribute` and is not overridden in this class. As it is not overridden here, it returns the same value that the `Equals` method would return.

```
public virtual bool Match(object obj);
```

SoapHeaderAttribute Class Protected Methods

❑ `Finalize` – inherited from `System.Object`, see Introduction for details

❑ `MemberwiseClone` – inherited from `System.Object`, see Introduction for details

SoapHeaderAttribute Class Public Properties

❑ **Direction**

❑ **MemberName**

❑ **Required**

❑ `TypeId` – inherited from `System.Attribute`, not implemented in this class

Direction

This property indicates the intended recipient of the `SoapHeader`: that is, whether the service is received from the web client, or the Web Service, or sent and received by both of them. The property uses the `System.Web.Services.Protocols.SoapHeaderDirection` enumeration value to represent the intended recipient.

The values of this enumeration are:

❑ `In` – the header is sent to the Web Service method only; this is the default value

❑ `Out` – the header is sent from the Web Service method to the web client

❑ `InOut` – the header is sent to and received from the Web Service

```
public SoapHeaderDirection Direction {get; set;}
```

MemberName

This property refers to the `memberName` of the `SoapHeader` derived class, in the Web Service. It returns or assigns a string object and there is no default value for this property. The SOAP header will be held within an XML element name, and this property allows you to assign exactly what that element name will be. Note that this value must be the same as the locally declared variable that contains the SOAP header, and also correspond to the SOAP header name given to the ASP.NET Web Service method.

```
public string MemberName {get; set;}
```

Required

This property determines whether the `SoapHeader` must be understood and be processed in the `SOAP` message sent by the Web Service or the web client.

This determines that the ASP.NET Web Service must either understand (`true`) the SOAP header before continuing or does not need to understand (`false`) the SOAP header. This property makes sure that ASP.NET does not ignore a Web Service header if it does not understand it.

```
public bool Required {get; set;}
```

SoapHttpClientProtocol Class

This class defines the mechanisms for calling Web Services using the HTTP-POST protocol. The HTTP-POST method of communication is similar to HTTP GET, except that parameter name-value pairs are transmitted as part of the actual body of the HTTP request, rather than being appended to the URL request line. This class defines the means for sending SOAP requests to the server using the SOAP communication technique.

This class can customize a Web Service method by using attributes assigned to either the Web Service method or to a client proxy class. The client proxy class should inherit from `SoapHttpClientProtocol` to call the web method in the Web Service using HTTP POST. The `wsdl.exe` .NET Framework tool helps in the automatic creation of a client proxy class by passing the `WSDL` reference of the Web Service and setting the protocol switch to the desired protocol. SOAP is the default protocol when the protocol switch is not mentioned while running the `wsdl.exe` tool. For example:

```
wsdl /protocol:SOAP /l:cs ⌐
http://localhost/systemWebServicesProtocols/IsbnQuery/IsbnQuery.asmx?wsdl
```

or:

```
wsdl /l:cs ⌐
http://localhost/systemWebServicesProtocols/IsbnQuery/IsbnQuery.asmx?wsdl
```

SoapHttpClientProtocol Class Public Methods

- ❑ **Abort**
- ❑ **CreateObjRef**
- ❑ **Discover**
- ❑ **Dispose**
- ❑ Equals – inherited from System.Object, see Introduction for details
- ❑ GetHashCode – inherited from System.Object, see Introduction for details
- ❑ **GetLifeTimeService**
- ❑ GetType – inherited from System.Object, see Introduction for details
- ❑ **InitializeLifeTimeService**
- ❑ ToString – inherited from System.Object, see Introduction for details

Abort

The Abort method stops any currently executing synchronous SOAP request from the client. This method can be helpful when you start a long-running web method synchronously on the server such as creating a report for annual sales analysis. If it seems to be taking too long, since the call may block the thread, you can stop it from running by executing this Abort command on a separate thread. For example, you might attach the abort to a button on your client form and call the Abort method on the click event of the button. A WebException is thrown when an Abort method is called and its Status property will have the value WebExceptionStatus.RequestCancelled. It is inherited from the System.Web.Services.Protocols.WebClientProtocol class.

```
public virtual void Abort();
```

CreateObjRef

This method is used to create an object that contains information on how to generate a proxy. This proxy will be used for communicating with remote objects. The parameter passed to this method is the Type that the return object would refer to. The method throws a RemotingException if the object created is not valid for remote communication. It is inherited from System.MarshalByRefObject class.

```
public virtual ObjRef CreateObjRef(Type);
```

Discover

The Discover method is used to dynamically discover the Web Service location with the help of the discovery document referenced by the Url property. This location is different from the location referenced in the proxy class. The method throws an exception if the discovery document does not have the same binding and namespace as defined in the proxy class. For more information about dynamic discovery, refer to the section titled *Web Service Discovery*, earlier in this chapter.

```
public void Discover();
```

Dispose

The `Dispose` method is used in order to flag resources for clean up and liberation by the periodic garbage collection service. It is inherited from the `System.ComponentModel.Component` class.

```
public void Dispose();
```

GetLifeTimeService

This method gets the lifetime service object of the current instance as an `ILease` object. This object is used to control the lifetime of a remote object. In the case of a high-traffic web site, the automatic garbage collection won't scale well. You can instead use this `LifeTimeService` object to specify the lease time for your remote object. The remote object will be removed when the lease expires; this way you can have fine control over your remote object's lifetime. This method is inherited from `System.MarshalByRefObject` class.

```
public object GetLifeTimeService();
```

InitializeLifeTimeService

This method gets the lifetime service object of the current instance as an object of `ILease` type. If no object already exists for this instance then it will return a new instance of `ILease` type that is initialized with the value of the `LifeTimeServices.LeaseManagerPollTime` property. This object is used to control the lifetime of a remote object. In the case of high-traffic web site, the automatic garbage collection won't scale well. You can instead use this `LifeTimeService` object to specify the lease time for your remote object. The remote object will be removed when the lease expires; this way you can have fine control over your remote object's lifetime. The default value of `LifeTimeServices.LeaseManagerPollTime` property is 10 seconds, which means that leases are inspected and cleaned every 10 seconds. This method is inherited from `System.MarshalByRefObject` class.

```
public virtual object InitializeLifeTimeService();
```

SoapHttpClientProtocol Class Protected Methods

❏ **`BeginInvoke`**

❏ **`Dispose`**

❏ **`EndInvoke`**

❏ `Finalize` – inherited from `System.Object`, see Introduction for details

❏ **`GetService`**

❏ **`GetWebRequest`**

❏ **`GetWebResponse`**

❏ **`Invoke`**

❏ `MemberwiseClone` – inherited from `System.Object`, see Introduction for details

BeginInvoke

The `BeginInvoke` method starts an asynchronous communication link to a remote Web Service.

```
protected IASyncResult BeginInvoke(methodName, parameters,
                                   callback, asyncState);
```

The `methodName` parameter specifies a `String` object referring to the name of the web method expected to run asynchronously. The `parameters` parameter specifies an array of `Objects` containing the parameters to be passed to the web method. The order of values in the array must correspond exactly to the order of the parameters that the web method is expecting. The `callback` parameter specifies an `Object` containing the method/delegate to call on the client once the event for completion of the asynchronous message is performed. If `callback` is nothing then no process is called on completion of the Web Service. The `asyncState` parameter specifies a parameter type container object for holding useful information about the client responsible for using this asynchronous SOAP request.

An `AsyncResult` object is returned that can be used within your code while the asynchronous communication continues. This object can be used to retain any state values you wish to retrieve at the end of the asynchronous communication process. Once the Web Service completes its processing the `AsyncResult` object is passed back into the `EndInvoke` method to obtain the return values. Typically, you would not call the `BeginInvoke` method directly, unless you were building your own proxy class for a Web Service. The method throws a `SoapException` if the SOAP request reached the server machine, but failed to process successfully.

Dispose

This `Dispose` method flags all the unmanaged resources for release by the periodic garbage collection service. It also flags for release the managed resources based on the `Boolean` value passed as the parameter. It is inherited from the `System.ComponentModel.Component` class.

```
protected virtual void Dispose(bool);
```

Passing in the parameter `true` indicates that the managed resources should also be released and `false` that they should not. This method is called by the `Finalize` method, with `false` as the parameter value. The public `Dispose` method discussed above also calls this method with the parameter value set to `true`.

EndInvoke Method

This method is called to complete the asynchronous invocation of a Web Service method. This method will be called on completion of the Web Service call to the SOAP server by the method identified as the callback delegate in the `BeginInvoke` method or simply from the client code.

```
protected object[] EndInvoke(asyncResult);
```

The parameter `asyncResult` specifies the `AsyncResult` object instantiated by the `BeginInvoke` method that initiated this Web Service request. An `ArgumentException` is thrown when the `AsyncResult` parameter does not match the one created by `BeginInvoke`.

An array of objects is returned that matches the return values produced by the Web Service in question; it also includes "by reference" or "out" arguments. This is functionally similar to returning multiple return values from the same method.

GetService

The `GetService` method returns an object that representing the Web Service. It returns `null` if the object does not provide the specified service. It is inherited from the `System.Componenet.Model.Component` class.

```
protected virtual object GetService(service);
```

The parameter `service` specifies the Web Service.

GetWebRequest

The method returns a `WebRequest` instance for the specified URI. This method overrides the default `WebRequest` specified by `System.Web.Services.Protocols.HttpWebClientProtocol`. The new instance of the `WebRequest` class can then be used to further customize by adding additional values as a custom header to the `Request` object.

```
protected override WebRequest GetWebRequest(uri);
```

The parameter `uri` specifies a valid and existing URI to create a `WebRequest` object for. If the `uri` parameter passed is `null` then an `InvalidOperationException` occurs. This method returns a `System.Net.WebRequest` object.

GetWebResponse

This method is inherited from the `System.Web.Services.Protocols.HttpWebClientProtocol` class and is overridden here. This method returns a `System.Net.WebResponse` object for a `System.Net.WebRequest` object passed to it as its parameter.

This method has two overloads basically to get `WebResponse` objects both for synchronous and asynchronous web method calls. Let's see them one by one:

The following method is only valid for **synchronous** communication:

```
protected override WebResponse GetWebResponse(request);
```

The parameter `request` refers to the `WebRequest` object associated with this connection to the server. The `WebResponse` object returned can be interrogated to determine the values returned by the server. You can use instances of this class to perform customization such as adding headers.

The following method is only valid for **asynchronous** communication:

```
protected override WebResponse GetWebResponse(request, result);
```

The parameter `request` refers to the `WebRequest` object associated with this connection to the server. The parameter `result` specifies the `AsyncResult` object that was instantiated by the `BeginInvoke` method.

Again, a `WebResponse` object is returned, which can be interrogated to find out the return values for the Web Service call.

Invoke

This method initiates synchronous communication with the web method. The proxy then communicates with the remote Web Service synchronously, meaning the client must wait for a response before continuing.

```
protected object[] Invoke(methodName, parameters);
```

The parameter `methodName` specifies a `String` containing the name of the method you are attempting to run synchronously on the Web Service. The parameter `parameters` specifies an array of `Objects` containing the parameters to pass to the web method. The order of values in the array must correspond to the exact order of the parameters expected by the Web Service. A `SoapException` occurs if the request reached the server machine, but was not processed successfully.

An array of objects containing the return value and the "by reference" or "out" parameters returned by the web method is returned.

SoapHttpClientProtocol Class Public Properties

- ❏ **AllowAutoRedirect**
- ❏ **ClientCertificates**
- ❏ **ConnectionGroupName**
- ❏ **Container**
- ❏ **CookieContainer**
- ❏ **Credentials**
- ❏ **PreAuthenticate**
- ❏ **Proxy**
- ❏ **RequestEncoding**
- ❏ **Site**
- ❏ **Timeout**
- ❏ **Url**
- ❏ **UserAgent**

AllowAutoRedirect

The SOAP standard allows for the transfer of SOAP messages from a client to a SOAP server, but because it also allows for the redirection or "daisy-chaining" of SOAP servers, messages may be processed by a different server from the one you originally opened up communication with. This property helps you in either allowing or preventing the automatic redirection of the client proxy to another server by setting it to `true` or `false` respectively. This property is inherited from `System.Web.Services.Protocols.HttpWebClientProtocol` and returns or assigns a `Boolean` object.

For security reasons, when the client proxy needs to send sensitive data like authentication information or financial information, then this property can be set to `false`, which will prevent the server from redirecting. If a redirection is attempted when this property is set to `false`, a `WebException` is thrown. The `Response` object will contain `StatusCode` and `Headers` properties which will show the location where redirection was attempted and the HTTP status code of the redirection (301, 302 and 307).

```
public bool AllowAutoRedirect {get; set;}
```

ClientCertificates

Certificates are digital documents that allocate unique public keys to identify an individual or other entity. They allow verification by ensuring that a public key does in fact belong to a given individual.

This property returns the collection of valid certificates for the current communication session by returning an `X509CertificateCollection` object. This property allows you to add client certificates to this collection object, which can be used to verify the identity of the client. These client certificates can then be used by the Web Service to authenticate the client proxy. It is inherited from the `System.Web.Services.Protocols.HttpWebClientProtocol` class.

```
public X509CertificateCollection ClientCertificate {get;}
```

ConnectionGroupName

This property enables you to associate a SOAP request with a specific and unique group name within your application session. This can be useful when your application makes requests to a server regarding different users, such as a web site that retrieves customer information from a database server.

Under normal circumstances, when a connection is opened to a .NET server, the connection pooling mechanisms built into .NET kick in. This is designed to save network latency by reusing already established connections rather than creating new ones. Problems can, however, occur if the connection requires a secure connection, and a user-specific authentication occurred between the client and the server. This creates a gray area when you then try to reuse a pooled secure connection for a non-secure user. By using `ConnectionGroupName` when establishing the connection, you create a new connection that is unique to that user, and will not be pooled for reuse by any other user.

Note that each connection group creates an additional connection with the associated server. This may not be the same server for all connection groups. If many connection groups are used then this may result in exceeding the `ServicePoint.ConnectionLimit` (specifying the maximum allowed) for that server.

This property is inherited from the `System.Web.Services.Protocols.WebClientProtocol` class.

```
public string ConnectionGroupName {get; set;}
```

Container

This property returns the `IContainer` object encapsulated in the component. This property returns `null` if the object is not encapsulated in the component. It is inherited from the `System.ComponentModel.Component` class.

```
public IContainer Container {get;}
```

CookieContainer

The client proxy uses this property to get or set the cookies collection associated with the SOAP request.

Cookies in Web Services can be used in a similar fashion to how cookies are used within web sites: to allow for the automatic retrieval of relevant data that can be stored on the client computer instead of the server. Note that this method of storing stateful data relies on many things, such as the client having cookies turned on, the client being able to understand cookies (non-cookie systems include most PDAs and WAP devices). It also invokes an additional roundtrip to retrieve cookie information that may significantly lengthen the time to run that Web Service.

If a Web Service supports session state, then a cookie is sent to the client in the response header to identify the session of the Web Service client. It is inherited from the `System.Web.Services.Protocols.HttpWebClientProtocol` class.

```
public CookieContainer Container {get; set;}
```

Credentials

This property contains authentication information to identify the client for a SOAP request. When using the `Credentials` property, a Web Service client must instantiate the `NetworkCredential` class, and then set the client credentials according to the authentication mechanism employed. This information will then be used to authenticate your connection to an ASP.NET server or any server supporting basic, digest, NTLM, or Kerberos authentication mechanisms.

Credential authentication is possibly the most important authentication technique available. It allows us to use the existing methods of username and password authority, which have over past years been tried and tested. Even though some are not encrypted, such as basic authentication, with the addition of SSL connections this becomes a significant security addition for transferring SOAP messages between client and server. It is inherited from the `System.Web.Services.Protocols.WebClientProtocol` class.

```
public ICredential Credentials {get; set;}
```

PreAuthenticate

When using the `Credentials` property and connecting to the ASP.NET server, the default behavior, with this property being `false`, is to send authentication information to the server only if that server returns a 401 HTTP access denied error to the client. This happens when anonymous access to the Web Service is not allowed and the server requires authentication information. However, by setting the `PreAuthenticate` property to `true`, you can send authentication information in a `WWW-authenticate` HTTP header with the SOAP request. This will save any latency arising from the server having to request authentication information. It is inherited from the `System.Web.Services.Protocols.WebClientProtocol` class.

```
public bool PreAuthenticate {get; set;}
```

Proxy

If your local network setup requires that you process SOAP requests through a firewall, then you need to use this property to configure firewall authentication information. This can be used to bypass the default proxy settings for your machine.

This property allows you to assign and interrogate the proxy settings. It contains information like URL, port, username, password, and so on necessary to connect to the proxy server. To pass in authentication information you must create credentials and assign them to the proxy class, before assigning the proxy class to your instantiated class. It returns a `WebProxy` class object implementing the `IWebProxy` interface. It is inherited from the `System.Web.Services.Protocols.HttpWebClientProtocol` class.

```
public IWebProxy Proxy {get; set;}
```

This property can be used within the Web Service's proxy class. Below we have some example code that shows how the proxy class (which we built previously) can be altered to allow proxy connections:

```
public double GetPrice(string Isbn As String)
  [System.Xml.Serialization.XmlRootAttribute("double",
  [Namespace]="http://localhost/IsbnQuery/", IsNullable=false)]
{
  //Create a proxy object with your details
  WebProxy proxyObject = new WebProxy("yourproxyservername", 80);

  //Assign the object to the proxy property
  this.Proxy = proxyObject;
  return ((System.Double)(this.Invoke("GetPrice",
                    (this.Url + "/GetPrice"), new object[] {Isbn}))); 
}
```

As well as using it from within the proxy class you can also use it within the client code, for example:

```
private void BtnProxy_Click(object sender,
                            System.EventArgs e)
{
  IsbnQuery Isbn = new IsbnQuery();

  //Create a proxy object with your details
  WebProxy proxyObject = new WebProxy("yourproxyservername", 80);

  //Assign the object to the proxy property
  Isbn.Proxy=proxyObject;

  LblPrice.Text = Isbn.GetPrice(TxtIsbn.Text);
}
```

RequestEncoding

This property allows you to get and set the character encoding method to be used for serializing SOAP request messages. The default value is the default encoding value of the transport protocol. In the case of `SoapHttpClientProtocol` it is UTF-8. You must use and populate the `Encoding` class appropriately, and pass it into this property. The response returned by the ASP.NET server will then reflect the encoding method given by `RequestEncoding`. It is inherited from the `System.Web.Services.Protocols.WebClientProtocol` class.

Valid encoding types are:

- ❑   `ASCIIEncoding`
- ❑   `UnicodeEncoding`
- ❑   `UTF7Encoding`
- ❑   `UTF8Encoding`

```
public Encoding RequestEncoding {get; set;}
```

Site

This property returns the site of the component indicating that a component is to be added to the container. It is inherited from the `System.ComponentModel.Component` class. This property returns `null` if the component has not been added to the container, or is being removed from the container, or is not associated with `ISite`.

```
public virtual ISite Site {get; set;}
```

Timeout

This property denotes the time period in milliseconds that the Web Service client proxy waits for a synchronous web request to complete before the request is timed out or aborted. The default period is 100,000 milliseconds or one minute and forty seconds. Setting it to -1 sets this property to `Timeout.Infinity`, which means that the request doesn't timeout at all, waiting indefinitely at the client proxy side. It is inherited from the `System.Web.Services.Protocols.WebClientProtocol` class.

```
public int TimeOut {get; set;}
```

Url

This contains the base or listener URL of the Web Service that the client is requesting. You can use this property to specify an alternative Web Service listener, for example to redirect the request to an alternative mirrored server in the event of failure on the main server. It is inherited from the `System.Web.Services.Protocols.WebClientProtocol` class.

```
public string Url {get; set;}
```

This value includes a definitive URL address location, as well as a port number when relevant.

UserAgent

This property is used to return or assign the value of the user agent header sent with each SOAP request to the server. The user agent is a value in the HTTP header that identifies the client. By default, this is MS Web Services Client Protocol *x.x.xxxx.x*, where *x.x.xxxx.x* is the version of the Common Language Runtime. You can change it to uniquely identify your client either by type or even by location, for example "dotNET client in New York". It is inherited from the System.Web.Services.Protocols.HttpWebClientProtocol class.

```
public string UserAgent {get; set;}
```

SoapHttpClientProtocol Class Protected Properties

- ❏ **DesignMode**
- ❏ **Events**

DesignMode

This property indicates whether the container is in design mode. It is inherited from the System.ComponentModel.Component class. This property returns false if the component does not have a site or is not in design mode.

```
protected bool DesignMode {get;}
```

Events

This property returns an EventHandlerList object representing all the event handlers attached to this component. If there are any event handlers associated with the component, they will be accessible through the EventHandlerList object. You can call various methods of the EventHandlerList object on the return value. It is inherited from the System.ComponentModel.Component class.

```
protected EventHandlerList Events {get;}
```

SoapHttpClientProtocol Class Public Events

- ❏ **Disposed**

Disposed

The Disposed event can be used to add an event handler for when the Dispose method is called. This event handler is invoked whenever the Disposed event on the proxy occurs. It is inherited from the System.ComponentModel.Component class.

```
public event EventHandler Disposed;
```

SoapRpcMethodAttribute Class

The `SoapRpcMethodAttribute`, when applied to any web method, changes the web method's default encoding to RPC formatting style for request and response messages. This class defines the requirement to use RPC methods to encode a message. RPC style refers to encoding the Web Service method according to the SOAP specification for using SOAP for RPC, otherwise known as Section 7 of the SOAP specification. It specifies that all the parameters should be encapsulated within a single element. This element is named after the web method. Within this element each XML island represents a parameter that is named after the parameter it is representing.

You can use this attribute for overriding the default encoding, if any, applied to the Web Service. A web method can have only one attribute applied, `SoapDocumentMethodAttribute` or `SoapRpcMethodAttribute`.

It is inherited from `System.Attribute` and it cannot be further inherited.

The following code shows how you can define your own `Request` and `Response` namespaces that will override the default definitions during the creation of the WSDL file:

```
[System.Web.Services.Protocols.SoapRpcMethodAttribute(
  RequestNamespace="http://www.wrox.com/ThisIsATest",
  ResponseNamespace="http://www.wrox.com/ThisIsTestToo"), WebMethod()]
public string HelloWorld()
```

SoapRpcMethodAttribute Class Public Methods

- ❏ `Equals` – inherited from `System.Object`, see Introduction for details

- ❏ **`GetHashCode`**

- ❏ `GetType` – inherited from `System.Object`, see Introduction for details

- ❏ **`IsDefaultAttribute`**

- ❏ **`Match`**

- ❏ `ToString` – inherited from `System.Object`, see Introduction for details

GetHashCode

The `GetHashCode` method returns the hash code for the current instance of the object. It is inherited from `System.Attribute`.

```
public override int GetHashCode();
```

IsDefaultAttribute

The `IsDefaultAttribute` method, if overridden, is used to indicate whether the values of the current instance are equal to the values of the default instance of the object. It is inherited from `System.Attribute` and is not overridden in this class. As it is not overridden here, it always returns `false` irrespective of the current object holding default values or not.

```
public virtual bool IsDefaultAttribute();
```

Match

The `Match` method, if overridden, is used to compare the current instance with another object. It is inherited from `System.Attribute` and is not overridden in this class. As it is not overridden here, it returns the same value that the `Equals` method would return.

```
public virtual bool Match(object obj);
```

SoapRpcMethodAttribute Class Protected Methods

- ❑   `Finalize` – inherited from `System.Object`, see Introduction for details
- ❑   `MemberwiseClone` – inherited from `System.Object`, see Introduction for details

SoapRpcMethodAttribute Class Public Properties

- ❑   `Action`
- ❑   `Binding`
- ❑   `OneWay`
- ❑   `RequestElementName`
- ❑   `RequestNamespace`
- ❑   `ResponseElementName`
- ❑   `ResponseNamespace`
- ❑   `TypeId` – inherited from `System.Attribute`, not implemented in this class

Action

The `Action` property can be used to get or set the SOAP `Action` header for the message. The SOAP `Action` specifies a `String` object representing a URI that indicates the intended business processing end point for the SOAP request. It can be used to indicate to the SOAP server that this message must be passed to another server or it can simply indicate that the next server receiving this SOAP message should process it.

SOAP places no restrictions on the format or specificity of the URI, and doesn't even require that it be resolvable. This property is used during SOAP, HTTP-GET, and HTTP-POST transfers, and is placed inside the HTML wrapper's header, not within the SOAP message.

```
public string Action {get; set;}
```

Binding

This property represents or assigns the `Binding` that links the Web Method with the assigned binding. The binding is assigned using `WebServiceBindingAttribute` customization. This will allow you to alter the binding and introduce advanced features such as describing a new communication end point that is not described in the WSDL schema.

This property identifies the binding a Web Service method implements during an operation. The `Binding`, as its name suggests, forms the namespace or interface that brings together different items within the WSDL schema to form a complete set of operations.

A `Binding` is an XML definition for attaching Web Services to a known end point or communication technique. This property can be used to create a new a `Binding` for a Web Service that was not included within the original WSDL schema definition.

When assigning a `Binding` name you must first of all create a new binding XML construct using the `WebServiceBinding` attribute at class level. This will create the XML within the WSDL schema; you can then use this binding construct by simply assigning its name to the Web Service with the `Binding` property.

```
public string Binding {get; set;}
```

OneWay

This property indicates whether the Web Service client will receive a response back from the web server or not when calling a web method. It assigns or returns a `Boolean` object. When this property is set to `true`, then the client need not wait for the server to finish executing the method, as it does not want to receive a response back from the server. However, the client needs to know that the server has started executing its request, and this is indicated when the client receives the HTTP 202 status code. The server sends this message after the server de-serializes the message request and starts working on the request. Web methods with the `OneWay` property set to `true` do not have access to intrinsic objects like `Context`, `Application`, `Session`, `Cache`, `User`, and so on.

This property can only be set to `true` for Subroutine procedures as they do not return a result to the client. This property is useful for instructing the server to initiate a task where the result is not required or there
is no result.

One potential use of one-way methods is to create an asynchronous message queuing system, where you create methods that do not return SOAP messages, but simply process requests. After you have asked for a Web Service to run, you can send another SOAP message to the server to find out the status of the previous Web Service. All state however will be controlled within the server using database activity.

```
public bool OneWay {get; set;}
```

RequestElementName

When `ParameterStyle` is set to `Wrapped`, this property can be used to get or set the element name used for the element wrapper around the parameters of the SOAP Request. The default value is the name of the Web Service method being called. It assigns or returns a `String` object. If the `ParameterStyle` is `Bare`, then this property will be ignored.

```
public string RequestElementName {get; set;}
```

RequestNamespace

Each SOAP request has an XML namespace associated with it. The default namespace for all .NET Web Services is `http://tempuri.org/`. This property allows you to declare an alternative namespace for a web method for its SOAP request. It assigns or returns a `String` object.

```
public string RequestNamespace {get; set;}
```

ResponseElementName

As you may have guessed, this property serves the same purpose as `RequestElementName`, except that it defines parameter names for the SOAP Response. So, for a `ParameterStyle` of `Wrapped`, this property defines the element wrapper to use for the parameters of the SOAP Response. Again, the default value is the name of the Web Service method used. It assigns or returns a `String` object. If the `ParameterStyle` is `Bare`, then this property will be ignored.

```
public string ResponseElementName {get; set;}
```

ResponseNamespace

This property mirrors the `RequestNamespace` property for the SOAP Response. Again, the default namespace for the response is `http://tempuri.org/`. This property lets you specify a different namespace for a web method for its SOAP response. It assigns or returns a `String` object.

It should be noted that the `ResponseNamespace` does not have to be different from the `RequestNamespace`. Namespaces are simply used to identify a particular SOAP message to a Web Service (if on the server) or match a request with a response message (if on the client).

```
public string ResponseNamespace {get; set;}
```

The following code is taken from `SoapRpcMethodAttributeUsage.asmx.cs`, an ASP.NET Web Service class in the code download for this chapter, detailing how you can set some of the properties of this class to override the default definitions during the creation of a WSDL file:

```
//Override the default Document Style of encoding for this web method
//by using SoapRpcMethodAttribute
[WebMethod(), SoapRpcMethod(RequestElementName="IsbnQueryGetPrice",
RequestNamespace="http://localhost/SoapRpcMethodAttributeUsage/IsbnQuery",
ResponseElementName="IsbnQueryGetPriceResponse",
ResponseNamespace="http://localhost/SoapRpcMethodAttributeUsage/IsbnQuery",
Action="http://localhost/SoapRpcMethodAttributeUsage/GetPrice")]
   public double GetPrice(string Isbn)
```

SoapRpcServiceAttribute Class

This class is used to customize SOAP Requests or SOAP Responses for a particular Web Service. Any changes made using this class will be reflected in the WSDL schema definition file produced by the `wsdl.exe`. Unlike the `SoapRpcMethodAttribute` class, these values are set at service level using a service-level attribute. This attribute sets the default encoding style for all the web methods in the Web Service to RPC formatting. The web methods if need be, can override the default behavior set by this attribute using `SoapRpcMethodAttribute` or `SoapRpcMethodAttribute`.

It is inherited from `System.Attribute` and it cannot be further inherited.

SoapRpcServiceAttribute Class Public Methods

- ❑ `Equals` – inherited from `System.Object`, see Introduction for details
- ❑ **GetHashCode**
- ❑ `GetType` – inherited from `System.Object`, see Introduction for details
- ❑ **IsDefaultAttribute**
- ❑ **Match**
- ❑ `ToString` – inherited from `System.Object`, see Introduction for details

GetHashCode

The `GetHashCode` method returns the hash code for the current instance of the object. It is inherited from `System.Attribute`.

```
public override int GetHashCode();
```

IsDefaultAttribute

The `IsDefaultAttribute` method, if overridden, is used to indicate whether the values of the current instance are equal to the values of the default instance of the object. It is inherited from `System.Attribute` and is not overridden in this class. As it is not overridden here, it always returns `false` irrespective of the current object holding default values or not.

```
public virtual bool IsDefaultAttribute();
```

Match

The `Match` method, if overridden, is used to compare the current instance with another object. It is inherited from `System.Attribute` and is not overridden in this class. As it is not overridden here, it returns the same value that the `Equals` method would return.

```
public virtual bool Match(object obj);
```

SoapRpcServiceAttribute Class Protected Methods

- ❑ `Finalize` – inherited from `System.Object`, see Introduction for details
- ❑ `MemberwiseClone` – inherited from `System.Object`, see Introduction for details

SoapRpcServiceAttribute Class Public Properties

- ❑ **RoutingStyle**
- ❑ `TypeId` – inherited from `System.Attribute`, not implemented in this class.

This property gets or sets how SOAP messages are routed. It specifies whether the `SOAPAction` header should be populated or not. It assigns a routing style as one of the two values of the enumeration `System.Web.Services.Protocols.SoapServiceRoutingStyle`: either `RequestElement` or `SoapAction`.

The default is `SoapAction`, which means the message is routed on the basis of the `SOAPAction` header. When it is set to `RequestElement`, the message is routed on the basis of the first child element of the `<Body>` element and the `SOAPAction` header can be left blank.

See the `SoapServiceRoutingStyle` enumeration section later in this chapter for further explanation.

```
public SoapServiceRoutingStyle RoutingStyle {get; set;}
```

The following code is taken from `SoapRpcServiceAttributeUsage.asmx.cs`, an ASP.NET Web Service class file, detailing how you can set some of the properties of this class that will override the default definitions during the creation of the WSDL file for all operations in the Web Service:

```
[WebService(Namespace="http://localhost/SoapRpcServiceAttributeUsage/"),
SoapRpcService(RoutingStyle=SoapServiceRoutingStyle.RequestElement)]
  public class SoapRpcServiceAttributeUsage : System.Web.Services.WebService
```

System.Web.Services.Protocols Enumerations

LogicalMethodTypes

This enumeration specifies the method by which the current Web Service was invoked.

It applies to the following member of the `System.Web.Services.Protocols` namespace:

❑   `LogicalMethodInfo`

Member Name	Description	Value
Sync	The current Web Service was invoked synchronously	1
Async	The current Web Service was invoked asynchronously	2

SoapHeaderDirection

This enumeration specifies the intended recipient of the attached `SoapHeader`.

It applies to the following member of the System.Web.Services.Protocols namespace:

❑   SoapHeaderAttribute

Member Name	Description	Value
In	The intended recipient for this header is the Web Service. The client should therefore ignore this header.	1
Out	The intended recipient for this header is the client. The Web Service should therefore ignore this header.	2
InOut	The current header contains information that is required by both Web Service and client.	3

SoapMessageStage

On trapping an event during the processing of a SOAP message, this enumeration determines the stage that the current SOAP message has reached.

The meaning of the enumeration depends on whether the event was trapped on the server or client, and therefore the table below contains two descriptions for each value.
Applies to the following members of the System.Web.Services.Protocols namespace:

❑   SoapClientMessage

❑   SoapServerMessage

❑   SoapMessage

Member Name	Description	Value
BeforeSerialize	CLIENT: Occurs after a client calls a Web Service, but before the SOAP request has been serialized. SERVER: Occurs after the Web Service returns results, but before the SOAP response has been serialized.	1
AfterSerialize	CLIENT: Occurs after a client call to a Web Service is serialized, but before sending the SOAP request to the server. SERVER: Occurs after the results from a Web Service are serialized, but before sending the SOAP response to the client.	2

Table continued on following page

Member Name	Description	Value
BeforeDeserialize	CLIENT: Occurs after the network response for a Web Service has been received, but before the SOAP response has been de-serialized. SERVER: Occurs after a network request for a Web Service is received, but before the SOAP request has been de-serialized.	4
AfterDeserialize	CLIENT: Occurs after the network response for a Web Service has been de-serialized, but before the client receives the results. SERVER: Occurs after a network request for a Web Service has been de-serialized, but before the Web Service has been called.	8

SoapParameterStyle

Indicates the position of SOAP parameters during transfer. Using this enumeration, you can fine-tune exactly where the parameters for SOAP Requests and Responses are to be contained.

Applies to the following members of the `System.Web.Services.Protocols` namespace:

- ❑ `SoapDocumentServiceAttribute`
- ❑ `SoapDocumentMethodAttribute`
- ❑ `SoapRpcServiceAttribute`
- ❑ `SoapRpcMethodAttribute`

Member Name	Description	Value
Default	Indicates the default value for the Web Service. The default will either be `Wrapped`, or the value declared by `SoapDocumentServiceAttribute` if any.	0
Bare	The Web Service method parameters are not wrapped by a container element, and instead appear unadorned directly after the Body element of SOAP Requests and Responses.	1
Wrapped	The Web Service parameters will be wrapped within container elements, which are in turn held inside the SOAP Body element.	2

SoapServiceRoutingStyle

Applies to the following members of the System.Web.Services.Protocols namespace:

- ❑ SoapRpcServiceAttribute
- ❑ SoapDocumentServiceAttribute

Member Name	Description	Value
RequestElement	Indicates that the SOAP message should be routed according to the value set in the first child element following the Body element in the SOAP message.	1
SoapAction	Indicates that the SOAP message should be routed according to the value set in the Body element in the SOAP message.	0

Data in ASP.NET

The .NET Framework provides robust data access mechanisms collectively called ADO.NET. As the name implies, ADO.NET is the "next generation" incarnation of ADO and the latest in the *very* long line of Microsoft data access APIs, solutions, and technologies that precede it. This chapter will provide high-level coverage of ADO.NET. For a full reference to this topic, you may want to look at the *ADO.NET Programmer's Reference*, ISBN 1-86100-558-X.

Using the Examples

A note about the examples in this chapter: while the intention of the examples is to provide a clear understanding of connecting to and working with a variety of data sources, there is also a need for some consistency in the examples. To that end, there are several examples of connecting to different databases, but many of the examples will use a simple example database on SQL Server, which holds information about movies and actors. Attempts will be made throughout the chapter to point out the differences in working with different data sources as they pertain to .NET. In order to use the examples, either set up the database manually, or use the script file included in the source code download (`wroxmoviedb.sql`) to create the database on SQL Server or the Microsoft Data Engine (MSDE).

The structure of the database used for the examples is shown overleaf and is extremely simple. The database consists of four tables: `Movie`, `Actor`, `Genre`, and `MovieActor`. Movies have a genre `ID` that relates them to a genre, while the `MovieActor` table acts as a go-between to connect `Actors` to `Movies`:

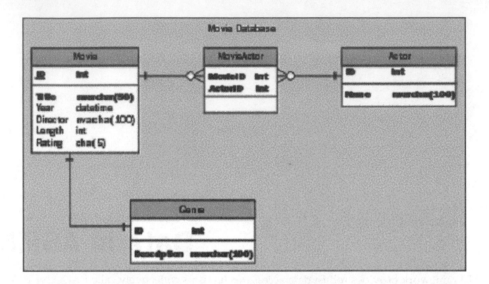

System.Data Namespace Overview

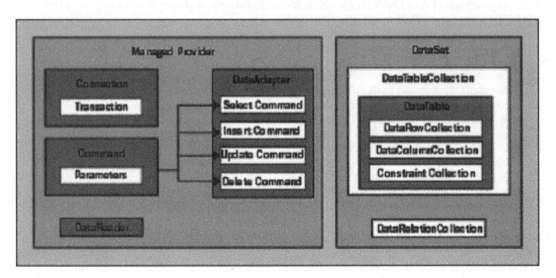

ADO.NET is the most recent culmination of Microsoft's efforts towards "Universal Data Access", wherein a single API provides data access and management to heterogeneous sources including Exchange, databases, Active Directory, text, and, perhaps most importantly due to its growing ubiquity, XML. The System.Data namespace contains the classes related to data access in .NET. These classes can be divided into three logical partitions:

❑ Common base classes

❑ .NET Managed Providers classes

❑ The DataSet and related classes

The common base classes provided functionality to both the managed providers and the `DataSet` and related classes. Managed providers serve as the command and control link between your application and a data store. The `DataSet` and related classes abstract and provide a persistently *disconnected* instance of the data you are working with within the data store. Working in concert, your application, the managed provider, and the `DataSet` synchronize the disconnected data with the data store. The advantage of this perpetually disconnected model is that all ADO.NET applications are inherently more scalable and "distributed application" friendly, as opposed to traditional applications that maintain a persistent connection to a data store like a SQL database.

The namespace itself is further divided to partition the included classes and interfaces. The namespace breaks down as follows:

❑ `System.Data` – this is the root of the namespace and holds the definition for the majority of the interfaces and classes used when accessing data, including the `DataSet` and `IdataReader`.

❑ `System.Data.Common` – contains classes that provide base functionality to .NET managed provider implementations such as Data Adapters and Table Mappings.

❑ `System.Data.Odbc*` – contains the classes necessary to work with data using ODBC drivers. This namespace constitutes the managed provider for ODBC.

❑ `System.Data.OleDb` – contains the classes necessary to work with data from OLEDB-compliant data sources. This namespace constitutes the managed provider for OLEDB.

❑ `System.Data.SqlClient` – contains the classes necessary to work with data from SQL Server. This namespace constitutes the managed provider for SQL Server.

❑ `System.Data.SqlTypes` – provides classes that map directly to native data types in SQL Server to enhance performance when working with data from SQL Server.

> **Note: The `System.Data.Odbc` namespace is a separate download available from Microsoft. It is useful for those connecting to ODBC-accessible data, but it is not part of the default reference .NET Framework.**

As you can see, each managed provider has its own namespace within the `System.Data` hierarchy. As future providers are written, they too will have their own namespace. For example, an Oracle Managed Provider would likely live in the `System.Data.Oracle` namespace. As the chapter progresses we will be using classes from all of the namespaces contained within the `System.Data` namespace.

Because managed providers will need to support a base level of functionality and expose standard interfaces, switching from one provider to another will not be difficult. In fact, using interfaces and configuration information, applications should theoretically be able to have the data source switched with no code changes. Of course, things never go this smoothly and every data source will have its intricacies and differences, but this makes for a very easy-to-use framework, with a gentle learning curve for new data sources.

A managed provider represents a set of classes whose purpose is to communicate with and control a data source. This involves connecting to the source, executing commands against it, and extracting data from it. A managed provider includes the following classes to accomplish this:

❑ Connection – the Connection class is responsible for opening and managing the physical connection to the data source.

❑ Command – the Command class represents a command to be executed against the data source such as an INSERT, UPDATE, DELETE, or SELECT. A command uses the connection to execute against the data source.

❑ DataReader – the DataReader class is responsible for providing a fast, forward-only, stream of data from the data source. Its sole responsibility is to read the data out as fast as it can.

❑ DataAdapter – the DataAdapter class is responsible for the communication between a DataSet and the data source. The DataAdapter uses command objects to execute commands against the data source on behalf of a DataSet, and the DataAdapter is used to fill a DataSet with data.

❑ Parameter – the Parameter class represents a parameter for a command. An example would be a parameter to be passed to a stored procedure in a database. Not all commands have parameters.

❑ Transaction – the Transaction class represents an executing transaction against the data source. Because the Connection class is responsible for communication with the data source the Transaction class is tied to the connection.

In addition to those classes provided by each of the managed providers, the ADO.NET framework provides a base set of classes for working with data, which includes the following:

❑ Constraint – the Constraint class represents constraints placed on the data in a DataTable or DataSet that force the data to meet certain requirements. A typical example would be a constraint that indicates that a DataColumn must have unique values in each of its rows.

❑ DataColumn – the DataColumn class represents a specific column of data in a DataTable and provides the type information for all items in that column, such as whether they are an Integer or a String.

❑ DataRelation – the DataRelation class represents a relation, or connection, between two DataTables. This relation can then be used to extract data from one table that is related to the data in another.

❑ DataRow – the DataRow class represents a single row of data in a DataTable.

❑ DataSet – The DataSet class is responsible for managing data outside of a data source. In fact, this object has no knowledge of the source of its data and can be used to manage data independent of any physical data source.

❑ DataTable – the DataTable represents a collection of rows and columns of data. Its structure is similar to that of a table in a relational database. The DataTable is often housed in a DataSet but can be used on its own as a collection of data.

As you can see, there is a rich set of objects that provide a great deal of power in working with data.

Connections and Transactions

Connections provide the mechanism for opening and maintaining communication with the data source. In addition, the `Connection` class is responsible for starting transactions and, optionally, creating `Command` objects. There is no concrete base class for a `Connection`; rather an interface, `IDbConnection`, is defined in the `System.Data` namespace. This interface is then implemented by managed providers on *their* connection classes. Using interface inheritance in this way helps ensure that all managed providers support a base set of features.

In the examples below, we open connections to a variety of data sources using the various managed providers. Full namespace qualifications are given for the items to help make it clear which provider is being used. These samples can be run in almost any function, but can be found in the `ConnectionsAndCommands.aspx.cs` files in the source code for the book.

> In order to use the **Microsoft.Data.Odbc** classes, you will have to download them from Microsoft first at:
>
> **http://support.microsoft.com/default.aspx?scid=kb;EN-US;q310985#2**
>
> Follow the installation instructions on that page.

OdbcConnection.Open

```
private const string ExcelConnStr =
  @"Driver=Microsoft Excel Driver (*.xls);DBQ=c:\DataAppendix\sales.xls";

...

OdbcConnection ExcelConnection = new OdbcConnection(ExcelConnStr);

...

ExcelConnection.Open()
```

OleDbConnection.Open

```
string conString = @"Provider=Microsoft.Jet.OleDb.4.0;" +
                    @"Data source=c:\DataAppendix\grocertogo.mdb;";
//OleDb Connection open
//NOTE the path to the grocer to go sample database
OleDbConnection AccessConnection = new OleDbConnection (conString);

try
{
  AccessConnection.Open();
```

As you can see, the only real difference that comes into play when opening connections is the connection string we pass to the constructor of our `Connection` class. This information points the provider to the database using the appropriate driver where necessary.

Connecting to a SQL Server database using the SQL Server Managed Provider is slightly different from the ODBC and OLEDB connection methods:

SqlClientConnection.Open

```
private const string SqlPubsConnStr =
              @"Data Source=(local);database=pubs;uid=sa;pwd=";

...

SqlConnection SqlServer = new SqlConnection(SqlPubsConnStr);

...

SqlServer.Open();
```

Once we have a connection open to the data source, the other actions we take are very similar regardless of the provider. For that reason, the rest of the examples in this chapter will use the various providers at different points rather than showing all three providers for each example.

Now that we have a connection open, we can create a transaction in which our actions can be ensured to all complete or all fail. We do this by calling the `BeginTransaction` method of the connection object, which returns an object implementing the `IDbTransaction` interface. We then use this object to either commit or roll back our transaction.

Example: Carrying Out Transactions

This code is in the `ConnectionsAndCommands.aspx.cs` file in the code download.

```
...
private void SqlOpen()
{
  SqlConnection SqlServer = new SqlConnection(SqlPubsConnStr);
  IDbTransaction PubsTransaction = null;    //SQL Transaction

  //implement our logic in a try, catch, finally block to properly
  //catch exceptions in our code
  try
  {
    SqlCommand PubsCommand = SqlServer.CreateCommand();
    PubsCommand.CommandText = "select * from authors;select * from titles";

    //open the connection
    SqlServer.Open();

    //get a connection object back as we begin the transaction
    PubsTransaction =
        SqlServer.BeginTransaction(IsolationLevel.ReadUncommitted);
    PubsCommand.Transaction = (SqlTransaction)PubsTransaction;
    PubsCommand.ExecuteNonQuery();

    //if there were no errors, commit the transaction
```

```
        PubsTransaction.Commit();
        Response.Write(SqlServer.ServerVersion.ToString() + "<br>");
    }
    catch(SqlException SqlEX)
    {
      Response.Write("Error opening connection to local server.  Be sure " +
                     "the username and password are correct.");
      Response.Write(SqlEX.ToString());

      //rollback our transaction if there was an error.
      PubsTransaction.Rollback();
    }
    finally
    {
      //close the connection whether we succeeded or failed
      SqlServer.Close();
      //call dispose to release resources in the connection
      SqlServer.Dispose();
    }
}
...
```

In this example, we open a connection and begin a transaction. We would then execute the code we want to have transacted and commit the transaction. Notice that in our error handler we roll back the transaction to ensure that all of our actions are reversed because they did not all complete successfully if there was an error.

When working with transactions, it is important to begin the transaction as late as possible and commit or roll back as soon as possible. Because the items in a transaction need to be able to revert to their original state, the resources involved are often locked to other users, which can cause performance problems in your application. Likewise, when working with database connections, it is best to open the connection as late as possible and close it as early as possible to allow your application to scale appropriately.

Commands and Parameters

A command allows us to define a function for the data source to perform. Using a connection, we execute a command against the data source which may, or may not, return results. Commands have a CommandText property that defines the command action, which might be a SQL statement. The CommandText is interpreted based on the CommandType set for the command. If the command type is "StoredProcedure", then the command text is interpreted as the name of a stored procedure. If the type is "Text", then it is interpreted as a direct command. The two examples below show these two properties; we've defined one command with text for SQL, and one with a stored procedure.

> Note that in order for a command to be executed, it must be associated with a
> connection that is open at the time the command is executed.

We associate a command with a connection by passing the Connection object to the constructor of the command, or by setting the Connection property of the command.

777

In this C# example we open a connection and execute a stored procedure with the `ExecuteReader` method of the command object:

Example: Executing a Stored Procedure

This code is in the `ConnectionsAndCommands.aspx.cs` file in the code download for this chapter. The `AuthorTitles` stored procedure was created when we ran the `wroxmoviedb.sql` file.

```
...
private void UseCommandProc()
{
  //dimension connection and command objects as well as a reader
  SqlConnection PubsConnection =
  new SqlConnection(SqlPubsConnStr);

  SqlCommand PubsCommand;
  SqlDataReader PubsReader;

  //create the command object from the connection which associates the
  //command with the connection (this is equivalent to setting the
  //connection property on the command)
  PubsCommand = PubsConnection.CreateCommand();

  //identify the name of the stored procedure as our command text
  PubsCommand.CommandText = "AuthorTitles";

  //identify the type of the command as a stored procedure
  PubsCommand.CommandType = CommandType.StoredProcedure;

  //open connection right before needing it
  PubsConnection.Open();

  //execute the command put the resulting data into a data reader we
  //identify the command behavior to close the connection when the reader
  //is closed so that we don't have to explicity close it.
  PubsReader = PubsCommand.ExecuteReader(CommandBehavior.CloseConnection);

  //DO WORK WITH READER'

  //close the reader when we are done with it
  PubsReader.Close();

  //clean up our variables.
  PubsReader = null;
  PubsCommand = null;
  PubsConnection = null;

  Response.Write
  ("<br>Stored procedure AuthorTitles called<br>");
}
...
```

We first have to define our connection and command objects. Next, we set the properties on our command object for the command text and command type. Finally, we execute our procedure, returning the results into a `DataReader` object. Notice that we specify the `CommandBehavior.CloseConnection` parameter to the `ExecuteReader` method, which tells the provider to close the connection when the `DataReader` is closing rather than waiting for an explicit command to close the connection as well.

In this next example we use the ODBC provider to query an Excel spreadsheet using a `Text` command. The primary differences are in the connection string used to connect to the data source and the command text and the type set on the command object.

Example: Executing a Text-Based Command

This code is in the `ConnectionsAndCommands.aspx.cs` file in the code download for this chapter.

```
...

private void UseText()
{

  //dimension command and connection objects along with reader
  OdbcConnection ExcelConnection = new OdbcConnection(ExcelConnStr);
  OdbcCommand ExcelCommand;
  OdbcDataReader ExcelReader;

  //create connection from command and set its properties
  ExcelCommand = ExcelConnection.CreateCommand();
  ExcelCommand.CommandText = "SELECT * FROM SalesFigures";
  ExcelCommand.CommandType = CommandType.Text;

  //open the connection
  ExcelConnection.Open();

  //execute the command and retrive the data into a reader
  ExcelReader =
          ExcelCommand.ExecuteReader(CommandBehavior.CloseConnection);

  //'''DO WORK WITH READER HERE'''

  while(ExcelReader.Read())
  {
    Response.Write(ExcelReader.GetString(0));
  }

  //close the reader and therefore the connection
  ExcelReader.Close();

  //clean up our variables
  ExcelReader = null;
```

```
        ExcelCommand = null;
        ExcelConnection = null;

    }
    ...
```

In both of the above examples, we used the `ExecuteReader` method of the `Command` object to return an object implementing the `IDataReader` interface. This is the method to use if you are returning rows of data from a data source. There are three different methods to execute commands, however, each with its own purpose. They include:

❑ `ExecuteNonQuery`

❑ `ExecuteReader`

❑ `ExecuteScalar`

The `ExecuteNonQuery` method is used when the command you are executing will not return rows of data. You can still have output parameters available to retrieve data and the method will return the number of rows affected. The `ExecuteScalar` method is used to return a single value, such as a sum or average. It returns the first item in the first column of the resulting records from the command. In addition, the SQL Server managed provider adds another version of this method, `ExecuteXmlReader`. This method is used when querying SQL Server for XML data and can be consumed by the `ReadXml` method of the `DataSet`.

In the example above, we used a stored procedure to return data. In many cases, a stored procedure will require input or output parameters. Input parameters can be used to pass information into the stored procedure, and output parameters can be used when you need to retrieve discrete values rather than whole rows. In order to pass parameters along with a command, we first create and define the parameters, and then add them to the command object's parameters collection. In the example below we call a simple stored procedure to return all movies with an R rating:

Example: Executing a Parameterized Procedure

This code is in the `ConnectionsAndCommands.aspx.cs` file in the code download for this chapter.

```
    ...
    private void CommandWithParameters()
    {

        //create connection and command objects
        OleDbConnection MovieConnection =
                        new OleDbConnection(OleDbConnStr);
        OleDbCommand MovieCommand;
        OleDbDataReader MovieReader;

        //set the properties for the command object
        MovieCommand = MovieConnection.CreateCommand();
        MovieCommand.CommandText = "GetMovieByRating";
        MovieCommand.CommandType = CommandType.StoredProcedure;
```

```
           //create an input parameter and add it to the collection
           OleDbParameter MovieParam = new OleDbParameter
                           ("@rating", OleDbType.VarChar, 5);
           MovieParam.Direction = ParameterDirection.Input;
           MovieParam.Value = "R";
           MovieCommand.Parameters.Add(MovieParam);

           //open the connection when we need it, and not before
           MovieConnection.Open();

           //fill the reader with the movie details.
           MovieReader = MovieCommand.ExecuteReader
                       (CommandBehavior.CloseConnection);

           //do some work with the data reader here
           while(MovieReader.Read())
           {
             Response.Write(MovieReader["title"] + "<br>");
           }

           //close the data reader, and thus the connection
           //based on the command behavior specified when we executed
           MovieReader.Close();

           //clean up variables
           MovieReader = null;
           MovieCommand = null;
           MovieConnection = null;
         }
         ...
```

In this example we created an input parameter by specifying ParameterDirection.Input as the Direction property of the parameter class. We then also created a return value parameter, which has its own direction enumerated value specifying it as a return value only. We then open the connection and run the stored procedure, placing the results in the DataReader. We could have used an output parameter to retrieve information from the database as well.

Another item to notice is the parameter we passed to the ExecuteReader method of the Command object. This command behavior parameter allows definition of specific behaviors about how the command will execute. In our example, we have specified CommandBehavior.CloseConnection, which closes the database connection as soon as the associated DataReader is closed. This helps prevent problems that may arise from forgetting to close a connection.

A stored procedure may only need to return a few values, and not rows of data. In these cases we can use parameters to get data out of a data source. An example of using an output parameter is shown next. In this example, we query our database for the genre of a given movie and its rating. Rather than return a reader, we simply return the data in two output parameters to our stored procedure:

This code is in the `ConnectionsAndCommands.aspx.cs` file in the code download for this chapter.

```
...
private void OutputParameters()
{

  //create connection and command objects
  SqlConnection MovieConnection = new SqlConnection(SqlConnStr);
  SqlCommand MovieCommand = new SqlCommand("GetGenreRating",
                                           MovieConnection);

  //set command type to stored procedure
  MovieCommand.CommandType = CommandType.StoredProcedure;

  //create and add all of the parameters for the stored procedure
  MovieCommand.Parameters.Add(new SqlParameter("@title",
                                         SqlDbType.VarChar, 50));
  MovieCommand.Parameters.Add(new SqlParameter("@genre",
                                         SqlDbType.VarChar, 100));
  MovieCommand.Parameters.Add(new SqlParameter("@rating",
                                         SqlDbType.VarChar, 5));

  //set the direction attribute for all of the parameter and the value for
  //the input parameter
  MovieCommand.Parameters["@title"].Direction = ParameterDirection.Input;
  MovieCommand.Parameters["@genre"].Direction = ParameterDirection.Output;
  MovieCommand.Parameters["@rating"].Direction = ParameterDirection.Output;
  MovieCommand.Parameters["@title"].Value = "Matrix";

  //open the connection
  MovieConnection.Open();

  //execute the query getting the number of rows affected
  int RecordsAffected;
  RecordsAffected = MovieCommand.ExecuteNonQuery();

  //write out the parameters, we could also put them in variables
  Response.Write("Matrix<br>");
  Response.Write("Rating: " +
                 MovieCommand.Parameters["@rating"].Value + "<br>");
  Response.Write("Genre: " +
                 MovieCommand.Parameters["@genre"].Value + "<br>");

  //close the database connection as soon as we are done with it
  MovieConnection.Close();

  //clean up our objects
  MovieConnection = null;
  MovieCommand = null;
}
...
```

In this example we were able to get data from the database without getting an entire rowset, and thus gained better performance. We created our connection and command objects as before and then created the individual parameter objects and added them to the parameters collection of the command object. Next, we had to set the direction for the parameters to indicate those items that are our output parameters. Finally, we executed the query and accessed the parameters through the parameters collection of the command to get the output.

> If the data coming back from a query is a single row, consider using output parameters and the **ExecuteNonQuery** method to achieve the best performance. Because a **DataReader** does not have to be created, this method provides better performance.

DataReader

The DataReader provides read-only, forward-only, access to a data stream coming from a data source. A DataReader is not created directly; instead it is created by using the ExecuteReader method of the Command object. Once a DataReader has been retrieved by executing a command the Read method moves the reader to the next record in the ResultSet. Usually, when looping through the results syntax similar to the following will be used:

```
while(Reader.Read())
{
   'access the values in the row
   Response.Write(Reader.Item("title"))
}
```

The Read method returns a Boolean value indicating whether or not the cursor was moved to the next record. A value of false indicates that the reader has reached the end of the ResultSet.

Once the DataReader is positioned on a row, there are a variety of methods that allow retrieval of items from the row in their native data type such as GetString and GetDateTime. In addition, using the Item property we can get an item from the row using the name or index of the field. Remember, when performance is a consideration, the methods that allow access to the native types should be used, as they do not require the returned value to be cast.

In the case where multiple Resultsets are returned in one query, the NextResult method allows movement to the next ResultSet. The following example loops through the ResultSets and the records within them outputting the values to the ASP.NET response.

Example: DataReader

This code is in the `ConnectionsAndCommands.aspx.cs` file in the code download for this chapter.

```
...
private void ReaderMultipleResultsets()
{
  //dimension variables
  SqlConnection MovieConnection = new SqlConnection(SqlConnStr);
  SqlCommand MovieCommand;
  SqlDataReader MovieReader;
  int Counter;

  //create command and set properties
  MovieCommand = MovieConnection.CreateCommand();
  MovieCommand.CommandText = "Select * from actor;select * from movie";
  MovieCommand.CommandType = CommandType.Text;

  //open the connection to the data source
  MovieConnection.Open();

  //execute command create reader
  MovieReader =
            MovieCommand.ExecuteReader(CommandBehavior.CloseConnection);

  //output the results to table in HTML
  Response.Write("<table>");

  //loop through the resultsets, being sure to execute at least once
  do
  {
    //create headers for the table using the schema table information
    //from the datareader object.  We get the column names from the first
    //column of the table returned.
    Response.Write("<tr>");
    for(Counter = 0; Counter < MovieReader.FieldCount; Counter++)
    {
      Response.Write("<th>" +
              MovieReader.GetSchemaTable().Rows[Counter][0] + "</th>");
    }

    Response.Write("</tr>");

    //loop through the fields and write out their value in a
    //table cell element as long as there are more values
    while(MovieReader.Read())
    {
      Response.Write("<tr>");
      for(Counter = 0; Counter < MovieReader.FieldCount; Counter++)
        Response.Write("<td>" + MovieReader[Counter] + "</td>");
    }
    Response.Write("</tr>");
  }
```

```
        //loop as long as their are more resultsets
        while(MovieReader.NextResult());

        //close the reader which closes the connection because of the
        //parameter we passed to the ExecuteReader method
        MovieReader.Close();

        //close the table and cleanup
        Response.Write("</table>");

        MovieReader = null;
        MovieCommand = null;
        MovieConnection = null;

    }
    ...
```

In this example we executed a command that, because it had multiple SQL statements in it, returned multiple `ResultSets`. Because of this, we were able to use the `NextResult` method of the `DataReader` to move to the second `ResultSet` and get its values as well. We loop through the `ResultSets` and, within that loop, we also loop through the rows and then the fields to build an HTML table. This approach is for demonstration purposes only as databinding, covered later in this chapter, provides a much easier way to achieve the same results.

DataAdapter

The `DataAdapter` serves as the communication mechanism between a managed provider and the `DataSet`. As can be seen from the figure earlier in the chapter, the `DataAdapter` is essentially a set of command objects. It uses these command objects to execute commands against the data source on behalf of the `DataSet`. There is a separate command for each of the four actions that can typically be performed against data: `SELECT`, `INSERT`, `UPDATE`, and `DELETE`. Each of these commands can be manipulated and configured independently of the others.

When creating a `DataAdapter`, the constructor optionally allows passing in information about the `SELECT` command and the connection. This allows easy creation of a `DataAdapter` that can extract data from a data source, but with no ability to update the data source.

In order to update the data source, we would have to create the `INSERT`, `UPDATE`, and `DELETE` commands. This can be done in one of two ways: one can manually define and assign the various commands, or use a `CommandBuilder` to automatically build the other commands based on the `SELECT` command and the table schema. In the following examples, we show both the manual process of setting up the commands and the automatic process.

This code is in the `ConnectionsAndCommands.aspx.cs` file in the code download for this chapter.

```
...
private void CommandBuilderManual()
{
  //create data variables
  SqlDataAdapter MovieDataAdapter =
               new SqlDataAdapter("select * from actor", SqlConnStr);
  DataSet MovieDataset = new DataSet();
  DataRow MovieDataRow;

  //create an textbased update command with parameters
  MovieDataAdapter.UpdateCommand = new SqlCommand();
  MovieDataAdapter.UpdateCommand.CommandText =
                          "UPDATE actor SET name=@name WHERE id=@id";
  MovieDataAdapter.UpdateCommand.CommandType = CommandType.Text;
  MovieDataAdapter.UpdateCommand.Connection =
                           MovieDataAdapter.SelectCommand.Connection;
  MovieDataAdapter.UpdateCommand.Parameters.Add
          (new SqlParameter("@name", SqlDbType.VarChar, 50, "Name"));
  MovieDataAdapter.UpdateCommand.Parameters.Add
                  (new SqlParameter("@id", SqlDbType.Int, 4, "ID"));

  //create an insert command to add new records to the
  //database when they are added to the data set.
  MovieDataAdapter.InsertCommand = new SqlCommand();
  MovieDataAdapter.InsertCommand.CommandText =
                             "insert actor(Name) values(@name)";
  MovieDataAdapter.InsertCommand.CommandType = CommandType.Text;
  MovieDataAdapter.InsertCommand.Connection =
  MovieDataAdapter.SelectCommand.Connection;
  MovieDataAdapter.InsertCommand.Parameters.Add
      (new SqlParameter("@name", SqlDbType.VarChar, 50, "Name"));

  //create the delete command and set its parameters
  MovieDataAdapter.DeleteCommand = new SqlCommand();
  MovieDataAdapter.DeleteCommand.CommandText =
                                    "delete actor where id=@id";
  MovieDataAdapter.DeleteCommand.CommandType = CommandType.Text;
  MovieDataAdapter.DeleteCommand.Connection =
                          MovieDataAdapter.SelectCommand.Connection;
  MovieDataAdapter.DeleteCommand.Parameters.Add
              (new SqlParameter("@id", SqlDbType.VarChar, 50, "ID"));

  //fill the dataset creating a table named "Actor"
  MovieDataAdapter.Fill(MovieDataset, "Actor");

  //add a new row to the dataset
  MovieDataRow = MovieDataset.Tables["Actor"].NewRow();
  MovieDataRow["name"] = "Geena Davis";
```

```
      MovieDataset.Tables["Actor"].Rows.Add(MovieDataRow);

      //update the database with the new changes.
      MovieDataAdapter.Update(MovieDataset, "Actor");

      Response.Write("Adapter built manually");
    }
    ...
```

In this example we have created the command objects, on their own, by manually assigning command text, command type, and parameters to the UPDATE, INSERT, and DELETE commands. Remember that the SELECT command can be specified in the constructor as demonstrated. We will touch on the Fill and Update methods in a bit, but first we will look at another way to build the commands using the CommandBuilder object. The CommandBuilder is a class that works with the DataAdapter to automatically build INSERT, UPDATE, and DELETE commands for the DataAdapter. CommandBuilder can be used as long as the source data is coming from a single table, and the schema information is known. The example below does just what we saw in the last example, but with much less code:

Example: Using the CommandBuilder Object

This code is in the ConnectionsAndCommands.aspx.cs file in the code download for this chapter.

```
...
private void CommandBuilderAuto()
{
  //create data variables
  SqlDataAdapter MovieDataAdapter = new SqlDataAdapter
                                ("select * from actor", SqlConnStr);
  DataSet MovieDataset = new DataSet();
  DataRow MovieDataRow;

  //create a new SqlCommandBuilder to build our commands for us
  //and pass in the data adapter to provide the select command and
  //allow the function to create the other command
  SqlCommandBuilder MovieCommandBuilder =
                          new SqlCommandBuilder(MovieDataAdapter);

  //fill the dataset creating a table named "Actor"
  MovieDataAdapter.Fill(MovieDataset, "Actor");

  //add a new row to the dataset
  MovieDataRow = MovieDataset.Tables["Actor"].NewRow();
  MovieDataRow["name"] = "Jeff Goldblum";
  MovieDataset.Tables["Actor"].Rows.Add(MovieDataRow);

  //update the database with the new changes.
```

```
        MovieDataAdapter.Update(MovieDataset, "Actor");

        Response.Write("<br>Adapter built automatically");
    }
    ...
```

The highlighted text in the above example takes the place of all the code we had to write in the previous example. The CommandBuilder can greatly reduce the task of creating commands when dealing with a single table. However, it is confined to working with a single table and is therefore limited in application.

The CommandBuilder uses the SelectCommand to get schema information about the table and uses that information to build the other commands, and you must therefore have a primary key defined on your table, and your data source must support the retrieval of schema information. In order to update and delete properly, the command must be able to reference a key for the row, or you need to build the command yourself to ensure that the proper rows are updated. The need to get schema information necessitates an additional call to the data source, which can also impact on performance. Keep these things in mind as you consider whether to use the CommandBuilder, or to write the code yourself. Additionally, the commands built by the CommandBuilder are SQL statements executed as text commands. With data sources such as SQL Server, a large performance gain can be achieved by using stored procedures. In order to use stored procedures for these commands, you must define the commands manually.

In the previous examples, we also used two other methods of the DataAdapter: Fill and Update. Both take a DataSet object and an optional table name as input parameters. There are several overloaded versions of these methods.

The Fill method actually executes the SelectCommand and loads the resulting data into the specified table, or a table with the name "Table1" if no name is specified. Internally, what this means is that the DataAdapter executes the SELECT command and gets a DataReader object back, which it then uses to create the structure of the DataSet. When updating, the DataSet and an optional table name are provided. The DataAdapter then uses information in the DataSet about the current state of the rows to call the UPDATE, INSERT, and DELETE commands to make sure the data in the data source matches that in the DataSet. The DataAdapter will open the connection associated with the SELECT command if it is not already opened. The DataAdapter will also close the connection after it is done, but only if it opened it in the first place.

If we need the schema of the data source in our DataSet or DataTable, then we can use the FillSchema method, which will create the schema for the DataTable to match that of the data source. This provides a quick way to build the DataTable structure without having to write all the code. However, this does require a trip to the server so there is a performance cost. For most applications, it is best to define the table schema directly if the code does not already require a trip to the data source.

Mapping

Another concept related to the DataAdapter is **mapping**. The DataAdapter provides the ability to create **table mappings** and **column mappings**. As it is the job of the DataAdapter to synchronize the DataSet and the data source, the DataAdapter needs to be able to relate, or "map", the tables and columns in the DataSet to the tables and columns in the data source. Having a mapping between the DataSet and data source tables and columns also allows the developer to use names for the tables and columns in the DataSet that differ from the names of their source table in the data source. Using mappings the DataAdapter can successfully execute the commands against the database using column and table names other than those specified in the data source.

In the example below, we query our movie database for the list of movies and map the table name and several columns to make them easier to reference in the code:

Example: Querying a Database

This code is in the Mapping.aspx.cs file in the code download for this chapter.

```
public class Mappings : System.Web.UI.Page
{
  private void Page_Load(object sender, System.EventArgs e)
  {
    Mapping();
  }

  private void Mapping()
  {

    //create connection, adapter and dataset
    SqlConnection MappingConnection = new SqlConnection
        (@"User ID=sa;Initial Catalog=WroxMovieDB;Data Source=(local);");
    SqlDataAdapter MappingAdapter = new SqlDataAdapter
                            ("SELECT * FROM MOVIE", MappingConnection);
    DataSet MappingDataSet = new DataSet();

    //create a new table mapping and then add new column mappings
    MappingAdapter.TableMappings.Add("movie", "Favorite_Movies");
    MappingAdapter.TableMappings["movie"].ColumnMappings.Add
                                            ("Length", "Minutes");
    MappingAdapter.TableMappings["movie"].ColumnMappings.Add
                                        ("Year", "Release Date");

    //fill the dataset passing in the name of the table mapping above
    //to indicate that we want to use this mapping for our schema
    MappingAdapter.Fill(MappingDataSet, "movie");

    //write out the table name and the columns to an html table by
    //looping through the columns for the headings and then through
    //the rows for the data.
    Response.Write("<Table border='1'><caption>" +
                MappingDataSet.Tables[0].TableName + "</caption><tr>");

    //column headings
```

```
      foreach(DataColumn c in MappingDataSet.Tables
                                ["Favorite_Movies"].Columns)
        Response.Write("<th>" + c.ColumnName + "</th>");

      Response.Write("</tr>");

      //table cells
      foreach(DataRow r in MappingDataSet.Tables["Favorite_Movies"].Rows)
      {
        Response.Write("<tr>");
        foreach(object item in r.ItemArray)
          Response.Write("<td>" + item.ToString() + "</td>");

        Response.Write("</tr>");
      }

    }
    ...
}
```

After defining the connection and query information, we create a table mapping to map the source table, Movie, to the local table named Favorite_Movies. Two column mappings are added as well, mapping year to Release Date and Length to Minutes. After filling the DataSet, we write the data out to an HTML table to show that the names changed.

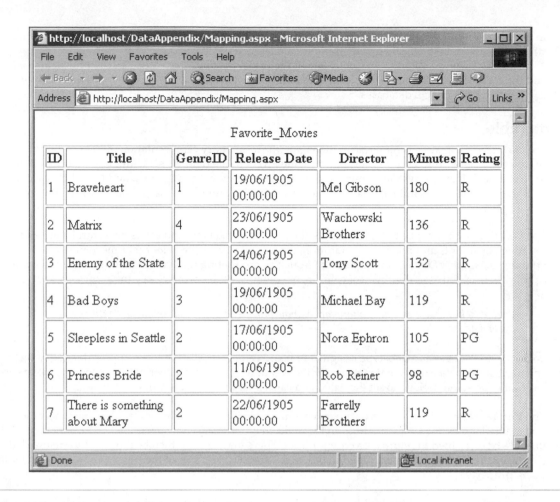

DataSet

The `DataSet` is the core of the ADO.NET framework. It acts as the local storage mechanism for data. The `DataSet` can be kept in synchronization with a data source using a `DataAdapter`, or it can be used as a standalone data storage object. In today's Internet-dominated world, user interaction with systems is typically stateless and disconnected, occurring one request at a time. In order to address this change, the `DataSet` has been developed to operate *independently* of any data source. The difference between working with a `DataSet` and the disconnected options when using an ADO `RecordSet` object is straightforward: **a DataSet cannot, *ever*, be connected.**

With XML making a significant impact on how we manage data today, one of the most important features about the `DataSet` is its ability to work with XML. In fact, the `DataSet`'s native serialization format is XML so that loading, reading, saving, and writing XML data are native operations and require less memory and processor overhead than similar methods in traditional ADO. (Using the `DataSet` to work with XML is covered in detail in Appendix B *XML in ASP.NET*.)

In order to best mimic the data source from which it is loaded, the `DataSet` provides a framework for structuring the data in a fashion that resembles a relational database. `DataTables` and `DataRelations`, are the two components that make this possible. `DataTables` hold the data itself, and the `DataRelations` allow for tying these tables together that is analogous to primary and foreign key relationships in SQL databases.

DataTable

The `DataTable` plays a central role in managing the in-memory representation of data. A `DataTable` represents a set of rows and columns that provide access to the data. Its structure is similar to that found in a relational database system. While the `DataTable` uses the `DataColumn` and `DataRow` classes to help manage the data within, it acts as the central point for gaining access to data for the `DataView` and `DataSet`.

The `DataColumns` in a `DataTable` define the schema of the table and act as the central element in defining constraints and relations. In addition, the `DataColumn` provides other mechanisms for defining the limits of data in the `DataTable` such as prohibiting null values in a column, marking a column as read-only, or identifying a column, or columns, as the primary key for a `DataTable`.

> *A primary key indicates that a column or columns provides a value that uniquely identifies each row of data.*

Each `DataColumn` has a data type assigned to it and can optionally have constraints defined, which ensure that the data exists within certain limits. A `DataColumn` can either hold a specific value or can have an expression defined to set the value to a calculated or aggregate value.

The `DataRow` provides access to data elements in a table. Each row in the data table must meet the schema defined by the `DataColumns` in the table. In order to add new data, the `NewRow` method of the `DataTable` is called to return a `DataRow` object. This `DataRow` can then be modified to ensure that no constraints will be violated and added to the `DataRowCollection` of the `DataTable` exposed by the `Rows` property.

The example below manually builds a `DataTable` by adding columns and rows. The web form for this example is simply a declaration of the code running behind the page:

Example: Building a DataTable

This code is in the `BuildTable.aspx` file in the code download for this chapter.

```
Page language="c#" Codebehind="BuildTable.aspx.cs"
    AutoEventWireup="false" Inherits="AspProgRefDataCs.BuildTable" %>
```

This code is in the `BuildTable.aspx.cs` file in the code download for this chapter.

```
...
private void BuildDataTable()
{
  //create a new data table object
  DataTable GenreTable = new DataTable("Genre");
```

```
//add two data columns to the datatable indicating name
//and type
GenreTable.Columns.Add(new DataColumn
                                ("ID", Type.GetType("System.Int32")));
GenreTable.Columns.Add(new DataColumn
                        ("Description", Type.GetType("System.String")));

//create a DataRow object
DataRow Row;

//set the row object to a new row created by the table
//this gives a new row with the schema of the table
Row = GenreTable.NewRow();

//set the values of the data
Row["ID"] = 1;
Row["Description"] = "Drama";

//add the row to the table
GenreTable.Rows.Add(Row);

//generate a new row as before
Row = GenreTable.NewRow();
Row["ID"] = 2;
Row["Description"] = "Action";

GenreTable.Rows.Add(Row);

//write out the table name and the columns to an html
//table by looping through the columns for the headings
//and then through the rows for the data.
Response.Write("<Table border='1'><caption>"
                + GenreTable.TableName + "</caption><tr>");

//column headings
foreach(DataColumn c in GenreTable.Columns)
  Response.Write("<th>" + c.ColumnName + "</th>");

Response.Write("</tr>");

//table cells

foreach(DataRow r in GenreTable.Rows)
{
  Response.Write("<tr>");
  foreach(Object item in r.ItemArray)
    Response.Write("<td>" + item.ToString() + "</td>");
  Response.Write("</tr>");
}

Response.Write("</table>");

}
...
```

We create a `DataTable` object and then add two columns to it using the `Add` method of the `Columns` property. These columns provide the schema for our table by defining the data types of the columns. We then use the `NewRow` method of the `DataTable` to return a new row, which we edit and then add into the table using the `Add` method of the `Rows` property. Once we have added a couple of rows, we write the data out to the response stream, creating an HTML table.

DataView

The `DataView` class provides a means for presenting and working with different views of a `DataTable`. In this sense a data view is analogous to a view or join in SQL in that it is a dynamically generated "view" of one or more tables. Moreover, several different `DataViews` can be pointing to a single `DataTable` and provide different views on the same data. For example, the first view could show a sorted view of all the rows still containing the original data while a second view could be a view of the rows that have been added, sorted into a different order.

The `DataView` is also used to bind data to user interface (UI) controls such as a `DataGrid` on a Windows Form or on a Web Form because the `DataView` implements a variety of interfaces allowing it to be easily enumerated and bound to other items. Remember, **if you want to bind part of a `DataSet` to a UI element, the `DataView` will be the class to use to bind to the control.**

The `DataTable` object has a `DefaultView` property, which provides a starting view on the data. This view, or a customized view of the data, can be used not only to view data, but to edit it as well. The `AllowDelete`, `AllowEdit`, and `AllowNew` properties on the `DataView` indicate the actions that can be performed on the `DataView`. These changes are then reflected in the `DataTable` that serves as the data source for the `DataView`.

The example below exhibits how to use the `DefaultView` property of a `DataTable` to retrieve a view of the data. This view is then sorted and filtered to provide a distinct look at the data and several values are edited. In addition, we create a second view, which only shows the newly added items from the table.

Example: Using the DefaultView Property of a Data Table

The web form for this example is a simple page containing two `DataGrid` controls, which will display the two views. These items are marked to run at the server so that we can use them in the code-behind page.

This code is in the `ViewSort.aspx` file in the code download for this chapter.

```
<%@ Page language="c#" Codebehind="ViewSort.aspx.cs"
        AutoEventWireup="false" Inherits="AspProgRefDataCs.ViewSort" %>
<!DOCTYPE HTML PUBLIC "-//W3C//DTD HTML 4.0 Transitional//EN" >
<HTML>
  <HEAD>
    <title>ViewSort</title>
    <meta name="GENERATOR" Content="Microsoft Visual Studio 7.0">
    <meta name="CODE_LANGUAGE" Content="C#">
    <meta name="vs_defaultClientScript" content="JavaScript">
    <meta name="vs_targetSchema"
        content="http://schemas.microsoft.com/intellisense/ie5">
```

```
    </HEAD>
    <body ms_positioning="FlowLayot">
      <form id="Form1" method="post" runat="server">
        <asp:datagrid id="MovieGrid" runat="server"></asp:datagrid>
        <br>
        <asp:datagrid id="MovieGrid2" runat="server"></asp:datagrid>
      </form>
    </body>
  </HTML>
```

The code behind is then implemented as follows:

This code is in the `ViewSort.aspx.cs` file in the code download for this chapter.

```
public class ViewSort : System.Web.UI.Page
{
  protected System.Web.UI.WebControls.DataGrid MovieGrid;
  protected System.Web.UI.WebControls.DataGrid MovieGrid2;

  private void Page_Load(object sender, System.EventArgs e)
  {
    ExampleView();
  }

  private void ExampleView()
  {

    //create connection dataAdapter and dataset
    SqlConnection ViewConnection = new SqlConnection
                          (@"User ID=sa;Initial Catalog=WroxMovieDB;"
                                          + "Data Source=(local);");
    SqlDataAdapter ViewAdapter = new SqlDataAdapter
                              ("SELECT * FROM movie", ViewConnection);
    DataSet ViewDataSet = new DataSet();

    //fill dataset
    ViewAdapter.Fill(ViewDataSet, "movie");

    //create a dataview and set it equal to the default view
    //of the movie table we have filled
    DataView MovieView = ViewDataSet.Tables["movie"].DefaultView;

    //sort the view on the Title column
    MovieView.Sort = "Title";

    //filter the rows to only show those movies with an R rating
    MovieView.RowFilter = "Rating='R'";

    //add a new row to the view, which adds it to
    //the underlying table as well.
    DataRowView NewRow = MovieView.AddNew();

    //begin editing the new row
    NewRow.BeginEdit();
    NewRow["ID"] = 8;
```

```
        NewRow["Title"] = "Traffic";
        NewRow["Director"] = "Barry Sonnenfeld";
        NewRow["Year"] = "1/1/2000";
        NewRow["Rating"] = "R";
        NewRow["GenreID"] = 4;
        NewRow["Length"] = 180;

        //end edit of new row
        NewRow.EndEdit();

        //create a new view which shows only added items
        DataView NewView = new DataView(ViewDataSet.Tables["movie"]);
        NewView.RowStateFilter = DataViewRowState.Added;

        //display the movies on the page, the first grid will show all
        //R rated movies sorted by title while the second will show
        //only the added item
        MovieGrid.DataSource = MovieView;
        MovieGrid2.DataSource = NewView;
        DataBind();
    }

...

    }
```

After filling a `DataSet` with data from the `Movie` table in our database, we use the default view as a starting point and define, sort, and filter clauses to arrange the view. We then add a new row to the view and edit it, adding it to the `DataTable` as well. Once this is complete, we create a new view based on the `Movie` table and set the `RowStateFilter` option to show only newly added rows. When displayed, the first grid contains only 'R' rated movies sorted by their title. The second grid contains only the new record that was added in the code.

Constraints and Relations

In most relational database systems, there are the concepts of constraints and relations. A **constraint** defines a rule by which the data must abide in order to be valid. For example, a `UniqueConstraint` can be created on a column of data to indicate that all rows must have a unique value in that column. This is often used for columns that need to uniquely identify a row and might be an employee ID, a Social Security number, or a machine-generated identifier or number. Constraints provide a means for ensuring the integrity of the data by keeping a user or application from inserting, updating, or deleting data that would violate the constraint. If a new record would violate the `UniqueConstraint`, most databases will throw an error to be caught by the calling application.

Relations provide another means to ensure data integrity, as well as a mechanism for finding items that are connected to one another. Relations allow a data item in one table to be associated with data items in other tables. The idea of related data is at the heart of relational database systems. As an example, the sample movie database we have been using in this chapter contains a `Movie` table. In this table there is column named `GenreID`. The `GenreID` column is related to the `ID` column of the `Genre` table to allow looking up the specific genre of a given movie. This provides a reduction in data redundancy because we do not need to specify the full genre name in the movie table, but can give a simple numeric ID. It also allows easier management of data, as we can change the name of the genre in one place and all of the movies specifying that genre, by its ID, will then reflect the change.

The `DataSet` is intended to provide a local, disconnected, copy of the data found in a data source. Having the data local provides many benefits, but the downside to this disconnected approach is that the data source is not able to enforce constraints or relations on the local data defined in the data source. Any data or relational integrity problems will not be known until an attempt is made to update the data source. Fortunately, the `DataSet` object has a `DataRelations` collection and the `DataTable` has a collection of `Constraints`. By mimicking the constraints and relations of the data source, we can ensure that the data, when updated, will be more likely to successfully integrate back into the data source. In addition, we can create constraints or relations that do not exist in the data source, but which ensure that data entered into the `DataSet` meets certain runtime or business rule requirements.

The .NET Framework provides two constraints: `ForeignKeyConstraint` and `UniqueConstraint`. The `UniqueConstraint` was described above and ensures that a data column contains unique values. The `ForeignKeyConstraint` is used to constrain values in two different `DataTable` objects. This constraint is used when a relation exists between the two tables, though this does not have to be a defined `DataRelation`. The `ForeignKeyConstraint` identifies what action should be taken in a related table when a value in one of the specified `DataColumns` is updated or deleted.

Developers can define their own constraints by simply inheriting from the `System.Data.Constraint` class and implementing the abstract methods defined in the base class. For example, a constraint could be created that ensures that values in a particular column are valid US phone numbers.

> In order for constraints to be enforced, the **EnforceConstraints** property of the **DataSet** must be set to **true** (this is the default value).

`DataRelations` allow a developer to define relationships between two `DataTables` in a `DataSet`. In this way, a parent-child relationship can be created. In our example using the `Movie` database, the `Movie` table would be the parent and the `Genre` table would be the child. The `DataRelation` allows access to related data in the parent table from a row in the child table, and vice versa. Given a specific row in the `Movie` table, we can access the related row in the genre table using the `DataRelation` defined between them.

Remember, in order for a `DataRelation` to be created, the data types of the data columns in the respective data tables must be the same. It is not possible, for example, to relate two tables if the column in the first table is a `String` type, and the column in the second table is an `Integer` type. Regardless of whether the values in the `String` column are always numbers, the relationship cannot exist unless the actual types are the same.

Example: Constraints and Relations

This code is in the `ConstraintAndRelation.aspx` file in the code download for this chapter.

```
<%@ Page language="c#" Codebehind="ConstraintAndRelation.aspx.cs"
         AutoEventWireup="false"
         Inherits="AspProgRefDataCs.ConstraintAndRelation" %>
<!DOCTYPE HTML PUBLIC "-//W3C//DTD HTML 4.0 Transitional//EN" >
<HTML>
  <HEAD>
    <title>ConstraintAndRelation</title>
```

```
      <meta name="GENERATOR" Content="Microsoft Visual Studio 7.0">
      <meta name="CODE_LANGUAGE" Content="C#">
      <meta name="vs_defaultClientScript" content="JavaScript">
      <meta name="vs_targetSchema"
            content="http://schemas.microsoft.com/intellisense/ie5">
    </HEAD>
    <body ms_positioning="FlowLayout">
      <form id="Form1" method="post" runat="server">
        <asp:DataGrid id="MovieGrid" runat="server"></asp:DataGrid>
      </form>
    </body>
</HTML>
```

This code is in the `ConstraintAndRelation.aspx.cs` file in the code download for this chapter.

```
using System;
using System.Collections;
using System.ComponentModel;
using System.Data;
using System.Data.SqlClient;
using System.Drawing;
using System.Web;
using System.Web.SessionState;
using System.Web.UI;
using System.Web.UI.WebControls;
using System.Web.UI.HtmlControls;

namespace AspProgRefDataCs
{
  /// <summary>
  /// Summary description for ConstraintAndRelation.
  /// </summary>
  public class ConstraintAndRelation : System.Web.UI.Page
  {
    protected System.Web.UI.WebControls.DataGrid MovieGrid;

    private void Page_Load(object sender, System.EventArgs e)
    {
      ConstrainAndRelate();
    }

    private void ConstrainAndRelate()
    {
      //create connection, adapter and dataset
      SqlConnection MovieConnection = new SqlConnection
                          (@"User ID=sa;Initial Catalog=WroxMovieDB;"
                                     + "Data Source=(local);");
      SqlDataAdapter MovieAdapter = new SqlDataAdapter
            ("select * from movie;select * from genre", MovieConnection);
      DataSet MovieDataSet = new DataSet();

      //create two table mappings
      MovieAdapter.TableMappings.Add("movie", "movie");
      MovieAdapter.TableMappings.Add("genre", "genre");
```

```
            //fill the dataset using the first mapping
            MovieAdapter.Fill(MovieDataSet, "movie");

            //name the second table to match our mapping
            MovieDataSet.Tables[1].TableName = "genre";

            //create a unique constraint on the "ID" column of the movie table
            DataColumn[] ConstrainedColumn =
                new DataColumn[] {MovieDataSet.Tables["movie"].Columns["id"]};
            UniqueConstraint UniqueActorID =
                    new UniqueConstraint("UniqueActorID", ConstrainedColumn);

            //create a relation between the movie and genre tables on the genre
            //id
            DataRelation MovieRelation = new DataRelation
                ("MovieGenre", new DataColumn[]
                {MovieDataSet.Tables["movie"].Columns["genreid"]},
                 new DataColumn[]
                {MovieDataSet.Tables[1].Columns[0]}, false);

            //add the constraint to the table and the relation to the dataset
            MovieDataSet.Tables["movie"].Constraints.Add(UniqueActorID);
            MovieDataSet.Relations.Add(MovieRelation);

            //display the data on the page
            MovieGrid.DataSource = MovieDataSet.Tables["movie"].DefaultView;
            DataBind();
        }

        ...

    }
}
```

In this example, we first load a `DataSet` with `genre` and movie information using table mappings to provide our internal tables with names. We then create a new `UniqueConstraint` object and indicate that the `ID` column of the movie table should be constrained. A `DataRelation` is defined between the movie and genre tables specifying `genreID` as the column that relates the two tables. Finally, we must add the newly-created constraint and relation to their respective collections on the `DataTable` and `DataSet`. Now, any attempt to add a row to the `Movie` table with an `ID` that already exists will result in a `ConstraintException` being thrown. We also have the ability to use the `genreID` to get related records in one table from the other.

DataBinding Examples

`DataBinding` allows a user interface element to be provided with a data source and then instructed to bind to that data. It is up to the control itself to manage this binding and determine how and where to display the data. This behavior is similar to the data-bound controls that became popular in the client-server world. An example of these controls is the `DataGrid`, which presents data in an HTML table. As an example, the following code sample shows creating this type of output. We use the `DataGrid` server-side control and use an `SqlDataReader` to extract data and bind it to the `DataGrid`.

This code is in the `readgrid.aspx` file in the code download for this chapter.

```
<%@ Page language="c#" Codebehind="readgrid.aspx.cs"
        AutoEventWireup="false" Inherits="AspProgRefDataCs.readgrid" %>
<!DOCTYPE HTML PUBLIC "-//W3C//DTD HTML 4.0 Transitional//EN" >
<HTML>
  <HEAD>
    <title>readgrid</title>
    <meta name="GENERATOR" Content="Microsoft Visual Studio 7.0">
    <meta name="CODE_LANGUAGE" Content="C#">
    <meta name="vs_defaultClientScript" content="JavaScript">
    <meta name="vs_targetSchema"
        content="http://schemas.microsoft.com/intellisense/ie5">
  </HEAD>
  <body>
    <form id="Form1" method="post" runat="server">
      <asp:DataGrid id="dgReader" style="Z-INDEX: 101; LEFT: 14px;
                                         POSITION: absolute; TOP: 8px"
                 runat="server"></asp:DataGrid>
    </form>
  </body>
</HTML>
```

As you can see, this is a standard ASP.NET web page with a single `DataGrid` server control element declared. This control is marked to run at server so that the data can be bound to it in the code-behind page.

This code is in the `readgrid.aspx.cs` file in the code download for this chapter.

```
using System;
using System.Collections;
using System.ComponentModel;
using System.Data;
using System.Drawing;
using System.Web;
using System.Web.SessionState;
using System.Web.UI;
using System.Web.UI.WebControls;
using System.Web.UI.HtmlControls;
using System.Data.SqlClient;

namespace AspProgRefDataCs
{
  /// <summary>
  /// Summary description for readgrid.
  /// </summary>
  public class readgrid : System.Web.UI.Page
  {
    protected System.Web.UI.WebControls.DataGrid dgReader;
```

```
private void Page_Load(object sender, System.EventArgs e)
    {
    //declare database variables
    SqlConnection MovieConnection = new SqlConnection
                           (@"User ID=sa;Initial Catalog=WroxMovieDB;"
                                          + "Data Source=(local);");
    SqlCommand MovieCommand = new SqlCommand
                              ("select * from movie", MovieConnection);

    SqlDataReader MovieReader;

    //open the connection to the database and get our reader
    MovieConnection.Open();
    MovieReader =
        MovieCommand.ExecuteReader(CommandBehavior.CloseConnection);

    //set the datasource of the grid to our reader and bind them
    dgReader.DataSource = MovieReader;
    dgReader.DataBind();

    //close the reader, and thus the connection based on the
    //parameter used to get the reader

    MovieReader.Close();

    }

    ...
    }
}
```

If you run the code, you can see how this operates:

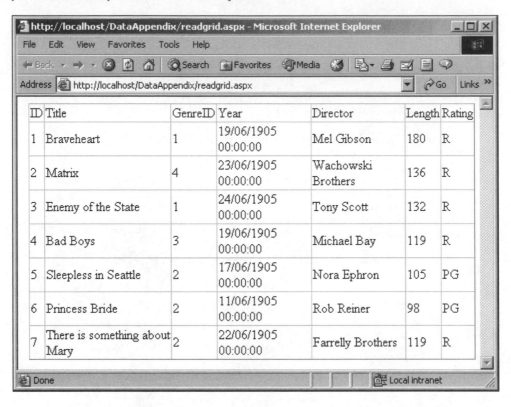

In the `Page Load` event we connect to the data source and use a command object to get a `SqlDataReader`. We then pass this `DataReader` to the `DataGrid` as its `DataSource` property. Calling the `DataBind` method on the `DataGrid` causes it to go through the `DataSource` and create the HTML output. If we just call `DataBind` within the page scope, all controls on the page will have their `DataBind` method called. This can be used as a shortcut, rather than trying to remember to call `DataBind` on each control.

The `SqlDataReader` is not the only object that can be passed to the `DataSource` property of a bound control. Any object that properly exposes the `IEnumerable` interface can be bound to a control. The `IEnumerable` interface allows for the `foreach` syntax in accessing items of a collection. Many of the base classes in the .NET framework implement this interface including `Array`, `ArrayList`, `DataView`, and `Hashtable`. In fact, a single `DataSet` could have several of its tables loaded from one call to the data source and then views of each of those tables could be bound to different controls on the page.

In the rest of this section, we'll walk through building an ASP.NET page containing several data controls. We will work with a variety of the functions of the `DataSet` in order to provide a hands-on look at working with the `DataSet` in ASP.NET. Many of the functions have been described earlier in the chapter, and this example brings them together. As this example is intended to provide insight on working with data in relation to the controls, attention is focused on the functionality of the page and not the layout.

The final web form is shown in the figure below. The page consists of several controls on the left-hand side for sorting and filtering. In the main portion of the page is a `DataGrid` containing the various genres of movies in our sample movie database. Below this grid is another grid showing movies. The page is set up such that when sort and filter criteria are selected, the genres grid reflects these criteria. Upon clicking on any one of the genre ID values, the movie grid is updated to show only those movies that are in the specified genre.

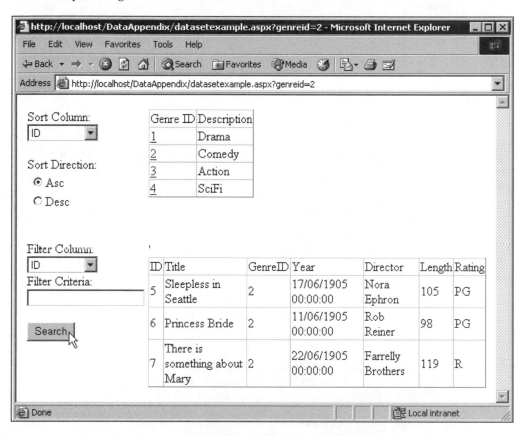

Example: Using the DataSet with Server Controls

This code is in the `DataSetExample.aspx` file in the code download for this chapter.

```
<%@ Page language="c#" Codebehind="DataSetExample.aspx.cs"
        AutoEventWireup="false"
        Inherits="AspProgRefDataCs.DataSetExample" %>
<!DOCTYPE HTML PUBLIC "-//W3C//DTD HTML 4.0 Transitional//EN" >
<HTML>
  <HEAD>
    <title>DataSetExample</title>
    <meta name="GENERATOR" Content="Microsoft Visual Studio 7.0">
    <meta name="CODE_LANGUAGE" Content="C#">
    <meta name="vs_defaultClientScript" content="JavaScript">
```

```
      <meta name="vs_targetSchema"
            content="http://schemas.microsoft.com/intellisense/ie5">
</HEAD>
<body ms_positioning="FlowLayout">
  <form id="frmExample" method="post" runat="server">
    <table>
      <tr>
        <!--Sort section -->
        <td rowspan="5" valign="top">
          Sort Column:
          <br>
          <asp:DropDownList id="sortcol"
                            runat="server"></asp:DropDownList>
          <br>
          <br>
          Sort Direction:
          <br>
          <asp:RadioButtonList id="sortdir" runat="server">
            <asp:ListItem text="Asc" value="ASC"
                          selected="True"></asp:ListItem>
            <asp:ListItem text="Desc" value="DESC"></asp:ListItem>
          </asp:RadioButtonList>
          <br>
          <!--End Sort Section -->
          <!--Filter Section -->
          <br>
          Filter Column:
          <br>
          <asp:DropDownList id="filtercol"
                            runat="server"></asp:DropDownList>
          <br>
          Filter Criteria:
          <br>
          <asp:TextBox id="filtercriteria" width="150"
                       runat="server"></asp:TextBox>
          <br>
          <!--End Filter Section -->
          <asp:Button id="postbackbutton" runat="server"
                      text="Search"></asp:Button>
        </td>
        <td>
          <!--Genre grid definition -->
          <asp:DataGrid id="genre" runat="server"
                        autogeneratecolumns="false">
            <Columns>
              <asp:HyperLinkColumn headertext="Genre ID"
                                   datatextfield="id"
                                   datanavigateurlformatstring=
                                     "datasetexample.aspx?genreid={0}"
                                   datanavigateurlfield="id">
              </asp:HyperLinkColumn>
              <asp:BoundColumn headertext="Description"
                               datafield="description"></asp:BoundColumn>
            </Columns>
```

```
          </asp:DataGrid>
          <!--End Genre Grid-->
          <br>
          <br>
          <br>
          '
          <!--Movie Grid-->
          <asp:DataGrid id="movies" runat="server"></asp:DataGrid>
        </td>
      </tr>
    </table>
  </form>
  </body>
</HTML>
```

We use an HTML table to lay out our page, providing a framework for organizing the various elements. The drop-down list and radio buttons for the sorting selection are defined and we indicate that these should run at the server so that we can get access to their values from the code behind our page. We do the same thing with the filter criteria and follow them with a button that we can use to post our form the web server. We then define a DataGrid element to hold the genres, which we provide with some custom layout instructions for the columns to allow the ID to act as a link.

Finally, we create a simple DataGrid to hold the movie information. Next, we take a look at the code behind this page in C#.

This code is in the DataSetExample.aspx.cs file in the code download for this chapter.

```
using System;
using System.Collections;
using System.ComponentModel;
using System.Data;
using System.Drawing;
using System.Web;
using System.Web.SessionState;
using System.Web.UI;
using System.Web.UI.WebControls;
using System.Web.UI.HtmlControls;
using System.Data.SqlClient;

namespace AspProgRefDataCs
{
  /// <summary>
  /// Summary description for DataSetExample.
  /// </summary>
  public class DataSetExample : System.Web.UI.Page
  {
    protected System.Web.UI.WebControls.DropDownList sortcol;
    protected System.Web.UI.WebControls.RadioButtonList sortdir;
    protected System.Web.UI.WebControls.DropDownList filtercol;
    protected System.Web.UI.WebControls.TextBox filtercriteria;
    protected System.Web.UI.WebControls.Button postbackbutton;
    protected System.Web.UI.WebControls.DataGrid genre;
    protected System.Web.UI.WebControls.DataGrid movies;
```

```
private void Page_Load(object sender, System.EventArgs e)
{
    SqlConnection MovieConnection = new SqlConnection
        (@"User ID=sa;Initial Catalog=WroxMovieDB;Data Source=(local);");
    SqlCommand MovieCommand = new SqlCommand
            ("select * from genre;select * from movie", MovieConnection);
    SqlDataAdapter MovieAdapter = new SqlDataAdapter();
    DataSet MovieDataSet = new DataSet();

    //set the select command and fill our dataset
    MovieAdapter.SelectCommand = MovieCommand;
    MovieAdapter.Fill(MovieDataSet, "genre");

    MovieDataSet.Tables[1].TableName = "movie";

    //set the datasource for our drop down lists to get the column names
    sortcol.DataSource = MovieDataSet.Tables["genre"].Columns;
    filtercol.DataSource = MovieDataSet.Tables["genre"].Columns;

    //if we are posting back to this page, then create a new view on our
    //data to bind to the grid
    if(IsPostBack)
    {
        //set the sort value in the format: column ASC|DESC
        MovieDataSet.Tables["genre"].DefaultView.Sort =
                                sortcol.SelectedItem.ToString() + " "
                                + sortdir.SelectedItem.ToString();

        //if we have filter criteria specified then filter the view
        if(filtercriteria.Text != "")
            MovieDataSet.Tables["genre"].DefaultView.RowFilter =
                                filtercol.SelectedItem.ToString() + "="
                                + filtercriteria.Text;


        //set the genre grid to have the new view as the datasource
        genre.DataSource = MovieDataSet.Tables["genre"].DefaultView;
    }
    else
    {
        //no postback so we use the default view of the genre table
        genre.DataSource = MovieDataSet.Tables["genre"].DefaultView;

    }

    //if we get a request for a genre, display the child rows of the
    //movie table
    if(Request.QueryString["genreid"] != "")
    {
        //create new view and set the filter based on the
        //item selected
        DataView MovieView = new DataView(MovieDataSet.Tables["movie"]);
        MovieView.RowFilter = "genreid="
                        + Convert.ToInt16(Request.QueryString["genreid"]);
```

```
            //MovieView.RowFilter = Request.QueryString["genreid"];
            //MovieView.RowFilter = "Rating='R'";
            //set datasource of movie grid to the new view
            movies.DataSource = MovieView;
        }

        //bind all of our controls
        DataBind();

    }

    ...

    }
}
```

First, we define our objects and then start by filling the `DataSet` with movie and genre information. We then set the data source for the drop-down controls to be the `Columns` property of the `Genre` table. Since the `DataColumns` collection is enumerable, these will be filled automatically when we call `Databind`. We next check to see if the request for the page is a postback. If it is, then we create a new view of the data and set the sort and filter properties accordingly, using this view as the source for the main grid on the page. Next we check to see if a specific genre ID was sent with the request, and if one was, then we filter the movie table's default view to show only movies with that genre ID. If no ID was sent with the request, we hide the grid altogether.

In a real application, we would not load the data on each request and would implement some form of caching (see `System.Web.Caching`). The repeated trips to the server in this scenario would not be acceptable for a high volume site, but this example serves to provide an example of using `DataSet` and `DataView` to view data.

Binding Templated Controls

In addition to those controls that allow binding simply by setting the data source, there are controls that can be bound, but that also require direction on layout as well as where to insert data items. These "templated" controls include the `DataList`. Here we'll show a simple example using the `DataList` and take a look at how we can bind data to the control using different databinding methods, which will be explained in more detail after the example. This example utilizes the `GrocerToGo` database, which comes as part of the Framework SDK for the .NET Framework. Having the images associated with that sample provides for a much more impressive example when run in a browser.

Example: Databinding

This code is in the `databind_template.aspx` file in the code download for this chapter.

```
<%@ Page language="c#" Codebehind="databind_template.aspx.cs"
        AutoEventWireup="false"
        Inherits="AspProgRefDataCs.databind_template" %>
<!DOCTYPE HTML PUBLIC "-//W3C//DTD HTML 4.0 Transitional//EN" >
<html>
<head>
    <title>databind_template</title>
```

```
            <meta name="GENERATOR" Content="Microsoft Visual Studio 7.0">
            <meta name="CODE_LANGUAGE" Content="C#">
            <meta name="vs_defaultClientScript" content="JavaScript">
            <meta name="vs_targetSchema"
                  content="http://schemas.microsoft.com/intellisense/ie5">
    </head>
    <body>
        <form id="Form1" method="post" runat="server">
            <asp:DataList id="dlProducts" runat="server"
                          RepeatDirection="Horizontal" RepeatColumns="3">
                <ItemTemplate>
                    <table>
                        <tr>
                            <td rowspan="5">
                                <img src="<%# DataBinder.Eval(Container.DataItem,
                                          "ImagePath") %>">
                            </td>
                            <td>
                                <b>
                                    <%# DataBinder.Eval(Container.DataItem, "productname")%>
                                </b>
                                <br>
                                <font style="FONT-WEIGHT: bold; FONT-SIZE: smaller">from
                                    <%# DataBinder.Eval(Container.DataItem, "manufacturer")%>
                                </font>
                            </td>
                        </tr>
                        <tr>
                            <td>
                                <%# DataBinder.Eval(Container.DataItem,
                                                    "productdescription")%>
                            </td>
                        </tr>
                        <tr>
                            <td>
                                Servings:
                                <%# DataBinder.Eval(Container.DataItem,"servings")%>
                            </td>
                        </tr>
                        <tr>
                            <td>
                                Serving Size:
                                <%# DataBinder.Eval(Container.DataItem,"servingsize")%>
                            </td>
                        </tr>
                        <tr>
                            <td>
                                Price:
                                <%# DataBinder.Eval(Container.DataItem,"unitprice")%>
                            </td>
                        </tr>
                    </table>
                </ItemTemplate>
```

```
      </asp:DataList>
      </form>
   </body>
</html>
```

This code is in the `databind_template.aspx.cs` file in the code download for this chapter. In order to run this code, it is necessary to import the `grocertogo` database into your SQL Server. This can be done by selecting **import data** by right-clicking on your Server icon in Enterprise Manager. This will open a wizard that will take you through the rest of the steps.

```csharp
using System;
using System.Collections;
using System.ComponentModel;
using System.Data;
using System.Data.SqlClient;
using System.Drawing;
using System.Web;
using System.Web.SessionState;
using System.Web.UI;
using System.Web.UI.WebControls;
using System.Web.UI.HtmlControls;
using System.Data.OleDb;
using Microsoft.Data.Odbc;

namespace AspProgRefDataCs
{
  /// <summary>
  /// Summary description for databind_template.
  /// </summary>
  public class databind_template : System.Web.UI.Page
  {
    protected DataList dlProducts;

    private void Page_Load(object sender, System.EventArgs e)
    {
      OleDbConnection GrocerConnection = new OleDbConnection
          (@"Provider=Microsoft.Jet.OleDb.4.0;" +
           @"Data Source=C:\inetpub\wwwroot\AppendixA\grocertogo.mdb;");
      OleDbDataAdapter GrocerAdapter = new OleDbDataAdapter
          ("SELECT productid,productname, productdescription,unitprice, " +
           "servingsize, servings, manufacturer,imagepath FROM products",
           GrocerConnection);
      DataSet GrocerDataSet = new DataSet("dsProducts");

      GrocerAdapter.Fill(GrocerDataSet, "Products");

      dlProducts.DataSource =
                  GrocerDataSet.Tables["Products"].DefaultView;
      dlProducts.DataBind();
    }

    ...
  }
```

```
    }
```

The first thing we do is to add a `DataList` item to the page and set its attributes to have three columns of repeating templates. Then we define the `ItemTemplate` and in it we build a table to display our data. As we define the template we indicate where the data should go for the given item. We do this though ASP.NET's declarative data binding syntax.

Declarative data binding in ASP.NET uses the `<%#...%>` tag syntax. Items within these tags are only evaluated when the `DataBind` method is called on the containing control, in this case the control serving as the container for the `ItemTemplate`. When the `DataBind` method is called on a control, including the page, all contained controls have their `DataBind` method called as well.

In our example, we have used two different methods of binding. The first, explicit binding, looks like the following:

```
<%# Container.DataItem("manufacturer") %>
```

This syntax explicitly casts the data item to a `DataRowView` object and then accesses the `"manufacturer"` item. Because this item is a string value, there is no need to cast it as well. If it were another type of object we could use the `ToString` method in order to be able to output it to the screen.

The other method for declarative binding involves the use of a static method on the `DataBinder` class. This method uses reflection to allow for using late-bound objects in the data-binding declarative output. For example we used this syntax on the price of the item in our page:

```
<%# DataBinder.Eval(Container.DataItem,"servings")%>
```

While this method is easier to write, it comes with a performance penalty. Because the information is late bound and reflection is used, this method will cost you and should only be used in Rapid Application Development (RAD) environments where performance is not a major concern, such as prototyping or small internal applications with few users.

Summary

In this appendix we saw how the `DataReader` and `DataSet` objects allow us to access data in a variety of data sources. We discussed how the Managed Providers take care of communicating with the data source and managing our connections for us. We also took a look at some of the data binding fundamentals.

The ADO.NET framework is extremely powerful and is geared towards a disconnected architecture like that found in web applications, which makes it a perfect complement to ASP.NET. With the improved XML features that are an integral part of the ADO.NET framework, transmitting data between applications, and even platforms, is a simple operation.

In this appendix we have covered:

- ❏ `Connection` and `Transaction` classes – these classes provide the actual communication mechanism with the database and manage the context of that connection

- ❏ `Command` and `Parameter` classes – the command and parameter classes work in conjunction to allow the developer to execute commands against a data source to `SELECT`, `INSERT`, `UPDATE`, or `DELETE` data

- ❏ `DataAdapter` – the `DataAdapter` manages the interaction between the data source and the `DataSet` object to keep the two in synch

- ❏ `DataReader` – the `DataReader` provides fast, forward-only, read-only access to data in a data source

- ❏ `DataTable`, `DataColumn`, and `DataRow` classes – these classes work together to manage the schema and editing of data

- ❏ `DataSet` – the core of the disconnected architecture in ADO.NET, the `DataSet` serves as a local data storage mechanism

- ❏ `DataRelation` and `Constraint` classes – these classes allow constraint of the data in the `DataSet` in order to provide data integrity when keeping the local copy of the data in synch with the data source

- ❏ ASP.NET data binding – presenting data to the user through the ASP.NET framework utilizes the server controls and a binding framework that allows binding many different collections to UI elements

XML in ASP.NET

Extensible Markup Language (XML), as the name suggests, is a markup language that provides an extensible way to describe information. Information can be represented in XML using customized tags and attributes; there are no predefined tags to represent information. These tags can be grouped together, with the rules that determine how they inter-relate, to form an XML dialect, which is defined by a Document Type Definition (DTD) or an XML Schema. XML was developed in 1996 by the World Wide Web Consortium's (W3C) XML working group to function as an open-standard and platform-independent way of representing information. Ever since then, XML has been widely adopted and is becoming increasingly popular for storing data that needs to be transferred between applications, especially over the Internet.

XML has a very important place in the .NET Framework. The Framework not only provides you with the ability to effectively use XML in your applications but it also utilizes XML extensively within itself, in configuration files, serializing objects, ADO.NET, Web Services, SOAP and source code documentation, to name but a few. The use of XML helps the Framework to meet a considerable number of its goals like extensibility, scalability, reliability, performance, high-end productivity, multi-lingual support and standards.

The .NET Framework provides a wide range of useful classes for working with XML documents and resources, belonging to the System.Xml namespace hierarchy. This includes support for the W3C XML DOM (Document Object Model) interface, and extensions to facilitate a wide variety of common tasks.

System.Xml Namespaces Overview

There are three namespaces that implement the main XML features of the .NET Framework. Note that the XML namespaces discussed in this chapter refer to the .NET class groupings, and should not be confused with namespaces in XML documents, which are used to distinguish XML tags within a particular XML dialect.

Namespace	Description
System.Xml	The primary namespace, containing the W3C-compliant XML document objects and the ancillary objects for working with XML documents. These include W3C-compliant objects that represent the nodes that make up any XML document, reader and writer objects for accessing XML disk files or streams, and a class for validating XML documents against an XML schema or DTD.
System.Xml.XPath	The XML Path Language (XPath) allows you to access and manipulate specific parts of the XML documents. You may create expressions that find nodes in an XML document based on name, type, value etc. These expressions are called XPath queries. This namespace includes a pull-model Navigator object that can be used to iterate through XML documents, plus objects to represent XPath expressions and collections of elements selected by an XPath expression. It does not support the W3C XML DOM interfaces, so cannot be used where this type of access to the content is required.
System.Xml.Xsl	XSL (eXtensible Stylesheet Language) is an XML vocabulary for formatting XML data. The classes in the System.Xml.Xsl namespace provide objects that can be used to perform XSL transformations (also known as XSLT) on an XML document. XSLT is the process of creating formatted text-based documents from an XML document. This namespace also includes a class for passing arguments to an XSLT stylesheet, allowing conditional transformations to be applied.

This chapter concentrates only on these three namespaces, however, there are two other namespaces available for more specialized XML tasks:

Namespace	Description
System.Xml.Schema	Contains a series of objects to represent the various parts of a W3C-compliant XML Schema, allowing them to be manipulated directly. This namespace also provides objects to represent collections of schemas and the event-handler objects required when validating XML documents against a schema or DTD.
System.Xml. Serialization	Contains a series of objects that can be used to serialize XML documents in a range of ways. It includes objects to represent SOAP messages, and also allows control over the encoding of the XML when serializing to a stream. Generally used only when building custom Web Services and when communicating XML-format in other non-standard ways.

This appendix will provide an overview of how to accomplish some of the most common XML-related tasks, such as:

- Creating XML documents using `XmlTextWriter`
- Reading XML documents using `XmlTextReader`
- Validating XML documents using `XmlValidatingReader`
- Working with XML using `XmlDocument`
- Working with XML using `XPathDocument`
- Transforming XML Documents
- ADO.NET Synchronization

Creating XML Documents Using XmlTextWriter

`XmlTextWriter` helps in writing well-formed XML data that conform to W3C XML 1.0 standard with complete namespace support. It provides a no cache, forward only (cursor style) way of writing XML data to files, streams and `TextWriter` objects. It is faster and uses less memory than using DOM, because only one node resides in memory at a particular point of time; it creates XML documents node by node, and sends the output, as it is created, to a stream, another object, or a disk file.

This class is inherited from the `XmlWriter` abstract class and it belongs to the `System.Xml` namespace. Each element and attribute, comment, text node or other node type can be created in the required order using code. It can also be used as the output for another object, whereupon that object calls the methods of the `XmlTextWriter` to create the output.

Example: Using the XmlTextWriter

The following code example, from `XmlTextWriterUsage.aspx.cs`, generates XML data using an `XmlTextWriter` object into an XML file:

```
using System;
using System.Collections;
using System.ComponentModel;
using System.Data;
using System.Drawing;
using System.Web;
using System.Web.SessionState;
using System.Web.UI;
using System.Web.UI.WebControls;
using System.Web.UI.HtmlControls;
using System.Text;
using System.Xml;
using System.IO;

namespace XMLUsageCs
{
    /// <summary>
    /// Summary description for XmlTextWriterUsage.
```

```
///   </summary>
public class XmlTextWriterUsage : System.Web.UI.Page
{
  protected System.Web.UI.WebControls.Label LblMessage;
  protected System.Web.UI.WebControls.Label LblFile;

  private void Page_Load(object sender, System.EventArgs e)
  {
    //create physical path for the new file (in same folder as ASPX page)
    string strCurrentPath = Request.PhysicalPath;
    string strXMLPath = BuildPath(strCurrentPath, "writerbooklist.xml");

    //declare a variable to hold an XmlTextWriter object
    XmlTextWriter objXMLWriter = null;

    try
    {
      //Create a XmlTextWriter object to write in the XML file
      objXMLWriter = new XmlTextWriter(strXMLPath, null);

      //turn on indented formatting and set indent to 3 chararcters
      objXMLWriter.Formatting = Formatting.Indented;
      objXMLWriter.Indentation = 3;

      //start the document with the XML declaration tag
      objXMLWriter.WriteStartDocument();

      //write a comment element including the current date/time
      objXMLWriter.WriteComment("Created using an XMLTextWriter - "
                                  + DateTime.Now);

      //write the opening tag for the <BookList> root element
      objXMLWriter.WriteStartElement("BookList");

      //write the opening tag for a <Book> element
      objXMLWriter.WriteStartElement("Book");

      //add two attributes to this element's opening tag
      objXMLWriter.WriteAttributeString("Category", "Technology");
      int intPageCount = 1248;    //numeric value to convert
      objXMLWriter.WriteAttributeString("Pagecount",
                                          intPageCount.ToString("G"));

      objXMLWriter.WriteElementString("Title", "Professional Video
          Recorder Programming");
      DateTime datReleaseDate = new DateTime(2000, 03, 03);
          //03/03/2000#;
      objXMLWriter.WriteElementString("ReleaseDate",
                              datReleaseDate.ToString("yyyy-MM-dd"));
      int intSales  = 17492;
      objXMLWriter.WriteElementString("Sales", intSales.ToString("G"));
      bool blnHardback = true;
      objXMLWriter.WriteElementString("Hardback",
                                  blnHardback.ToString());
```

```csharp
      //write the opening tag for the <AuthorList> child element
      objXMLWriter.WriteStartElement("AuthorList");

      //add two <Author> elements
      objXMLWriter.WriteElementString("Author", "Francesca Unix");
      objXMLWriter.WriteElementString("Author", "William Soft");

      //close the <AuthorList> element
      objXMLWriter.WriteEndElement();

      //close the <Book> element
      objXMLWriter.WriteEndElement();

      //close the root <BookList> element
      objXMLWriter.WriteEndElement();

      //flush the current content to the file
      objXMLWriter.Flush();

      LblMessage.Text = "Written file: " +
         "<a href=\"writerbooklist.xml\"><b>writerbooklist.xml</b></a>";
    }
    catch(Exception objError)
    {
      //display error details
      LblMessage.Text = "<b>* Error while writing document</b>.<br />"
                        + objError.Message + "<br />" + objError.Source;
      return;   // and stop execution
    }
    finally
    {
      if(objXMLWriter != null)
      {
        // close the file associated with the XmlTextWriter object
        objXMLWriter.Close();
      }
    }

    //now open the new XML file and read it into a string
    string strXMLResult;
    StreamReader objSR = File.OpenText(strXMLPath);
    strXMLResult = objSR.ReadToEnd();
    objSR.Close();
    objSR = null;

    //and display the results in the page
    LblFile.Text = "Reading back from file:<pre>"
                   + Server.HtmlEncode(strXMLResult) + "<pre>";
}

private string BuildPath(string current, string extension)
{
  StringBuilder builder = new StringBuilder(current);
  int u = current.LastIndexOf("\\")+1;
```

```
            builder.Remove(u, current.Length-u);
            builder.Append(extension);
            return builder.ToString();
        }

        #region Web Form Designer generated code
        ...
    }
}
```

The above code makes use of many of the `XmlTextWriter` properties and methods to create well-formed XML. (A full definition of what constitutes a well-formed XML is given by the World Wide Web Consortium (W3C) at www.w3.org). At the time of writing the document, the code is written inside a `try-catch-finally` construct to catch any errors occurring. The code first creates an `XmlTextWriter` object passing the output XML file path as its parameter, and then the code sets the `Formatting` property of the `XmlTextWriter` object. There are only two possible values, `Formatting.Indented` or `Formatting.None`, and the number of indentation characters are set using `Indentation` property. The `WriteStartDocument` method is called to write the `<?xml>` declaration element-indicating version 1.0 and then the comment is included in the output file by calling `WriteComment` method with the comment's text as its parameter.

The code then starts writing out elements using the `WriteStartElement` method, with the element name as its parameter, to write the opening tag of the element and the `WriteEndElement` method to close the last open element tag. The `WriteStartElement` method is overloaded and gives you the option to specify the namespace and namespace-prefix associated with the element name. Attributes are created using the `WriteAttributeString` method, which takes the attribute name and the value of the attribute as its parameter. This method escapes special characters by using entities helping in the creation of well-formed documents. The `WriteElementString` method writes the element with the specified value passed as the parameter. After creating the whole file the `Flush` method is called which flushes the write buffer to the underlying stream or file. The file associated with the object is closed in the `Finally` block by calling the `Close` method.

Here is a screenshot displaying the contents of the newly created output file:

```
http://localhost/XMLUsageCs/writerbooklist.xml - Microsoft Inter...

File   Edit   View   Favorites   Tools   Help

⇐ Back  ▾  ⇒  ▾  ⊗  ⊠  ⌂   ⚲Search  ⊞Favorites  ◍Media  ☺   »

Address ⬀ http://localhost/XMLUsageCs/writerbooklist.xml  ▾  ⌁Go   Links »

   <?xml version="1.0" ?>
   <!-- Created using an XMLTextWriter - 30/05/2002
   13:32:22  -->
 - <BookList>
   - <Book Category="Technology" Pagecount="1248">
       <Title>Professional Video Recorder
         Programming</Title>
       <ReleaseDate>2000-03-03</ReleaseDate>
       <Sales>17492</Sales>
       <Hardback>True</Hardback>
     - <AuthorList>
         <Author>Francesca Unix</Author>
         <Author>William Soft</Author>
       </AuthorList>
     </Book>
   </BookList>

⬀ Done                                   ⬚ Local intranet
```

Reading XML Documents Using XmlTextReader

XmlTextReader provides a fast way to parse XML data efficiently and has low memory requirements. Only the current XML data node, which is being read, is cached in memory; the previous elements that are already parsed no longer exist in memory and as a result they cannot be accessed again unless the XML data is read again from the beginning. XmlTextReader reads data in forward-only manner, ensuring that the data read from the streams, files and other objects is well-formed This class is inherited from the XmlReader abstract class and it belongs to the System.Xml namespace.

The XmlTextReader ensures the integrity of the XML data using Document Type Definition (DTD), which formally declares names and types in XML syntax that will be included in the document; it does not, however use a Document Type Definition for validating. As XmlTextReader does not spend time in validation, it provides the fastest way to read XML data; however, it may be used with an XmlValidatingReader when validation on an XML document is needed. Being a forward-only parser has some drawbacks too. To begin with, you will need to track the point where the reader is positioned in the document structure and, also, if you want to read data in a non-orderly fashion then this method is not recommended, as the data is read sequentially and the access to previously parsed data is not available.

The following code example, from `XmlTextReaderUsage.aspx.cs`, generates XML data using an `XmlTextReader` object:

```
using System;
using System.Collections;
using System.ComponentModel;
using System.Data;
using System.Drawing;
using System.Web;
using System.Web.SessionState;
using System.Web.UI;
using System.Web.UI.WebControls;
using System.Web.UI.HtmlControls;
using System.Text;
using System.Xml;

namespace XMLUsageCs
{
  /// <summary>
  /// Summary description for XmlTextReaderUsage.
  /// </summary>
  public class XmlTextReaderUsage : System.Web.UI.Page
  {
    protected System.Web.UI.WebControls.Label LblMessage;
    protected System.Web.UI.WebControls.Label LblFile;

    private void Page_Load(object sender, System.EventArgs e)
    {
      //create physical path to booklist.xml sample file
      //(in same folder as ASPX page)
      string strCurrentPath = Request.PhysicalPath;
      string strXMLPath = BuildPath(strCurrentPath, "booklist.xml");

      //declare a variable to hold an XmlTextReader object
      XmlTextReader objXMLReader = null;

      try
      {
        //create a new XmlTextReader object for the XML file
        objXMLReader = new XmlTextReader(strXMLPath);

        //now ready to read (or "pull") the nodes of the XML document
        string strNodeResult = "";
        XmlNodeType objNodeType;

        //read each node in turn - returns False if no more nodes to read
        while(objXMLReader.Read())
        {
          //select on the type of the node (these are
          //only some of the types)
          objNodeType = objXMLReader.NodeType;
```

```
            switch(objNodeType)
            {
              case XmlNodeType.XmlDeclaration:
                //get the name and value
                strNodeResult += "XML Declaration: <b>" + objXMLReader.Name
                                + " " + objXMLReader.Value + "</b><br />";
                break;
              case XmlNodeType.Element:
                //just get the name, any value will be in next (#text) node
                strNodeResult += "Element: <b>" + objXMLReader.Name
                                + "</b><br />";
                break;
              case XmlNodeType.Text:
                //just display the value, node name is "#text" in this case
                strNodeResult += "  - Value: <b>" + objXMLReader.Value
                                + "</b><br />";
                break;
            }

            //see if this node has any attributes
            if(objXMLReader.AttributeCount > 0)
            {
              //iterate through the attributes by moving to the next one
              //could use MoveToFirstAttribute but MoveToNextAttribute does
              //the same when the current node is an element-type node
              while(objXMLReader.MoveToNextAttribute())
              {
                //get the attribute name and value
                strNodeResult += "  - Attribute: <b>"
                                + objXMLReader.Name
                                + "</b>   Value: <b>"
                                + objXMLReader.Value
                                + "</b><br />";
              }
            }

          }
          //and display the results in the page
          LblFile.Text = strNodeResult;
          LblMessage.Text = "Opened file: <b>booklist.xml</b>";
        }
        catch(Exception objError)
        {
          //display error details
          LblMessage.Text = "<b>* Error while reading document</b>.<br />"
                          + objError.Message + "<br />" + objError.Source;
          return;  // and stop execution
        }
        finally
        {
          if(objXMLReader != null)
          {
            // close the file associated with the XmlTextReader object
```

```
                objXMLReader.Close();
            }
        }
    }

    private string BuildPath(string current, string extension)
    {
        StringBuilder builder = new StringBuilder(current);
        int u = current.LastIndexOf("\\")+1;
        builder.Remove(u, current.Length-u);
        builder.Append(extension);
        return builder.ToString();
    }

    #region Web Form Designer generated code
    ...
    }
}
```

The above code makes use of the `XmlTextReader` properties and methods to read well-formed XML. The whole code is inside a `try-catch-finally` construct to catch any errors occurring at the time of reading XML.

The code first creates an `XmlTextReader` object, passing the input XML file path as its parameter, and then the code calls the `Read` method in a `do-while` loop. The `Read` method reads the next node (of any type) and returns `true` if it succeeds, or `false` if there are no more nodes left to be read (in other words, the reader is positioned at the end of the document). As each node is read, the code examines the `NodeType` property of the `XmlTextReader` object to find the type of the node where the reader is positioned. In this example, we're only handling three node types (`XmlNodeType.Declaration`, `XmlNodeType.Element` and `XmlNodeType.Text`) in a switch-case block.

For each type, we display the appropriate `Name` property or the `Value` property of the `XmlTextReader` object. The `Name` property displays the qualified name (namespace and the local name) of the current node and the `Value` property displays the value of the current node. The `XmlTextReader` fetches a complete element node when it encounters an opening tag, and this contains any attributes that are declared on that element. The code then checks whether the current node has any attributes by calling the `XmlTextReader.AttributeCount` property. The `AttributeCount` property returns the number of attributes contained in the current node. If the `AttributeCount` property returns more than zero, then the `MovetoNextAttribute` method of the `XmlTextReader` object is called. This method returns `true` if it is able to move to the next attribute node. The `MoveToNextAttribute` method is called in the `do-while` loop to iterate through all the attributes of the current node displaying the `Name` and `Value` properties. The file associated with the object is then closed in the `finally` block by calling the `Close` method.

Here is a screenshot displaying the contents of the newly created output file:

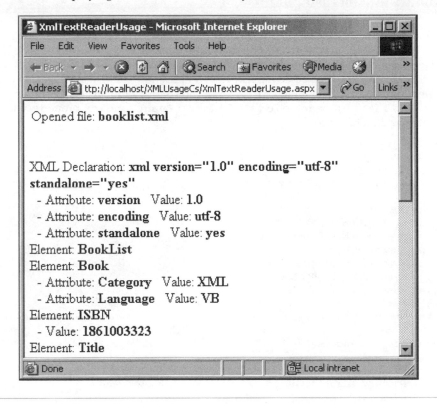

Validating XML Documents Using XmlValidatingReader

XmlValidatingReader is a special reader class that allows the validation of an XML document, or a set of nodes taken from an XML document, against an eXtensible Schema Definition Language (XSD) schema, Document Type Definition (DTD) or XML-Data Reduced (XDR) schema. This class is inherited from the XmlReader abstract class and accesses the data in a non-cached, forward-only manner. It belongs to the System.Xml namespace. The XmlValidatingReader class inherits the properties and methods defined by the XmlReader class, and adds the validation properties to manage the validation process. It can be created from an existing XmlTextReader or XmlNodeReader object and it raises events as the document is read to indicate any validation errors that may be encountered.

Example: Using XmlValidatingReader

The following example, taken from `XmlValidatingReaderUsage.aspx.cs`, demonstrates the `XmlValidatingReader` object, which is created from an `XmlTextReader` object. The code creates an `XmlSchemaCollection` and loads an XSD schema into it, then attaches the `XmlSchemaCollection` object to the `XmlValidatingReader`. The XML is read one node at a time using the `Read` method of the `XmlValidatingReader`, and an event handler that is attached to the `XmlValidatingReader` object's `ValidationEventHandler` property, which outputs details of any validation errors.

```
using System;
using System.Collections;
using System.ComponentModel;
using System.Data;
using System.Drawing;
using System.Web;
using System.Web.SessionState;
using System.Web.UI;
using System.Web.UI.WebControls;
using System.Web.UI.HtmlControls;
using System.Text;
using System.Xml;
using System.Xml.Schema;

namespace XMLUsageCs
{
  /// <summary>
  /// Summary description for XmlValidatingReaderUsage.
  /// </summary>
  public class XmlValidatingReaderUsage : System.Web.UI.Page
  {
    protected System.Web.UI.WebControls.DropDownList selXMLFile;
    protected System.Web.UI.WebControls.Button BtnGo;
    protected System.Web.UI.WebControls.Label LblMessage;
    //declare a variable to hold an XmlTextReader and one to hold the
    //number of errors found. They have to be global because we need
    //to access them within the event handler as well as Page_Load
    XmlTextReader objXTReader;
    int intValidErrors = 0;


    private void Page_Load(object sender, System.EventArgs e)
    {
      //create physical path to booklist sample files
      //(in same folder as ASPX page)
      string strCurrentPath = Request.PhysicalPath;
      string strXMLPath = BuildPath(strCurrentPath,
                                    selXMLFile.SelectedItem.Value);
      string strSchemaPath = BuildPath(strCurrentPath,
                                       "booklist-schema.xsd");

      //create the new XmlTextReader object and load the XML document
      objXTReader = new XmlTextReader(strXMLPath);
```

```
if(selXMLFile.SelectedItem.Value != "not-there.xml")
{
  LblMessage.Text = "Loaded file: <b><a href=\n"
                    + selXMLFile.SelectedItem.Value
                    + "\">" + selXMLFile.SelectedItem.Value
                    + "</a></b><br />";
}
else
  LblMessage.Text = "Loaded file: <b>"
                    + selXMLFile.SelectedItem.Value + "</b><br />";

//create an XMLValidatingReader for this XmlTextReader
XmlValidatingReader objValidator = new
                              XmlValidatingReader(objXTReader);

//set the validation type to use an XSD schema
objValidator.ValidationType = ValidationType.Schema;
```

The above code creates two global variables, then loads the XML source document into a new instance of an `XmlTextReader` object, and from this creates an `XmlValidatingReader` object with the validation type set to `Schema`. The `ValidationType` property can be set to any of the values from the `ValidationType` enumeration, which are listed below:

❑   `Schema` - to validate XML Schemas

❑   `XDR` - to validate XML Data Reduced schema

❑   `DTD` – to validate Document Type Definition

❑   `None` – if choose not to validate

❑   `Auto` – validates if schema

❑   `DTD` – information is found

Then a new `XmlSchemaCollection` is created, and the schema we're using is added to it.

```
//create a new XmlSchemaCollection
XmlSchemaCollection objSchemaCol = new XmlSchemaCollection();

//add the booklist-schema.xsd schema to it
objSchemaCol.Add("", strSchemaPath);

//assign the schema collection to the XmlValidatingReader
objValidator.Schemas.Add(objSchemaCol);

LblMessage.Text += "Validating against: <b>"
        + "<a href=\nbooklist-schema.xsd\">booklist-schema.xsd</a>"
        + "</b><p />";

//add the event handler for any validation errors found
objValidator.ValidationEventHandler += new
                          ValidationEventHandler(ValidationError);
```

The `XmlSchemaCollection` object is then attached to the `XmlValidatingReader` and the code specifies the event handler that will be used to detect any errors encountered during validation. Finally we read all the nodes of the document one-by-one by calling the `Read` method of `XmlValidatingReader` class in a `do-while` loop.

```
try
{
  //iterate through the document using the contents as required
  //we simply read each element here without using it for anything
  while(objValidator.Read())
  {
    //use or display the XML content here as required
  }

  //display count of errors found
  LblMessage.Text += "<b>* Validation complete - "
                    + intValidErrors + "</b> error(s) found";
}
catch(Exception objError)
{
  //in case of a read error or the document unable to be parsed
  LblMessage.Text += "<b>* Read/Parser error:</b> "
                    + objError.Message + "<br />";
}
finally
{
  //must remember to always close the XmlTextReader after use
  objXTReader.Close();
}
}
```

We're not actually doing anything inside the loop here; however, this same format could be used to display output, or could be used in the same way as in the other examples in this section of the chapter. The reading is done within a `try...catch` construct, which means that any errors thrown from a document that is not well formed will be trapped here and displayed.

The event handler specified for the `ValidationEventHandler` property of the `XmlValidatingReader` is shown next, and because this exists, validation errors won't stop the document from being read from disk. If we don't set up an event handler, the validation errors are caught by the `try...catch` construct around the `Read` method instead, and so the first validation error would stop the document from being read any further.

```
public void ValidationError(object sender, ValidationEventArgs args)
{
  //event handler called when a validation error is found
  intValidErrors += 1;   //increment count of errors

  //check the severity of the error
  string strSeverity = "";
  if(args.Severity == XmlSeverityType.Error)
    strSeverity = "Error";
  else if(args.Severity == XmlSeverityType.Warning)
```

```
                strSeverity = "Warning";

            //display a message
            LblMessage.Text += "<b>* Validation error:</b> " + args.Message
                            + "<br /> Severity level: '<b>"
                            + strSeverity + "</b>'. ";

            if(objXTReader.LineNumber > 0)
                LblMessage.Text += "Line: " + objXTReader.LineNumber
                                + ", character: "
                                + objXTReader.LinePosition + "<br />";
        }

        private string BuildPath(string current, string extension)
        {
            StringBuilder builder = new StringBuilder(current);
            int u = current.LastIndexOf("\\")+1;
            builder.Remove(u, current.Length-u);
            builder.Append(extension);
            return builder.ToString();
        }

        #region Web Form Designer generated code
        ...
    }
}
```

Whenever an error occurs during validation, the Validation event handler is called; here it is
ValidationError. The procedure accesses the ValidationEventArgs object to get the details
of the error. The code displays the severity of the error; that is, whether it is error or warning based on
the value of the Severity property. It then displays the error message and also displays the position
at which error occurred with the help of the XmlTextReader properties.

In this example, there are three appropriately named documents you can experiment with. The
options are available in a drop-down list to select the appropriate document.

The following screenshot displays the error messages generated when an invalid document was passed:

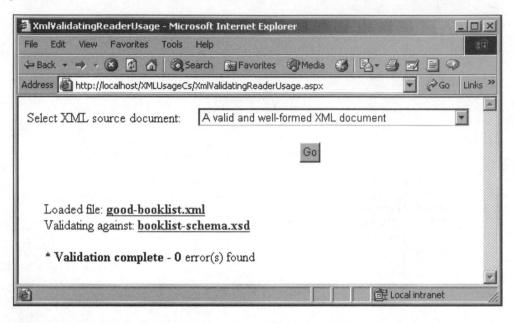

Working with XML Using XmlDocument

XmlDocument implements the W3C Document Object Model (DOM), providing an in-memory representation of an XML document. XmlDocument loads the entire XML data in the memory in a hierarchical tree structure using DOM. This allows efficient access to any node of data in any fashion, therefore it is very efficient when the XML data needs to be inserted, updated, deleted or moved. DOM provides a flexible approach in allowing access to any required node when compared to the forward-only approach used by the XmlTextWriter or XmlTextReader objects. However, the biggest drawback is that since the whole XML data is loaded into memory, depending on the size of the document, it can consume a huge amount of memory. Therefore, if memory is a constraint then it is better to use the forward-only approach; unless the XML data needs to be modified.

The XmlDocument class is inherited from the System.Xml.XmlNode abstract base class that represents a single node and has basic properties and methods to enable working with nodes. XmlDocument has added some more properties and methods to enable working with the root element that is the XML document. It belongs to the System.Xml namespace and implements W3C DOM (Document Object Model) Level1 Core and Core DOM Level2.

This is the standard class for storing and manipulating XML documents. It provides objects such as `XmlElement`, `XmlEntity`, `XmlAttribute`, `XmlComment`, `XmlNode`, `XmlNodeList`, and so on that expose W3C-compliant interfaces for working with the document content. All of these objects have additional Microsoft-specific extensions that make common tasks such as persisting data to disk and copying nodes from one document to another much easier. The `XmlDocument` class provides methods to create new nodes in an `XmlDocument` instance using either W3C standard approaches, or Microsoft's own proprietary extension mechanisms. This gives the developer much more choice over how they work with the objects.

This class provides the nearest equivalent to the MSXML parser, supplied with Internet Explorer, and the Microsoft Data Access Components (MDAC) for use with unmanaged code outside the .NET Framework.

Example: Writing XML Documents

The following code example from `XmlDocumentWritingUsage.aspx.cs` generates XML data using an `XmlDocument` object into an XML file:

```
using System;
using System.Collections;
using System.ComponentModel;
using System.Data;
using System.Drawing;
using System.Web;
using System.Web.SessionState;
using System.Web.UI;
using System.Web.UI.WebControls;
using System.Web.UI.HtmlControls;
using System.Text;
using System.Xml;

namespace XMLUsageCs
{
  /// <summary>
  /// Summary description for XmlDocumentWritingUsage.
  /// </summary>
  public class XmlDocumentWritingUsage : System.Web.UI.Page
  {
    protected System.Web.UI.WebControls.Label LblFile;
    protected System.Web.UI.WebControls.Label LblMessage;

    private void Page_Load(object sender, System.EventArgs e)
    {
      //create physical path to booklist sample files (in same folder as
      //ASPX page)
      string strCurrentPath = Request.PhysicalPath;
      string strXMLPath = BuildPath(strCurrentPath,
                                    "documentbooklist.xml");

      //create new empty XmlDocument object
      XmlDocument objXMLDoc = new XmlDocument();

      //create a new XmlDeclaration object
      XmlDeclaration objDeclare;
```

```
objDeclare = objXMLDoc.CreateXmlDeclaration("1.0", "UTF-8", "yes");

//and add it as the first node in the new document
objDeclare = (XmlDeclaration)objXMLDoc.InsertBefore(objDeclare,
                                    objXMLDoc.DocumentElement);

//create a new XmlComment object
XmlComment objComment;
objComment = objXMLDoc.CreateComment("New document created " +
                                    DateTime.Now);

//and add it as the second node in the new document
objComment = (XmlComment)objXMLDoc.InsertAfter(objComment,
                                            objDeclare);

//create a new XmlElement object, including namespace and prefix
XmlElement objRootElem;
objRootElem = objXMLDoc.CreateElement("wx", "BookList",
                                    "http://wrox.com");

//and add it as the root element in the new document
objRootElem = (XmlElement)objXMLDoc.InsertAfter(objRootElem,
                                            objComment);

//create another new XmlElement object
XmlElement objBookElem;
objBookElem = objXMLDoc.CreateElement("Book");

//and add it as a child of the root element
//don't need to save the returned reference
objRootElem.AppendChild(objBookElem);

//create a new XmlAttribute object
XmlAttribute objAttr;
objAttr = objXMLDoc.CreateAttribute("Category");

//set the attribute value
objAttr.Value = "Computing";

//and add it to the <Book> element
//don't need to save the returned reference
objBookElem.SetAttributeNode(objAttr);

//create some content for the <Book> element
string strContent;
strContent = "<Title>Professional ASP.NET</Title>"
            + "<ISBN>1-861004-88-5</ISBN>"
            + "<Pages>1287</Pages>";

//put it into the element using the InnerXml property
objBookElem.InnerXml = strContent;

//display the contents of the new document
LblFile.Text = "Created new XML document:<br />"
```

```
            + Server.HtmlEncode(objXMLDoc.OuterXml);

        //write the new document to a disk file
        objXMLDoc.Save(strXMLPath);

        //display a link to view the updated document
        LblMessage.Text += "<br /><b>* Saved updated document: "
            + "<a href=\"\documentbooklist.xml\">documentbooklist.xml</a>"
            + "</b><br />";
    }

    private string BuildPath(string current, string extension)
    {
        StringBuilder builder = new StringBuilder(current);
        int u = current.LastIndexOf("\\")+1;
        builder.Remove(u, current.Length-u);
        builder.Append(extension);
        return builder.ToString();
    }

    #region Web Form Designer generated code
    ...
    }
}
}
```

The above example uses a mixture of W3C-compliant and Microsoft-specific code techniques to create a new XML document within an XmlDocument object, and then saves the new document to a disk file using the Save method. The code starts by creating an empty XmlDocument object, then creates an <?xml> declaration element by creating an XmlDeclaration object. The XmlDeclaration object is created by calling the CreateXmlDeclaration method of the XmlDocument class, passing the version of the document encoding and standalone attribute value as its parameter. The XmlDeclaration object is added as the first node in the document by calling the InsertBefore method; here the XmlDeclaration object is placed before the root element of the document. The InsertBefore method needs two parameters; an XmlNode object is passed as the first parameter representing the new node, and an XmlNode object representing an existing node in the document is passed as the second parameter.

This method returns a reference to the new node after it has been inserted. The root element is accessed by the DocumentElement property of the XmlDocument class. Next, the CreateComment method is used to create an XmlComment object that needs the comment's text as its parameter. This object is now placed after the <?xml> declaration element by calling the InsertAfter method. The code then creates an XmlElement named <BookList> and makes it the root element of the document, and another XmlElement named <Book>, which it inserts within this element as a child element. It also creates a new XmlAttribute object named Category, assigns it the value "Computing", and adds it to the <Book> element. To create content for the <Book> element we use a Microsoft-specific shortcut technique. We can create a string that is an XML document fragment and then set the value of an element's InnerXml property to that string, effectively adding several elements and their values in one go. Then we can save the new document to disk by calling the Save method.

Here is a screenshot displaying the contents of the newly created output file:

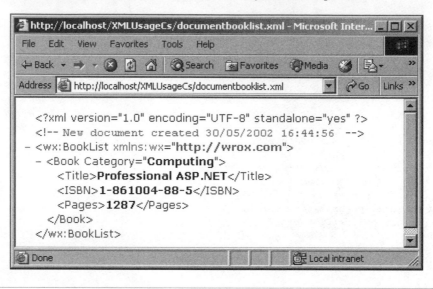

Other Options for Writing XML Documents

Other options for writing XML, to disk or to another object or stream, are:

❑ Using the Save method of an XmlDataDocument object derived from the XmlDocument class.

❑ Using the WriteTo or WriteContentTo methods of an XmlDocument or XmlDataDocument, or any individual XmlNode within the document.

❑ Extracting XML from a document or node using the InnerXml or OuterXml properties of the XmlNode class and writing it to a disk file or stream. Remember that the ASP.NET Response object (from which many other specialized classes are also derived) can accept a Stream object to output XML to the client directly.

Reading XML Documents

Example: Using an XMLDocument object

The following code example is taken from `XmlDocumentReadingUsage.aspx.cs` and parses XML data using an `XmlDocument` object from an XML file:

```
using System;
using System.Collections;
using System.ComponentModel;
using System.Data;
using System.Drawing;
using System.Web;
using System.Web.SessionState;
using System.Web.UI;
using System.Web.UI.WebControls;
using System.Web.UI.HtmlControls;
using System.Text;
using System.Xml;

namespace XMLUsageCs
{
    /// <summary>
    /// Summary description for XmlDocumentReadingUsage.
    /// </summary>
    public class XmlDocumentReadingUsage : System.Web.UI.Page
    {
        protected System.Web.UI.WebControls.Label LblMessage;
        protected System.Web.UI.WebControls.Label LblFile;

        private void Page_Load(object sender, System.EventArgs e)
        {
            //create physical path to booklist.xml sample file
            //(in same folder as ASPX page)
            string strCurrentPath = Request.PhysicalPath;
            string strXMLPath = BuildPath(strCurrentPath, "booklist.xml");

            //create a new XMLDocument object
            XmlDocument objXMLDoc = new XmlDocument();

            try
            {
                //load the XML file into the XMLDocument object
                objXMLDoc.Load(strXMLPath);
                //now ready to parse the XML document
                //it must be well-formed to have loaded without error
                //call a recursive function to iterate through all the nodes
                //in the document creating a string that is placed in the <div>
                //above
                string strNodes = "";
                LblFile.Text = strNodes + GetChildNodes(objXMLDoc.ChildNodes, 0);
                LblMessage.Text = "Loaded and parsed file: <b>booklist.xml</b>";
            }
```

```
    catch(Exception objError)
        {
        //display error details
        LblMessage.Text = "<b>* Error while accessing document</b>.<br />"
                    + objError.Message + "<br />" + objError.Source;
        return; // and stop execution
        }
    }
```

The code above reads the file by loading the XML into an `XmlDocument` object and parsing it into an XML DOM "tree" internally by calling the `Load` method. It ensures that the XML data is well formed. The whole code is inside a `try-catch-finally` construct to catch any errors occurring at the time of loading or parsing document. The code then uses recursion to follow all the branches of the tree and display details about each node.

The recursive function is listed next:

```
    string GetChildNodes(XmlNodeList objNodeList, int intLevel)
    {
      string strNodes = "";

      //iterate through all the child nodes for the current node
      foreach(XmlNode objNode in objNodeList)
      {
        //display information about this node
        strNodes = strNodes + GetIndent(intLevel)
                   + GetNodeType((int)objNode.NodeType)
                   + ": <b>" + objNode.Name;

        //if it is an XML Declaration node, display the 'special'
        //properties
        if(objNode.NodeType == XmlNodeType.XmlDeclaration)
        {
          //cast the XMLNode object to an XmlDeclaration object
          XmlDeclaration objXMLDec = (XmlDeclaration)objNode;
          strNodes = strNodes + "</b>  version=<b>"
                     + objXMLDec.Version
                     + "</b>  standalone=<b>"
                     + objXMLDec.Standalone
                     + "</b><br />";
        }
        else
        {
          //just display the generic 'value' property
          strNodes = strNodes + "</b>  value=<b>" + objNode.Value
                 + "</b><br />";
        }

        //if it is an Element node, iterate through the Attributes
        //collection displaying information about each attribute
        if(objNode.NodeType == XmlNodeType.Element)
        {
          //display the attribute information for each attribute
```

```
      foreach(XmlAttribute objAttr in objNode.Attributes)
        {
          strNodes = strNodes + GetIndent(intLevel + 1)
                   + GetNodeType((int)objAttr.NodeType)
                   + ": <b>" + objAttr.Name
                   + "</b>  value=<b>"
                   + objAttr.Value + "</b><br />";
      }
          }

          //if this node has child nodes, call the same function recursively
          //to display the information for it and each of its child nodes
          if(objNode.HasChildNodes)
            strNodes = strNodes + GetChildNodes(objNode.ChildNodes,
                                                intLevel + 1);

      }

      return strNodes;     //pass the result back to the caller
      }

      string GetIndent(int intLevel)
      {
        //returns a string of non-breaking spaces used to indent each line
        string strIndent = "";
        int intIndent;
        for(intIndent = 0; intIndent <= intLevel; intIndent++)
          strIndent = strIndent + "      ";

        return strIndent;
      }

      string GetNodeType(int intType)
      {
        //returns the node type as a string
        switch(intType)
        {
          case 0: return "NONE";
          case 1: return "ELEMENT";
          case 2: return "ATTRIBUTE";
          case 3: return "TEXT";
          case 4: return "CDATA SECTION";
          case 5: return "ENTITY REFERENCE";
          case 6: return "ENTITY";
          case 7: return "PROCESSING INSTRUCTION";
          case 8: return "COMMENT";
          case 9: return "DOCUMENT";
          case 10: return "DOCUMENT TYPE";
          case 11: return "DOCUMENT FRAGMENT";
          case 12: return "NOTATION";
          case 13: return "WHITESPACE";
          case 14: return "SIGNIFICANT WHITESPACE";
          case 15: return "END ELEMENT";
          case 16: return "END ENTITY";
```

```
            case 17: return "XML DECLARATION";
            case 18: return "NODE (ALL)";
            default: return "UNKNOWN";
        }
    }

    private string BuildPath(string current, string extension)
    {
        StringBuilder builder = new StringBuilder(current);
        int u = current.LastIndexOf("\\")+1;
        builder.Remove(u, current.Length-u);
        builder.Append(extension);
        return builder.ToString();
    }

    #region Web Form Designer generated code
    ...
    }
}
```

This functions in a similar way to the XmlTextReader code, though now the source is an XmlNodeList object that is created by calling the function with the ChildNodes property of the XmlDocument object. This XmlNodeList contains all the nodes at the root of the document (basically the XML declaration and the root <BookList> element). For each node in the XmlNodeList, the code examines the type of node and adds display details for the appropriate values to a string named strNodes. When it encounters an XmlElement node, it also iterates through the attributes collecting their values.

The magic comes at the end of this function, where it then recursively calls the same function again for each set of child nodes of this node. Finally, the cumulative result is passed back to the previous instance of the function in a string.

There are a couple of other functions in the page that accomplish the peripheral tasks like getting a text representation of the element type and building up a string with the correct number of   characters to provide the indenting seen in the screenshot below:

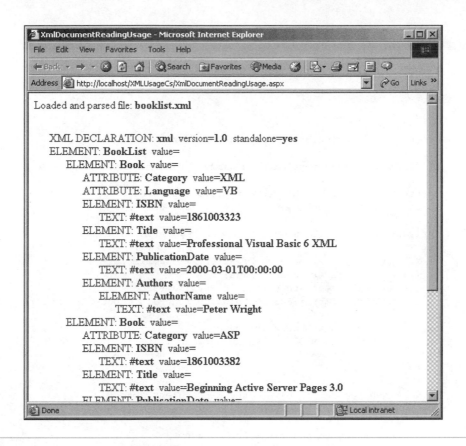

Searching XML Documents

This section presents information on how to use the W3C-compliant DOM methods with an
`XmlDocument` object to navigate XML data and search for a particular node. The example below loads
the XML document into an `XmlDocument` object, and then uses the `GetElementsByTagName`
method to locate all the `<AuthorName>` elements.

Example: Searching Through an XML Document

The complete code for this example can be found in
`XmlDocumentSearchingUsage.aspx.cs`:

```
using System;
using System.Collections;
using System.ComponentModel;
using System.Data;
using System.Drawing;
using System.Web;
using System.Web.SessionState;
using System.Web.UI;
using System.Web.UI.WebControls;
```

```csharp
using System.Web.UI.HtmlControls;
using System.Text;
using System.Xml;

namespace XMLUsageCs
{
  /// <summary>
  /// Summary description for XmlDocumentSearchingUsage.
  /// </summary>
  public class XmlDocumentSearchingUsage : System.Web.UI.Page
  {
    protected System.Web.UI.WebControls.Label LblFile;
    protected System.Web.UI.WebControls.Label LblMessage;

    private void Page_Load(object sender, System.EventArgs e)
    {
      //create physical path to booklist.xml sample file
      //(in same folder as ASPX page)
      string strCurrentPath = Request.PhysicalPath;
      string strXMLPath = BuildPath(strCurrentPath, "booklist.xml");

      //create a new XMLDocument object
      XmlDocument objXMLDoc = new XmlDocument();

      try
      {
        //load the XML file into the XMLDocument object
        objXMLDoc.Load(strXMLPath);

        //now ready to parse the XML document
        //it must be well-formed to have loaded without error
        //create a string to hold the matching values found
        string strResults = "<b>List of authors</b>:<br />";

        //create a NodeList collection of all matching child nodes
        XmlNodeList colElements;
        colElements = objXMLDoc.GetElementsByTagName("AuthorName");

        //iterate through the collection getting the values of the
        //child #text nodes for each one
        foreach(XmlNode objNode in colElements)
          strResults += objNode.FirstChild.Value + "<br />";

        //then display the result
        LblFile.Text = strResults;   //display the result

        LblMessage.Text = "Loaded and parsed file: <b>booklist.xml</b>";
      }
      catch (Exception objError)
      {
        //display error details
        LblMessage.Text = "<b>* Error while accessing document</b>.<br />"
                        + objError.Message + "<br />" + objError.Source;
        return;  // and stop execution
```

```
        }
    }

    private string BuildPath(string current, string extension)
    {
        StringBuilder builder = new StringBuilder(current);
        int u = current.LastIndexOf("\\")+1;
        builder.Remove(u, current.Length-u);
        builder.Append(extension);
        return builder.ToString();
    }

    #region Web Form Designer generated code
    ...
    }
}
```

The code in this example is quite simple. After creating the `XmlDocument` object and loading the XML from disk, it uses the `GetElementsByTagname` method to create an `XmlNodeList` containing the matching element nodes. This returns all the elements that have `AuthorName` as the `tagname`. Then it is just a matter of iterating through the list and displaying the values from the child `XmlText` node from each element by accessing it through the `FirstChild` property.

Here is a screenshot showing the name of all authors:

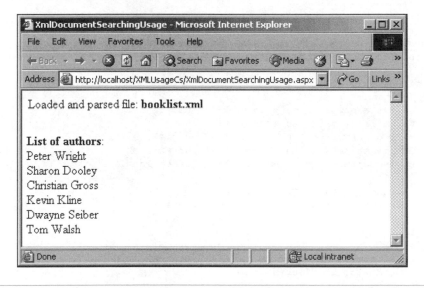

Editing XML Documents

This section explains how to perform a mix of operations like insert, remove and copy nodes from one document to another using the following techniques; using W3C-compliant DOM methods with an `XmlDocument` object, using an `XPathNavigator` and utilizing the `XPathDocument` object to do an `XPath` search. Also refer to the next section: *Working with XML using XPathDocument*, as some information presented there will help you to better understand the material in this section.

839

Example: Editing XML Documents

The example below in this section is somewhat more complex. It demonstrates four different techniques. The complete code is available in `XmlDocumentEditingUsage.aspx.cs`. The code for the page is fully commented, and broken down into the four sections shown:

```
using System;
using System.Collections;
using System.ComponentModel;
using System.Data;
using System.Drawing;
using System.Web;
using System.Web.SessionState;
using System.Web.UI;
using System.Web.UI.WebControls;
using System.Web.UI.HtmlControls;
using System.Xml;
using System.Text;

namespace XMLUsageCs
{
  /// <summary>
  /// Summary description for XmlDocumentEditingUsage.
  /// </summary>
  public class XmlDocumentEditingUsage : System.Web.UI.Page
  {
    protected System.Web.UI.WebControls.Label LblMessage;
    protected System.Web.UI.WebControls.Label LblFile;

    private void Page_Load(object sender, System.EventArgs e)
    {
      //create physical path to booklist sample files
      //(in same folder as ASPX page)
      string strCurrentPath = Request.PhysicalPath;
      string strXMLPath  = BuildPath(strCurrentPath,"bookdetails.xml");
      string strNewPath  = BuildPath(strCurrentPath, "newdetails.xml");

      //create a new XMLDocument object
      XmlDocument objXMLDoc = new XmlDocument();

      try
      {
        //load the XML file into the XMLDocument object
        objXMLDoc.Load(strXMLPath);
        //now ready to use the XMLDocument object

        //****************************************************************
        //*** 1: Select a Node, display content and then remove it   ***
        //****************************************************************

        //specify XPath expression to select a book element
        string strXPath = "descendant::Book[ISBN=" + "\x22"
```

```
            + "1861003234" + "\x22" + "]";

//get a reference to the matching <Book> node
XmlNode objNode;
objNode = objXMLDoc.SelectSingleNode(strXPath);

//then display the result
LblFile.Text = "XPath expression '<b>" + strXPath
               + "</b>' returned:<br />"
               + Server.HtmlEncode(objNode.OuterXml) + "<br />";

//delete this node using RemoveChild method from document element
objXMLDoc.DocumentElement.RemoveChild(objNode);
LblFile.Text += "<b>* Removed node from document.</b><br />";
```

Here it first selects a node using the `SelectSingleNode` method of the `XmlDocument`, and removes it using the `RemoveChild` method. The `SelectSingleNode` method selects just the first node that matches the `XPath` expression (here it gets a book node containing ISBN=1861003234) and returns an `XmlNode` object that represents the book node selected. The selected node is then deleted by calling the method `RemoveChild` referring to the `DocumentElement` (that is the root element) of the document.

Next, the code creates a new empty XML document and adds the XML declaration and a comment to it:

```
//****************************************************************
//** 2: Create empty XML document, add declaration and comment ***
//****************************************************************

//create new empty XML Document object
XmlDocument objNewDoc = new XmlDocument();

//create a new XmlDeclaration object
XmlDeclaration objDeclare;
objDeclare = objNewDoc.CreateXmlDeclaration("1.0", null, null);

//and add it as the first node in the new document
objDeclare = (XmlDeclaration)objNewDoc.InsertBefore(objDeclare,
                                    objNewDoc.DocumentElement);

//create a new XmlComment object
XmlComment objComment;
objComment = objNewDoc.CreateComment("New document created "
                                    + DateTime.Now);

//and add it as the second node in the new document
objComment = (XmlComment)objNewDoc.InsertAfter(objComment,
                                        objDeclare);
```

The above code segment starts by creating an empty `XmlDocument` object. We create an `<?xml>` declaration element by creating an `XmlDeclaration` object. The `XmlDeclaration` object is created by calling the `CreateXmlDeclaration` method of the `XmlDocument` class passing the version of the document, encoding and the standalone attribute value as its parameter. The `XmlDeclaration` object is added as the first node in the document by calling the `InsertBefore` method; here the `XmlDeclaration` object is placed before the root element of the Document. The `InsertBefore` method needs two parameters; an `XmlNode` object is passed as the first parameter representing the new node, and an `XmlNode` object representing an existing node in the document is passed as the second parameter. This method returns a reference to the new node after it has been inserted. The root element is accessed by the `DocumentElement` property of the `XmlDocument` class. Next, the `CreateComment` method is used to create an `XmlComment` object that needs the comment's text as its parameter. This object is now placed after the `<?xml>` declaration element by calling the `InsertAfter` method.

Then, in the third section:

```
//*********************************************************************
//*** 3: Select node in original document and import into new one  ***
//*********************************************************************

      //change the XPath expression to select a different book
      strXPath = "descendant::Book[ISBN=" + "\x22" + "1861003382"
                 + "\x22" + "]";

      //get a reference to the matching <Book> node
      objNode = objXMLDoc.SelectSingleNode(strXPath);

      //create a variable to hold the imported node object
      XmlNode objImportedNode;

      //import the node and all children into new document (un-attached
      //fragment)
      objImportedNode = objNewDoc.ImportNode(objNode, true);

      //insert the new un-attached node into document after the comment
      //node
      objNewDoc.InsertAfter(objImportedNode, objComment);

      //display the contents of the new document
      LblFile.Text += "Created new XML document and inserted "
              + "into it the node selected by<br />"
              + "the XPath expression '<b>" + strXPath + "'</b><br />"
              + "<b>* Content of new document is</b>:<br />"
              + Server.HtmlEncode(objNewDoc.OuterXml)+ "<br/>";
```

The code selects a single `<Book>` node in the original document, copies it into the new document using the `ImportNode` method, and inserts it as the root element of the new document. The contents of this document are then displayed in the page.

Finally, in section four:

```
//*********************************************************************
//*** 4: Select and edit/insert new content into ISBN elements   ***
//*********************************************************************

    //change the XPath expression to select all ISBN elements
    strXPath = "descendant::ISBN";

    //get a reference to the matching nodes as a collection
    XmlNodeList colNodeList;
    colNodeList = objXMLDoc.SelectNodes(strXPath);

    //display the number of matches found
    LblFile.Text += "Found <b>" + colNodeList.Count
                + "</b> nodes matching the"
                + "XPath expression '<b>" + strXPath + "'</b><br />"
                + "<b>* Editing and inserting new content</b><br />";

    string strNodeValue, strNewValue, strShortCode;

    //create a variable to hold an XmlAttribute object
    XmlAttribute objAttr;

    //iterate through all the nodes found
    foreach(XmlNode objnode in colNodeList)
    {

      //create an XmlAttribute named 'formatting'
      objAttr = objXMLDoc.CreateAttribute("formatting");

      //set the value of the XmlAttribute to 'hyphens'
      objAttr.Value = "hyphens";

      //and add it to this ISBN element - have to cast the object
      //to an XmlElement as XmlNode doesn't have this method
      ((XmlElement)objnode).SetAttributeNode(objAttr);

      //get text value of this ISBN element
      strNodeValue = objnode.InnerText;

      //create short and long strings to replace content
      strShortCode = strNodeValue.Substring(strNodeValue.Length-4, 4);
      strNewValue = strNodeValue.Substring(0,1) + "-"
                + strNodeValue.Substring(1, 6)
                + "-" + strNodeValue.Substring(7, 2) + "-"
                + strNodeValue[strNodeValue.Length-1];

      //insert into element by setting the InnerXml property
      objnode.InnerXml = "<LongCode>" + strNewValue
                    + "</LongCode><ShortCode>"
                    + strShortCode + "</ShortCode>";

    }
```

```
                //write the updated document to a disk file
                objXMLDoc.Save(strNewPath);

                //display a link to view the updated document
                LblFile.Text += @"<br /><b>* Saved updated document: "
                    + "<a href=""newdetails.xml"">newdetails.xml</a></b><br />";

                LblMessage.Text = @"<b>* Loaded file: "
                    + "<a href=""bookdetails.xml"">bookdetails.xml</a></b><br />";
            }
            catch(Exception objError)
            {
                //display error details
                LblMessage.Text = "<b>* Error while accessing document</b>.<br />"
                                + objError.Message + "<br />" + objError.Source;
                return;   // and stop execution
            }


        }

        private string BuildPath(string current, string extension)
        {
            StringBuilder builder = new StringBuilder(current);
            int u = current.LastIndexOf("\\")+1;
            builder.Remove(u, current.Length-u);
            builder.Append(extension);
            return builder.ToString();
        }

        #region Web Form Designer generated code
        ...
    }
}
```

The code selects all the <ISBN> nodes using the SelectNodes method with the XPath expression "descendant::ISBN", and edits and inserts new content into these nodes. It creates a new XmlAttribute named Formatting in the ISBN element using the CreateAttribute method. It also inserts two more elements inside the ISBN element representing the LongCode and ShortCode of the ISBN element.

You can view the original and the edited documents using the links in the page:

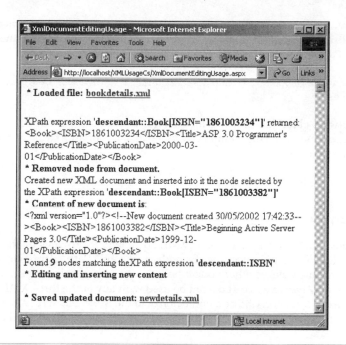

Working with XML Using XPathDocument

XPathDocument

This class is used to store an XML document but unlike the `XmlDocument`, `XmlDataDocument` classes in .NET Framework class library it does not support the W3C XML DOM interface; instead, all access to the content of the document is made through an `XPathNavigator` that can be attached to it. This class is inherited from `System.Object` and belongs to `System.Xml.XPath` namespace. To create an `XPathDocument`, we must provide details of the XML document that will be loaded. There is no `Load` or `LoadXml` method that can be used to load the XML. The source of the XML can be a stream object, disk file, a `TextReader` object, or an `XmlReader` object such as an `XmlTextReader` or `XmlNodeReader`.

```
XPathDocument objXPathDoc = new XPathDocument(@"c:\temp\test.xml");
```

Or using an `XmlTextReader`:

```
XmlTextReader objXMLReader;
objXMLReader = new XmlTextReader(@"c:\temp\test.xml");
XPathDocument objXPathDoc = new XPathDocument(objXMLReader);
```

When using a disk file or an `XmlReader` as the source a second optional parameter can be used to specify how white space should be handled. It must be one of the values from the `XmlSpace` enumeration (`Default` (1), `None`, (0) or `Preserve` (2)).

```
XPathDocument objXPathDoc = new XPathDocument(@"c:\temp\test.xml",
XmlSpace.Preserve);
```

The `XPathDocument` object has only one method that is commonly used, which is the `CreateNavigator` method. This method creates an instance of an `XPathNavigator` object based on the `XPathDocument` object.

```
XPathNavigator objXPNav = objXPathDoc.CreateNavigator();
```

XPathNavigator

This class provides "push-model" access to an XML document. It provides methods that can be used to iterate through a document, and select specific nodes using an XPath expression. It can be used to move to a specific element, attribute, or other node type, or to move to a sibling, child, or parent of the current element. Note that an `XPathNavigator` can be used with **any** of the three XML document objects. This class is inherited from `System.Object` and belongs to the `System.Xml.XPath` namespace. Although located in the `System.Xml.XPath` namespace, it is not specific to the `XPathDocument` object.

Parsing XML Documents

The example below parses an XML document using `XPathDocument` and an `XPathNavigator` class in the `System.Xml.Xpath` namespace. The `Move` methods of the `XPathNavigator` are used to access each node recursively and output the information about the nodes. Note that the value of a node in an `XPathNavigator` is actually a concatenation of the text in all the child nodes. In an `XmlDocument`, when using the DOM methods, the value is just that of the node itself or the appropriate child text (`XmlText`) node.

Example: Parsing XML documents

The code example below is taken from `XpathDocumentReadingUsage.aspx.cs`:

```
using System;
using System.Collections;
using System.ComponentModel;
using System.Data;
using System.Drawing;
using System.Web;
using System.Web.SessionState;
using System.Web.UI;
using System.Web.UI.WebControls;
using System.Web.UI.HtmlControls;
using System.Text;
using System.Xml.XPath;

namespace XMLUsageCs
{
/// <summary>
```

```
/// Summary description for XPathDocumentReadingUsage.
/// </summary>
public class XPathDocumentReadingUsage : System.Web.UI.Page
{
  protected System.Web.UI.WebControls.Label LblMessage;
  protected System.Web.UI.WebControls.Label LblFile;

  private void Page_Load(object sender, System.EventArgs e)
  {
    //create physical path to booklist.xml sample file
    //(in same folder as ASPX page)
    string strCurrentPath = Request.PhysicalPath;
    string strXMLPath = BuildPath(strCurrentPath, "booklist.xml");

    //declare a variable to hold an XMLDocument object
    XPathDocument objXPathDoc;

    try
    {
      //create a new XpathDocument object and load the XML file
      objXPathDoc = new XPathDocument(strXMLPath);
      //now ready to parse the XML document
      //it must be well-formed to have loaded without error
      //create a new XPathNavigator object using the XMLDocument object
      XPathNavigator objXPNav = objXPathDoc.CreateNavigator();

      //move the current position to the root #document node
      objXPNav.MoveToRoot();

      //call a recursive function to iterate through all the nodes in the
      //XPathNavigator, creating a string that is placed in the <div>
      //above
      LblFile.Text = GetXMLDocFragment(objXPNav, 0);
      LblMessage.Text = "Loaded and parsed file: <b>booklist.xml</b>";
    }
    catch(Exception objError)
    {
      //display error details
      LblMessage.Text = "<b>* Error while accessing document</b>.<br />"
                        + objError.Message + "<br />" + objError.Source;
      return;   // and stop execution
    }
  }
}
```

After creating an XPathDocument based on the XML source document, it creates an XPathNavigator, by calling the CreateNavigator method. Then the MoveToRoot method of the XPathNavigator class is called to move the current position in the document to the root element. The code then calls a recursive function named GetXMLDocFragment passing in the XPathNavigator just created.

The recursive function follows next:

```
string GetXMLDocFragment(XPathNavigator objXPNav, int intLevel)
{
  string strNodes = "";

  //display information about this node
  strNodes = strNodes + GetIndent(intLevel)
             + GetNodeType((int)objXPNav.NodeType)
             + ": <b>" + objXPNav.Name + "</b>  value=<b>"
             + objXPNav.Value + "</b><br />";

  //see if this node has any Attributes
  if(objXPNav.HasAttributes)
  {
    //move to the first attribute
    objXPNav.MoveToFirstAttribute();

    do
    {
      //display the information about it
      strNodes = strNodes + GetIndent(intLevel + 1)
                 + GetNodeType((int)objXPNav.NodeType)
                 + ": <b>" + objXPNav.Name + "</b>  value=<b>"
                 + objXPNav.Value + "</b><br />";
    }
    while(objXPNav.MoveToNextAttribute());

    //then move back to the parent node (i.e. the element itself)
    objXPNav.MoveToParent();

  }

  //see if this node has any child nodes
  if(objXPNav.HasChildren)
  {
    //move to the first child node of the current node
    objXPNav.MoveToFirstChild();

    do
    {
      //recursively call this function to display the child node
      //fragment
      strNodes = strNodes + GetXMLDocFragment(objXPNav, intLevel + 1);
    }
    while(objXPNav.MoveToNext());

    //move back to the parent node - the node we started from when we
    //moved to the first child node - could have used Push and Pop
    //instead
    objXPNav.MoveToParent();
  }

  //must repeat the process for the remaining sibling nodes (i.e.nodes
```

```
        //at the same 'level' as the current node within the XML document
        //so repeat while we can move to the next sibling node
        while(objXPNav.MoveToNext())
        {
          //recursively call this function to display this sibling node
          //and its atributes and child nodes
          strNodes = strNodes + GetXMLDocFragment(objXPNav, intLevel);
        }
        return strNodes;  //pass the result back to the caller

}

string GetIndent(int intLevel)
{
      //returns a string of non-breaking spaces used to indent each line
      string strIndent = "";
      int intIndent;
      for(intIndent = 0; intIndent <= intLevel; intIndent++)
        strIndent = strIndent + "      ";

      return strIndent;
}

string GetNodeType(int intType)
{
      //returns the node type as a string
      switch(intType)
      {
        case 0: return "NONE";
        case 1: return "ELEMENT";
        case 2: return "ATTRIBUTE";
        case 3: return "TEXT";
        case 4: return "CDATA SECTION";
        case 5: return "ENTITY REFERENCE";
        case 6: return "ENTITY";
        case 7: return "PROCESSING INSTRUCTION";
        case 8: return "COMMENT";
        case 9: return "DOCUMENT";
        case 10: return "DOCUMENT TYPE";
        case 11: return "DOCUMENT FRAGMENT";
        case 12: return "NOTATION";
        case 13: return "WHITESPACE";
        case 14: return "SIGNIFICANT WHITESPACE";
        case 15: return "END ELEMENT";
        case 16: return "END ENTITY";
        case 17: return "XML DECLARATION";
        case 18: return "NODE (ALL)";
        default: return "UNKNOWN";
      }
}

private string BuildPath(string current, string extension)
{
      StringBuilder builder = new StringBuilder(current);
```

```
        int u = current.LastIndexOf("\\")+1;
        builder.Remove(u, current.Length-u);
        builder.Append(extension);
        return builder.ToString();
    }

    #region Web Form Designer generated code
    ...
    }
}
```

The recursive function here carries out the navigation through the document using the special methods of the `XPathNavigator` object. The technique is to display information about the current node, see if there are any attributes and, if so, iterate through these collecting the name and value of each one. Then the function iterates through all the children of this node. For each node, it recursively calls the same function to get information about the child nodes and their children. Finally, it moves to the next sibling node of the start node and does the same again.

Here's a screenshot showing the parsed data:

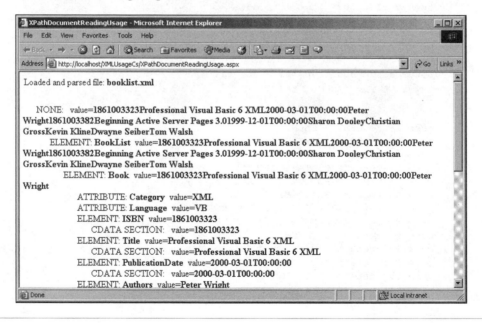

Searching XML Documents

The `XPathNavigator` object has methods that help in the searching of a particular node in the XML data. The node to be searched is encapsulated using an `XPath` expression object.

Example: Using XpathNavigator to Search Documents

The following example, from `XPathDocumentSearchingUsage.aspx.cs`, searches for all nodes having `<AuthorName>` as the element and displays their values:

```csharp
using System;
using System.Collections;
using System.ComponentModel;
using System.Data;
using System.Drawing;
using System.Web;
using System.Web.SessionState;
using System.Web.UI;
using System.Web.UI.WebControls;
using System.Web.UI.HtmlControls;
using System.Text;
using System.Xml.XPath;

namespace XMLUsageCs
{
    /// <summary>
    /// Summary description for XPathDocumentSearchingUsage.
    /// </summary>
    public class XPathDocumentSearchingUsage : System.Web.UI.Page
    {
        protected System.Web.UI.WebControls.Label LblMessage;
        protected System.Web.UI.WebControls.Label LblFile;

        private void Page_Load(object sender, System.EventArgs e)
        {
            //create physical path to booklist.xml sample file
            //(in same folder as ASPX page)
            string strCurrentPath = Request.PhysicalPath;
            string strXMLPath = BuildPath(strCurrentPath, "booklist.xml");

            //declare a variable within current scope to hold an XPathDocument
            XPathDocument objXPathDoc;

            try
            {

                //create XPathDocument object and load the XML file
                objXPathDoc = new XPathDocument(strXMLPath);
                //now ready to parse the XML document
                //it must be well-formed to have loaded without error
                //create a new XPathNavigator object using the XPathDocument object
                XPathNavigator objXPNav = objXPathDoc.CreateNavigator();

                //create a string to hold the matching values found
                string strResults = "<b>List of authors</b>:<br />";

                //select all the AuthorName nodes into an XPathNodeIterator object
                //using an XPath expression
```

```
        XPathNodeIterator objXPIter;
        objXPIter = objXPNav.Select("descendant::AuthorName");

        //iterate through the nodes. Each "node" in the XPathNodeIterator
        //is itself an XPathNavigator, so Name and Value properties are
        //available
        while(objXPIter.MoveNext())
        {
          //get the value and add to the 'results' string
          strResults += objXPIter.Current.Value + "<br />";
        }

        LblFile.Text = strResults;    //display the result
        LblMessage.Text = "Loaded file: <b>booklist.xml</b>";
      }
      catch(Exception objError)
      {
        //display error details
        LblMessage.Text = "<b>* Error while accessing document</b>.<br />"
                        + objError.Message + "<br />" + objError.Source;
        return;   // and stop execution
      }
    }

    private string BuildPath(string current, string extension)
    {
      StringBuilder builder = new StringBuilder(current);
      int u = current.LastIndexOf("\\")+1;
      builder.Remove(u, current.Length-u);
      builder.Append(extension);
      return builder.ToString();
    }

    #region Web Form Designer generated code
    ...
  }
}
```

After creating an XPathDocument based on the XML source document, the code creates an XPathNavigator object by calling the CreateNavigator method. The code executes the Select method of the XPathNavigator with the XPath expression "descendant::AuthorName", which returns an XPathNodeIterator object containing the matching elements. It's then just a matter of iterating through this list and displaying the values.

Here is a screenshot displaying the author names:

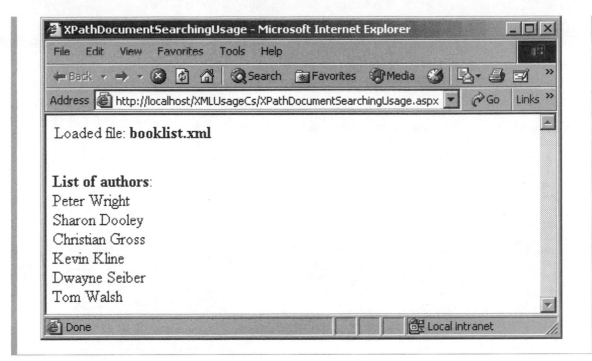

Transforming XML Documents

Extensible Stylesheet Language Transformation (XSLT) helps in transforming the data contained in an XML document to another document in different structure or format. For example, an XML file may be transformed using style sheets to an HTML file.

The `System.Xml.Xsl.XslTransform` class helps in transforming XML documents with the help of XSLT stylesheets. This class provides features for performing XSL or XSLT transformations. The input XML document can be a single XML node, an `XPathNavigator`, or the path and name of a disk file. The resulting transformed document can be specified as any of the XML "reader" or "writer" objects, a stream, or the path and name of a disk file.

We've provided two examples of transforming XML documents using the `XslTransform` object. The first transforms the XML into HTML using the simplest technique, and the second demonstrates several different ways of managing the transformation and the different objects that are available to handle the source and result documents.

The following example takes an XML source file and an XSL stylesheet, and transforms the XML directly to a disk file in HTML format (the format is, of course, governed by the contents of the stylesheet).

This is taken from `XslTransformSimpleUsage.aspx.cs`:

```
using System;
using System.Collections;
using System.ComponentModel;
using System.Data;
using System.Drawing;
using System.Web;
using System.Web.SessionState;
using System.Web.UI;
using System.Web.UI.WebControls;
using System.Web.UI.HtmlControls;
using System.Text;
using System.Xml.Xsl;
using System.Xml;

namespace XMLUsageCs
{
  /// <summary>
  /// Summary description for XslTransformSimpleUsage.
  /// </summary>
  public class XslTransformSimpleUsage : System.Web.UI.Page
  {
    protected System.Web.UI.WebControls.Label LblMessage;
    protected System.Web.UI.HtmlControls.HtmlGenericControl outXMLURL;
    protected System.Web.UI.HtmlControls.HtmlGenericControl outXSLURL;
    protected System.Web.UI.HtmlControls.HtmlGenericControl outHTMLURL;

    private void Page_Load(object sender, System.EventArgs e)
    {
      //create physical path to booklist sample files
      //(in same folder as ASPX page)
      string strCurrentPath = Request.PhysicalPath;
      string strXMLPath = BuildPath(strCurrentPath, "booklist.xml");
      string strXSLPath = BuildPath(strCurrentPath, "booklist.xsl");
      string strHTMLPath = BuildPath(strCurrentPath, "booklist.html");

      try
      {
        outXMLURL.InnerHtml = "<a href=\"booklist.xml\">booklist.xml</a>";

        //create a new XslTransform object
        XslTransform objTransform = new XslTransform();

        //load the XSL stylesheet into the XSLTransform object
        objTransform.Load(strXSLPath);
        outXSLURL.InnerHtml = "<a href=\"booklist.xsl\">booklist.xsl</a>";
```

```
            //perform the transformation using the XSL file in the
            //XSLTransform and the XML file path in strXMLPath
            //the result is sent to the disk file in strHTMLPath
            objTransform.Transform(strXMLPath, strHTMLPath);

            outHTMLURL.InnerHtml =
                            "<a href=\"booklist.html\">booklist.html</a>";

            //------------ error handling code -------------
        }
        catch(Exception objError)
        {
            //display error details
            LblMessage.Text = "<b>* Error while accessing document</b>.<br />"
                            + objError.Message + "<br />" + objError.Source;
            return;   // and stop execution
        }
    }

    private string BuildPath(string current, string extension)
    {
        StringBuilder builder = new StringBuilder(current);
        int u = current.LastIndexOf("\\")+1;
        builder.Remove(u, current.Length-u);
        builder.Append(extension);
        return builder.ToString();
    }

    #region Web Form Designer generated code
    ...
  }
}
```

The code creates the three path and filename combinations for an .xml document that needs to be transformed, the .xsl document that contains the stylesheet and the HTML file that will contain the transformed HTML document. Then the code creates the XslTransform object and calls its Transform method by passing the .xml file path and .xsl file path. This method takes an XML document and transforms it using the loaded stylesheet, the result being an output HTML file.

You can use the links in the page to open the XML document and the stylesheet, as well as to display the resulting HTML document.

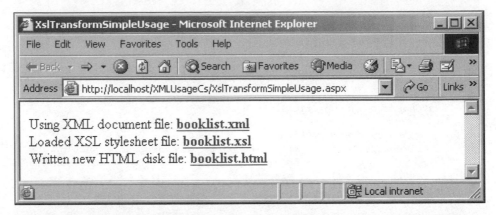

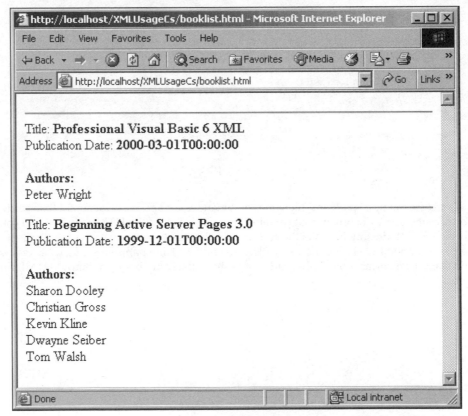

Example: Converting XML Documents to Different Formats

In the second example, we use the `XslTransform` object to transform the source XML document into another XML document of a completely different format. We also use several different techniques to handle the process.

The following code example is taken from `XslTransformMultipleUsage.aspx.cs`:

```
using System;
using System.Collections;
using System.ComponentModel;
using System.Data;
using System.Drawing;
using System.Web;
using System.Web.SessionState;
using System.Web.UI;
using System.Web.UI.WebControls;
using System.Web.UI.HtmlControls;
using System.Xml.XPath;
using System.Text;
using System.Xml;
using System.Xml.Xsl;

namespace XMLUsageCs
{
  /// <summary>
  /// Summary description for XslTransformMultipleUsage.
  /// </summary>
  public class XslTransformMultipleUsage : System.Web.UI.Page
  {
    protected System.Web.UI.WebControls.Label LblMessage;
    protected System.Web.UI.HtmlControls.HtmlGenericControl outXMLURL;
    protected System.Web.UI.HtmlControls.HtmlGenericControl outXSLURL;
    protected System.Web.UI.HtmlControls.HtmlGenericControl outXML;

    private void Page_Load(object sender, System.EventArgs e)
    {
      //create virtual path to booklist.xml and authors.xsl files
      //(in same folder as ASPX page)
      string strCurrentPath  = Request.PhysicalPath;
      string strXMLPath = BuildPath(strCurrentPath, "booklist.xml");
      string strXSLPath = BuildPath(strCurrentPath, "authors.xsl");
      string strOutPath = BuildPath(Request.PhysicalPath, "authors.xml");

      try
      {
        //create a new XslTransform object to do the transformation
        XslTransform objTransform = new XslTransform();

        //load the XSL stylesheet into the XSLTransform object
        objTransform.Load(strXSLPath);
        outXSLURL.InnerHtml = "<a href=\"" + strXSLPath
                             + "\">authors.xsl</a>";
```

857

```csharp
        //create a new XmlTextReader object to fetch XML document
        XmlTextReader objXTReader = new XmlTextReader(strXMLPath);
        outXMLURL.InnerHtml = "<a href=\"" + strXMLPath
                            + "\">booklist.xml</a>";

        //create a new XPathDocument object from the XmlTextReader
        XPathDocument objXPDoc = new XPathDocument(objXTReader);

        //create a new XPathNavigator object from the XPathDocument
        XPathNavigator objXPNav;
        objXPNav = objXPDoc.CreateNavigator();

        //create a variable to hold the XmlReader object that is
        //returned from the Transform method
        XmlReader objReader;

        //perform the transformation using the XSL file in the
        //XSLTransform and the XML document referenced by the
        //XPathNavigator. The result is in the XmlReader object
        objReader = objTransform.Transform(objXPNav, null);

        //display the contents of the XmlReader object
        objReader.MoveToContent();
        outXML.InnerText = objReader.ReadOuterXml();

        //create an XMLTextWriter object to write result to disk
        XmlTextWriter objWriter = new XmlTextWriter(strOutPath, null);

        //write the opening <?xml .. ?> declaration and a comment
        objWriter.WriteStartDocument();
        objWriter.WriteComment("List of authors created " + DateTime.Now);

        //transform the XML into the XMLTextWriter
        objTransform.Transform(objXPNav, null, objWriter);

        //ensure that all open elements are closed to end the document
        objWriter.WriteEndDocument();

        //flush the buffer to disk and close the file
        objWriter.Close();
        LblMessage.Text = "<a href=\"authors.xml\">authors.xml</a>";
    }
    //------------ error handling code --------------

    catch(Exception objError)
    {
        //display error details
        LblMessage.Text = "<b>* Error while accessing document</b>.<br />"
                        + objError.Message + "<br />" + objError.Source;
        return;   // and stop execution
    }
}
```

```
      private string BuildPath(string current, string extension)
    {
      StringBuilder builder = new StringBuilder(current);
      int u = current.LastIndexOf("\\")+1;
      builder.Remove(u, current.Length-u);
      builder.Append(extension);
      return builder.ToString();
    }

    #region Web Form Designer generated code
    ...
  }
}
```

After creating the paths and filenames required (as in the previous example) the code creates a new
XslTransform object and loads the stylesheet by calling the Load method and passing the
stylesheet file name as its parameter. Next it demonstrates how an XmlTextReader and an
XPathDocument can be used to load the source XML document. This would allow an
XmlValidatingReader to be added if the document required validation against a schema.
The code next creates an XPathNavigator based on the XPathDocument. The XPathNavigator
is used in the call to the XslTransform object's Transform method, which returns an XmlReader
object. It then uses the MoveToContent and ReadOuterXml methods of the XmlReader to display
the result of the transformation in the page.

Next, the code creates an XmlTextWriter object and uses it to write the opening <?xml>
declaration and a comment element to a disk file. Then the Transform method of the
XslTransform object is used to send the result of the transformation direct to the new disk file.

Here is a screenshot showing the output:

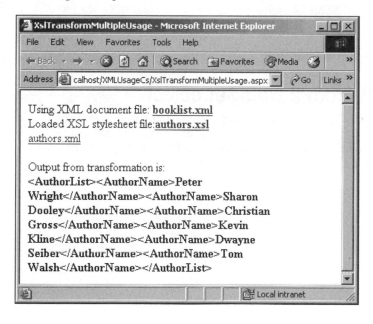

XML and ADO.NET Synchronization

One of the biggest strengths of the new .NET data management classes is the inherent synchronization and interoperability between ADO.NET relational data access techniques and XML-based document management methods.

The ADO.NET `DataSet` object can be used to read and write XML documents in a pre-defined format. There is also a feature of the ADO.NET "command" objects that allow an XML "reader" object to be used to connect to the SQL Server XML output that is produced from a SQL "`FOR XML`" query statement (though we're not going to explore this aspect here).

However, the `System.Xml` namespace provides another useful way to integrate XML and relational data: the `XmlDataDocument` object. This is an extension of the `XmlDocument` object that provides three Microsoft-specific (non W3C-compliant) members that allow synchronization of relational and XML-formatted data. It allows you to access the same instance of the XML data using ADO.NET relational methods or XML techniques.

This class is inherited from the `System.Xml.XmlDocument` class and inherits all its properties, adding an extra `DataSet` property that makes it so useful. Therefore `XmlDataDocument` can be loaded with an XML document in the same way as an `XmlDocument` object, but it exposes a "relational" view of the data through its `DataSet` property.

The `DataSet` property returns a reference to a normal ADO.NET-style `DataSet` object containing the data in the XML document that is currently loaded into the `XmlDataDocument` object. Changes made to the XML document within the `DataSet` are immediately reflected in the `XmlDataDocument` object itself, and vice versa.

We've provided examples in this appendix that demonstrate how these methods are used. For example, we can create an ADO.NET `DataView` object from the first table in a `DataSet` referenced by `objXmlDataDoc` using:

```
DataView dv = new DataView(objXmlDataDoc.DataSet.Tables[0]);
```

Writing XML from a DataSet object

This section uses ADO.NET relational data manipulation techniques to create a `DataSet` and `DataTable` object, and add rows to the `DataTable` object. After creating the required dataset object, the `DataSet` object is written on to the XML disk file. The `DataSet` object has certain handy methods that help in writing the content to the XML file.

Example: Writing XML from a DataSet Object

The following code example, taken from `XmlDataDocumentWritingUsage.aspx.cs`, shows how the desired `DataSet` object is created. This shows the ADO.NET code used to create the `DataSet` object:

```csharp
using System;
using System.Collections;
using System.ComponentModel;
using System.Data;
using System.Drawing;
using System.Web;
using System.Web.SessionState;
using System.Web.UI;
using System.Web.UI.WebControls;
using System.Web.UI.HtmlControls;

namespace XMLUsageCs
{
  /// <summary>
  /// Summary description for XmlDataDocumentWritingUsage.
  /// </summary>
  public class XmlDataDocumentWritingUsage : System.Web.UI.Page
  {
    protected System.Web.UI.WebControls.Label LblMessage;

    private void Page_Load(object sender, System.EventArgs e)
    {
      //create a new empty Table object
      DataTable objTable = new DataTable("Books");

      //define four columns (fields) within the table
      objTable.Columns.Add("ISBN", System.Type.GetType("System.String"));
      objTable.Columns.Add("Title", System.Type.GetType("System.String"));
      objTable.Columns.Add("PublicationDate",
                          System.Type.GetType("System.DateTime"));
      objTable.Columns.Add("Quantity",
                          System.Type.GetType("System.Int32"));

      //declare a variable to hold a DataRow object
      DataRow objDataRow;

      ///create a new DataRow object instance in this table
      objDataRow = objTable.NewRow();

      //and fill in the values
      objDataRow["ISBN"] = "1234567800";
      objDataRow["Title"] = "Professional Video Recorder Programming";
      objDataRow["PublicationDate"] = "2001-03-01";
      objDataRow["Quantity"] = 3956;
      objTable.Rows.Add(objDataRow);

      //repeat to add two more rows
```

```
objDataRow = objTable.NewRow();
objDataRow["ISBN"] = "1234567801";
objDataRow["Title"] = "Professional WAP Phone Programming";
objDataRow["PublicationDate"] = "2001-06-01";
objDataRow["Quantity"] = 29;
objTable.Rows.Add(objDataRow);

objDataRow = objTable.NewRow();
objDataRow["ISBN"] = "1234567802";
objDataRow["Title"] = "Professional Radio Station Programming";
objDataRow["PublicationDate"] = "2001-04-01";
objDataRow["Quantity"] = 10456;
objTable.Rows.Add(objDataRow);

//create a new empty DataSet object and insert table
DataSet objDataSet = new DataSet("BookList");
objDataSet.Tables.Add(objTable);
```

The above code first creates a `DataTable` object with the desired columns. It then uses `DataRow` object to add rows to the `DataTable` object. The `DataTable` object is now added to the `DataSet` object by calling `DataSet.Tables.Add` method. Now that the ADO.NET `DataSet` object is created, we can write its content into XML file.

```
//now we're ready to save the DataSet contents to an XML disk file

try
{
   //use the path to the current virtual application
   string strVirtualPath = Request.ApplicationPath
                           + @"/XML-from-DataSet.xml";
   string strVSchemaPath = Request.ApplicationPath
                           + @"/Schema-from-DataSet.xsd";

   //write the data and schema from the DataSet to an XML document on
   //disk
   //must use the Physical path to the file not the Virtual path
   objDataSet.WriteXml(Request.MapPath(strVirtualPath));
   LblMessage.Text = "Written file: <b><a href=" + "\x22"
                  + strVirtualPath
                  + "\x22" + ">" + strVirtualPath
                  + "</a></b><br />";
   objDataSet.WriteXmlSchema(Request.MapPath(strVSchemaPath));
   LblMessage.Text += "Written file: <b><a href=" + "\x22"
                  + strVSchemaPath + "\x22" + ">"
                  + strVSchemaPath + "</a></b>";
}
catch(Exception objError)
{
   //display error details
   LblMessage.Text = "<b>* Error while writing disk file</b>.<br />"
                  + objError.Message + "<br />" + objError.Source;
   return;  // and stop execution
}
```

```
    }

    #region Web Form Designer generated code
    ...
  }
}
```

This code creates the path and filenames required. It then calls the `WriteXml` method of the `DataSet` object to write its content into an XML file. The entire writing process is encapsulated by this method. Similarly it calls the `WriteXmlSchema` method to write the schema into an `.xsd` file. This shows how closely XML is integrated with ADO.NET.

The standard (and only) persistence format for the ADO.NET objects is XML, and so they are well suited to transferring data from XML to relational format and vice versa. The page writes both the XML data itself, and the XSD schema for that data to the disk as two separate files. The XML representation of the data can be seen in the following screenshot:

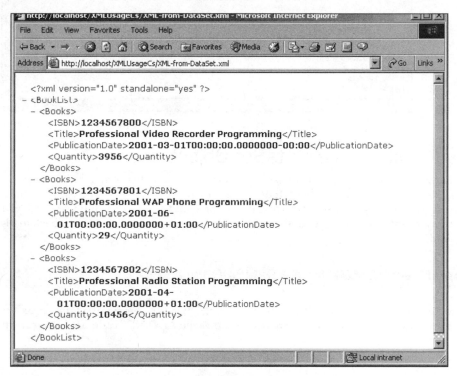

You can see that this is a very natural format, and relates well with the formats we've been using for XML documents throughout this chapter. The `DataSet` object is created as the root element.

The schema produced from the `DataSet` (and, therefore, the schema for this XML document) is shown in the next screenshot:

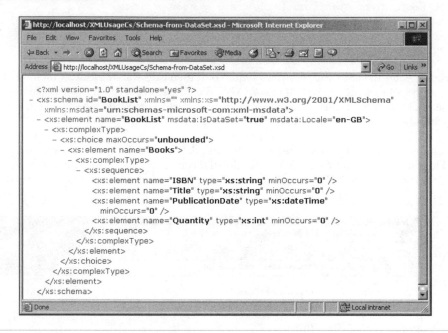

```
<?xml version="1.0" standalone="yes" ?>
- <xs:schema id="BookList" xmlns="" xmlns:xs="http://www.w3.org/2001/XMLSchema"
    xmlns:msdata="urn:schemas-microsoft-com:xml-msdata">
  - <xs:element name="BookList" msdata:IsDataSet="true" msdata:Locale="en-GB">
    - <xs:complexType>
      - <xs:choice maxOccurs="unbounded">
        - <xs:element name="Books">
          - <xs:complexType>
            - <xs:sequence>
                <xs:element name="ISBN" type="xs:string" minOccurs="0" />
                <xs:element name="Title" type="xs:string" minOccurs="0" />
                <xs:element name="PublicationDate" type="xs:dateTime"
                  minOccurs="0" />
                <xs:element name="Quantity" type="xs:int" minOccurs="0" />
              </xs:sequence>
            </xs:complexType>
          </xs:element>
        </xs:choice>
      </xs:complexType>
    </xs:element>
  </xs:schema>
```

Reading XML from a DataSet Object

Now that we've written the files to disk in the previous section, this section talks about how to read the XML file back into a `DataSet` object. It demonstrates that if we have a valid XML document and (optionally) a matching XSD schema, we can load them into a `DataSet` and use ADO.NET relational data access techniques to work with the data; and, of course, export it or write it back to disk again if required.

Example: Reading XML from a DataSetObject

The following code example, taken from `XmlDataDocumentReadingUsage.aspx.cs`, shows how the desired `DataSet` object is created. It shows the ADO.NET code used to create the `DataSet` object:

```
using System;
using System.Collections;
using System.ComponentModel;
using System.Data;
using System.Drawing;
using System.Web;
using System.Web.SessionState;
using System.Web.UI;
using System.Web.UI.WebControls;
using System.Web.UI.HtmlControls;
```

```
namespace XMLUsageCs
{
  /// <summary>
  /// Summary description for XmlDataDocumentReadingUsage.
  /// </summary>
  public class XmlDataDocumentReadingUsage : System.Web.UI.Page
  {
    protected System.Web.UI.WebControls.Label LblMessage;
    protected System.Web.UI.WebControls.DataGrid dgrTables;
    protected System.Web.UI.WebControls.DataGrid dgrValues;

    private void Page_Load(object sender, System.EventArgs e)
    {
      //create a new DataSet object
      DataSet objDataSet = new DataSet();

      try
      {

        //use the path to the current virtual application
        string strVirtualPath = Request.ApplicationPath
                            + @"/XML-from-DataSet.xml";
        string strVSchemaPath = Request.ApplicationPath
                            + @"/Schema-from-DataSet.xsd";

        //read the schema and data into the DataSet from an
        //XML document on disk
        //must use the Physical path to the file not the Virtual path
        objDataSet.ReadXmlSchema(Request.MapPath(strVSchemaPath));
        LblMessage.Text = "Reading file: <b><a href=" + "\x22"
                        + strVSchemaPath + "\x22"
                            + ">" + strVSchemaPath + "</a></b><br />";

        objDataSet.ReadXml(Request.MapPath(strVirtualPath));
        LblMessage.Text += "Reading file: <b><a href=" + "\x22"
                        + strVirtualPath + "\x22"
                        + ">" + strVirtualPath + "</a></b>";
      }
      catch(Exception objError)
      {
        //display error details
        LblMessage.Text = "<b>* Error while reading disk file</b>.<br />"
            + objError.Message + "<br />" + objError.Source + "<br />"
            + "Run the previous example to create the disk file";
        return;   // and stop execution
      }

      //now we can display the DataSet contents
      //assign the DataView.Tables collection to first the DataGrid control
      dgrTables.DataSource = objDataSet.Tables;
      dgrTables.DataBind();  //and bind (display) the data

      //create a DataView object for the Books table in the DataSet
```

```
            DataView objDataView = new DataView(objDataSet.Tables["Books"]);

            //assign the DataView object to the second DataGrid control
            dgrValues.DataSource = objDataView;
            dgrValues.DataBind();   //and bind (display) the data

        }

    #region Web Form Designer generated code
    ...
    }
}
```

The code first creates a new `DataSet` object and then builds the paths and filenames for the schema and XML data files. Like the `WriteXml` and `WriteXmlSchema` methods of the `DataSet` used to write contents to XML, there are `ReadXml` and `ReadXmlSchema` methods to read the XML contents into a `DataSet` object.

The page first loads the schema using the `ReadXmlSchema` method, followed by the `ReadXml` method to load the XML data, and then it displays information about it. It shows the contents of the `DataSet` object's `Tables` collection (the table named `Books` that is created from the XML schema and data), and the content of this table:

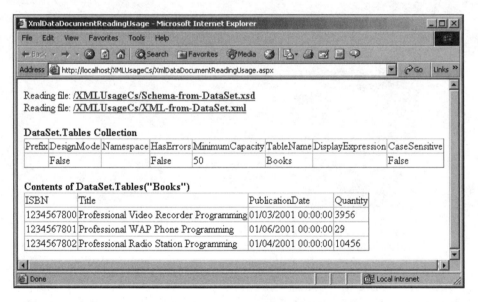

XML data can be loaded into a `DataSet` object without first loading a schema, and the `DataSet` will use its built-in solutions to figure out the structure and build the appropriate tables. However, this may produce unpredictable results if the data is not uniform. If a schema is loaded first, the `DataSet` will allocate the values in the XML data to the appropriate pre-defined tables and columns, leaving null values in any that it can't fill.

Synchronization of the XmlDataDocument and DataSet Objects

The synchronization between the `XmlDataDocument` and `DataSet` is achieved by the `DataSet` property. The `DataSet` property returns a reference to a normal ADO.NET-style `DataSet` object containing the data in the XML document that is currently loaded into the `XmlDataDocument` object. Changes made to the XML document within the `DataSet` are immediately reflected in the `XmlDataDocument` object itself, and vice versa.

Example: Data Synchronization

The final example below demonstrates how an `XmlDataDocument` object's `DataSet` property, and the corresponding synchronized `DataSet` object that this property exposes, can be used.

The code example shown below, is taken from
`XmlDataDocumentSynchronizationUsage.aspx.cs`:

```
using System;
using System.Collections;
using System.ComponentModel;
using System.Data;
using System.Drawing;
using System.Web;
using System.Web.SessionState;
using System.Web.UI;
using System.Web.UI.WebControls;
using System.Web.UI.HtmlControls;
using System.Xml.XPath;
using System.Xml;
using System.Text;

namespace XMLUsageCs
{
  /// <summary>
  /// Summary description for XmlDataDocumentSynchronizationUsage.
  /// </summary>
  public class XmlDataDocumentSynchronizationUsage : System.Web.UI.Page
  {
    protected System.Web.UI.WebControls.Label LblMessage;
    protected System.Web.UI.WebControls.DataGrid dgrResult;
    protected System.Web.UI.HtmlControls.HtmlGenericControl outDOMResult;
    protected System.Web.UI.HtmlControls.HtmlGenericControl outXPNavResult;
    protected System.Web.UI.HtmlControls.HtmlGenericControl
                                                 outFromRowResult;

    private string BuildPath(string current, string extension)
    {
      StringBuilder builder = new StringBuilder(current);
      int u = current.LastIndexOf("\\")+1;
      builder.Remove(u, current.Length-u);
      builder.Append(extension);
      return builder.ToString();
    }
```

```
private void Page_Load(object sender, System.EventArgs e)
{
  //create physical path to booklist sample files
  //(in same folder as ASPX page)
  string strCurrentPath = Request.PhysicalPath;
  string strXMLPath = BuildPath(strCurrentPath,"booklist-dataset.xml");
      strCurrentPath.Substring(0, strCurrentPath.IndexOf(@"\"))
      + "booklist-dataset.xml";
  string strSchemaPath = BuildPath(strCurrentPath,
      "booklist-schema.xsd"); //strCurrentPath.Substring(0,
      strCurrentPath.IndexOf(@"\")) + "booklist-schema.xsd";

  //create a new XMLDataDocument object
  XmlDataDocument objXMLDataDoc = new XmlDataDocument();
  try
  {
    //load the XML schema into the XMLDataDocument object
    objXMLDataDoc.DataSet.ReadXmlSchema(strSchemaPath);
    LblMessage.Text = @"Loaded file: <b><a href="
        + ""booklist-dataset.xml"">booklist-dataset.xml</a></b><br />";

    //load the XML file into the XMLDataDocument object
    objXMLDataDoc.Load(strXMLPath);
    LblMessage.Text += @"Loaded file: <b><a href="
        + ""booklist-schema.xsd"">booklist-schema.xsd</a></b><br />";
  }
  catch(Exception objError)
  {
    //display error details
    LblMessage.Text = "<b>* Error while accessing document</b>.<br />"
                    + objError.Message + "<br />" + objError.Source;
    return;  // and stop execution

  }

  //now ready to use the XMLDataDocument object
```

The above code creates a new `XmlDataDocument` object and loads the schema using the path and filename created at the start of the code. As the `XmlDataDocument` object does not have a method for loading a schema, it does it by calling the `ReadXmlSchema` method of the synchronized `DataSet` object - via the `DataSet` property of the `XmlDataDocument` object. Then it loads the XML data itself using the `Load` method of the `XmlDataDocument` object.

Once the XML schema and data are loaded, the page performs four separate operations to show how the data can be accessed in different ways:

```
//****************************************************************
//*** 1: Extract the author names using the XML DOM methods ***
//****************************************************************

    string strResults = "";
```

```
            //create a NodeList collection of all matching child nodes
            XmlNodeList colElements;
            colElements = objXMLDataDoc.GetElementsByTagName("LastName");

            int Dummy = colElements.Count;

    //***********************<<<<<<<< error if removed

            //iterate through the collection getting the values of the
            //child #text nodes for each one
            foreach(XmlNode objNode in colElements)
              strResults += objNode.FirstChild.Value + "   ";

            //then display the result
            outDOMResult.InnerHtml = strResults;
            strResults = "";
```

The first uses the GetElementsByTagName method of the XmlDataDocument. As the XmlDataDocument is an extension of the normal XmlDocument object, these XML DOM techniques work just the same as in the earlier examples.

Next, it creates an XPathNavigator for the XmlDataDocument, and uses this to search for the <LastName> nodes that contain the author names. This is accomplished through a recursive routine defined at the end of the code in the page. It is very similar to that used in earlier examples of reading an XML document, and so that routine code isn't repeated here:

```
    //*******************************************************************
    //*** 2: Extract the author names with an XPathNavigator object ***
    //*******************************************************************

            //create a new XPathNavigator object using the XMLDataDocument object
            XPathNavigator objXPNav;
            objXPNav = objXMLDataDoc.CreateNavigator();

            //move to the root element of the document
            objXPNav.MoveToRoot();

            //and display the result of the recursive 'search' function
            outXPNavResult.InnerHtml = SearchForElement(objXPNav, "LastName");
```

To demonstrate that the DataSet property of the XmlDataDocument exposes a standard DataSet object, the third section is to bind the DataSet to an ASP.NET DataGrid server control. The code does this by creating an ADO.NET DataView object based on the table in the DataSet, and then assigning this to the DataGrid control's DataSource property. To display the contents of the DataView it can then simply call the control's DataBind method:

```
    //*******************************************************************
    //3: Display content of the XMLDataDocument object's DataSet property
    //*******************************************************************
```

```
        //create a DataView object for the Books table in the DataSet
        DataView objDataView = new DataView(objXMLDataDoc.DataSet.Tables[0]);

        //assign the DataView object to the DataGrid control
        dgrResult.DataSource = objDataView;
        dgrResult.DataBind();  //and bind (display) the data
```

Finally, the code uses the GetElementFromRow method of each row in the DataTable object to retrieve an XML representation of the data for that row. This simply involves iterating through each member of the Rows collection of the table and calling GetElementFromRow to return that row as an XML element. It then displays the XML from that element by accessing its OuterXml property using Server.HtmlEncode so that the individual elements within each <Book> element are visible:

```
    //***********************************************************************
    //4: Extract XML elements from the XMLDataDocument object's DataSet ***
    //***********************************************************************
        //create a DataTable object for the Books table in the DataSet
        DataTable objDataTable = objXMLDataDoc.DataSet.Tables[0];

        XmlElement objXMLElement;

        //iterate through all the rows in this table
        foreach(DataRow objRow in objDataTable.Rows)
        {
          //get an XML element that represents this row
          objXMLElement = objXMLDataDoc.GetElementFromRow(objRow);

          //HTMLEncode it because it contains XML element tags
          strResults += Server.HtmlEncode(objXMLElement.OuterXml) + "<br />";
        }

        //display the result
        outFromRowResult.InnerHtml = strResults;

    //***********************************************************************
      }

      //recursive function used by step 2 - using an XPathNavigator
      string SearchForElement(XPathNavigator objXPNav, string strNodeName)
      {
        string strResults = "";    //to hold the result

        do
        {

          //see if this node is an element that we're looking for
          if(objXPNav.Name == strNodeName)
          {
            //move to the the first child (i.e the #text) node
```

```
            objXPNav.MoveToFirstChild();

            //get the value and add to the 'results' string
            strResults += objXPNav.Value + "   ";

            //move back to the parent of this node (i.e. the element node)
            objXPNav.MoveToParent();
        }

        //now check if the current node has any child nodes
        if(objXPNav.HasChildren)
        {

            //move to the first child node
            objXPNav.MoveToFirstChild();

            //recursively call this same function to search the child nodes
            strResults += SearchForElement(objXPNav, strNodeName);

            //move back to the parent of this node
            objXPNav.MoveToParent();
        }

        //then move to next sibling of current node (if any)
    }
    while(objXPNav.MoveToNext());

    return strResults;  //return the result
    }

  #region Web Form Designer generated code
  ...
  }
}
```

The format of the XML that is returned for each element looks like this:

```
<Books><ISBN>1861003323</ISBN><Title>Professional Visual Basic 6
XML</Title><PublicationDate>2000-03-01T00:00:00</PublicationDate>
<FirstName>James</FirstName><LastName>Britt</LastName></Books>
```

Here is a screenshot showing the output page:

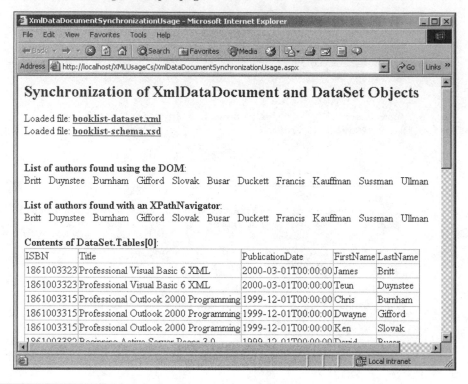

Summary

In this appendix, we've examined some of the main features of the three namespaces: `System.Xml`, `System.Xml.XPath`, and `System.Xml.Xsl`. These are most often in ASP.NET when working directly with XML documents, XML Schemas, and related document formats.

We looked at techniques for writing and reading XML documents, validating XML documents against a schema, creating new XML documents, searching for information within XML documents, and modifying them using a range of methods. We also looked at how we can perform XSL or XSLT transformations on XML documents using stylesheets.

Finally, we briefly looked at how the ADO.NET and XML-based data manipulation techniques available within the .NET Framework can provide a boundary-free and synchronized approach to managing data.

wrox

Programmer to Programmer™

Index

A Guide to the Index

The lists of methods, properties and events shown under individual classes omit most of those which are inherited from other classes, unless they are overridden. Comprehensive lists are found in the book content, under the individual classes.

Many "*see also* references" are to classes where start of the class name hides its functionality. The listings of methods, properties and events under each class should assist you in locating those whose name you are uncertain of.

"*See also* references", where applicable, will go from general to specific, but not specific to general, for example "**browsers**:*see* downlevel browsers", but not "**downlevel browsers**:*see* browsers".

You will find that greater detail is often available by following a second-level entry to its first-level equivalent, for example "**directories**:virtual directory" leads to "**virtual directory**:holding page or server control".

Classes at first-level (bold) are followed by their namespace, omitting the word namespace, for example "**WebControl class, System.Web.UI.WebControls**".

Use of 'Xyz' – Whenever the string '*Xyz*' is used within a name, it indicates that there are multiple similarly named objects, all occurring on the same page. For example "**DataGrid*Xyz* classes**" indicates "**DataGridColumn class**", "**DataGridColumnCollection class**," and seven other classes all commencing "**DataGrid**". The full list of class names is found under the namespace entry "System.*NamespaceName*", in this case "System.Web.UI.WebControls".

Use of '/~' – The '/~' characters indicates the initial part (normal font) is followed by the italicized parts preceding and following the '/~'. For example "**FormsCookie*Name*/~*Path* properties**" indicates both the "**FormsCookieName property**" and the "**FormsCookiePath property**". If no italicized part precedes the first '/~', then the initial (normal font) part exists as well. For example "**Fill/~*Schema* methods**" indicates that the index entry applies equally to both the "**Fill method**" and the "**FillSchema method**".

B

883

H

RangeValidator class, System.Web.UI.WebControls (continued)
  protected properties, 401
  public events, 402
  public methods, 399
  public properties, 400
  validating input against range of values, 401
RawUrl property
  HttpRequest class, 63
Read method
  DataReader classes, 783
  ServiceDescription class, 683
ReadOnly property
  TextBox class, 422
ReadXml method, DataSet class
  reading XML into DataSet object, 866
ReadXmlSchema method, DataSet class
  reading XML into DataSet object, 866
  synchronizing DataSet and XmlDataDocument
  objects, 867
Redirect method
  HttpResponse class, 77
RedirectFromLoginPage method
  FormsAuthentication class, 586
redirection
  forwarding when unhandled page exceptions, 166
  programmatically redirecting user to alternative
  page, 35
references to web sites
  ECMA, 26
  MIME types, 50
  PICS, 77
  UDDI, 606
  W3C WSDL v1.1 draft specification, 627
  Web Services standards, 602
Regional Options settings
  overriding, 547
**Register*ArrayDeclaration/~ClientScriptBlock/~HiddenF
ield* methods**
  Page class, 151–52
registering
  client-side registration example, 153
  determining if client-side script registered, 150
  determining if startup script registered, 150
  registering hidden fields, 152
RegisterOnSubmitStatement method
  Page class, 152
RegisterRequiresPostBack method
  Page class, 152
RegisterRequiresRaiseEvent method
  Page class, 153
RegisterStartupScript method
  Page class, 153
RegisterValidatorCommonScript method
  BaseValidator class, 292
RegisterValidatorDeclaration method
  BaseValidator class, 293
RegisterViewStateHandler method
  Page class, 153
registry key
  Passport based security, 594
regular expressions
  list of common regular expressions, 403
**RegularExpressionValidator class,
  System.Web.UI.MobileControls, 448**
**RegularExpressionValidator class,
  System.Web.UI.WebControls, 280, 402**
  properties
    ValidationExpression property, 403

protected methods, 402
protected properties, 405
public events, 405
public methods, 402
public properties, 403
validating input against regular expression, 404
Relations property
  DataSet class, 797
relationships, database
  Relations property, 796
remote methods
  calling for current service, 670
  multiple communication end-points for handling, 678
Remote Procedure Calls
  see RPC.
Remoting
  Web Services compared, 603
Remove method
  Cache class, 526
  HttpApplicationState class, 18
  HttpSessionState class, 99
Remove*All/~At* methods
  HttpApplicationState class, 18
  HttpSessionState class, 99
RemoveOutputCacheItem method
  HttpResponse class, 78
Render method
  Control class, 126
  Page class, 162
Render stage, control lifecycle, 109
RenderBeginTag method
  WebControl class, 428
RenderChildren method
  Control class, 127
  Page class, 163
RenderControl method
  Control class, 115
RenderEndTag method
  WebControl class, 428
rendering
  device specific rendering, 456, 462
  TextBox controls, 448
RendersBreakBeforeWmlSelectAndInput property
  MobileCapabilities class, 472
RendersBreaksAfter*Xyz* properties
  MobileCapabilities class, 472–73
RendersWmlDoAcceptsInline property
  MobileCapabilities class, 473
RendersWmlSelectsAsMenuCards property
  MobileCapabilities class, 473
RenderUpLevel property
  BaseValidator class, 295
RenewTicketIfOld method
  FormsAuthentication class, 586
RepeatColumns property
  CheckBoxList class, 320
  DataList class, 355
  RadioButtonList class, 396
RepeatDirection property
  CheckBoxList class, 321
  DataList class, 355
  RadioButtonList class, 396
Repeater class, System.Web.UI.WebControls, 405
  description, 280
  properties
    Items property, 406
  protected methods, 406
  protected properties, 407

S

917

ASP Today

The daily knowledge site for professional ASP programmers

ASPToday brings the essence of the Wrox Programmer to Programmer philosophy to you through the web. Every working day, www.asptoday.com delivers a new, original article by ASP programmers for ASP programmers.

Want to know about Classic ASP, ASP.NET, Performance, Data Access, Site Design, SQL Server, and more? Then visit us. You can make sure that you don't miss a thing by subscribing to our free daily e-mail updates featuring ASPToday highlights and tips.

By bringing you daily articles written by real programmers, ASPToday is an indispensable resource for quickly finding out exactly what you need. ASPToday is THE daily knowledge site for professional ASP programmers.

In addition to our free weekly and monthly articles, ASPToday also includes a premier subscription service. You can now join the growing number of ASPToday subscribers who benefit from access to:

- Daily in-depth articles
- Code-heavy demonstrations of real applications
- Access to the ASPToday Living Book, our collection of past articles
- ASP reference material
- Fully searchable index and advanced search engine
- Tips and tricks for professionals

Visit ASPToday at: www.asptoday.com